CRASS STRUGGLE

Crass Struggle

Greed, Glitz, and Gluttony in a Wanna-Have World

R.T. NAYLOR

McGill-Queen's University Press

Montreal & Kingston • London • Ithaca

© McGill-Queen's University Press 2011

ISBN 978-0-7735-3771-2 (cloth)
ISBN 978-0-7735-4172-6 (paper)

Legal deposit second quarter 2011
Bibliothèque nationale du Québec

First paperback edition 2013

Printed in Canada on acid-free paper that is 100% ancient forest free
(100% post-consumer recycled), processed chlorine free

This book was first published with the help of a grant from the
Canadian Federation for the Humanities and Social Sciences, through
the Aid to Scholarly Publications Program, using funds provided by the
Social Sciences and Humanities Research Council of Canada.

McGill-Queen's University Press acknowledges the support of the
Canada Council for the Arts for our publishing program. We also
acknowledge the financial support of the Government of Canada
through the Canada Book Fund for our publishing activities.

Library and Archives Canada Cataloguing in Publication

Naylor, R. T., 1945–
    Crass struggle : greed, glitz, and gluttony in a wanna-have world /
R.T. Naylor.

Includes bibliographical references and index.
ISBN 978-0-7735-3771-2 (bnd)
ISBN 978-0-7735-4172-6 (pbk)

1. Wealth – Moral and ethical aspects. 2. Wealth – Social aspects.
3. Rich people – Conduct of life. 4. Consumption (Economics) – Moral
and ethical aspects. 5. Consumption (Economics) – Social aspects.
I. Title.

HB835.N39 2011   178   C2010-907464-5

This book was typeset by Jay Tee Graphics Ltd. in 10.5/13 Sabon

Contents

CRASS STRUGGLE

Preamble: Bacchanalian Adventures with the Ultra-Rich

This is a book about big money, the kind that today just about everyone finds gratuitously shoved in their face but rarely in their wallet, unless they work for Goldman Sachs. However, it is a book about big money with a difference. Rather than worrying about how people at the top of today's income and wealth heap "earned" their oodles of boodle – although a little of that is also essential to the story – this book deals primarily with how those who have megabucks spend them and, more importantly, with the costs to everyone else.

This book investigates how the steady growth of the affluence-influence-effluence gap in the last few decades has caused markets catering to the whims and fancies of the very rich to bubble up to – or sometimes beyond – the point of explosion. It demonstrates how crooks, con artists, and counterfeiters flourish in the overheated ambiance that results when too much money chases too few objects that confer acclaim and prestige – even if the acclaim is phony and the prestige misplaced. And it shows how so much done in today's luxury trades compounds the already appalling burden humans collectively inflict on nature.

Modern überclass excess cascades down through the social ladder and spreads across geographic space. The result is that today in much of the world the visible trappings of great wealth have reached obscene proportions; the "middle classes" have exploded in numbers and appetites for what they define as fine living, usually a pathetic emulation of upper crust ostentation; and the poor continue to explode only in numbers that, alas, also translate into mass appetites, albeit for a rather different set of "goods." The combined result is a natural world being literally devoured alive.

In unscrambling the consequences, the book takes the reader to some of the greener pastures where big money goes to graze at least vicariously: to gold mines and diamond fields; to purveyors of luxury seafood and galleries peddling high-end art and antiquities; to merchants offering top-vintage wines and tobacconists with Cuban cigars on display (or not on display if they are located in the USA); to companies running five-star trophy-hunting expeditions and dealers in exotic pets; and much more. What stands out from these commercial safaris into the modern jungle of extravagant spending is the extent to which today's top-priced items reveal a schizoid streak – glittering on the outside, yet with more than a spot of rot at the core.

In short, this book deals with the low side of the high life, the bad side of the good life, or, more poetically, the underbelly of the potbelly. But first it is necessary to ask: how did that potbelly manage to get so distended?

Unless someone has chosen to live in a monastery on a secluded mountaintop where the monks take vows of silence as well as poverty, they are presumably aware that recent financial manipulations have produced not just a string of speculative bubbles but a fabulously rich club of speculators and bubblers who celebrate their success with a spendathon of epic proportions.[1] And if the intrepid mountaineers don't know, they will find out soon enough once the monastery is seized for unpaid debts, then converted into luxury condos with dazzling vistas, surveillance cameras, and machinegun-toting guards.

Credit for this state of affairs is commonly given to the free market's "invisible hand," whose fingers seem to come rather clearly into view to grab fat rewards on the way up or a big chunk of public bailout money on the way down. A more convincing explanation would be that much of the recent run-up of wealth is the result of a gigantic swindle, far beyond anything to which Bernie Madoff could have aspired and with the advantage of being (more or less) legal. The blame, though, lies not with some agoraphobic computer geek deep in the bowels of a major Wall Street or City of London financial house (a useful hobgobblin to divert attention from a more uncomfortable reality). Instead the foundations were set firmly in place over three decades by decisions at the highest political levels.[2]

At the end of World War II a senior North American corporate executive earned on average maybe forty times as much as a production worker, a ratio down from the roaring twenties and dirty thirties, although the numbers are too sketchy to be absolutely sure by how much. Governments in the West, haunted by the twin spectres of a Great Depression in the recent past and a Communist Bloc very much in the present, maintained that kind of spread, even narrower in Western Europe, with laws to protect collective bargaining, with progressive taxes, and with tight financial regulations. Those at the top were certainly well-off during the early postwar decades, but for the most part not obscenely so. And those who were extremely rich generally kept a low profile as they frittered away their family fortune.

Then came the mid-1970s. Governments, led by those in English-speaking places, started to adopt what John Kenneth Galbraith, one of the few North American economists who valued social reality ahead of mathematical mumbo jumbo, called the "horses-and-oats" principle – feed a horse enough oats and it will leave something behind on the road for the sparrows to eat.[3] Over the next thirty-plus years "globalization" (a polite term for big companies setting up in places free from environmental restrictions or pesky unions), "fiscal reform" (AKA tax cuts for the rich balanced for the sake of fairness by welfare cuts for the poor), and "liberalization" (i.e., turning financial predators loose to do what they wanted with other people's money) interacted to pave the way for a new parasitocracy.[4] By the time crisis hit in 2007–08, those on the top rung of the pay ladder in North America, led by but certainly not restricted to the financial sector, carted home compensation packages equal to perhaps as much as 1,750 times the mean (in both senses) wage that was itself moving in real terms in the opposite direction.[5]

But maybe they deserve it? Just ask Leo Hindery Jr, billionaire sports broadcasting tycoon and racing-car enthusiast, who modestly remarked during the upswing: "I think there are people including myself … who because of their uniqueness warrant whatever the market will bear."[6] That was a view shared by Sanford Weill, who was heralded as a genius for creating Citigroup and who counted as one of his most prized possessions the pen President Bill Clinton used to sign the deregulation bill that made Weill's corporate goliath possible – or at least prevented it from being prosecuted for violating previous US laws intended to prohibit exactly that kind of financial supermarket. In 2007, in conformity with the central principle of modern economic theory that high wages for labour lead to sloth while high rewards for capital stimulate entrepreneurial effort, Weill rationalized compensation that had pushed his wealth, too, above the $1 billion point with the claim that "the results our company had … justified what I got."[7] Yet scarcely a year later, when Citigroup became the biggest financial failure in history, Mr Weill made no offer to return his previous merit pay. Of course, if most of it was in Citigroup stock, there may have been little left to give back.

Plenty of ink has already flowed arguing over just what factors coalesced to produce a situation in which the top 1 percent of the world's population wound up owning maybe 50 percent of the wealth, and the bottom 50 percent about 1 percent, a rough symmetry seeming to suggest divine ordination.[8] Even more energy is likely to go into debating just what combination of forces, systemic or random, internal or external, caused the system to come crashing down, even if temporarily.[9] And there will be an outpouring of outrage, at least on paper, when the truth finally dawns about the massive bailouts that amount to perhaps the greatest involuntary transfer of treasure from the weak to the strong since the Spanish sacked Peru and Mexico.[10] However, the main point of this book is not how today's super rich amassed their colossal wealth but what happens when they decide that the time has come to party.[11]

Granted, the two sides of the coin – a mountain of wealth on one and a bacchanalian spending spree on the other – can't be fully separated. Obviously how much people "earn" affects how much they spend. Even more important, though, just how they get it, and how fast, can affect how much and on what they spend.[12] One study of prostitutes in the 1980s provided a useful insight: the ladies of the night carefully budgeted money from legal jobs or from welfare to use for their families, while frittering away anything they got from turning tricks on booze, drugs, and fancy clothes. Of course, the analogy is not perfect: unlike derivatives traders, for example, prostitutes render a genuine service and stay on the job even later into the dark hours.

It is true that rarely in history – the immediate post-World War II period was one possible exception – did those who have hesitate to make a public display of what others have not. Certainly American tycoons of the late nineteenth century, like the European old money they tried to ape, were shameless in their displays of wealth and their abuses of the political power it conferred. But perhaps because financial manipulations of the last few decades have produced so many multi-millionaires, and not a few billionaires, on both sides of the Atlantic and across the world, today's hyper-rich have distinguished themselves by a level of conspicuous presumption that might have shocked even Thorstein Veblen, the most prescient US analyst of a previous gilded age.[13]

Certainly, too, in even earlier times, great fortunes had less than glorious foundations: looting nature, dispossessing and slaughtering native peoples, or plundering the public purse. But at least in the nineteenth century (some of) their founders left behind a growing industrial complex, at a time when factories fouling the air and poisoning the water were almost universally worshipped as symbols of prosperity and progress rather than loathed for spawning human misery and environmental blight.[14] US steel magnate Andrew Carnegie, for example, although himself from an impoverished mill-hand background, crushed his workers, savaged his competitors, and profiteered from the US Civil War's inflated demand for his oil (after he paid someone else to take his place in the army) while reducing politicians to their preferred state of fawning servility. But unlike platinum-class members of today's super-rich, who seem to get off more on stripping financial assets than building up physical ones while rewarding themselves handsomely for the "value" they create, Carnegie preferred running a business to shorting shares. He also lived modestly, given his means, and at the end of the day was dedicated to giving back to the community what it had (however unwillingly) given to him. Calling for confiscatory taxes on his peers to prevent dynasties of privilege and sloth, he handed over to trustees most of his money along with broad guidelines as to how it was to be spent, then left them to their own devices. However appalling the story of how his money was earned, including a major scandal over faulty nickel-steel armour supplied for naval vessels in the 1890s, it merits a grudging respect for how it was used: schools, libraries, universities, and even a modest pension plan for former employees, although presumably not those he had sent Pinkerton detectives to gun down during frequent strikes at his steel plants. However, today's "captain of industry" is more likely sitting on the bridge deliberately steering the S.S. Enterprise toward shoals where scavengers wait to sell off the wreckage, on the rationale that the bits and pieces will fetch in total more than the "market value" of the ship as a whole.

With modern money that seems to rain down like manna from a bond-futures trader's heaven, to the delight of those lucky enough to be caught outside with a bucket rather than an umbrella, the guiding principle seems to be: easy come, easy blow. Like the late Michael Jackson dwelling both on and off stage in a Neverland of his own creation, today's super-rich apparently have an irresistible urge to spend both as quickly and as publicly as possible. They seem to unload their money fast out of a combination of guilt and fear: guilt that they maybe they don't deserve it, something that is generally true; fear that someone will take it away from them, something that is certainly false if the suspect is one of today's governments, who define their main responsibilities as gutting social security on one side and bailing out mega-financial interests on the other. They lavish it publicly, too, to one-up rivals from their own ranks or to challenge old wealth for a higher rung on the social ladder, or maybe just to remind the Great Unwashed of their proper place in the larger scheme of things. However, to some, no doubt, extravagant enjoyment simply reflects a deep sense of entitlement, captured brilliantly by Ray Dalio, the hedge-fund manager whose take-home pay hit $780 million in 2008. "How much money people have earned," he observed as bankruptcies, foreclosures, and layoffs were soaring, "is a rough measure of how much they gave society what it wanted."[15] Presumably how much they spend is similarly just a reflection of how much society owes them back.

Take, for example, the house that Ira built. Despite a rocky early history in which he was stripped by regulators of his license to trade securities, Ira Rennert made it big during the junk-bond rage of the 1980s and early 1990s. He would target ailing and failing companies in the metals business, buy them cheaply with borrowed money, strip the assets, lay off workers, and use the profits to reward himself for his entrepreneurship. Out of this came a business empire made up, according to a fan of his at Fortune magazine, of "pollution-belching, lawsuit-ridden, money-mulching metals and mining properties."[16] Still, one jewel continued to shine in his corporate crown: he had also bought the company that produced both civil and military versions of the Hummer. Perhaps to celebrate his success in both thumbing his nose at ecofreaks and flipping the finger to peaceniks, he built a home-to-almost-end-all-homes in the ultra-tony Township of Southampton near New York City. Although in that locale dimensions and bank accounts alike were already far from modest, his 66,395 square foot Italianate mansion sporting twenty-nine bedrooms, three dining rooms, three swimming pools, a 164-seat theatre, and a recreational pavilion with basketball court, gym, and bowling alley on sixty-three acres of waterfront land was so large that it obscured the ocean view of other houses. Outraged neighbours tried unsuccessfully through legal action to prevent him from occupying what a pilot flying over the site described as "some huge industrial project …. with … fields around it."[17]

Mr Rennert himself dismissed the complaints as coming from "a few people with emotional and psychological problems."[18] No doubt he knew of what he spoke. In the past he had had to deal with delusional bondholders in his enterprises who claimed to see $1.5 billion in holdings shrinking to half that value well before the recent market collapse, along with deranged environmentalists and hysterical federal regulators who launched lawsuits against his steel, coal, and heavy-metal businesses, tarring them as some of the country's worst polluters.[19]

Of course, domicilius elephantiasis is far from just a North American or even a Western affliction.[20] In India, for example, one billionaire forty-three times over, Mukesh Ambani, who heads the petrochemical giant Reliance Industries, decided to mark his success with a home that in different location might have caused Ira Rennert to apply for a restraining order. The result in downtown Mumbai is a twenty-seven-storey skyscraper – actually sixty normal levels, but with elevated ceilings – for which his architects reputedly presented to the world's fifth richest man a $1–2 billion bill for services rendered.[21] That seems not unreasonable for a home spread over 44,000 square feet to accommodate three helipads, a six-story garage with its own service centre for the family's 168 imported cars, nine elevators in the front lobby, a ballroom with silver railings and a ceiling 80 percent covered with crystal chandeliers, a retractable showcase for the art collection, a health spa, and, because the founder insists on Indian cultural motifs wherever possible, its own yoga studio.[22] The tower will allow the family to rise above Mumbai's foul air and, in a country where 700 million still defecate in the open, avoid contact with water whose fecal contamination in places reaches hundreds of times "normal." In fact, from the top floor the family might on a clear day be able look down on a million people crammed into the 175-hectare Dharavi slum, one of whose main industries is recycling garbage from the rest of the city.[23] None of this seems exactly what Mohandas Gandhi had in mind with his calls for simplicity, self-sufficiency, and control of the senses.

The überclass spendathon shows up, too, in other kinds of "consumer durables" that any self-respecting family requires. Private planes with solid gold bathroom fixtures may seem the kind of thing best left to "Arabian oil sheiks." Crude begets crude, the *sophistiqué* might sniffle through noses nearly at the altitude of the corporate jets in which the CEOs of the US Big Three automakers flew to Washington to make the case that their industry was running out of cash. But no one seems particularly shocked at a naval battle fought to see whose yacht is biggest. Roman Abramovich's $600 million Eclipse – with two helipads, home cinema screens in every guest cabin, multiple hot tubs, plus essentials like bulletproof glass, motion detectors, a missile detection system, and, in case those fail to do their job, its own miniature submarine – wins the size sweepstakes. At 557 feet it is longer than the ex-Russian oil oligarch's other two mega-yachts combined.[24]

To be sure, not everything the super wealthy seek has to be grandiose. They also need those day-to-day necessities to keep body and soul together. Gold (and platinum) jewellery by the kilo is a no-brainer; and the main subject of the first section of this book. Every gram of gold, the product of perhaps the most wasteful extractive process on Earth, that adds razzle-dazzle to a socialite's soirée leaves behind on average about a ton and a half of mine tailings full of mercury, cyanide, arsenic, and cadmium for the rest of humanity to enjoy. Gold is also the mining sector probably most riddled with fraud, albeit the offenses of shysters who salt assay samples seem minor compared to the legal, politically endorsed, and often tax-deductible crimes of the corporate giants that run the real business. Meanwhile the high-end gemstones so often set in that gold have no competitor for the human misery associated with their production, the commercial duplicity accompanying their trafficking, the political mayhem that the scramble for them leaves behind, or the vulgar glitz in their marketing. This reached its perky pinnacle (or two) in Victoria's Secret bras, especially the 2008 Black Diamond Fantasy Miracle ("Cleavage like this could only be a Miracle") with about 3,500 black diamonds, 117 1-carat round diamonds, and 34 rubies. For today's sleazure class, it seems, nothing exceeds like excess.[25]

For the truly blasé, though, the ultimate conspicuous consumption trick was likely stopping at the bar in New York's Algonquin Hotel that, prior to the crash, offered a $10,000 "martini on a rock" featuring a diamond at the bottom of the glass. That achievement could only bested, possibly, by ordering the Frrrozen Haute Chocolate dessert, deemed the world's most expensive by the Guiness Book of Records, something that has probably replaced Gideon's Bible at the bedsides of many of the new rich. This delectable concoction – the dessert, not the Bible – containing twenty-eight types of cocoa from around the world plus 5 grams of edible 23-karat gold, was laid on by the Serendipity 3 Restaurant until that place was closed by health inspectors who found in its kitchen "a live mouse ... fruit flies, horse flies and more than 100 live cockroaches," a fitting metaphor for the times.[26]

Of course, those little accessories – and many more ranging from a Classical Billionaire Touribillon watch at $998,000 to a bottle of Imperial Majesty, a "Clive Christian signature scent," at $215,000 – can serve their social function only if they are "genuine." Imagine the discomfiture of a hedge-fund boss bending over to sign off on a deal to buy credit default swaps on the equity tranche of a batch of collateralized debt obligations secured by the discounted present value of the estimated future flow of user fees from the privatization of aquifers in a drought-ravaged sector of sub-Sahara Africa. Just as the 18-karat gold point of his rhodium-coated solid silver pen set with more than five thousand diamonds reaches the paper, his counterparty hauls out a jeweller's loupe to declare that the stones are really cubic zirconiums set in nickel-plated stainless steel.[27] Today it is that pen, not the "securities" involved or the people making the deal, that represents fraud in the eyes of the law.

The spread of businesses making fake luxury products today complicates considerably the social responsibility faced by the ultra-rich to keep up appearances in the face of so much competition from both their peers and wannabes from the Great Unwashed. In ages past the überclass was assisted by sumptuary laws that forbad lower orders from imitating the ornamentation – be it clothing, jewellery, food, wine, even furniture – of their social superiors. True, the parasitocracy today get some legal protection from intellectual property laws that give to corporations controlling luxury lines exclusive rights to stamp their goods with particular trade names. Granting those companies the right to enclose, privatize, and eventually "securitize" humanity's linguistic commons simultaneously assures wealthy buyers that few from outside their class will be able to display the stuff in public. But even if serious penalties were easy to obtain and enforce, which they are not, "intellectual property" laws punishing the producers of fakes are a weak substitute for being able to order the axe man to hack off offending hands wearing jewellery restricted to the upper nobility or to chop off heads that dared to wear hats made from the wrong fur.

Apart from consumer luxuries, of which gold and gemstones form the dazzling core, another way in which the überclass consumania shows up is in a zeal for fine living, a subject also treated extensively in this book. That showed up, for example, back in 2004, when markets were still boiling and the then-chief executive of NASDAQ, the big computerized securities-trading system, decided to salute his own professional success by hiring Tours of Enchantment to manage a homecoming party in the Ireland of his forefathers. The splash featured, apart from goose hunts for the daring or a visit to Dublin zoo for the more sedate, string quartets, horse-drawn carriages, four butlers and two nannies to tend twenty guests, not to mention satin pillows for the ladies to rest their feet during dinner – a nine-course chef-competition feast judged by two professional food critics and spiced up further by sommeliers and cigar experts.[28]

Whatever else was served, it seems a reasonable guess that dinner included a course or two of things like beluga caviar, wild Pacific oysters and bluefin tuna, or other types of seafood that used to be naturally abundant until humanity's short-sighted greed toward sea creatures and criminal irresponsibility toward the sea itself turned those creatures into avidly sought rarities. All of those "delicacies" are probably slated in the not too distant future to vanish forever, whatever the feeble laws and regulations intended (in theory) to conserve them happen to say. Their very present scarcity, raising their attractiveness to both rich consumers and enterprising poachers, all but guarantees their future absence.

No doubt the wine was also equal to the occasion, in price if not quality, despite evidence from neuroscience that (as with most "luxury" goods) appreciation increases with price paid rather than vice versa, and despite evidence from fraud squads that there is a good chance the only thing genuine about a trophy wine is the bottle, recycled from a fancy restaurant or dug up at the back of an antique store before being refilled with Château de New Jersey Waterfront. As to the cigars, the Western world is now dotted with clubs full of preening clients of both sexes, though still mainly male, oozing self importance as they competitively blow into each other's faces expensive smoke from boxes with fake *Hecho en Cuba* stamps on the outside.[29]

Granted, the Irish event was a small, private party; and it happened when times were good. But well after a market crash that supposedly wiped out 40 percent of world "wealth," the principality of Monaco (35,000 people, 350,000 bank accounts) decided to launch its Concept URI (ultra-rich individual) program. Facing the threat of being black-listed by the G–20 group of rich countries as a "predatory tax haven," Monaco planned a charm counter offensive for a select group whose political clout matched their personal wealth. Each URI would receive a "key to Monaco" card that opened twenty-four-hour private shopping in local Prada, Christian Dior, Yves St Laurent, and Cartier outlets with the guarantee that "ordinary" clients would be cleared out in advance. Each URI would be feted, too, with a helicopter tour of the environs capped by a reception in a "private home" to study the local way of life, no doubt with the same enthusiasm as an anthropology student doing doctoral field research among exotic cultures. A visit to the Royal Palace (big chief's hut?) got tossed in for good measure.[30] After all that excitement, guests were bound to be famished. Time to join natives in a tribal feast at the Louis XV restaurant complete with a tour of its 600,000-bottle wine cellar to help diners select the appropriate accompaniment to their "farm piglet caramelized with sage, vegetable garnish, shoulder and head in vinaigrette sauce, condiment with mustard and eggplant/piglet ear."[31] Better than stewed leg of missionary served in a coconut shell any old day.

Yet another way by which the ultra-rich raise a crystal champagne flute to their own fame and fortune is by their passion for the creations of nature. That ardour takes them to strange and wonderful destinations abroad, even if back home their bulldozers and cement mixers are busy turning wildlife habitat first into powder, then into urban sprawl and agro-industrial blight. Sometimes it is just a matter of closing up the MacMansion, double-locking the garage holding the Pagani Zonda (at $1.2 million) or the McLaren F–1 (whose rarity assured that a used one sold in 2009 for $4.1 million, four times the original retail price), then heading off to a place offering "sustainable tourism." They might book, for example, for $6–8,000 per night Soneva Kiri reserve ("combines the best of luxury design with cutting edge eco-concepts") on the tropical island of Kood off Thailand, to get a 1001 square metre wooden villa with its own 209 square metre pool and a treehouse for the children.[32] The "reserve" can be enjoyed without qualms about its ecological footprint since it grows its own organic vegetables.[33] Hopefully guests remember to dump the empty *foie gras* jars into the recycling bins.

Since that kind of thrill is hard to top anywhere on Earth, other URI types might seek a truly out-of-this-world experience. For example,

Charles Simonyi, the US billionaire ex-Microsoftie who went from cyberspace-cadet to intrepid explorer of the real thing, splurged $60 million on two trips in a Russian rocket. Before climbing aboard in his space suit, he blew a kiss to his wife standing at the launch pad with, to guard against the Kazakhstan chill, a floor-length fur coat (possibly sable; certainly not a polyester imitation).[34]

Some mean-spirited souls, of course, might criticize this as just the ultra-rich racing for the space-boats to escape an Earth looted and polluted to the point of collapse, leaving the rest of humanity stranded. Others might laud Mr Simonyi as a pioneer in search of new worlds full of resources to exploit, the only way to maintain a system that, to offer an average North American living standard to everyone presently alive, would require six to eight planet Earths. (The mind boggles at the planetary bill for allowing every loving upper-crust couple on Earth to enjoy a weekend on the dark side of the moon – although it might be offset at least a little if some of them decided to stay there permanently.)

Of course, those space-capades took place before Hollywood roundly criticized human excess in the $500 million blockbuster Avatar. That film's devastating depiction of corporate greed and bloody-mindedness in scrambling for mineral wealth is predicted to set off a rush to convert not just cinema technology but even home computers and cellphones to 3D mode.[35] That will accelerate the already existing race to extract rare metals from deep in the Earth, further fouling surrounding areas with mountains of toxic tailings while pushing electronic equipment rendered obsolete onto heaps of e-waste poisoning ecosystems in places too poor or ignorant to refuse the honour of receiving the effluent world's dangerous trash. But no one can say that Hollywood didn't warn them, in 3D no less.

Doubtlessly, too, Mr Simonyi's blastoff served as great advertising for a plan by Biglow Aerospace to launch a space hotel. In the interest of fuel economy, the company proposed that the building be inflatable on arrival in orbit, unlike its prospective clientele who, as people like Leo Hindery or Sandy Weill so well demonstrated, were quite capable of inflating themselves while still on Earth.[36]

In the meantime back on that Earth, while much of the world struggles (or at least puts on a show of so doing) to protect endangered species provided they are sufficiently photogenic – honey bees and horned toads just don't cut it – a subspecies of the world's wealthy, mainly white males, sets off on things like a Grand Slam Safari into deepest, darkest Africa to bag elephants, hippos, giraffes, buffaloes, and leopards, perhaps under the auspices of organizations like Safari Club International that stand tall for wildlife conservation. After all, if too many of those great beasts get killed off, what will members of the club have left to shoot at? Illegal immigrants in Arizona, maybe?

The impulse to possess as private property bits and pieces of nature takes many other forms apart from hunting trophies featuring the biggest horns, sharpest claws, or most dangerous teeth. There are, for example, Lana Marks ("offers the ultimate fashion experience in sophisticated elegance"[37]) handbags fashioned from ostrich and alligator skin – cheapos at $5,000, better quality at $100,000. There are (still) fragrances extracted from endangered species ranging from musk deer to civet cats. There are exotic pets, now popular not just among the rich but also with a growing number of "middle-class" emulators. That category (exotic pets, not middle-class emulators) embraces everything from Madagascar hissing cockroaches to Australian sugar gliders, or even to the Burmese pythons now proliferating in the Florida Everglades, to the consternation of alligators already under siege from falling water levels and agro-chemical sludge.

The rarer and/or odder is one of nature's creations, as shown so vividly with luxury seafood, the more coveted it will be; and, to the super rich, not only is price not a barrier, it is an added attraction. Each time a member of some endangered species ends up gracing the wall of a hedge-fund tycoon's private study or a private-equity partner's dinner table, the resulting notch-up in degree of biological rarity increases the attractiveness of the remaining specimens to human predators, aided and abetted by poachers, smugglers, and crooked dealers who would make a mockery out of existing treaties and conventions designed to stop the traffic if they were not already a bad joke in their own right.

However, most collectaholism manifests itself in more conventional forms, the main concern of the middle sections of this book. These can include everything from Van Gogh paintings to Greco-Roman antiquities, from Byzantine coins to eighteenth-century navigation maps, perhaps even trophy wives or, on occasion, husbands. Except for the last set, these categories represent pinnacles of human achievement in arts and crafts – the exception seems more a monument to modern plastic surgery. Properly speaking they are part of a collective heritage; and many of the most coveted examples survived the decline and fall of their respective times and places because someone understood their importance enough to preserve them for posterity. That, of course, is not really possible with trophy spouses, short of cremating them, then crystallizing them into synthetic diamonds.

Of course, there is nothing new about those amply endowed with money and power seeking rare works of art as personal playthings. And part of the appeal of collectibles like antique jewellery or jade vases has long been that they are easy to toss into a suitcase ahead of cops, tax inspectors, or a hungry mob – although that doesn't work quite so well with Louis Philippe marble-top mahogany commodes. However, more recently, several other factors coalesced to drive prices of collectibles to dizzy new heights.

One, obviously, is the recent accumulation of financial assets, increasing as fast as computers can add zeros to balance sheets, facing a (by definition) limited or even falling physical stock of collectibles. A second driving force is that along with the trend to rapidly rising wealth in the hands of the already rich has come a quantum leap in sheer numbers of those loaded with loot. The emergence of this band of socially insecure parvenus vying for status with an established überclass dramatically intensifies the traditional competition for "bragging rights" that propels the market for collectibles (and other luxuries) forward.

Not to be neglected in keeping prices frothing is a third development – the conversion of collectibles into "non-correlated assets," i.e., things expected to move in a different direction than markets for stocks and bonds. That is why after the 2008 crash Old Master paintings shot up to record highs.[38] Today some collectibles are even "securitized," then traded through offshore mutual funds and tax-haven investment companies, making it impossible to trace the chain of ownership or to collect taxes due. With those kinds of incentives, who wouldn't want to take an equity position in something like a Jeff Koons sculpture, perhaps the one depicting his imaginative sex life with his porn-star-turned-member-of-the-Italian-Parliament paramour?[39]

Those developments also mean that if, not so long ago, true aficionados amassed first-edition books, old musical instruments, or ancient pottery shards as a pleasure in itself, while building up a fund of knowledge that could be tapped for cultural and educational purposes, today the main thing collected might well be speculative gains from a quick flip of an item upon which the owner might never have cast eyes except in a sales catalogue.

On the other hand, maybe it makes more sense for a buyer today not to look too closely. When prices soar for things whose physical availability is strictly limited, clever souls inevitably apply modern crafts to ancient arts in an effort to bridge the gap between demand and supply.

There is nothing new about what would today be viewed as crooked activities in the high-end collectibles business, although in times past they might have been regarded as just one more day at the atelier. When ancient Greek statuary became the rage in imperial Rome, contemporary sculptors quickly learned how to knock the odd hand or even an arm off their creations, then roll them in dirt to age them suitably. Early modern

Europe saw a plague of ecclesiastical entrepreneurs who wandered the town-fair circuit peddling vials of Christ's blood. Peter Paul Reubens was so notorious for having his students do the work that some of his clients insisted on written contracts that he at least dab a few details on canvases for which they were paying top rates. The early twentieth century saw boatloads of American upstarts off to England to buy for their homes eighteenth-century furniture (all by Thomas Chippendale, of course) that had probably been hammered together a week or so before they docked. And so forth.

However, the recent long boom sending prices to dizzy heights induced what seems to be an epidemic of fakery, of theft from private and public collections, of forging authentication documents, of looting archeological sites, and of smuggling the results with help from people who know how to apply the collectible world's equivalent of plastic surgery to an item on the run. In effect, the illegal end of the collectibles market seems like a distorted mirror image of the legal one (or is it the other way around?), and those responsible for the games can count themselves as simply the ultimate servants of the same "market forces" their ultra-rich clientele did so much to bring to fruition.

This is not to suggest that every high-end art or antiquities dealer is a crook. Far from it; that characterization cannot even be applied to most investment bankers, harder to believe though that may be. Apart from the fact that the lower-price ends of those and similar trades also have their share of shysters and charlatans, the point is that, in an economy where wealth accrues so rapidly to an upstart class, the bidding war for choice items that convey social status, and the way that such a contest inspires hordes of wannabes and wanna-haves, creates an atmosphere in which the shades of grey (normal enough in any business where personal trust at least partially displaces written contracts and where professional judgments are highly subjective) tend to darken enough to periodically spill over into the black end of the spectrum. In a sense all participants are joint captives not just of the emergence of parallel bubbles and the sky-high returns they promise but simultaneously of today's dramatic shortening of the time horizons over which financial and commercial decisions, legal and illegal alike, are made and their outcomes valued. Also at play is the general triumph over a broader sense of social responsibility of a dog-eat-many-smaller-dogs mindset, cheered on from both the gilded pulpit and the ivory tower as their respective occupants invoke either the will of god or the magic of the market as a rationalization for a gross and growing disparity of income and wealth.

Whatever the actual extent of theft, fakery, or smuggling in the high-end collectibles business, the biggest racket today will almost certainly lead to a flattering press release rather than a stern "wanted" poster. It involves bidding up prices, securing inflated appraisals, donating acquisitions to museums or other public collections for fat tax deductions, then using the profits to repeat the process, all quite legally of course. After all, isn't that what the "free market" is all about?

Idolatry aside, there is actually nothing inherently wrong with "the market" per se as a system for allocating goods and services, provided certain things are understood about it and certain constraints are imposed upon it. The market system is just a practical device chosen by (or forced on) some people in some places at some times, including now the great majority of humanity, for which there have been plenty of alternatives tried with various degrees of success by different peoples in different places at different times. Contrary to academic fantasies, markets have no intrinsic self-regulatory properties, except to the extent that left unchecked they routinely self-regulate into disaster, taking countless innocent bystanders down with them. Markets, too, need to be restricted to those spheres of activity in which they can "deliver the goods" in a fair and equitable way. No one, for example, ought to be permitted under the pretense of freedom of the marketplace to extort money from the public for use of what was once common property or for what ought to still be collective services. Yet that is precisely what happens when public infrastructure is sold off or mineral and timber rights given away or the very air waves handed over to communications conglomerates. Nor ought any market participant be allowed to privatize, enclose, and ultimately "securitize" things that the market had no role in creating. Yet the spread of just that practice has led to efforts to commodify in bits and pieces preparatory to sale to the highest bidder just about everything on the grounds that, for example, the most effective way to protect a country's cultural heritage is to have it locked in a display case with a state-of-the-art security system in some billionaire's mansion – or, in a similar spirit, that the most "efficient" way to protect marine biodiversity is to auction off the oceans, one cubic metre at a time, to fish-finger manufacturers.

Not least, no market of any scale or significance ought to be left free of the scrutiny of a genuinely independent and properly informed regulatory authority. Too bad that in an era increasingly marked by the proliferation of fact-free policies and brain-free politicians independent and informed regulatory systems are becoming something that would fetch a fine price on markets specializing in rare collectibles or endangered species.

To be fair to the movers and shakers of Generation-B (for Bubble) and their dependents – be they movie stars, pop idols, upscale clothing

designers, purveyors of luxury accessories, golf pros, top-end restau-
rateurs, private helicopter pilots, art consultants, high-priced fashion
models, sports legends flaunting the latest branded gimmicks, exotic pet
suppliers, interior decorators, plastic surgeons (exterior redecorators?),
trophy spouses, and politicians on the make and the take – do more
than just throw away money in an orgy of selfish exhibitionism. Some
are deeply concerned about helping the world's less fortunate, if only by
reducing their birthrate.[40] That kind of commitment shines through in
events like the one in Britain's Old Royal Navy College in June 2008,
when 1,100 people, including the cream of London's hedge-fund crowd,
paid up to £10,000 each for a "war child" charity dinner featuring performances by Stevie Wonder (later named a UN Messenger of Peace)
and Tony Blair (later accused of war crimes that created a fair share
of the event's nominal beneficiaries). After champagne and a gourmet
meal featuring typical war-child fare like "poached Shetland ray wings
on a cushion of Kent apple tapioca," guests bid for thrills donated by
prominent supporters of the occasion. These included a new work of
art by Damien Hirst (a heart-shaped collage of wings torn from but-
terflies) that brought in nearly a million pounds. That item bested by
a factor of five the winning bid of £200,000 for a Fiat 500 decorated
by Tracey Emin, star of the Young British Artists school and creator
of, among other famous works, "I've Got It All."[41] This features the
creatrice sitting with legs spread, apparently shoving handfuls of money
up her private parts, perhaps a dress rehearsal for her recent decision to
move to the continent to avoid British income taxes on her contributions
to global culture.[42]

But there was much more: for example, a weekend cliff-top "shooting party" that the area's birds must have found particularly charitable,
and a tour by private jet of France's Château Cheval Blanc and Château
d'Yquem vineyards. And fetching £450,000 at auction was a bit part in a
new movie featuring Uma Thurman, girlfriend of the French hedge-fund
billionaire who organized the event.[43] That gentleman himself at one
point took centre stage to remind guests of their obligations as "keepers
of the world's wealth," however the world whose wealth was being kept
felt about it. Those assembled, he noted, had a "responsibility to come
together and give to our common humanity."

Perhaps it was an unfortunate error of syntax by someone whose
first language was other than English. However, referring to recipients
of charity as "common humanity" at a time of massive looting of the
public purse by a financially flatulent class trying desperately to keep
more stale air from being let out of its over-inflated spare tire, might con-

jure up memories of another French resident's dismissive outburst: "Let them eat cake!" Now, though, the advice might be to chow down on the "truffle ice cream with hazelnut pane cotta and chocolate gnocchi" that ended the feast portion of the gala evening.[44]

PART ONE

Razzle Dazzle

1

The Gold Diggers: Precious Metal, Poisoned Chalice

Imagine a City of London hedge-fund manager en route to work one morning in the back seat of his chauffeured Rolls-Royce Phantom. It's actually a modest car, only $450,000. To maintain appearances in difficult times, today the financier decided to leave at home the Bugatti Veyron (sold by invitation only) that, at full throttle, will empty a 100 litre tank in a little under twelve minutes. As the cityscape rushes past the side windows, he seems to take no heed of all the history embodied in the old buildings, so attentive is he to numbers flashing on his 24 karat MacBook Pro.[1] Fascinating though the rows and columns racing across the screen might be as Tokyo shuts down and Frankfurt opens, he cannot resist the impulse to close the computer lid periodically and stare reverentially at his own reflection on a solid gold case that he lovingly burnishes with a velvet cloth several times a day.

Objects fashioned from gold are more than simple luxuries; they are passports to another world – perhaps because gold, both the lust to possess it and the technology to extract it, has done so much to turn the present one into a hellhole.[2] The very word "gold" conjures up dazzling images: a medieval alchemist muttering incantations over a bubbling cauldron while his hushed audience awaits a glittering transmutation; Spanish conquistadores slaughtering America's aboriginal peoples, plundering their temples, then melting stunning artifacts into crude bars; masked highwaymen waving down gilded carriages at pistolpoint to relieve passengers of purses bursting with coin; shifty Levantine traders sitting cross-legged before heaps of dazzling gold chain while water pipes gurgle in the background; big-city sharpies in top hats hawking claims to empty sand while gold fever rages in the boondocks. And who, stuck in a minimum-wage job in a dumpy town with foul weather, doesn't fantasize about dipping a tin plate into a babbling brook surrounded by pristine rain forest to haul up gravel laced with nuggets the size of pigeon eggs?

Today, despite new goldfields coming onstream and modern alchemical arts extracting more from old ones, every ounce finds a ready market. The historical images have merely been airbrushed with modern tones: gold-scam artists troll middle-class suburbs for suckers; Brazil's garampeiros, participants in history's greatest gold rush, massacre Yanomani Indians in the Amazon; robbers in a record bullion heist truss up guards in the Brinks warehouse at London's Heathrow Airport; Dubai gold dealers stuff smuggling boats with "ten-tola" bars (rounded to avoid damaging delicate parts of the courier's internal anatomy) for a quick run across the Indian Ocean to feed the ravenous gold market on the other side; and stock touts hyperventilate over yet another rediscovery of King Solomon's mines, the most peripatetic motherlode in history.[3] Meanwhile the only stuff those wide-eyed dreamers manning cash registers at the local discount mall are likely to get their hands on has been crushed, milled, smelted, poured into bars, melted down again, further refined, cast into smaller bars, stamped and numbered, then adulterated with tin, silver, or copper, before being molded into tiny wedding bands – while the rain forest has been flattened by bulldozers and the brook now bubbles with mercury or cyanide.

In days gone by, it was easy to explain the attraction of gold. To the ancient Egyptians gold was their supreme god, Ra (the sun), come down from the heavens. Silver from the moon embodied a lesser deity. Since the pharaohs were descendants of Ra, they staked the first claim, both at home and in territories they conquered and plundered.[4] In the Inca Empire, too, thousands of years after and thousands of kilometres distant from ancient Egypt, the sun was number 1, gold was its terrestrial embodiment, and the Lord Inca and his family, being divinely born, commandeered as their birthright all the gold – and all the silver, the tears of the moon.[5]

More prosaically, great empires intent on conquest saw gold and silver as "the sinews of war," the strategic reserve to consolidate and expand state power. From ancient times, too, leaders fearing overthrow took pains to accumulate a nest egg of precious metals to ensure a comfortable exile or finance a comeback. In recent decades stories about (usually mythical) hoards have swirled around deposed potentates ranging from Indonesia's Achmed Sukarno to Ethiopia's Haile Selassie, from the Philippines' Ferdinand Marcos to Ghana's Kwame Nkrumah, who led the country to independence in 1957, only to be ousted in a 1966 coup. That kind of mystique stirs ever more interest in gold, sparks treasure hunts around the world, and gives con artists a great selling point.

Take, for example, John Ackah-Blay Miezah, who claimed to have been close to the president of Ghana through his years in exile. During those dark days, Nkrumah trusted his protegé with a secret: Nkrumah in his later years in office had lost faith in the people around him and sent for safe-keeping enormous amounts of the country's legendary gold and diamond wealth to Swiss and Liechtenstein bank accounts held in the name of the Cayman Islands-based Oman-Ghana Trust Fund. John, it seemed, was named sole custodian of the trust. Initially worth $150,000,000, by the time John began pounding pavements, the value had swollen to about $1.5 billion. John needed investors, he said, to cover the expenses of meeting the terms of the trust, particularly to bribe politicians back home to secure a Ghanaian diplomatic passport with a special number that was the key to opening the vaults. In return investors received "notes" drawn on the fund promising a 1,000 percent return; and John put whatever money he coaxed out of them to good use in his London exile, riding around in luxury limos with private security guards and running up bills at fancy hotels.

For John to be at Nkrumah's deathbed would have been quite an honour for a teenager. But at that moment he was actually serving time in a Pennsylvania prison for posing as a diplomat and stiffing a hotel for a $2,644. A few years later he again faced charges, this time for using a fraudulently obtained university degree and trying to cash $250,000 in stolen bank drafts. He fled the US ahead of the new arrest warrant. Back home he was sentenced to seven years for fraud and bribery. Released under curiously shaded circumstances, he jetted off to London to resume high living, this time, he said, with the coveted Ghanaian diplomatic passport. After reassuring his investors that the banks were about to unlock the vault doors, he "died," vanishing from the face of the Earth.[6] Too bad. Today his "notes" promising fat returns from a future share in a nonexistent treasure might be hot items on markets that specialize in things like synthetic collateralized debt obligations.[7]

Of course, unlike Ghana's fabulous horde, today most gold extracted from a stingy and jealous Earth doesn't just get stuffed back underground into the secret bank accounts of former heads of state. A small, declining part is used by industry, the only function for gold that may even partly justify the misery and destruction its production causes. By far the biggest chunk ends up in jewellery, and an increasing proportion gets squirreled away by prudent individuals with no aspiration for high office. To some, gold is just an extra layer of financial security for tough times. (Witness the booming business of Swiss smelters in melting down gold jewellery and watches sold off in the wake of the 2008 market crash.[8]) Others may see gold as a means to collect handsome (preferably tax-free) capital gains, although over the long haul baseball cards have probably done better. Some others afflicted by possessive-compulsive disorder may want nothing more than to descend into a secret, well-sealed room after dinner each night to roll around on a heap of gold coins. Then there are those, burdened with a prosecution complex, who figure that a secret cache of precious metals could help them to beat a hasty retreat when cops instead of opportunity come knocking on the door. Not least are those cautious souls who hide a little stash under the floorboards of their log cabin in the hills, along with shotgun shells and a year's supply of Hamburger Helper, while awaiting Armageddon. And how often have dinner guests in elegant homes been regaled with tales of their hosts escaping death and despoilation by fleeing across borders with several generations of family silver along with a strong-box packed with gold jewellery? The real explanation for their opulence, and for their abrupt decision to decamp – that for decades they rent-racked the peasantry, cheated on their taxes, and smuggled cash to Switzerland in body bags – might not sit so well with the Château Lafite Rothschild Pauillac premier grand cru.

Some buyers of gold today may even be seduced by the old mystery of its celestial origins, albeit translated into terms appropriate to a secular age. At the start of the millennium, when the market was not exactly sparkling, the World Gold Council, the main industry lobby, decided to revive gold's fortunes with a media blitz that claimed, in blatant disregard for basic physics, that gold simultaneously captured the warmth of the sun and represented "the new cool." Gold, the council also declared, embodied nothing less than the sheer "joy and happiness derived from human experiences."[9] Tell that to the untold millions who, over the millennia, endured miserable lives and agonizing deaths moiling for the stuff.[10]

INHUMAN EXPERIENCES?

In ancient Egypt, criminals, war captives, and others who offended the regime (along with their kin) were chained in the mines to work day and night, guarded by mercenaries whose foreign language was a safeguard against conspiracy or corruption. The Romans, too, initially relied on captives made slaves but came to prefer a permanent hereditary subclass of people who were born, lived, and (shortly) died in the mines. The Inca Empire was more benign – commoners had to work the mines only part of the year although shirking was a capital offense. When the Spanish conquered the Americas, they showed much more imagination. They stole gold trinkets from the natives; robbed tombs; forced aboriginal chiefs under threat of mutilation or death to pay a fixed tribute in gold; herded native peoples en masse into mines to extract silver and gold; and when the supply of Indians seemed exhausted, replaced them with black slaves.[11]

Of course, it would be quite wrong to equate the barbarism of primitive societies and the bloodthirsty lust of their warrior-kings for gold and silver with the actions of the overseas pioneers of European civilization. As people whose sense of morality equals their knowledge of history so often contend, Europeans did not conquer and pillage – they "discovered" and, just incidentally, liberated sterile hordes of treasure, transforming it from the inert stuff of idols adorning heathen temples into healthy bank balances pulsating with the magic of compound interest.[12]

Gold most commonly starts as a deposit from superheated water into a quartz vein a few miles below the Earth's surface, forming a motherlode. Over time, wind and water free the gold, then break it into ever smaller particles that sink into the sand and mud of a riverbed. With more time, rock debris accumulates on top, eventually turning the alluvial into a fossil deposit. Whether the gold is embedded in hard rock, buried under a pile of gravel, or just precipitated shallowly into mud and sand dictates the difficulty of extraction. That in turn determines in good part who does the extracting, and how.

At the start, native peoples may quietly exploit a living riverbed, perhaps for centuries, taking out visible gold with shovels, sieves, and pans, to fashion into ornaments or to trade for corn and beans. Over long periods of time nature may replace some of the lost gold with material freshly eroded from a motherlode.

Then come outsiders, alone or in small partnerships, to sweep away indigenous peoples by force or disease, then deploy sluicing machinery that fouls rivers and poisons the surrounding ecosystem to extract perhaps 30 percent of the available gold, mainly in gold dust, out of the sand and gravel. They lead an ephemeral existence. If not carried off by malnutrition, malaria, or mercury poisoning, they fall prey to bandits, claim jumpers, or debt collectors. The pay is usually lousy, too.

After "free miners" come junior companies, happy to ride out market spikes and plunges, or even to make them happen by salting the occasional ore sample in order to raise capital to finance a risky, if potentially lucrative, venture.[13] Convincing the host government that their techniques will retrieve far more gold, they arrange for the national military, local police, or their own security forces to chase away alluvial miners and expropriate nearby farmers. Extending their search beyond the river to try to locate fossil deposits buried long before, they tear off the "overburden" (of living soil full of micro-organisms, plants and insects), grind rock into gravel, then drench it with toxic chemicals to amalgamate tiny, invisible gold particles.

Finally, giant international corporations may muscle in. Financially well connected, the majors announce finds just fast enough to keep their stock price steadily rising and their investors happy. Politically conservative, they try to avoid public scandal – better to put members of the president's family on the payroll than to take the chance of being caught bankrolling a coup d'état. They might simply buy out the juniors; or they might promise the host government a bigger cut of the spoils for public coffers or private retirement accounts – or both. Big companies alone have the financial resources and technical means to follow the trail back through geological history to (maybe) find a motherlode in hard-rock formations that might be hundreds of miles away and thousands of metres deep.[14]

FIELDS OF DREAMS

The struggle pitting natives against newcomers, independent miners against companies, juniors against majors, with the government (if there is one) content to cheer the victors and collect a small cut of the loot, occurs across the contemporary world. However the modern multisided struggles over control of gold fields probably first showed up in modern guise in eighteenth-century Brazil. There goldfields in jungle areas were so far-flung that efforts by Portugal, the imperial power, to keep a lid on things quickly broke down. Even properly licensed miners (whites only) sold gold to unlicensed buyers (who paid no taxes) and bought contraband goods (that paid no customs duty), while officials went into business with the miners they were supposed to regulate. Trafficking was made easier by priests who, despite repeated edicts from their bishops, added illegal gold trading to their other duties like usury, embezzlement of tithes, overcharging for clerical services, trafficking in slaves, and selling contraband supplies. Apart from operating illegal smelters, they were notorious as couriers. Exempt from customs searches and ignoring the supposed advice of Jesus on fiscal propriety, they saw tax evasion as so much a part of their ecclesiastical duties that some allegedly preached the virtues of it from their pulpits.[15] If they boarded a ship with gold (or diamonds), they could claim to be trustees for estates of well-to-do members of their flocks who had died in Brazil, or to be taking back dowries sent by successful businessmen to accompany their daughters to convents back home.[16]

Meanwhile miners and their black slaves – compared to the Spanish colonies, surviving local Indians were fewer and widely scattered in deep jungle – died in droves from starvation, leprosy, and malaria; and a lush, verdant area had its watercourses choked and diverted, its trees chopped down, and its soil eroded and poisoned.[17]

The next century witnessed a series of epic gold rushes – California, the Fraser, Western Australia, Siberia, the Klondike, and South Africa. The political and geological context differed in each, but the consequences were much the same. Each major site became an ecological disaster zone; each rush produced clashes with native peoples leaving a legacy of distrust that continues to poison relations to this day; and each saw the calloused hands of free miners steadily displaced by the manicured grip of ever-bigger companies.

Generally a rush starts with the discovery of alluvial gold, then graduates to fossil deposits or perhaps shallow quartz mines. The shift means much higher capital costs. That squeezes out individuals or small partnerships, reducing miners to wage labour, putting more power in the hands of financiers, and opening mining areas to swindles by company promoters. The beneficiaries might also include a plague of lawyers to "litigate" over mining claims using perjury and blackmail.[18]

The nineteenth century, too, saw the emergence of a class of itinerant prospectors who, as easily accessed gold disappeared from one location, moved on to another, bringing their challenges to constituted authority and notions of quick "justice" with them.[19] But for a brief flurry in the Klondike, last in line was South Africa's Witwatersrand. There the gold-bearing material was of low quality but spread over an enormous area. The rush petered out fast; but the giant companies that replaced free miners became and remained the dominant players in the world gold market until late in the twentieth century. At that point they were challenged by new behemoths from the US, Australia, and even Canada. That is not because the latter struck some hitherto unknown motherlode of entrepreneurial talent. Rather it is because its stock exchanges have long been more open to precious-metal mining swindles than those of the US, and because its mining companies are so powerful that, apart from lavish government subsidies, they have long benefitted from laws and legal procedures bent in their favour to intimidate and silence critics.[20]

When the string of great nineteenth-century rushes ended, sages insisted that the world would never see their like again. Then in Brazil in the 1970s, alluvial tin miners, pushed out of their diggings by US mining companies, moved deeper into the Amazon and discovered gold nuggets of record-breaking size. History's greatest rush was on, peaking at perhaps a million miners in about two thousand different camps, spilling over to Venezuela, Colombia, and Guyana and touching off a new epidemic of gold fever that still ravages the world from Australia to Zimbabwe.[21] It shows up in Indonesia's Sulweisi, where free miners, thrown off their diggings by Australian multinationals, surround the area on motorcycles waiting for blasts, then rush down to swipe chunks of conveniently broken-up gold-bearing material. It shows up in northern Nigeria, where hundreds of children have been poisoned from villagers unearthing lead-contaminated ore.[22] It even shows up in contemporary South Africa. After many long decades of virtual slavery in the country's gold fields, the end of Apartheid seemed to promise to the black proletariat freedom to be full participants in the emerging free-market economy – although the "illegal" miners gunned down by police at a corporate gold mine owned by relatives of Nelson Mandela and current president Jacob Zuma might have a different view of what the transition to "black majority rule" really meant.[23]

Although alluvial gold attracts independents all over the world, for sheer numbers none of the other modern gold rushes can hold a candle to that of Brazil. Most of its garampeiros (informal miners) operate alone or in small partnerships, using little beyond shovels and sluice boxes: others graduate to steam-powered machinery and diesel-fuelled bulldozers. Some remain independent; some form coops; most end up working for those who either staked claims first or hit it lucky enough to buy out others. Either way few see more than survival money. As always, the real beneficiaries of a gold rush traffic in claims, supply food and capital equipment on credit, buy gold, run brothels, peddle booze and drugs, or hire out private armies as enforcers.[24] As always, the main losers are, apart from nature itself, native peoples, particularly in this case the Yanomani, the last major unassimilated tribe in Latin America. Miners used to brag that they learned how to deal with Indians by watching American cowboy movies.[25]

Initially Brazil's government was delighted. With the country mired in economic crisis, the rush drew off desperate farmers and unemployed workers, held out the lure of hard currency to placate foreign creditors, and promised to consolidate Brazil's claims on the vast Amazon region, much the way the Siberian rush had for czarist Russia in its Asian interior. But soon the government looked askance at the ultimate free-market economy in the heart of the Amazon. Miners made their own law and kept it scant. Gold-rush country saw thousands of landings and takeoffs per month without radar or emergency equipment or safety inspections. The same light planes that brought in cocaine, booze, and tax-free tobacco smuggled out most of the gold.[26] Some left via Paraguay, premier contraband centre of Latin America; enough passed through Uruguay, the continent's main bank-secrecy haven, that it was

soon exporting annually twenty to thirty tons without risking the ecological consequences of a single mine on its turf.[27]

Typically garampeiros use technology that in principle has not changed
radically since Roman, perhaps even ancient Egyptian, times, and one so
appalling in terms of health and environmental impact that even the
Romans briefly banned it. Water pressure forces mud and sand from
riverbeds and banks through mercury-coated sieves. Gold dust bonds to
the mercury, while the rest of the material washes into rivers, depleting
the sunlight and oxygen necessary for fish and plant life. Then miners
heat the amalgam to vaporize the mercury, leaving flecks of gold behind.
Dealers who buy the product may submit the gold to another burning for further purification. Leakages are common; and open containers
vent most of the mercury into the air. It blows around, dissolving in rain
before falling back to the ground. Biologically converted into methyl
mercury by the action of sulfate-reducing bacteria or other microbes in
low oxygen environments, it enters the food chain to be absorbed by
animals, fish, and people, the concentration increasing by a factor of
about ten each step up the food chain. Meanwhile bigger players use
high-powered water cannons to blast away surface soil along with its
thin layer of vegetation to expose gold-bearing rock. Apart from fouling
waterways with waste oil and forming pools of stagnant water as breeding grounds for malaria- and dengue-carrying mosquitoes, the practice
washes into streams mercury accumulated naturally in the soil over
thousands of years.[28]

Watching all this were/are big mining companies who, in exchange
for Brazil kicking out independent miners from prime territory (only to
move deeper into the Amazon to repeat the cycle), promised to treble gold
yields, pledged to pay (some) taxes, guaranteed that their gold would follow official channels, and supported from the depths of their ecologically
sensitive souls a worldwide campaign to end to the mercury plague. After
all, they had something else up their gold cufflinked silk sleeves.

PICK YOUR POISON

Early in 2003, more than 1,000 delegates from 130 countries at a UN
environment conference in Nairobi endorsed a global crackdown on
mercury use modelled on the Montreal Protocol that phased out ozone-
depleting substances. By then, gold mining was directly releasing about
460 tons of mercury per year, about two thirds into the atmosphere,
the rest into soil and water.[29] Even though data from the Center for
Disease Control in the US indicated that one in twelve American women

of child-bearing age had unsafe mercury levels, the Bush regime blocked efforts for binding restrictions.[30] True, the Obama Administration joined 139 other countries to pledge cooperation in stopping atmospheric emissions.[31] However its main concern was mercury from coal burned to generate electricity, and the US change of heart may have reflected lobbying from the western US coal industry, whose product emits less mercury than its eastern rivals. Not only did the meeting sidestep the threat from mercury released indirectly from the soil, rather than directly from retorts during gold mining, but it made no attempt to address the continued leakage from old mines, tens, perhaps hundreds of thousands of which are scattered over the US, encouraged by an 1872 law that permitted companies and inviduals to buy public land for next to nothing, mine it to their wallet's content, and pay no royalties to the state. Needless to add, back then there were also no environmental restrictions. California alone in a century of production used about 1,300 tons of mercury. And there are many thousands more mines abandoned in Canada, Australia, Russia, and South Africa.[32]

Anyway, this time no one could fairly impute the reluctance of successive US regimes to address the issue seriously just to cozy relations with mining companies. Canadian governments long ago sold their political souls, for what they were worth, to big metal. Australia, probably the only country where billionaires wearing pearl necklaces join street demos to protest higher taxes, may now be worse. It recently capitulated before threats from Big Gold (that described the "discussions" as "very constructive") to largely shelve a proposed new tax on mining companies.[33] However, to be fair to Big Gold, when it comes to wreaking environmental havoc and ruining human health, corporate miners genuinely dislike mercury – they prefer cyanide.

As shallow alluvial deposits are depleted, attention shifts to deeper sources where gold is present only microscopically. First, mining companies strip off perhaps seventy tons of overburden per ounce of gold ultimately recovered. Next, they haul out actual ore (about thirty more tons per ounce) to be crushed and ground, with particles physically separated in a giant gravity concentrator. Then crushed ore is sprayed with sodium cyanide that amalgamates the gold. The amalgam runs into collection tanks, leaving heaps of tailings in which exposed metal sulfides react with the ambient humidity to form acid runoff. The gold is separated; and the cyanide solution is drained away. The gold is smelted and cast into crude ingots that are later refined to reduce impurities to acceptable limits. The cyanide process is popular because it removes (so the companies claim) up to 99 percent of the gold; it can extract formerly inaccessible gold from tailings abandoned on older sites; and the cyanide solution can be reused or neutralized.[34] That part of the theory was tested at the Baia Mare mine in Romania in 2001 when melting snow and ice raised the level of a tailings pond enough to overflow a dam and spill into a river flowing into the Danube. The cyanide-laced water reached 1,600 miles, killing thousands of tons of fish and threatening the water supply of millions of people.[35] Just to improve things further, in autumn 2010 yet another tailings pond (dimensions 300 by 450 metres) burst, this time in Hungary holding back the heavy-metal contaminated red sludge from an alumina plant, sending it down towards the Danube.[36]

Cyanide-based technology was invented in Scotland in the late nineteenth century for use in South Africa, and later perfected by the US Department of Mines. However, its true commercial pioneer was Newmont Mining Corporation. Active around the world, its most important recent venture has been in Peru, a country that may now surpass Brazil as Latin America's leading gold producer. Like Brazil, Peru had plenty of informal miners drawn from the ranks of the urban poor, the rural dispossessed, or the refugees from areas torn by nearly two decades of civil war. As in Brazil, they were often poisoned by mercury, and their meagre earnings enriched thieves and swindlers along with drug peddlers, pimps, and bootleggers. As did Brazil's, Peru's government decided that big companies were more "efficient." So it allowed transnationals to extract potentially billions in revenues without the nuisance of royalty payments.[37] To clear their way, the government sent security forces to chase away free miners, then seized land with derisory compensation from local farmers, some later protesting that they thought they were lending, not selling the land, and that they had been assured they would be able to continue farming. Everything was ready but for a bitter legal fight between Newmont and a French competitor over who would secure the concession. When Newmont won, its rival released tapes showing Peru's ex-spy chief and long-time CIA asset, currently in prison for drug trafficking and gunrunning, telling one of the judges to decide in favour of Newmont. The US Justice Department launched a bribery investigation, then dropped it when the Peruvian government refused to cooperate.[38]

In short order, Newmont's Minera Yanacocha, covering 22,000 acres, achieved the status of second largest gold mine in the world. (Gold majors compete not just for profitability or total production, but for who can claim to have dug the biggest hole, destroyed the most rainforest, and created the largest heap of toxic tailings.) Showing a profit rate double the industry average, Newmont blasted apart mountains held sacred by local peoples, hauled ore to giant heap-leach facilities, dissolved it in cyanide solution, then drained the residue into collection ponds, leaving

behind the usual mountains of toxic tailings. Runoff fouled local waterways, killing fish or even horses and cows who drank from them; while
the site was littered with old cyanide containers that some uninformed
residents used to store water. Although the mine uses cyanide to amalgamate gold, mercury is its secondary product. In 2000, badly sealed
containers spilled 150 kilograms, poisoning about one thousand people.
When Newmont tried to expand onto an adjacent tract, it met mass
protests, busted up by police with tear gas. In subsequent forays its sur-
veyors had to be protected by police wearing black masks (to prevent
reprisals) and toting automatic rifles.[39]

Of course, not all governments were as accommodating. In Indonesia,
Newmont faced charges of dumping mercury and arsenic into a bay in
the Indonesian state of Sulweisi, a place where the company once had
to evacuate its personnel because "irresponsible people" forced off their
land to make way for the mining company set up roadblocks.[40] But a
court acquitted the company. When the government appealed the decision, Newmont threatened to stop investing if the judgment finally went
against it.[41] The next year it lined up with other transnational giants in
the country to warn that passage of a new mining law might lead to a
collective shut down. In other circumstances, the first threat might be
called obstruction of justice, the second blackmail; in the gold mining
world, they are sound corporate strategy to protect shareholder interests.

Of course, it is necessary to protect business reputations. As a
result in 2007, after its acquittal in Indonesia, a senior executive of
Newmont sued the New York Times and one of its major reporters for
claiming that the company had grossly polluted the bay with its by then
defunct mine.[42]

Newmont also owned as a joint venture with Toronto's Barrick Gold,
Kalgoorie Consolidated, Australia's biggest gold mine – AKA the Super
Pit. Built to take in more than one hundred old underground mines,
Super Pit is among the largest holes ever dug by human enterprise. Into
and out of it, 240 ton trucks run 24 hours a day, 365 days a year. While
blasts shatter the walls of the local population's houses – those the company had not already bought and bulldozed – the industry thrived, turning out 700,000 ounces in 2009 alone. As to the impact of the world
economic crisis, Superpit's general manager was upbeat. "Global financial crisis?" he observed. "We watched it on our new plasma-screen TVs
and heard about it as we drove to work in out big new cars."[43]

Despite industry threats to close operations, repeated cyanide spills
finally forced the government to act, inflicting on a company a $37,000
fine – "the equivalent of two 240-tonne trucks loaded with low-grade
ore."[44] Still, big miners can claim in their own defense that they follow the

International Cyanide Management Code, whose main purpose seems to be to insulate companies from civil lawsuits and regulatory action.[45]

Although Newmont was a leader in the commercialization of the cyanide process, Robert Friedland brought it the most notoriety. An ex-hippie who came of age with the LSD generation, with an interest in Oriental mysticism, tree-farming, and primal-scream therapy, he started his mining career on borrowed money with a Nevada gold mine named after Hanuman, the Hindu monkey god, then folded it into Galactic Resources, a shell he picked up from a company broker on the Vancouver Stock Exchange, back when the VSE was struggling hard to live up to its reputation as the mining scam capital of the world. His Nevada mine was a bust, but Galactic had another asset, Colorado's Summitville Mine, a property that had a history of actually producing gold. Although another company had already rejected further exploitation as uneconomic, investors put up tens of millions, Galactic stock soaring from pennies to $36.00 before collapsing again to pennies, then to nothing. Before that happened, Galactic set up the largest cyanide facility then in existence, on a mountain no less, ignoring advice that severe winter conditions would play havoc with its operation. The first cyanide spill came five days after startup. After six years of cyanide leaks along with dumping nearly a ton of heavy metals daily into the Alamosa River, killing all aquatic life over a distance of seventeen miles, Summitville achieved the official status of being one of the top ten toxic waste sites in the US. Colorado authorities took no action for fear of loss of jobs and tax revenues. But the federal Environmental Protection Agency slapped Galactic with a cleanup bill that might have gone over $200 million if the company had not taken the precaution of declaring bankruptcy. Friedland had already resigned; so clearly he was not to blame. Instead, Friedland himself sued ten companies involved in the design, engineering, construction, and financing of the mine, along with the historic owners for contamination dating back to the late 1880s. Eventually the former environmental manager for the site was indicted for intentionally dumping lead and cyanide directly into streams.[46] Friedland, for his part, insisted he could no more be expected to know what had been going on at Summitville than the chairman of Exxon about some "pipe breaks in an oilfield in Azerbaijan."[47] Friedland eventually settled with the EPA, receiving immunity from further liability in exchange for $27.5 million paid into a cleanup fund.[48] He could afford it.

After leaving Galactic, Friedland staked a claim in Newfoundland to what he modestly called "the richest nickel, cooper and cobalt deposit on the planet Earth," boosting his shares from $4 to $167 in two years by luring two mining giants into a bidding war, to the subsequent regret of the winner. He also made a brief foray into Venezuelan gold that saw five thousand indigenous people protesting an invasion of their land. And his Golden Star Resources helped to develop what was claimed for a time to be yet another second largest mine in South America.

In Guyana as in Brazil, Amazon gold attracted independent miners using simple tools and mercury-based technology. As in Brazil, almost everything collected was smuggled out of the country.[49] So Guyana's government created a state monopoly to buy all gold, collect taxes, and license miners. Then, under pressure from the IMF and World Bank to open the interior to transnational gold and timber companies, it invited in Omai Gold Mines Limited, a joint venture of Cambior, a Canadian multinational with 60 percent of the shares, Friedland's Golden Star Resources holding 35 percent, and the Guyana government taking a princely 5 percent. So much gold flowed from the Omai site that it soon became the country's single largest export earner. So much cyanide flowed back into the ecosystem that rivers essential to the lives of aboriginal peoples showed counts well above allowable North American standards even before 1995. That year 3.2 million cubic metres of effluent from the tailings pond broke though a badly constructed dam. A Commission of Inquiry insisted that there was no criminal negligence by the company, while consultants who investigated after the fact, having apparently missed seeing newspaper photos of dead fish floating on the river, insisted that the cyanide-laced water had posed no serious danger. That would have been a tough sell to the People's Temple, an American religious cult, of whom nine hundred members committed suicide by drinking cyanide in Guyana in 1978.

True, sodium cyanide is photodegradable. But much ends up under tropical canopies or in deep water where the sun's rays cannot penetrate. Furthermore when sulfides in crushed rock are exposed to water and air, the resulting acid, along with heavy metals it dissolves, flows into the same rivers and lakes, destroying aquatic life. That assumes, of course, any fish have survived the suspended solids from the tailings heaps that clog gills, reduce oxygen supplies, smother eggs, and disrupt feeding.

Of course, big mining companies may take preventive action: for example, they might run giant pipes to carry toxic solutions away from the mine site and dump them, along with contaminated solid tailings, into the ocean, wrecking the coastal ecology instead of or in addition to the interior one, something that the Indonesian government accused Newmont of doing in the Bay of Buyat in Sulweisi. Meanwhile their refineries, both onsite and further afield, vent sulfur dioxide and nitrous oxides into the atmosphere, which fall again as acid rain.

Back in Guyana, Cambior offered each local plaintiff a compensation package of G$10,000, the equivalent of about $100, in exchange for a waiver freeing the company of further claims.[50] An attempt by 23,000 of them to obtain legal redress failed in Québec in 1997 when a judge declared the proper legal forum to be Guyana. But in 2006 a $2 billion class-action suit in Guyana was thrown out by a court that awarded costs to Cambior's Omai subsidiary. Anyway, Robert Friedland had sold his shares long before and gotten busy, first in Burma working out gold-mining deals with the ruling generals, then in Mongolia where his gold projects led to protestors burning him in effigy and camping out in the capital for three weeks.[51]

PARADISE LOST?

The little bit of gold all this energy and effort yields contrasts remarkably with the amount of debris left behind. At South Africa's West Wits mine, for example, workers descend 2–3,000 metres, braving heat and pressure, accidental explosions and collapsing tunnels, to extract enormous quantities of ore – the deeper the mine and the poorer the grade of ore, the greater the volume of material to be broken into workable pieces, then hauled ever greater distances at ever greater cost to the surface. Once there, material is milled into powder in giant steel drums before amalgamation. That process, too, is not without risk. In 1999 four thieves broke into an ore crusher to scoop up gold dust inside, only to be blended with the mix when the mill somehow got turned on.

But today the great majority of major gold mines are open-pit. They pose fewer direct hazards to miners, and are much cheaper (financially speaking) than dropping mine shafts deep into hard rock. However they produce even more destruction of surrounding landscape. Nowhere is that clearer than in Bougainville.

That former Pacific Island paradise lived under a double curse. The first was political. Seized by Germany in the late nineteenth century, the island was taken over by Australia in the First World War, grabbed by Japan in the Second, restored to Australia as a UN trust territory after that conflict, then in 1972 merged with Papua New Guinea (PNG) even though its population seemed to prefer independence or union with the ethnically related Solomon Islands. The result was a twenty-year insurrection.[52]

The second curse was geological: massive deposits of copper, silver, and gold. Conflicts between mining interests and landowners dated back to the 1960s, but matters got very nasty after Rio Tinto Group took control to create what was at its time the world's largest open-pit mine. The company brought in ten thousand workers to build from scratch a port, a highway system, an electrical grid, and a capital city, slashing jungle and demolishing villages. The island passed in a mere decade from a virtual Stone Age existence to modernity in its most blighted form.

At peak the mine set world records for copper and gold production. Since it accounted for nearly half of PNG's total exports, prospects for Bougainville's peaceful separation dropped close to zero. During the mine's term of operation, the central government collected about $1 billion in royalties while its opponents claimed it paid out perhaps $20 million in social services to locals.[53] By 1989, when rebellion forced its closure, the mine had metastasized into a hole 6 kilometres wide, 4 kilometres long, and 0.5 kilometres deep, surrounded by about 1 billion tons of waste, with toxic tailings spread over 486 square kilometres.

Initially the company and government tried to buy off opposition leaders. And the original resistance movement split into armed factions. The most serious demanded a referendum on independence, half the profits immediately to be used on the island, local ownership of the mine within five years, strict environmental controls, and $11.5 billion compensation for past damage. Weaponry in the hands of the most militant faction led by Francis Ona, a former mine surveyor, went from bows and arrows, shotguns, and stolen dynamite to World War II vintage arms sent by sympathizers in the Solomon Islands (a place littered with old US stuff), then to modern equipment bought or stolen from the PNG military.[54] When the rebels captured the mine site, its closure cost the government more than $1,000 a minute in lost revenue. When direct repression failed, the PNG government imposed on the island an economic blockade, then hired a British mercenary firm, fresh from supplying "security forces" to fight diamond wars in West Africa, to try to restore its authority. It also wooed away local businessmen and landlords by promising autonomy and a better royalty split. Meanwhile the mining equipment rusted away in the encroaching jungle.

In 2001, local powers and the PNG government reached an accord. But Ona and his followers, who still controlled the mine site, denounced any attempt to compromise on their claims to independence and restitution. Two months after Ona had himself crowned by a local shaman as hereditary ruler of the island, the man who would be king died, apparently of malaria. Shares of the Rio Tinto subsidiary jumped nearly 20 percent.[55]

In one respect, the people of Bougainville had more in common with co-citizens on the main island than perhaps they realized. While the Bougainville mine started in copper and branched into gold, the Ok Tedi mine in western PNG, did the reverse. Or rather it did so after the country's prime minister ordered in police to suppress native grievances because, he said, they threatened "investor confidence." It worked. After the police moved in, he bragged that "the investors know that the government is firm."[56] Majority-owned by the ironically named Broken Hill Proprietary (later BHP Billiton), one of Australia's majors, the mine, located high in rainforest-covered mountains among people who lived a subsistence existence, was such an economic success that by the late 1990s it generated 10 percent of the country's GNP and 20 percent of its export revenues, desperately needed with the closure of Bougainville. With the government pushing its rapid development, the mine also produced similar results.[57]

There was supposed to be a barrier to stop Ok Tedi's tailings from washing down out of an earthquake-prone area that gets regularly drenched by tropical downpours. After the half-built dam collapsed, the government let the company dump waste directly into the river. Soon nearly 70 kilometres of the main river was "almost biologically dead," 130 kilometres "severely degraded," and both the Gulf of Papua and the Torres Straits fed by the river poisoned. Fish stocks declined between 50–80 percent, destroying the livelihood of downstream landholders. Since the immunity applied to past as well as future destruction, that stopped enforcement of early court judgments holding the company liable for destruction of properties and wiped out injunctions protecting villages. BHP Billiton transferred majority ownership to a newly created Singapore-based company with the Orwellian name PNG Sustainable Development Program Ltd, owned by the PNG government. The price the company extracted was full indemnity against all claims arising from its previous environmental depredations.[58]

Meanwhile, the usual suspects were busy at work in eastern Papua, the part controlled by Indonesia. They had help. From the time of its independence from the Dutch after World War II until 1965, Indonesia was run by Achmed Sukarno's nationalist government, committed to self-reliance and, even worse in the eyes of the West and its resource companies, to non-alignment. That year a US-sponsored coup by General Suharto led to the slaughter of hundreds of thousands of "Communists" – mostly union leaders, peasants who had irritated their landlords, or Chinese traders suspected of having goodies hidden away. Shortly after, a group of major western corporate interests met with the new regime to dictate the terms on which foreign capital would enjoy the tropical fruits.[59] Among those pouring was Freeport-McMoRan Copper & Gold, which moved into Papua province to run, in partnership with Rio Tinto and with the eager assent of the Indonesian government, the Grasberg Mine, winning the further agreement of traditional leaders of a virtually

Stone Age people on terms that, at least to outside observers, would be more akin to the Manhattan Purchase than to the Marshall Plan.[60]

For a while the world's largest producer of gold and third largest of copper, the mine transformed both society and ecology. That made the Indonesian government happy. It helped to water down the distinct ethnic character of the area; and the government got cut in for 10 percent of the profits. Equally pleased were members of the Indonesian military, almost all outsiders, who were paid to keep mining operations free from labour organizers, NGO observers, independence activists, and people upset that their land had been seized, water sources polluted, and sago palms (the main indigenous food source) buried under mountains of waste. In the first twenty-five years of operation, the mine produced 1.3 billion tons of tailings on its way to the estimated total of six billion tons before the commercially viable ore ran out, much of it poured into rivers, leaving dead trees sticking out of the silt like ecological tombstones. Not surprisingly the disgruntled natives included independent prospectors forced from their traditional diggings. Some who tried to continue small-scale mining in the region were buried in mudslides from mountains of tailings that periodically broke through makeshift levies. But, of course, unlike the company, the independent miners were operating illegally. ·

Even though the two partners in the Grasberg mine could show that, prior to beginning operations, they had a careful environmental assessment done by the same company that had given Papua New Guinea's OK Tedi mine a clean bill of health, locals apparently were not very impressed. Hundreds of them rioted in 2006, hacking to death three Indonesian riot police and forcing a brief Grasberg shutdown. Three years later, some of the guilty parties were arrested; investors could breathe a sigh of relief that justice was finally done.[61]

THE ALCHEMY OF FRAUD

Major mining companies have a number of serious advantages over their competitors: cozy relations with big banks, boards of directors blinking with well-connected bright lights, and discrete understandings with host governments. That translates into, among other things, better access to start-up capital and lower tax or royalty payments to reduce operating costs. The ever-increasing financial requirements for mining gold (like most minerals) reflect the fact that the easily accessible gold in large fields has already been found and exploited. So gold diggers must explore ever more out-of-the-way places and apply ever more sophisticated, energy-intensive, and expensive technologies.

Sometimes majors do the initial exploration in-house; sometimes they wait for upstarts to assume the risks and take the heat before making their own move. That leaves junior companies to look for investors prepared to gamble in a stock-market ambiance as superheated as the water out of which gold was initially deposited. Since shares of start-up ventures are issued for pennies, small changes in the world price of gold, real or merely anticipated, or wild rumours about another bonanza, can cause enormous swings in "value." Whichever way the market moves, the change is for a time self-sustaining: as the stock price rises, speculators scramble to get in before it goes up further, pushing it still higher; as it falls, they rush to be first into overcrowded lifeboats, making fortunes for those who shorted the stock. Of course, these movements can be all the wilder if the invisible hand guiding the free market takes time off to dial numbers on sucker lists and to write hyped prospectuses, bogus geological reports, or phony assay results.[62]

Some claims made to attract investors are purely fraudulent. Con artists may buy a dummy company, feed the market with phony geological reports, then wait for prices to shoot up before dumping and running. More elaborately, they may use complicit brokers to wash stock back and forth on legitimate exchanges. Or they may peddle it through boiler rooms whose operators are skilled in promising that the streets outside an investor's home will soon be paved with gold.

Nor is there any need to be modest about claims. In the mid-1970s Pier Luigi Torri, an Italian scam-and-scram artist, claimed in the brochure of his Metal Research SA (incorporated discreetly in Panama with a Cayman Islands address) to have rights to an area of British Columbia holding nearly 900 million ounces of gold, silver, and platinum worth $288 billion – no mean feat for a property that consisted of a tumbledown shack on a small piece of logged-out scrubland. Metal Research, the brochure claimed, was poised to haul out twenty-four tons of ore daily, enough to yield investors a return on each dollar of $346 per year. For reassurance the prospectus included pictures of gold nuggets from the site. They actually came from a 1968 issue of National Geographic. Further proof that it was a hot property came when its shares rose from $1.00 to $32.00 in a matter of weeks on the basis of trades through a backstreet London brokerage house owned by two offshore banks that in turn were owned by Pier Luigi Torri. Jailed in the US, Torri granted himself leave of absence through the roof ventilator of his cell. Picked up again in New York and shipped back to Britain for trial, he eventually copped seven years.[63]

Still, modesty is sometimes the best policy, even if it doesn't alter the final outcome. The owner of Dynapac Inc., a former furniture salesman and TV commercial pitch artist, had a ranch that hosted the Golden Gulch Mine, located near the New Mexican town of Truth or Consequences. The truth was that Dynapac did not have mining rights, but that might be merely the consequence of the fact that the mine had no gold. Besides there were always ways to rectify inconvenient facts of local geology – for example, slipping a few extraneous nuggets into ore samples or hauling in copper ore from another property (that the promoter did not own), processing it on site into shiny burnished pyramids, and telling would-be investors that each pyramid, including the one proudly displayed at the front door of the promoter's home, contained $90,000 worth of gold. There would be, the promoter promised, much more once engineering studies on a 160 ton per hour processing plant were completed. Anyone doubting his bona fides might be reassured by a letter full of glowing praise written by a prominent lawyer who held 5 percent of the stock. "I am proud to be a major shareholder and member of the board of directors of Dynapac," declared Melvin Belli, less affectionately known as Melvin Bellicose, King of the Torts. Born, appropriately enough, in an ex-California Gold Rush town and representing, among others, a coterie of Hollywood celebs, disgraced evangelical ministers, and coke-addled rock stars, Belli over his career racked up from his law office in a former Gold Rush-era brothel over $600 million in judgments, celebrating them by flying the Jolly Roger after each success. His endorsement, along with Dynapac's claims of a magical machine to extract gold from formerly unproductive ores, its accounting error that turned an annual income forecast into a monthly one, and the energetic efforts of a trio of Denver stockbrokers puffing the stock, kept the ostensible gold-mining company's shares listed for a year on NASDAQ. Facing a civil suit, the intrepid entrepreneur decamped to Vancouver to try his hand once more in the furniture business, then fled again leaving behind a string of debts. Next stop, Oregon, where he opened a credit repair service for people having trouble securing credit cards. Eventually found guilty of racketeering, securities fraud, and criminal solicitation, he disappeared before he could start serving a 19.5-year sentence. His wife later claimed that he had died of cancer, presenting a certificate from a doctor who had not been present at the time of death, and telling authorities that the body had been cremated.[64]

Although Dynapac seems to have been an unqualified scam, most of the time promoters genuinely, even if desperately, believe that with enough capital, success will follow. So it seemed when Richard Silberman and associates took over Yuba Natural Resources. When he described its flagship, Yuba Goldfields, as a "natural resource bank," few, if any, of the other investors realized that it would specialize in overdrafts.[65]

Certainly the context seemed good: world gold prices were on the rise. And Silberman looked like he was made of the right stuff. Son of an immigrant Russian-Jewish junkman, his personal fortune came from smart investments like a chain of fast-food restaurants across the USA. He also began cultivating an image as a patron of the arts and developing political connections, sufficiently so to attend the coronation of George Bush I.

Silberman's partners also had experience in investments. J. David Dominelli, who owned 20 percent of Yuba's shares, ran a commodity fund out of Montserrat that promised a 40 percent return. He reputedly attracted $120 million from 1,200 investors across the US, carefully investing their money in luxury cars, fancy parties, and real-estate loans to friends. After the operation crashed with $80 million missing, Dominelli was given twenty years of penal leisure to improve his knowledge of high finance. Another early Yuba investor was a penny-stock artist who later pleaded guilty to selling worthless shares to a British pension fund.[66]

Despite such assistance, Silberman had a problem. After a brief rise, gold prices refused to budge. But Yuba was an old high-cost operation that would dredge up huge amounts of conglomerate from the bottom of the Yuba River, sift through the debris, then attempt to amalgamate the gold with mercury. During its six years, Yuba registered a profit only once, thanks to accounting alchemy. With one creditor after another suing for unpaid bills or defaulted notes, local tax collectors threatening proceedings, and the US Bureau of Land Management pressing for payment of a fine from a mineral trespass complaint, by late 1988 Silberman was desperate. He approached a bookie. The bookie introduced him to someone claiming to be a money-mover for Colombian cocaine barons. To impress his new benefactor, Silberman bragged that he had been pulling off laundry jobs for fifteen years. The initial deal involved a shoe box with $100,000 in cash in exchange for which Silberman gave the money mover fifty thoushand shares in Yuba Goldfield's Canadian affiliate, then wired the funds to Switzerland. The next deal was for $200,000 stuffed in a hotel laundry bag in exchange for Treasury bonds. A third for $1.1 million was in the works when the Mafia money mover offering the cash transmuted himself into an undercover FBI agent.[67] Somehow or other, in the US justice system, it became Silberman, not the FBI agent, who was guilty of trying to launder money.

Often the lure for investors is a dramatic technological breakthrough – a modern Moses-turned-Midas striking a rock with a geological divining rod so that liquid gold pours out, or a magical machine that turns sand into silver. These gain credibility from a combination of technological

fact and geological oddity. Methods of extracting unconventional gold
(or silver or platinum) take a lot of time to develop but are potentially
dramatic in impact. Gold, in addition to turning up in alluvial deposits,
quartz veins, and pyretic ores, occurs in extremely low concentrations in
everything from peat bogs to coal deposits, from seawater to sand.

Attempts to mine the sea date at least back to the 1920s, when Fritz
Haber, the Nobel Prize-winning chemist and main architect of Germany's
poison-gas program in World War I, tried to help Germany make its
huge postwar reparations to the Allies by extracting gold from seawater, a project abandoned because the concentration of gold in seawater
was too low for available technology.[68] Half a century later, two McGill
University professors who had discovered how the human body stores
iron to protect itself from disease, tried to see if the same biochemical
mechanism would extract other metals, like gold, from seawater or from
the cyanide sludge left after gold-bearing rock is crushed. Desperate for
research money, they were introduced to a Montreal promoter named
Irving Kott, who already had a conviction for stock fraud on his CV.
After Kott decamped to Amsterdam with securities investigators on his
tail, he continued to peddle shares in a company to exploit the technology. After a raid by Dutch regulators, his venture collapsed with investors losing everything – as they would likely have done anyway, just a
little later. Then, in the early 1990s, an online brokerage house again
began selling shares in a Kott company that claimed to possess the salt-
water-into-gold secret. Kott himself pleaded guilty to two felony charges
in California in 2004.[69]

Where there is seawater, presumably there is also a beach or two. In
1981, Florida-based Tarsands Petroleum exchanged two million shares
for two gold concessions in Costa Rica and officially became Goldcor
Incorporated. The scheme was backed by both faith and experience: its
president and chairman, Richard Brown, was the founder of an evan-
gelical outreach based in Daytona Beach, while his two closest business
associates had already been convicted in securities cases. Goldcor's most
attractive asset was a secret chemical process, acquired along with the
gold sites from their previous owner, Chem-Tech International Mining
(that Brown also happened to own), that was able to recover gold from
black volcanic sands, abundant on the coasts of Costa Rica. The claims
were suitably modest – one beach alone contained merely $540 billion
worth. Soon the promoters were flying down reporters, brokers, and
investment counsellors, taking them past armed security officers and
snarling guard dogs to a lab where chemists were busy at work while
outside trucks (hired only on the days potential investors were present)
hauled black sand to the lab. By 1987 the stock had hit $11.25, giving

Goldcor a peak market valuation of $210 million – at a time when it was briefly unable to pay its $500 Delaware corporate tax. Undeterred, President Brown called a meeting of would-be investors to exhibit four hunks of gold from the site – he had bought 209 ounces of gold in the US and melted them into lumps that to the untutored eye could pass as giant nuggets. By then Costa Rica had already refused Goldcor the right to mine the beach. When the company proceeded anyway, local authorities shut it down. In 1988 the shares collapsed and the company went into receivership. While the Securities and Exchange Commission (SEC) in the US was investigating, Brown reported that he had been kidnapped by men who beat him, then faxed to his son a ransom note demanding the $3.5 million that, they claimed, their boss had lost in the Costa Rica scheme. In 1991, three days before he was to appear at a pre-trial hearing on criminal charges, Brown died. Initially the police blamed a heart attack. Then the verdict was suicide – until someone discovered a bullet hole in the back of his head.[70]

Of course, the wise but conservative investor may try to avoid the highly speculative plays associated with developing a new gold field. Fortunately there are ways to invest in gold after the basic mining has already been done, but the product has not yet entered the complex refining, manufacturing, wholesaling, and retailing chain. That kind of opportunity was offered, for example, in Arizona in 1993 by a group of entrepreneurs who took control from its aging owners of a played-out mine on a long-abandoned property whose tunnels had collapsed and equipment decayed beyond repair. Even better, they got it for nothing, using fraudulent trust certificates from an offshore entity they had created for the job. Over the next five years they sold a sort of gold future, promising clients that they could buy in advance gold from the mine for a 10 percent discount over the world price in minimum lots of $100,000. It seemed a safe investment: there was plenty of security in the form of piles of valueless old tailings that they claimed to contain $26 million worth of gold on top of all the gold they planned to extract from 2.65 million tons of ore still underground. And the claims were backed by documents valuing the property at up to $353 million. Supposedly they collected $100 million before the gold mine, figuratively speaking, caved in around the investors' ears.[71]

Even better was the operation pulled off by Oreo Mines in combination with Orex, its processing and refining arm (no relationship to Orex Exploration or Orex Minerals Inc. or Orex Gold Mines Corporation or …). The very name, Shadow Valley Development Project, seemed to invoke something divinely ordained. And the men who ran it were competent. Its sole disadvantage seemed to be that its main promoter had to remain out of sight, lest he be held criminally liable for violating his court-imposed ban on securities activity. But that was compensated by the president whose own conviction for securities fraud attested to his experience.

The math seemed simple, and irresistible. Each investor would buy a minimum of one hundred tons of gold-bearing ore for $50.00 per ton, with a guaranteed minimum yield of one ounce per ton. If the particular pile of gravel did not produce that much, Orex would make up the difference free of charge. At the time the world gold price was hovering around $450. Hence a $5,000 investment in one hundred tons would produce a guaranteed minimum of one hundred ounces, worth a total of $45,000 – minus the fee of only $10,000 for Orex to do the processing. But the brochures assured would-be investors that the costs were tax deductible. As further security, any investor was entitled to a guided tour of the site at any time within sixty days *after* purchase and, if not satisfied with the results of the tour, could request a full refund. It seemed a great idea, particularly to the salesmen who pushed it over the phone in exchange for 20 percent of what they brought in plus a 5 percent override on earnings of any other salesmen they recruited. It probably seemed an even better idea to the promoter who managed to maintain his reputation for keeping a low profile by disappearing before the court-appointed bankruptcy receivers arrived at his office.[72]

SALT AND PEPPER?

Although techno-wizardry and abiding faith can suffice to lure potential investors, the classic swindle involves a salt job.[73] Antecedents no doubt long predate Martin Frobisher. However that Elizabethan adventurer may have presided over the modern world's first great example.

The "investment climate" was certainly right. Other European states were acutely aware that sixteenth-century Spain's super-power status was built largely on the plunder of the Americas. Hence England's Queen was ready to listen to Frobisher's plan to find both the Northwest Passage to Asia and new sources of precious metals. In 1576 his first effort to breach the Arctic ice ran afoul of bad weather. But he returned to England with a chunk of black rock that was sent in pieces to three different assayers. Two declared it worthless; the third claimed it would yield gold at the rate of twenty-five ounces per ton. In words so many modern promoters might be inclined to echo in a final appeal to the jury, that assayer later justified the discrepancy with the observation: "Nature had to be coaxed." Happily, he coaxed it well enough to ensure sufficient capital for a second voyage, the queen herself becoming a major investor.

That expedition returned with yet more ore for study and set off an epidemic of gold fever.[74] A third, larger venture hauled back 1,200 tons of ore, only to find material from the previous voyage declared worthless. This was confirmed four and a half centuries later when up-to-date techniques used on ore samples from the same area revealed gold concentrations only 1/10,000th of what Frobisher's initial assayer reported. Although Frobisher himself may have been innocent of anything but overenthusiasm, he had the distinction of being perhaps the first goldmine puff artist to go to prison. Not that he was any stranger to such an environment: before signing on as a naval officer he had a long career, first as a privateer, then as a bona fide pirate, miraculously escaping the noose. Still, there was a happy ending. With England facing the threat of the Spanish Armada, Frobisher was soon sprung to take his place as second-in-command to Sir Francis Drake, a man who had more primitive but ultimately more effective ideas about how to dig for gold and silver in the Americas.[75]

Today the normal procedure for assessing a mine's potential is to drill several test holes, crush the drill cores and send the pulverized material to a lab for analysis. To salt the sample, sometimes an intact core is sprayed with a solution containing gold – the solution evaporates leaving only the gold. Sometimes a drill core is switched en route with a sample from a different, well-proven site. Sometimes gold, in solution or in powder, is added after the core has been crushed. Credibility is enhanced if added particles are premixed with sand or gravel from the actual site. Most labs, unless specifically requested, merely confirm the presence of gold, whatever its origin; and sometimes evidence of tampering is destroyed by the very process of chemical analysis. Some labs, too, are lax or complicit. Technicians might be paid to add gold to the powdered core or to the test solutions, or just to falsify reported results. Assuming the truth does emerge, it may still be difficult to tell if inflated results resulted from a salt job or sloppy test procedures.[76] But, once the results exist, promoters tout and shout; brokers gush "buy" recommendations; and business reporters do enough heavy breathing to drive the market wild. At that point the schemers dump their own shares and catch a plane to Panama with the cash in a suitcase.

Salting sometimes takes place not to con investors into buying stock in a fake project but to keep money flowing into a genuine one whose architects are convinced will, given time and resources, rival Witwatersrand. That was how, for example, within three years Bre-X's billing changed from the greatest gold discovery in history to the greatest mining fraud of the century. Alas, it did not deserve either distinction; it was just another bush-league salt job that happened to get out of hand.

The story begins in 1968, when John Felderhof, using a novel geological theory about the location of the world's gold, was credited with
finding major deposits of copper and gold in Papua New Guinea. The
mining world was delighted – the local people subsequently devastated
by Ok Tedi can be forgiven a different opinion.[77] A few years later, after
the US-sponsored coup in Indonesia, one of the majors hired Felderhof
to check out the place. He arrived to proclaim that Indonesia would
soon rival South Africa as a gold producer. That project foundered after
the 1987 stock-market crash. A few years later he was back. This time
the theory that had apparently worked in Papua New Guinea led his
team in rapid succession into the jungles of Kalimantan, the swamp of
Indonesian politics, and the sewer of Canadian stock exchanges. Thus
was Bre-X born.[78]

Kalimantan does have gold. For centuries indigenous peoples panned
the riverbeds. But that gold was nowhere near the site pinpointed by the
Bre-X theories. Nonetheless, drilling began. In charge was Michael de
Guzman, a Filipino geologist recently fired from another job for buying
presents for a girlfriend with company money. After the first few drill
holes came up empty, de Guzman decided to buy more time with one
currency everyone accepted. Over the next three years he acquired sixty
ounces of river gold from merchants who had bought it from alluvial
miners. By day he carefully supervised the extraction of core samples: at
night he carefully measured alluvial gold, matching it to ground-up rock
from the drill cores. The assay results went from negative to wildly optimistic, apparently without raising suspicions among senior management.

The initial objective seems to have been simply to keep development
money flowing until gold was actually found. But, when one disappoint-
ment followed another, de Guzman, and whoever else was in the know,
was caught in a trap: there was no way to halt optimistic assay reports
without exposing the original deception. Yet not only were wild stories
(for example, that the site might contain 200 million ounces of gold)
bound to attract covetous rivals, but, if there were any basis to them,
everyone knew a junior company could never hope to develop such a
site. The question was: which senior would it team up with and on what
terms? A number of those seniors watched and plotted.

In 1996, Toronto's Barrick Gold, soon to win (briefly) the title of
the world's largest gold-mining company, made its move.[79] It was well
placed politically – its board of directors glittered with, among other
luminaries, ex-US president George Bush I. (Canada's former prime
minister, Brian Mulroney, was tossed in as a ten-watt extra.) Barrick
got President Suharto's eldest daughter to persuade daddy to issue an
edict granting 70 percent ownership to Barrick and a mere 20 percent

to Bre-X, the government taking the residual 10 percent. But Bre-X held tough. The possibility that banks would be leery about funding mining ventures in Indonesia if the government changed rules in mid-match led Suharto to back-track. Then Bre-X offered one of Suharto's sons 10 percent plus $1 million per month in "consultancy fees." Faced with an impasse, Suharto called on Mohamed "Bob" Hassan, the country's number 1 timber baron, notorious for turning great tracts of Sumatra's jungles into environmental wastelands. As partner for Bre-X, "Bob" recommended Freeport-McMoRan, who had already done such a fine job in Grasberg and whose boss was a chum of both "Bob" and Suharto. The new idea was give Bre-X 45 percent and Freeport 15 percent, then divide the remaining 40 percent among the Indonesian government and the two rival offspring of the president.[80]

Meanwhile all the fuss served to consolidate the Bre-X claims in the public mind. Stock touts boosted the potential to 400–500 million ounces, a mere 16–20 percent of the world's supply, worth $154 billion at then-current prices. And what could go wrong? Bre-X, they pointed out, was headed by people of experience and success. Nor was there any need to trust the word of promoters: lab results existed from more than 250 drill-hole samples. The only problem was that, in analyzing the cores, the labs had managed to overlook not just the occasional red flag but a field full of frantically flapping crimson banners.

The finer an ore sample is ground, the higher should be the concentration of gold revealed in tests – in this case the proportions remained constant. While alluvial gold appears in grains visible to the naked eye, underground deposits are almost always in flecks so small they cannot be seen – those in the Bre-X samples could be. Since the deposit was supposedly of volcanic origin, the gold should have been firmly embedded in the bedrock – in these samples gold literally fell right out of the crushed matrix when it was run through a gravity concentrator. Gold and silver occur together in nature. With surface gold, the silver leaches out; with underground gold, it remains. In the Bre-X samples, there was no associated silver. While underground gold may retain some features of its original crystalline structure, alluvial gold, present in the Bre-X samples, is rounded by the action of water.[81]

Still, the shares still rose to dizzy heights before Freeport, as a precondition of buying into the claim, reran the tests and reported it could find only 0.01 grams per ton in samples from which Bre-X had reported 1.80–3.70. Shortly after, de Guzman fell out of a helicopter deep in the jungle. When his body was found, gutted by wild pigs, it was recognizable only by his jeans. Falling even further was the stock price. By the time the carnage ended, some C$5 billion in stock "value" had disappeared.[82]

THE ETERNAL METAL?

After each scandal industry spokesmen lament the damage done by the unscrupulous and predict that recovery of mining stocks will be a long time coming. That prognosis reveals a remarkably poor sense of history. Gold fever is a disease that occasionally goes into remission but is never cured. A more sensible forecast would have been that, given a little time for memories to fade, any such a disaster, like countless before it, will be rationalized as the aberration rather than the rule, or as a near miss that failed to deliver only because investors lacked faith in a scheme to extract the gold from goldfish. In fact, less than a decade after the Bre-X debacle, one of Bre-X's former boosters claimed that the remote Indonesian island of Lembata hosted the world's third largest gold reserves, perhaps 70 million ounces in an area that an Australian company had already explored to find virtually nothing.[83]

That will be the ultimate fate of all gold mining ventures. However in the meantime there are plenty of attractions. South Africa's Witwatersrand, which has already yielded half a trillion dollars worth, may hold at least that much more deep below its current diggings – or so its mining companies claim as they watch production in other countries leap ahead. All that is necessary to keep the gold coming is to drill down far enough to blast apart, haul up, crush, grind, and leach ever-greater masses of rock. Gold, too, exists dissolved in both salt and fresh water. What is required is a way to run it in sufficient quantities through an extractive process that will obliterate all life forms before dumping the sterilized and toxified residue back into the river, lake, or sea. Trees and bushes draw gold up through their roots and concentrate it in their biomass with the result that ashes of burnt stumps yield detectable amounts of gold, along with silver and platinum. What better example of economic efficiency than for gold miners to not merely uproot vegetation from the Amazon and other parts of the world's remaining but rapidly shrinking rainforests but – rather than just burn it, releasing its carbon into the atmosphere – to first extract its stores of precious metals.[84]

Still, whoever does the digging, wherever it takes place, whatever the technique used, whichever swindles are employed to raise capital, and however much corporate greenwash about "sustainable mining" is spewed out to try to cover up the damage, the fact remains that as the "quality" of ore progressively falls, the result is a simultaneous increase per ounce recovered in the physical amount of waste, the hazardous nature of extractive technologies, the energy required to drive ever-larger machinery, the volume of fresh water run through the processing stages to re-emerge as a river of poison, and the number of independent prospectors displaced or farmers uprooted who lack the skills or connections for an alternative job in a modern mining operation.

What is most necessary for future prosperity of the gold diggers is a way to ensure that the price remains high enough and rising fast enough to compensate for increased costs. That requires finding some means to offset the impact of falling industrial demand – even dentists have switched from gold to ceramic material for crowning teeth. Therefore success of the gold diggers depends ever more on human stupidity, venality, and vanity.

The first takes the form of buying, then burying, precious metals back in the earth – if not via an underground bank vault, then at least in a back garden – as a safeguard against military, environmental, or financial Armageddon. So important is that reflex today that gold industry tycoons probably get together from time to time to at least symbolically pray for a repeat appearance of one of the Four Horsemen in modern guise – a spectacular son-et-lumière show by the US Air Force, a worldwide failure of bioengineered grain crops, the meltdown of both Greenland and Antarctic ice sheets, or a massive Wall Street collapse that spreads economic chaos across the world. They have to hope also that the population never wakes up to the fact that to guard against those four great calamities, people would be better off relying on lead sheeting to cover their house, an excellent sailboat with a well-stocked bar tied up at their wharf, a hefty stash of canned food in the root cellar, and a policy of assiduously avoiding any contact with the institutionalized crap shoots with odds bent way in favour of the house that constitute today's financial markets.

The second factor, venality, is similar but simpler. It boils down to the hope that, once financial markets implode and paper currencies collapse, those who put their money in gold will emerge from under the economic debris with an even broader smile pasted across their self-satisfied faces – until one of the bands of brigands likely to thrive in the resulting chaos wipes off their smirks with a shotgun blast.

As to the third source of demand, human vanity, that seems the surest base on which gold diggers can stake their future. After all, while the alchemists of old took pains to point out that gold is the metal most impervious to biogeochemical processes of decay, they failed to add that it is probably the one most conducive to corrosion in its moral, political, and financial forms.

2

Vulgari: Flawed Beauty in the Gemstones Business

Queen Elizabeth II is reputed to have so much jewellery that she keeps her personal trinkets in a special room the size of an indoor skating rink forty feet below Buckingham Palace. That's in addition to the Crown Jewels – those, being state property, are housed separately in the Tower of London.[1] Although that division of the royal spoil dates back centuries, its wisdom was perhaps confirmed recently by the queen's attempt to dip into public funds intended for poor relief to heat her palaces, rather than drawing down her enormous personal wealth for such mundane purposes. Pinching and pawning a few of the Crown Jewels might have gone a long way.[2]

Still, the story about the awesome dimensions of the royal horde is no doubt a gross exaggeration put about by the jewellery trade to puff public interest in its wares. Nonetheless the queen's collection is the most fabulous in the world.[3] The French royal jewels, never as grand, were almost all sold off at auction in 1887 – at least those remaining after the great thefts that followed the 1792 overthrow of the monarchy. The stupendous pile of gold, silver, gems, jewellery, and jewelled brocades seized by the Bolsheviks from the Crown, aristocracy, and Church of the old Russian Empire was largely dissipated long ago. Some was entrusted to Russian museums; much was melted into bullion or broken up and quietly sold abroad.[4]

Although most of the British queen's own playthings came from gifts or inheritance, questions about where and how the persons who gave the jewels to her, or to her ancestors, got their hands on the stuff to begin with are rarely asked. It would most likely preclude an invitation to tea at the palace to speculate in public about the itinerary followed by the 352-carat Timur Ruby, one of the highlights of her collection. Apart from the fact that it is actually a spinel, a much less valuable stone, the jewel is inscribed with the names of its previous owners, several Mughal emperors of India, a breed not generally known for freely sharing their treasures with friends, admirers, or fellow royals.[5]

To be sure, there were exceptions. For example when Nizam Ali Khan, ruler of Hyderabad in the late eighteenth century, sent the 101 carat Hastings diamond to King George III as a diplomatic overture toward Great Britain – an act about as sensible as sending the vestal virgins to Jack the Ripper to coax him into a more respectable pattern of social interaction.

To be fair to the queen, a probe of the origins of any other royal collection, and not a few private ones, might prompt the same kind of questions and elicit the same kind of evasions. And India's various princes hardly earned a reputation at home for respecting each other's portable property when they could get away with it, in both senses. Nonetheless, the British monarchy's lead is no accident. After all, what other collector in history has had the advantage of the world's greatest collection agencies, the British Army and Navy, to help with the selection process over several centuries?

Throughout the ages and across the continents, gemstones, jewels, and jewellery have been bought and bartered, coveted and collected – and frequently stolen – for their magical, magisterial, or medicinal properties. They warded off evil, conferred or confirmed status, and even cured strange ailments. In fourteenth-century Europe, for example, swallowing a pearl powdered into distilled water was reckoned by some physicians a sure cure for insanity instead of another form of it.[6] Nor do only females collect precious baubles with the same passion that Imelda Marcos, former first lady of the Philippines, once showed for shoes. On his death, Henry VIII of England left 234 rings and 324 broaches in addition to cupboards full of necklets, collars, and gem-studded clothes, although not many surviving wives to squabble over them.[7]

Granted that today probably few still believe (as did Spanish doctors in the sixteenth century) that touching their abdomens with an emerald while carrying another inside their mouths will cure a bad case of the runs – Kaopectate is a lot cheaper and perhaps a little more effective. But the lure of gemstones is stronger than ever. As demand has skyrocketed, so have prices. Partly that is because a growing population faces a limited geological stock. But the main thing driving the market for high-end gems, like so much else, is the pileup of riches by members of a nouveau gauche class trying desperately to convince others, and perhaps even more so themselves, of a social status appropriate to their financial success. Again, far from exclusively female, the heaviest buyers today might well be males, some of whom may feel that offering expensive looking jewellery to "significant others" is the only way, short of rape, that they will get to satisfy their most basic biological urges.

On top of public showpieces, a large share of current demand is for single, unmounted "investment" stones – mainly diamonds, but also rubies, emeralds, sapphires, and a host of others, all destined for a safety deposit box or perhaps a shoebox under the bed, a more fitting choice given what so many are actually "worth." Yet as financial assets (some) gemstones do have desirable characteristics: high in value in relation to bulk, they are easy to hide, smuggle, and liquidate through worldwide marketing networks whose members share an affinity for "discretion."[8]

On the other side of the market, gemstones have been since ancient times (and usually still are today) the product of appalling working conditions; and they impose, much like gold if not so extensively, a heavy toll on nature – mounds of tailings, fouled water-courses, and blighted landscapes.[9] Nor is the process by which they, once dug up, get redistributed across the face of the Earth exactly benign. Although peaceful trade in gemstones may predate other forms of commerce, how often over thousands of years has one motive for military conquest been treasure in the form of gemstones and jewels along with precious metals, or, more precisely, the prospect of arranging a transfer of ownership without the modern risk that lawyers will make off with most of the loot? Furthermore, because of faith in the afterlife or lack of faith in security arrangements in the existing one, members of materially exalted classes throughout history have had their treasure entombed with them. So to the redistributive handiwork of marauding armies must be added less spectacular but more persistent efforts of generations of graverobbers. And that brings into sharp relief the fundamental paradox of the business.

For thousands of years an elite among artisans has laboured to turn rough stones that to ordinary eyes might be indistinguishable from common gravel into exquisite objects to entrance people of all ethnic divisions, geographic locations, or political creeds even if only a small subset delineated by social status and/or income level was in a position to personally enjoy the finest of them.

Today, of course, some things are different. The market is far broader; and sophisticated machinery has largely displaced manual skills – although for actually matching a gem to a setting, there will never be a substitute for a talented eye and long experience. Supposedly commercial standards have improved, too, although that is hard to see in the trajectory an expensive gemstone follows on its passage from the depths of the Earth to the heights of fashion. En route it passes from

mines that are either illegal per se or, if legal, rife with theft; crosses borders in smugglers' pouches; wends its way through cutting and polishing
centres whose practitioners grant themselves a universal tax exemption;
heads back into underground channels through deals done in cash and
sealed with a handshake; then arrives in a marketing nexus replete with
commercial fraud, the real gem mixed with others that have been oiled
to hide cracks, irradiated to change colour, flux treated to fill fissures,
grown in a modern crystal lab, or totally faked. During its voyage, that
same gem might have been handled by impoverished diggers and backwoods traders, aspiring warlords and corrupt bureaucrats, intelligence
agents and ragtag insurgents, gunrunners, and mercenaries, professional
smugglers and black-market moneychangers, drug-money launderers
and telemarketing scam-artists, before coming to rest around an elegant
neck or a languorously beckoning finger, at least until an enterprising
jewel thief thinks differently.

All of this goes to support a proverb frequently quoted by gemologists: that the best way to find precious stones is not to rely on rock
picks, chrome chisels, and streak plates but on the front page of a good
newspaper, something now rarer than many of the stones gemologists
seek. Search for a place sufficiently plagued by war, disease, and acute
deprivation, and fine stones are likely to abound. Of course, what those
gemologists rarely add is that the objects of their frenzied search are
often a direct cause of the very matrix of crime, violence, and misery in
which the stones, especially the much coveted green, red, and blue ones,
are embedded.

GREEN GOODS, BLACK MONEY

The contrast is stark. On the one side, take the Chopard collection's
33-carat solitaire emerald, set with half-moon diamond shoulders in a
platinum band, thus creating a cocktail ring valued at $2.14 million. On
the other, take the sight, virtually in the shadow of Colombia's Banco de
la República, of leather-jacketed men gathering to flash at passersby the
contents of envelopes they draw covertly from inside pockets. But for
the absence of dirty trench coats, the first thought of someone who has
strolled rue St Denis in Paris might be that these dudes are peddling the
latest in kiddie porn.[10] Actually they are offering what a hyperventilating
journalist once called "the most precious stones in the world," a quality of reporting about on a par with that of the gems hawked on that
Bogotá street. Certainly Colombia long produced the finest (and most)
emeralds in the world, although that status is much challenged today.
The top ones, carat by carat, beat the best diamonds in the price sweep-

stakes. But the finest are snapped up at source and smuggled abroad, while the poorest, along with fakes, get unloaded in that street on unsuspecting tourists and gullible reporters for Bloomberg Business News.[11]

For thousands of years virtually all the world's emeralds came from the slave-worked "Cleopatra Mines" in Upper Egypt until the site was abandoned around the end of the first millennium AD.[12] For the next several centuries the "civilized" world faced an emerald drought – until the Spanish arrived in what is now Colombia to find that Indians had been digging and trading emeralds for centuries. Conquest and slavery in the mines created a tradition of resistance to authority that persists to this day. Smuggling was rife; taxation almost impossible. With independence the Colombian government faced the same problems. After over a century of frustration, it nationalized the mines, then abandoned them as the country slid into a long civil war. Peace put the mines under control of the country's central bank, more or less – with the daily open-air flea market near its main office in Bogatá speaking volumes about how far its writ really ran. But by the early 1970s the mines were so bled by theft, and the region so wracked by renewed violence, that the government officially closed the area again, leaving it to illegal gem lords or cocaine traffickers – or both. Illegal miners might be former coca planters and vice versa; money from one business might finance the other; and the products of both took similar clandestine routes out of the country.

The best-known entrepreneur straddling the two businesses was José Gonzalo Rodríguez Gacha, allegedly number 2 man in the so-called Medellín Cartel. Members of that closely controlled, hierarchically structured transnational of drugs supposedly accounting for 80 percent of world cocaine used to celebrate their talent for clandestine criminal conspiracy by murdering one another in public bloodbaths or ratting out each other in private deals with US narcs, all the while driving down prices by competitively flooding the market with their product. Rodríguez Gacha – or "el Mexicano," as he was popularly called because of his zeal for mariachi music – got started as a bodyguard to an emerald millionaire, took control of his own mines, then moved his money into cocaine. Still, emeralds kept their allure sufficiently for Rodríguez Gacha to seek outside help to re-establish himself in the gemstone business.

At the time Israeli mercenaries, veterans of "anti-terrorism" work in Lebanon and Occupied Palestine, were fanning out across Latin America in competition for the "private security" business with the likes of former British SAS men and veterans of white Rhodesia's elite anti-guerrilla forces. The Israelis usually came out on top – others were more likely to be genuine mercenaries whereas the Israelis retained professionally useful ties to the army and intelligence apparatus back home and doubled as arms salesmen on behalf of their government. So Rodríguez Gacha, in preparation for his return to emerald country, hired Israeli reserve colonel Yair Klein to show his men how to do their job and to supply them with Israeli weapons so they could outgun the opposition.[13]

They were good students. A promotional videotape (later broadcast on US TV news) showed the trainees going through manoeuvres in front of their Israeli teachers while the eager students shouted, "We are thirsty to drink the blood of Communists." After graduation they displayed their proficiency in a more dramatic way, by gunning down a reformist presidential candidate during an election rally, then followed up by murdering a judge who had ordered Rodríguez Gacha's arrest.[14] Some time later Rodríguez Gacha himself was killed in an army raid on his ranch, aborting rather decisively his hopes to get back into business peddling the gemological symbol of eternal life. His sidekick, Yair Klein, had already fled back to Israel. Once comfortably reinstalled in a house he had built on land seized from the Palestinians in the West Bank, he applied his talents to training "civil administrators" for the occupied territories while promoting a company to sell Bibles and Holy Water to Christian fundamentalist pilgrims.[15] Eventually his own fascination for gemstones lured him to Liberia and Sierra Leone, seeking in the midst of their ugly civil wars contracts to supply arms and buy diamonds, only to be arrested again. When Colombia sought his extradition, somehow or other he escaped from jail and returned to safety in Israel once more, only to be rearrested in Russia in 2007 on an Interpol warrant. But Klein, whose protegés in Colombia routinely run drugs, traffic arms, and commit mass murder, won a judgment against extradition from the European Court of Human Rights on the grounds that he ran the risk of being ill-treated in a Colombian prison.[16]

Meanwhile, back in Colombia's emerald country, would-be miners – mainly peasants displaced elsewhere by ecological disaster, overpopulation, or conversion of farmland into pasture – needed someone already in the business to vouch for them. With that guarantee, gem traders provided them with basic supplies and primitive equipment in return for a pledge of their production. Then the stones were sold to buyers from Bogotá. Since couriers using the roads were prey to rivals, bandits, insurgents, or moonlighting soldiers, big producers and dealers started a helicopter service. Back in Bogotá those who bought stones from miners had three options – place the poorest in the street; sell the medium quality to local outlets; or smuggle the best to the US or beyond.[17]

In the early 1980s, the government had officially reopened the mines, licensing them to private operators and setting off a six-year *guerra verde* that left maybe 3,500 people dead. With the tacit backing of the government, one gem lord, Victor Carranza, put together a private army to wipe out rival *esmeraldistas*, intruding drug dealers, and left-wing guerrillas. He reacted to the bodies that police later dug up on his property with the observation that, when people die in that region, they are usually buried quickly to avoid spreading disease. Besides, Carranza later added, the place where the bodies were found was far from his own farm. When the US accused him, too, of cocaine trafficking and operating a private army, Colombia was forced to arrest him.[18] He spent a few years directing business from prison, then was released by a judge who pronounced the accusations against Carranza too horrible to be believed. A grateful government granted him a fifty-year monopoly on sites he controlled, free from taxes, regulations, or police presence, in return for bringing peace and stability to an emerald sector hurt by bad reputation and increasing competition from abroad. The nature of that peace and stability was well illustrated early in 2009 when five of his bodyguards were killed in an attack on his armoured land cruiser, and another attack followed the next year, although Carranza himself escaped both unscathed.[19]

With the new arrangements, contraband did not disappear; it just took different forms. First, licensed mine owners report only part of the yield. Those stones are inspected, classified, and taxed by a government agency; the rest are sold on the black market at home or smuggled abroad. Second, mine workers typically are paid not a wage but a percentage of the stones they find. They turn over some to suppliers to repay advances of food, equipment, or money, then sell the rest to itinerant buyers for cash. Third, at the main sites, bulldozers scrape off overburden and dig out huge amounts of rock that miners bust apart with dynamite and jackhammers. Official mineworkers find large crystals that survived the blasts, while smaller stones are caught up in the enormous amounts of tailings washed down into the valleys to be picked up by informal miners. They are at the bottom, financially as well as geographically, earning bare subsistence but dreaming of a big score. They, too, sell their finds to local traders in exchange for supplies and equipment or to agents of big Bogotá emerald dealers. As before, low-quality material goes to the street; and the finest is exported, legally or illegally, mainly to the US. to be grabbed up by jewellery manufacturers, private collectors, and gem merchants who, in turn, move some to Israel, India, or Thailand.

Emeralds, alas, are not forever. After centuries of digging, top-quality gems from Colombia's older mines steadily dipped. That meant more effort, more investment, and more garbage in the form of mounds of tailings per carat of results. So other places began to fill the gap. One was Afghanistan, whose mines had long been known well enough for industry insiders to mislabel their stones as Colombian in origin, then sell them at a premium. They attracted more attention during the long war between the country's Soviet-supported regime and US-sponsored "freedom fighters" combating the Communist government's more appalling forms of oppression – like mandatory female education and a ban on peasants settling debts by giving their pre-teen daughters to landlords and money-lenders. The most mediagenic of these rebel leaders, the late Ahmed Shah Ma'soud, helped to finance his war effort, first against the USSR (when it was not just paying him off), later against the Taliban, by a tax on emeralds and lapis lazuli coming out of his fiefdom. Ma'soud himself rose to greater things after the Soviet withdrawal, democratically contesting political power with his former allies by joining them in blasting sections of the capital city of Kabul to smithereens, along with a lot of its civilian population. After his assassination and the subsequent fall of the Taliban government, the new US-installed regime appointed his multilingual brother to ferry suitcases of Afghan gemstones to the Gulf States to open new markets. After all, what is freedom for if not freedom to trade?

Today Afghan miners blow apart bedrock with old shells and bombs, then, braving accidental explosions, gas buildups, and collapsing tunnels, burrow into mountains to gather stones that survive the blasts. Those who do the hardest and most dangerous work naturally collect the smallest part of the reward. Miners get a pittance; merchants who advance money and equipment a lot more. Then itinerant traders buy the stones, pay taxes to local warlords, and haul gems along a well-worn contraband trail to Pakistan's Northwest Frontier Province, facing the new danger of random US airstrikes plus extra transit fees charged by Pakistani officials as their contribution to the War on Terror. Once across, emeralds, lapis lazuli, rubies, spodumene, tourmaline, and aquamarine mixed with synthetics and fakes are sold to buyers from all over the world.[20]

Now other places, too, challenge Colombia's lead. In the 1970s, emerald deposits were found in Zambia close to the copper mines that were long its economic backbone – even though that backbone has suffered increasingly from herniated disks and is now effectively broken. Formerly run by the state, the copper mines, the biggest single non-agricultural employer, provided some income security even if their toxic emissions threatened the health of workers and their families as well as blighting the surrounding countryside. In came US-run international financial agencies to tell the government that prices were going to stay much the same and that, to lock in the benefits as well as get desperately needed debt relief, it needed to privatize the mines. So in a secret deal with the Zambian president, since charged with embezzling $500,000 in public funds, the sites were sold at a bargain price to transnational mining companies. After privatization, unions were busted, towns near the smelters periodically smothered in sulfur dioxide, and armed company goons replaced police in ensuring security. Then the price of copper, supposedly slated to remain stable, plunged, employment along with it. The result is a plague of illegal miners now mining rubbish dumps for bits of copper, manganese, or cobalt ore to sell on the black market.[21]

On the other hand, emeralds destined for the world's wealthy thrived. Stolen with equal enthusiasm by miners and managerial personnel, they are hauled by professional smugglers by road past easily bribed police and customs officers or by air, assisted by corrupt airport officials and cooperative airline staff, to the Kenyan capital of Nairobi, regional hub for gemstone trafficking. There the government rolls out the welcome mat for gems smuggled from neighbouring countries but has the cheek to expect these gems pay taxes when they try to leave again. Not to worry. An enterprising dealer might go to the Department of Mines, declare a parcel of low-grade stones, and pay the small tax due. Once government appraisers seal the parcel and clear it for export, the dealer reopens it on the sly to substitute high-quality stones. Or he might give a batch in a coffee bag to an airport official who passes it to a helpful sales clerk in a duty-free shop. On departure day, a gem courier, like so many tourists, buys a souvenir bag of Kenyan "coffee," recouping the gems along with an invoice. Even better, since passengers and luggage bound for Israel are cleared on departure rather than on arrival, Israeli security personnel, given free run of Nairobi's main airport to keep an eye out for "Arab terrorists," set aside particular bags for "further inspection," then, just before departure, rush them onto the plane, bypassing their Kenyan counterparts. In Israel the stones are welcomed by customs, appraised by officials from the local diamond exchange, then sent to government-subsidized cutters to help them beat out rivals from places like Thailand.[22]

BEHIND THE CORUNDUM CURTAIN

Thailand is renowned for steamy, languorous days and red-hot nights, at least in Bangkok's celebrated sex district. Actually, compared to a lot of major cities in Asia, Bangkok's red-light area is quite small – two streets of clubs and bars with some spillover to nearby sidestreets. The claim that the city hosts ten thousand sex change clinics sounds like the kind of fantasy expected from fat, middle aged white men who spend their days swilling beer and their nights leering at prostitutes they are too scared to actually proposition. Still, in districts that sell sex, if not in the act itself, size doesn't matter too much.

However there is something else that Thailand has in abundance. It is the source of about 80 percent of the world's cut and polished rubies (the red form of corundum, a very hard aluminum oxide), plus a fair chunk of its sapphires (corundum of any colour except red). The secret lies not in geology so much as sociology – a tightly knit, extremely wealthy Chinese community from an ethnolinguistic minority whose sense of intragroup mutual obligation takes precedence over written codes of law.[23] These Thai Chinese, survivors of wars, revolutions, and pogroms, have decades of experience manipulating local politics, handling (and doctoring) gem crystals, controlling international networks to smuggle goods and money, and locating underground sources of raw material. Since the richest mines in Thailand itself were depleted decades ago, supply lines now run deep into Burma-Myanmar, Cambodia, and Vietnam, and further afield to Sri Lanka and East Africa, in the face of long-standing efforts by their governments to stop, limit, or tax the outflow.

Rubies from Burma-Myanmar have been known for centuries, even millennia, as the finest. Most coveted are "pigeon-blood" stones unique to the Mogok area; their unique pinkish-red fluorescence is due to tiny needles of "silk" (titanium oxide) that scatter light onto facets that would otherwise be dark.[24] Mogok stones rise in value the closer they come to exhaustion. In fact today most Burmese rubies are from a much newer mine site at Mong Hsu whose stones are smaller and have their colour artificially hyped before they can be sold, perhaps with paperwork claiming they come from Mogok.[25]

Historically Burma's rubies were prized for much more than their beauty. Most local people used the stones for religious offerings, encasing them in pagoda relic chambers and burial mounds of Buddhist saints. Rubies, too, supposedly cured ills involving inflammation or bleeding while warding off bad luck and enhancing sex appeal. Rubies were also a favourite way for warlords who fought for control of the producing region to levy tribute on their underlings. When Burmese kings finally brought the area more or less under their rule, they implemented a royal reserve on all stones above a certain value; concealment was punishable by slow death, sometimes for an entire village. Others in more modern times appreciate rubies for rather different reasons.

In a 2007 roster of the world's most expensive necklaces, H. Stern's Venus scored $3.17 million, beaten by the De Beers Marie-Antionette at $3.7 million and the Neil Lane at $4 million. All of them featured diamonds, but all of them were left in the dust by Garrand's Heart of the Kingdom ruby necklace featuring a 40-plus carat Burmese pigeon-blood stone that could double as a tiara – it bore a price tag of $14 million.[26]

Rubies from Burma started to reach Europe via India in early modern times, first through trade, later and more reliably through plunder. As the British grabbed India by bits and pieces, they bought cheaply or stole at gunpoint most of the great rubies there. Then they went to the source. Taking as a pretext Burmese efforts to stop British-Indian companies from stealing rare hardwoods, in the 1880s the British invaded, deploying for the first time in one of their conquests the new Maxim gun that mowed down defenders in rows. After victory they set out to loot the king's palace. The story goes that its legendary rubies were saved by female servants who hid the finest under their sarongs.[27] However that tale perhaps underestimates the seriousness with which British forces took their collection duties during empire-building, or the propensity of marauding armies to be curious about what might be hidden beneath female undergarments. The less patriotic reality seems to be that, not only did retainers flee carrying what they could ahead of the British but hundreds of women from outside (the British had banned men from entering or leaving the royal compound) joined the fun, taking everything of value they found.

Still, even if the British missed a lot of palace treasure, they got to ransack about one thousand pagodas, then decide what to sell on behalf of the government of British India and what to send home. Queen Victoria got the Burmese king's best crown; the prince and princess of Wales two carved ivory tusks and a gold Buddha. Showing their usual respect for archeological sites, the British turned parts of the royal palace into a chapel and clubroom with billiard table and bar and razed hundreds of teakwood upper-class houses in the then-capital of Mandalay to make room for a parade ground and prison. Since they had already burned the archives and palace library, there was no longer a formal record of the lineage of the nobles who had formerly lived in those places.[28] Of course, the British also seized the ruby mines.

After Burma became independent in 1947, the British, as they had in India and parts of the Middle East, left behind conflicting promises to various groups and, either through duplicity or indifference, left different ethnicities at each other's throats. When a Burmese military government nationalized the mines, demanding that the finest stones go to Yangon for state-controlled auction, those edicts came at the same time it tried to clamp down on restless minorities who constitute perhaps a third of the population and, by happy coincidence, are concentrated in border areas bountifully endowed with rubies, jade, rare hardwoods, and opium. Contraband became a matter of political urgency as well as private profit. Stones liberated from the mines ended up mainly in Thailand.[29]

A miner could just pocket his find or hide it to return at night, paying off the guards. He might smuggle the stone himself, facing a rough trip to Thailand. More likely he would turn it over to professionals working with Chinese-Thai dealers. Either way the stone made its way along the ruby trail through country controlled by opium dealers or guerrilla groups or both, paying "transit fees" at various points, including to both Myanmar and Thai border guards. Even when stones were dutifully turned in to government sorting stations, the finer ones might be diverted by managers and security personnel before they, too, were sent to Thailand. There skilled cutters could compensate themselves for low wages by replacing good stones with poor-quality, fake, or synthetic ones. Since cutting changes the shape and heat treatment the colour, a switch can be difficult to prove. Finally, cut gemstones enter mainstream trade circuits via Bangkok.[30]

Now, nearly two decades after Myanmar liberalized mining and gem-dealing, high quality stones are still stolen by alluvial miners, officials in government mines, and private partners, to end up in Thailand. If border agents seize contraband, the main result, unless there are too many witnesses, is just to change the identity of the person collecting most of the money. In Thailand, tourists, amateur collections, and pros alike try to snatch up rubies, sapphires, and jade, along with lesser stones like amethysts and agates, from street vendors who may try to pass off stones that are fake, enhanced, or seriously flawed, from jewellery stores that may do the same at a higher price, or from wholesale merchants who might sell the genuine article but at whatever price the combined depth of a buyer's knowledge and pockets will bear.[31]

Elsewhere in the region, too, Thai dealers adapted remarkably to political circumstances. In Cambodia, for a time source of most of the world's raw rubies by bulk, not by quality, Thai arch-capitalists comfortably cut deals with Khmer Rouge ultra-leftists when that insurgent organization controlled the ruby-producing areas. Once ideological dissent and corruption tore apart the rebel group, Thai dealers smoothly switched to negotiating with the government – when that was necessary.[32] Collapse of Khmer Rouge authority sparked a secondary ruby rush relying heavily on child labour that, along with indiscriminate logging, ravaged an area already rendered dangerous by millions of landmines and cure-resistant malaria and pushed thousands of people off their land.[33] Similarly Vietnam's recently discovered ruby mines disgorged a steady stream of contraband to transit into Cambodia – where ex-guerrillas, moonlighting army units, and corrupt officials demand compensation – before crossing into Thailand along with endangered wildlife bound for the exotic pet trade in the West or for use in traditional medicine in the East.

The Thai hold on the coloured gemstone trade even extends into East Africa. In Tanzania, home of the region's finest gems, Thai companies control the most prolific mines, tightly supervising workers to guard against theft and, allegedly, periodically placing synthetic stones in the mines to ruin the reputations of thieves among black-market dealers. This display of virtue seems to work only in one direction – by exporting ruby still in its rock matrix, Thai miners can undervalue the loads and reduce taxes.[34]

Tanzania also has alluvial deposits where professional dealers skin miners on prices, then resell stones to amateur buyers under the name Burma or pigeon-blood rubies.[35] To avoid taxes, these stones might leave Tanzania by road or air into Kenya, paying the usual unofficial transit fees, then set off to their final destinations, probably in Israel or India, along with Zambian emeralds and perhaps some of Kenya's own small ruby production.

In the early 1970s a US geologist named John Saul stumbled across a rich-looking ruby deposit in the Tsavora region. He understood enough about Kenya to offer several senior politicians, their business cronies, and the wife of the president 51 percent. They demanded 80 percent. When he balked at going beyond 72 percent, they charged him with smuggling, declared him a national security risk, and gave him 2.5 hours to leave the country. By coincidence, the claims books at the Department of Mines and Geology were lost. When new books were opened, the first entry was a claim to that ruby mine filed by a member of the inner ruling circle. An international scandal and the threat of capital flight by foreign investors forced the government to repudiate that claim and nationalize the mine.[36] A few years later the US geologist was quietly welcomed back, the Kenyan government paid some compensation, and the mine began production again.[37]

Further afield, Sri Lanka, too, produces rubies but is better known for sapphires. For decades the unchallenged leader at the highest end of that market was Kashmir. However its mines were long ago played out. Anything left now is in an area overrun by competing guerrilla groups variously seeking independence, union with Pakistan, or Islamic rule, in the face of a vicious Indian counterinsurgency campaign. Although the Kashmiri brand name still sends the market soaring – in 2007 Christie's auctioned a 22-carat Kashmiri sapphire for more than $3 million, about $135,000 per carat – the real action long ago switched to other places, of which Sri Lanka is number 1. Every night its alluvial fields fill with illegal miners; every day the streets of the main town in the gem-mining area abound with buyers. Low-quality stones along with fakes get unloaded on tourists, while the finest are snapped up by professionals and snuck out to Hong Kong, Singapore, and especially Bangkok, secure in diplomatic pouches, hidden in spice and tea packets, stuffed into corpses supposedly being sent home for burial, even mixed with loads of live lobsters exported to Bangkok restaurants.[38]

In more recent years the Thai grip on the world's gem-quality corundum has extended even to Madagascar, host of perhaps the largest previously unexploited deposits, not just of sapphires and rubies but of emeralds, garnets, aquamarines, tourmalines, and even some diamonds.[39] Most mining is done by impoverished locals on an island that was already a grossly overpopulated, deforested environmental wasteland before the gem rush made matters worse. Miners use the most basic kind of equipment, like children who can wriggle into smaller holes, reducing the required digging, unless they are unable to wriggle out again. Those who find stones may get ripped off by buyers, have their money stolen by police, or spend what little they get on booze, prostitutes, or overpriced supplies. Cash deals are the norm, with a parallel banking system ready to covert foreign to local currency for a small discount over official rates. The iron rule here, as almost everywhere on the gemstone frontier, is that amateur buyers and foreign tourists must be cheated. When the government recently tightened up, the main result seems to be a drop in smuggling by unlicensed traders who were vulnerable to airport searches and an increase in invoice fraud by licensed Thai buyers who underdeclare quantity, quality, or weight on stones officially bound for Bangkok.[40]

Back in Thailand, Chinese entrepreneurs have made the country second only to India as an exporter of gemstones and second only to Italy as an exporter of finished jewellery. Of course, they had help from the government – zero tariffs on imported raw materials about whose origins no one asks, low income taxes, absence of real anti-trust laws so that manufacturers can make deals not to hire away each other's skilled workers, free use of the country's burgeoning prison population for unskilled jobs, subsidized credit, and government encouragement of a second business for which Bangkok is now world renowned. American, European, and Israeli wholesalers, along with countless thousands of retail customers, can combine the pleasures of gem-buying with tours of Bangkok's legendary sex district, something that grew up to service US soldiers on R&R during the Vietnam war and today offers buyers a choice of all possible shapes, sizes, and ages, much as do the country's gemstone dealers. And Thailand's gem industry has another distinction, albeit one about which it is unlikely to brag, at least in public. As to what the country's gem business, like its sex trade, did behind closed doors, that was strictly its own affair, as long as clients didn't complain too much.

SKIN DEEP?

Pliny the Elder, the great Roman senator, naval commander, and naturalist, carefully studied the geological processes from which beautiful gemstones are formed – although not thoroughly enough to prevent himself from being buried under ash when Mount Vesuvius erupted in 79 AD. Before that unfortunate event, he ventured an opinion that still resonates today. "There is no fraud or deceit in the world," he opined, "that yields greater gain and profit than that of counterfeiting gems."[41] Of course, he wrote before the modern tobacco, petroleum, or "defense" industries existed. But he still had a point.

Treatments to enhance or change colour, improve clarity, or hide flaws long predate Pliny. Ancient Egyptians substituted coloured glass for real minerals, glazed over ordinary material to make it appear gem-like, and dipped hot rock crystal in cedar oil mixed with sulphur to create a semblance to ruby. Lapidaries discovered how to put foil behind stones to increase lustre and soak them in vinegar to liven up colour. And traders misrepresented the provenance of stones to buyers who, even back then, might value place of origin as much or more than physical and optical properties.[42]

By today's standards these processes were crude: chemicals were rudimentary, and not until the end of the nineteenth century were ovens able to reach temperatures now used for heat treatments or creating synthetics. Still, the results could be impressive. In 1758, Joseph Strasser of Vienna developed a glass with a high refractive index that could be ground to look like diamonds. Although banned from sale, his handiwork achieved a cult following; today there is a cottage industry faking his fakes.

There were also genuine mistakes. Henry V's renowned Black Prince Ruby is actually a spinel, a much less valuable stone; and in Charlemagne's Talisman, one "sapphire" is glass, the other quartz. There are no doubt many other pretenders to aristocratic status whose ancestry is basely common. However it was standard practice until the nineteenth century to refer to any deep-red stone, for example, as a ruby. Today there is no such excuse. Yet some curators of historic collections seem slow to correct the record, possibly because the misclassifications are useful to coax admission revenues out of visitors who remain blissfully unaware that they could satisfy their parvenu aspirations just as easily by a trip to the local flea market.

Today manipulation ranges along a spectrum from imitations with no geochemical relationship to the supposed gemstone at one extreme to synthetic reproductions of natural forces at the other. In between lie assembly jobs, artificial colouring, oiling, irradiation, heat treatments, fissure filling, surface-colour diffusion, and patching with synthetic material. Even the two extremes contain subdivisions. On the imitation end, the gambit runs from simple plastic reproductions to complex manufacture of lookalike materials; on the synthesis end, techniques exist to cook up everything from rubies out of tiny seed crystals to diamonds from Jack Daniels whiskey.

Treatments can be applied to rough stones or to polished gems. Partly it depends on the nature of the treatment: partly it reflects who is on the receiving end – bedazzled newlyweds, seniors with failing eyesight, greedy tax evaders, or gemstone pros with state-of-the-art detection gear. Although particular types of stones are amenable to particular forms of "enhancement," with some almost anything goes. Lapis lazuli, for example, on closer examination can turn out to be: the real thing dyed to deepen the colour; another mineral whose natural blue is close enough to fool a casual buyer; a completely unrelated stone artificially coloured; or a synthetic substitute. True, the lapis might even turn out to be as nature made it. But today the cautious buyer will presume any expensive gemstone guilty until proven innocent.

With an assembly job, two or more pieces are stuck together to mimic a genuine stone. In general, one or more parts are natural, the other(s) fake or synthetic, with coloured adhesive to bind them. The usual method of detection is to look for colour differences on the two sides of the separation plane. But if stones are carefully put together, with genuine material on top and seams covered by a setting, they are difficult to recognize. The colour variation can be eliminated, too, by melting together splinters of genuine precious stone to produce pieces of a larger size.[43]

The simplest forms of treatment of a single stone focus on colour, easiest if a stone is amorphous (non-crystalline) in structure. Turquoise is impregnated with paraffin, sodium silicate or plastic to "colour-stabilize" it. Dyes and bleaches "improve" lapis, alabaster, pearl, even coral and ivory.[44] But opal is perhaps in a class by itself in terms of the imaginative way its appearance (and price) is enhanced.

Australia's Lightning Ridge is reputedly a place where people go by first names or aliases, keep no records, conduct business in cash, guard inventory with heavy-duty firepower, and settle disputes the old-fashioned way – although most of this, whatever its historical basis, is now put about mainly to titillate tourists.[45] More than a mining town, it is also a cutting centre, particularly renowned for black opals. They could be the result of nature. They could also be the result of putting a stone in a hot sugar solution, then immersing it in sulphuric acid to release carbon from the sugar into the stone's open pores. Alternatively the opal might be smoked, much as a ham is cured, over burning wood, although in some cases, allegedly, the preferred fuel is sheep manure, suggesting that the usual test, touching the stone to the tongue to try to detect sugar, may not always be a good idea.[46] The danger is that the smoke tint will wash or wipe off. So the technique might be enhanced by infusing the stone with wax or plastic. And it is always possible to just use glass – it has much the same hardness as opal.

Since simple enhancement techniques like that don't work with crystals, one alternative dating back hundreds, perhaps thousands of years, is to use oil to hide inclusions or occlusions (fragments of alien substances or minute cavities filled with gas or liquid), fissures, and cracks, and therefore improve surface lustre. This is particularly popular with emeralds. Because of the geological processes by which they are formed, emeralds have more flaws than other precious stones, marring appearance and making them prone to cracking and chipping. The simplest way to hide flaws is to place the emerald in a machine to suck out the air, then fill cracks with an organic oil – the effect can be enhanced if the oil is tinted an appropriate green shade. Subjected to hot lights in a shop window, or even to the dry air of a charter flight heading home with a load of happy suntanned tourists, the oil may dry up and the stone return to its original, flawed appearance. More recent practice is to fill cracks and fissures with polymer or epoxy resin, along with a hardener to seal the surface. The closer is the filler's refractive index to that of the natural stone, the better it hides flaws and therefore jacks up the price.[47]

Many rubies and sapphires are also oiled, and subjected to more elaborate manipulation. Irradiating a gem improves clarity and colour, though only temporarily.[48] Heating (practiced for millennia, but at much lower temperatures than now attainable) is more reliable. Applied to rubies, "low" temperatures eliminate the blue that tends to give a stone a purplish hue. Higher heat melts the "silk" to clarify the stone. The result of both is a clearer, richer red. Whether done in crude charcoal-heated crucibles or computer-controlled electronic ovens, the technique is so widely used that today almost all stones coming out of Thailand are heat treated.

Heating can be combined with more aggressive techniques. Burma's Mong Hsu rubies that today dominate the market are both weakly coloured and physically flawed. So some Thai "burners" paint the surface with silica gel, then melt the glass into cracks and fissures. For a better job they "heal" the stone by using lasers to drill out inclusions, then fill the holes with glass or synthetic corundum.[49]

With sapphires, heat treatment can be supplemented by surface diffusion. Stones are packed in a crucible with iron, titanium and perhaps cobalt, then heated to near melting point (about two thousand degrees Celsius), until the stones absorb the chemicals. Originally used by Union Carbide for industrial gemstones, in the 1970s a Swiss company licensed the technology to colour and sell geuda, a naturally colourless sapphire. It disclosed the process to wholesale clients, but what wholesalers told retailers or retailers related to their customers was, of course, out of its hands. After the method was picked up in Thailand, treated stones quietly entered the general trade, initially with no one the wiser. By the late 1980s, instead of just using the technique on pale stones, Thai burners applied it to those whose colour was already good but uneven, to improve quality and increase price. Since the colour diffuses shallowly, it is done only to already cut stones. But if a buyer subsequently wants a sapphire cleaned and restored, the artificial colour could still be polished right off. However the temporary effect can be spectacular, commercially speaking, changing, for example, colourless geuda that used to be purchased wholesale in Sri Lanka for cents per carat into deep blue that could retail for thousands of dollars.[50] And that trick is complemented by another.

Around the millennium, when a rare and extremely valuable orange-pink sapphire ("padparadscha") from Sri Lanka became the latest gemstone rage, Thai burners discovered that a much cheaper Madagascar stones could be coated with borax and heated in the presence of oxygen to created an orange rim around the surface of the stone. The results were almost indistinguishable from the real thing, particularly with the additional precaution of moving the finished stones to Sri Lanka before sale.[51]

In all of these cases, the stone starts as a pure product of geology, then is subjected to an array of interventions, leaving open to debate the point at which the gem properly qualifies as fake or artificial. To those who make a living by trading gems, it also leaves open to debate the point at which the desire to avoid lawsuits or a visit from the fraud squad suggests that the customer be told in advance. However with the "queen of gems" the industry answer seems settled – tell the client nothing.

SHELL GAME

Pearl is the only "precious stone" not just of organic origin (also true of amber) but the product of living rather than fossilized nature. If a piece of alien matter, or a parasite, gets inside a mollusk and can't be expelled, the mollusk coats the invader with nacre, the same calcium carbonate material from which it constructs a shell. With a bit of luck, a pearl is born, or at least a lump of pearl-like material that can be used to assemble composites or do mother-of-pearl inlay work.[52]

Pearls, probably discovered by accident by fisher folk, have long been treasured across Asia. For centuries great pearl fisheries in the Persian Gulf and off Ceylon sufficed to meet Eastern demand. Then came rising popularity in the West, a function of war and conquest on the supply side and the usual mix of magic, medicine, and mercenary instinct on the demand. The Romans looted massive amounts in their Eastern campaigns; then the Crusaders brought back from the Holy Land both defeat and a taste for, among other luxuries, the pearl's lustrous beauty, sufficiently for early sumptuary laws to prohibit the lower classes from wearing them.[53]

Although Europe knew freshwater pearls, they were not as striking as Eastern saltwater ones. Portugal briefly conquered pearl-producing areas in the Indian Ocean but was bested by Spain when Christopher Columbus "discovered" a great pearl fishery off the coast of Venezuela. One of his successors, Hernando de Soto, also spotted aboriginals wearing pearls in Florida and decided that robbing graves to strip corpses of pearls was easier than diving for them. When Vasco Nuñez crossed Panama to the Pacific side, he found Indians there were willing to trade pearls for trinkets. The local cacique even pledged one hundred pounds of them a year as tribute to the Spanish rulers, an early case of casting pearls before swine. Until the silver mines opened in the mid-sixteenth century, pearls were Spanish America's most valuable export.[54] But they were not to last. The Spanish so plundered the seabed that the fishery collapsed within a few decades. In the meantime aboriginal slaves were forced into the water until they died, reputedly attracting so many sharks that they hindered the fishery and led to edicts demanding not an end to forced labour but that bodies be immediately retrieved. When aboriginal labour became scarce, black slaves were substituted, though the military had to put down periodic rebellions. The Spanish American fisheries were ostensibly royal prerogatives, leased to private individuals provided they paid an initial 5 percent, eventually to rise to 20 percent, to the Crown. Naturally the entrepreneurs preferred to sell to itinerant smuggling ships or to carry the finest pearls to European markets by themselves.[55]

By contrast, the fishery in the Persian Gulf lasted for thousands of years and was always decentralized. From Bahrain until comparatively recently hundreds of small boats set out each season with a captain who was often the owner (although in debt to a merchant who provided supplies and took the catch), a couple of divers, some rope-tenders, and an extra hand or two to relieve the others during prayer times. Divers leapt in with virtually no gear except nose plugs and thirty- to fifty-pound stones to drag them quickly to the bottom, facing sharks, sawfish and giant clams on the one side, lung disease, arthritis, early blindness, and long-term brain damage from oxygen deprivation on the other. Sometimes thousands of oysters had to be taken to secure a decent pearl. Extracting it from layers of encrusting mother-of-pearl required great skill, lest the pearl be damaged and devalued. Perhaps because of the uncertainties, pearl-boat captains might have another occupation – piracy. Later as the pearl fishery declined, their night job was more likely smuggling whiskey, Swiss watches, porno movies, ivory, or gold between East Africa, the Arabian peninsula, and the Indian subcontinent.

Ultimately the impact of oil – high wages in the oil fields drew off workers, and pollution from the wells ravaged oyster beds – combined with a flood of cultured pearls to devastate the Gulf fishery. Today remaining crews are aging; traditional skills are disappearing; and oyster beds declining further, something that recent wars have accelerated. The little remaining catch is gobbled up by dealers from London, New York, and Geneva. The rarer natural pearls become, the higher their price. That, of course, opens interesting possibilities for pulling a bait-and-switch on untutored clients.

Fake pearls can be made from glass, ceramic, or plastic, then covered with varnish or lacquer and ground fish-scales. But they are generally smooth, while real pearls feel gritty. Fakes, too, tend to be more homogenous in colour, while real ones come in a variety of hues and tones. Fakes are likely uniform in shape, while the genuine are varied. Still, the real challenge lies not in differentiating genuine from fake but natural from cultured.

Although reports of seeding oysters go way back, the big breakthrough came at the end of the nineteenth century, when the Japanese learned to open an oyster without destroying the abductor muscle: insert beads along with a piece of mantle tissue from a living mollusk to stimulate nacre secretion, then let it close; the oyster was returned to its habitat for long enough that, if the oyster did not die or expel the intruding object, a pearl might form. When cultured pearls first appeared, the traditional industry fought efforts to pass off them off as natural. But demand for pearls, combined with the cheapness of the cultured product, defeated resistance. During the roaring twenties the industry took off, only to crash during the Depression and subsequent war. By the 1950s it was airborne again to spread, almost totally under Japanese control, across the South Pacific in pursuit of unpolluted water. Today the cultured have overwhelmed the natural.

Finding natural pearls is a matter of luck; with cultured, barring environmental problems, every seeded oyster ought to produce. Natural pearls form in oysters clinging to rocks in normal feeding grounds; cultured take shape in oysters dangled back into the water in mesh bags. In fact today, instead of pulling up wild oysters, seeding them, then returning them to their natural habitat, cultivators might hatch oysters in glass tanks in an onshore laboratory, seed them, then transfer them to baskets hung in saltwater. Because the shape of the nucleus is controlled, cultured stones are more reliably rounded; and because the size of the nucleus is predetermined, they can be harvested much faster. A natural pearl takes about four years to reach commercial size: a cultured one much less. No doubt someday somewhere someone trained in the modern beef or poultry industries will figure out how to inject a mollusk with growth hormones, then program it to spit out giant pearls in a manner of days, maybe already trademarked and strung on pre-inserted plastic fibre.

According to industry claims, there is no real difference between cultured and natural. Both are produced by the same biochemical process and given the same treatments after "harvest." Most emerge with a yellowish sheen removed to enhance lustre by soaking them in chemical bleaches, then subjecting them to UV light and heat. Poorly rounded ones are artificially tumbled. Sometimes people drilling holes for stringing could peer inside or examine drill dust to find out if the nucleus consisted of a bit of shell or an artificial bead; but certainty required an X-ray. Even that no longer works. The industry learned to seed a mollusk without a bead so that the resulting pearl is pure nacre, then muddied the distinction, too, between fresh- and saltwater pearls by taking tiny, imperfect pearls from one, tumbling them to assure a round shape, and using them as nucleating material in the other.[56]

While the industry claims they are all the same, it belies its own propaganda with its marketing strategy, setting a price hierarchy of natural saltwater, natural freshwater, cultured saltwater, and cultured freshwater, with further subdivisions based on place of origin. Given the price differences, freshwater pearls get marketed as saltwater, and pearls cultured in China are sold as Japanese. Yet top place actually goes to the Caribbean queen conch. About one in ten thousand produces a pearl. Of those few, the vast majority are mediocre; but the finest can retail for $10,000 a carat. Added to the pressure from giant trawlers and millions of tourists who insist on trying conch chowder even though they usually dislike the fishy taste, or who further insist on hauling home beautiful new conch shells to make kitschy ashtrays and lamps, the queen conch pearl rush has hastened the conch's march, together with kinfolk like the oyster and the abalone, along the path toward extinction in the wild, while "science" proclaims breakthroughs in the potential to raise that great gastropod, too, like it does diseased salmon in polluted fish farms.[57]

REALITY CHECK

As stones advance along the chain of human interventions – irradiated, heated in electronic ovens, colour diffused with added chemicals, then "healed" with synthetic substances – the obvious question becomes: why not go all the way? Early twentieth-century efforts to synthesize gem crystals were too expensive and time-consuming to threaten the market. The turning point came in World War II, when the US needed a domestic source of synthetics to make jewelled bearings for military equipment. Today more and more synthetic gemstones are available at cheaper and cheaper prices. Some are non-crystalline. But the most important are single crystals grown in controlled conditions to mimic geological processes. Unlike simulates or imitations or even enhanced stones, they have the same physical properties as those formed by nature.

While most synthetic crystals still go to industrial use (abrasives, watch movements, lasers, aerospace technology, even missile nosecones), some end up on the gemstone market, perhaps with certificates from "laboratories" attesting to authenticity. Not only is the price trend downward, but the capacity to fool the beholder has improved over time. When synthetic spinels first hit the market in 1915, they were easy to detect; but today's synthetic rubies and emeralds can look perfect. In fact that may be the best way to detect what they really are – nature never produces a perfect ruby or emerald.[58] However some modern synthesizing techniques result in stones with tiny flaws. And even with those that emerge unnaturally flawless, clever fakers, rather than just filling natural stones to hide flaws, might induce fissures and cracks in synthetic ones.[59]

Of course, synthesis produces only rough material. Before it can be cut into gems posing as natural, it has to enter regular trade channels – some will be cooperative; others must be fooled. Synthetic crystal can be broken, burned, artificially stained, or buried for a while to make it seem natural. One way is to introduce synthetic rough at a mine site, for example, stuck onto local rock or mixed with natural gem material.[60] This occurs now with tanzanite, a blue variant of the mineral zoisite that only true collectors wanted until it played a starring role around the neck of an otherwise naked Kate Winslet in the Hollywood hit *Titanic*. That so much "tanzanite" on the market is actually common green zoisite coloured blue by heat treatment is a secret the industry rarely chooses to share with its trend-obsessed clientele.

The tanzanite story actually begins in Kenya several decades ago with Campbell Bridges, a British gemologist who first made his name by finding a commercial deposit of a rare green garnet, since named tsavorite, in an area of Kenya (Tsavora) that now hosts one of its largest game parks. Later venturing across the border, he came across the blue mineral whose name reflects its (so far) sole geological location, a small area of Tanzania where it is mined and sold under the same conditions that prevail in most of that country's gemstone ventures. Independent prospectors using primitive equipment – including children to get in and sometimes out of small holes and narrow tunnels that have a propensity to flood or collapse – then sell tanzanite to informal dealers, either directly to their scouts on site or in the nearby city of Arusha. Those dealers dump some of low quality on Western tourists who flock to Arusha to join "safaris" bound for the Tanzanian game reserves, and smuggle more of it, using Massai tribesmen who can cross the Kenyan border with impunity, to Nairobi. From there it goes, partly to Bangkok, mainly to Jaipur in India for manufacture. Meanwhile synthetic stuff made in Russian gem labs can be snuck into mine sites with the cooperation of local miners. There it is mixed with loads of genuine material heading to the US, still its leading market, complete with the best kind of fake certificate of origin, one issued by a government-approved agency.[61]

As to the man who found the first commercially exploited deposits, as economic times in Kenya got tougher, he, like other white landlords whose present-day holdings date back to forced seizures during British colonial rule, found more and more desperate black Kenyans encroaching in search of gemstones. When he tried to get police to clear them off, the officer in charge was ordered by his superiors to let them go. Bridges followed up by pressing trespassing charges against another group of illegal miners who responded by hacking him to death.[62]

JAILHOUSE ROCKS

Some experts claim not just to spot synthetics but to pinpoint production technique using nothing more than a loupe. However truly effective detection requires lasers to fingerprint gemstones, too expensive for most retail jewellers, let alone individual buyers. Anyway, by the time a stone reaches a properly equipped lab, the perpetrator of a con may be lying under a palm tree recovering from plastic surgery. Furthermore, if a jeweller discovers he has been had, he may do like a merchant stuck with counterfeit money – just pass it on to a client. In fact that may have been the intent all along.

Take, for instance, Jack Hasson, a West Palm Beach gem dealer who relished a lifestyle – with a fleet of boats, two private jets, a mansion in an elite section of Key West, a $7 million ranch, and private schools for his children – appropriate to the reputed status of the goods he sold. Operating in a resort where almost everyone was a multimillionaire, over the course of a decade he bilked his tony clientele for about $160 million in overpriced, altered or fake jewels, stashing money in foreign, offshore, and US accounts under false names.

More than his gems were fake. He backed up sales with do-it-yourself certificates from Cartier, Tiffany, and Van Cleef. Even his credentials from gemology school proudly mounted on his wall were phony. So, too, were a bevy of appraisal forms, receipts, purchase orders, checks, and stories about his business. He told clients that he had people like Bill Gates, Stephen Spielberg, and Elizabeth Taylor queuing for his merchandise and that he was in competition with the Smithsonian Institute for some particularly fine specimens. If clients were still unsure, Hasson would recommend they take the stones to an "independent" appraiser with whom he had a side deal, while advising them to always beware of outside appraisals lest some unscrupulous soul try to switch their stones. That warning was based on experience. Sometimes when clients brought in jewellery for repair or appraisal, Hasson and his nimble assistant could in 30 seconds, the assistant bragged, remove the real stones and plug in synthetics or fakes.

To be fair to Hasson, some of his gems were genuine, barring minor embellishments like irradiation to enhance colour or cracks filled with oil or epoxy. On occasion he sold a quality real one, then persuaded the client to have it genuinely appraised – that way he built up credibility in preparation for a major con.

While Hasson had a long list of well-known, well-to-do clients including golf stars like Jack Nicklaus and Greg Norman, his biggest customer was a former media mogul who had sold his TV station for $175 million and decided to plunk $80 million into Hasson's fine gems.[63] Hasson had told the savvy investor that the richest man in the world, the Sultan of Brunei, wanted to buy Hasson's rare blue diamonds, some from the collection of an imaginary Walmart heiress. If the prospective client got these stones first, Hasson claimed, he could sew up the market. To make it more credible, Hasson dressed up one of his employees to pose as the Sultan of Brunei's nephew and hired a hooker to get pictures of the client in compromising positions. The ex-media mogul passed on the hooker but, after a scene on a private plane where he was introduced to two beautiful escort-service employees in diaphanous *I Dream of Jeannie* outfits, bought the story about the nephew and, with it, the diamonds, most of which turned out to be cubic zirconiums, then the most popular diamond simulant, that Hasson himself had tinted blue. But despite the time and effort he spent to sell "diamonds," Hasson was no snob – he was equally willing to peddle citrines, tourmalines, low-quality topaz, and mediocre sapphires at a price high enough to swell a client's chest(s) with pride. In fact, the collection he peddled to the media mogul included a blue topaz for $3 million, or $10,000 for each carat later optimistically valued at $10.[64]

Hasson's usual MO if he was caught was to blame the mix-up on a disgruntled employee who had already been fired. If a client became testy, Hasson would settle out of court for less than the client had paid, then resell the items to someone else, protected by a confidentiality agreement. If there was a hint that the client violated the agreement, Hasson would sue. It didn't always work. When the wife of Jack Nicklaus discovered through a routine insurance appraisal that her $35,000 ruby was synthetic, Hasson obligingly replaced it – with another fake. Nicklaus then had appraisals done on all the jewellery he had obtained from Hasson. His $500,000 investment turned out to be worth so little that Hasson settled out of court for a $380,000 refund and an agreement that Nichlaus would keep quiet. However the news got to Greg Norman, who, on the basis of Nicklaus's recommendation, had parted with $450,000 for jewellery that included a cluster of coloured diamonds Hasson had supposedly hauled personally from South Africa. In reality he had sold to Norman a pile of synthetic and irradiated stones worth about $7,000, all obtained locally. The end result was a forty-year sentence for fraud, money-laundering, and obstruction of justice and a court order to pay nearly $80 million in restitution, the largest penalty ever imposed on a jeweller in the US. The judge tossed in three years for Hasson's lawyer as a penalty for helping to hide the loot.[65]

Of course, those stuck with grossly overvalued gemstones need not abandon all hope. There is at least a chance they can successfully recoup a fair chunk, perhaps all, of the purchase price by following the example of a smooth-talking, polo-playing Spaniard. He set up four Liechtenstein companies and used them to borrow $45 million from several banks, pledging as collateral emeralds, rubies, and sapphires "worth" $90 million. When the loans went into arrears and the custodial institution in Switzerland finally brought in appraisers, they discovered that the stones were US shopping-mall models worth 5–10 percent of their declared value.[66]

GEMSTONES AND PET ROCKS

If the sole reason for buying a stone were its inherent beauty, there would be little reason to worry whether it is natural, artificially enhanced, or even totally synthetic. Since beauty is in the (so often myopic, astigmatic, or cataract-afflicted) eye of a beholder, some people would be just as happy with pet rocks. Even if the purpose is to flaunt a gem (or many) in front of jealous peers, origin and constitution ought not to matter, provided it cost enough. In that case it would make more sense to leave the gem at home in a safe and just wear the invoice. Subtle differences between various qualities or between natural stones and good fakes are generally impossible to detect by the naked eye, and few people bring a laser fingerprinting machine to cocktail parties. "Authenticity" becomes important when the insecurity that drives high-end demand is more financial than sexual in nature. That is why purchasers of "investment grade" stones insist on a certificate and, if they are really smart, take considerable interest in who issued it.

Until the 1980s if a stone had the qualities typically found in those from a certain location, it was so classified. If customers did not realize that Muso or Mogok or Kashmir were brand names rather than place names, the vendor was unlikely to disabuse them. But with new technology to pinpoint optical, physical, and chemical properties along with the nature and pattern of inclusions, the trend became to insist on geographic accuracy. So now all rubies legally purchased in Thailand, for example, exit with certificates attesting to Thai origins. With that they may pass customs back home, especially in places like the US, which impose sanctions on Myanmar. Once inside the country of destination, new certificates may miraculously appear attesting to Burmese provenance – even if the rough stones really came from Cambodia, Vietnam, Sri Lanka, Madagascar, or Afghanistan, a double con. In fact the claim that while Burma produces 90 percent of the world's rubies, only 3 percent of those entering the US are so identified was one pretext for the introduction into the US Congress of the Block Burmese JADE (Junta's Anti-Democratic Effects) Act – publicity value trumping grammar and logic in the choice of name.[67] The purpose of the legislation was to tighten existing sanctions and so further isolate a military regime whose obsession had always been to find more ways to close the country off from the rest of the world.[68]

Despite advances in forensic geology, the results even in reputable labs are far from perfect. It is difficult to attest accurately to the provenance of very small stones. Besides, given the cost of investigation and the fact that most are diverted to jewellery rather than to the investment market, they are rarely tested. Even for large stones there are obstacles. New locations with stones of different geochemical makeup are constantly found. As digging proceeds to new depths or fresh areas within established locations, characteristics also change. No matter how hard a lab tries to keep its range of samples updated, it will inevitably lag. Once stones have been altered, particularly by high temperatures, it becomes more difficult, sometimes impossible, to pinpoint origin.

Nor can the industry be trusted to adequately disclose treatments. It has to balance its desire to maintain autonomy against the threat of external regulation while also fending off the danger of lawsuits from clients angry that they were sold stones that have begun to resemble modern US cuisine – wrapped in plastic, stuffed with preservatives, covered with oil, cooked in an oven or nuked in a microwave until the colour change suggests it is well done, then served sprinkled with artificial colorants, with the additional possibility that the raw material might have been grown in a gemological greenhouse from a geochemically modified seed-crystal.

The prevailing view is that only temporary fixes, like oiling, zapping with X-rays, or plugging holes with glass or plastic, need be revealed – even though there is no way of ensuring that they are. Since more long-term measures like heat treatment are "normal trade practice," that information is best kept discretely in house.[69] After all, the claim goes, heat treatment simply completes nature's job. The argument about completing nature's handiwork certainly has merit provided that: geological forces remain constant over eons; the relative presence or absence of trace elements never changes in response to natural pressures; the particles inside the stone do not themselves shift state and position or even pick up alien intruders in response to artificially applied heat; and the person doing the treatment would have been prepared to hang around for several million years to retrieve the naturally finished stones.

Disagreements over show-and-tell-how-much combined with different national standards also mean that information even on proper paperwork is vulnerable to exploitation. Thus, the most important US lab ascertains if stones have been heat-treated; the biggest Swiss one does not. A smart gem dealer might insist on seeing the US lab report to knock down the purchase price, then, once a heat-treated stone is bought, resell it with a Swiss certificate at the higher price of an unheated one.

If there were total disclosure, the only sane policy, the industry would be free to serve up a gemstone coloured and cut to resemble a cheese-mushroom-and-pepperoni pizza, if that suited consumer tastes – given today's standards, it would likely be a big hit. After all, if clients know what they are buying, there is no reason to be any more hesitant about an oiled stone than an oiled antique chest of drawers. In fact, if demand were driven purely by aesthetics, gem treatment ought to enhance not reduce value. And those concerned about the ecological or human devastation that gemstone mining can cause ought to prefer a synthetic. But, alas, the fundamental problem is that today high-end gemstones have ceased to have much to do with mystery, medicine, or magic – except the magic of the market; and aesthetics now take second place to short-term profit, one thing that has trouble coexisting with honesty or openness or much else of genuine value. Of course, looking on the bright side, the situation with diamonds is worse.[70]

Icecapades: The Diamond's Darker Facets

The most expensive diamond engagement ring in the world, declared ex-gambling czar turned luxury real-estate promoter (and recent US presidential hopeful) Donald Trump when he gave a $2 million 12-carat rock to supermodel Melania Knauss – who was also honoured with the task of ringing the closing bell for NASDAQ to celebrate the Fifth Annual National Love Our Children Day.[1] She may have gotten her ring in the nick of time. When the big crisis hit, Trump, facing insolvency – his serial bankruptcy record may be his best preparation for the US presidency – pleaded in court that his inability to pay off his major creditors on his latest condo project was an Act of God, not of personal hubris. Besides, he further charged, his main backer, Deutsche Bank, had caused him $3 billion worth of reputational damage for daring to ask for the return of $40 million that Trump had personally guaranteed.[2] A victory for Trump (at least in court) would presumably buy a lot more big rocks for Melania.

On the other hand, perhaps his bride no longer needs his generosity, given the success of her own jewellery business. Back in autumn 2005 when she was hosting the Vacheron Constantin 250th anniversary party at the New York Public Library, Melania flashed for the cameras the Swiss brand's $600,000 44-carat Lady Kalla silhouette watch. "The sparkler," her website comments demurely, "turned almost as many heads as the model herself." A few years later came the launch of her "unbelievably well-received" *Melania™ Timepieces & Fashion Jewelry* on QVC, allowing her to expand her own description of her professional accomplishments to include "super model, entrepreneur and international jetsetter."[3]

Although the French adventurer Jean-Baptiste Tavernier would probably have objected to being called a supermodel, he qualifies as much as Melania as an international jetsetter, barring the fact that back in the seventeenth century he had to travel by sailing ship. When he reported on his visit to India, then the world's sole producer of diamonds, he stressed one reason for the stone's commercial success that may also shed light on Donald Trump's preferences: "All the Orientals are very much of our taste in matters of whiteness .... (T)hey prefer the ... whitest diamonds, the whitest bread, and the whitest women."[4] Tavernier also had a few things to say about how diamond traders contrived to keep the stones scarce: they spread stories that mines were "situated in barbarous countries to which one could not travel except by the most dangerous routes"; they tightly supervised a bonded labour force to reduce pilferage; they dealt with each other in a code that they alone understood; they handed out fine stones to appease tax officials; and they offered the bulk to foreign buyers in sealed parcels that had to be accepted or rejected as a whole.[5] Any similarity, in spirit and in fact, to industry practices of recent decades is not just coincidental.[6]

However there is at least one big difference now. Before the mid-nineteenth century few would have suggested that diamonds were beautiful. Cutting and polishing was done mainly to hide flaws, for example by grinding off damaged faces.[7] Even after the perfection of methods to bring out internal fire, the stones were (are) bland compared to the splendour of a fine star-ruby or even the fascinating variegations of a common agate.[8] For a long time their main appeal was in the magic they represented and a hardness appreciated for industrial or even medical uses. Convinced that the legendary durability of diamonds could be passed on to people, the sixteenth-century Pope Clement VII, on his doctor's orders, began to sprinkle diamond powder on his food. Two weeks later and 40,000 ducats poorer, he died.[9]

Another difference was that in former times diamonds were worn exclusively by men, closely guarded within families for generations, and rarely seen by outsiders – unless they stole them. Witness the trajectory of the Koh-i-Noor, which passed through conquest from Hindu to Mughal to Persian to Afghan to Sikh rulers while remaining in pristine condition, only to be finally ceded to the British after the conquest of the Punjab. It was then so carved up (losing over 40 percent of its bulk) as to turn a historical treasure into a glittering bauble to pander to a British queen's vanity. That is an apt metaphor for the greater transformation of diamonds as a whole. The main purpose of possession today is to publicly one-up largely female social rivals, culminating in those two perky pinnacles so tastefully celebrated in Victoria's Secret bras, featuring diamonds in the thousands and price tags in the millions.

Alternatively the purpose might be just to cash in stones when the market gets hot. And who could be more familiar with hot markets than professors of economics? For decades, during a student's first immersion in the magic of supply-and-demand, the profs insisted on the importance of the water-diamond paradox. Why, the instructor would ask, eyes as full of fire as a brilliant-cut Jager (pale, steel-blue) diamond, is something as useful as water free, while diamond, so useless, is so expensive? A more sensible riddle would have been the hot air-diamond paradox. Why is methane gas, whether emitted through biological decay or intellectual flatulence, so cheap when it can be converted into everything from Space Age plastic to nitrogenous fertilizer, while diamond is so expensive even if it, too, may be nothing more than methane geochemically transformed into something fit only for fobs and fools?

Apart from a few that fell literally from the heavens to be forged at the site of meteorite crashes, diamonds result when carbon-bearing material was subjected at least one hundred miles below the surface of the Earth to sufficient heat and pressure to crystallize it. Although most diamonds brought to the surface transform en route into graphite, the other naturally occurring form of pure carbon, any shot up sufficiently fast by an eruption, if not shattered by the force of the explosion, retain their crystal structure. Thus the most concentrated deposits are found in volcanic pipes that acted as conveyor belts from the depths, although many more end up scattered in alluvial deposits far from the source. Such an origin produces the intriguing possibility that there are still within the Earth billions of tons of diamonds, some perhaps the size of watermelons, waiting for someone to figure out how to get them to the surface, and then find a true supermodel capable of carrying them around a neck or finger.[10] Needless to say, that possible discovery fills today's diamond business with trepidation. Even worse, what if intrepid space explorers make their way to the Centaur constellation 50 light-years distant to land on a rock made up of solid diamond 2,500 miles in diameter, then figure out a way to haul it back to Earth?[11]

Nonetheless, the down-to-earth truth is that once India ceased to be the sole source, the entire history of the diamond trade became a long struggle against the nasty effects on the market (i.e., steady downward pressure on prices) of the fact that the diamond trade faced not a looming deficit of supply, something that hangs over the gold business as ore quality declines and costs rise, but a potential glut. The response came on both sides of the market. On the supply side, the diamond trade deployed its considerable political power to stop independents from flooding the market. On the demand side, the movers and shakers of the diamond world steadily moved what was once the most aristocratic of gems step by step down the social scale, from class market to mass market to crass market, a process that, if it continues, will culminate in a tiny diamond sparkling on the top of every Big Mac.

THE CRUCIBLE

When Tavernier arrived in India, then visited the diamond centre of Golconda, he described something that might have inspired a scene from the Arabian Nights. Great workshops handled not just diamonds but Burmese rubies, emeralds probably from what is now Afghanistan, and an array of lesser stones like spinels and chrysoberyls, while fashioning everything from jewelled scimitars to gold bindings of rare and sacred books, mainly copies of the Qur'ān. The city's wealth supported a good life for the rich, perhaps best captured by the image of more than twenty thousand registered courtesans who took turns dancing for the Sultan every Friday – assuming that story was not just the figment of the French traveller's fevered imagination after a long sea voyage deprived of female company.[12]

Yet, ironically enough, Tavernier made his observations about the abundance and splendour of India's diamonds just a few decades before they began to run out, sending prices soaring. However, for a diamond hungry world, or at least a privileged part of it, salvation was soon at hand.

Early in the eighteenth century, garampeiros hunting gold in Brazil turned up what was at first thought to be quartz crystals until a Portuguese trader familiar with India recognized them.[13] For a while the governor of the area kept the news quiet so he could scoop up diamonds for himself. Once the Crown found out, it scrambled to enforce its right to 20 percent of the production, slapped a head tax on miners and their slaves, and raised customs duties on goods heading into the area. But, as with gold, illegal mining and smuggling were epidemic. So the Crown kicked out of the diamond region any business not directly necessary to supply the mines, closed the area to entrepreneurial priests, and even briefly banned mining to push up prices. Over time it replaced licensed free-miners with monopoly companies using slave-labour forces, and it sold exclusive rights to buy diamonds to contractors whose convoys en route to official ships bound for Portugal were guarded by elite military units. It even paid a bounty to special militias to shake down anyone caught on forest trails. Variants of most of these became standard practice in diamond rushes to come.

In spite of the Crown's efforts, unlicensed mining, diversion from official mines, clandestine trading, and smuggling persisted. They, too, set precedents for the future. Foreign buyers haunted areas of Brazil where illegal stones were sold; foreign sailors, especially British and Dutch, were happy to act as couriers. Some traffickers infiltrated their own slaves into bush militias; priests, despite the ban, ran their usual rackets; and ship captains licensed to take the official product home also carried unlicensed stones to divert to foreign buyers. Phony provenance, too, figured early. Those with a stake in Indian stones spread stories that Brazilian ones were too soft, or fake, leading some merchants to take cheap Brazilian diamonds to Goa, the Portuguese enclave on India's west coast, to sell as Indian in origin.[14] For those stones that arrived officially in Lisbon, the Crown tried to create a major cutting centre. But further diversion occurred, mainly to London and Amsterdam, with an increasing number of stones ending up in Antwerp, the city that had dominated the diamond business when India was the source and eventually would again displace rivals as the capital of the European cutting and dealing business when Brazil was played out.

At the start of the Brazilian rush, Portugal sold fine stones to the European aristocracy. Then falling prices brought the ability to buy diamonds to the bourgeoisie, with the primary clientele shifting from male to female. The new zeal for diamonds meant faster depletion. Production was already falling sharply in the early nineteenth century, when Napoleon Bonaparte overran the Netherlands, still the main place where diamonds were cut and finished stones traded. Once he also invaded Spain, he was well placed to put the squeeze on Portugal, demanding a huge indemnity to refrain from military action. The Portuguese Crown managed to pay by borrowing in Britain but had to send a large part of its diamond inventory as collateral to London, the city's first step to an eventual lock on the business of trading rough stones. When Napoleon invaded anyway, the Portuguese king fled to Brazil, taking the remaining royal stockpile back to its geological home, while inside Portugal French officers and functionaries made off with diamonds aplenty as taxes, bribes, or "gifts."[15]

By mid-century, with Brazil in rapid decline, the world faced another diamond famine. Then came an even more dramatic discovery in South Africa that opened not just new alluvial fields but volcanic pipes to exploitation. By then workshops with horse- or steam-powered machinery were replacing traditional hand skills in working rough stones. The perfection of cutting techniques made dazzling visual effects rather than myth and magic the foundation of the stone's appeal. Thus the formerly regal diamond took another big step down the social ladder on its eventual way to Wal-Mart, although it had to await the automobile age and mass suburbanization to finish the trip, a transformation with far-reaching effects on the lore as well as the lure of diamonds.

The source of raw material for this modern-new glittering abundance was, for a long time, mainly South Africa, a country on which the impact was revolutionary. Until the late 1860s, the British had viewed the area mainly as a base to defend trade routes with India, leaving the interior largely to native peoples and old Dutch settlers. The Suez Canal threatened to diminish the country's strategic significance; but the discovery of diamonds, followed by gold and, later, key industrial minerals, did the reverse.[16] The first alluvial strike flooded the country with prospectors, many of them veterans of the California or Australia gold rushes who brought their techniques, common law, and con artists. At first African tribal leaders tried to collect royalties from miners and rent out workers who were expected to pay tribute in cattle, guns, or sometimes gold back to their chiefs. But chiefs quickly lost control of both the land and their young men. Soon Boer farmers, too, found their position marginalized. The British annexed the producing areas, then replaced its (white male) miners' democracy with a (even whiter male) colonial autocracy, one spectral development that Tavernier failed to anticipate. At the start of the twentieth century, that helped to spark another diamond rush as disbanded British soldiers, finding that control of the main diggings was in the hands of the same big companies that had pushed for the land seizures that contributed to the onset of the Boer War, poured in to mine river diggings. The most notorious were members of irregular units who had been paid not just a daily wage during the war but a bonus for all the cattle and horses they could steal from Boer farmers, and who invested their wartimes spoils in mining equipment.[17]

When South African diamonds had first begun appearing en masse on the market the trade establishment balked, either denying their existence or insisting that Brazilian ones were superior. Just as Brazilian stones initially masqueraded as Indian, in the early years South African were sold as Brazilian. (Faking place of origin, too, has deep roots in the diamond trade.) But sheer abundance won again, causing prices to fall rapidly at the same time that, back in the diggings, costs moved steadily up.

In the early years, the small miner faced a multiple squeeze. Black labour was scarce enough to bargain for decent (by the standards of the time and place) wages and working conditions. Since few miners had collateral to borrow from banks, private money-lenders soaked them with high interest costs. Landlords, too, could gouge on rents. When it came time to sell, miners faced a ladder of increasingly powerful commercial interests, each rung intent on getting the best for the least. Diggers had to sell to local dealers who sold to agents of big exporters who sold to London mercantile houses who sold at auction to brokers who sold to the cutting-and-polishing industry in Antwerp and Amsterdam.

Diggers even faced competition from their own claims. Workers pilfered stones, sometimes independently, sometimes on behalf of traffickers who planted their own people in the diggings. Receivers might resell under the table to agents of licensed dealers who could commingle stolen stones with legal, or to smugglers who could arrange covert shipment to Europe where the next set of buyers would introduce them quietly onto the market. A more sophisticated operation would involve buying a claim as a front for purchase and resale of illicit stones.[18] As alluvial sources were exhausted, the switch to volcanic pipes worsened the problem. Each pipe might host hundreds of independent diggers, each with hired hands. With the flood of production driving down prices, white miners responded with an equal-opportunity lynch law – black thieves were brutally punished, but any white man who bought stones from an African risked having his possessions destroyed and possibly his ears cut off before being tarred, feathered, and pilloried in the market square.[19]

In the 1880s, the mining sector tried a different strategy to ward off a glut. Cecil Rhodes, backed by big London diamond merchants, created De Beers Consolidated, which, over the next few decades, reacted to each crisis by buying up and closing down mining properties, the initial step toward a de facto monopoly that embraced not just diamonds but gold and strategic minerals, creating the corporate giants that came to dominate the entire South African economy.[20] Along with efforts at corporate concentration came the 1882 Diamond Trade Act. It shifted the burden of legal proof, forcing those found with diamonds to explain their origins. Since juries had been lenient to illegal dealers, it introduced special courts presided over only by judges. It created a special diamond department in the police force. It imposed much more severe penalties. And it approved the use not just of sting operations run by police, until then frowned upon by British courts, but of secret operatives drawn from the margins of society to entrap would-be traffickers in exchange for a percentage of the take, an open invitation to corruption that was a trailblazer for "drug war" tactics about a century later.

Theft, as mine owners sometimes admitted, was probably less a source of loss than sloppy technique. But it was easier to blame blacks for stealing. That also provided the rationalization for a third response to the glut, pushing down labour costs by increasing the supply and reducing the independence of black workers through measures that ultimately formed the foundations of the Apartheid system. Pass laws stipulated that any black found near a mining camp without a pass signed by his master or a magistrate could be arrested without warrant, lashed, or imprisoned, possibly with hard labour. And the labour force was penned up in closed compounds modelled on earlier convict-labour stations:

that greatly reduced both the chances of competitors bidding up wages and the desertion rate. Black workers were marched to and from work behind barbed wire under the eyes of club-wielding Zulu guards, strip-searched on entering and leaving, and subjected when terms of service ended to body probes, including forced purges. Closed compounds, too, reduced alcohol-induced absenteeism and gave companies additional profits from selling supplies to workers for more than independent merchants charged.[21] It is doubtful if any of these measures seriously reduced trafficking but highly probable that they drove down wage costs and guaranteed a docile labour supply.

Increased corporate control extended beyond production into the wholesale market. In 1892 De Beers created its first stockpile, its central instrument for stabilizing and steering the market for a century to come, from which it could leak or withhold particular types of diamonds to steer prices. Then it created the Central Selling Organization to collect and pool diamonds from participating producers before offering them to selected dealers and cutters at a "sight," something that could have been better named a "sight unseen." Like buyers in India in centuries past, those invited were offered a sealed box with no bargaining over price or content. If they refused, there was a good chance they would never be invited back. However for this strategy to be viable over the long haul, De Beers had to control the flow of rough stones not only from South Africa but from everywhere else on the continent where diamonds were subsequently found in abundance.[22]

PLAYING THE ACE OF DIAMONDS

By the 1920s consolidation was about complete, just in time for a further crisis. First the Great Depression, then World War II, largely shut down the gem market. But invention of the diamond grinding wheel started a long series of technical uses for small, malformed diamonds previously stockpiled or discarded. The strength, hardness, and heat-conductivity of diamonds and their capacity to take an extremely smooth polish meant that they would soon be essential for stone and metal cutting, drilling and mining (including oil wells), and especially precision work in war industries.

At the start of the war the Allies seemed to hold, if not all the trump cards, at least the Ace of Diamonds. All mines were in either Africa, where De Beers largely ran them, or South America, the USA's backyard. Early in the war the British sent a destroyer to Antwerp, world centre of diamond cutting, to pick up stocks before the Germans arrived. Diamonds the Nazis did grab in Europe were mainly gem quality. So in the years before the US became a declared belligerent, gems were smuggled by diplomatic pouch via Lisbon and Rio to New York, and the money used to pay spies or finance strategic purchases in the then-neutral country.[23] The Germans also set up trafficking rings or just negotiated with existing criminal bands to smuggle them from places like the Belgian-ruled Congo. Partly that came through leakages in security systems at the De Beers-controlled mines. More importantly, and an omen for the future, high prices and war-weakened colonial control encouraged illegal alluvial mining by natives who sold to dealers who passed the stones on to couriers who flew them to neutral areas where German agents were waiting.[24] In 1944, three years after the US entered the war, Chase National Bank was criminally indicted and a prominent New York diamond merchant jailed in a racket to sneak industrial diamonds into Germany via Panama. The German smuggling apparatus worked well enough that until the end of the war Germany turned out plenty of advanced weapons – it just didn't have the fuel to operate them. Still, the lessons learned during the war had a big impact on how De Beers in the years to come would try to defend its lock on the diamond business.

If that war directly goosed the industrial diamond market in the 1940s, preparation for the next one indirectly buoyed the gemstone market in the 1950s and beyond. The permanent war economy along with cheap oil, massive highway construction, and suburbanization transformed the social landscape, particularly in the US. Cookie-cutter couples drove cookie-cutter cars to and from cookie-cutter suburbs where they raised cookie-cutter kids after, thanks to a phenomenally successful PR campaign launched by De Beers, the process had been solemnized by cookie-cutter engagement rings. And what Hollywood starlet dared to appear in any even moderately successful movie without the warmth of her smile highlighted by the ice on her finger? Once the association of diamonds with eternal love was turned into a globetrotting road show, diamond rings became as much a part of the Americanization of tastes around the world as Coca-Cola – whose bottles could have been ground into something almost as flashy. But success still required a firm grip on the flow of rough stones onto the market.

GETTING ROUGH

De Beers owned outright the major mines in South Africa, shared with the country's government responsibility for the mines in Botswana (soon the world's biggest producer), controlled all mining in South African-controlled Namibia, had purchase monopolies with several West African countries, set up long-term exclusive sales arrangements with Central and East African governments, and had a "secret" agreement with the USSR, the first major producer to emerge outside of Africa, to jointly market its prodigious output. Ironically the Soviet deal grew out of a failed attempt by De Beers to do the opposite.

Claiming that the Soviet Union (which had just lost twenty million people and half of its industry in World War II) was intent on world-wide expansion, NATO launched an economic war, including an embargo on industrial diamonds. De Beers publicly refused to sell directly to the USSR and threatened to cut off raw material to manufacturers who supplied the enemy-of-the-day with diamond tools. The USSR responded by discovering enormous diamond deposits right at home.[25] By the mid 1950s Siberian gem-quality material flowed in such quantities that De Beers had to admit the USSR as junior partner in its schemes, hiding the link through Switzerland and Luxembourg.[26]

The willingness of the USSR to ignore ideology in favour of shared profit from restricting the diamond supply was true of all governments of diamond-producing states. As it had for the USSR, De Beers set up affiliates in corporate-secrecy havens so that governments in black Africa, nominally at loggerheads with white-ruled South Africa, could pretend to be dealing with, for example, a Bermuda company. Offshore transactions also made easier diversion of a country's diamond revenues into personal retirement accounts of presidents and their families and friends. If there were carrots for the carats, there were also big sticks. Because of close relations with major international banks, De Beers could turn the financial spigot off and on, both directly through a phone call and indirectly through its ability to wreck the finances of any economically weak country that dared to strike out on its own. It could use its stock-pile not just to steer prices of this or that type of stone but to massively dump the sort in which a particular country specialized. And from time to time its buyers, strategically located in contraband centres, could, by raising prices, encourage a drain from a target country, denying it export revenues while capturing the stones for its own stockpile.[27]

The other form of complicity required was a government impervious to the environmental consequences of diamond mining whose impact, while not as great as gold, nonetheless, like other forms of open-pit operations, strips off vegetation and soil, permits waste like diesel fuels to seep into ground water, and piles up mounds of tailings full of toxic heavy metals that induce acid runoff. Sea-bed mining, as in Namibia, produces its own range of environmental horrors, like the mass destruction of benthic colonies of starfish, oysters, clams, urchins, sea cucumbers, and anemone.[28]

It was not enough to have governments in its pocket: De Beers also had to ensure security at mine sites, control "illegal" buying of stones that escaped, stop smugglers getting them out of the country, and intimidate dealers trying to sell to independent cutters abroad. Diamonds exit mine sites up anal cavities, hidden under bandages, secreted in the knots of ties worn by white-collar personnel, stuffed inside vehicle gas tanks, fired by sling shots over security fences, even strapped to the legs of carrier pigeons, a strategy that once backfired badly when the bird turned stool pigeon, alighting on the windowsill of a police station. The response depends on a mix of politics, geology, and geography.

Where production is concentrated, heavy security (electric fences, computerized cameras, X-rays of miners leaving the sites, and serious penalties) can reduce although never stop the drain.[29] It helps, too, if De Beers controls the mine sufficiently to insist on state-of-the-art recovery and sorting methods that minimize human intervention, as in the big Botswana mines today. But where De Beers had minimal control of a local government, especially in countries cursed with widespread alluvial deposits, De Beers and its affiliates had to resort to paid informants, infiltration of smuggling rings, buy-and-bust ops, "low-intensity warfare" (paying gangs of brigands to ambush smugglers, then steal their stones), and outbidding black-market dealers onsite, at ports of exit, or even at points of sale in Europe.[30] One way or another, De Beers at the peak of its powers ensured that up to 80 percent (so it claimed) of the world's raw diamonds ended up in its London offices to be offered to 250 (later greatly reduced in number) sight-holders (all large-scale dealers or cutters) in pre-assigned lots at fixed prices ten times a year. After buying the boxes, sight-holders were free to resell to other dealers directly or via any of the world's diamond bourses, although those of Antwerp remained the largest. At that point the very free market took over the route to Melania Trump's ring finger.

TRADING PLACES

During World War II, Antwerp lost its position as the world centre for diamond-cutting, partly to New York, partly to Tel Aviv, where the British created an alternative under their control. After the war the government of Belgium rebuilt the city's pre-eminence, exempting it from import duties on raw material or sales taxes on finished product, encouraging local banks to finance rough purchases from London and ensuring that the diamond district was policed against theft but otherwise unregulated. In addition to being the most important participants at a Central

Selling Organization "sight," the ten-times-annual meetings to which select dealers and cutters were summoned to receive their allotments, Belgian-based dealers were prominent recipients of stones snuck out of producer countries. Supposedly people turning up with rough stones at a Belgian embassy or consulate in Africa would leave again with a visa for each of their (probably multiple) passports, an Antwerp city guide, the names and addresses of diamond dealers, and a consular official's card.[31] The city handled so much hot material that for a time the biggest De Beers anti-smuggling operation consisted of its buyers purchasing "submarines" (smuggled stones) off the Antwerp black market to repatriate to London. From there they might end up resold to a Belgian dealer during a sight, and sold again either to Belgian-based cutters or onto Antwerp's rough-diamond exchange to dealers and cutters abroad. Once cut and polished, many returned to pass through Antwerp's finished-diamond exchange to be sold one more time onto the world wholesale market. Antwerp traders had a reputation for providing the purchaser with whatever invoice was needed to placate an importing country's customs and revenue services. All this had the implicit endorsement of a government fearful that a serious crackdown (including on the diamond district's casual attitude toward income taxes) would send cutters fleeing to Israel or India.[32]

India's 1980s return to prominence in diamonds, this time as a cutting centre, reflected the steady social descent of the diamond to something peddled by American jewellery chains in shopping-mall outlets, by telemarketing networks, by televised sales pitches, and eventually by the internet. The Indian government eased regulations and taxes and provided cheap credit from state-run banks to a business run by a tightly knit network of Jain families. Members of an ancient, pacifist sect, Jains had the social bonds necessary to compete on a worldwide basis with closed communities of Hassidic Jews and Armenians.[33] India had another advantage. Tens of thousands of boys coveted for their sharp eyesight came from impoverished villages near the squalid cutting centre of Surat to breathe diamond dust ten hour days, seven days a week in the same rooms in which they lived in groups of ten to fifteen for the equivalent of about $50 per month. Bad press from organizations as varied as the Anti-Slavery Society and the International Labour Organization eventually forced the industry to cut back on child labour; but the children were just shifted to other sweated industries like carpet-weaving or to smaller gem-cutting centres less in the public eye.[34] Besides, as wages in India for adult workers got pushed down, the financial advantage of using children diminished. Anyway, by the late 1990s, India's cutting facilities were under attack from places like Sri Lanka and Thailand that offered even cheaper labour that was similarly uncontaminated by unions or enforceable work codes.

Next, cut diamonds enter international channels via major dealers in big cities who are members of diamond bourses (now twenty-six worldwide), sometimes taking circuitous routes to reduce the nuisance of exchange controls, import duties, or luxury taxes. The most common technique is to commingle valuable with poorer stones and under-declare the lot. If invoices provided by the exporter read for less than the actual amount of the load, the importer might pay the specified amount by formal bank transfer and the balance in cash or out of secret offshore accounts. If a manufacturer or dealer wants to reduce income taxes in the purchasing country, invoices can read for more than the value of the stones, the exporter depositing the extra in the importer's foreign account.

If traders have particularly exotic stones that would stand out if commingled, or if small manufacturers try to keep their very existence secret from tax authorities, there are other tricks. A local manufacturer or broker phones a dealer in Antwerp, Tel Aviv, or Surat. The manufacturer or broker receives a call back from a "bagman" (almost always male) indicating in which hotel he is staying. After the transfer of an inconspicuous parcel, the bagman departs on an already reserved flight. The service charge is about 1–2 percent of the value of the load.[35] The actual couriers could be anyone from airline pilots to career diplomats. That particular phase of the underground diamond business is an equal-opportunity employer. Not only do women have more places to hide the stones but often don't have to do so. Stones, too, could be painted, disguised with foil backing, or even sewn into cloth while purporting to be rhinestone sequins.[36]

Smuggling is not without risks as twenty-one Indian dealers attending a Shenzhen diamond fair discovered. Surat dealers had a problem: the world financial meltdown had cut into their business so badly as to prompt a wave of suicides. But this group found a way to alleviate the pain. China encourages its only diamond exchange by allowing members to import stones for a 4 percent duty – non-members pay 18 percent. But Hong Kong allows free import and export. So the Surat dealers sent their stones to Hong Kong, then had them smuggled into China for black-market sale, only to find China's Anti-Smuggling Bureau waiting. Back home the families of the jailed dealers were sufficiently concerned over their fate to gather at the local temple to pray for their safe return. To expedite that, they put the idol of the Swami Narayan on one side of a scale and 4,200 carats of precious stones on the other. "We always wanted," they explained, "to offer diamonds ... to the Lord ..."[37] No US televangelist could have phrased it better.

At the receiving end of most diamond smuggling operations are wholesalers, perhaps linked by sect or family ties to the exporter. They function in an environment where written records have traditionally been the exception and reneging on verbal commitments rare – it would lead to expulsion, not merely from the guilty party's own diamond club but from those around the world. Clan loyalty, a wide geographic spread, mobility, and tradition combine to permit goods, money, and information to flow seamlessly, secretly, and securely from country to country. However recent money-laundering scandals may be changing that.

For many years, it seems, Hasidic networks using yeshivas (schools of Jewish religious teaching) as fronts would place money in the New York branches of Israeli banks, claiming it was from cash donations to religious institutions. The yeshiva collected a commission of 0.5 percent, while the organizers took 9.5 percent. The money whizzed off to Panama, Colombia, the Cayman Islands, and Israel. Queried by a reporter on the morality of the business, particularly since some of the money came from drugs, one of the launderers, then hiding in Israel, noted: "Only the laws of the Torah dictate our conduct, and there is nothing in them which prohibits laundering money."[38]

Investigations were difficult. The FBI was petrified of being denounced for anti-Semitism, and there were problems finding informants. One participant noted: "If a Jew would dare to speak to Gentiles about Jewish money laundering, he knows that he would be ostracized for his entire life." The first attempt to break the system collapsed in 1991 when a Hebrew translator, advised by his rabbi that taking down a drug-money-laundering ring would constitute an attack on Israel, tipped off the targets.[39] When the net finally closed, it might have encouraged others to add another level of security by working the laundering cycle through diamond dealers.

For example, Abraham Low, head of an ultra-Orthodox sect in Los Angeles, had borrowed large sums from wealthy members of his congregation, ostensibly to build a Talmudic academy. When property values collapsed, he couldn't repay. Angry, some of his creditors began leaving the congregation. Perhaps because Rabbi Low acquired extra-curricular skills working with Rabbi Joseph Prushinowski, the notorious "robbing Rabbi" who took off to Israel ahead of warrants for his involvement in passing $300 million in fake bank paper, Low sought financial salvation by buying and depositing in his wife's account cashiers' checks stolen from a branch of Bank of America, then refusing to return the money. However the man who sold him the stolen cashiers' checks, arrested on unrelated charges, confessed to the police that Low had paid him $30,000 cash plus two diamond rings. So the FBI floated in an under-cover agent posing as a drug trafficker to see what other financial tricks Low had up his sleeve. Low bragged to the agent of a money-laundering network that could handle up to $5 million a week. His couriers could fly cash to New York to Hasidic diamond dealers who deposited it in their accounts, then wired it to Switzerland. The money could return to the US via payments into the accounts of Low's religious institutions. Low first offered his services for a modest 30 percent, then suggested instead that he would buy the drug money outright from the agent using checks forged on the bank accounts of a local insurance company.[40]

Three years after Rabbi Low's arrest, the FBI busted two Brooklyn rabbis and a group of Colombian drug dealers in the same kind of caper. The rabbis met the drug dealers in the diamond district, took their cash, broke it into sums below the reporting threshold, and put it into yeshiva accounts, offering the drug dealers in exchange checks drawn on those accounts. The proceeds were either used to purchase aircraft to haul drugs or sent to safety in Switzerland.[41]

The string of scandals didn't end there. After the US Securities and Exchange Commission filed civil fraud charges against several executives of a health-care corporation, its boss offered evidence of a scam involving diamond merchants in exchange for leniency. This led to the 2007 arrest for tax evasion and money laundering of the grand rabbi of the Spinka Hasidic sect. The rabbi and his chief assistant solicited "donations" from members, issued them tax slips, and secretly refunded up to 95 percent of the money either in cash they could collect in the Los Angeles jewellery district (presumably from other members of the con-gregation) or in funds wired nominally for religious work in Israel, where a cooperative bank would deposit it in secret accounts for the "donors." Meanwhile "donors" filed tax returns claiming full deductions.[42]

That affair engendered considerable debate among the faithful. Some were of the opinion that the government got what it deserved for taking so much money from (certain) citizens in taxes and that "anyone who can save *yiddishe gelt* from going down that toilet is doing a *mitzvah* [i.e., act of human kindness]." To some, the real issue was how to handle a *moser* [informant], given that Jewish religious law supposedly forbids one Jew from ratting out another to any secular government, particu-larly in a financial case where there is no danger to others.[43]

Actually the Rabbi got off fairly easily, with a two year sentence. Partly that may be because shortly after his arrest, the media was abuzz with tales of his illustrious ancestor, a great uncle who was also the sect's leader and who died in Auswitz. But it also reflected the government's and the court's conviction that the scheme long predated the current rabbi and in fact was so widespread as to be almost normal activity.[44]

Although repeated scandals put pressure on diamond wholesalers to rely more on regular bank instruments, their financial inventiveness did not end. In 2003 several of them got together to kite checks for tens of millions made out to each other supposedly to cover nonexistent diamond sales; the checks were all deposited on the same day so that banks phoning each other for verification would confirm the existence of funds; and the inflated deposits were used either draw cash or to serve as collateral for increased lines of credit. The scheme collapsed when some of the checks failed to clear.[45]

Diamond clubs used to be renowned, as well, for intra-group trust. How far those features had deteriorated was illustrated in 2007 when forty-five wholesalers sued A. Taub Diamond Co., run by recent Israeli immigrants, for $3.3 million on the grounds that the company slowly built up an appearance of creditworthiness, then took dozens of stones on consignment and never paid – for the diamonds, for invoices already outstanding, or for rent on its premises. The company president insisted that the delay was because he had been robbed of $1 million worth of diamonds, then lost $2.4 million when a client paid with bum checks. But a police raid turned up some of the purportedly stolen diamonds on which insurance claims had already been filed, drawing the lament from the president of one of the USA's diamond clubs that "the trust factor in the industry is fading away."[46]

UNDER THE COUNTER?

From wholesalers, diamonds (like all other gems) move through the manufacturing and retailing stages. In fact diamonds are the core of the modern jewellery trade, far exceeding other stones in volume and value. For a long time, too, diamonds seemed relatively impervious to fakery. Although substitute materials have been used since time immemorial, they failed the easy-to-apply hardness test; and once cutting techniques were perfected in the mid-nineteenth century, the internal fire of genuine diamonds also seemed a guarantee, at least to the experienced eye. But panic swept the trade three times in the late twentieth century.

The first came in the 1970s, when new ovens able to reach 2750 degrees Celsius could grow cubic zirconium crystals with a fire similar to diamonds. Some jewellers were conned into purchasing them; some, no doubt, took the occasion to dump them on clients. However the storm blew over quickly. The stone's brilliance may be comparable to diamond, but its specific gravity is very different; and by the early 1980s a cheap thermal-conductivity meter could differentiate it from the real thing. By then most halfway competent jewellers were able to spot cubic zirconium anyway.

Then in 1996 came the perfection by a US company of gem-quality moissanite (AKA carborundum), originally created as industrial abrasive. When it first hit the market, it could easily pass for diamond in terms of refraction, hardness, and specific gravity. It even breezed through the thermal-conductivity test. For a short time people approached jewellers to unload "family diamonds" cheaply, but only for cash.[47] However, the stone is doubly refractive and its fire is actually much greater than diamonds. Although the company producing the moissanite gems also started to market a detector for several hundred dollars a pop, after a little time jewellers could spot the difference with nothing fancier than a $10 magnifying glass. Within a year or so of the big rush, the producing company was laying off staff.[48]

The third source of panic was much more serious, and it had much deeper roots. By the 1950s technology to create synthetic diamonds out of everything from peanut butter to Kentucky bourbon was perfected at much the same time in the USA and the USSR. Initially gem-sized crystals were slow and expensive to produce; so synthetics were purely for industrial use. However there were recurrent tales of Soviet breakthroughs followed by the USSR sneaking, with the cooperation of De Beers, gem-quality synthetics onto the market. These fears increased in the 1980s with the perfection of a much cheaper method using methane gas as a feedstock. In 1993 Russian stones, detectable as synthetics only because they were so marked, made their appearance at a US trade fair. Today, smaller US companies have purchased old Soviet machinery to make near-perfect (some claim actually perfect) synthetics for much less than naturals. One of the companies, to the horror of the diamond trade, markets them as "cultured diamonds" on the rational that they are no more "artificial" than most of today's pearls.[49]

Synthetics also have a special market niche. Someone losing a loved one can have the body cremated, then the ashes converted into gemstones to be worn "forever." The more ancestors whose souls go to meet their maker, the more diamonds grace the finger or neck of their earthly survivors – until a bad run at the slot machines greatly shortens the bearer's own time horizon, necessitating a trip to a pawnshop to unload the remains of Uncle Bill and Auntie Ruth, and maybe those of Rover along with them.[50]

Simultaneously came big improvements in techniques to repair imperfections or change colours.[51] Appearance can be hyped crudely with everything from fingernail polish on the outside to foreign optical materials inserted within. At the end of the 1980s an Israeli firm filled cracks and holes with a material so hard it could be removed only by boiling the stone in acid, applying the method to stones whose large fissures were previously impossible to hide or repair. The process required a microscope to detect. Although the firm promised full disclosure, in 1988 the Gemological Institute of America, the country's foremost appraiser, discovered treated stones sold covertly through the Israeli Diamond Exchange.[52] The Israeli firm's successors promised to laser print any such stones and sell them with a certificate stating what had been done. However certificates have a habit of getting lost or faked; and, if a stone is large enough, there is little problem grinding off an imprinted warning. Today, drilling out imperfections not in a straight line that looks artificial but in a way that mimics natural flaws, then filling the hole with synthetic diamond, is well nigh undetectable.

Changing colour is now routine, too. Although there were always exceptions, historically the closer to colourless a diamond, the higher the price, as Tavernier so poetically noted. But, as diamonds became increasingly commonplace, colour became a mark of rarity. That led to experiments, for example, to change yellow and brown tints into "fancy colours" by high pressure and temperature or by irradiation, something also undetectable if done well. Since some purists insist that a perfect diamond has to be free of the trace minerals that account for the tint, in 2000 a subsidiary of jewellery giant Lazare Kaplan International announced the advent of "enhanced natural diamonds" in order to return "certain rare, off-color diamonds to their natural colorless origin."[53] It seems that "nature" was being redefined for diamonds much as for breakfast cereals, most of whose nutritional value comes from eating the box.

CERTIFIABLE?

Not every stone's fate is to be set in precious metals. A typical dealer purchases stones in a job lot and, before selling to jewellery makers, separates out those suitable for the "investment" market, which sprang into existence in the 1970s as diamonds came to be appreciated as an instrument for capital flight, a supposedly sure-fire investment, and even as an underground currency, performing all those functions as dependably as its role in guaranteeing eternal love. At times in the past, too, diamonds played similar roles. Baroness Rothschild is reputed to have fled Paris ahead of the Nazis to arrive in New York in 1940 with $1 million worth of fine stones.[54] However, before the war she probably visited Monaco regularly with at least that much.

What makes today's investment diamond different from the kind used by flight capitalists in the past is that it (like other precious stones and rare gold coins) is sold single, unmounted, and in a plastic bubble with a certificate of authenticity explaining type, origins, and weight, but saying nothing about price. Until the 1930s, appraisals of diamonds were done by the same people handling the sale, using their own criteria – a little like embezzlers asked to audit their own books and permitted to make up the accounting rules while they were at it. (Not so different, come to think of it, from the racket run by the big investment banks with the main Wall Street rating agencies in the run-up to the subprime scandal.) However, massmarket sales of diamonds that come in thousands of subvariants seemed to call for a more "objective" mechanism. In 1931 big US dealers founded the Gemological Institute of America, a nonprofit trade association that, among other things, invented the Four Cs (Cut, Caratage, Clarity, and Color) criteria along with a very-much-for-profit lab to do the appraisal job. The numbered certificate and plastic bubble followed later, along with several major competitors. In 1976 even the Diamond High Council of Antwerp began issuing certificates, albeit mainly to grease the wholesale trade. While the certificate was touted as a means to cut costs of repeat appraisals and to reduce theft, in reality someone in possession of a stolen stone could simply have it altered slightly, then pay a small fee for recertification. Arguably, certification made stolen stones easier, not harder, to unload by eliminating the need for any serious queries about provenance, not that some diamond dealers have ever been reputed to be very fussy about the origins of the goods they handled. But the certificate also paved the way for retail "investment diamonds," something established dealers had treated with suspicion until the inflationary 1970s.

Today there are several large players in the appraisal and certification business, as well as dozens of smaller ones, some genuine, some fake, giving highly variable results. That produces an obvious temptation for people selling stones to shop for the most accommodating lab much the way those peddling shares in start-up gold mines look for the most obliging assay office. Rumours abound in the trade, never proven, that paying double the standard fee to certain labs guarantees a suitably inflated report, although presumably more subtle means ranging from expensive gifts to a nocturnal visit from a high-class hooker will also do (or turn) the trick. However GIA is by far the largest, appraising a million stones a year. Many turn to it because its imprimatur may facilitate resale, particularly now that stones it appraises are lasered, recorded in a worldwide database, and sent home with certificates protected by serial numbers and holograms.

Still, there have been problems – apart from the fact that even legitimate labs can differ widely in their appraisals.[55] Moti Weisbrot, an Israeli dealer operating out of Italy, managed to take the image of a GIA certificate off the internet, manipulate it by computer, then use copies to sell enhanced diamonds as well as cubic zirconia as the real thing. He got away with it for years until one alert jeweller in Australia tipped off the police. A police raid found Weisbrot's house full of low-grade stones and dozens of fake certificates.[56] Then came a scandal over how much faith could be put even in an official GIA certificate.

The issue blew up after Max Pincione, a prominent US retailer, bought from a wholesaler two expensive pieces of diamond jewellery, complete with GIA certificates, then resold them to members of the Saudi royal family. The clients had them reappraised, only to return them, demanding a refund and refusing future business. Pincione sued the wholesaler and GIA. After a secret investigation, GIA fired four appraisers and undertook other confidence-rebuilding changes. One theory is that some major dealers, seeking to corner the market in certain large stones, overpaid substantially to squeeze out competitors, safe in the knowledge that they had already bribed those GIA staff members to exaggerate appraisals so the stones could be resold at a much higher price than normal.[57] But that could be simply a smear story spread by a dissatisfied customer or an enterprising competitor.

Price depends on negotiations between dealer and client and can vary greatly depending on the same factors that affect all speculative markets. When the surge of interest began in the early 1970s, some diamond merchants grossly overcharged, scam artists unloaded fakes and synthetics, and diamond mutual funds formed in the usual sunny places for shady people to sell stones or even shares in upstart (sometimes undiscovered) diamond mines. If one especially clever operation peddling overpriced stones stumbled across people who already had some, it asked them to send in the stones for possibly resale. If they did, they never saw the stones again. As with so many of these rackets, the best marks are those whose money's origins would not bear close scrutiny and who are therefore unlikely to call the cops. Sometimes, though, the cops are already on the case for quite different reasons.

CROWNED HEADS AND MANACLED WRISTS

Most losers in diamond swindles fit the general profile of telemarketing scam victims – seniors worried about stretching pensions or small-town dentists who pulled in a little gold on the side. But the investment diamond frenzy also infected some distinctly upper-crust participants and

led to the downfall of Chaumet frères, the tenth generation of a family of
jewellers whose clients had included Queen Victoria and the Romanoffs
and whose handicraft extended to the crown that graced Napoleon's
imperial head. The firm's collapse in 1990 cost the late King Hassan II of
Morocco some 225 million French francs he badly needed to maintain
his five palaces and permanently floodlit golf course and knocked 100
million francs off the heritage fund president-for-life-who-is-now-dead
Mobutu Sese Seko of Zaire was building for future generations.[58]

The problem was that while part of the Chaumet business was traditional (providing for the conspicuous consumption needs of the beautifully rich), part was not (catering to the inconspicuous financial needs of
the discretely wealthy). In the 1970s, when the investment market was
hot, the brothers had invited a few trusted old clients to join them in a
speculative play. The client's cash would be used to purchase diamonds,
and the stones kept in the Chaumet safe for one year. At that point the
client could sell them to the jewellers at a guaranteed 20 percent markup,
then repeat the exercise with the same guarantee. It worked as long as
prices kept rising. When prices collapsed in 1981, the firm, already facing a soft market for its orthodox business, had to cover the guaranteed
markup. Desperate for cash, it solicited loans from clients to pay interest
on previous commitments.

Some clients consigned to the firm pieces of jewellery to sell on their
behalf, then left the proceeds with the brothers to invest, again on their
behalf, in the speculative diamond market; and they might occasionally add extra money in cash or by check or bank transfer. Those balances drew 11–14 percent interest that clients could have deposited in
their bank accounts, paid to them in precious stones, or reinvested with
Chaumet. Names were kept openly on the books, and interest payments
faithfully reported to the tax authorities. No one seemed too concerned
that the scheme represented a double violation of French law: only
licensed banks could operate what were in effect checking accounts, and
checking accounts could not bear interest. However, there was a second
set of clients, their identities protected by codes, who deposited larger
amounts, mainly in cash, and were issued phony invoices supposedly
for jewellery or precious stones left for possible sale. On these accounts
interest ran at 12–22 percent, payable in cash or in gems, with no reporting. For such extra-special clients, the brothers offered another service,
thanks to the happy accident that the firm's main foreign affiliate was
in Geneva.

Even before the Revolution it was *de rigueur* for a wealthy Frenchman
to have both a mistress and a Swiss bank account. Desire for the second

was certainly not dampened when a Socialist government introduced a wealth tax. But for most of its recent history France has had stringent controls on the export of money. A lot of itinerant funds simply moved to Geneva in suitcases. But for its elite clientele, the Chaumets arranged something more elegant. They would "buy" gemstones from their Swiss affiliate, hiding deals via shell companies, then send money to Switzerland on behalf of clients disguised as payment for the stones. Once in Switzerland, the money simply moved to the client's bank account. If a client needed money back home, the Chaumets reversed the process. They established an account at a Swiss bank in the name of a front-company and gave the account number to the client. The client shifted money from personal Swiss accounts into the Chaumet account, and the money was transferred publicly back to France reported as "payment" for nonexistent purchases by the Chaumet Geneva affiliate of precious stones from the Paris branch. French customs caught on that something was amiss. But two years after an investigation began, it was closed on orders from the top – apparently someone with clout had decided that customs had better things to do.

As the investment market still continued to fall, and the hole in the accounts grew, the Chaumets began desperately seeking bank loans. Of course, bank loans require collateral. So the brothers produced false invoices showing "sales" to the Geneva affiliate, pledging the nonexistent funds to the banks to cover the loans. Since the sales had never really occurred, they could also offer the same stones as direct collateral. Not only was that double dipping, but some of the stones so used were the property of clients or other jewellers left with the Chaumets for potential sale or just for safekeeping. With such solid collateral from a firm of sterling reputation, enough loans were approved to assure that, when the end came, some twelve banks took a 700 million franc bath. Along with losses to clients and suppliers, the total hole in the firm's books came to about 1.5 billion francs.

In the aftermath many people came calling: bankers anxious to realize on their "collateral"; professional dealers who had left stones with the Chaumets, only to find some vanished; and police who inflicted on one brother the humiliation of sharing a jail cell with a jewel thief. Missing from the visitor roster were large-scale depositors who preferred to remain at home praying that the fiscal authorities would be unable to crack either the Chaumets or the secret codes they had used to record the names of customers, accounts, and banks. However, the identity of at least one was soon public knowledge. France's minister of Justice found himself in the interesting position of simultaneously controlling the investigation and explaining why he had been depositing cash at and drawing interest from a jewellery firm when French banking law, of which he was the ultimate overseer, clearly forbade it.

OUT OF THE CLOSET

About the same time, other regal gemstones, including some that might have been sold to the Romanoffs by ancestors of the two Chaumet brothers, were weaving a different geographic path to end up similarly immersed in international scandal. It all started with a plan by political kingpins to help Russia, then producing about 25 percent of the world's diamonds, operate outside restrictions imposed by De Beers, while the cabal of con artists they hired to do the job decided to help themselves to part of Russia's treasure trove of gemstones, precious metals, and dazzling objets d'art.[59]

Russia's formal relations with De Beers date back to 1957, when the company boss, desperate to keep the USSR from flooding the market, made a not-very-secret deal to turn a monopoly into a duopoly. In 1989 that deal went public with De Beers getting control of the great bulk of Russian diamond output in exchange for a guaranteed $1 billion annually. Some people, including Yevgeni Bychkov, head of the Committee of the Russian Federation on Precious Metals and Gems (Komdragmet), were convinced that Russia was being hosed. So was Finance Minister Boris Fyodorov, a close confidant of President Boris Yeltsin. The answer, they decided, was to overtly respect the De Beers deal while covertly violating its intent by creating joint-ventures to cut Russian stones in India and Israel and by setting up an operation in the US. The American affiliate would receive Russian rough to be cut and polished for the US market, something permitted (within limits) under the De Beers agreement, but also to serve as a conduit to divert even more Russian rough diamonds onto the world parallel market in violation of that deal.[60]

Bychkov dispatched Andrei Kozlenok, a Russian businessman and political crony, to San Francisco, where he connected with two recent émigrés, Ashot and David Shagirian. The three partners set up Golden ADA, the name drawn from the first initials of their first names, then won the glittering endorsement of the mayor and senior officials in San Francisco by promising to bring to that city some of the business hitherto controlled by Los Angeles. It was good timing – LA was still reeling from a huge money-laundering scandal involving its Armenian-dominated diamond district.[61]

To break into the US market, Golden ADA claimed to need a line of credit from a major US bank. So in 1992 Bychkov, with Fyodorov's approval, dipped into The Closet, Russia's remaining stash of old gold coins, platinum bullion, silver ornaments, gemstones, jewellery, and valuable artworks from massive expropriations just after the Revolution. The first load consisted of 26,000 carats of diamonds, plus crates of silver, gems, gold coins, and artwork. ADA diverted the diamonds for sale in Europe for $20 million and had the gold coins melted down, then sold through a Los Angeles bullion broker for about $50 million – much less than their value to collectors, but the partners were in a hurry. The rest fetched perhaps $20 million more.

Of course, the partners needed a lot of the money for business essentials – $11 million for a $6 million building as headquarters for their firm, fancy homes (Kozlenok's boasted paintings by Rembrandt and Picasso, even some Fabergé eggs), luxury cars and yachts, an $18 million private jet, and a huge Russian military helicopter given to the San Francisco police force on the condition that it be available, along with off-duty police officers, whenever ADA had a shipment of valuables to ferry from airport to office. They also purchased prime sites for future condos, supposedly vacation homes for Russian diamond-mining executives. Of the remaining money, some was used to buy state-of-the-art polishing equipment and control of a New York jewellery retailer that quickly went broke; some went into Bank of America, then out again to Switzerland and the Bahamas.

So much for start-up cash. Now it was time to get serious. In 1993, Golden ADA created a Russian subsidiary, Star of the Urals, to which Komdragmet boss Bychkov consigned $88 million worth of rough diamonds. Star shipped the diamonds to ADA for "polishing." A few were worked; most were diverted to Antwerp with fake invoices stating that they were from Zaire. Part of the money found discrete homes in Liechtenstein, Israel, and Belgium; part was wired back to Moscow. There, some was used by Star of the Urals to diversify into banking, weapons production, luxury real-estate, and mineral exporting. Some may have helped finance Boris Yeltsin's re-election campaign. Meantime Bychkov was reporting to his superiors that ADA was running a loss.[62]

Three sets of eyeballs were watching these events unfold. One belonged to sleuths working for De Beers to find out how so many Russian stones were finding their way onto the parallel market at a time of market glut. Another belonged to the FBI wondering about Russians on a big spending spree in San Francisco. A third belonged to police in Russia. Despite being repeatedly stymied by officials, late in 1994 tax cops raided Star of the Urals, arresting its boss for tax evasion, freezing its accounts, and unearthing details about the $88 million shipment. Kozlenok, in a panic, told his partners, the Shagirian brothers, to scram.[63]

Early in 1995, personnel from Russia's largest private security firm, mainly comprised of ex-KGB and Special Forces musclemen, turned up in San Francisco. Kozlenok afterwards claimed he had been kidnapped to Central America and forced to sign over control of ADA. It was placed under the care of a "financial consultant" from Delhi who arrived waving two university degrees – a B.Eng from MIT and an MBA from the Wharton School – that, on closer scrutiny, turned out to be a single degree issued by a small technical college. Over the next few months, the "consultant" consulted $500,000 out of ADA and sold off $20 million worth of remaining diamonds to feed the money into accounts around the world. At this point, the IRS, alarmed at the steady drain of money, swept in to seize the remaining $44 million in assets. At the end of the day Komdragmet was disbanded; responsibility for diamond sales and The Closet was transferred to the Ministry of Finance; and Russia signed a new De Beers deal in which it pledged to wind up not just ADA but also the other joint ventures with Israel and India that had been designed to give Russia greater freedom of action in the world diamond market.[64]

THE EMPIRE STRIKES BACK

For a time it seemed that De Beers could continue the magic. It neatly sidestepped the fall of white rule in South Africa by transferring control of its major assets to offshore companies.[65] It kept a lock on Namibia's diamonds after independence. It faced down the challenge when a cooperative Soviet junior partner transmuted into a restless and hungry Russia.[66] But Australia defected from the cartel; and new diamond strikes in Canada's northwest threatened a flood. Synthetic diamonds continued to spook the market. And traditional measures to control alluvial diamonds in Africa were faltering in the face of civil collapse and multisided wars – rebel movements and regional warlords proved harder to deal with than corrupt or thuggish governments.

All this was occurring as the world economy shifted from a medium-to-high inflationary post-World War II to a low-inflationary post-Cold War environment, as new diamond bourses and cutting centres proliferated, promising fresh opportunities for dealers to connect with producers, and as new mines began vertically integrating with large jewellery concerns, bypassing the De Beers apparatus. In the face of market glut and a falling share of the world's total rough diamonds, down from 80 percent to 60 percent by the early 1990s, De Beers found that the stockpile, the key instrument for price control, was a drag on the company's finances. Meanwhile its US shareholders were pressing De Beers to settle a long-standing anti-trust investigation (into claims De Beers and General Electric had colluded to rig the synthetic diamond market) in the US. Things became more pressing when the US Justice Department blocked De Beers from selling directly into the ($10 billion per year) US diamond market.[67] Just when things looked blackest, along came the uproar over conflict diamonds.

Actually it was an old story, dating back at least half a century. It started in Sierra Leone after World War II, when native soldiers who had been with British Special Forces returned home to find a country still under colonial rule and its leading industry still in the grip of a British monopoly. Most diamond mines produce a majority of industrial-grade stones, but in Sierra Leone an exceptional proportion were (are) gem quality and in widely dispersed alluvial fields rather than concentrated in deep mines, where security is easier. Initially the main problem was in company-run areas: miners would steal stones to sell to local merchants who would then pass them on to smugglers. But by the early 1950s more native diggers ventured into fresh territory. While the British regularly sent the police and army to try to clear illegal diggings, the miners applied skills they (or leaders of their mining coops) had learned in British irregular warfare units during World War II to evade capture. For every informer kept by the company in the illegal mining camps, the miners seemed to have at least one in the local police. Illegal production also required illegal trade. Those facilities were provided by descendants of early waves of Lebanese immigrants who dominated the retail trade even deep into the countryside.[68] They advanced to diggers equipment and supplies, then arranged to move the diamonds to Liberia, which had low taxes and a financial system based on the US dollar.

To strike back, De Beers fed newspapers with claims that smuggling was sufficient to threaten the British balance of payments when the country had still not fully recovered from World War II; and it sent "John Blaize," a self-proclaimed undercover agent for the International Diamond Security Organization, the De Beers private policing affiliate, to chat to former Naval Intelligence officer Ian Fleming, who had already published *Diamonds Are Forever*, in which the dashingly decadent James Bond foils international smugglers working on behalf of Terror International. Who better to write the "true story" of the underground diamond trade than someone with the right political credentials and a proven capacity to concoct fantasies with the desired political spin?[69]

The problem De Beers faced was that existing methods to control trafficking in West Africa were failing. Within its own mining concessions it had traditionally relied on X-rays to stop miners from stealing stones. But, as John Blaize explained to Fleming, "You can't go on X-raying men, even if they're black...." Other techniques included planting irradiated stones, then trying to pick them up with Geiger counters as miners passed the turnstiles, or to trace them to buyers. That, by definition, caught only the irradiated stones – of little use if large numbers of miners lifted large numbers of gems. Nor could the company irradiate en masse. That would mean trying to plant back into the diggings stones already found and officially in company stores. And presumably there might be fear of a skin cancer epidemic on the ring fingers of the blushing brides who were the primary clientele. In the alluvial fields outside direct company control, the problem was worse. Here the company's most important technique was to plant its own agents to outbid the illicit buyers. While that permitted the company to control where the stones went, it drove up the price and encouraged more illegal production. For a time De Beers combined that strategy with a buy-and-bust approach. But judges kept throwing out the cases – most of those entrapped were amateurs with no previous history who were lured into the traffic, then arrested in a blaze of publicity to try to scare away others. So John Blaize appealed to Fleming's patriotic sentiments to help them publicize "the biggest racket being operated anywhere in the world."[70]

According to the story, the Evil Empire (at that time Atheistic Communism rather than Islamic Terrorism) ran the traffic for two purposes. One was to obtain industrial diamonds (in the face of a NATO embargo) to aid the Soviet nuclear weapons program. John Blaize assured Fleming that "our man in East Berlin" reported the USSR taking 25 percent, China 25 percent, the rest going to various places in Eastern Europe, "all presumably for the various armaments industries."[71] This was some accomplishment given that stones from Sierra Leone were largely gem quality, and that the USSR was already producing so many diamonds of its own that De Beers had entered a secret agreement to sneak them onto Western markets in violation of anti-Soviet sanctions then in force.[72]

The second purpose, so the account went, was to use gemstones to finance Arab "terrorist" activity in Syria (which had just kicked out the French), Iraq (shaking off the British), and Algeria (where the first shots of an insurrection against French rule had been fired). Reports of the Soviet-Weapons-of-Mass-Destruction-cum-Arab-Terrorist plot sent a shudder through the British spook agencies who endorsed a covert program, jointly with De Beers, to use British secret intelligence funds to infiltrate Lebanese smuggling rings, snare traders, and, where necessary, assassinate ringleaders.

Therefore, apart from alerting the public to these early conflict diamonds, De Beers arranged for Sir Percy Sillitoe, former head of Britain's

MI–5, where he had made a reputation as a Commie-hunter, to be hauled from a pleasant retirement selling chocolates, to spearhead the counterinsurgency. Among the means employed was a turned Lebanese storekeeper who put together a gang of petty criminals to ambush convoys of smugglers, steal their diamonds, and collect a reward of one third their value.[73] But Sir Percy soon realized that the real point was to permit De Beers to consolidate its monopoly with the British taxpayer picking up the tab. Not only had the Soviet Union already discovered enormous supplies of natural diamonds but it was at the forefront of world synthetic-diamond research. The notion that it would buy black-market diamonds to fund guerrilla groups made no financial sense. And the only traceable flow of smuggled diamonds into Arab hands ran from Lebanese traders of West Africa to Lebanon, then across the ceasefire line into Israel in defiance of the Arab League Embargo against the Zionist entity.[74]

Fast-forward to Sierra Leone in the late 1990s, when the world's curiously selective conscience was shocked by images of an insurgent group, fond of hacking off hands and feet with machetes, that funded its war by exploiting slave labour in diamond fields, smuggling gemstones via complicit (Lebanese, naturally) dealers to Liberia, then onto world markets. Horror stories from Sierra Leone (and Liberia, soon facing its own bloodbath) were added to those already around from Angola, where the government was locked in battle with the CIA-created UNITA guerrilla movement, then multiplied further from the Congo (AKA Zaire) on which neighbouring countries descended in a multisided scramble for spoil after the death of its US-sponsored president-for-life. What to do about African "conflict diamonds" became one of the hottest topics discussed by the New York cognoscente as they puffed contraband Cuban cigars and sampled poached Russian caviar while seated at tables made from illegally cut Brazilian big-leaf mahogany in elegant rooms embellished with looted Chinese, Peruvian, and Iraqi antiquities. Thus, conflict diamonds (later reincarnated as "blood diamonds" to heighten the shock value) were already high on the international agenda before the discovery that behind the trade could be found the evil hand of Usamah bin Lāden.[75]

Action had begun even before that shocking revelation. In 1998 the UN had imposed sanctions on purchase of diamonds from UNITA in Angola. Hitherto all diamonds from Angola were to be accompanied by government-issued certificates of origin. This had the happy effect of creating work for skilled forgers and an opportunity for corrupt functionaries to commingle UNITA's with official stones. A short time later the

UN imposed sanctions on Sierra Leone's gemstones, too. Zaire, wracked by civil war, was next. NGOs eager for the spotlight kept up the pressure while the mass media hyperventilated.

The last pockets of resistance to controls on "conflict diamonds" crumbled, sending the diamond trade on a scramble to placate consumer countries when, in 2002, the world learned that Usamah bin Lāden's al-Qā'idah had not simply been profiting from sales but had rushed, after 9/11, to convert its assets into more easily hidden forms, including rough diamonds – something that would have done more than all the world's anti-terrorist financing laws to strip Usamah of his reputed fortune. In vain, people who had some inkling about the realities of illegal markets, the ins-and-outs of the diamond trade, and how so-called Islamic terrorist groups really operate protested. Yet the UN followed up with a demand to ban not just of "conflict diamonds" but of all "illicit" stones. Member states and the diamond industry began negotiating conventions to shut out of the market not the 3 percent of the world's gemstones that came from conflict-ridden areas of Africa but the 15–30 percent (depending on definition) that bypassed official marketing agencies. And the fuss gave officials of corrupt and repressive governments a pretext to knock out independent miners to turn concessions over to kin and cronies.[76]

To the extent that the bans actually worked, their impact was to open space for De Beers to unload onto the market identical stones from its own stockpile. That stockpile, long a drag on its finances, shot up in value. The drive to eliminate stones that had bypassed formal government monopolies (most still marketed through De Beers) further enhanced the company's power. It piously declared that it would no longer sell any diamond that did not come from mines it controlled or governments and companies with which it formally partnered, as if that were a guarantee of good behaviour. Not least, the changes in international rules came (just by coincidence) while De Beers was drastically revising its marketing strategy.[77] It set out for the first time to sell cut and polished ones to the retail trade under its own brand name. To do so, it set up a joint venture with the French luxury purveyor LVMH (derived from Louis Vuitton and Moet-Hennessey), a firm that had already acquired the defunct Chaumet frères, for a series of high-end retail outlets in trendy neighbourhoods of major cities. The pitch was to sell stones laser-printed (invisible to the naked eye but eminently readable through a device De Beers was also happy to sell) with the De Beers logo and ID numbers guaranteeing a stone to be "conflict free." Even more sternly, it demanded of remaining sight-holders a guarantee that any stone they bought from anywhere else, like various freewheeling diamond bourses, came with a proper certificate attesting to the same thing or else risk being cut off by De Beers. It was a brilliant public-relations coup.

In fact the conventions held as much water as a leaky sieve; and no one was better positioned to violate them than De Beers itself. Potentially it could, if it wanted, collect stones from the Congo at Zurich airport, export them nominally to Russia, then "re-import" them to Switzerland and sell them as Russian in origin without them leaving the duty-free facilities. Anyway, it is very difficult to be sure of the origins of a rough stone. Trace materials like thorium or uranium, detectible by impressive-sounding means like "laser ablation inductively coupled plasma mass spectrometry," may occur in some areas in higher concentrations than others, but they are not unique to any particular type of diamond or region – they provide at best a clue, nothing that would stand serious scrutiny in a criminal court. Once a stone is cut and polished, its origins can't be determined.

However, if few De Beers competitors would ever handle a "conflict diamond," even fewer would to be able to convey the same assurance that their stones were "conflict free." The logo soothed a market further spooked by the spread of sophisticated fakes, simulates, or synthetics, particularly once old Soviet technology for making them turned up cheaply in the US.[78] Not least, by becoming a full-fledged ally in the "war on terror," pleading guilty to a few charges, and accepting a trivial $10 million fine, De Beers settled the anti-trust suit that would have prevented it from selling directly under its own name in the US market.[79] These changes in its commercial strategy were firmly cemented into place once reporters hungry for a scoop in alliance with NGOs peddling a mishmash of unsubstantiated rumours, anti-Arab stereotypes, and spook disinformation successfully sold the "Usamah-sells-conflict-diamonds" fable.[80]

Once that fable's mediaworthiness had passed, most of the pressure on the diamond trade to clean up its act disappeared, leaving the NGOcrats desperate for something else with which to restore their place in the limelight, and De Beers sitting pretty with its new strategy. The diamond, freed of association with the Muslim hordes, could get back to business as usual – fouling the environment, corrupting politicians, evading taxes, exploiting child labour, getting its political cronies to send in the army and police to beat up "illegal" miners, and conning buyers with claims about "ethical diamond rings" or jewellery that allows people to "wear your commitment."

Meanwhile as the millennium unfolded, so did new devices to take diamonds another step up in terms of energetic marketing and another leap down in terms of good taste. Victoria's Secret diamond-encrusted brassieres were complemented by matching jewel-fronted panties, both to be delivered by armoured car. (No credit cards, please. Only bank wire transfers.)[81] And a South Korean company in 2007 announced a way to use diamonds to truly flash the cash – a line of diamond-studded credit cards to attract "vvip" clients.[82] That same year Damien Hirst, celebrated for his "high art provocation" with things like collages made from butterfly wings, created *For the Love of God* – a platinum cast of a human skull and set it with 8,601 flawless diamonds including one weighing in at 52 carats. The diamonds, of course, were certified "conflict-free."[83]What a relief that must have been to the troubled conscience of potential buyers at the Sotheby's auction in Hong Kong in autumn 2007, when a single blue hue, quality-cut 6-carat stone went for $7.89 million.[84]

PART TWO

Pack Rats

4

Sketchy Business: On Art Connoisseurs and Con Artists

Some paleolithic troglodyte may have invented visual art about 38,000 years ago.[1] However, it took more than 37,000 years for that first artist's descendants (an apt phrase given humanity's current condition) to create a truly international market in which to sell the stuff.[2] Although some trade in art dates back millennia, the usual pattern in post-classical times was for artists to put their talents directly at the disposal of a wealthy patron who sought to bask in the reflected glory of spectacular works. Only after the Renaissance did independent artists operating under their own name become the norm in Europe. Even then, remuneration was negotiated directly by artist and patron, not by professional dealers.

Yet artists in early modern Europe were certainly not indifferent to commercial considerations. Rembrandt Harmenszoon van Rijn, for one, was a notorious moneygrubber who rigged bids for his prints and whose students painted coins on the floor to see if he would try to pick them up. And Peter Paul Rubens, never one to refuse fat fees from the biggest aristocratic collectors of his day, supervised apprentices to turn out "Rubens" en masse with the result that some clients insisted on a written agreement that he would paint at least a few of the actual figures.[3]

Nor was there anything exceptional about the tastes of aristocrats. As prone to fad and fashion as any social climber today, they were likely to judge quality by how flattering a picture it painted, literally or figuratively, of themselves. A portrait of an individual in an elegant, expensive frame symbolized that he (and occasionally she by virtue of he) had truly arrived, until some busybody invented photography and radically democratized the process.[4] However, artworks tended to remain within aristocratic families – or inside religious institutions to which they had been willed as a literally last-gasp attempt to expiate multiple earthly sins – unless lost through theft or accident or, more dramatically, through the misfortunes of war.[5]

ART OF WAR OR WAR FOR ART?

Ancient civilizations celebrated military triumphs by parading through the streets back home looted effigies of their rivals' gods – much as did Julius Caesar after his conquests in Greece, setting off a fad for antique Greek statuary among Rome's elite that the era's forgers were delighted to satisfy.[6] In more modern times, Napoleon Bonaparte, seeking to make Paris the cultural capital of the world, sent collectors to pick up choice items across conquered Europe. His biggest coup came with his threat to invade the papal territories. The Vatican bought him off with part of its massive hoard. Some items were sold for cash; the rest formed the seed from which sprouted the current collection in the Louvre – although its holdings of looted artworks pale compared to the plunder of China, Egypt, Iraq, and Greece that subsequently graced the British Museum, to the glory of empire, queen, and country.

While a helpful start, wholesale transfers at gunpoint could not create a modern art market. Individual pieces first had to become commodities bought and sold like pork bellies or orange-juice futures – indifferent to the fact that artworks, including personal portraits, were originally produced in a context that gave them a cultural and historical significance that could not be reproduced on some upstart's drawing-room wall or even in an art museum. Then, in more recent times, they had to be further transformed into assets traded like stocks and bonds, and for the same reasons. Those shifts in the way art was regarded in turn depended on a more fundamental social change.

Although old aristocrats held major collections over generations, they were not dependable customers for new material. They might control great tracts of land and the attached peasants, but they were usually short on cash. However, in countries like England and the Netherlands in the seventeenth and eighteenth centuries, business tycoons piled up liquid wealth while aspiring to a social status to equal their economic one. Rich merchants, when no longer blocked by inheritance or sumptuary laws, aped the rolling estates, fancy clothes, and art acquisitions of the landed class.[7] Elsewhere the elevation of money over inherited status was often bloody. But in Britain the two tended to merge: the nouveau riche bought blue blood, while surplus sons of old families headed abroad to loot India, kidnap slaves from Africa, or ruin the ecology of West Indian islands with sugar and tobacco. Thus the British landed class, more flush than its continental rivals, became and remained until the late nineteenth century the white world's most dependable art buyers, rivalled only briefly by the Russian aristocracy in the late eighteenth.

It was still largely a one-way flow. Material acquired by established families was held in trust for future generations. A modern high-end art market required, in addition to the triumph of liquid over landed wealth, a major political and economic upheaval, maybe a whole string of them, to make the settled aristocracy and aspiring gentry cough up their hordes, along with dealers able to pull off with sharp business practices what Napoleon had accomplished at bayonet point.[8]

The transformation began in the late-nineteenth-century US, home of great fortunes, first from Civil War profiteering, then from plundering the public patrimony during the westward expansion, then from creating giant monopolies and trusts.[9] Robber barons, happy to fleece the government on public contracts, cheat their suppliers, cut throats of their competitors, and gun down striking workers, could subsequently launder their reputations by posing as patrons of the arts. Simultaneously, cheap US grain and beef so undermined the financial position of Britain's landed elite that its government revised the law to permit old families to sell on the open market treasures previously held in trust. Of course, some managed to survive by hanging on to their art, then opening parts of their homes to paying visits from the Great Unwashed. The masses, including increasing numbers of insecure North Americans, were allowed for a fee to stare in wide-eyed wonder at cavernous rooms full of heavy furniture or to gawk at portraits of the ancestors of their social betters – even though the first were probably just as damp and cold as their own shacks and the second just as sour looking as their own forefathers.

Barring such a recourse, the law of comparative advantage kicked in: art treasures of old British families moved west across the Altantic into nouveau-riche mansions; the daughters of US parvenus moved east into aristocratic, if not necessarily holy, matrimony. And the contagion spread elsewhere. So much art fled France for the US that the French government took over Church properties, the main repositories; and Italy imposed in 1903 harsh anti-export laws that Benito Mussolini's regime later tightened into their current form. But the drain continued underground. In fact the flow across the Atlantic to private collectors and, a little later, to great US museums, became a flood with the Bolshevik Revolution.[10]

In the chaos, artworks from personal hordes, museums, or Orthodox churches became for fleeing aristocrats and rich bourgeoisie a way to move assets to safety, a practice only partly arrested once the new regime nationalized the museums, banned exports of cultural patrimony, and confiscated art and antiquities along with a stupendous pile of gold, silver, gems, jewellery, and jewelled brocades.[11] The government then sold abroad much of the official horde to finance industrialization. Private

exports had favoured France, where fleeing Russians – the higher their
social status the more francophile their pretensions – preferred to take
up residence. But the Soviet state preferred the US, where the sale of
Russian art could finance machine-tool purchases, build political sympathy, and avoid legal trouble that exiles in Europe might cause if they
spotted their former property in an auction house. The flow was lubri-
cated by US carpetbaggers who came to Russia during the Revolution
to pick up goodies cheaply from desperate families, then cultivated close
relations with ministries handling sales. Among them was a soon-to-be
oil billionaire named Armand Hammer who sent back to the US, among
other things, fake Fabergé eggs, using an exiled prince to shill for them.
At home he pioneered the department-store approach to peddling artworks to wealthy US women who envied their European sisters their
sophistication and wanted to distance themselves from their own comparatively uncouth social origins.[12]

Those rooting in the rubble of revolution were not just *arrivistes* like
Hammer. There were also the *arrivés*. As the USSR began to dump raw
materials to increase its foreign-exchange earnings, Andrew Mellon, oil
and banking tycoon and secretary of the treasury to five US presidents
(where his main responsibility was engineering tax breaks for oil companies), responded to the laments of US producers by slapping an embargo
on Soviet timber and minerals, then cashed in on the financial difficulties
his actions caused by collecting Russian art cheaply, in violation of the
exchange regulations he had imposed on everyone else.[13]

The job of bringing together the two sides of the market fell to a
clique of ambitious, mutually suspicious high-end dealers. They bribed
hotel staff to report movements of competitors, spread rumours that
other dealers dealt in fakes, and, if engaged by customs as appraisers,
overvalued stuff brought in by rivals to get them slapped with heavy
excise taxes – assuming those rival dealers actually reported their goods.
Their talents for smuggling were equally useful in evading export restrictions or import taxes. That could be risky. But high-end dealers regularly consorted with the rich and powerful. Like foreign correspondents,
they were among the few professions with an excuse to turn up in distant and disturbed places where their intelligence networks could also
serve their home (or politically adopted) countries for political espio-
nage. For example Anthony Blunt, the so-called Fourth Man in a Soviet
ring inside British Intelligence, used his art dealership as cover to run
a network of dealer-spies across Europe – as well as to make off, on
orders from the British monarch, with the Hanoverian Crown jewels
to prevent victorious US soldiers from stealing them first. Nor did he
emerge from a professional vacuum. Perhaps the most celebrated of the

early-twentieth-century dealers, Joseph Duveen put his Paris, London, and New York galleries at the disposal of British Intelligence during both world wars.[14] Well-placed dealers could also recruit an occasional consul or ambassador to move stuff around for them in the diplomatic pouch. Back home, they assured their upper-crust clients of supposedly gilt-edged art investments and offered special financial terms to sweeten the pie, figuring that they would likely have the chance to buy the material back cheaply from the estate and resell it elsewhere. Duveen was so cocky that he would sell works he didn't have, then afterward negotiate with their real owners.[15]

The golden age (prior to the present) was likely the 1920s, with income and wealth rising sharply for a privileged few. Although in the 1930s dealers could pick up prime pieces at distress prices, there were few buyers. The war years were worse – at least for the "free market." In postwar years enormous attention would be paid to artworks stolen by the Nazis from Jews and virtually none to artworks stolen by Allied military personnel from anyone else.[16]

Of course, interest in "Holocaust art," too, is somewhat episodic. Its recent revival perhaps reflects not just outrage over the atrocities of the war era but also dramatic price increases. These in turn draw attention to the fact that some of the prime pieces restored with great fanfare to heirs of their previous owners in Europe were quickly flipped to end up in the hands of rich US collectors who had been prime agitators for "recovery."[17] Morality, at least with respect to art, seems not only ethno-politically selective but rises and falls with the market.

CASH OR CACHET?

In the decades right after the war, that market was relatively calm. Tastes were less ostentatious, the distribution of income not so widely skewed, the tax system more progressive, financial markets better regulated, and inflation low. Although things began to pick up in the 1960s, the real change was in the next decade when the art market began to soar. The popular explanation is that fear of inflation drove investors to seek safety in durable goods. But the real reasons in the US, heartland of this second modern art-market transformation, are more profound. They really lie in a shift in attitudes toward celebrating instead of excoriating conspicuous wealth combined with the dismantling of social security, which, along with the demise of union power and the slashing of upper-income tax rates over the next few decades, turned the discretely rich into the flagrantly super-rich. Add to that the impact of bubble economics in creating hundreds, even thousands of pretenders to a social status to match their decidedly unearned wealth.[18] The emergence of this new parasitocracy helped to convert artworks, along with everything from antique furniture to vintage wines, into speculative assets, flipped quickly from one buyer to another and arbitraged across national markets or even between auction houses.

With the old aristocracy of Europe, the commercially minded gentry in Britain in the eighteenth and early nineteenth centuries, and the nouveaux riches of the US in the late nineteenth and early twentieth, the objective had been to acquire expensive art as a mark of status. But as the 1960s evolved into the 1970s, and accelerating in the decades beyond, the logic increasingly worked in reverse.[19] Certainly a collection of high-end art remained a symbol of wealth; but it also became a tool to obtain yet more – even though, in reality, art as a whole, as distinct from a few spectacular pieces, has performed even more poorly than government bonds, the ultimate conservative investment, over the long term.[20]

For the next several decades, despite occasional setbacks, prices of some items did skyrocket. For example, a painting purchased by David Rockefeller in 1960 for $8,500 sold in 2007 for $73 million in a particularly frenzied market.[21] And Damien Hirst's tiger-shark-in-formaldehyde, originally commissioned by advertising magnate Charles Saatchi for £50,000, sold fourteen years later to hedge-fund tycoon Steven Cohen for $12 million – albeit Hirst agreed to first replace the rotting original shark with a new one and to increase the strength of the formaldehyde. Publicity from such spectacular individual sales attracted new buyers, making the movement self-sustaining. So, too, did the titillation from events like when the ex-spouse of mega-fraudster Marc Rich kidnapped his Van Gogh until he agreed to a $200 million divorce settlement – whose unwritten clauses may have included her influence with the Clintons to secure for Rich a pardon for offenses that might have carried several centuries of prison time.[22] No doubt all the excitement even gave the struggling unknown artists some faint hope that a work in which they had invested years of study and effort might rise in price enough to pay the rent on an unheated garret.[23]

ARTFUL CRAFTS ... ?

Today's prestige art market is much more liberal than its noble ancestor: it welcomes a diversity of clients with a variety of motives provided only that they have enough money to paint the town red – or blue or green or even purple with pink polka dots, a guaranteed bestseller in the current climate. As in the past, but even more so now, some participants are rich collectors who seek through ostentatious display formerly associated with aristocratic wealth to disguise (or, in a manifestation of equal insecurity, sometimes to celebrate) their own ascent from more modest social ranks. Take, for example, US billionaire Norton Simon, who, when he decided to buy Rembrandt's *Titius*, wanted to set a record for the highest price ever paid for a work of art. So at the auction he actually bid against himself several times for something that, as matters turned out, was probably painted by one of Rembrandt's students.[24]

Other buyers may be simply people with no particular interest in the items other than the fact that they both cost a lot now and are expected to cost a lot more in the near future. For example, two French dealers, convinced that the Art Deco furniture creations of André Sornay, hitherto dismissed as a provincial by the Paris-dominated French art scene, were ready to be manipulated into a takeoff, began quietly buying and stockpiling. If at an auction two Sornay pieces were on the block, they would bid energetically (by telephone to keep their identities secret) for the poorer one, stopping just before victory, to push up the price in order to exhaust the winning bidder's resources before the really fine piece came up. Then, to coincide with publication of a book on the long-dead Sornay, a signal in the art world that someone is about to "make it," they announced that their huge inventory was for sale at outrageous prices. After a pause, the stampede began. One English banker phoned to ask if he could buy the most expensive piece they had, no matter what it was, in expectation that the market would continue to skyrocket – exactly the logic that played out so brilliantly for England's bankers in the property bubble.[25]

Yet others seek not the ego boost from personal possession but the accolade from public donation provided they can arrange an inflated appraisal and a fat tax write-off, and maybe dictate the press release. Yet others are speculators betting on the course of prices, a game rendered more attractive by opportunities to hide capital gains from the revenue authorities. Some seek a de facto corner on the market for particular artists and invest so heavily that they act, as one gallery owner described, less like gamblers than owners of the casino. By withdrawing a large inventory into their private stock, they steer the market upward at each successive auction until they are ready to sell.[26] That works best with old items by long defunct artists. Yet, by the curious economics of the art market, the same result can be achieved with works by new, living artists. It suffices that dealer and artist agree to make something quietly available at a discount to a prominent collector. The news that the collector has acquired the item sets off a buying frenzy. And once a modern artist is hot, the greater the artist's production, the higher rather than the lower the price the work will command as parasitocrats stumble over themselves to catch up with each other. This, of course, is not commercial fraud but the magic of the market at work.[27]

Most buyers are private; but some customers are corporations seeking to dress up their public image. Who cares if they were caught dumping carcinogenic wastes into a municipal water supply as long as they are publicly acknowledged as boosters of the arts? Art has also proved an excellent tool to pay bribes or evade price controls. In Japan in the late 1980s, when the government tried to clamp a lid on a property bubble, corporate buyers might write a cheque for a sum that conformed to the legal limit for a purchase, give a multimillion-dollar piece of art to the vendor, then buy it back a short time later for several times its supposed value, neatly transferring the extra money to the seller of land while simultaneously pushing the high-end art market up further.[28] Then there are museums and public galleries whose appetites, whether satisfied by direct donations or by cash gifts to finance their own choices, vary from the hearty to the voracious, without them being too fussy about the origins of the stuff they consume.[29]

In keeping with the public Puritanism of the late nineteenth and early twentieth centuries, US museums and public galleries were set up by the super-rich as places not for a cultural elite to rhapsodize over venerable masterworks or the wonders of lost civilizations – the ladies did that in their own drawing rooms while the gentlemen gathered to grouse elsewhere over brandy and cigars – but to morally uplift the masses, trying to keep them out of saloons and brothels where they might have had a lot more fun. Instead the Great Unwashed were allowed from a respectful distance to look at but not to touch things that their social betters had discarded from their dining-room walls, perhaps after a skillful restorer had hidden the slashes and stains resulting from glasses broken on the painting during some drunken carousal. That way both underclass and überclass had their sense of proper place in the social order reinforced.

Therefore, compared to major European museums, most originally endowed by high-ranking aristocrats, success in North America depended on mass rather than class appeal. While great European museums built reputations on stable collections of well-known works, those in the US needed a constant influx of new, preferably sensational material.[30] They still do, perhaps more so now, to keep attendance climbing in the face of intense competition from video arcades and reality TV. Hence the zeal to exhibit trendy material. That also helps the museum peddle knicknacks emblazoned with images from the display, a practice that has spread to big European museums. Today even the Louvre has "thematic trails" to take patrons to crowd-pleasers like the Mona Lisa where they might jostle with the rest of the mob for a digital photo before decamping to a gift shop to buy for their screaming three-year-old something like a plastic mug featuring that enigmatic sidelong glance.

However, European museums are usually forbidden to resell, while North American ones can dump older acquisitions, already milked for their entertainment value, on the secondary market. In Europe, too, because most major museums are now funded directly by the state, they are accountable like other public institutions. That, in theory, makes them more wary about the origins of material they put on display – unless it was stolen abroad by a senior officer in the line of duty so long ago as to no longer appear on anyone's hot list. Once they have an item, they, unlike US museums, are generally stuck with it unless relieved of that obligation by an embarrassing court order.[31]

By contrast, US museums rely overwhelmingly on what now passes as private philanthropy. In the past, the super-rich set up museums to hold personal collections, perhaps also endowing them with operating capital. Then came major tax changes in the 1950s, one of the seminal events in the evolution of the modern speculative art market. It was fortuitously timed for an era when Western Europe was still reconstructing from the war, and many of its old holdings in private hands were again available for sale at bargain prices. Not only did any donation of an art object become tax deductible against income (as well as reducing future estate-tax obligations), but the deduction was set at current "market value" rather than acquisition cost. Thus someone could pick up a Picasso in Europe on the cheap, hold it for several years, then donate it for many times the purchase price, getting a fine tax deduction for up to 30 percent of their total tax due that year. Even better, until removed in tax reforms in 2006, it was possible in the US to make a "fractional gift" – i.e., to donate an artwork for public display for only part of a year and still claim the full deduction. If the deal was arranged as a "remainder trust," the artwork could remain in the possession of the donor until their death while the donation was immediately credited against taxes.[32] All this had the same kind of impact in uprooting European art hordes, even if not as great, as flooding the world market with American grain and meat did in the late nineteenth century. In Canada, too, a donation is appraised at so-called fair-market value; and, while most types of charitable giving cannot exceed 20 percent of taxable income, for cultural properties the sky is the limit.[33]

In other words, "private philanthropy" in North America (and in Britain, where the rules are comprehensible only to tax lawyers and forensic accountants) is just a backhanded form of state subsidy in which the government cedes to rich private citizens the right not to pay a certain amount of taxes, the privilege of deciding which charitable, religious, or educational cause gains the benefit, and the power to shape just how the endowed institution will use the bequest. Inevitably these practices also affect how much care a museum or public gallery will put into vetting potential acquisitions. After curators have buttered up a billionaire to coax him to donate an artwork, they are less likely to ask questions about its origin.

Of course, that opens up grand opportunities to scam the system. One way is for someone in the inner circle, perhaps a trustee, to give to their art museum a cash donation, then quietly sell to the museum artworks for the same sum, getting the money back. That avoids an outside appraisal of the artwork. Donors get a full tax write-off for the donated cash and can use the "sale" as proof that they were in the art business and therefore able to claim expenses as a further deduction.[34]

Probably more common is the practice of donors creating consortia to buy works en masse at well below the unit price they would normally expect to pay, have them re-evaluated sharply upward, then give them to museums or public galleries for a 100 percent write-off. In the event of "an honest difference of opinion," tax authorities, to avoid tortured screams from the "arts community," usually accept the higher appraisal, particularly since the panels that advise them are stacked with representatives of the very professions most benefiting from the tax dodge.[35] The curator of the acquiring institution, too, has every incentive to concur with an inflated appraisal – the cost falls on taxpayers at large. Even better, the museum can resell the stuff it originally got for free, possibly using the exaggerated appraisal to set a base price, with no tax obligation. By contrast, continental European museums never seem to lack for donations without donors receiving a tax write-off.[36]

Granted, in the mid-1980s, the Reagan regime tried to blunt criticism of its tax cuts for the rich (lowering the top marginal rate from 50 percent to 28 percent) by restricting donor deductions to acquisition cost rather than appraised value. That left collectors with the option of selling rather than donating their holdings, and paying capital-gains tax, part of the pain of which Reagan charitably removed by also cutting the capital-gains rate. Donations supposedly plummeted, at least according to the afflicted institutions. Yet overall donations by individuals to all forms of charity actually rose; and even if the rich cut back their contributions to culture palaces, they probably did so because reduced tax rates reduced incentives to seek a deduction.[37] Then in 1991 the Clinton cabal, while imposing a small income-tax hike on the rich, restored full deductibility. The Bush gang decided that both of its predecessors had been right – it further slashed taxes at the top while letting rich donors continue to deduct at "market value."

Yet, even during the brief Reagan hiatus, the art market flourished, private demand expanding more than enough to compensate for any, largely exaggerated, public shortfall. In fact, rich private buyers, their purchasing power bolstered, were probably delighted not only to be free of competition from museums but to see public institutions deaccession inventory, selling it off to finance new purchases.

By the time of the tax changes, not only had art recovered its 1920s sparkle, but it gained new speculative potential, thanks in part to a revolution in art financing. In the past, a bank got involved only to lend money to a dealer with ample independent collateral; the dealer in turn might give credit to favoured clients. With the art-market explosion came professional financiers to front the money, then collect interest and a share of capital gains on subsequent sale. Deals could also be backed by art mutual-funds headquartered in financial havens where secrecy laws cloaked transactions against probes by customs, cops, or tax collectors. These funds were first established by Swiss private banks to permit their elite international clientele of tax and exchange-control evaders invest collectively in batches of art and antiquities.[38] They were imitated in the next decade in places like Liechtenstein and Panama. Participants could smuggle money to a haven bank to buy art in the name of the fund; the fund sold the item; the purchaser sent payment to the haven bank; and the bank divided proceeds secretly among the shareholders without the nuisance of taxes in their places of legal domicile. That was on top of the usual games of shifting assets back and forth between shell companies.[39]

All of these fiscal dodges take place in the context of an ever-broadening definition of what constitutes "art," which, in the name of expanding humanity's cultural horizons, serves ably in shrinking the state's fiscal frontiers. After all, if Andy Warhol could urinate on copper-coated plates, then sell the results, corroded by uric acid, as great art, or if César Baldaccini could delight the European art market by compressing old cars or refrigerators into metal blocks hard to differentiate from the normal output of a metal scrapyard, who could object when an Ulster paramilitary thug, who had already served twelve years for multiple murders, tried to force his way into the Belfast parliament with a small arsenal to kill IRA leaders, then insist that it was not terrorism but "an act of performance art?"[40] Certainly that seemed just as worthy of that name as a recent exposition at the Museum of Modern Art in New York where *Sitting in Silence* was judged to be the longest (seven hundred hours) piece of performance art on record. In fact it so moved at least one of the viewers as to induce a bout of projectile vomiting all over the seated creator. On the other hand, the same artist has reputedly plunged a knife between her fingers at high speed, brushed her hair until her scalp bled, and taken pills to induce seizures, all in the name of art.[41] So maybe the claims of that Ulster gentleman aren't so far-fetched after all.

As the market grew stronger and art easier to liquidate, financial institutions were happy to feed the mania. Commercial banks would still not lend to individuals to buy art for personal possession, but they accepted artwork from existing owners as collateral. That way unrealized capital gains on previous purchases could be used to finance new ones. Citibank in particular, as part of its big push to compete with private Swiss and British institutions for the business of "the high net-worth individual," began lending against art collections in 1979.[42] By early in the new millennium, it was common for big banks to have art-investment advisory services, while new investment funds, the joint ventures of ex-auction house executives and Wall Street bankers, spread. Collectors who borrowed against their art preferred to keep the collateral hanging on their living-room walls, with the bank simply taking a lien on the painting. But some banks demanded physical possession. If so, a piece of art might end up in a bank vault, perhaps for many years. On occasion when the bank finally took a look at its collateral, it got a rude surprise.

... AND CRAFTY ARTS?

When the market goes up, the taste of art thieves heads down.[43] If they steal a renowned painting, the media immediately attach to it a sky-high value, scaring off potential buyers but delighting art-market touts. A problem for artnappers, too, is that both insurance adjusters and cops have underworld informants who may resent the heat from all the publicity generated by a major score. So the thieves will have taken a huge risk for little or no return.

Granted, if a heist was planned directly by a would-be collector, rather than by thieves or fences, it might target a masterwork.[44] If the instigator gets caught, they will no doubt claim that the motive was to appreciate the work's aesthetic rather than financial value. But if enjoyment of the painting (rather than ego enhancement) were the real objective, the individual could buy a season's ticket to the museum and turn up every day at noon with a box lunch. And if a work originally stolen for private enjoyment potentially commands a high price, appreciation of its merits on a wall may well give way to appreciation of its merits in a bank book.[45] In general the image of the solitary eccentric sipping Château d'Yquem '62 while thrilling to the sight of Edvard Munch's *The Scream* hanging in a sealed room in the basement is the stuff of bad Hollywood remakes – and may account for the fact that *The Scream* was recovered both times it was stolen. And the twenty paintings supposedly worth $500 million taken from the Van Gogh Museum in Amsterdam in 1990 were all found in an abandoned car not far from the place. Perhaps the thieves were intimidated by their own success; perhaps they had just heard that in the opinion of some art experts as many as one hundred known Van Goghs are fakes.[46]

The most likely motive to steal something of that genre is to ransom it to an insurance company.[47] Even that might prove disappointing. Arranging a ransom requires repeated contacts, and insurance companies might cooperate with the police. Not always, though. As one insurance veteran explained elliptically: "we are able to be more flexible in getting the stolen items returned than the authorities." Of course, they don't offer ransom, merely "rewards for the safe return of stolen material."[48]

Even so, insurance companies try to keep payments down. Hence high-value artnapping may be directed more to quietly selling items back to private owners who prefer to avoid publicity about the origins of prized pieces in their collections, or of the money used to acquire them.[49] If an uninsured museum is the target, it may cost less to ransom than to replace a painting. Even if it is insured, a ransom may be cheaper than a big increase in premiums (or a major investment in new security systems) that the insurance company might demand in response to a reported theft.

Although a museum provides a bigger selection, particularly among the stuff stored in its vaults, most reported art thefts occur in private homes. They might be inside jobs. The owner first takes out a hefty insurance policy. A broker may be greedy for the sale; an appraiser may be coaxed to inflate the value; or the insurance company may decide that high premiums are enough compensation for the low risk of a big payout. Besides, if it does pay, a recovered painting becomes the property of the company, which might be able to sell it on a hot market for even more. With a policy in place, the owner can steal their own artwork, selling it on the black market or hiding it until it seems safe to resurface, while pocketing the insurance money. However, things do not always work as planned.

In 1992 Steven Cooperman, a California ophthalmologist with a keen eye for both the money he could earn from renting his professional credentials to class-action lawyers and the pricey artwork he could buy with his fees, lent a Picasso and a Monet to a local museum, claiming they were "worth" $12.5 million – their "market value" was closer to $2 million. The museum drew up a loan agreement based on his valuation. Cooperman used the first page (a subsequent page noted that the museum had nothing to do with the appraisal) to update his policy. After the paintings were returned to his home, he arranged a break-in. With no sign of forced entry, the police were suspicious; and the insurance company balked. But Cooperman, experienced in such matters, threatened to sue for $12.5 million plus punitive damages (possibly three times that sum), extorting from the insurance company nine times the market value of the not-actually-stolen art. Five years later the ex-girlfriend of the man who hid the paintings for Cooperman got angry at her former beau and told the police. To reduce his sentence, Cooperman traded information on a racket run by his lawyer friends that paid secret kickbacks (including to Cooperman himself) to phony plaintiffs and witnesses in multibillion dollar class-action suits.[50]

Along with stolen artworks has come a reputed deluge of fakes – copies of existing works or, more commonly, of previously unknown paintings passed off as the work of known artists. Theft and fakery can go together. In the late nineteenth and early twentieth centuries, when French churches were being plundered by US dealers, one ploy was to create a replica of the work to replace the real one, gaining time until discovery of the theft. A smarter version would involve taking a picture of the real thing, selling it in advance of delivery to a greedy collector, then sticking him with a fake. That may account for the uncertainty that now hangs over some items in US museums that originated in the collection of J.P. Morgan, whose zeal for overt collection of US cash was matched by his enthusiasm for the covert acquisition of European art.[51]

Then there is the tale of a bankrupt Argentine aristocrat and a crooked painter friend who in 1911 got into the Louvre on a Sunday afternoon dressed as maintenance men, hid until the next day when the museum was closed for repairs, then left through the front door with the Mona Lisa. The idea was to knock off some copies, peddle them for several hundred thousand dollars each, then return the original, confident that the heat would quickly die down once it was back and that no one who thought they had bought the real thing would have the gall to complain to the police. However, after the artist turned over six copies to his partner, the partner vanished. Three years later the contrite artist contacted the authorities to return the original. Or so one story goes. Another version is that the thief was an Italian working in the Louvre who was reputedly incensed over Napoleon's hijacking of this masterpiece from his homeland. He returned it only after he could not interest an Italian dealer.[52]

However, not all fakes were created with intent to defraud. In post-Renaissance Europe, master painters turned out copies of their own successful works to double, treble, or multiple dip; and they trained students to imitate them. The result can be supreme embarrassment as in 2008 when Francisco de Goya's *el Coloso*, one of his most renowned creations and the pride of Madrid's Prado Museum, was revealed to be likely the handwork of a student in his studio.[53] Masters, too, sometimes finished or simply signed the paintings of their protegés, knowing that would enhance the price. When protegés struck out on their own, they might replicate the master's signature as well as style.[54] The result was a supply of near-misses of the right age and materials so that today with masterworks in multiple copies expert opinion may be divided as to which is phony.

Furthermore, since master painters were quite capable of turning out less than masterful works, sometimes in multiple copies, it is distinctly possible that the best get attributed to the master even if done by a disciple, while responsibility for the mediocre gets sloughed off on others of lesser or unknown name even though these paintings are more "genuine" than the "great" works.[55]

Today, too, not all imitations are intended to defraud a buyer. Some clearly indicate that they are reproductions, sold to people happy to decorate their homes with a legal copy of a Monet or Picasso. After all, how many of their snooty friends will know the difference? The copies might also be intended to fool thieves – with the real thing safely stashed under lock and key. Because admitted fakes of well-known works can today be very expensive, there is even a legal business of faking fakes. However, paintings that start as acknowledged fakes of expensive works with the real artist's signature displayed on them might end up, with a minor touchup, posing as the genuine article somewhere else.

If the intent is to defraud, rarely does someone today copy a well-known piece by an old master. Too much information exists about their life's work; the style is well known; and materials (pigments, canvas, frame, etc.) that can pass muster are tough to get. The painting, too, must have a credible explanation as to why it has suddenly come on the market. Hence cases more likely involve a hitherto unknown work of that master rather than a reproduction of a known one. Catalogues raisonnés of an artist's work used for reference may be incomplete. Academic experts, too, wrangle incessantly about what ought to be included, not necessarily because there is real doubt but because that is what academic experts do reflexively to justify their existence. And there might be exploitable gaps in the record.

An apparent ten-year hiatus in Johannes Vermeer's known output led in the 1920s to scholars speculating about more paintings forgotten in dusty basements or on walls of old castles. So Hans Van Meegeren, a Dutch painter, eager to avenge himself on critics who refused to acknowledge his talent, decided to prove those scholars right. He hand-ground his pigments to simulate the types used in Vermeer's era. He used gum instead of oil as a medium to make the paint resistant to alcohol. (Pouring alcohol on a spot of paint to see if it dissolved was one of the main techniques then employed to detect forgeries.) He used the same kind of porcupine-hair brush as had Vermeer. And he added to his paint an industrial plastic to make the colours more vivid once they were heated in an oven. By scraping most of the old paint off a seventeenth-century canvas and painting over the remnants, his new work acquired the cracks a canvas gets over time.

Any new Vermeer, not to mention a whole series, required authentica-tion and a good story about its discovery. After completing his first fake, Van Meegeren told an acquaintance well known in the art world that Van Meegeren's mistress was forced by the death of her father to start selling off family antiques, among which he had discovered what he thought was a Vermeer. The acquaintance informed an elderly half-blind Vermeer scholar who had long advocated the existence of missing Vermeers. With the expert's endorsement, Van Meegeren was on his way to a brilliant, if anonymous, career, including several works that ended up in the hands of Andrew Mellon, then trying to make society matrons forget his social origins as a lumber and coal merchant. Donated to the National Gallery in Washington, the Mellon paintings were only exposed in the 1960s.[56] The real question, of course, is not why they were revealed as fakes, but why the gallery took so long to look carefully at them when alarm bells about Van Meegeren had been ringing for years.

During World War II, one of his fake Vermeers had fallen into the hands of an avid art collector named Hermann Goering. After the war Van Meegeren was accused of collaboration, a capital offense. To defend himself, he publicly produced another "Vermeer." Though sentenced to only a brief prison stint, he died soon after in a rehab clinic before start-ing his sentence, two decades before the National Gallery reviewed its Vermeer holdings.[57]

Today's forgers might be not disgruntled artists but accomplished restorers. To do their day job well, restorers must mimic styles and simu-late materials. There is always a question of when a painting ceases to be "restored" and becomes de facto a new work that ought to be attributed more to the restorer rather than the original painter. But if so, it would not fetch anywhere near the same price.

A forger might start with a sketch by the original artist, maybe found in books or files of art libraries. Then materials are reproduced, per-haps following instructions in the artist's notes, and applied to canvas.

Success is not just a matter of technical skill. The original artist was free to create – the forger is constrained to duplicate at least the style. Although buyers may initially see the work through the forger's eyes, over time to the experienced observer fakes seem stilted – or so claim the experts, particularly those seeking to reaffirm their expertise after a fake over which they had publicly drooled for years gets exposed. However, by then, the forger may have also forged a new identity.

Given the money involved, modern detection techniques use all manner of sophisticated devices with jaw-numbing names: macro-, X-ray- and ultraviolet-photography, infra-red scans, X-ray diffraction, fluorescence spectrometry, emission spectroscopy, differential thermal analysis, even electron microscopes that project three-dimensional images, etc. They are used to examine the pattern of cracks that develop with age, detect underdrawings, uncover alterations in signatures, show up areas of restoration, help identify and date pigments, and trace the progress of micro-organisms feeding on the canvas or locate worm galleries in old frames to help establish age. Dendrochronology can cross-match patterns in the wood with a piece of known age. Carbon–14 dating works on the principle that, when an organism is alive, the amount of carbon–14 is constantly replenished; once it dies, radioactive decay will steadily diminish it. Similar is the practice of checking paints for lead-210, with its short half-life – any substantial concentration in an "old" painting is a strong warning. Dust particles deep in cracks can be analyzed for their composition. It might seem odd if a seventeenth-century masterwork just discovered in a ruined castle in the Loire Valley has buried in its worm holes traces of Paris Hilton perfume or crumbs from some Chicken McNuggets.

None of these techniques is perfect. It took a combination of microscopic, infrared, and X-ray examination for the Cologne art museum to discover in 2008 that its precious Monet (*La Seine à Port Villez*) was a 1920s fake, artificially aged with a transparent glaze.[58] Most detection methods can be beaten with care and commitment. Efforts to establish the age of the frame, for example, can be countered by stripping wood from an old building or just using a frame from a not-so-valuable painting of about the desired age. Lead from an antique grandfather-clock's pendulum can be added to paint. A fake, too, has to be tested against a control group that itself may be replete with reproductions. Still, the need to defeat fancy detection methods raises the cost of making a good fake. As a result, fakes, like thefts, are more likely at lower price ranges, where buyers rarely bother with tests nor take serious action if they are scammed.

Fakes are also more common with modern art. Styles are easier to mimic. They might consist of just a few dabs or lines of paint plus the occasional slash from a deftly wielded box-cutter, one of the artistic tools employed by the venerable and venerated Lucio Fontana, whose works have been persuasively described as possessing "an undeniable intuitive sense of resolution, a feeling of wholeness through negation."[59] Today, too, there are likely many more pictures by a modern artist than by an old master in which to immerse the new work. Materials that can pass detection are easier to obtain; and any "aging" required might be done just by baking the painting in an oven, then sticking it in a fridge to crack the paint. Faking modern stuff is also easier because there are usually fewer experts on the particular artist to pass judgement. Furthermore, a smart forger paints what is "hot," since it will be grabbed faster with fewer questions asked. The downside is that the artists may still around to identify what passes for their work. That was what ended the brilliant career of the late David Stein.

Actually it was his second career. He had been sentenced by French courts for theft so often that his decision to start life anew as an art forger was a big step up. Stein would psych himself to believe he actually was the artist, then paint with great speed in the artist's style, assuring his works of a spontaneity that a laboriously copied painting lacks. He and his wife, who was in charge of aging paper with tea and sometimes handled sales to various galleries, travelled Europe unloading Chagalls and Van Dongens, though Stein later developed a taste for Picassos as well. The galleries were delighted. Some owners must have been suspicious, but they realized that the works were good enough to sell as the real thing, and since they were not party to the actual production, they were legally in the clear. In Europe, though, there was danger of flooding a local market. So the Steins decamped to New York, where it was easier to sell en masse. In four years, his wife claimed, he turned out "thousands" of fakes, though that may have been spousal pride speaking. (By contrast, in her memoirs she was silent about his similarly impressive record of passing bum checks and skipping out on hotel bills.) But perhaps she was right. Thomas Hoving, long-time director of the Metropolitan Museum of Art, indirectly lent some support to her claim when he revealed that he received his own training in how to detect fakes from a restorer who could turn out a passable Renoir in two hours, a Manet or Cézanne in three to four – only Monet defeated the faker's talents.[60]

For David Stein the downfall came when a buyer asked a dealer for authentication of a couple of Stein's "Chagalls." Stein promised to obtain the certificate from a prominent Paris gallery whose stamp (among others) he had already copied. He produced the document on a typewriter with a French keyboard he kept for that purpose. But the dealer was suspicious over the speed with which the certificate arrived, given normal post and processing time. Worse luck, the dealer bumped into Marc Chagall himself, then on a visit to New York. Stein was convicted even without the assistance of art dealers, who didn't want to appear in public as dupes or co-conspirators, or of collectors who refused to believe, or didn't want the public to believe, that their prize acquisitions were phony. Even in prison, Stein continued to turn out fakes. As art they were equal to any he had produced – but with only his signature, they were worth only a tiny fraction of the prices he used to command. However, he earned the ultimate accolade. Not only did his reputation as a forger allow him to develop a thriving legal business, but, at one exhibit of his fakes, someone set up an easel outside to fake David Stein fakes.[61]

Fakes also abound, rumour has it, in the market for modern sculpture. Take, for example, César Baldaccini squashing old cars, fridges, even cutlery into blocks or giant thumbs and the like in an effort, he said, to "disown consumer society" – an argument that would have been more convincing if he had stolen Lambroghinis and Breuget watches, pounded them into pieces in a well-publicized fit of rage, then sold the wreckage to a scrap dealer and donated the money to an orphanage. His artwork was apparently so unique and difficult to replicate that after he died two brothers (of each other, not of Baldaccini) in France were accused of making 130 "César compressions" that were authenticated at reputable art auction houses and even by the artist's mistress. The fraud was revealed after a police investigation prompted, it seems, by a dispute between the mistress and wife over the sale of his works while the battle over his will was still in front of the courts.[62]

The sector of the art business where manipulation is easiest is probably prints. That began in the early twentieth century when US museums were looking for easy money. In theory an artist arranges for a master plate to be made, authorizes a fixed number of reproductions with serial numbers, signs them, then destroys the plate. In practice there could be unauthorized overruns at the print shop with faked signatures added, or subsequent reproductions of reproductions by old-fashioned photolithographic or more modern electronic means. The scam is easier if artists are sloppy, complicit, or indifferent. One of the most notorious cases involves Salvador Dalí prints, with tales of fakes "worth" anywhere from $625 million to $3 billion, numbers as dubious as the prints they supposedly represent. Reputedly from the mid-1960s to the late 1970s, Dalí supplied watercolours for publishers to use in limited edition prints but also gave his assistants pre-signed paper on which prints could be made while he was travelling. On his deathbed, news of his pending demise stoked a buying frenzy. Counterfeiters, including close friends in the art retail and publishing businesses, figuring Dalí would not live long enough to denounce them, got to work with a vengeance. Dalí may not have cared. In his view, so his lawyer claimed, those who make and those who buy lousy reproductions "deserve each other."

That opinion was not shared by police, who in the late 1980s and on into the 1990s busted dealers from New York to Hawaii for selling "Dalí" prints, misrepresenting values, and refusing to honour buy-back guarantees.[63] Nor were the artist's prints the only things affected after his demise. In January 2009, Spanish police seized at a purported Dalí auction on the Costa del Sol, eighty-one lithographs, textiles, sculptures, and bas-reliefs along with twenty certificates of authenticity of statues attributed to Dalí, charging the French dealer with fraud and forgery.[64]

Although the motive for fraud is generally money, pure and simple, some soon-to-be-con artists, like the wannabe Vermeer in the 1930s, claim to be seeking revenge on an art world that refuses to acknowledge their genius. That was the alibi, too, of a young man in Bolton, England, who found himself brushed off by the establishment and unable to sell his own work or even attend art college. So, with the help of his brother (who handled the money) and his aging parents (who arranged phony provenances), from 1989 to 2006 he managed, using simple household equipment, to produce 120 fake modern paintings along with antiquities that passed the scrutiny of experts – although it was ultimately flaws in some "Assyrian reliefs" that ended his career. While newspapers claimed the "value" of his creations to be £10 million, the family collected about £850,000, with £350,000 still in bank accounts at the time of their arrest. Money may not have been the sole reason for their activities, but there is no sign that they took strong objection to it.[65]

THE ART OF THE DEAL

Whether a painting is real and legitimate, genuine but stolen, or flat-out fake, it passes through the same set of intermediary institutions to reach the same set of final buyers. But the role of those institutions has changed over time, adding fresh risks to anyone venturing onto the art-market minefield.

Originally, auction houses handled large lots, perhaps from estates or bankruptcy sales, rarely taking ownership but simply earning commissions for acting on behalf of sellers. Their customers might be collectors, museum curators, buyers for smaller auction houses, and dealers. Dealers, by contrast, were usually merchants, buying to resell at a higher price to the "public" – i.e., to rich collectors and well-endowed museums. But once the market took off, major auction houses raised their profiles and prices, targeting the general market in competition with dealers and marketing art, as the Detroit real-estate tycoon who took over Sotheby's in 1983 described it, the same way they would root beer.[66] This strategy met with so much success that today publicity around spectacular sales by Christie's and Sotheby's rather than by top dealers sets the tone of the market. Auction houses have also muscled in on another role on which dealers used to have a lock – selling on credit. In fact, making loans to buyers is one of their biggest sources of revenue even if, with "Mickey" Cohen, it was a practice they came to regret.

Michel Cohen was a "runner." Runners grease the wholesale market. They exist because high-end dealers try to isolate clients and guard sources to avoid poaching. Since runners generally don't have the cash to hold pricey items until a deal can be closed, they rely on outside money; and, with low commission rates, they thrive on volume. Cohen's business was enough to support a lavish lifestyle until he discovered stock options. To cover mounting debts, he once sold a painting to two different clients. That was bad enough. That the painting had been lent to him by the Metropolitan Museum of Art made things a little worse. At another time he borrowed $8.4 million from Sotheby's to buy five Picassos and Chagalls, claiming he had buyers waiting to fork over $10 million. Then he sold the paintings at less than cost, using the money to try to keep his stock brokers from legal action. When Sotheby's threatened to sue, Cohen bought some time by writing a couple of checks, then stopped payment and vanished along with his family. In 2004 he was arrested in a ritzy part of Rio. Held pending extradition to the US, he faked illness and escaped from an ambulance never to be seen again, leaving (so it was claimed) anywhere from $50 to 100 million in debts behind.[67]

However, sometimes a runner, rather than assuring anonymity, lands buyer and/or seller in a public legal spat. Such a saga began when a runner approached Phoenix Capital Reserve Fund, a Bermuda based hedge fund, with news that Paul Gaugin's *Paysage aux trois arbres* was for sale. It was hot stuff – another Gaugin had just sold for $40 million. At the runner's suggestion, the would-be buyers obtained an appraisal of $15–17 million from New York's Wildenstein Art Gallery, one of the world's wealthiest and most discreet houses, most of whose inventory is reputed to be stored in a nuclear-proof bunker in the Catskill Mountains of New York. To keep things properly at arm's length, the same family's Wildenstein Institute in Paris, world experts on Gaugin, issued a certificate of authenticity. Since the subsequent legal case never reached discovery stage and everyone involved worked through proxies, what happened next remains murky; but the sequence appears to be roughly as follows.

First, Phoenix appointed an agent called Mandarin Trading to handle the purchase. Then Calypso Fine Art, an intermediary for the seller, issued an invoice. This contained the news that the Wildensteins had once owned the painting; but it had since passed into a private collection – that seemed to make the Wildensteins all the better placed to judge its value objectively. So Mandarin sent $11.3 million to Calypso. Calypso kept $2.2 million as a "transaction fee" and passed on $9.1 million to another company called Peintures Hermès. Since it, too, was an intermediary, it pocketed $700,000 and paid Allez la France Ltd, the putative corporate owner, $8.4 million. All seemed well until Mandarin, on behalf of Phoenix, the Bermuda hedge fund, tried to flip the painting via Christie's, putting in a reserve bid of $12 million only to find the highest bidder offering a mere $9 million. Several years later, convinced that the Wildensteins had not only owned the intermediary, Peintures Hermès, and used it to skim a big commission, but they also had secretly continued to own the painting itself on which they had supplied a grossly inflated appraisal, Mandarin sued. But the New York Supreme Court dismissed the complaint.[68]

That must have been welcome news for the Wildensteins. Their public image had already been battered by accusations of trafficking confiscated art with the Nazis in wartime France and by a media frenzy over the divorce of Alex Wildenstein, late head of the house, from a lady whose frantic efforts via plastic surgery to pander to her hubby's exotic wildcat fetish had earned her the title "Bride of Wildenstein." His unhappy spouse lamented in court that she needed $1 million per month for maintenance because her abilities to take care of herself had been ruined by luxurious married life. She didn't even know, she claimed, how to boil an egg. So the judge advised that she buy a microwave. He also ordered the knife-happy lady to pay for her own mutilations, another charge she tried to load on her soon-to-be ex. Still, she had the satisfaction of getting maintenance of $2.4 million per annum, the townhouse in New York where she had caught her beloved in bed with his teenage mistress, a 150-year-old château outside Paris, and a 66,000 acre ranch in Kenya with 55 artificial lakes.[69]

Whatever games dealers play directly with clients, auction houses also witness their share of dirty tricks.[70] Sellers can employ agents to enter phony bids to puff prices, but that is usually unnecessary. The auction house has enough incentive to do the job itself. Although auction houses collect commissions from the seller, they make even more by charging a buyer's premium on top of the winning bid – with the total then reported as the "market price." That is one reason buyers form rings whose members agree not to compete, except perhaps at the start for the sake of appearances. One is designated to win; and the piece is later privately re-auctioned within the group or collectively resold with the profits split.

There is plenty of scope for the auction house itself to manipulate. Auctioneers can announce nonexistent bids or trot out confidentially presubmitted bids at strategic times to keep the excitement building. If a bidder gets carried away, then defaults, the house can use the winning bid, even though it was never paid, to advertise when it resells the piece. Even the giants of the high-end market have been caught fixing commission rates, faking sales volume to attract more clients, and organizing smuggling from countries that restrict art exports. The practice of lending to buyers – and charging them not only the principal and interest but also a percentage of profits on resale – is very lucrative and helps keep upward pressure on prices.[71] For a time big houses would even lend to a hopeful client to finance up to half the purchase price of an item they wanted to sell. But stung badly by a "high net worth" client whose net worth proved to be largely imaginary, Sotheby's (for one) backed off. But it still would lend on security of existing items in someone's collection to help them acquire something else that the auction house was peddling.[72]

However the greatest scope for shady dealings is probably how goods are described. Generally items are sold as shown, with neither house nor seller taking responsibility for "errors of description." A major house, to defend its reputation, may grant some de facto guarantees, perhaps for too short a period to permit a buyer to get a proper outside evaluation. Anyway, catalogues deliberately use terminology to provide the house with a chance to claim it never meant what the catalogue copy implied. As to how closely they check the provenance of their goods, not only are the volumes passing through a successfully auction house large but legally it has a fiduciary relationship with a seller not with a buyer, including an obligation to keep a seller's identity secret. That can be especially useful when the seller is a dealer who handles merchandise of dubious origins and who decides to sell via an auction house with its rapid turnover rather than through their own business, where the buyer can get a closer, calmer look. Either that, or somebody decides to go public with unusual revelations, whether about paintings or any of the other expensive collectibles in which auction houses specialize.

For example, in June 2008, Sotheby's pulled from its Important European Furniture & Decorations sales roster "a fine pair of German neoclassical ormolu-mounted mahogany commodes c.1800." Its catalogue had hinted they would go for $200–300,000, normal enough (in today's world of pricy antique furniture) for something made in Berlin for the imperial Russian market by a cabinet-maker trained in one of the great London workshops. But suddenly the pieces were withdrawn, the head of the house's English and European furniture department slightly modifying his description of the commodes to "convincingly made and with an intention to deceive."[73] The prominent English restorer (and supplier to dealers who were the toast of the London and New York high-end antique furniture trades) proudly said of his creations that the commodes had been made in the early 1990s from old wardrobes combined with new wood from local timber merchants. And he claimed with apparent professional pride: "We turned out hundreds of pieces from carcasses or from scratch. Most people think 18th or 19th century craftsmanship is dead, but we've been doing it here." But, he insisted, he never knew that the dealers he had been supplying were selling his handiwork as if it were genuine. Apparently one of Britain's busiest and ablest restorers never bothered in the course of more than twenty years in business to read auction catalogues or trade magazines.[74]

As the affair sent shockwaves through the antique-furniture world, the editor-in-chief of *House Beautiful* commented, "everybody knows this kind of thing goes on ... but the story never comes out." Presumably "everybody" in his books meant trade insiders, not their clients who, but for the affair exploding into the public domain, might have paid up to $870,000 for an "18th Century Louis XVI Bureau Plat with Marquetry and gold bronze mounted by G Haupt, Stockholm 1770 including cartonnier." This was, said the restorer, really a late twentieth-century reproduction, based on a photo, using wood from a dismantled pre-1760s French oak-timbered barn and reconditioned leather recovered by divers from a shipwreck.[75] On the other hand, if those clients had enough spare cash to fork out that much for what could have been less pretentiously called a writing table with some decorative veneer and a couple drawers on top, they probably deserved to be fleeced. In a perverse way, they probably wanted to be – they just didn't want anyone else to find out.

As to the dealers who were caught up in the affair, one of them, taking note of the terrible toll the scandal took at a time when, because of the great financial crisis sweeping through its client base, the expensive antiques business in general was in trouble, announced that he and his partner were considering alternative commercial careers: "We're thinking of going into modern art."[76] That was a fair choice for, unlike what may have transpired in some antique furniture deals, with modern art what people see is generally what they get; and what they get is pretty much what they deserve.

Although most buyers of high-end paintings seem to get a bigger kick out of spending the money in public than enjoying the painting in private, others prefer anonymity. They can work through art advisors who act as discrete salaried agents to locate and negotiate private sales. Or they can rely on their friendly auction house. In a normal auction the house may protect the identity of the seller or even sometimes the buyer, but the item itself is on public display. In a private sale, the very existence of the deal is kept quiet, providing an excellent milieu for speculative flips and, quite likely, for unloading items that might not benefit greatly from public scrutiny.[77]

Dealers operate quite differently from auction houses. They may buy from private sellers or auction houses, from each other, or directly from artists whose works they have undertaken to hype, particularly if that artist is in debt to them to support a sex, drugs, or booze habit. As merchants rather than agents, dealers supposedly stand behind their goods – although that did not prevent the owner of two New York galleries from buying French masterworks, arranging to have duplicates made, then selling both the fakes and the originals.[78] Dealers also offer personalized service – sometimes at a client's considerable expense. For example, during the early 1980s, one regular visitor to two New York galleries owned by the late Armand Hammer was Imelda Marcos, first lady of the Philippines. On a single day she purchased twelve paintings for $3 million, a special price arranged for her by the tycoon whose oil company had just submitted to President Ferdinand Marcos an application for a new drilling project with special tax incentives. On another occasion she walked out of his galleries with fifty-two paintings by a little-known French impressionist whose work had been occupying space in the gallery's basement, at a price that set the New York artsy crowd to snickering. Even happier, reputedly, was a Florentine dealer who sold her an $8.3 million lot of "Old Masters" that, according to wags, he had arranged for some clever nuns to paint a short time before. After the first lady and her husband fled the Philippines in 1986, the new government discovered that of Imelda's collection of seventy-five Old Masters, sixty were the work of unknown provincial eighteenth-century artists or nineteenth-century fakes.[79]

A high-ranking dealer revels in publicity, since the gallery's reputation is usually more important than any particular painting in establishing the price. That reputation also makes possible sale of things over the telephone sight unseen to modern collectors who then might pose before the media to brag of their artistic taste and discretion.[80] A dealer's search for a highly publicized niche to plant the kind of work they are selling assures that some things on display in today's public galleries or beaux-arts museums make those institutions difficult to differentiate from *Ripley's Believe It or Not*.[81] One of Damien Hirst's first big hits, for example, was a glass case with a cow's head in one section, flies breeding on the other, and an electric zapper killing off the flies as they tried to migrate from one side to the other, the pile of dead flies neatly synchronizing its growth with the decomposition of the cow's head. But maybe he was just trying to demonstrate the laws of thermodynamics in action.

All these transactions hinge on authentication and appraisal, two distinct things that may done by the same person. One possible reason why art galleries and private collections are vulnerable to fakes is that authenticators who also appraised in the past were sometimes paid by rich collectors not a fixed fee but a percentage of the appraisal. Sometimes a living artist may be called upon to authenticate his own work prior to resale. If it is true that Pablo Diego José Francisco de Paula Juan Nepomuceno María de los Remedios Cipriano de la Santísima Trinidad Ruiz y Picasso (AKA Pablo Picasso) was once so taken by an imitation of his style by Jean Cocteau that he insisted on signing the painting himself, what he would have done if later called upon to authenticate it?[82] On the other hand, artists, angry that their work initially sold for so little, only to reappear on the resale market at a huge mark-up, might be tempted to exact revenge by authenticating a fake and charging a healthy fee for the service. If the artist is dead, a known scholar can do the job. So can a dealer. In one case, a dealer sold a copy of a Gaugin to a Japanese collector accompanied by a genuine letter of authentication, while unloading the original painting in New York, where it was so well known it did not require any documentation.[83]

On occasion the dealer can be both authenticator and appraiser or even a collector at the same time. Members of the same self-selected group can further recycle themselves into critics in the media, curators for galleries and museums, or art consultants to help people make their choices, perhaps receiving kickbacks from galleries. Obviously appraisers can fundamentally disagree even with each other, perhaps even with their own previous opinions, in a market that is subject to rapid changes of mind and mood.[84] An appraiser, too, can help to defraud banks or insurance companies and to sell stolen or fake art. Since a banker is more familiar with compound-interest tables and flow charts than easels and brush strokes, the most important document required to pledge a painting as collateral for a loan is the appraisal. Apart from seeming to guarantee repayment, it may open the door to an insurance policy that further reassures the lender. The collateral might then be stashed in the vault along with all the stolen and counterfeit stocks, bonds, and bills the institution has already taken as security for its commercial loan portfolio and only subjected to a second look when the borrower takes the money and runs. On the other hand, if a stolen item is potentially very valuable, the thief (or the buyer) may decide to just let the bank hold it securely, renewing the loan until it is safe to unload the artwork on the open market.[85]

When that date comes depends on countries of origin and of sale. Technically in places following a British common-law tradition, including the US and Canada, no one can obtain legal title to a stolen work even if bought in good faith, a situation that potentially hurts an innocent buyer. However, that is modified by statutes of limitation and a requirement of due diligence by the previous owner. If someone left a painting in the tool shed of a country cottage they had not visited since the death of a maiden aunt twenty years before, they might have no legal grounds to protest if it turned up in someone else's collection. The practice in European Civil Code countries, and in Japan, though, is that good title does pass to a bona fide purchaser at point of purchase. The previous owner can only regain possession, again within a statutory period that varies from place to place, by compensating a good-faith buyer. The result is plenty of opportunities for legal arbitrage.[86] In an effort to find a compromise, the Unidroit Convention proposed that victims retain full title but had to compensate good-faith buyers to reclaim their property. However the UK and the US, who dominate the international art market refused to sign, making the convention a dead letter.[87]

While some clients may be naïve or indifferent, generally if a work of art carries a hefty price tag, especially if it is marketed as in some way antique, it requires a credible record of previous ownership and of voluntary sale. But police are (sometimes) informed right after the theft; and, unless it was taken directly on orders of the person planning to acquire it, media attention might scare off potential buyers. By contrast, a fake generates no pre-emptive alert – it must merely pass through a business where volume is everything and where dealers or auction houses are inclined to assume all is well unless someone shoves in their face a blaring headline with a large colour photo.

However, sometimes the issue of provenance never arises. It didn't, for example, with Russian avant-garde paintings that became the rage among New York trendies starting in the late 1970s. In fact these paintings were treasured precisely because they had no official documentation.

After the Bolshevik Revolution, the internal market in the USSR was carefully controlled. The state provided materials directly to officially sanctioned artists; and their product, however good, was automatically written off by the outside art world as just regime-pandering propaganda. On the other hand, official disapproval was taken in the West as a sign of that the artist was truly a talented and free spirit, setting off a search for regime-taunting artists producing religiously inspired or scatological art – the kind that Soviet premier Nikita Krushchev typified as "some messy yellow lines which looked, if you will excuse me, as though some child had done his businesses on the canvas when his mother was away and then spread it around with his hands."[88] In New York such paintings, perhaps smuggled out by the US embassy in its diplomatic pouch, could generate the same kind of thrill as hosting a refusenik for dinner without the same qualms about hanging the exhibit permanently on the wall. The flow also provided cover for fakes. Forgers, with Berlin their main locus operandus not only created paintings but sometimes entire biographies of nonexistent artists.

While all this was happening, the intelligence agencies in the West, led by the CIA, were celebrating the kind of freedom of artistic expression their societies offered by sponsoring artists to turn out works, especially abstract expressionism, that celebrated the glories of life under capitalism and, with the indispensable aid of New York's Museum of Modern Art, sponsoring worldwide exhibitions that would show how backward and boring was the "socialist realism" coming out the East Bloc – and they did that even as neanderthals in the US Senate were publicly denouncing emerging US abstract art as a Communist plot.[89]

After the end of Communism, there was no longer any need for secrecy about Russian avant-garde paintings, something that might have detracted from their appeal. On the other hand now documentation could flow abundantly, written with old typewriters on official looking stationary or churned out by Russian art experts eager to sell authentications.[90]

Many tricks can increase credibility. An item may be introduced through a location seemingly beyond suspicion, perhaps on display in the home of a well-known collector or in the window of a ritzy store. It might go through an auction house that cares about little except its commission. It might be passed through a few pseudo sales among collaborating dealers before arriving in an upscale art mart where a connoisseur or curator "discovers" it. On the other hand, it might have full authentication by experts drawing on the best archival sources that the art world has to offer.

MASTERS AND MASTERMINDS

In 1986 John Myatt, a minor British pop musician, discovered a talent for imitating modern masters. Abandoned with small children by his wife and in desperate financial shape, he advertised in *Private Eye*, a British satirical weekly, copies of nineteenth- and twentieth-century paintings for £150 each. One client he attracted was John Drewe, whose own life as a faker went back to a childhood in a banal lower-class home, concocting stories about his aristocratic origins. Even the name "John Drewe" was an invention. He told Myatt that he was a professor of nuclear physics and an agent of British Intelligence and asked him to do some fakes to decorate his house. Initially it was legit. When Drewe had one of the paintings appraised by Christie's for $38,000, the impecunious Myatt was persuaded to cross the line.

Rather than fake existing works, Myatt invented new ones imputable to known artists, all dead. He worked with an emulsion paint developed in the 1960s, decades after most of the paintings he was creating were supposed to have been made, to knock off "lost works" in a matter of days. His masterpieces eventually totalled two hundred, almost all targeted at the mid-price (less than £10,000) market to avoid too much attention. His partner Drewe faked signatures, aged appearances with mud or the contents of a vacuum cleaner bag, located old wood for frames, and wetted nails to cause them to rust. And he had a more important job.

Drewe bought his way into the archives holding correspondence between twentieth-century artists, collectors, and curators, exhibition catalogues, photographs, receipts, and bills of sale of the three institutions (the Tate Gallery, the Victoria & Albert National Art Library, and the Institute of Contemporary Art) that potential buyers might use for verification, by donating fake paintings or cash. His applications were accompanied, too, by letters of reference that he wrote for himself.[91] Once inside, he created notes on an old typewriter identifying photos of forged paintings to stick into relevant catalogues, using a forged stamp for authentication. He also wrote to families of artists to trick them into authenticating the works. At one point Drewe, by passing himself off as a professional archivist working for a phony art research company, provided the authentication himself.

It was also necessary prior to sale to establish a current owner. So Drewe coaxed friends to pose for the role or just invented owners and documents. Given the modest price range of most of the paintings and the market's conviction that fakes abound anyway, even if documentation did not always seem perfect, it was easy to find someone to sell them. Taking care to use runners so that his face would not become too familiar, Drewe peddled all two hundred, most through Sotheby's and Christie's, others through dealers. Although experts later declared them to be amateurish and replete with errors, Drewe collected perhaps as much as £2.5 million, most of which, barring a measly £100,000 for Myatt, was stashed tax-free in Swiss bank accounts.

The downfall would have been familiar to Steven Cooperman, the California eye doctor who did not see danger from a woman one of his confederates had scorned. Drewe's embittered ex stumbled across the evidence and tipped off the authorities. The police dropped in on Myatt, who agreed to help nail his former partner. Drewe went to jail still fabricating – claiming that he was under orders from British Intelligence to sell four thousand fakes to finance illegal arms shipments to Iran, Iraq, and Sierra Leone.[92]

When the scandal broke, dealers blamed auction houses for sloppy verification; the auction houses blamed their advisors and authenticators. The truth was that dealers and auction houses alike were greedy for sales at a time of market slump and would probably have handled anything short of a kindergarten child's finger-painting (even the one that Nikita Krushchev had graphically described) if someone told them it was a newly discovered Monet.[93] Of the two hundred works sold, seventy-three were recovered, the rest following the same fate as other successful fakes.

If the buyers have no cause for suspicion, the painting will never be reported. If they do have such cause, the painting may still never be reported. A private buyer realizing they've been scammed might hide the item out of embarrassment or arrange a "theft" or a fire to dump the cost onto their insurance company. The really clever ones might donate it to a public institution and (in some countries) collect a tax deduction as a reward for their civic-mindedness. Besides, an ordinary buyer (with extraordinary money) has the burden of proof and may have trouble finding experts ready to stick out their necks to pronounce something counterfeit for fear that it will eventually turn out to be a genuine, previously unknown work by the accredited artist.

If the buyers are dealers, they might arrange, much as do merchants paid in counterfeit currency, to quietly unload the item onto unsuspecting clients. Alternatively the dealer may lend the painting to a museum, then follow up by donating it, assured that it will be subject to much less scrutiny than an item coming from a nonprofessional source. Dealers commonly make donations to museums – it helps relieve temporary market gluts of particular types of items at public expense, simultaneously setting market trends for the same stuff and pushing up the prices while building good will for possible future sales to the same institution.[94] The other options – for the dealer to swallow the loss or have their professional competence questioned – would be too much to countenance.

If, on the other hand, buyers are museums or public galleries, they, too, might just keep mum and hope no one notices. After all, their professionally trained curators did not. And, in the final analysis, it's not their money.

That, of course, raises the question that bothered Hans Van Meegeren, David Stein, John Myatt, and others like them. Why does it matter? The answer, alas, is not because of the need to defend a real artist's reputation, important though that ought to be, or because of a desire to protect humanity's cultural commons, something even more vital. In today's high-end art world, artistic merit is a function of price, not vice versa. Certainly fakes can play havoc with the reputations of art historians and, more to the point, undermine the social pretenses of today's parasitocrats; but it is never clear why the rest of society needs to weep over either eventuality.

The real problem is that a proliferation of excellent fakes means that there are a lot more people of talent than a market thriving on contrived scarcity and professional incest can accommodate. Even worse, if the public ultimately decides that it wants paintings because of their aesthetic qualities or their ability to capture larger-than-life truths rather than because they bear famous autographs, prices of grossly overblown stuff from which intermediaries make their money and on which art experts base their reputations would sink like New Orleans waterfront luxury condos built just before Katrina blew through. About the only thing the high-end art business can say in its own defense is that things are just as bad in the antiquities trade.

5

The Chiselers: From Tomb-Raider to Curator

During the Cold War (and after) the "free market" probably ranked in importance as a strategic weapon just behind the intercontinental ballistic missile – and did a lot more damage. It was the battering ram to smash open weak economies for looting, the wrecking ball to crumble social support programs in the name of "efficiency," and the heavy artillery to blast away any value except "market price."

Yet most countries still persist in regarding archeological relics and vintage artworks as collective property to guard for posterity. They face no lack of advice to the contrary. It comes from battalions of academic economists who menace holdouts with asymmetric non-zero sum games, indecomposable homothetic utility functions and Fisherine separation theorems to prove that the best way to combat the insidious effects of the free market is to legalize its most malicious results.[1] It comes from high-end dealers and rich collectors in the West who insist that any attempt at restriction will just lead to an epidemic of theft and smuggling, an opinion that, given the business practices of so many members of that cabal, must be accorded the status of expert.[2] It comes from detached, scientific observers writing on the op-ed page of the Wall Street Journal who counsel that the best way to preserve a country's archeological heritage is to put it under the care of those who appreciate it most – with the corollary proposition that the more money they are willing to pay, the greater must be their cultural and aesthetic sensitivity.[3]

In spite of that advice, most countries still impose restrictions. Some ban private possession in favour of public collections; some demand registration of individual holdings; some insist on state control of excavations along with public ownership of everything the Earth disgorges; some forbid certain types of exports while requiring licenses for others; and all of these are reinforced by international conventions preventing free export and import.[4]

Of course, they do so even if what they call their national history is a self-glorifying fable based, as the old saying goes, on a collective dislike of their neighbours and a common misconception about their ethnopolitical origins.[5] They do so even if they see the main function of antiquities as creating "ancestor myths," not to illuminate the past but to rationalize the present, no matter how much nonsense, dishonesty, and injustice it represents. They do so, too, even if a fair amount of stuff in their own national collections was likely stolen from someone else, somewhere else, assuming it isn't just fake.

SHROUDED PAST, SHADY PRESENT?

Properly speaking, an "antiquity" is at least 1,500 years old, neatly coinciding in popular consciousness with the fall of Rome to the (pre-Islamic) barbarian hordes. The ensuing Dark Ages of Europe (when the rest of the world was remarkably well illuminated) spelled the end of the empire's flourishing trade in cultural artifacts.[6] Yet trade was not the only way that things moved around in Roman times. Following Greek precedent, statues erected to the gods of conquered peoples were picked up by triumphant generals, along with animal and mineral curiosities, to be preserved in treasuries that the Romans called Museums, because they were dedicated to the Muses. (Given the methods of acquisition, a more suitable name might have been Pilleums, a somewhat ungrammatical derivative of "pilleus," Latin for "pillage.") In another telling sign of a post-Roman end of history, nomadic tribesmen, although eager for plunder, preferred useful, portable things like cattle, fertile young women, or bags of gold rather than waste time and energy trying to haul off, for example, one of Cleopatra's Needles – those twenty-one-metre-high red-granite obelisks were left in Egypt to be appreciated by proper gentlemen centuries later and now grace the urbane centres of London, Paris, and New York. Back then, too, no one, Roman general or barbarian warrior-chief, was likely to search very hard for ancient sites to "study." Although graverobbing had a long history, the targets were more likely precious metals or jewels buried with their owners rather than "antiquities," unless, by good fortune, the latter were fashioned from the former.

Even in early modern times European manifestations of what would grow into the contemporary antiquities trade had more a practical than an aesthetic bent. Once alchemy crossed the Pyrenees from Arab Spain into Western Europe, the frantic search for an elixir to extend life led to a demand for Egyptian mummies from which to wring, sometimes literally, the secrets of how to resist natural forces of corruption and decay: the bodies were boiled down into a thick black fluid reputed to do the job. Tomb raiders responded to what economists now call "market incentives" by fleshing out, so to speak, their inventories with recent corpses suitably aged in the desert sun. Their spirits lived on in current times at a recent auction in Christchurch, New Zealand, when the winners forked over $2,000 for a pair of glass vials with stoppers dipped in Holy Water containing the ghosts of two dead people. Useful for exorcisms, the owner declared, referring to evil spirits inside living persons rather than to toxic portfolios of dead assets inside today's post-crisis zombie banks.[7]

Even before the mummy business peaked, European religious institutions competing for the pilgrim trade collected relics supposedly from the dawn of Christianity. The leading example, in more ways than one, was the Turin Shroud, proven – except to true believers fresh from watching statutes of Mary shedding bloody tears – to be a fake only in 1998.[8] A similar fate may eventually be shared by a hefty chunk of displays in today's great museums once they work up the courage to run proper age tests.[9] In the meantime those relics will continue to be exploited shamelessly by the institutions that hold them, much as the House of Savoy did with the Turin Shroud for centuries and the City of Turin does to this day. In spring 2010, it attracted millions of visitors to its cathedral to gawk at the "burial cloth of Jesus" ten years after its last display, even though tradition holds that the shroud is only supposed to so manifest itself every twenty-five years. That abbreviated holy hiatus was the result less of a miracle than of two more worldly forces: lobbying from an industrial town hard hit in the downturn that hoped to rake in €121 per religious daytripper (€225 if they stayed overnight); and pressure from the city's archbishop who wanted to mark his retirement with a paroxysm of pure faith.[10]

Although private as distinct from institutional collecting fell out of favour in post-Roman Europe, it was revived in Renaissance Italy with an infatuation for classical artifacts. The trend gathered strength along with the general art market as rich merchants began to compete for bragging rights with old aristocratic families. Institutionalized collecting, though, still had its fan clubs. When great museums began to emerge in Europe in the late seventeenth century, they were closed to the Great Unwashed. The first truly public one was probably the Louvre, opened during the French Revolution to display treasures seized from the aristocracy. With Napoleon's accession its role shifted from educating the masses about the inequities of the *ancien régime* to propagandizing the virtues of the *nouvel ordre*. Then other governments began competitively to support public museums on the assumption that the size of archeological haul complemented the extent of geographical conquest in determining whose empire was highest and mightiest.

Even then collection came in waves, imperial reach igniting geographic fad. By the late eighteenth and early nineteenth centuries, ancient Egypt was the rage, especially after Napoleon's brief and highly qualified conquest; he shipped off loads of loot, but lost, first his navy, then his army. He also lost his last consignment of antiquities, grabbed by the British to start their own Egyptian artifact collections. (The crown jewel of the looted loot was the Rosetta Stone, whose return Egypt is now demanding.[11]) With the spread of colonialism later in the nineteenth century, the interlocking professions of collector and archeologist, smuggler and businessman, diplomat and spy fanned out to the far corners of the globe to dig furiously, or more accurately, to sit under an umbrella in a pith helmet sipping gin and tonic while the fellahin grunted and heaved, then to haul the booty triumphantly home.[12]

To be fair, acquisition of fine antiquities can sometimes require enormous time and effort on the part of acquisitors, including the logistical cost of moving great armies around the world. Take for example all of those Ethiopian relics, including gorgeous old Christian manuscripts, now so carefully protected in major British collections.

In 1868 a British military expedition landed in Ethiopia to free Europeans held captive by the country's lunatic emperor. After they slaughtered the emperor's army without the loss of a single British soldier, and the defeated emperor killed himself, a mob of British soldiers and officers gathered around his body to tear off souvenir pieces of his clothing, a prelude to the mass looting of Magdala, the imperial capital. The targets there were not just the emperor's palace but also the houses of wealthy individuals along with all the city's churches. The result was heaps of jewellery, fine cloth, crystal- and silverware, altars, and other sacred items. The US journalist Henry Stanley, present at the event, spoke of "an infinite variety of gold, silver and bronze crosses" and of "heaps of parchment royally illuminated." That was a reference to about four hundred Ethiopian sacred manuscripts, some embossed with precious metals and dating back to the fifteenth century, which afterwards came to grace British libraries and private collections.[13]

In this and other imperial campaigns, soldiers gave the locals – via their portable property – a shining example of the principles of unfettered free enterprise in action. The soldiers were required to turn in all stolen items (including, in this instance, locks of the dead emperor's hair) for auction, with proceeds distributed to the looters according to rank. At the auction the top bidders were usually senior officers buying (for resale) on behalf of their units, private collectors, and official purchasers from institutions that, like the representatives of the British Museum, tended to follow British armies to exotic places. In Ethiopia, the final step was to haul the stuff on fifteen elephants and two hundred mules back to waiting ships, although before they left the British set fires and triggered explosions that destroyed the city, claiming at least three thousand houses. It was not entirely clear if they were trying to hide the evidence or were just leaving behind their usual imperial calling card.[14]

The net result was that, apart from the British Museum itself, other great British institutions came to house the booty, including the Victoria and Albert Museum, Oxford and Cambridge Universities, the Royal Library in Windsor Castle and now the British Library, legally separated from the British Museum in 1973. In fact, that latter institution's share was the target of an early attempt at rather indirect repatriation when, in the 1980s, a senior Rasta (member of the ganja-smoking cult from Jamaica that accords the defunct emperor of Ethiopia divine status) got himself tossed in prison in Britain from trying to "liberate" books from London collections, including the British Library, to return them to Ethiopia. Since the world takes strong objection to attempted theft of a country's cultural properties, that Rasta gentlemen much later found himself arrested by US Immigration agents while en route to an event to the Smithsonian Institute to which he had been officially invited. To anyone suggesting that the Rasta gentleman had simply been trying to liberate purloined property, the British Library could point out that it had proper authority to protect its Ethiopian treasures under the terms of the 1972 British Library Act, which banned institutions from "de-accessioning" any items unless they received an explicit order from the British government itself – which has been too busy in other matters like invading and destroying Iraq to take up the Ethiopian issue. Yet, curiously, any similar concerns about the integrity of its collections of antiquities did not prevent Italy from returning to Ethiopia items stolen by its forces during their invasion of Ethiopia nearly a century after the British one.[15]

Although the phrase "antiquities" ("historical artifacts" is a better term) still conjures up images of Greco-Roman glory, as it was meant to do, in today's commercial jargon it is used for, apart from fifteenth-century Ethiopian manuscripts, everything from a piece of Sumerian alabaster allegedly from the fourth century BCE to a Malian terracotta supposedly from a millennium or more later, both possibly fakes.[16] The supply to feed institutional and private collections is concentrated heavily in countries that were, at least until recently and sometimes even now, financially poor but historically rich: China, India, Turkey, Iraq, Egypt, Greece, Southern Italy, and parts of Latin America. West Africa got itself included after dealers found that they could profitably add "primitive" to their "ancient" and "oriental" stock-in-trade. The only real requirements to qualify for the trade's attention seem to be that an object be three dimensional, apparently older than the collector, damaged sufficiently to give it credibility but not enough to keep it from attracting collector attention, and potentially saleable for large sums of money.

However, modern demand comes mainly from cash-rich, history-poor (provided aboriginals don't count) industrialized countries, the US well in the lead. (Japan's anomalous position as a major world buyer is a tribute to the recent McSushification of its billionaire class.) Within key market-countries, the driving force making the high-end market work is a small set of dealers who, while eager to cut each other's commercial throats, maintain both a collective wall of protective silence worthy of any gunrunner or drug smuggler when faced with potentially embarrassing probes from outside and a capacity for self-justification that would make a tobacco-company executive blush.[17] Much like high-end art dealers with whom they often intersect, upscale vendors of historical artifacts enjoy an incestuous connection with collector-donors, museum curators, auction-house staff, art historians, and professional appraisers, and a mutually suspicious relationship with tax collectors, insurance adjusters, fraud-squad cops, and customs agents.[18] Perhaps the major difference is that those who traffic in historical artifacts today, unlike in times past, add to their burn list "dirt archeologists" who denounce looting of historical sites to feed the vagaries of the "fine art" market – although, no doubt, some of their colleagues, as true academics, prefer to duck behind the nearest midden or press their noses against the closest petroglyph whenever any controversy erupts that might weaken their sinecures or threaten their grants.[19]

ARTIFACT OR ARTIFAKE?

Not surprisingly, private-sector crimes (as distinct from officially prescribed ones) involving historical artifacts parallel those in paintings.[20] Apart from insurance frauds and inflated tax claims, they fall into three broad categories. The most sensational is theft for ransom or resale. Sometimes a buyer is fully aware; sometimes a buyer is unaware; sometimes, if an object is especially desirable, a suspicious buyer is afflicted by moral myopia. While thefts from private homes are, as with paintings, no doubt more common than from institutions, the Corinth Archeological Museum set a record in 1990 (only surpassed, dramatically, in Baghdad in 2003) when four men smashed through the roof of the atrium, trussed up the sole guard, and made off with 271 objects, mainly vases and statuary, along with the cash. The first sign of the stolen objects came in 1997 when Christie's sold six to New York dealers. Prior to reselling, one dealer contacted an Oxford University professor for authentication, was informed of the theft, then phoned the FBI. Apparently that dealer had used the same care in checking the provenance of his acquisitions as he had in proofreading an art magazine of which he was editor-in-chief: shortly after the theft, it had carried photos of some of the stolen objects. In 1999, virtually the entire horde was discovered packed in crates under a load of fish in a Miami warehouse. When the search also turned up a separate shipment of "$30 million worth" of cocaine, this became proof that "Colombian cartels" were masterminding the illegal art and antiquities trade – although a conniving cabal of crab fishermen might have been a more logical, if less newsworthy, suspect. The heist was actually the work of a Greek gang, possibly with high-level political connections.[21]

The second major form of historical-artifact crime involves forgeries. These, like copied paintings, have legitimate roots. Sculptors, just as did master painters, trained apprentices; and in most countries aspiring artisans learned by imitation – what happened later to their work was none of their business. Even when the motive for reproduction was (is) commercial fraud, political or theological prestige could also be a factor.

In 801 CE, Charlemagne of France reinstated the Church canon (in abeyance for centuries) that required a holy relic in each church altar. Churches and monastic orders, too, used relics both to one-up the competition – the more impressive their relics, the greater their ability to shake down the local faithful as well as to collect a larger share of revenues from the pilgrim trade. A priest accompanied armies into the battle; and the more prestigious the relic he brandished at the enemy, the greater the presumption that the Almighty would bless the enterprise. All that zeal unleashed a plague of clerical scavengers, sometimes working on orders from Crown, nobility, or top clergy, sometimes freelancing. The more enterprising headed to Rome to raid the Catacombs. Others made off with choice material from neighbouring monasteries, sometimes by infiltration and embezzlement, sometimes by direct theft. Naturally some peddlers of piety offered the same relics of the same saints to different institutions. Although the clergy themselves played a role similar to some of today's professional authenticators, judging the legitimacy of various pieces of cloth or bone or even the odd dried-up foreskin on the basis of pure faith, credibility could be enhanced (also like today) by faking provenance. Monasteries who pinched stuff from rivals might plant in their libraries (and, if possible, in the libraries of their victims) "aged" parchment accounts of how the relic came legiti-mately into their hands.[22]

With the Crusades, trafficking in relics moved from the regional to the international in scope and shifted from the entrepreneurial to the corporate in form. The Knights Templar, apart from pioneering methods for moving money to finance other Christian terrorist organizations run-ning amok in Syria and Palestine, handled much of the return flow of looted relics, including the Turin Shroud.[23] Alas, the man who actually brought it back was burned at the stake with the rest of the chivalric order's leadership. Among the charges against them was worship of false relics. Their ashes were scattered on a river to prevent them, in turn, from being adored as holy remains.

Nor is this just a matter of historical interest. The Vatican today, despite Napoleon's successful shakedown, still holds one of the world's greatest art and antiquity collections, deeded over centuries by wealthy patrons in a last-ditch effort to buy their way past heavenly gatekeepers. It also has a place in the Apostolic Palace full of remnants of early saints and martyrs. This is more than just sanctimonious necrophilia. Much of the Holy See's income comes from the maintenance of cults. The most important is probably the cult of St Peter. In Rome his alleged remains act as a magnet for religious tourists and the revenues they bring in, while helping the Vatican vaunt its theological superiority over rivals, especially the Eastern Orthodox Church. Similar but less renowned cults at other holy sites also generate cash that can be siphoned off to Rome to cover its budget deficits, a racket that became all the more impor-tant after the Vatican was forced by Italy in 1984 to renounce its highly profitable capital-flight and tax-evasion business – although the recent launching of an investigation into Vatican Bank money-laundering by Italy's Financial Guard may point to somewhat of a delay in implemen-tation of the agreement.[24] Even now bits and pieces of various saints are put on display across Christendom despite the fact that if they were ever reassembled, they would come out like a cross between Frankenstein's monster and a science-fiction writer's concept of life after a nuclear holocaust. Across Italy alone four ears of St Procopius, nine breasts of St Eulalia, three heads of St John the Baptist, and twenty-eight thumbs and fingers of St Dominic, not to mention hundreds of thorns from the crown worn by Christ, have been put on display. Yet even the Vatican recognizes limits: the bones of one saint were destroyed when they were determined to belong to a large dog.[25]

The Vatican, of course, has no intention of turning any of St Dominic's spare digits over to Christie's for auction. But the same kind of ambiguity of origin hangs over plenty of items in the holdings of major museums; and not a few likely end up deaccessioned with their former status as museum exhibits sufficing for authentication. Some even seem of impeccable origin. At the start of the current archeological age, expeditions paid local workers a bonus for prime specimens they unearthed. That inspired the entrepreneurial to make deals with local artisans, miffed that their creations were ignored in favour of dirty, broken old stuff. Craftsmen learned to pick the right materials and suitably age them. For example, since genuine gold artifacts from pharaonic Egypt often had a slight reddish tint from trace minerals, artisans simply embedded the right impurities into their own creations. They knew, too, that sand from the Mediterranean shore had minute shell fragments; from Aswan; granite particles; from the Nile, additional silica; and from the deep desert, more lime.[26] The workers planted the fakes and split their bonuses with the artisans, leaving European expeditions to proclaim a triumph and scholars to rush into print with laudatory accounts. With each subsequent generation of archeologists "publishing" the artifacts, art historians extolling their aesthetic qualities, fine-art magazines enhancing their snob appeal, and dealers extolling their investment value, their authenticity became so widely accepted that any suggestion to the contrary was dismissed as ignorance or professional jealousy, or treated with the haughty silence it was presumed to merit – until the final embarrassment. That occurred, for example, in 2008 when the curator of the Brooklyn Museum of Art admitted that about a third of its Coptic sculptures and reliefs were fakes.[27] Fortunately for Benito Mussolini, he was long dead before his cherished symbol of the New Rome, the Lupa Carolina (a bronze statue of a she-wolf suckling two human infants) was proven that same year to date not from the fifth century BCE but from about a millennium and a half later.[28]

Struggling to avoid that ignominious fate, the museum in today's Arles, France, site of a major Roman city, insists stubbornly in the face of skeptics on its conviction that the bust hauled up from the slime of the Rhône River in 2007 really is the first portrait of Julius Caesar.[29] But then, it has plenty of precedents on which to draw – for example, the Louvre holds near and dear its ability to play host to the world's most famed piece of classical Greek statuary, even if the Venus de Milo was actually done by an Antiochan sculptor long after the Greek classical age had ended.[30]

As in the ancient world, so in the modern. Once easily available sites in Mali, for example, were exhausted of old terracottas, local artisans turned out replicas, aged in everything from animal dung to industrial acid, for local dealers to market through international channels. They now grace all manner of private and museum collections.

Although collectors and curators may insist that they "know" if an object is real by how it "speaks to them," wiser souls let a thermoluminescence test do the talking. By measuring energy output from radioactive decay, it can approximate the age of the object. But since the test has a margin of error of at least 20 percent, it is useful only for detecting large age discrepancies; and it requires extraction of a piece of the object. Smart forgers have long known to insert real material in some inconspicuous area whence the sample is likely to be removed. Even taking several samples is not foolproof. In Mali there are so many fragments of ancient terracottas lying around, it is possible to construct a new one almost entirely from genuine old material, or even to grind the fragments into powder, then cast it in a mould.[31] Besides, to reduce chances of a TL test, a useful precaution is to fake as well a certificate of authenticity. The more prestigious the name of the issuer on the document, the higher the credibility and price the illicit material will command.[32]

Nor is "expert" appraisal always a safe guide. The gentleman in Bolton who, with the help of his brother and aging parents, unloaded on the British market 120 modern master paintings of his own creation actually specialized more in antiquities. His first coup consisted of dumping on Manchester University a silver container purportedly bearing an Old English inscription. Although it was deemed not original, the wood inside was possibly genuine; so the university paid £100 for a fake that later became the subject of a student's thesis. Others included an "Egyptian statue" supposedly 3,300 years old that was authenticated by experts at the British Museum and sold to the Bolton Museum for £440,000. His pièce-sans-résistance, not in price but in audacity, was likely Le Faune, a Paul Gauguin sculpture of a half-man, half-goat endorsed by the Wildenstein Institute of Paris, sold via Sotheby's to a dealer for £20,000 in 1994, then resold for £61,000 to the Art Institute of Chicago, which declared the work one of its most important acquisitions in decades. By the time the Gaugin sculpture was revealed a fake in 2007, there were already questions about spelling mistakes on some "Assyrian reliefs" that led to a police investigation and the breaking of the ring.

The vagaries of professional opinion were also something that luxury-brand billionaire (Gucci, Château Latour, etc.) François Pinault found out about to his regret while trying to safeguard his reputation as France's number one art collector. At one point Pinault was expecting for dinner no less a personage than then-president Jacques Chirac, whose passion for "primitive art" extended to hatching a deal with a president of Nigeria to overrule the Nigerian export-control body so that French museums could "legally" acquire banned terracottas and who had personally bought others from Belgian dealers, safe in the realization that Belgium had refused to ratify the UNESCO convention on the return of misappropriated cultural property. So M. Pinault looked for something appropriate to put in the middle of the dining-room table besides fine food and excellent wine. Apparently Christie's, which he happened to own, didn't have what he needed; so he sent his wife to Hôtel Drouot, France's most prestigious auction house, to bid on a statue of a Twelth Dynasty pharaoh. Curiously it went for only €770,000, mainly because of a general alert about the statue's dubious parentage. Back in 1981, when it had been acquired by Berlin's Egyptian Museum, a leading scholar had disputed its authenticity; and when he heard it was being reauctioned, he alerted the antiquities world that its latest manifestation was missing the fake hieroglyphics that had been one of the original tip-offs. None of that moderated the Drouot sales pitch. Eventually twenty-five international experts concurred that it was a fake, but they were opposed by two from the Louvre, who contended that, although the statue did not depict the pharaoh that the sales blurb claimed, it was a genuine commemorative statue of a slightly more recent Egyptian king.

Pinault took that judgment as evidence of a faulty sales description. But the lower courts rejected his efforts to have the sale rescinded. Interestingly enough, although the Louvre experts were the key to the court judgement, that institution, which, thanks to the nimble fingers of Napoleon's collectors, had begun the European rage for Egyptian collections, politely declined his offer to donate the thing. When Pinault finally coughed up the money and took possession 3.5 years after the auction and had the statue formally tested, the lab detected marks from steel, chrome and diamond tools, and declared it a modern fake. But the courts now ruled that he had waited so long that the new evidence was inadmissible. Pinault, it seems, was stuck by court order with something widely denounced as a fake, probably to the delight of Bernard Arnault, the art-collecting billionaire boss of the Louis Vuitton Moët-Hennessy luxury goods dynasty, Pinault's biggest rival.[33]

Several years later, M. Pinault may have had the last laugh as agents from the French Office central de lutte contre le trafic des biens culturels converged on Hôtel Drouot. The seventy auctioneer-owners of this monument to France's early days as world centre for the fine art and collectibles trade still account for half of the country's auction traffic; and their collective political power has long been sufficient to block English rivals, like M. Pinault's Christie's, from participating directly in the French market. However the art cops were not there to round up Drouot auctioneers, notorious for introducing fake bids to push up prices, their commissions along with them. Nor were they even there to collar its assortment of dealer-clients, equally renowned for creating cabals to hold bids down, then redistribute the goods among themselves. Rather their target was some members of its 110-man labour force, the famed *cols rouges*. These workers, taking their name from the red collars on their black vests, were all drawn from certain impoverished villages in the Savoy region. In the mid-nineteenth century, villagers there were given privileged access to jobs inside France to blunt nationalist agitation after France annexed the area from Italy. (Mussolini's invasion of France during the opening years of World War II was really just an attempt to take the Savoy back again.) The Savoyards, as they were also called, formed a tightly closed workers' cooperative, perhaps the last of its kind in France, whose members could pass on their jobs to family or fellow villagers. Paid not a wage but a share of the house profits, their main job was pickup and delivery of up to 800,000 items for 2,000 annual sales, storing the items until they were due on the block, then presenting them during auctions, although they sometimes served as proxies for long-standing customers, especially antique dealers, in the bidding sessions. All these tasks provided some among the *cols rouges* with unique entrepreneurial opportunities and the distinction of being later designated an organized crime cabal. When they were sent to collect from wealthy estates items for auction, parts of the load had a habit of falling off the trucks, while other pieces ended up officially forgotten in containers that the Savoyards themselves kept in a suburban warehouse. If a theft was spotted by heirs to an estate, the item magically reappeared. If not, commonplace items were diverted directly to antique dealers; more expensive ones might end up sold via complicit auctioneers in the house with the funds diverted. Another of their reputed tricks was to remove parts of a choice antique in transit, arrange for a stand-in to buy the apparently damaged item cheaply, then sell the restored whole to a happy dealer a few months later.[34] Although the arrests sent shockwaves through the French art and antiquities scene, one of Drouot's regular customers, an antique dealer from Champagne, figured that it was just business as usual. "It's a racket," he observed. "But that's the job."[35]

Theft may be common in the fine arts trade, fakery is likely more so – although just how frequent either of them are is impossible to say. After all, if fakes are really so all-pervasive as some suspect, they may end up protecting each other. For experts may well end up declaring items authentic on the basis of the characteristics of all the fakes they inadvertently studied during their training on the assumption that they were genuine.[36]

However, what makes the historical artifacts subdivision of the fine-art market unique is the plundering of ancient sites for genuine (but, by definition, previously unknown) items.[37] This, too, is hardly new. For decades archeological digs facing legal restrictions might hand over a few pieces to national museums, then make off with prime stuff as well as bushels of small items like scarabs, beads, and bits of pottery, hoovered up to peddle to the hoi polloi once museums began to establish gift shops.[38] For every Gertrude Bell, the British archeologist and author committed to keeping inside early twentieth-century Iraq the astounding record of its historical predecessors, or every Auguste Mariette, the French archeologist who repented his early role as an official looter to fight energetically against the drain from Egypt, there were more like Sir Wallis Budge, the great benefactor of the British Museum, who looted Egypt from top to bottom, the British army lending him the services of the engineering corps. His standing was so good among local black-market dealers that he picked up items on credit, sent them to England, and reimbursed suppliers after he received payment. When arrested, he bribed his way out of custody, stole back from police confiscated material, and smuggled it home. However, it would be unfair to accuse Sir Wallis of lack of ethical standards. He was once deputed to Iraq to stop the leakage of cuneiform tablets from British Museum-controlled sites onto the London private market. Looting was only acceptable to Sir Wallis if intended for public display.[39]

Nor was that just a British phenomenon. In the 1870s, the US Consul in Cyprus dug up 35,000 objects to sneak home in defiance of Turkish law. Although most were lost at sea, the rest were acquired by the Metropolitan Museum of Art, along with the light-fingered diplomat who became its first director.[40] Early the next century, after Canada's most powerful banker joined with the University of Toronto to create the Royal Ontario Museum, in addition to sending wealthy boosters to Egypt to have their pictures taken on the backs of camels, the museum world's new entrant arranged for Bishop William Charles White in China to combine religious with archeological conversion. When donors back home began to balk at his demands, he reassured the museum of the scholarly importance of his work: "One bronze jar which cost the Museum $1200 if returned to me here could probably sell for $10,000." When the Chinese, angry over foreign depredations, prohibited the drain, the incensed bishop declared the law "selfish" and "anti-foreign." After the bishop returned to Canada, the museum, to flesh out its world-famous collection of ancient Chinese artifacts, had to resort to purchasing on the secondary market. No doubt it was greatly relieved when Canada followed the US lead in giving tax deductions to donors. Subsequently acquisition became more a matter of plundering the public purse at home than looting archeological sites abroad. Just in time, too. The Communist victory in China brought not just a more severe attitude toward archeological theft, for a while anyway, but also an ability to enforce it. Henceforth the job was best left to professional graverobbers and career smugglers.[41]

Today, most important source countries have their own archeological services. Even with major museums that still sponsor their own digs, the real problem lies not in their policy on excavations but their practice on acquisitions. Now, dodgy market action more likely starts with private collectors and dealers who may be openly complicit in acquiring plundered material – the risk is generally limited to loss of the object after a legal wrangle. Of course, some may plead that it was a misunderstanding, as did a US collector-dealer who "fell in love" with mosaics from a sixth-century church in Cyprus. After the 1974 Turkish invasion, these ended up in the hands of a Turkish dealer operating out of Munich. The Turkish dealer alerted a Dutch one with impressive credentials – he was once convicted of forging Marc Chagall's signature on a painting and claimed descent from both Rembrandt and Reubens. The Dutch dealer contacted a US agent who enticed the collector-dealer. She hired a lawyer to check things out. He came back with the story that the Turkish dealer who had the item was official archeologist to the emerging Turkish republic of North Cyprus and that the mosaics came from a church ruined in the fighting. Apart from the facts that only Turkey recognized the "state" erected after its invasion and that the famed old church was still standing, intact but for the mosaics, an official archeologist would hardly be openly peddling the very wares he was responsible for protecting. But the collector accepted the story. Equipped with an appraisal setting their value in the $3–6 million range, she obtained a loan for $1,200,000 from the bank that normally backed her purchases, $1,080,000 for the material and the rest for restoration, insurance, and similar necessities. Further attesting to her faith in the legitimacy of the deal, she drew out the money in $100 bills, stuffed them into two valises, and flew to Geneva to meet the others in a transit lounge. The Turkish dealer got $350,000; the man-who-would-be-Chagall, $280,000; the US art dealer, around $275,000; a British lawyer acting for that dealer, $70,000; and the collector's US lawyer, another $80,000. Then she went to the Getty Museum, offering to sell for $20 million the mosaics she loved so much. However, the curator of the classical collection knew that the Cyprus government was looking for these mosaics. When that government sued for their return, the new owner pleaded good-faith purchase. The judge ruled against her on the grounds that she had shown no evidence of due diligence in researching the provenance, and she was ordered to return them without compensation. The Turkish dealer was later arrested in a sting arranged by his former Dutch partner.[42]

If a collector-dealer succeeds with an acquisition, they could donate it to a museum, putting another layer of insulation between any original theft or smuggling operation and the museum's conscience.[43] As with paintings, the advantage of donation is that the appraisal (at least in North America) can be inflated so that the tax deduction greatly exceeds the money laid out to buy the item. Alternatively, rather than buying directly, museum curators may steer a collector onto a particular item, attesting to value and authenticity in the hope that it will then be donated, perhaps further assuring that result by appointing the collector as a museum trustee.

On the other hand, the advantage to the collector of a direct sale to a museum is cash in hand without the threat of a disagreeable tax review. In fact, one thing can lead to the other. Once a museum has used public money to bid up the price of a piece, it not only may raise prices of similar works but can set off a bidding war with other publicly funded institutions for that particular one, leading to a further drain from taxpayers into the pockets of rich collectors and dealers.[44] With the "fair-market price" duly puffed, the dealer or collector might be able to donate another example of the same genre of artifact for a higher deduction, then use the tax savings to start the process again with something else, perhaps looted from an archeological site or foreign museum. To complete the deal, the seller might draw on the services of an academic art historian or archeologist for the "authentication" that substitutes for a proper accounting of origin and ownership. People who pull off such coups are referred to respectfully as "patrons of the arts."

Of course, collector-donors and curators have their own justifications. They might pose rhetorical questions. Why does the Metropolitan Museum of Art in New York not have as good a claim to Hittite relics as the government of Turkey, representing an ethnic group that invaded Asia Minor long after Hittite civilization collapsed? How much connection does today's Greece really have to ancient Athens or Sparta, let along to Alexandria? The idea that source countries have no exclusive claim to the material under their ground is articulated with particular vehemence by dealers in the US, one of the few places in the world where landowners (except in a few US states) have absolute property rights to anything they dig up – some even advertise the probable presence of Amerindian relics to raise the resale value of their land. However, one prominent US dealer, André Emmerich, may have found a way out of that contradiction when he asserted that, since the US contains a mix of peoples from all over the world, Americans "surely have a moral claim to reasonable access to the buried treasures of our common ancestors."[45] That kind of rationalization may be joined with another: that limits on the free flow of cultural property impede education about and appreciation of other cultures. After all, Wall Street-High Street billionaires are renowned for welcoming busloads of ghetto kids for tours of their drawing rooms.

On the other hand, some countries use antiquities to establish just the opposite, their ethnopolitical uniqueness, including one place whose national museum lauded André Emmerich on his death because "he was always there for us!"[46] (Apparently some places have a greater moral claim to Emmerich's "reasonable access" than others.) In 1948, the victorious Israeli army emptied hundreds of Palestinian towns and villages of their inhabitants, confining hundreds of thousands to an eternity of exile in refugee camps; looted homes and businesses; gave the demographic deserts thereby created ancient Jewish names; then repopulated them, initially with European refugees.[47] After this, came another invasion seeking archeological "evidence" to rationalize the deeds as well as to attract more immigrants, usually American, and their money. As an Israeli Museum press official later explained about the effects of viewing such ancient relics: "It is very exciting, very emotional, very Jewish feelings."[48]

While the museum official's sentiments were likely intended to be general, he had particularly in mind an ivory pomegranate believed to have come from Solomon's temple that the Israel Museum obtained in 1988 from the "free market" using the advanced archeological technique of paying $550,000 into a Swiss bank account. The item was hailed as the only surviving evidence of the First Temple, the holiest of Jewish religious sites, whose exact geographic position seems to vary with whichever Palestinian homes or institutional structures happen to be inconveniently located. Alas, in 2005 the item was exposed as a fake. It may have been the handiwork of a major ring including a prominent collector, a university expert in inscriptions, and a dealer who was a former agent of the Shin Beit, the Israeli internal intelligence service. That group may have been responsible for thousands of fakes now clogging institutions or personal collections. Asked why the museum would accept items off the "free market" with no verification, the director replied: "Because the objects are very special, and so they can be placed in a museum setting and benefit the public. You wouldn't want to miss an opportunity like that."[49]

Not missing opportunities also appears to have been the operational philosophy of the eye-patched Israeli warlord, the late Moyse Dayan, who matched personal enthusiasm for ethnically cleansing Palestine with a "hunger" (as he himself put it) for plundering conquered areas of their archeological treasures. He began his career with friends who included professional antiquity thieves in the parts of Palestine seized in 1948, then expanded to the post-1967 conquest areas, including the Sinai Peninsula, from which he shipped home four loads of antiquities. Only one batch was returned to Egypt some thirty years later. The best pieces (described by Egyptian archeologists as "priceless") remain in Israel, perhaps to be used later to bolster a claim that the Sinai, too, is part of historical Israel. Much of Dayan's collection was sold by his widow to the Israel Museum for a mere $1 million, perhaps because he had been denounced as a criminal – not for stealing from the Palestinians, but because he broke an Israeli law that reserves relics of previous societies for the Israeli state. Another batch that had been donated by Dayan to a US leader of the United Jewish Appeal went on auction in the US in 2007 at a "bargain" price.[50]

Museums, to justify their holdings, may also rely on a slightly different type of claim; for instance, the insistence by the British government that the decision of its ambassador to the Ottoman Empire, Lord Elgin, in 1806 to make off with the choicest marble sculptures from the Parthenon kept them from being lost to humanity. The British could cite the seedy history of the site, converted first to Christian churches, then to mosques, then used by the Ottomans as a fortress. Although "saving the marbles" was hardly the reason Elgin lifted them in the first place (in the face of an order to the contrary by the supposedly indifferent Ottoman authorities), given modern Greece's record of putting short-term tourist revenues ahead of long-term protection of the Parthenon, the argument seems to contain a touch of truth. On the other hand, Greece not only paid to have copies made scarcely twenty-five years after the marbles were taken but more recently set up an Acropolis Museum that sits partly empty as a rebuke to Britain for its refusal to release the loot.[51] Furthermore, the fact that the British Museum turned the marbles over to elite art dealer Joseph Duveen to clean – only to have him destroy their patina with acids and metal tools – suggests that the notion of Britain as a better custodian of the world's archeological heritage may need some rethinking.

It is certainly true that local rulers may be indifferent to, or destructive of, archeological treasures. The Mamelukes, who long ruled Egypt, had no respect for ancient relics. And the Albanian royal house that the British and French contrived to put in their place was happy to smash up old temples into building stone. However, both could be dismissed as alien oppressors. That argument does not work with the Egyptians themselves, who tend to think of their real history as starting with the Islamic era, while senior clergy regard many ancient statutes as idolatrous. However, the spirit of envisioning a country's cultural past through rather all-encompassing lenses can affect even places that have been repeatedly victimized. When, in autumn 2010, a Van Gogh painting was stolen from Cairo's Mahmoud Khalil Museum, the Interior minister announced that it necessitated a "review of all security measures in places that hold the treasures of Egyptian civilization."[52]

Nor is the problem restricted to Islamic countries. In Cyprus for centuries dust from the courtyard of the church that hosts the tomb of St Agapitikos was supposed to stimulate romantic interest if slipped by a lovelorn thief into the drink of the target of his unrequited affections. But, when the belief spread that a hunk of rock from the tomb worked much better, the entire structure seemed to be in danger of disappearing.[53]

It is also indisputable that a major motive for Egypt (or Cyprus or so many others) to get back "its" archeological heritage is not just a desire to protect evidence of "their" past but the potential tourist money. However, Europeans who plundered the East were similarly more interested in current money than ancient history. In fact they still are, even with leading relics of their own past. In 2008 Italy's minister of the Environment, backed by its minister of Culture, gave the green light to a huge gas-storage and -flaring facility a few minutes walk from a site in Sicily that hosts some of the finest surviving Doric temples in the Mediterranean.[54] And Turkey, long one of the major victims of international antiquities traffickers, has launched a project to dam the Tigris that will flood out a town that, apart from thousand year old churches and mosques along with a castle and ancient bazaar, is also reputed to host the tomb of Iman Abdullah, a close relative of the Prophet Mohammed.[55]

To be sure, some museums in recent years have greatly improved their scrutiny of acquisitions. Some have formal (but not legally binding) codes of ethics, even if they are full of weasel words.[56] The British Museum recently upgraded its avowed standards sufficiently that if it had applied them during its long history, it would have little to display, except the latest paint job on its walls. Still, that didn't prevent Britain's prime minister from answering another request for the return of the Koh-i-Noor diamond to India by claiming that, if Britain acceded to that and similar demands, "suddenly we would have the British Museum empty."[57] In any event, the change in policy associated with acquisitions usually comes only after a particularly malodorous scandal and does not seem to apply to smaller, privately owned institutions, or even a few of the big ones who continue to display the moral standards of pawnshops with less public oversight.[58] If a major museum wants a piece badly enough, it will perform semantic handstands and moral somersaults to justify the acquisition. And the "free market" will gladly oblige.

THE REAL UNDERGROUND ECONOMY

The script is much the same from one source area to another. At the bottom, in both senses, are the diggers. In the early stages they may be drawn from local peasants, perhaps facing loss of land to cattle ranchers or agribusinesses, repeated crop failures, or absence of marketing infrastructure. Their finds at first may be opportunistic, sold for a pittance to local dealers. Over time those dealers may take the initiative to organize nighttime forays into known or (officially) undiscovered archeological sites, still paying diggers minimally. With experience, diggers might become more specialized, perhaps working in families who have exploited particular areas for generations. Although some finds may still be windfalls, diggers may work with client wish lists or even photographs. While they continue to collect only a small percentage of final market value, what they get depends on their knowledge of that market. The common claim that they receive on average a mere 1 percent of retail price is probably a fantasy of critics eager (for good reason) to highlight the pivotal role of intermediaries and anxious (for less convincing reason) to present people who may have been professional tomb-raiders (with power tools and dynamite) for generations as simply exploited or misunderstood.

Another excuse for tomb-raiding is that those who do the dirty deed are motivated not just by money but by lack of pride in their country's past. Yet anyone truly cognizant of the past of most countries will find little enough about which to be proud. In fact the more a country generates chest-swelling pride among its citizens, the more things it has in its history of which it really ought to be embarrassed, and the more things it will probably have in its future of which to feel ashamed. Besides, it usually makes more sense for a poor peasant to take genuine pride in his ability to put a chicken in the family pot today than to contemplate the probably fabricated glories of some bloodthirsty warrior-king or blood-sucking high priest in centuries past.

A final category of digger is the pro with fancy equipment hired on a long-term basis, perhaps with bonuses for particularly valuable finds, who may have originally learned the trade working for legitimate archeological expeditions. Some move from place to place on command, perhaps scaring off with a show of muscle security personnel who cannot be squared off with a show of cash. But most are probably local, thriving because of experience, knowledge of an area's conditions, and good relations with its population. Southern Italy, for example, has been plagued for hundreds of years by *tomberoli*, interfacing with networks of crooked dealers and protected by corrupt politicians. It is even renowned for fake archeological sites planted with things like freshly minted "Etruscan vases" to be unloaded on collectors whose subsequent laments are unlikely to be heard outside a confession box. The frequent coupling in the pop press of these professionals with "the Mafia" certainly makes for a good story; but it is really the art-crime world's version of the Turin Shroud. Like almost everything important done on modern stock markets, archeological plundering is very much an inside job.

After passing through intermediary layers from local to regional, material might be collected in large cities with international access, likely via legitimate-looking dealers who can disguise an item's origins and sweeten officials. These dealers resell to smugglers or undertake themselves to move out the item using a variety of deceptive or corruptive tools. The first stop abroad may be a jurisdiction where title can be easily laundered. Switzerland has long been a favourite in the West, Hong Kong in the East. Then the material seems to move on in two major ways. One is via major auction houses, particularly in London or New York, although Geneva or Hong Kong also have active auction markets. If an item has been privately ordered or is particularly hot, the dealer may sell directly to a final buyer, bypassing the minimal scrutiny of an auction-house sale but also foregoing a possible higher return. From dealer or auction house, the artifact makes its way into collections, private and public, mainly (though certainly not exclusively) in the US, Japan, and Western Europe. At point of retail sale, the price is further inflated, not just by notions of inherent "value" or prospects of capital gains on the demand side, but by the expense of clandestine movement, including costs of faked documents, multiple layers of intermediation, and bribed officials on the supply side.[59] It is inflated further when tax codes give wealthy donors handsome write-offs, making governments of some countries of final repose unindicted co-conspirators in the racket.

There appear to be two distinct although interrelated dimensions to waves of enthusiasm that periodically sweep the historical-artifacts market – a sudden passion for particular types of artifact, or a new zeal for old things from particular places. It can be both – as with the "antique" West African sculptures that now bring fortune but no fame to some of the area's contemporary artisans. These fads may result from internal factors in the market countries, like breaking news (stoked by dealers and auction houses) about a trend in sales. But influences of that sort are unlikely by themselves to lead to a wave of archeological crime unless accompanied by precipitating events in the source country: tomb-raiders striking gold in one sense or another; sudden access to an area long suspected of being replete with relics after a government removes barriers; or a formerly well protected treasure trove suddenly thrown open by war and conquest.

CULTURAL CONQUISTADORES

The first of these onsite factors, a literal and figurative gold rush, played out dramatically in Peru in the 1980s when its badly protected sites (previously assumed to be depleted by centuries of plunder) became for collectors a new El Dorado. In spirit the trade in pre-Columbian artifacts has changed little since the Spanish grabbed mounds of beautifully wrought gold and silver ornaments then melted them into money. The Spanish were honest enough to plunder at gunpoint, torture Indians to reveal hiding places, then brag of their deeds while offering a share to the Pope in exchange for indulgences. Today's cultural conquistadores pillage vicariously, then pose as saviours of humanity's collective heritage while collecting public accolades and tax deductions if they contribute part of the loot to a grateful museum.

Collectors en masse rediscovered pre-Columbian artifacts in the 1960s, first filling shelves with cheaply acquired Mayan material even though both Mexico and Guatemala forbad its export.[60] The US was the main (though hardly the sole) destination. The overt traffic was curbed after the US belatedly signed the 1970 UNESCO Convention. This bound each signatory to protect its own cultural heritage, establish an export permit system, prohibit the import of material stolen from museums and public monuments, and take steps for recovery and return if the state of origin paid just compensation to an innocent buyer. Since the convention was only useful for material already in a public inventory, not fresh stuff from archeological sites, the US also passed a law barring entry of any pre-Columbian artifact without certification from the relevant government, then added bilateral agreements for repatriation with some governments in the hemisphere. Mexico, the main source of Mayan relics, was the first. But to this day Mayan sites are ransacked for gold, jade, pottery, and inscribed stones, sometimes opportunistically, sometimes by gangs working to order. After material is hauled out of the immediate area, it runs into the US, hidden in regular cargoes or dressed up to look like normal tourist schlock.

However, the real gold rush is further south. Both Peru and Colombia prohibit export of relics more than one hundred years old; and both have bilateral agreements with the US that require importers to show export licenses from the country of origin. However, since both allow private ownership of artifacts, their collectors can finance illegal digs, buy material for a pittance, register it, then sit on it while it appreciates, immune from legal sanction – only diggers face the music. Then they may find some pretext to ship it out for auction, perhaps replacing it in the private collection with a clever fake.[61] Furthermore, apart from having hosted long-running insurgencies, both countries are notorious centers for contraband in everything from endangered species to coffee to cocaine heading out, and US tobacco, booze, and electronic goods coming back in, a situation not exactly conducive to close control of archeological sites or the artifacts trade.[62]

The process of unearthing and selling off underground treasures may begin when farmers stumble across sites while planting, which yields mainly commonplace material to peddle around town squares and tourist centres, perhaps interspersed with not-very-clever fakes – although quality does improve with practice, as does the skill employed to disguise origins. To get genuine items, local buyers hire experienced teams to scour an area selected on the basis of both indigenous and scholarly knowledge. Those buyers pass finds to dealers from big cities. Things of minor value get sold off to local customers or tourists, while the priciest go to international distributors.

No doubt a lot of material leaves the country as personal luggage or hidden in commercial cargoes heading directly to point of sale. Some, though, might go out disguised as non-controlled items – perhaps with a coating of fresh plaster or mixed with a shipment of present-day artifacts simulating past designs. Sometimes real material could be openly presented with fake paperwork. Or bent officials might provide bona fide export licenses. It may be possible, too, to get permission to send an artifact abroad for scientific or educational purposes for a specified time – the paperwork vanishes, or the artifact is declared lost or destroyed, with the insurance company covering the cost of any bond the exporter had to post. An alternative is to physically smuggle the stuff to some neighbouring country, then to a point of sale. Since ancient cultures straddled current borders, logically the item could have originated in any Andean country. The best route is probably to sneak material to Europe, particularly to Switzerland, park it in an airport free-trade zone, establish a fake history by selling it back and forth between shell companies, then wash it through London before shipping it back across the Atlantic into a US collection. And there are countless subvariant scenarios.

In the mid 1980s, the market was electrified by news of a magnificent find full of gold artifacts in the impoverished Peruvian village of Sipán.

The source was a necropolis of the Moché, arguably the most artistically advanced of ancient Peruvian civilizations as well as the most skilled in metallurgy. The Moché era lasted from 250 to 750 AD, at peak covering hundreds of square miles with vast irrigation works, palaces, and pyramids. Unlike the Maya, the Moché had no written records. What is known had to be reconstructed from a few monuments. After the initial discovery, local peasants, facing a bad sugar harvest and high unemployment, scrambled to dig. That find sparked imitative rushes for archeological gold across the country plus, inevitably, fakes and material from other locations passed off as Sipán in origin.

When the loot first started to turn up on the Lima market, a California upscale ethnic-art dealer with a financially challenged British sidekick was there to buy colonial furniture. Then their path crossed that of another Californian dealer, a veteran smuggler with a network of couriers – airline staff were his top choices. Backed by a group of private investors from back home, the team started outbidding rivals for black-market Sipán ceramics and gold. The original plan was to fly material to Vancouver, then have the California dealer drive it south. Deterred when Canada Customs stopped a couple of shipments, they snuck some over the border to Bolivia. There it was coated in clay, stamped *Hecho en Bolivia*, and flown to London along with other Sipán material moved directly from Lima. Held in transit, it was not subject to inspection. Then the British partner arranged to bring it to the US, declaring it as part of the estate of his recently deceased father, an avid collector. On arrival the booty was sold to rich industrialists, corporate executives, and self-styled philanthropists. But the British gofer got cold feet, offering the authorities information in exchange for immunity. After that, sixty heavily armed, flak-jacketed customs agents burst into the office of the main dealer as well as the homes of investors and customers, seizing two thousand items – of which only a small number turned out to be Sipán gold. While the senior partner did six months, the others took a walk. When Peru tried to retrieve some of the gold from a prominent collector-dealer, a judge ruled that the collector had bought in good faith, that there was no evidence that the material came from Peru (rather than Colombia or Ecuador), that Peru could present no proof that the material had been the property of the government (since Peru also permits private local ownership), and that Peru's laws were too fuzzy and had changed too often to merit a ruling in its favour. The defendant was also able to recover costs.[63] Back in Sipán supposedly unsophisticated peasants lacking pride in their past fumed that local people ought to be able to harvest antiquities from their own ancestors on their own land, that archeologists were the real thieves, and that any stuff sent to Peruvian museums would just be stolen and replaced with fakes.[64]

JADED TASTES

If Peru was subject to a new gold rush, the initiating factor reopening China, with perhaps 350,000 historic sites and a couple thousand museums, to mass looting was huge infrastructural projects that since the mid-1990s exposed the resting places of thousands of years of artifacts. As with Peru, there were ample precedents.

For decades after its forcible first opening in the mid-nineteenth century, China was plundered by European armies and their local henchmen, the Japanese completing the job. A Communist victory in 1949 led to a clampdown. Subsequently no item more than two hundred years old could be exported; looting and smuggling could bring a death sentence. Initially the government left private hordes intact. However, the Cultural Revolution brought massive confiscations and a huge pileup of poorly catalogued artifacts in state hands. In the late 1970s the government, like that of the USSR about fifty years earlier, invited in selected foreign dealers and began official sales. That piqued market interest. Underground outflows, previously sporadic, allegedly became strong enough by the 1980s to depress prices in Hong Kong, the major outlet. By then the parallel market had bifurcated – really good stuff went via private dealers to well-heeled collectors, poorer quality along with fakes to tourist shops.

As China progressively opened to trade and tourism, it also liberalized antiquities law. By the 1990s, export was legal provided material was pre-appraised by heritage officials, purchased from a licensed dealer, declared at customs, and sent abroad with officially stamped copies of permits. With rising wealth, too, came sufficient internal demand that, even when private trading was still banned, the rich patronized black-market dealers. After legalization of private trading, China developed its own auction houses and private museums. Although restrictions on exports remained, they seemed to do little to hamper the outflow from private hordes, public museums, and archeological sites.

While peasants unearth graves, temples, and settlements, and fishermen blow apart ancient wrecks, in many places the late 1990s saw a quantum leap in illegal excavation activity around major projects. Once completed, the Three Gorges Dam, for example, will submerge 1,300 official heritage sites and displace 750,000 people. After bulldozers strip off upper layers, diggers make their move. In theory construction companies are supposed to report anything unearthed; in practice they may put their equipment at the disposal of the better organized tomb-raiders in exchange for a share.

Yet more material flows to market from official depositories and local museums left by the central government in the care of regional authori-ties – the poorer the region, the weaker the security. Small museums, too, may deliberately keep incomplete records to prevent their best items being requisitioned by big provincial or national institutions, a practice making theft harder to monitor.[65] Stolen material is sold to local antique dealers linked to professional smugglers who move it, still mainly to Hong Kong. Starting its career in Chinese artifacts after 1949, that former British colony is today home to hundreds of dealers in every form from family-run shops to big auction houses.[66] Getting the material over the border is no problem. Chinese border guards and customs officials long ago noted the enthusiasm with which their leaders had embraced capitalist ethics. With travel restrictions gone, masses of commercial vehicles and people coming and going to work cross every day; while Chinese ships ranging from fishing smacks to cargo carriers call regularly.

Sometimes Hong Kong dealers tell Chinese suppliers what they want. Sometimes suppliers fax to Hong Kong dealers what they have available. For greater security they can communicate via encrypted email, includ-ing digital photographs of choice items. Hong Kong dealers can send couriers to bring the stuff back. There are no restrictions on the subse-quent outflow from Hong Kong. Its facility with instant corporations and coded bank accounts, precisely what long made it the main entrepôt for China's legal trade, eases passage of contraband; while legitimate trade provides cover. The unique legal position of Hong Kong in China is slated to remain in place until fifty years after its 1997 reintegration with the mainland.[67] By then there may be little left to steal.

Of course, not all buyers leave happy. Hong Kong shops are crammed full of stuff that sales personnel introduce as Qing, Song, Yuan, or even Chicken Chow Mien, depending on how they size up the motive and means of the buyer. It is hardly a surprise if the culture that first cre-ated porcelain thousands of years ago did not also master techniques of artificial aging. Freshly minted material might have its shine dulled with animal urine or industrial chemicals, then be rubbed with dirt (perhaps from the supposed site of the artifact) and strategically cracked. And its craftsmen know how to simulate the effects of ancient tools on the surfaces of old carvings.[68]

Originally most of the antiquities traffic revolved around pottery. It probably still does. But the really prize targets are bronze, gold, and especially jade.[69] To the ruling classes of imperial China, jade was a harbinger of a long life and a symbol of heaven; Han rulers were buried on sheets of jade to ensure revival of the corpse and eternal life.[70] For millennia the practice of jade carving was limited by raw material supply. But in the eighteenth century, Emperor Qianlong seized present-day Xinkiang, doubling China's size and taking control of the only known (at the time) source of nephrite, a whitish silicate of iron, magnesium, and calcium that maintains its integrity when carved into delicate shapes so thin as to be translucent. Soon his camel trains were hauling it, even in the face of almost continuous rebellion, to Beijing to supply carvers. His successors made a concerted effort to also consolidate supplies of jadeite from Burma. Much rarer, jadeite had the desirable traits of nephrite plus a waxy lustre and unique green hue. It was and is far more valuable: in 2000 a small jadeite gemstone could sell for $2 million, the same thing in nephrite for $2,500.[71] (The fact that in the trade both are referred to as "jade" increases confusion and the scope for a con job.) On the other hand, to Europeans jade was, apart from a "cure" for kidney complaints, simply a curiosity – until the Opium Wars.

In its trade relations with China from the late eighteenth to the mid-nineteenth centuries, Britain faced a dilemma. Europe had a huge demand for tea, porcelain, and luxury fabrics, while China looked with disdain at consumer trash offered by the West (only getting its revenge by reversing the flow in the late twentieth century). The result was a massive drain of silver from West to East to cover the trade deficit – until the British found a magic solution. In Bengal, initially the richest of Britain's Indian conquests, the British East India Company converted large tracts of land to growing opium, processed it in official factories, packed it in sizes convenient for hiding, then sold it at auction (on credit) to smugglers to run into China, protected by British gunboats. There it was resold for silver that was used to pay for tea. Back home an excise-tax on tea in turn helped Britain to abolish import duties and proclaim to the world the superiority of "free trade."

However, China resisted the influx of opium that corrupted its civil service, fed the rise of regional warlords, and drained its monetary silver. The Opium Wars, intended to persuade the Chinese of their ideological error, culminated in one of the most outrageous acts of cultural barbarism in history when an Anglo-French military expedition looted and burned the Old Summer Palace (actually a complex of gardens and palaces) in Beijing. Its jade carvings converged on London, Paris, and later New York, to turn up as prestige pieces in almost every major Chinese art collection founded in the mid to late nineteenth century.

Soon the British were also busy in Burma, looting palaces, monasteries, and public buildings of jade, gems, ivory carvings, and the like, then

razing many of the structures. In 1886 they formally annexed Burma
to British India. Two years later they sent an expedition into the jade-
producing area. Although jadeite continued to flow into imperial collections in China, court officials siphoned it off to feed black-market
dealers who in turn shipped jadeite and nephrite to Europe and the US.
Much of what remained was stolen at the end of the nineteenth century
when the major powers again marched into China in a campaign disguised, of course, as a humanitarian intervention to protect foreign (but
not Chinese) lives.[72]

After the Revolution, the Communists frowned on jade carving.
The business decamped to Hong Kong, drawing its raw material out
of Burma, partly through auctions run by the military government,
more through a network of smugglers who, in cooperation with anti-
government insurgents, moved blocks of raw jade through Thailand.[73]
As the Hong Kong carving industry reoriented toward feeding Western
tastes, standards degraded. Materials like serpentine marble, chalced-
ony, chrysophrase, some types of granites, or doctored low-quality jade
(artificially stained or painted to brighten the colour) were substituted
for increasingly rare and expensive raw material; and a cottage industry emerged to fake antique jade carvings complete with certificates of
authenticity for gullible collectors. Galleries in Hong Kong mixed fake
and real material, although from time to time the failure of authentication services to spot pricey fakes causes a scandal that temporarily dries
up the market.

So it was with Steven Ng Sheong Cheung, a man with impeccable credentials to make a practical demonstration of the virtues of the free market. A graduate of the University of Chicago and a friend (he claimed)
of Milton Friedman, high priest of laissez-nous-faire, Steven was later
president of the Western Economics Association, founder of the School
of Economics at Hong Kong University, financial columnist, and public
advocate of capitalist reform in China. In his free time he opened a gallery in a ritzy part of Seattle to sell antiques from China. As long as they
were more than one hundred years old, they could enter the US duty
free. Although he also sold porcelain and bronze, he was renowned for
old jade that he obtained, so he claimed, from Asian collectors selling
out after the big financial meltdown of 1997. He provided certificates
of authenticity from a Hong Kong laboratory that he happened to own;
and buyers who complained received letters from "experts" guaranteeing
the quality of Steven's merchandise. Meanwhile he invested his money
around the world in real estate, stocks, art from Christie's, and even a
California airplane-parts manufacturer. Charged with tax evasion in the
US and later sued for commercial fraud, he ran off to China, claiming to

be victim of a frame-up.[74] He might have won more sympathy if instead he had insisted that he had been simply exacting revenge for more than a century of looting of China's finest artifacts.

In 2005 UNESCO counted 1.67 million Chinese relics in two hundred museums of forty-seven countries around the world, to which China added a guesstimate of ten times that amount in private hands.[75] After the indignity of having Sotheby's and Christie's ignore its warning not to put on the auction block material stolen from the Summer Palace 150 years before, China began a major buy-back scheme, supported by some of its new billionaires and major corporations and operated by an arm of the People's Liberation Army. It also sent teams to examine the contents of American and European museums.[76] The buyback is perhaps unique in the history of the antiquities trade. Instead of Western nouveaux riches competing for relics stolen from ancient civilizations, the upstart Eastern ultra-rich outspent their Western confrères at auction to bring home at least a few of the lost treasures.[77] The peak was a successful bid by an anonymous Chinese buyer of a 2.4 inch white-jade seal created to mark the repudiation of Emperor Quinlong in 1796 that sold for $5.92 million. On the other hand, an anonymous bidder, who was later identified as a collector, auctioneer, and consultant to China's Lost Cultural Relics Recovery Program, managed a brilliant coup-de-théâtre by entering a $40 million bid for two eighteenth-century bronzes at the Paris auction of the Yves St Laurent collection, then publicly refusing to pay.[78] Several thousand miles away, custodians of another ravaged archeological treasure house were probably hoping that the opportunity might emerge for them to do likewise.

MESOPOTAMIA AND THE NEW MONGOLS

Sometimes, as in Peru, a gold rush excites collector greed; sometimes, as in China, "development" opens sites to plunder. But, in the case of Iraq, the trigger, literally and figuratively, was its fate at the hands of the armed forces of two countries, one the most important world centre for trafficking in historical artifacts, the other the principal final destination for the world's looted material. For Iraq, too, there was an element of déjà vu.

Under British rule, Iraq (hosting, among others, Sumerian, Akkadian, Babylonian, and Assyrian ruins) was plagued by peasant diggers working for European collectors. On independence, it created a Department of Antiquities to supervise exploration, banned exports, required private owners to register artifacts and to secure approval for further acquisitions or transfers of ownership, and reserved relics still in the ground for the state.[79] Of course, other countries also had laws that were tough on paper, to little avail. But when the art market's appetite started to turn voracious in the late 1960s and early 1970s, Iraq was ruled by the strong-armed Ba'ath Party, ready to defend the cultural heritage. Its archeological service, charged with supervising about 10,000 sites (only 1,500 really explored) and a string of museums, remained effective during the Iran-Iraq war of the 1980s. But, much the way the Mongol hordes from the East in the thirteenth century had reduced Mesopotamia's infrastructure to rubble, destroyed its urban civilization and opened the door to massive looting, so the neocon hordes from the West did likewise at the end of the twentieth and start of the twenty-first.[80]

There was actually a dress rehearsal in Lebanon a couple decades before.[81] Like Iraq, historical Syria (embracing modern day Syria, Lebanon, and Palestine) is an archeological treasure house. Unlike Iraq's, Lebanon's archeological service had been small and badly under-funded, and its political class more interested in collecting graft than protecting the public interest. Still the Lebanese antiquities department succeeded over the years in building up interesting collections and coop-erating with foreign archeological services for important digs. But from the mid-1970s until the early 1990s, the country saw a series of mul-tisided civil wars interspersed with repeated acts of Israeli brigandage culminating in a massively destructive invasion in 1982. In that context militias of various persuasions proliferated, usually financing them-selves from rackets: bank heists, ransom kidnappings, and smuggling through pirate ports along the coasts everything from drugs to stolen cars to weapons. Antiquity storehouses and archeological sites, too, were ripe for looting.[82]

Granted, the best pieces in the National Museum were protected, partly by the foresight of staff in hiding them behind concrete walls, partly by the fact that the place was located at the crossroads between East and West Beirut and hence always under the scrutiny of at least two rival militias. At one point the Communist Party sent its forces, among the strongest in the country, to protect the museum. However, smaller caches like the museum storehouse in Byblos or the entire contents of the Ottoman citadel in Sidon were emptied. The Israeli army, too, walked off with prize pieces to back up claims that southern Lebanon was for-merly part of ancient Israel. During Israel's long occupation of the south, scavenging continued. Then, under pressure from Hizbu'allah, the Israeli military pulled back step by step, exposing various southern locations to local looters who were, as always, underpaid, operating out of despera-tion in a collapsed economy, and sometimes directly under the orders of local dealers. Masses of material vanished – for example, allegedly up to twenty thousand Phoenician terracotta figures from Tyre, sold on a glutted market, so the rumour has it, for only $60 each while fetching many thousands abroad.[83]

There was no mystery about the itinerary. Material by the ton went by ship to Cyprus, where representatives of international dealerships set up shop. From there it ended up in Britain, Western Europe, Japan, and the US, the latter particularly well served by New York dealers. Some smaller items went out through Beirut airport when it was operating. All of this was supplemented by material, probably even more than from Lebanese sites, looted from Syria, routed through Damascus, then carried by truck to Lebanon, and out on the same ships and planes. Even after peace more or less returned, the archeological sites remained plagued by looters while powerful business and political figures proudly displayed stolen antiquities in their fancy Beirut apartments. In the unlikely event anyone had the nerve to ask questions, the likely response was that the antiquities were inherited or purchased legally in good faith.[84]

In fact the looting has continued even in a reunified Beirut free of Israeli attention, except for the occasional bombing of a poor Shia' suburb or Palestinian refugee camp. During "reconstruction," the company with a monopoly of choice projects did its own bombing attack, demolishing things like the charming old souq to replace it with a Westernized glitzy upscale shopping mall to cater not to ordinary citizens but to visiting petro-princes and the wives of Lebanese war profiteers. Little or any artifacts unearthed made it into the hands of the antiquities service. Not to fear. As one local archeologist enthused: "They are going to do some flashy things ... There will be lights everywhere. It will be beautiful, fantastic. They will make you forget that a lot has gone."[85] All too true.

By contrast, the downfall in Iraq began not with civil collapse – that came later – but with its 1990 invasion of Kuwait. Iraq stripped Kuwait's national museum, but kept the items intact, catalogued and protected, and (grudgingly) returned them after its defeat in the subsequent war – even though valuables ranging from Rolls Royces to Rolex watches grabbed from individual Kuwaitis were never recovered. Under UN sanctions imposed on Iraq just before, during, and long after the 1991 war, cultural exchanges were forbidden, including, in theory, the purchase of Iraqi antiquities – although the British and US governments seemed too busy holding up shipments to Iraq of food, medical supplies, and fertilizer to enforce that part of the sanctions. After the war, state authority collapsed in large areas. Archeological work stopped; and sites, along with regional museums, became free-enterprise zones.

At first it was random: unpaid soldiers, farmers, and Bedu tribesmen looted sites while the urban poor raided regional museums, selling to local dealers who peddled the relics abroad. On top came a massive, illegal selloff of private collections by people rendered desperate as the economy collapsed or anxious to get assets (along with themselves) to safety abroad. Since Iraq technically had no legal antiquities trade, antique dealers, jewellers, and carpet merchants stepped into the breach. News of the availability of Iraqi artifacts after so many decades of dearth spread among Western dealers and collectors. Working through agents in neighbouring countries, they provided digger teams with wish lists. Locals could be hired for a pittance, and the few remaining guards easily bribed or intimidated. There was little the regime could do besides close afflicted provincial museums and move their remaining valuables to Baghdad. The only improvement came in 1998 when the regime, permitted some extra oil revenues by the sanctions authorities, began to again fund its antiquities services, hiring local people to reopen some diggings and providing armed guards to keep freelancers at bay.

After the 2003 invasion and fall of the regime, the first impulse of people traumatized by more than a decade of medieval economic siege and repeated wars was to seize the moment – and whatever else was at hand.[86] Major cities faced an epidemic of looting – of homes, stores, factories, and public infrastructure. The target was not just food and consumer goods, but anything that could provide at least temporary relief by direct consumption or sale.[87] Worst hit was Baghdad itself. To simulate a popular uprising, US forces had brought in a rent-a-mob from Sadr City, the sprawling Shi'a slum, which went on to trash parts of the city centre while US soldiers watched and encouraged it.[88] While 158 official buildings in Baghdad were looted and burned, US forces took care to protect the headquarters (and records) of the ministries of the interior (i.e., secret police) and oil. Not so the Koranic Library of the Ministry of Religious Endowments and the National Library and Archives that held, along with documents, old manuscripts and antiquarian maps dating back hundreds of years.[89] Elsewhere the scene was repeated. The university library in Mosul, celebrated for its ancient manuscripts and cuneiform tablets, was robbed despite appeals from minarets for people to stop destroying their own city.[90]

No doubt these were mainly acts of desperation by locals, reflecting as well indifference by US soldiers who had no orders to protect the sites and were probably confused as well as delirious over the rapidity of their victory over nonexistent opposition – it was like a video-game come to life. However, alongside random looters were gangs with the knowledge to make off with valuable items for sale outside of Iraq. Their targets included the country's historical artifacts.

Iraq's remarkable abundance had long attracted two distinct sets of foreign admirers – archeologists and private collectors. While archeologists stress the central importance of context in interpreting the meaning of relics, to dealers, collectors, and sometimes curators, they are detachable items that can fetch fabulous prices. Hence Iraq's severe restrictions against the export of cultural property were admired by (modern) archeologists and excoriated by collectors. In the run-up to the invasion, the first tried to provide the Pentagon with coordinates of major sites in hopes of sparing them from bombs and missiles. On the other hand, William Pearlstein, treasurer of the American Council for Cultural Policy, a set of wealthy and politically influential collectors and curators who lobby against laws that hamper the free flow of art and antiquities, blundered his way to infamy when, in a meeting at the Pentagon, he described Iraq's cultural heritage laws as "too retentionist."[91]

Those who descended on the national museum seemed to agree. The mob seized equipment, trashed displays, and grabbed relics from public galleries. Under cover of the chaos came experts who knew what they wanted and had keys to storage places. Only the foresight of museum staff in moving many of the best, including most of those made from gold, to vaults in the Central Bank prevented a worse cultural catastrophe. Similarly the Mosul Museum was sacked in two stages, though in reverse sequence: first came pros who knew where the best items were and ignored replicas or things of lesser value, then came a second wave who grabbed or trashed at random.[92]

Although the total number of items lost was much smaller than initial shocked reports, and tales of professionals with forklift trucks turned out to be bogus, the museum heist led to worldwide revulsion, forcing even Switzerland to finally ratify the UNESCO Convention and Britain to pass a law criminalizing any conscious act of trafficking in stolen artworks. When scholars around the world demanded an independent assessment of the damage, the US refused to cooperate unless the investigation was under US control and used US consultants. To the victor, it seemed to insist, goes the spoils, one way or another. But facing bad press, the US announced an emergency deployment of FBI, customs, and CIA agents to locate stolen material, ignoring thousands of experienced Iraqi officers who knew the local black market and would have asked for much lower rates of pay – that itself was probably sufficient to disqualify them.[93] The Marine colonel in charge of recovery claimed that US forces had been unable to protect the museum because the Iraqi military had been illegally using it as a fortress – a handful of irregulars had been there for a short time, then vanished. He insisted that the US, unlike Iraq, was obeying international law by refusing to send troops to a museum – just as the US was so observant of normal rules of war by showering the country with cluster bombs, white phosphorus, and depleted uranium. After all, he contended, US troops in their tanks would have been vulnerable – apparently to looters threatening them with cuneiform seals. Anyway the real brigand had been Saddam (who had previously ordered looters executed on sight); and the main mistake of the US military had been to not realize "the extent to which Iraqis viewed the museum not as housing the priceless cultural heritage of their country" but "as Saddam Hussein's gift shop." That officer's no doubt genuine distaste for the illegal trade in antiquities was clarified further by his claims that its other sin was to help finance the Iraqi resistance against a benign US occupation.[94]

Meanwhile back home, others quickly moved to reassure the public that there was really a silver lining in every battlefield smoke cloud. André Emmerich, the US art dealer who had been a pioneer in introducing Mayan art to the US market in the face of export bans in Mexico and Guatemala and the man who had articulated the opinion that the US, because of its multinational character, is the natural repository of the world's great art, wept great tears in, appropriately enough, the Wall Street Journal. But, he insisted, the museum tragedy was further proof of how the world's cultural heritage was better preserved if private enterprise dispersed it to more secure places, no doubt including his New York galleries.[95]

Following a public appeal from the Grand Ayatollah, many objects were recovered. Key items, too, were found abandoned. The Occupation authorities claimed that its fast action had made those too hot to handle. But all that the heat would really do would be to temporarily reduce the price while heightening future expectations. The sensational recovery in New York of the Entemena statue of a Sumerian king, the largest item stolen, may have been less a law-enforcement triumph than a publicity stunt. By one theory, the statue had been hauled to Beirut to show to an art dealer with galleries in New York and Geneva, who, later arrested in a different case, traded the information for leniency; and the original thieves were paid to return it.[96]

Not so lucky was Joseph Braude, a US federal government "terrorism consultant" who had written a book about "building the new Iraq" in the course of applying for a job with the Washington gang plotting to destroy the old one. Jetting off to war-torn Baghdad to have a look around, he was caught on his return to New York with three cylinder seals still bearing Iraqi national museum identification marks, even though he initially denied to customs ever being there. Fortunately he had a good lawyer, one famed for his "fierce" courtroom attitude, which also came to the fore when speaking about the world's "intellectual dishonesty" on the Middle East, particularly its failure to just kill the Palestinian leadership. To the lawyer the five hundred Jewish settlers who occupy parts of the Palestinian city of Hebron in defiance of international law, and ride through the streets harassing and abusing its rightly inhabitants, are "the greatest heroes of our generation."[97] Duly moved, the judge agreed with Braude's lawyer that the defendant's behaviour represented a "marked deviation from an otherwise law-abiding life" and sentenced Braude to six months home confinement. A few years later the New York Times celebrated the rehabilitation of a man whom it fondly described as able to "eavesdrop on an Arabic-speaking [taxi] driver's phone conversation" with glowing coverage of his wedding to a young Jewish lady he had met in the courthouse. "It's a textbook case of divine intervention," the happy groom beamed at the nuptials. "If I had not sought to recover these antiquities, I would have been working in Baghdad for as long as I lived."[98] Apparently the Iraqis would have had no say about that either.

At the time of the nuptials, eight thousand of seventeen thousand items taken from the museum were still missing, not counting those trashed in mob violence.[99] They no doubt paled compared to the flow onto the world black market from archeological sites whose contents were undocumented and were therefore, apart from representing a dead loss compared to items already studied, usually impossible to trace and recover. Starting the very day of the invasion, those sites were worked by gangs of unofficial diggers, including people previously hired by the official antiquities service. Former farmers, they just moved from digging fields to digging ruins, and from working for the state to hiring on with private employers, a neat metaphor for the planned US remake of the country. Some of their work was opportunistic; no doubt some was done on commission for buyers after the few poorly armed guards were chased off, paid off, or simply co-opted. In another part of the US program to turn Iraq into the Arab world's first "free-market economy," the occupation regime also allowed Iraqi landlords to buy up sites with archeological significance, then dig for artifacts – just like in the U.S. of A.[100]

However, there was good news: parts of two of the most important sites were protected from (Iraqi) looters by the simple fact that they were inside the spreading network of US military bases. Thus Tallil air base, the largest in the Middle East, contained within it the ruins of Ur (possible birthplace of Abraham), the main gate of the new base built on top of the principal suburb of the ancient city. The site was barred to the head of Iraq's antiquities board but open to US Air Force personnel.

Similarly "the hanging gardens of Halliburton" (AKA Babylon) became a huge armoured base, its 2,500 year old structures damaged by tanks, its soil (full of relics) bulldozed to fill sandbags, some areas dug out like open-pit mines, others compacted for helipads and car parks using gravel hauled from elsewhere to be gratuitously mixed with local material, and all contaminated by diesel and gasoline runoff. Besides, its famed Ishtar Gate was a fake anyway – created by the Iraqi antiquity service, much like the imitation marbles in Greece's Acropolis Museum, when Iraq was unable to get back the real thing sitting since the late nineteenth century in a Berlin museum.[101]

To be fair to the US forces, they did try to make amends. For example, when the 101st Airborne division captured what became its operating base at Marez, its tanks blasted apart a side wall of the St Elijah's Monastery, which had stood without damage for the previous thousand years. In 2009, the US military decided that it ought to restore the crumpled side of that Christian redoubt. "G.I.'s in Iraq hope to Heal Sacred Walls" headlined the heartwarming pre-Christmas story in *The New York Times*.[102] It said nothing about healing any wounds in Fallujah, Iraq's glittering city of mosques, where US forces slaughtered thousands with flechette munitions, cluster bombs, and white phosphorus shells, condemning countless thousands more to a slow death by cancer, and reducing that major pilgrimage centre full of the tombs of Sufi saints to just another Mesopotamian archeological site.

Stealing from Iraqi museums and diggings was only the first step. Before being sold, material had to be moved to places where it could be laundered. After the museum heist, Syria and Jordan began returning to Iraq mainly small, not very valuable items confiscated from the hundreds of thousands of refugees fleeing the stricken country. Saudi Arabia and the UAE seized more valuable pieces, probably destined for international dealers.[103] Three other neighbours, though, seemed less enthusiastic about helping. One was Kuwait, perhaps seeking revenge for Iraqi looting a decade and a half before. A second was Israel. Its antiquities dealers, long the beneficiaries of loot from Palestine and neighbouring Arab countries, not only have a huge market of Jewish and Christian-fundamentalist religious tourists but also have privileged relations with the New York dealer community, giving Israel both a political and commercial interest in maintaining the status quo.[104] However, paucity of action from Turkey reflected something more complex.

Turkey shares with Iraq the status of hosting many former civilizations along with tough antiquities laws. It bans exports and requires that all artifacts be registered soon after discovery with the Ministry of Culture. Yet prior to the invasion of Iraq, it was also the world's largest

supplier of classical antiquities, thanks to an experienced class of smugglers, often from the Kurdish and Syriac minorities. Politically harassed
and culturally repressed, they repay Turkey by dealing in gold and
weapons coming in, along with drugs, refugees, and antiquities going
out. As usual, dealers hire locals to dig by night, paying a pittance, perhaps in basic goods, especially when the rainy season uncovers tombs.
International buyers congregate in Istanbul to dicker; then the material
heads abroad in sealed trucks through Bulgaria, with payoffs if needed
to officials in both countries. The prior existence of this contraband network to handle locally sourced material greatly simplified the job of
Turkey becoming a true transnational in the underground artifacts trade
once war provided the right conditions.[105]

Shortly after the 1991 war, Iraqi antiquities from the archeologi-
cally rich south began moving up through the Kurdish provinces,
where smuggling rackets run by local warlords were sheltered under
an Anglo-American air-force umbrella, then into Turkey, mixing with
sanctions-busting trucks full of consumer goods and tax-free cigarettes
coming in and tanker-loads of petroleum products going out. From
there they headed to Munich for distribution across Central Europe, or
to Switzerland to be laundered, then to England for auction, to end up
mainly in the US or Japan. With the 2003 war, it was open season.

Of course Iraq was not alone in facing this kind of "collateral damage" from the War on Terror. Like its Iraqi counterpart and unlike a
typical Western one, the Afghan national museum in Kabul had been
devoted not to the loot of the world but to material collected within
the country, thanks to a law that welcomed foreign archeologists but
banned the export of their finds. During the 1980s, the Soviet military
had protected the museum and helped with maintenance. After the Red
Army pulled out, the US-backed victors fell to slaughtering one other,
each faction celebrating temporary control of the museum area by cart-
ing off trophies. Within two years most of the collection was gone. The
looting stopped only with the victory of the Taliban, although it celebrated its own victory by destroying some of the museum's remaining
statues, deemed idolatrous.[106]

Among the most remarkable losses in those years of free-for-all were
the Begram ivories, two-thousand-year-old Indian panels from the ruins
of King Kanishka's capital. They began to turn up in the hands of wealthy
collectors, including a former Pakistani minister of the Interior.[107] In
addition, illegal excavations spread. One area hit hard was the Minaret
of Jam, which the Taliban, rightly excoriated for destroying the great
Buddhist monuments at Bamian, had protected as an Islamic shrine.
With the triumph of the US and its local allies in 2002, in swarmed

the diggers, smashing far more than they took out. Anything interesting could be sold to dealers from Herat, close to the Iranian border, or
from Peshawar in Pakistan, then sent to Europe to be offered on the
London market, duly disguised as Persian or Seljuk in origin.[108] On the
other hand, no one bothered to disguise the origins or nature of the
two-thousand-year-old manuscripts often referred to as "The Dead Sea
Scrolls of Buddhism," which vanished during the wars along with countless other ancient documents, only to come to light again in the British
Library in London, where they could sit proudly alongside those sacred
manuscripts from Ethiopia.[109]

Meanwhile back in liberated Iraq, by early 2008, with the country
still wracked by political and criminal violence and the remaining infrastructure collapsing, Iraqi officials put the total loss, museums and sites
combined, at roughly 100,000 items.[110] They could hardly expect trig-
ger-happy US troops with faulty body armour crouching in their badly
protected Humvees to go poking around for Sumerian vases. Anyway,
there was no place to put them. The national museum whose salvation
by the US crimebusters had been so widely broadcast, was bricked up
while Iraq's director-general of antiquities had fled abroad ahead of
death threats. It was reopened, against the wishes of Ministry of Culture
and its former director, as a sign of Iraqi "progress" early in 2009, with
over half its exhibition halls still shut, dark and in disrepair.[111]

As to the reassuring claim that the loot was too hot to handle, a major
antiquities heist is usually followed by silence, apart from a flurry of
internet offers of things that turn out to be fakes. Anyway, a stolen piece
of remarkable quality likely goes directly to a private collector to be
quietly admired by like minds. Alternatively it could make its way slowly
through the infrastructure of the underground trade to sit, perhaps for
years, in a high-end dealer's inventory. It is finally put on the market,
perhaps with some cosmetic alterations, accompanied by a suitably falsified provenance backed up by enough sham transfers to cloud the record
and blunt any legal challenge. As to those taken from the archeological
sites and therefore without prior record of existence, time alone suffices
to dull memories, alleviate suspicions, and raise potential prices enough
to make the wait worthwhile.

6

The Numismaniacs: When Big Modern Money Chases Little Old Coins

Today enormous progress has been made toward the fundamental goal of postmodern capitalism: creating a "market price" for just about anything while trashing the intrinsic value of just about everything. In that spirit, "securitization," something that worked magic in the mortgage market recently, has spread beyond conventional art forms to embrace at least tentatively other types of collectibles.

Today the stress is less on the appearance and more on the asset value of high-end collectibles. For example, one vendor of Persian carpets advises that "Even those indifferent to the aesthetic qualities of antique rugs can see the financial advantage ... [A]ntique rugs make a far more desirable and useful investment than a stock portfolio."[1] Besides, he failed to add, an eighteenth-century Sarouq looks a lot classier than a bunch of IBM certificates spread out on a living-room floor. Similarly dealers in antique furniture reassure would-be buyers that there is serious money to be made in the "small area of the trade commonly referred to as investment grade antiques." Collecting and holding them for the long haul will "add wealth to your estate" much as will investing in "big companies whose stocks are considered investment grade" like "General Motors" – although hopefully the antiques chosen will not be so badly in need of "restoration."[2] Not only are antique collectibles further examples of "uncorrelated assets," gaining value as stock and bond markets collapse, but financial progress/regress can be followed through things like the Antique Collectors' Club Antique Furniture Price Index.[3]

One prerequisite to full scale modernization of markets in these more esoteric collectibles is a grading system that first converts adjectival descriptions (semi-antique, superb, mint condition, and so forth) into ordinal rankings (i.e., 1,2,3, ..., 10, etc.), then transmutes ordinal rankings into discrete prices like $105,679, $345,004, $4,676,087 – or even $2.87. That last is probably the "fair market value" of a signed first edition of a classic text by a University of Chicago economics professor who carried off his discipline's "Nobel Prize," something as genuine as a lot of other items traded on the collectibles market today.[4] To the extent those modern evaluation methods work, old fuddy-duddies who appreciated Byzantine coins, Chippendale chairs, Turkish prayer mats, or Malian terracotta vases for the individual accomplishment by which, the romance of the era in which, and the cultural context for which they were conceived, and who gained their knowledge by studying parchment documents rather than Sotheby's catalogues, get shunted aside in favour of high-end investors, financial manipulators, and parasitocrats searching for "bragging rights." As W. Graham Arader III, the doyen of today's US antiquarian map dealers (whose prime clients are no longer university archivists but big corporations or big-money collectors) described his profession with a frankness that made his colleagues squirm – it consisted of "servicing the rich. Sycophancy."[5] The same could be said for the whole business of high-end collectibles, including rare coins.

COIN OF WHOSE REALM?

Most contemporary passions for objects of antiquity have historical precedents. Coins are no different.[6] Wealthy Romans fancied old Greek ones; Renaissance noblemen liked classical Roman issues. By the eighteenth century the Western European bourgeoisie had added coins to its growing interest in collectibles, to the delight of both counterfeiters and the emerging professional numismatists, the latter with hands full dealing with the former. In the 1800s, the practice became well established, too, in North America. However, in more recent years collecting rare coins has been converted from a pastime popularly viewed as suitable mainly for "golden age" eccentrics too gimpy to golf into perhaps the first sector of the antiques market to be properly "securitized" by Wall Street banksters. Of course, once upon a time rare old coins were real money; so, at least conceptually, the transformation isn't such a big deal.

Modern high-end "investors" reserve their greatest passion for antique coins fashioned from silver or gold. Originally chosen as monetary metals because of ease of working, inherent beauty, and myths about divine origins etc., precious metals had another advantage that they could pass without much loss of weight or value from dining room to counting house and back again simply by taking decorative silver plate to a mint for coining, or the reverse. Originally churches wrapped up that market. But by late medieval times in Europe, crown and nobility amassed ornamental objects fashioned from silver – until they became necessary to finance a war or bankroll a monarch's lecherous self-indulgence. The fact that coin and plate were so interchangeable also meant that the wiser among noblemen and rich bourgeoisie learned to keep their treasure in gemstones and jewellery, just as effective for display while less vulnerable to impecunious kings.[7]

Contrary to the claims of today's monetary cranks, usually trying simultaneously to sell shares in a new technology that turns iron rust into gold dust, monarchs in ages past were not constantly plotting to reduce the silver or gold content in their coins, then unload them on an innocent public at original face value. Official debasement happened mainly in periods of wartime emergency or civil breakdown, although subsequent generations of free-market ideologues made academic careers by claiming the former caused the latter rather than vice versa. The spread of coins with the monarch's face on them to the far corners of the then-known Earth was an important source of both political prestige and revenue from charging people to have their gold and silver coined at the royal mint. While an occasional official debasement might throw the monetary standard into confusion, most people knew what had happened, or soon found out, and could quickly adjust. Meanwhile private enterprise was busy subverting the coinage quietly and more or less constantly.

The easiest way to "make money" back then was to put a metal blank between upper and lower dies and "strike" (the term still used for quality of a coin's stamped features) them with a hammer so that each coin was slightly different in size, weight, shape, even precious metal content. While the dies were kept under close guard at the mint, this lack of uniformity even of official coins made easier both circulating fakes (since there was no sure basis for comparison) and "clipping" – i.e., shaving precious metal off real ones. The alternative of casting (i.e., pouring liquid metal into a mold) made for more uniform results, but was technically more challenging and expensive. Used by fakers, though, it allowed creation of coins with gold or silver on the surface while the inside was lead, bronze, or tin.

Originally (legal) minting was the exclusive preserve of emperors. Eventually every king or territorial potentate wanted to turn out coins emblazoned with self-glorifying images and self-edifying slogans. When those coins found their way into foreign countries, another trick used by private counterfeiters was to alter surface inscriptions in order to raise the apparent denomination (and exchange value) of unfamiliar coins. Representative examples of most of these counterfeit or altered coins are still floating around today, sometimes valued by collectors more than the bona fide equivalents, assuming they can figure out which is which.

Granted that punishments meted out for counterfeiting (e.g., being burnt alive, fed to wild animals, having eyes put out, or having hands or testicles lopped off) might have been something of a deterrent. They were especially vicious because faking coins was more than a crime; it was an affront to the sovereign power. Still, Emperor Justinian (responsible for codifying Rome's laws) proved himself worthy of his name with a response that anticipated the US government's treatment of top culprits in recent multi-trillion-dollar Wall Street swindles – he made the most notorious counterfeiter of the age the chief financial officer of his realm.

"Clipping" was eventually discouraged by milling (raising a uniform rim around) the edges, and fakery became more difficult once the screw press (which converts the circular movement of a handle into a stronger downward force) was adapted from squeezing grapes into wine to coining. Combined with a rolling mill that produced uniform metallic strips out of which blanks were cut, the eventual result was a currency whose very uniformity helped to deter counterfeiting. But, ironically, that also hastened the decline of metallic currency.[8] After Johannes Gutenberg adapted the screw press to mass printing, governments could shift from minting coin out of rare metals to churning out reams of paper money out of old rags. However, that changeover was still a couple of centuries away.

In principle two different sets of functionaries controlled opposite ends of the precious metals cycle. Goldsmiths – despite the name, they worked much more with silver – handled the manufacture of silver and gold articles for ornamental use; while the supreme political power controlled the coinage. Yet goldsmiths frequently ran the mint, too.[9] It was an honoured profession, if not always an honourable one. England, for example, saw repeated scandals over local goldsmiths producing silver plate of much lower standard than the coins they melted, selling it at full price, and diverting the excess metal to private sale, or, if they worked at the mint, stealing from the Crown. Monarchs responded with the death penalty for adulteration, and forced goldsmiths to work in public streets where everyone could keep an eye on them. Around 1300, King John invited to settle in England a group of Saxon goldsmiths (named Easterlings) whose reputation for a product unique in purity and uniformity during an age when coins were generally judged by their degree of debasement. In their new abode they (according to one theory) eventually dropped the first two letters of their name to form "Sterling," the mark of quality for both silver plate and a silver currency that set European standards in its day, and continues to set world standards today.[10]

However, England was not exactly blessed with precious metal mines – its silver deposits were by then seriously depleted and the mining profession had trouble recovering from the ravages of the Black Death. Most of its silver had to be earned by trade. And monarchs, to secure their needs, had to periodically impose on nobles or clergy mandatory loans technically repayable in silver plate, although they rarely were. Henry VIII temporarily solved the problem with a massive seizure of Church silver along with its lands. But most was frittered away by his successors in wars. The depletion of English silver coincided roughly with the Spanish conquest of the Americas, whose plunder transformed international finance.

At first the loot of the Americas came in short-lived lumps: theft from the living, then from the dead, of their existing gold and silver; enslaving Indians in their own placer mines; a pearl rush that dried up as oyster beds were ravaged; and a brief emerald boom. Then discovery of rich veins of silver ore at Potosí in Peru in 1535, followed by great strikes in Mexico, seemed to place the Spanish empire on a stable fiscal basis, Spain's capacity to project power across Europe along with it. The Spanish silver dollar quickly established itself as the first true world currency. However, that, too, was not to last. The system was ravaged from within by the closely related plagues of political dissent, administrative corruption, and tax evasion, not to mention simple depletion of prime silver deposits; and it was eaten away from without as other envious powers unleashed smugglers and privateers against Spain's economic lifeline while mounting ever more powerful challenges to its military and territorial might. High quality ore was smuggled from mines to illegal smelters; couriers (including, rather prominently, priests) ran untaxed silver bars to smuggling centres where British, French, and Dutch traders were happy to receive it; even silver that made the trip to the official mints was siphoned off; and local-made coin, although nominally forbidden to travel to anywhere but Seville, leaked across the globe. Even when the silver was captured by the Spanish official system for minting and coining, it poured out of Spain again in an ultimately vain pursuit of power and influence abroad. If the Spanish empire was built upon gross crimes against humanity, its fall was at least in part a consequence of widespread economic crimes against imperial authority – and even more a consequence of imperial overreach, something that the neocons running US foreign policy in the last couple of decades have had considerable problem understanding.[11]

By the late eighteenth century, the role of Spanish silver coins as the international standard was challenged by British gold, this time a reflection of British skills not in working metal so much as in plundering the globe. Gold from mines in Brazil, Russia, the US, Canada, Australia, Ghana, and South Africa ran through its mint to re-emerge in both coin and bar form. Although by the end of the nineteenth century, paper money was far more common than coin, the British gold sovereign remained the main standard of value; while silver was reduced in much of the world (but not in the US, thanks to the power of its silver-mining lobby) to a mere token, like copper.[12] When World War I wrecked the finances of its major participants, desperate governments increasingly replaced even private paper (usually exchangeable into gold or silver on demand) with public notes that were legal tender – in other words, they had to be accepted in payment for debts. There was no more need for gold or silver coin as a backstop. Although there were still holdouts, the age of precious metals as the financial cornerstone of world commerce was drawing to a close, leaving thousands of years of legacy for coin collectors to ponder.

Certainly coins did not disappear from circulation. But their importance became marginal, and their legal value ceased to bear any relationship to a metallic content that was now exclusively non-precious in nature. That has transformed the counterfeiting business. Faking coins that are actually in use today is rare – although the 14 million counterfeit one-pound coins allegedly turned out recently by a British engineer would buy a lot of bubblegum from a vending machine.[13] Rather, the purpose of faking coins is generally to create something to sell for a hefty price on the market dealing in rare coins that no longer circulate as money.

PRECIOUS COINS AND GOLDEN CALFS

Some factors transforming coin collecting from a hobby of amateur (yet often quite sophisticated) history buffs (who were sometimes pioneers, way ahead of professional historians, in researching how trade and financial flows worked in ages past) into a small form of big business are the usual ones – the search for an inflation hedge, the shift of today's barons of business from earning income to exploiting assets, and the emergence of a new parasitocracy with time and money to waste. However, with coins, unlike other collectibles, another factor at work is ideology-cum-theology in the form of a conviction that either god or the market, to the extent they are separable, has decreed that only gold and silver are genuine money. And there is another factor feeding the US part (by far the largest) of the coin market. Historically the US was an enormous producer of gold coins for circulation – of silver even more. But in 1933, in the midst of the Great Depression, the government stopped minting gold, demonetized existing coins, and banned private possession of bars or coins (except those deemed collectibles), demanding they be turned over to the government in exchange for paper. That ban, in place until 1974, left a two-fold legacy. One is that today a major selling point in the US for coin-artists trying to unload overpriced stuff is the idea that their goods are collectibles, therefore free of risk of another government confiscation. Second, the ban meant that, in the US market, any gold coin predating 1933 is considered rare. And that reflects another possible misapprehension – that the coins turned in by good citizens were melted into bullion, therefore permanently lost to the coin market.

At the time of the recall, gold coins ounce for ounce commanded a premium over bars – they almost always do. So when the US had to pay bills in Europe, rather than send bullion, it shipped gold coins to join millions already there. In fact, the combination in the 1930s of a US devaluation of its currency so that foreign gold could buy much more in the US along with rising political fears across Europe meant that the flow of gold bars went the other way, from Europe into US government hordes. Combined with the US systematically plundering Britain, its desperate "ally," in return for military assistance, the result was that the US emerged from World War II with a lock on most of the world's gold bullion; while rich Europeans and their banks held scads of US gold coins. By the early 1970s, a lot of the gold bullion had moved back out again, to Europe and parts of Asia, to cover a chronic US balance of payments deficit largely the result of military spending abroad. (Somehow the US elites convinced themselves that the USA was impervious to the British disease of periodically plunging into wars it could not afford, only to have its finances wrecked and its gold stocks drained.) But, once the ban was lifted, coins were moving the other way. The net result is that today old US gold coins, whatever their historic value to genuine collectors, are probably a lousy long-term investment, although few dealers are going to admit that to their clients.[14]

Items traded on the high end of the coin market today fall into two distinct categories. The first consists of modern "bullion coins" issued by mints of major gold-producing countries at a price well above the value of their metallic content – the expectation is that, as gold rises in the future, coins go up in price even faster. Issuing coins at a price significantly higher than the gold content means that minting them can be a neat source of public revenue. Of course, that doesn't always work.

In 1986 the Japanese government commissioned 10 million coins to commemorate the sixtieth year of Emperor Hirohito's reign. Given the momentous occasion, the government decided to make this first gold coin minted in Japan since the 1930s "risk free." It guaranteed that, although each coin issued at a price of ¥100,000 contained only ¥40,000 worth of gold, if the market price started to fall, the coin could be resold to the government at the original issue price, while, if the price rose, investors could sell the coin on the open market at its current value.

The scheme promised $3.5 billion in profits to the Japanese Ministry of Finance. Reputedly it also offered a literally golden opportunity for some private-sector entrepreneurs to arrange somewhere in the Middle East for two tons of gold to be stamped into counterfeits, each, like the originals, containing ¥40,000 worth of gold, and to sneak them back into Japan via foreign coin-dealers. The coins were then sold to banks for the full government-guaranteed price. The Osaka Mint that had created the coins shouted fraud; and the Ministry of Finance claimed it had forked over $70 million for the fakes. But the police hunt went nowhere. One British dealer to whom the alleged counterfeits were traced (although he had bought them from two Swiss dealers) even had a former chief metal-lurgist of the British mint attest to their veracity, a claim corroborated a few years later by a gold-fingerprinting test in the Western Australian government's minerals-science lab. No culprits were ever found. Possibly none existed. But, to be on the safe side, the government's next coin issue in 1991 to mark the start of Emperor Akihito's reign, was much smaller, contained 50 percent more gold, and was sold almost at the bullion price. A similar strategy was used in 1993 to honour Crown Prince Naruhito. Alas, even those more modest efforts were far from scintillating successes. Once the Asian Crisis of 1997 hit and people dumped gold to get cash to pay their bills, the government was again stuck with honouring the high guaranteed price in a rapidly falling market.[15]

Normally that market shows greater receptivity to officially issued bullion coins than the unfortunate Japanese experienced. There are lots of potential takers. Apart from tax and alimony evaders who squirrel them away in safety-deposit boxes, the regular clientele no doubt includes survivalists holed up in log cabins with boxes of ammunition, bags of dried beans, and a sack of US gold eagles, now that the USA is back in the gold-coin minting business. Gold coins might be favoured, too, by people in high-risk professions – one veteran gunrunner advises those entering his trade to carry a survival belt stuffed with them, an idea he probably got from a James Bond movie.[16] And, of course, some people have a special need for the discretion that gold can provide. In 1994, when police looking for evidence of corporate payoffs raided the home (one of several) of a former head of the Italian Ministry of Health's pharmaceuticals division, they found, in addition to one hundred small bars of gold, thousands of British gold sovereigns and South African krugerrands, along with old Russian and Roman coins – quite a haul in a country where private investment in gold had been illegal since 1936.

Then, of course, there are "ordinary" investors just seeking higher returns. They, especially old age pensioners trying to stretch their means, were/are sitting ducks for high-pressure telemarketing firms peddling gold and platinum bullion coins that either are badly overpriced or simply don't exist. Once the firm selling the stuff has run up enough charges on the client's credit card, it, too, might vanish.[17] There are also from time to time mass purchases by investors badly burned in orthodox financial markets who run to gold coins for cover – while others, facing a financial squeeze, unload their watches, rings, and necklaces on dealers who resell them to smelters turning out yet more coins. After the 2008 crash, big mints of the world along with a lot of new competitors greatly stepped up the flow (the Royal Canadian Mint by a factor of four) to cash in on the panic that financial mismanagement by their governments had helped produce, without anyone charging them with conspiracy, commercial fraud, or insider trading.

Because government mints almost always charge for new gold coins a price well above the market value of their gold content, some people look for different sources. One Nevada gold-mining scam, for example, promised to repay its investors not in cash, not in heaps of unprocessed ore, not even in the crude gold that ore would yield, but in coins minted from the refined gold bars it would eventually produce. The promoters kept their promise: the mine never produced any gold; so the investors never got any coins.

Other coin artists might invoke the Lord Almighty to sell their wares, something easier these days with wide acceptance of two religious trends. One is the popularity of prosperity theology that (apparently working from a version of the New Testament suitably abridged to lack any mention of the difficulties the rich supposedly had in the old days of getting into heaven) preaches the virtues of wealth, using as an earthly example the fancy clothes, big cars, private planes, and Hawaiian first-class cruises of the pastor of the parish. The parish itself assembles in a taxpayer-funded neon-lit plasticized cathedral more like a trendy Las Vegas casino than the old, cold, and austere stone edifice of yesteryear, with the word spread across the world through the wonders of modern electronic communication rather than through stern and stentorian tones from the pulpit amplified by little more than a bullhorn.[18] That occurs concurrently with search by the faithful for "Biblically sound" investments. Apart from generous donations to the work of the particular ministry, typically the stress is on things like gold, silver, land, and cattle, which "maintain a store of value over time and … offer an instant liquidity."[19] Not only will such choices have concrete substance and therefore likely persist after more ephemeral forms of wealth are consumed in the inevitable floods or fires, but gold and silver (although probably not cattle) can be safely buried in the ground until Satan, perhaps assuming the corporal form of tax inspectors, is driven off the premises. If anyone needs more encouragement, they can look up Revelations 21:21–23 where Jesus promised that the New Jerusalem would have streets made of gold and gates of pearl. Since he didn't say much about where the raw material was coming from, some of his followers took that as license to look around the world, including in rather unlikely spots. So it was with the investment strategy of the Greater Ministries International Church.[20]

Gerald Payne made a career peddling gold coins before founding a church whose central doctrine of "doubling" was based on Luke 6:38: "Give and it will be given unto you." Greater Ministries leaders told followers that it would take about a year and a half for their contributions to come back at 200 percent of the original. If God's blessing were not enough guarantee, additional collateral took the form of gold, platinum, and diamond mines – especially in Liberia. Untapped deposits were potentially worth $40 billion, ample to support a "Christian Social Security Plan." Church leaders held "road-show" meetings across the US, inducing the faithful to mortgage homes, run up credit-card debt, or cash out retirement savings to "give" in the truly modern Christian expectation of being given back doubly. In the interim their funds were held, they were told, in Cayman Island- and Nauru-based banks, safe from IRS scrutiny. If anyone questioned what happened to the money, they were accused of lack of faith.

Yet no amount of faith could conjure up Church-owned gold mines in the US; the one in Liberia was never operational; and the diamond deposit yielded only a handful of industrial stones. Also existing in holy spirit alone was the Cayman Island bank. By contrast the "Nauru" one was real, sort of – it just chose to manifest itself not on a mined-out wasteland way off in the Pacific but as a storefront in Tampa. Most of the funds actually went into a Colorado bank from which each director drew "gas money" in the form of 5 percent of the funds gifted by people they recruited to the cause and from which previous "givers" were occasionally repaid out of money put in by later donors. Payne also used part of the money to buy gold and silver bullion, then have it converted into celebratory coins emblazoned with the church logo to hand out to donors in commemoration of their good deeds.[21] After the Colorado bank crashed, wiping out $20 million of church funds, the church offered to its flock certificates redeemable in gold, silver, or cash at the Greater Church Storehouse that didn't have any gold, silver, or cash, or even a civil address. Payne was convicted on seventy-two counts of conspiracy, wire and mail fraud, and money-laundering.[22]

COIN JOB

The market for old and rare coins, the ones long sought by collectors, and now increasingly by investors, is quite different. Obviously not all are made from gold or silver – some from more humble metals are even more coveted. And in those that are gold or silver, bullion content is only a minor factor in determining market value. In recent decades the "market," as reflected in an index of coin prices published by Solomon Brothers, seems to have risen sharply, perhaps indicating that old coins are a hot new investment. A new world record was set early in 2010, when a 1794 one dollar silver coin, part of the first run authorized by the Congress of a freshly independent US, sold at auction for $7.85 million.[23]

Much credit for moving control of the coin market from near-sighted numismatists to the visionary field marshals of finance is given to Bruce McNall. Starting out in the 1970s, he boasted an Oxford University degree and control of the Numismatic Fine Arts company, boasting a clientele of five thousand and generating $2–10 million in net income per year. McNall also accepted credit for building great coin collections for industrial czar Howard Hughes and oil billionaire J. Paul Getty.[24] The degree didn't exist; the income and client base were grossly inflated; the Hughes connection was pure invention; and the closest he got to J. Paul Getty was when he teamed up with the antiquities curator at the Getty Museum to pull off tax scams on behalf of donors. McNall would locate items the curator wanted, then front a sale to a would-be donor, collecting a commission, while the donor got an inflated appraisal for a tax deduction that not only covered the purchase but turned a profit. McNall got so tight with the Getty that he was able to put his own stock on display there, then sell his "museum quality" pieces at much higher prices.[25]

Antiquities, though, were a sideline to his main business of smuggling old coins from the Middle East and Italy back to the US, hidden in his clothes and luggage. Sometimes he bought directly from black-market dealers, sometimes from Switzerland's Bank Leu, no doubt well stocked from its long history servicing tax evaders, flight capitalists, and insider traders. McNall himself noted that, "at some point, virtually every ancient coin on the market was smuggled, stolen or otherwise the subject of shady dealings."[26]

Among collectors, McNall's first big client was a Hollywood mogul who also turned his friends onto the coin craze. Of course, he got a share of McNall's profits. But what else are friends for? McNall made even more from selling that same mogul's collection to oil magnate Nelson Bunker Hunt, already a client for McNall's antiquities, a business association that almost ended McNall's career prematurely.

Nelson Hunt and his equally rich brother had inherited both gazillions and an ultra-right-wing political mindset from their father. Among their favourite causes was the remonetization of precious metals. A paper currency backed by gold (or silver) would, so the theory went, keep the government from engaging in deficit spending that had to be financed by printing paper money. Yet exactly the opposite seemed to be happening. With the US bogged down in an unwinnable war in Southeast Asia and its balance of payments under extreme pressure, President Richard Nixon suspended the historical link between the US dollar and gold. Freed from the constraints previously imposed by central banks, gold began to soar. Silver seemed primed to follow. Bunker's study of "history" and the Bible suggested that the appropriate relationship between gold and silver ought to be set at 1:5. Yet when the Hunts first began implementing their plan to corner the world's silver supply, the ratio was more like 1:25 and getting wider by the day as gold rose while silver stagnated.[27]

The main threat to a successful corner was the US government stockpile. Back in 1934, supposedly as a reflationary measure, a powerful lobby of western senators representing silver mining states persuaded the Roosevelt Administration to order the US Treasury to buy silver from western producers until the price rose to $1.29 an ounce; at the same time the government sequestrated all privately held bullion for $0.50 an ounce and closed the silver market. Purchases did not stop until 1963 when the price finally hit the legislated target. It held steady for a while, then softened when the US government started intermittent sales. Clearly success or failure of a corner would hinge on the US government remaining on the sidelines.

To corner a market in a commodity traded worldwide, initial purchases must be large enough to set off a price increase that in turn justifies financial institutions offering more credit to buy yet more of the commodity. However, the price hikes must be gradual enough not to trigger massive dishoarding or a collapse of demand. Once the job is done, those responsible must be able to realize their gains without identifying themselves or flooding the market – or ending up in prison. In the US, for example, people trying to corner a commodity risk not only charges under anti-trust law but also under the RICO (Racketeer Influenced and Corrupt Organizations) statute. Also to be avoided are civil suits from losers – speculators who shorted the market and industrial users who faced sharply higher prices.

In this case everything possible went wrong. Their first purchase of 20 million ounces telegraphed their interest and alerted copycat speculators. A scheme to take over a major silver producer to control the feed into the market collapsed when the manager director they had para-chuted into place lined up with dissident shareholders to force the Hunts out. Meanwhile they had been pledging personal assets for bank credits and searching the world for rich partners. After several disappointments, they manage to interest a consortium of fabulously rich Saudis. Working through the front of a Bermuda company, the group bought even more energetically. By the time it was over, if the silver in their contracts was added to the stuff they physically owned, they would have had over 200 million ounces, almost equivalent to the whole world's 1979 production. In the wake of gold prices soaring further in the late 1970s run-up, silver started to move sharply, peaking at $50 an ounce. But the Hunts were hit from just about all possible directions.

First, the dramatic rise in price led to drastic cutbacks in industrial use. Second, mine sites that had previously been uneconomic began pro-ducing. Third came a flood of silver from India. Although exporting silver was illegal, Indians who were the world's leading hoarders sold it en masse onto the black market to be smuggled, via Dubai, to Europe and America, and used the money to buy gold, which they preferred but had previously been unable to afford. Fourth, there was a rash of silver robberies, probably prompted by the price hikes, with bullion dis-cretely finding its way onto the market. Fifth, as the market rose to dizzy heights, people began hauling silverware and beautiful antiques, includ-ing doubtlessly a fair share of the world's antique silver coins, to be melted into bullion, just like old times, but now with collectors, numis-matists, and coin dealers gnashing their teeth in frustration. The silver nail in the coffin would have been the US government releasing part of its stockpile. That was just barely averted by the Hunts mobilizing in the US Congress a cabal of Southern segregationists, Born Again Christians, and even a representative of the loony right John Birch Society to force the government to buy, not sell, over $500 million worth of silver. But federal regulators, fearing the impact of a skyrocketing price, tightened trading rules. As the price began to slide, banks called for more collat-eral and brokers demanded higher margins that the Hunts could only meet by selling some of their silver, further softening the price. In the meantime in what might have been an inspiration for Goldman Sachs a couple decades later, the man managing their silver contracts began trading against his clients, liquidating his own position while everyone else was taking a hit and therefore aggravating the down cycle. And their Saudi allies, smelling legal and political trouble, bailed out. The Hunts were left bankrupt in what some unkindly souls called the biggest per-sonal financial reversal in US history, with the court cases stretching on for over a decade.[28]

To give the Hunts credit, they had realized early on that success of their silver play would rebound in other markets, including that for gold coins. So they had also decided to use Bruce McNall as agent to buy up all existing Byzantine gold coins. Since, like most modern big-time "collectors," their real interest was flipping, they didn't care if they actually saw their acquisitions. That gave McNall the opportunity to invent a new kind of coin future – he took their money and reported that he had acquired on their behalf some three hundred coins when he actually had only a couple dozen. When the brothers got into financial trouble with their silver play and asked banks for bailout funds, bank auditors demanded to see their assets, including the coins. That sent McNall scurrying around the world to find replacements.[29] Although the banks eventually fronted $1.3 billion, the Hunt brothers still went under. And just how well McNall understood the market of which he had pronounced himself a grand master was underscored in 1988 when Nelson Bunker Hunt's $50 million coin and antiquities collection was sold via Sotheby's for $34 million, although not before the world collector community shuddered at the potential for market collapse when all that stuff got unloaded.[30]

Before that unfortunate event, McNall's coin-dealer-to-the-stars reputation had enabled him to persuade Merrill-Lynch to set up under his management three limited partnerships for rich clients to invest in old coins. McNall could buy coins wholesale through his regular business channels and sell them to his funds at retail, claiming fees and commission while also cutting himself in for a chunk of the profits once the funds finally liquidated their holdings. But in 1994 the funds collapsed in scandal. Merrill-Lynch had to repay 3,500 investors $30 million to settle lawsuits charging that the brokers had misrepresented risks, rewards, and liquidity. Soon McNall himself was in front of the courts, eventually copping five years in a $300 million bank-fraud case.[31]

The changes in the coin market went far beyond simply the emergence of coin funds, and much deeper than the pioneering exploits of some intrepid entrepreneur over whom the popular press drools during the upswing and on whom it dumps during the down.[32] Probably the most fundamental were in grading procedures. Originally dealers themselves authenticated, dated, and typed a coin, and eyeballed it for general appearance, "strike" (the clarity of the impression from the minting process), colour, and tarnish, then described its condition as good, fine, or uncirculated, gradually adding other in-between categories like very fine or extra fine. That subjective grading system, reflecting the fact that each coin is unique, was still prevalent when the market began to take off in the 1970s. What had worked reasonably well in the old closed world of local dealers and hobbyists did not function so effectively in the emerging modern world of big-time traders and high-end investors. But help was on the way.

Back in 1948, a numismatist named William Sheldon had created a coin-grading system based on numeric scores from 1 to 70. The theory was that a "69" (a "70" could probably never exist) was worth 69 times as much as a "1." In the 1970s the principle won general acceptance. Then, as the market took off, other key changes occurred.

In the past, some dealers doing their own appraisals might pull a coin job on a client, claiming a piece was a higher grade when a client was buying and lower when the client was selling. But now independent services claiming greater objectivity emerged. The Professional Coin Grading Service (PCGS), for example, altered the Sheldon ordinal scale to give it a cardinal dimension.[33] This kind of change, by giving the illusion of an objective one-grade, one-price standard for old coins, allowed anyone with money to enter the market even if they thought a Septimius Severus was what happened to Jack Nicholson's nose in the movie *Chinatown*. Even better, pseudo-standardized ratings permitted coins to be bought and sold sight unseen. People like the Hunts could then aspire to grab all the world's Byzantine gold coins without knowing how they differed in appearance from subway tokens.

Furthermore new grading services returned a coin to an owner "slabbed" like an investment gemstone, with a certificate of authenticity and grade sealed along with the coin in a tamper-resistant (quite different from tamper-proof) plastic bubble, making them in theory far easier to resell.[34] Coins were triumphantly declared to be "securitized" – a curious description for something with retail-wholesale spreads of up to 50 percent, poor liquidity, and, despite the hype, big variations in grading.[35]

Since an assigned grade usually reflected a compromise among several of a particular service's graders, it could vary widely over time and place. The result was a floating population of coins for which the owner figured having a shot at getting a higher grade by busting the coin out of its plastic case and resubmitting, perhaps to the same service (happy to oblige since it collected a fee on each submission) or to a competitor known for higher grades, much like submitting a bond to the rating service with a reputation for giving out the most triple As. With genuinely rare coins in high demand, a few grade points could make a huge difference in price.[36]

That was happy news to, among others, William J. Ulrich, a man who in the early 1980s started an investment newsletter, *Money Advocate*, with two or three part-time employees. Soon he was running Central Coin Exchange Inc., which bought coins off the general market, graded them, and sold them to Security Rare Coin and Bullion Corporation. That company retailed at prices reflecting Central's grades while reassuring clients that the products were low-risk, high-return opportunities. After all, the coins came with buy-back guarantees. Scrutinizing the whole process was an investment newsletter called *Capital Gain$*, staffed by rent-an-economists who touted bullion and rare coins as ideal investments in inflationary times. The only thing wrong with the picture of a thriving set of arms-length enterprises is that Urlich ran them all. A court later declared that some coins were so inflated in price that the clients stood a good chance of being wiped out, that there was no money in the buy-back fund, and that Urlich had misrepresented the grading process as arms-length.[37]

That was still the story more than a decade later when Armand De Agnelis had his (second) date with the justice system. He started as a salesman in a New Jersey penny-stock operation, a career that ended when the police busted the firm. While awaiting a date with the judge, De Angelis proclaimed himself a Born-Again Christian and took off to Florida to bring the benefit of Biblically endorsed investment strategies to the broader Christian community. There he set up US Coin Exchange, a collectibles dealership, selling coins appraised by independent services while promoting himself as the leading Christian coin-dealer in magazines like *Christianity Today*.[38] In 1991 he returned to New Jersey to face a conviction in the penny-stock case for buying and selling without client permission, failure to follow customer instructions, and misrepresenting potential risk. "I feel terrible about what happened," he said at his sentencing hearing. "I truly thought that every person who ever bought stock could make money, but unfortunately, it doesn't work that way." Besides, he added, "I didn't really feel I was doing anything wrong." And he expressed regret that the thousands of others who had profited from his advice would not be able to "march in here" to speak on his behalf.[39] Indeed, the silence seemed deafening, especially to the judge who gave De Angelis a brief sentence and ordered him to pay $1.1 million (later cut on appeal to $600,000) in restitution.

Meanwhile, his coin business seemed to be thriving. It got a further boost when, just in time to take advantage of the Y2K scare, De Angelis set up Twenty First Century Grading Service along with Currency Clearing Corporation. He used the clearing company to buy coins from dealers and private collectors, then consigned them to his own grading service for objective assessment. Meantime his retail clients were reassured by his membership in the American Numismatic Association, the Certified Coin Exchange, and the World Gold Council – but in reality the first two had expelled him and the third accepts as members only major gold producers, not bush-league gold-coin dealers. Although all the coins were genuine and possessed a market potential above their bullion value, they were, claimed the prosecution, appraised sometimes at several times their "worth." After one persistent client drew the attention of the US Post Office and the IRS, De Angelis was sentenced to 97 months in prison and ordered to make approximately $1.3 million in restitution.[40]

Yet there was something curious about the sins of both Urlich and De Angelis. "Overvaluation" of the coins they sold seems an odd concept to be applied anywhere in a modern capitalist economy where getting the most for the least is the Golden Rule. Furthermore, misrepresentation of objectivity (or lack thereof) of a grading system was just business as usual. At one point the Federal Trade Commission had forced none other than Professional Coin Grading Service to stop overselling its presumed objectivity – not to protect widows and orphans but because, in the wake of the McNall debacle, the FTC wanted "to make sure Wall Street brokerages aren't lulled into a false sense of confidence about the degree of risk."[41] (Overconfidence on Wall Street in its own genius? The very idea!) Anyway, a couple of years after De Angelis had his second run-in with the law, an industry newsletter submitted thirty coins to top grading services, only to find that "in no case did the grading services agree on the grade of any given coin, and in some cases the difference in grading was as much as seven points off."[42] The usual discrepancy in the Urlich and De Angelis cases was two or three grades.

Nonetheless, the new "scientific" grading methods, along with the emergence of electronic trading systems, transformed the business in several ways. First, it created the preconditions for someone like McNall to launch Wall Street brokerage houses in the late 1980s into their coin market foray, with less than brilliant results. Second, it made life easier for boiler-room operators already peddling "investment-grade" gemstones and shares in shaky, defunct or nonexistent gold mines to branch into coins, perhaps using as bait that Solomon Brothers coin-investment index without informing their prospective clients that it was based on a handful of very rare and exceptionally successful coins.[43] Third, it redoubled efforts by tomb-raiders in the Middle East and Southern Europe to feed a hot new market in the US. In 1984, amid all the excitement, William Koch, the billionaire industrialist (and avid funder of right-wing causes ranging from the Cato Institute, a "free market" propaganda mill, to today's version of the mad hatter's Tea Party) managed, in conjunction with a couple friends, to obtain 1,900 old Greek silver coins unearthed by three Turkish peasants who had been hoeing their fields with a metal detector. His dream had been to own an ancient coin collection that might be called the hoard of the century while at the same time doubling or trebling his money. In a backhanded way his coin cache did earn the first part of that distinction.[44] A lawsuit by the Turkish government resulted in the coins (today known as the Elmali Hoard) now sitting in a museum near their place of discovery rather than competing for a visitor's eye beside Koch's world-famous collection of trophy wines – although that soon came to have a type of notoriety of its own. Fourth, the new pseudo-scientific grading system along with the entry of big money into the small-money world made the business of faking coins more lucrative.

Creating a complete fake that will pass scrutiny takes some skill. The simplest technique is casting with two molds, one of each side, joined before the metal is poured inside. But the result may be marred by a seam in the middle, pits from air bubbles, or raised lumps of metal so that the coins do not look or feel right. (More modern versions of the equipment at least partially reduce that risk at higher cost.) The lettering under magnification may show less wear than the rest of the coin – indicating it has been added afterward, perhaps to a genuine old coin of much less value. The weight may be off with a gold or silver coin, although that could also be due to someone filing or clipping the original. (Bronze coins whose value was dictated purely by law, rather than by precious metal content, can show wider variation.) The patina may be artificially enhanced. And counterfeiters sometimes get sloppy in reproducing the relative position of the figures on one side compared to the other. Nor might fakes "ring" properly when struck with a blunt object. Die-casting (forcing molten metal under pressure into a single mold) is better but, unless it employs a crude and easily detectable hand-cut die, is more expensive and demanding; and it requires the sacrifice of a real coin. Furthermore the results will show all the defects of the original on every copy. And if the body of the fake coin shrinks slightly while cooling, there will be a noticeable difference in measurement. However detection may require finding a real example of the same coin for close comparison.[45]

Whatever technique is used, the coin will likely require chemical aging to eliminate its freshly minted lustre. Ultimately, though, how good the counterfeit is depends on how much time and money the faker was/is ready to invest. That in turn has something to do with whether the coin was/is intended to fool the general public or experienced collectors. The most dangerous for that latter class is probably fakes that were struck from molds created out of genuine coins a long time ago – the older the fake, the harder it is to distinguish from the real thing. That early numismatists might have accepted them in days before more technical tests were possible may serve to collectors as sufficient proof of authenticity. Granted, the main problem serious collectors face is probably alterations of mint marks or dates rather than actual reproduction.[46] But complete fakes have occurred amply in the past, and apparently with even greater frequency today, with the fakery capitals shifting from Eastern Europe in the 1990s to present-day China. There "fake factories" allegedly sell facsimiles marked "replicas," yet stand ready to meet special orders for the same coins unmarked.[47]

On the other hand, maybe China feels it is just paying back the US in its own coin, so to speak. China today exports to the US enormous amounts of physical products of its labour, raw materials, and energy; while the US repays in pieces of paper (or just computer entries) churned out en masse by its Treasury and by Fannie Mae and Freddie Mac, the US government-sponsored (now -owned) mortgage-market institutions. So who is the real counterfeiter?

Of course, it is not enough to simply counterfeit a coin. Its appearance on the market, as with a fake painting, may require explanation. Is it being sold off by a prominent collector or "deaccessioned" by a museum or, best of all, has it recently come out of an archeological site, legally or not? Take, for example, the notorious Black Sea Hoard. According to one story, in 1988 a Bulgarian lifeguard discovered 150 ancient Greek coins and gave some to a German tourist to sell in the West. A German dealer then offered to buy them all. But when he shortchanged his intermediaries, they got angry. A Bulgarian diemaker then stepped into the story, producing fifteen false dies to strike approximately one thousand fakes. The lifeguard buried them in the Black Sea for a few weeks; the German tourist smuggled them out, and the dealer who had bought the original real ones took the entire "hoard" for a low price. From there they spread through trade circles.[48] Although the British Museum declared them forgeries, some retail vendors insisted on their authenticity, particularly after they passed examination by both electron microscope and neutron activation, one of the most sensitive methods of trace element analysis. Others, led by Wayne Sayles, publisher of the leading coin magazine in the US, preferred to put their faith in the "smell test," insisting, to considerable acrimonious criticism, that the styles were too deviant. Proof that they were fakes came only when a member of the anti-forgery committee of the International Association of Professional Numismatists bought a pair for a few dollars from the Bulgarian National Historical Museum, complete with a receipt identifying them as reproductions.[49]

That bit of bad luck aside, the early success of the coins to some degree reflected their also faked shady origin – they were marketed as smuggled rather than counterfeit objects. Much like "Etruscan urns" whose creators bury them in Italian made-to-measure "archeological sites," counterfeit coins that supposedly come illegally out of their ancient resting places not only automatically make a willing buyer a co-conspirator but severely hamper the ability to complain to the authorities after the fact. More likely the unfortunate purchaser just looks for another sucker. That is reputedly common, too, with another type of fake coin, one especially profitable because of public fascination with tales of sunken treasure ships.

FISHERS OF COINS

Treasure hunters are today attracted to several hot spots. The bottom of the Aegean Sea, for one, is littered with Roman wrecks, a particularly coveted item given the fondness of imperial Rome for hauling home treasures from its widespread conquests. How many more lie elsewhere around the eastern Mediterranean? Greece territorial waters alone must host thousands bulging with antiquities, to which that country's government reacted brilliantly in 2005 by opening the once-forbidden shoreline to maritime free-enterprise – a prelude, perhaps, to its recent post-crisis decision to try to stabilize its finances not by suing Goldman Sachs or just repudiating all the phony debts the banks foisted on it but by selling off bits and pieces of the Greek islands to the same class of financial sharks that caused the problem.[50] To the west, the Gulf of Cadiz, to which Spanish treasure ships from the Americas were usually bound, is another paradise for underwater scavengers seeking to loot the loot of earlier looters, though the Spanish government periodically swoops in to make arrests.[51]

The long-prevailing practice was that those who conducted salvage operations could demand compensation, but the cargo remained the property of the original owners or their legal successors. However growing appreciation of archeological significance led to the 2001 UNESCO Convention on the Protection of Underwater Cultural Heritage, stipulating that wrecks represented collective cultural heritage and demanding that archeologists be present at all salvage operations. Lacking support from the major powers – the US refused to sign; the UK balked, eventually declaring it would respect the convention without actually signing it – it has remained de facto another legal dead letter confined to the archives for future historians to puzzle about. What is left is a jungle of national regulations, claims, and counterclaims that, along with taxes, encourage salvers to do things on the sly.

In 1987, the US, hoping to relieve federal courts of the need to sort through a legal morass, passed the Abandoned Shipwreck Act, which

gave state governments jurisdiction over any commercial wreck if owners had failed to maintain their claims; *and* it gave title to the finder. In
practice that meant that a treasure hunter had to buy a license from,
submit finds to judicial review of, and pay a share to the state in order
to claim ownership, leaving the previous owners out in the cold. There
was an exemption for government or military property – its importance was shown in the late 1990s when a Spanish government claim
bested that of US scavengers for two nineteenth-century Spanish vessels off the coast of Virginia. However, there was no treasure involved,
merely artifacts. The situation was very different in 2002 when Odyssey
Marine Exploration of Florida thought that after a four-year search it
had located off the coast of Gibraltar the HMS Sussex, sunk in 1694
with ten tons of gold bound to buy the Duke of Savoy's allegiance in
one of Britain's wars against France. The British government, apparently
forgetting in the rush of other business that it had promised to respect
the UNESCO Convention, offered a secret deal to Odyssey that would
give the company the lion's share, so to speak, of the proceeds, only to
face protests from archeological institutes and an opposition motion in
Parliament. When Odyssey tried to go ahead anyway, it was blocked by
Spanish legal action. Finally it got permission from Spain, apparently
satisfied that the sunken ship was British, to proceed. However, in 2007,
in a completely separate case, US courts granted a salvage company title
to a 400-year-old wreck outside any country's territorial waters with a
cargo, according to the original excited claims, that might eventually
total 500,000 gold and silver coins. Spain, sure that the wreck was the
Spanish Crown's Nuestra Senora de las Mercedes, sent ships to seize the
research vessel. Just for good measure it also suspended cooperation
with the Sussex recovery.[52]

Today there is ample treasure hunting in Central America, especially
Panama, which in the sixteenth and seventeenth centuries served as a
transit route for precious metals heading to Spain. But the main centre
of action in the Americas is Florida's Key West, a place that first moved
from backwater to boomtown on the basis of what locals could plunder from shipwrecks before turning their talents to gouging the physiological wrecks who descend on the state every winter. Although today
there are obvious advantages from not reporting finds (avoiding taxes
and the state share), publicity probably drives up the price of treasures
(along with anything else retrieved) enough to offset much of the government's take. Still, there may be a strong temptation to sell off quietly
at least part of the haul, particularly coins that are easy to hide from
the authorities. Like antiquities from land-based archeological sites,
with shipwrecks there is little if any reliable record. Even a check of the

Spanish imperial archives in Seville is not much help since many, perhaps most, treasure ships were themselves carrying contraband to avoid the imperial *quinto*, the 20 percent share taken by the government. Claiming that a salvage operation is strictly off-the-books also creates an opportunity to con investors – they can hardly complain to the cops about being cheated. And it represents a chance to reproduce old Spanish-type coins, chemically age them, then unload them on tourists to whom the "low" prices of the stuff on offer are explained by the black-market nature of the deal. Although most such counterfeiting scandals involve small fry, one of them caught an unexpectedly large fish that had been diving in warm saltwater for decades.

The late Mel Fisher hit the news with his discovery of the Antocha, sunk in 1622, from which he allegedly retrieved $400 million in gold, silver, and jewellery – only to have Florida confiscate it, leaving Fisher to spend years in multiple legal hearings to win its return – minus 20 percent. That figure of $400 million must have been grossly inflated – if not, Fisher's subsequent need to scramble for outside investment to sustain his other treasure hunts would be hard to explain. Whatever the real number, the Antocha yield was the largest *reported* treasure haul to date, with choice items offered for sale at Christie's.[53] Some were purchased by the Spanish government, probably miffed that, although the Antocha had been sailing under commission from the Spanish crown, Spain had to purchase from a US scavenger via a British auction house Spanish historical relics – mindless of the fact that they were the product of plunder, enslavement, and mass murder far from home. But then, to the victor always goes both the spoils and the power to revise the historical record.

For Fisher this brilliant start was quickly bogged down in controversy – including wild accusations that the marine museum he set up as a tax dodge was full of fakes and that he had sold most of the Antocha treasure on the black market before hauling the cash to a secret bank account in the Bahamas. So many lawsuits followed that, when he decided to invest in a resort property complete with a dolphin training centre, he rationalized that not only would dolphins help him find more gold but "they won't sue, either." Archeologists excoriated him for destroying wrecks; environmentalists scored a victory against his habit of blowing holes in the seabed, destroying seabed grasses that form a crucial fish habitat; securities regulators asked questions about his technique of raising money by private subscription, then repaying investors with a share of the finds; Mexican experts decried as counterfeit some Mexican silver dollars he tried to sell at a coin show to raise more money; and the broader numismatic community was already shunning him before the accusations from the Florida attorney general that he had been selling fake Spanish imperial gold coins from his shop, which paid part of the costs of his treasure hunts.[54]

This last accusation started when a customer bought a $5,900 coin complete with a certificate of authenticity stating that it came from a Spanish fleet sunk in 1733 – only to be advised by a jeweller that the coin was fake. When the client demanded his money back, Fisher obliged, allegedly sight unseen, something that made the state attorney's office suspicious. (Something about the tale becomes at this point, no pun intended, a bit fishy.) At first Fisher insisted that the coins were real, only to have the government point out that he had never reported finding a 1733 wreck. Then he said he had gotten the suspect coins from an investor in his last big treasure find. Finally, while dying of cancer, he admitted (probably under duress) to selling the fakes inadvertently and promised in the future to deal only in coins from shipwrecks for which he had acquired proper salvage rights.[55] Fisher, of course, blamed his problems not on his disdain for the rules but on a plot by prosecutors and environmentalists. "This is a setup ... They're doing this to try to shut me down." The reason the government was out to get him, he insisted, was "billions and billions of dollars .... they're using the environment as an excuse to take away all the treasure and the shipwrecks."[56]

Others, somewhat sympathetic to Fisher's point of view, have contended, with some justification, that official aversion to maritime treasure hunting is based on the myth that the seas and oceans are undisturbed oases of biodiversity and history, instead of the liquid waste dumps overflowing with toxic chemicals and plastic detritus that they have really become – with the result that maritime scavenging ought to be encouraged before the artifacts are destroyed or just further buried under assorted poisonous and corrosive gunk. True to a point; but that scarcely seems to justify turning them into private property at prices determined by how much money the class of people most responsible for the devastation of the seabed have to spend on their collections.

Wayne Sayles, the "conservative Republican" founder of the Ancient Coins Collectors' Guild, expressed his opposition to regulations in more direct terms. In 2007, when the Republic of Cyprus, long drained by treasure hunters by land and sea, negotiated with the USA a ban on US imports of old coins from the island, Sayles denounced the action as "a major offensive" against collectors that threatened to turn the US "into an island of prohibition." The deal, he insisted, in language appropriate to an Air Force veteran who created and ran the 416th Bomb Group memorial website, was no less than "the Pearl Harbor of the Cultural Property War." (Interestingly, he did not call it the "Hiroshima.") By contrast, the Cypriot ambassador to the US may have landed a direct hit when he replied to collectors that, "It may be your hobby, but it's our heritage."[57]

On the other hand, there is a rather good chance that the ambassador's "our" was intended as a reference to Cypriots who claim descent from the Mycenaeans and therefore insist on being "pure Greek," rather than from the Hittites, Assyrians, Egyptians, Macedonians, Persians, Umayyads, Venetians, and Ottomans whose own contributions to both the physical archeology and the genetic architecture of the island are likely more abundant. Undoubtedly in future centuries a similar ethno-cultural mark will be made on Cyprus by its most recent set of invaders made up heavily of British tax evaders, sleazy international bankers, embargo-busters, gunrunners, and white-collar criminals from around the world. For decades they have been buying up the once beautiful and sedate island without any vocal protest from Cypriot government officials – or the country's senior diplomats. However, to assess the contribution to the island's heritage of that set of newcomers, future archeologists will have to work not by deciphering ancient scripts on cuneiform tablets but by studying encrypted balance sheets on discarded computer disks.

PART THREE

The Cost of High Living

7

The Winophiliacs: Uncorking the Secrets of the Wine Trade

Few things can cause someone's cup-of-life to brim over like descending into a cool, dark cellar, perhaps carrying a sputtering beeswax candle, to haul from a set of cedar racks a dusty old bottle with a label written in a language sufficiently foreign to convey an air of sophistication but not alien enough to risk a visit from their country's security and intelligence service. After extracting the cork and allowing the contents to breathe revitalizing air, hastened perhaps by a deft swirl of the wine in the glass, the eager epicure takes that exploratory sip, feeling a little *frisson* of delight as a bouquet of fruity and spicy flavours first caresses the tongue, then explodes against the palette. That ecstatically sensual feeling from fine wine in the mouth seems only a fair return after paying for it through the nose.

However, true enjoyment of great wine ought not to be a solitary pleasure. Acquisition of an exceptional modern vintage from high-end merchants, or, even better, of an old trophy wine from an upscale auction house, is better celebrated by a "tasting," the list of invitees to include both media-savvy wine gurus and the host's rivals for social standing. If none of the guests succumb to paralysis or death from the lead oxide (or worse) that crooked vintners in ages past used to tart up the taste of mediocre wines, the wine wizards depart to prose about the event in their columns, collecting their reward in repeat invitations from the host and/or frenzied requests from the host's jealous peers.[1]

Of course, the scribes have to be careful about what they write. No one really wants to know, for example, that the old family name on a bottle identifying a venerable vineyard is just a glorified modern brand-name attached to a piece of land that has changed owners many times through bankruptcy or speculation, recently fallen into the hands of a very successful retailer of kinky lingerie, shifted its borders by frequent buying and selling of adjoining parcels, and had any ecological connection to the original *terroir* further lost through erosion, chemical fertilization, and microclimate change. The crushed grapes were probably chemically treated to kill off temperamental natural yeasts before more commercially dependable bioengineered varieties were substituted. Then the "must" – the mix of juice, pulp, and skins, along with stray leaves, twigs, and any insects hardy enough to survive repeated doses of pesticides, about double the average for other forms of fruit farming and constituting a virtual what's what in the chemical poisons most unwanted list – gets laced with sugar to hype the alcohol level, perhaps sufficiently to permit the product to be stretched by adding water. (A charismatic fellow with hair as long as a hip California vintner is rumoured to have pulled off a similar scam in Palestine a couple of millennia ago.) The wine can be further jazzed up with fruit or spice extracts so that winophiliacs can one-up each other by rhyming off a list of subtle flavours they detect in the grape. And it can be laced with illegal additives to ensure better shelf-life. All this occurs before the bottler cuts the nominally fine wine with cheap commercial stuff rescued from a fate of being distilled into ethanol for biofuel. The Roman sage who made the observation that "in vino veritas" was, of course, referring to its effect on the consumer's brain, not to the contents of the bottle, much less the claims on the label.

SOMETHING TO WINE ABOUT?

What would today be regarded as wine fakery has an ancient pedigree. Wine may have originated, like so much else, in Sumer (AKA Iraq), a place rewarded in recent times for its enormous contributions to modern civilization by being systematically sanctioned, bombed, and looted back to a pre-Stone Age state. Beer also had its origins there. In fact the two were inseparable, literally: the Sumerians added crushed grapes to barley to guarantee fermentation, maybe with pomegranates and dates tossed in for good measure. Pure wine from grapes alone was likely reserved for priests as a sacrament, and later used for long-distance luxury trade.

From Sumer production spread, for example, to Phoenicia, whose wines received so many of the ancient world's equivalent of celebrity endorsements that Greece and Sicily launched themselves into the wine trade in the eighth century BCE by faking Phoenician varieties. The business was prone enough to racketeering that some Greek islands ordered wine to be sold only in sealed containers to prevent adulteration, prohibited watering the product, and banned selling it via futures contracts, probably for the common-sense reason that the buyer would not be able to physically inspect the product before paying.[2] The Romans, too, had to contend with adulteration to such an extent that the ever-observant

Pliny the Elder remarked: "So many poisons are needed to make it fit to drink and yet we are surprised that it gives us indigestion."[3]

Although the Romans shipped wine over thousands of miles in wax-sealed amphorae, the art was lost for many centuries. The wine trade of medieval Europe consisted of sending far-from-airtight barrels from southern producers to areas too far north to host grape. Back then there was no distinction between ordinary and fine wines; and the contents of barrels lasted at best a year before succumbing to the elements.[4] Yet, as time progressed, so did the importance of the business. Monastery-produced wines were especially blessed. During communion, believers were required to participate in the Dracula-like ritual of downing wine as a substitute for the blood of Jesus that was presumably in shorter supply – although no doubt some entrepreneurs working the fake religious relics trade managed to unload a few phials of an appropriately gory-looking substitute. Military monastic orders, too, could sell wine to raise money for their wars in the Middle East.[5] That side of the business got another boost when the pope celebrated the mass expulsion of the Moors in Spain by banning public baths and cannabis cultivation, the first because they were deemed unhealthy and lust-inducing, the second a perhaps incidental gift to grape-growing landlords who were the core of the papacy's military support. God, it seems, had decreed that good Christians, unlike evil Saracens, were to demonstrate their piety by appearing in public dirty and drunk.

In the seventeenth century, the glass bottle and the cork revolutionized the business.[6] They greatly extended the commercial life expectancy of wine, shifted the cost of holding inventory from the grower with his oak barrels to the merchant who bottled the stuff, and helped make a clearer distinction between fine wines and plonk, aided further by the spread among the elite of elegant dining and extravagant parties. Along with these developments came multiple forms of fakery – putting inferior wine must in casks with leftovers from fermenting higher quality material; adding sugar, raisins, or syrup to step up fermentation or sweeten the final product; blending cheap with expensive; watering down wines to stretch supply; changing or deepening colours with additives; tossing in fragrant herbs to make ordinary wines seem like rarer types; lacing wine with juices to give "fruity" tones; using a range of adulterants like ox blood and pigeon dung; and so forth.[7] Out of this reputed epidemic of fraud came calls for a way to guarantee quality, which growers and bottlers neatly diverted into a demand that their product be protected from outsiders even if foreign wines might be better and safer. Provenance protection was applied first in Portugal, then in a more complicated way in France, and later in Germany, where it reached truly baffling levels of complexity, before being picked up more recently by producers around the world.[8] None of this stopped the games so much as drove them deeper underground, tipping the advantage to industry insiders against upstarts.

Quantity and variety of production combined with tradition and geography allowed France to establish early dominance in the international trade. Especially favoured was Bordeaux, a river port that could tap the wine flow from its own large producing area as well as from more southern regions and direct it to the main foreign markets, England and the Netherlands – although the great Bordeaux fortunes were really built not on wine but slaves, about a million of them kidnapped to work on Haitian sugar plantations after the Arawak Indians were wiped out by guns and imported disease. Burgundy, the other great vine-growing region, was isolated inland to the east, barely able to make its wares known as far as Paris until a major program of road-building in the eighteenth century. Even then progress was uneven. For example, during the Napoleonic Wars, Britain cut off France's supply of sugar from the Caribbean; and France banned, among other things, exports of wine across the Channel, allowing the Portuguese to briefly wrap up the (legal) English market. When France responded to the consequent cane-sugar famine by investing heavily in beet sugar, the result was a long-term glut that encouraged more winemakers to boost natural fermentation by loading their product with cheap sugar. Originally popular in colder areas, over time the practice of heavy sugaring spread even to Burgundy and Bordeaux, whose growers always insisted that the fullness of their grapes, not additional sugar, accounted for the splendid results.[9]

The French industry fell on hard times again in the late nineteenth century. The problem was not foreign competition – stuff from Spain and Italy was viewed, then like now, as inferior. Rather, disease brought from North America along with its grape varieties virtually obliterated French vineyards. That prompted another epidemic of fraud as imported grape juice and raisin extracts, not to mention more inventive concoctions with little or no botanical relationship to the grape, were substituted. The process was no doubt aided by a nineteenth-century flood of publications with recipes for do-it-yourself imitation wine. The introduction of disease-resistant hybrids eventually led to recovery; and World War I helped to consolidate the gains, thanks to the radical difference in French and US official attitudes toward their country's favourite forms of tipple.

In the US, in the late nineteenth century, demands for a federal prohibition law came first from an alliance between teetotaling (so they claimed in public) Protestant ministers and bored middle-class housewives who concurred that alcohol made men lazy, inclined to crime, and prone to domestic violence – as well as keeping them out of churches on Sunday morning when they stayed home nursing hangovers. Although some municipalities and states went officially dry, the federal government resisted: excise taxes on alcoholic beverages were its single most important source of inland revenue, particularly given the key role of booze taxes in financing every major military operation from the Revolution to the Spanish-American War.[10] But others jumped on the anti-alcohol bandwagon. Small-town WASP USA protested the vices of big cities where immigrants (like the Irish with their noisy libations) concentrated. The Prohibition movement grew stronger once big-business interests became convinced that alcohol encouraged absenteeism and reduced job performance. And partisans of "political reform," along with union busters, targeted for closure saloons that functioned as working-men's clubs. In the saloons candidates bid for working-class votes by boisterously handing out a few dollars worth of booze; while in the salons they humbly solicited support from their social betters by offering commercial concessions worth millions – the first was corruption, the second nation-building.

Victory over the Demon Rum finally came when the US entered World War I. In 1917 the federal government, having introduced an income tax to cover its expanded revenue needs, banned distilling of grain into alcoholic beverages at home to cash in on a market in Europe expanded by mass conscription of its peasantry into the army. Emboldened by the prevailing patriotic fervour, US Prohibitionists insisted that beer-drinking was a German-inspired vice and that drunken soldiers could not shoot straight – although the real problem was more likely a general reluctance to fire at the "enemy," drunk or sober. Wartime restrictions were turned into an Act of Congress in 1919 and a Constitutional Amendment the next year.[11]

In France, the response to war was very different. Claiming that wine-drinkers were more valiant (i.e., had their judgement sufficiently impaired not to question suicidal orders), the government made massive purchases to distribute a generous ration to each soldier, partly offsetting damage to the industry from shortages of labour (recruited into the army), animals (used to haul supplies to the frontlines), chemical sprays (diverted to poison-gas production), and fertilizers (requiring the same raw material as explosives). Enough money flowed into major wine regions (except Champagne, ravaged by direct fighting) to banish memories of the traumatic 1880s.[12] In 1919, the same year the US Congress passed its prohibition act, France established national wine standards intended to reassure buyers that what was in the bottle might bear some semblance to what was on the label.

THE GAME OF THE NAME

The core of the *appellation d'origine contrôlée* system was a strict definition of place of origin of an agricultural product (originally wine, later cheese, honey, even lentils) and a ban on producers elsewhere from using the *appellation* (based on the name of the region or village) to sell their merchandise. The system also exercised control over types of grapes, quantity per hectare, alcohol content of wines, even some details of how wines are produced. For example, any blending of local with outside varieties required a wine be reclassified from *appellation* perhaps all the way down to ordinary *vin de table* without place of origin on the label.[13]

A particular *appellation* is in theory based not on ownership of a piece of land but on the ecological characteristics (collectively, the *terroir*) of an area that are presumed to confer unique qualities on its produce. Hundreds of *appellations* exist across France, though the highest number is in Burgundy spread over thousands of small vineyards that are sometimes criss-crossed with multiple ownerships. Enormous variations exist in what an *appellation* covers – that of Côtes du Rhône applies to thousands of hectares, yet contains within itself another distinct *appellation* of less than four.[14]

On top of this comes classification of wines from particular estates. In 1855, in preparation for the Paris International Exhibition, the emperor asked for a formal ranking of Bordeaux's greatest wines to display to the world. In response local brokers designated wines from eighty (out of thousands) of growers as *grands crus classés*. In reality wine from any vineyard can vary dramatically over time, or even according to which part of the vineyard the grapes come from in any given year; and particular vineyards improve or deteriorate because of ecological or economic change. Yet the classification has remained intact but for minor alternations ever since – to the delight of generations of counterfeiters assured of a long-term stable market. Unlike an *appellation*, this list reflects not *terroir* but the presumed superior qualities of a particular wine produced by a particular vineyard. As a result, a Bordeaux label gives the official *appellation*, the estate name, the 1855 classification (if any) of that estate, the year that 100 percent of the grapes were harvested, whether the wine was bottled at the *château* where the grapes were grown, and the alcohol content. Yet in theory that same vineyard could expand by buying inferior land and bring its product, too, under the *grand cru* classification, reaping a substantial increase in selling price.[15]

Nor does that end the potential for confusion. In 1955, the Bordeaux region of Saint-Émilion, whose vineyards had been snubbed a century before, created its own *classé* list in a bid to boost reputation, demand,

and price. The word *château* on labels can further mislead. In 1855 only four of Bordeaux's top eighty producers used that term to describe their establishments. By the turn of the twentieth century about fifty did; and the practice has spread to many other of Bordeaux's several thousand growers even if their operating premises are, literally, at the back of a garage.

Although the *appellation* system was codified in 1919, France did not create its Institut national des appellations d'origine to enforce it until 1935, on the eve of another war that would devastate the wine industry. This time there was no government bailout through mass purchase. Just the opposite. With France occupied and economically prostrate, the most lucrative domestic market for fine wines was among blackmarketeers or the German occupation authorities. Huge stocks were taken to Germany. At first they were just confiscated. But, once the Germans settled in for the long haul, they assigned control of wine-growing areas to officials with a background in the business. The local *weinführers* (as French growers snidely called them) were given quotas to purchase at prices kept low by rigging the exchange rate between German and French currencies at one third its prewar levels. However, since the officials had sometimes been prewar business associates of French growers and merchants, they usually tried to ensure adequate supplies of fertilizer, hay, and sugar to keep the industry going. Even Nazi Foreign Minister Joachim von Ribbentrop had represented French champagne houses in Germany before the war and had married the daughter of Germany's most prominent manufacturer of bubbly – although that did not stanch rumours that the stuff he sold was "jacked up" apple juice.[16]

Inevitably the postwar period saw stories of heroic efforts by growers and merchants to sabotage deliveries – of diverting the worst plonk to occupation forces; of top Parisian restaurants "aging" bottles served to their German clientele with old dust supplied by a Persian-carpet dealer; of vineyards meeting a personal order from Hermann Göring, second man in the Nazi hierarchy, for Château Mouton Rothschild, by pasting the great wine's labels on *vin ordinaire*, etc. No doubt some such tales are true, but a lot were probably invented after the war when newly patriotic Frenchmen claimed to have been active in the Resistance to hide their real record. No doubt, too, stories of duping the Germans were easier to create to the extent that they reflected what some members of the wine business had been doing to their regular clients all along.

As the war wound down, business slowly returned to normal. For example, the conflict had cut off the British supply of French wines. But after the Anglo-American invasion of North Africa in 1943, Algerian wines piled up in British warehouses waiting for the government to figure out how to ration them equitably among squabbling merchants. By the time a compromise was reached, the genuine French article was again available. So the British merchants secured permission to export the very cheap Algerian to Germany, then suffering a wine drought. German dealers were then happy to relabel some as burgundy and sell them back to the same English wine merchants who had refused to handle the presumably inferior Algerian wines once the French stuff started to flow again.[17] No doubt illegal blending and sugaring also returned to normal in both Burgundy and Bordeaux. No one there really knew how extensive were those practices – they were just sure that their competitors engaged in them routinely.

SOUR GRAPES?

In 1913, several years before the *appellation* system was codified, Bordeaux merchants, to bolster public confidence in the integrity of their product, agreed to sell no more under Bordeaux labels than they bought, an interesting comment on previous practices. But all that the agreement really meant was that as long as the totals in and out of their cellars balanced, no one asked questions about what went on inside. It was simple for a merchant to buy an inferior lot of what was in normal years a fine wine, decide that it was too poor to retail as it was, blend it with another full-bodied but non-*appellation* wine, perhaps from another region, then sell it under the name of the supposedly better one at a higher price, with the rest of the genuine but mediocre *appellation* wine diverted to the *vin ordinaire* market.[18] When, in the 1920s, top Bordeaux growers themselves began bottling their best-known products, turning over only inferior stuff to merchants to blend, bottle, and sell under other labels, that decision was prompted in part by a desire to protect their reputations should a major blending scandal occur. In 1973 it did.[19]

Pierre Bert was born into the wine trade, inheriting the business from his grandfather and father. The house had fallen into disrepute after World War II when his father was convicted of "economic collaboration," a rather expansively defined offense that served as cover in postwar France to settle a range of scores. When Pierre took over, the firm seemed burdened with both a heavy fine and steady losses. Puzzled, he asked his accountant how they stayed in business. The answer was simple: "*À Bordeaux, tout le monde fraude, et nous faisons comme les autres*" ("In Bordeaux, everyone cheats and we do the same as everyone else"). Growers underreported their harvests; winemakers added *vin de lune* (stuff sugared at night) to their inventory, watered their product, tossed in forbidden additives, and cut good wine with cheaper stuff from supposedly banned American-European hybrid grapes.[20] Duly encouraged, Bert launched a side business of *vin médicin*, a wine rich in alcohol, sugar, acid, or other things to tart up the regular stuff.[21] However he bought so much sugar from one supplier that he was denounced by an informant, drawing a suspended sentence both for oversugaring and for diluting his wine with pond water, and another big fine. That conviction posed a problem when he tried to set up his next, much bigger scam.

By the early 1970s, the wine market had been transformed. The US had displaced Britain as the premier market for fine Bordeaux. The giant auction houses, Christie's and Sotheby's, had begun selling, in addition to old trophy wines, top new vintages. Fine Bordeaux wines were increasingly favoured as a long-term investment, while the futures market attracted short-term speculators. Producers of *grands crus* held tastings two years in advance of bottling for merchants, critics, and connoisseurs (even though it is difficult to predict how a wine still in the barrel will turn out) as a prelude to selling wines for future delivery. They also learned to manipulate the market by selling in tranches, hiking prices with each release. But in 1973 the bottom fell out, and some merchants sought devious ways to hike revenues. One was to play the name game.

Supposedly the distinction between *appellation* and ordinary wines was maintained by a certificate-of-origin system. A load of *appellation* wine was accompanied by a green manifest, the rest by a white one. At destination, a leaf was detached from the manifest and returned by the buyer to the tax office nearest to the seller. The seller also sent its copy to that office. When the two were joined, delivery was deemed complete. However, at that time the paperwork did not indicate a specific *appellation* or whether wine was red or white. So there was no way for the tax office to know if the wine received by the buyer was the same as that sold by the seller.

Furthermore, to reduce the administrative burden, winemakers of good repute could apply to the tax office to rent a franking machine to themselves stamp the official seal on certificates of origin. Given that Bert had a previous conviction, he did not qualify for that honour. So he set up a front company with its own mock producing unit in the name of his chauffeur, then accompanied the chauffeur to the local tax office to vouch for the chauffeur's character and solvency. And he enlisted the prominent merchant house of Cruse et fils, then under pressure from US and Japanese clients to deliver more good Bordeaux. Bert and his confederates bought cheap, ordinary red from the Midi region of France for 270 francs a barrel, drove it to the Cruse warehouse, exchanged it for appellation white worth 350 francs a barrel, sold the appellation white as if it were ordinary white for 294 francs (losing 56 francs per barrel), then used the appellation paperwork to sell the Midi ordinary red for 825 francs, a profit of 555 francs per barrel. In total they sold enough mislabelled wine to fill four million bottles. Since, in conformity with the 1913 Bordeaux agreement, the totals in and out of the Cruse warehouses balanced, and since there had long been a tacit understanding with tax authorities that the big merchant houses would be warned of any pending visits, everyone assumed the system was largely risk-free. Besides, no customer ever complained.[22]

That a disgruntled insider tipped off the authorities would not necessarily have been a major problem, given the quiet understanding between regulator and regulated. However, the race to succeed an ailing French president pitted the minister of Finance, who wanted to grab the spotlight by a public show of cracking down on fiscal fraud, against another cabinet minister who was a close friend of the head of the Cruse firm. The ensuing raids turned up, in addition to the *appellation* paper switch, proof that the Cruse firm had been mixing ordinary and *appellation* wines to sell the blend as high-grade stuff, as well as replacing wine that evaporated from its higher-priced casks with lower-quality material. Topping up casks is necessary to prevent deterioration, but the law required that the replacement be the same wine as the original, certainly not an inferior one that would, after mixing, be sold at a premium price.

Yet, apart from a prison sentence for Bert, there were few penalties, and most were reduced on appeal after the scandal had died down. After all, even Bordeaux at its worst would be hard pressed to rival Italy where, a few years before, one of its largest producers was accused of selling "wine" produced in a few hours from a recipe that included sludge from banana boats, ox blood, tap water, and sugar; while another Italian winemaker a few years later managed to kill nineteen people and blind fifteen more by stiffening its wine with methanol. Parenthetically, both were dwarfed by a 2007 scandal involving 70 million litres of cheap "wine" that was 20 percent grape, the rest sugar, water, chemicals, even fertilizers, with sulphuric and hydrochloric acid tossed in to break the sucrose molecules into fructose and glucose and thereby disguise the sugaring from normal test methods. This time there were no deaths, although one investigator passed out from the fumes in the warehouse. Naturally blame was placed on "the Mafia."[23]

There were also epic scandals in Germany over mislabelling, illegal sugaring, and banned additives. In 1976 inspectors discovered in a warehouse seven million litres of "sparkling hock" composed of Bulgarian wine to which had been added extra alcohol, chemical flavouring, and preservatives, along with water to spread it further. A decade later, 1,800 growers, including the president of the German Winegrowers'

Association, and 200 sugar merchants were found guilty of diverting enough sugar to the wine industry to turn out 260 million bottles. Germany, with its northerly climate, permits only restricted sugaring in ordinary wines, and none in top-of-the-line Qualitätswein mit Prädikat.

This affair produced an unexpected casualty. In addition to sugar, German producers sometimes blended in sweet Austrian wine. But some Austrian winemakers had been artificially sweetening their own product with diethylene glycol, a petroleum derivative used in antifreeze and in brake or hydraulic fluid as well as for making polyester resins. It had the happy effect of softening the tannins, therefore improving the flavour of a poor wine, while helping to hide the fact that a wine has been watered. Nor could it be detected by then-standard tests for adulterants. The culprits were caught only because one tried to reclaim the value-added tax he had paid on the diethylene glycol, sparking suspicions in the local tax inspector's office. The result was a massive recall, along with huge demands by German buyers for reimbursements from Austrian suppliers.[24]

The victims of that scandal actually got off easily: there were no reported deaths. Not so in future uses of diethylene glycol. By the new millennium the industrial solvent could be purchased extremely cheaply in Asia and was soon turning up as a substitute or dilutant for far more expensive glycerin in cough syrup, pain relievers, fever medication, and toothpaste as well as in paint, textiles, tobacco, and various food products, leading to illnesses with possibly dozens of deaths around the world.[25]

LIQUID GOLD

Some practices banned in European countries are legal for New World producers. The leader in setting new standards is California. Although Spanish priests began making sacramental wines there in the eighteenth century, its commercial wine industry was an indirect product of the gold rushes of the 1850s, when a few European fortune-seekers put down roots, their own and those of the vines they imported or hybridized with native varieties. In the early years the wine – poorly aged, watered, sugared, and laced with additives – sold mainly because the whiskey and brandy peddled by San Francisco jobbers were worse. The few decent local wines were sold under imitation French labels, a practice that remained prevalent over the next few decades even as the industry expanded.[26]

Already suffering from bad reputation, then nearly obliterated by an infestation of phylloxera (an aphid-like insect), the US wine business had barely recovered before it took another hit with Prohibition. Covert "whiskey" production flourished. But surviving wineries, rather more conspicuous, had to hide behind the pretext of supplying communion or medicinal wines – albeit for several years they actually expanded their acreage. Others, of course, could easily ferment fruit juices at home. But the quality of black-market "wine" was so bad that the reputation of wine as rotgut persisted in the US for decades.[27] Even today a homeless person on a park bench with a bottle of cheap hooch wrapped in a brown paper bag is dismissed as a "wino." World War II meant further disruption for a nonessential industry. Not until the 1960s, when the US middle class began to develop a taste for wines, did the Napa Valley begin its steep ascent, albeit with the old natural techniques swept away by "professionalization," a flood of agrochemical poisons, and the extension of production onto marginal, often unsuitable terrain.

The rise of wine was probably aided by unionization drives among the poor, largely Mexican workers who picked table grapes. The difference was that table grapes had to be in stores across the country within a few days of ripening, and, since appearance was critical, picking could not at the time be consigned to crude mechanical devices. Because wine grapes gave growers a longer window within which to pick and then crush onsite, workers had less bargaining power and were harder to unionize. Nor was the example of the table grape pickers a consistent incentive. Their early strikes and boycotts, organized by the United Farm Workers, were a great success. But growers fought back, assisted by raiding by the rival Teamsters and by the election of a Republican governor with $1 million of campaign funds from big growers in his coffers, who then began to create legal obstacles to the gains the UFA had won. (A threat to switch from table to wine grapes is apparently still used in California today to ward off unions.[28])

Given a climate (biophysical rather than political) where grapes of almost any type were guaranteed to ripen fully, with the resulting wine aging faster than in Europe, California wine was at the start of the boom torrential in quantity and industrial in quality – in keeping with a rule understood since antiquity that the higher the grape yield, the worse the wine.[29] Yet by the mid-1970s some growers produced wines good enough to embarrass the French in a notorious blind taste-test in Paris.[30] After the results were revealed, some French judges tried to repudiate their own appraisals, while the French industry insisted that the match had been rigged.[31]

What they didn't know was how much of the high quality wines that California was beginning to make were based on smuggling from France. The US imposes a seven-year delay on legally imported vegetable

material to allow for testing. But not many customs officers were likely
to be alarmed at the sight of a few twigs mixed with a traveller's dirty
underwear. Once in California cuttings were cloned to replicate the success of the top French vineyards from which they had been stolen. If the
chickens did not come home to roost, at least the moths did a couple
decades later as a voracious grape-eater found its way in someone's suitcase along with more cuttings.[32] Not to fear – a few doses of nerve gas
(AKA modern high-strength pesticides) ought to do the trick, eventually.

While the French still pay at least lip-service to making a traditional wine based on grapes selected to suit the *terroir*, California has
mainly focused on mass production with state-of-the-art equipment –
although the high-tech stuff kicks in only after Mexican sweated labour
has endured exploitation by human traffickers, the brutality of border
patrols, harassment by immigration agents, backbreaking working conditions, cheating by labour-gang bosses, and inhalation of pesticides to
handpick the grapes. The industry abandoned wooden fermentation
vats in favour of stainless steel and relied on chemical magic to adapt
the wine to consumer tastes homogenised through mass advertising and
huge consumption of mass-produced soft drinks. While in France a wine
legally had to be made up 100 percent of the grapes advertised on the
label, in the US it is only 75 percent, leaving ample scope for unreported
blending that could radically change the taste from year to year unless
corrected for consistency by a longer list of additives than permitted in
Europe. Californian winemakers even modernized the practice of aging
in oak barrels. Normal barrels have a three-year working life. (Old oak
barrels could be sold off as collectibles or used to make trendy furniture,
presumably after the stink of decomposing wine residue had been chemi-
cally eradicated.) But Californians learned first to recondition the interior, then to use impermeable material while achieving an oak flavour
far more cheaply by inserting oak staves, passing oak chains through the
bung hole, or dangling in oak chips in a reusable nylon bag.[33]

Australia closely followed the US model, so much so that Yellow Tail,
a red wine with heavy residual sweetness and a chemical aftertaste, in
some years outsold in the US the total of all imports from France. Its
principal distributor neatly summarized the main reason for its success:
"Case one tasted the same as case one million."[34] Of course, another
reason for the rapid rise of Australia to the rank of fourth largest wine
exporter by volume in the world (a status fading in recent times as
drought, high wages, and consumer overload set in) was the way it was
peddled through classy outlets like British supermarket chains.[35]

As in Bordeaux, where most wines are quite ordinary while a small
fraction are reputedly epicurean marvels, in California, too, the industry

split into basic and high-end wines. However, in California none could command anything like the price of a top-ranked Bordeaux; and unlike Bordeaux, California had high-profile producers who sneered at the notion that expensive wines were so superior. None achieved the notoriety of Fred Franzia, whose enterprises can crush up to 60,000 tons of grapes a day to turn out 62 million gallons of wine a year. After riding out an early scandal in which he paid a $2.5 million fine for selling 5,000 tons of cheap grapes disguised as more expensive by dressing them up with Cabernet Sauvignon and Zinfandel leaves, his Bronco Wineries hit the big time selling via massmarket retailers Two Buck Chuck, a wine made by buying up and blending surplus from across California. "You put something in your mouth and enjoy it," he insisted. "If you spend $100 to buy a bottle of wine, how the hell are you going to enjoy it? ... There's no wine worth that kind of money."[36] Consumers of 400 million bottles (by mid-2009)of Two Buck Chuck seemed to agree – although the seventeen-year-old pregnant Mexican girl who passed out from heat exhaustion on a vineyard Fred Franzia co-owned, then died in the hospital, may not have.[37]

However the true cost of California wines went far beyond their modest price tag. Great tracts of field and forest were uprooted into vineyards. Soil erosion was exacerbated by nutrient exhaustion through continuous cultivation relying on chemical fertilizers, synthetic pesticides, diesel-driven machinery, genetically modified yeasts, and lab-produced enzymes, with sales aided by corporate massmarketing techniques inspired by the soft-drink business. Most notoriously, after methyl bromide, widely used as a soil sterilizer, fumigant, and general pesticide, was proven to be not only carcinogenic and toxic but sixty times worse than chlorine in its effects on the ozone layer, California wine (and strawberry) producers got the Bush regime to muscle the secretariat of the Montréal Protocol, the body that attempts to curb ozone-depleting chemicals, into granting to the state's use of 17 million pounds a year a "Critical Use Exemption." After all, the chemical, present in trace amounts in virtually all California wine, is also effective as rat poison.[38]

Certainly some growers attempt to protect the local ecology, and California certainly boasts wineries (good ones, too) whose products bear "organic" certification.[39] But, once a vineyard hits the big time, it usually carries a heavy burden of debt. That requires it to maintain a predictable cash flow and that in turn depends on constant output – or else resort, as so many Napa wineries have, to pandering to the tourist trade. (Today, Napa is second only to Disneyland as a US tourist destination.) When drought or pests or bank debt charges pose the choice between environmental integrity and possible business survival, there is little doubt about which way most growers will go – in California or in Europe, where EU bureaucratization and economic centralization have produced similar, if still less spectacular, results in terms of environmental degradation.

Today red wines in particular are touted as important for a life that is not just healthy but long, thanks to the magic of resveratrol, a phytoalexin manufactured by some plants to ward off pathogens that is particularly abundant in pinot noir. It is credited in humans with fighting cancer, lowering blood sugar, and combating heart disease. Perhaps; but the medical test results are, as usual, all over the map.[40] However, one thing that seems a lot clearer is the link between growing grapes coated with organochlorine pesticides and the incidence of brain cancer.[41] Even before that link was reasonably established among grape workers in France and Italy came studies of the pesticide residues in corks made from natural materials extracted from cork oaks.[42] Since the cork sits in the bottle sometimes for years, presumably it adds to any pesticide residues already in the wine. Still, there is also good news – ever more of the world's large vineyards are following the lead of big California producers in sealing their wines with extruded foam plastics made from things like metallocene polyolefin plastomer coated with a solid elastomer.[43] That must be quite safe. After all, the industry says it is.

Because US-style wine is heavier and stronger with more powerful flavours than its European competitors, it called forth a new breed of wine advocate. Until the 1980s, English-speaking fans relied on British winosaurs renowned for prose as purple as concord grapes that, when carefully dissected, said little except perhaps to tout wines in which some of the writers had a financial interest. New US critics like Robert Parker claimed greater impartiality and supposedly scientific scoring methods to reflect his philosophy that "Wine is no different from any other consumer product."[44] Parker was repeatedly denounced – by his competitors or by winemakers upset at his opinions – on the grounds that wines were so variable as to render precise numerical scores unreliable and that no one could really claim expertise on so many wines or make proper judgements on sometimes hundreds he claimed to taste in a single day.[45] Anyway, insisted critics of the critic, taste and smell preferences depend on a complex blend of cultural influences, psychological makeup, and personal experience.[46] What they did not add was that, according to one study by French neuroscientists, wine experts can actually be worse at selecting wines than ordinary consumers – they are influenced more by what they see, be it the label or the colour, than by what they taste. For example, the molecule that gives red wine the flavour that winophiliacs describe as currant or raspberry is identical to the one that gives white wine its alleged apricot or peach taste – the description by the taster changes in response to colour alone. More recently a test at CalTech and Stanford University using sophisticated brain-scanning technology verified that the more people paid, the higher their appreciation, even of exactly the same wine. These results, of course, also explain why wine fraud is generally detected not by taste, but by the condition of the bottle, cork, or label, or by a tip-off.[47]

However Parker hit the scene in the early 1980s just when big money was starting to consume more of and invest more in fine wines. It was an era when expansive snobs and expensive wines both started to come of age, a transformation typified by the twenty-five-year-old financial whiz-kid waxing eloquent over the bouquet of a 1945 Mouton-Rothschild or a 1947 Cheval Blanc in a glass he waved under a nose whose septum had been burned out by cocaine. As a result US methods began to infect even Bordeaux production; winemakers found that prices of their futures depended increasingly on the judgement of US critics; and, in response, more wineries began to hire technical consultants to make their products conform more closely to the kind of full-bodied wines that people like Parker favoured. Thus Parker came to appeal powerfully to several classes of interested parties. Consumers trusted him to tell them what to like; emerging producers (and some established ones) wanted him to tell them what to make: mass retailers relied on him to tell them what to stock; speculators in futures depended on him to tell them what to buy; and underground entrepreneurs might use his recommendations to tell them which wines were most propitious to fake.

FUTURE IMPERFECT?

High-end wines fall roughly into two categories. One consists of fine wines in short supply because of the rarity of the right soils and climate conditions, the impact of well-established names in reducing space for upstarts, and decisions by top growers to limit each year's production, then further restrict the amount bottled and sold, leaving them with barrels of prime stuff to drip into the market when financial conditions are ripe. These wines are sold to wealthy consumers via specialist wine merchants or auction houses, or to speculators via wine brokers or wine-investment funds.

The second category consists of old trophy wines, usually available only in single bottles from private sales by collectors or through top auction houses. These are in even shorter supply since, by definition, only counterfeiters continue to make them; and their availability inevitably falls further as some bottles get forgotten in old cellars, others succumb to elements and accidents, and a few may even be consumed by daring individuals. One such was a woman with both a big mortgage that she had trouble paying and a hefty insurance policy on her large collection. So she drank the lot, recorked them, and set fire to her house. Unfortunately the insurance company sent in fraud examiners who discovered that the corks were still in the bottles – if the bottles had been full when the fire occurred, the corks would have been pushed out as the bottles burst.[48]

Although there is a technical distinction, the two types of high-end wines are interrelated: expensive modern vintages evolve over time into trophy wines; trophy wines are sometimes drunk at well-publicized tastings, not just by pyromaniacs getting ready to light the fuse; and auction houses are involved with both. The difference is that, while the commercial appeal of a fine modern wine depends at least partly on its reputation as a consumable, trophy wines sell by the label, not by a taste that will in most cases be execrable, if not fatal. Since some people collect wine labels the way others obsess over classic comic books, auction catalogues pay special attention to the condition of the labels in making sales pitches. The often spectacular results from the auction of trophy wines then feed back to help keep the whole wine market sizzling.[49]

The result is to make high-end modern wines, too, not just a collector's item but a means for stashing wealth out of sight and sound of the tax authorities. Just how extensive is that practice became apparent, at least in France, in the wake of the 2008 crisis when the working class reacted by locking up bosses in their offices and launching huge protest marches through Paris, while the bourgeoisie responded by either pawning or selling off their hordes of *grands crus*.[50]

Although big international auction houses cater mainly to people with big international money who want to acquire top wines on the spot, either to drink or collect, more recently those customers have been joined by others whose motives are more crudely mercenary. They work through investment funds that trade fine wines like stocks or bonds on both spot and forward markets. If the wines actually exist, they might sit untouched in a bonded warehouse as title is bought and sold, safe from indignities like excise, customs, or value-added taxes, or even, for that matter, income and capital-gains taxes. It suffices for the buyer to persuade a revenue authority that wine is a "wasting asset," i.e., constantly depreciating – and for the revenue officer in charge to be too dumb to wonder why, then, the buyer bothered to lay out so much money to acquire it. If the wines do not yet exist, evading taxes is much easier. So, too, is cheating investors.

Originally the wine-futures market consisted simply of top Bordeaux producers, later embracing those of other producing areas, who sold to merchants while wine was still in the cask. For the grower-cum-bottler the advantage was cash in advance; for the merchant-dealer, it was the assurance of inventory at a price hopefully lower than what might prevail later on the spot market. The merchant in turn might resell futures to favoured clients. But by the 1980s, forward selling shifted from being purely a commercial arrangement inside the wine trade to a speculative venture in which outsiders ranging from metropolitan hedge-fund managers to small-town hardware-store owners could participate. Needless to say, the first were more common than the second.

Those lacking time or desire to learn the fine details of wine investment, or to develop inside contacts, might work through a wine broker who, for a commission, could link buyer and seller for either a futures contract or spot delivery. The alternative was to put money into a fund specializing in "blue-chip wines." It, too, could buy both future and spot. The attractions were enormous: from 1982 to 2003 the Fine Wine 50 Index (tracking fifty investment wines) showed a return of 12 percent per annum.[51] Alas, investors occasionally found out that a statistical average based on the past is no guarantee of any particular deal in the present, or of the integrity of any particular dealer.

Among the wine investment companies that left a bitter taste on the palettes of its clients was Rare LLC of Aspen, Colorado. Its founder and director was a go-getter who planted ads in the wine press and sponsored high-profile tastings. After Robert Parker praised the 2000 Bordeaux, Rare LLC collected many millions from clients to buy futures. The company boss claimed that, because of his special relationship with Bordeaux growers (none of whom he actually knew), he could use "early deposit" money to get priority access to the first tranche of the futures even before official release. After clients coughed up, he was forced to divert his attention, and their money, to more pressing needs – payments on his BMW, the cost of remodelling his house, dues at his country club, and bills from a flashy wine-tasting in a Beverley Hills hotel. After pleading guilty to multiple counts of wire and mail fraud, he was sentenced to five years of probation and ordered to pay $11 million in restitution.[52]

Aspen is hardly the world centre for wine trading; London still holds that honour, as it has for centuries. There, each time the market runs up, new wine brokers emerge, perhaps operating behind the screen of companies established in places like Gibraltar. That helps to disguise, among other things, instances where several new brokerage firms are actually run by the same people under different names to give the appearance of active trading. They might sell to the overeager and underinformed fine wines at far more than actual market price, divert a client's money to other uses, or sell "futures" on wine that doesn't exist, knowing they have up to two years before the client starts to demand delivery. From time to time the British Department of Trade and Industry clamps down on shady dealers; but they seem to return quickly under new names. One that is not likely to come back, though, was run by a former director of international wine sales of a major British auction house with money from private investors. It lured several hundred clients into the wine investment business in a pyramid scheme (money from later investors used to pay off earlier ones) that crashed in 2006.[53]

Obviously the distinction between future and spot markets for any particular consignment eventually vanishes – the future becomes the present. When whoever is last in the chain of claims to ownership (some claims are likely held by offshore companies in corporate secrecy havens) takes physical possession, they may find that during the time titles were flying back and forth some enterprising soul got into the warehouse to replace the contents of a wooden case of expensive wines with a dozen or so bottles of Château Plonc de Plonc or just coloured water. After all, there were plenty of precedents on which to draw.

NEW WINE IN OLD BOTTLES?

The division of the high-end market between top modern-vintages and old trophy wines affects counterfeiters, too. On the surface the task with an expensive recent wine does not seem easy. The bottle, perhaps made especially for the particular wine, bears a unique label, sometimes quite elegant and artistic, attesting to the origins and boasting of the attributes of the contents; the cork probably has the name of the chateau and the vintage carved in its side; the top is sealed with a custom-made metal-foil capsule; the bottles are shipped by the chateau in well-marked wooden crates to respectable and knowledgeable wine merchants or to auction houses with their own experts to inspect bottle, capsule, the part of the cork exposed through the glass, ullage (fill level), and label, as well as colour and clarity of the wine. In the event of doubt, the merchant or auction house may even insist on sampling a bottle chosen at random from the allotment, especially if the wine passed through several inter-mediate hands or spent part of its life in a bonded warehouse. All this appears to provide reasonable security. However appearances can be as deceiving as the contents of the bottle.

The first requirement for a fake is a bottle that will pass muster. The best, of course, are genuine, perhaps passed on by waiters from fancy restaurants, then refilled with cheaper (not the same as inferior) wine. While the cork is normally ruined when a bottle is opened, it could be replaced by another from the same chateau, extracted with care from the cheaper wine used to replace the contents, with the vintage shaved off

– its absence may never be noted, especially if the replacement capsule looks real. In the worst case, the old cork can be replaced with a new one bearing an engraving of the name of the chateau and the vintage of the wine being faked. The label can be approximated, provided the paper seems genuine. The case can be simulated by piecing together bits and pieces of genuine ones. And unless the contents are fit only to derust nails, once the wine has been decanted most clients are unlikely to know the difference, or say anything if they suspect for fear of being exposed as bumpkins unable appreciate a rapturous experience. Even experts can be fooled by a judicious blend of cheaper stuff that follows a formula that probably most knowledgeable wine merchants could provide.

There are many subvariants. For example, a fraudster can decide to enjoy both the top vintage and the income from selling it by extracting the contents of the bottle with a hypodermic needle, toasting the future sale, then refilling the bottle in whole or in part with a cheap substitute. Or the cork can be pulled with a tool that leaves along two sides only very slight groves that can be hidden by a good facsimile of the original capsule.

How large a fake lot needs to be depends on how expensive is the wine. For example, as the so-called Asian Economic Miracle drove tens of millions into dire poverty, plundered scarce natural resources, and turned huge areas into environmental wastelands, it added many thousands to the ranks of the world's super rich, ready to get hooked on fine wine, or at least on fine wine prices. In 2005, during the resulting fraud wave, cops in Guangzhou raided a shop run by ex-wine workers and found, along with a state-of-the-art label-making machine, thirty bottles of 1982 Lafite Rothschild, some types of which sell for up to $15,000 each. The bottles were real, recycled from expensive restaurants; but the contents were 1991 $97.00 Bordeaux, fine wine in its own right that was good enough to satisfy the vast majority of imbibers. The giveaway was the sale through confederates in a local wine-store of too many bottles of a very rare wine at too low a price.[54] However that did not seem to cool Asian ardour – wealthy Chinese continued to invest in wines at such a rate that by 2010 Hong Kong threatened to beat London for high-end auctions.[55]

Less conspicuous, and therefore more successful, is the racket with ice wines. Originating in Germany but today dominated by Canada, which almost alone among grape-growing countries has a sufficiently miserable climate to guarantee the results, ice wines are made from grapes frozen on the vine and picked at minus eight Celsius. They are expensive because the juice yield of vine-frozen grapes is about 10 percent of normal. That does not deter Chinese imitators who sugar ordinary white wine or even add alcohol to imported grape juice, invent labels that crudely depict "Canadian" winter scenes replete with geographic and orthographic errors, and put them on recycled or fake bottles for sale across Southeast Asia, enough, reputedly, to drive some Canadian producers out of the market.[56]

On the other side of the world, for some European producers, faking wine may be not so much a matter of profiteering as simply trying to survive. In recent years the European market has been glutted, partly because gross overuse of dangerous chemicals has obviated the old claims about wine being a health food and caused consumer revulsion, partly because progress of so-called free trade has permitted Californian and Australian mass-produced wine to flood into Europe, and partly because of overproduction encouraged by agricultural subsidies. As a result Europe's "wine lake" continues to expand even as governments subsidize its distillation into ethanol for biofuels. Since the market for higher-priced wine has remained stronger than for ordinary, the smart thing for a producer of a more banal wine is to dress it up with fake labels.

The year 2006 was particularly notorious for the Italian industry. One police raid netted twenty thousand bottles of counterfeit Sassicaia, modestly regarded by its producers as Italy's greatest wine. The fake stuff had been made with cheaper cabernet and Montepulciano d'Abruzza and poured into bottles that successfully copied the genuine ones, had labels with watermarked paper and an excellent replica of the capsule. They were then sold out of the trunk of the manufacturer's car. This occurred only one month after the anti-fraud unit unearthed fifteen thousand counterfeit Falaghinas. During that same year a Tuscan winemaker who had five hundred acres of which only sixty-five were classified as suitable for Chianti Classico, blended all of his production under that label, selling it to prominent bottlers. The result was a police investigation and confiscation of half a million bottles.[57] But the real sensation came from the Brunellogate affair.

Brunello di Montalcino is one of only twenty-four wines to receive top standing of Denominazione di origine controllata e garantita under Italy's classification system based, like that of France, on geographic origin with limits on production.[58] The wine, supposedly made from 100 percent Sangiovese grape produced in a small valley in Tuscany, is described by the regional regulatory body, the Consorzio del Vino Brunello di Montalcino, in prose much richer than the product itself, as "a visibly limpid, brilliant wine, with a bright garnet colour. It has an intense perfume, persistent, ample and ethereal. One can recognize scents of undergrowth, aromatic wood, berries, light vanilla and jam..." Over the course of the early twenty-first century, demand for the normally thin almost astringent wine exploded, particularly in the US, despite its Parkerized taste for thick, sticky stuff. Yet the very restricted producing area in Italy was able to keep up. That led to the Financial Guard's Operazione Mixed Wine investigation of seven wineries, the outcome of which was 6.7 million litres of Brunello di Montalcino impounded, of which 20 percent was reduced in classification, along with 1.7 million litres of Rosso di Montalcino, Chianti Classico, and Toscana Rossa, of which 40 percent was downgraded, while about 100,000 litres were just shipped off to be distilled. Yet, some asked, how else could the big wineries hope to pander to American and Americanized tastes. Anyway, what was the fuss? Everyone knew that the game of blending tart Sangiovese wine with sweeter ones from Merlot, Syrah, and Montepulciano grape was standard practice even for the Italian market.[59]

Of course, not all mass fakery occurs at the high end, and it may take place without the bottler knowing. E&J Gallo, for example, California's biggest family-owned producer, seemed to hit a series of homeruns when it introduced its pinot noir line in 2003, neatly coinciding with the opening the next year of the hit movie *Sideways*, in which pinot noir played a co-starring role. While there are plenty of California growers of the temperamental grape, Gallo began sourcing from the Languedoc region of France more than 3.5 million gallons, enough to fill 16 million bottles. Yet Languedoc had never managed to produce anything like that amount. Then an audit by the French financial police showed that one of the suppliers had been invoicing its pinot noir exports to Gallo at about two-thirds the regular price. The result was the indictment and conviction of several wineries, co-ops, and wine merchants for cutting their pinot noir with cheaper merlot and syrah. But the story got more complicated. In the US, it is permissible to sell a wine that is up to 25 percent blended with other grapes without informing the retail client. Although when Gallo introduced its "pinot noir," it was originally 100 percent from that grape, by the time of the scandal it had already cut that proportion in its "world acclaimed" wine to 85 percent, even as its popularity soared and winosaurs roared approval. Now came the discovery that the French suppliers, in response to a demand for a price cut, had themselves already preblended the wine that Gallo reblended. Could the final product then have been under the 75 percent lower limit of the US? On the other hand, as the French suppliers noted in their defense, no customer complained.[60]

The really spectacular counterfeiting cases, in terms of price per bottle, not total take, occur at the commercial rather than production level and focus on high-end or trophy wines. Some merchants or even primary producers make the counterfeiting job easier by reconditioning bottles. Over time the cork shrinks causing some wine to evaporate; and humidity makes the label fade. Yet today's wine collector may want the bottle to look perfect. So, at client request, the chateau or a licensed merchant would top it up, in theory with more of the same fine wine (although in practice no one can be sure), affix spiffy new labels, and replace old corks with new ones that bear the date of the original vintage, a disconnect that would attract suspicion if not accompanied by reassurance from the house doing the reconditioning.[61] The practice was supposed to have stopped some time ago. But no one apparently informed a Belgian specialist in old wines who, in 1999, bought some 1995 Lafite and Margaux wine, using it to recondition several hundred bottles of 1900 vintages produced by the same houses. He sold four hundred of them to fancy restaurants, many more via London auction houses, claiming that the wines had been reconditioned by Barton & Guestier with the agreement of the producing chateaux themselves, along with fake certificates of reconditioning, for an average price of €3,200 per bottle. The trick was exposed by applying a test that measures radioactive cesium in the wine – prior to 1945, the advent of the atomic age, that level would have been zero.

No one has a clue whether there is a veritable tsunami of fraud or merely an occasional undesirable bit of coloured froth on top of a boiling market. Although some wine experts insist fraud to be of epidemic proportions, their opinion needs be nuanced by the fact that repeatedly shouting "fire!" helps ensure that the person with the hose never lacks for someplace remunerative to spray it. Still, rumours grew intense enough to prompt in 2007 news of a big joint FBI-Scotland Yard investigation complete with subpoenas of wine sellers, major collectors, and auction houses suspected of peddling counterfeits. Christie's, of course, publicly welcomed the investigation as good for customer confidence.[62]

The response from the industry is the same kind of race to stay ahead of counterfeiters that governments run to protect their bank notes. Château Le Pin (a tiny Bordeaux plot working out of a garage to make California-style wines at grand Bordeaux prices) began printing its labels on currency paper. Château Pétrus started to emboss its name on the bottom of bottles and printing on its labels random line patterns only visible under a UV scanner. Château d'Yquem uses paper with watermarks. Producers in Rioja reacted to discovery of a million fakes produced at an industrial bottling plant three hundred miles south of the wine-growing region by attaching strips of metallized refractive paper to labels. Ciacci Piccolomini d'Aragona di Bianchini of Tuscany grafts holograms into the capsule and has experimented with microchips embedded in the label that can be read with an optical scanner. Some vintners number their bottles, and the pricier ones in California ask that the numbers be quoted at auctions. After two major scandals, Penfolds of Australia began laser-etching name and vintage into its bottles, along with an alphanumeric code. In 1998 BRL Hardy, Australia's supervintner, began placing on its Eileen Hardy Shiraz labels the genetic imprint of cuttings from the grapevines. Yet others speak of a future with thermochromatic inks and latent-image technology. Particle accelerators can direct ion beams at glass to determine the origin and age of glass. And in 2004, after the Rioja scandal, Spanish scientists unveiled a technique to use atomic spectrometry to measure sixteen trace elements in a wine, then compare the results to the fingerprint of other wines.[63] Most of these are expensive, and all can be beaten. However, as with bank notes, the real purpose is not to defeat a truly determined faker, but to raise the cost of mimicking label, cork, bottle, and contents to scare off the amateur. Yet perhaps London's Corney & Barrow, wine merchants who also run a string of wine bars, discovered a much simpler and more effective policy to stop their clients from being taken: they refuse to buy anything from an auction house, the Far East, or the US.[64]

LIQUIDITY CRISIS

No form of high-tech wizardry applied to deter faking of limited-edition modern can work for old trophy wines. But here the challenge is already considerable. Modern wine is immersed in a much larger flow of product with many wines that are at least reasonable facsimiles of each other; the materials are far more accessible; the wine (and therefore the evidence) is likely to be drunk fairly quickly; and, provided the contents are less than lethal, few will notice after a wine has been decanted. But someone intent on faking trophy wines has to reproduce the appearance of very old materials and face the suspicion that automatically results when yet another bottle emerges from some bankrupt nobleman's rotting cellar. On the other side, a trophy wine is less likely to be drunk at all, simply admired. If it is consumed, there is some cover in the fact that growers only started keeping good vintage records relatively recently. (Old catalogues of wine merchants can confirm a wine's existence but give no information about total production.) In addition, wines made decades, let alone centuries, ago varied much more from barrel to barrel and therefore potentially from bottle to bottle than new ones. Furthermore a single bottle can sell for an astronomical sum, then get easily lost in the collector circuit, sold privately from hand to hand, perhaps occasionally for cash, making tracing back to source very difficult – particularly since the first instinct of collectors who realize they have been stung is probably much like merchants who get stiffed with counterfeit money or dealers with fake art: let the next sucker beware.

The main challenge in faking a trophy wine is the bottle. Often something suitable can be found in an antique store – properly selected it could survive a particle accelerator test. Or it may be reproduced, a difficult (but not impossible) task given that old bottles were probably handblown (showing bubbles) or constructed with distinct seams, and each will be slightly different. However variation also increases the difficulty of determining if a bottle is wrong for the vintage. The older (and more precious) the wine, the greater the problem. Corks, of course, degrade; but most trophy wines have been reconditioned, perhaps several times. It does not take a genius to realize that an old wine ought to show a noticeably low ullage, or to know enough to tint the wine toward the brown end of the spectrum, something that happens naturally as wines age. Adding a few visible impurities helps, too. While reproductions of the label are easy to find in books or simply bought off eBay, the paper and ink have to be appropriately aged to show humidity damage. And there has to be credible provenance – i.e., who found the wine, when, where, and how?[65]

The response to the threat of fakery depends on the level of the wine trade involved. An auction house or high-end merchant (assuming they are not complicit) will fear the reputation loss from selling freshly brewed grand cru de Fresh Kills Landfill in an antique Lafitte bottle; and some collectors who deal back and forth, directly or via auction houses, like to sue each other publicly over egregious blows to their inflated egos.

Among the most successful of those collector-dealers is Germany's Hardy Rodenstock. Not only does he have a worldwide reputation for uncovering classics others could only dream about, but he periodically stages tastings of wines sometimes dating back to the late eighteenth century to which he invites world-renowned critics. The resulting publicity helps to sell others of similar type at auction for record prices. So it was when via Christie's Rodenstock sold to US publisher Malcolm Forbes for $157,000 an old Bordeaux bearing the initials "Th.J." – for Thomas Jefferson, known for his passion for fine French wine. The bottle came from a cache reputedly found in a boarded-up Paris cellar by an anonymous English collector. A year later US billionaire William Koch acquired from a dealer in Chicago four bottles from the same group of wines for $311,000. But when Koch tried to put the bottles on display in the Boston Museum of Fine Art, along with his Monet, Degas, and Dalí art, his Greco-Roman and American West artifacts, and his America's Cup-winning yacht, the museum asked for proof of origin. After the

Thomas Jefferson Foundation reported its doubts, Koch set off on a transatlantic forensic search in a perfect storm of accusations and counteraccusations. In explaining why he had spent more than double the price he paid for the wine in a so-far futile attempt to prove Rodenstock had defrauded him, Koch stated elegantly: "If someone robs you of ... bragging rights, you get pissed off."[66] His temper was further tested when his forensic team casts similar doubts on other prize items in his modest 35,000 bottle collection, leading to a barrage of lawsuits and countersuits. One was, ironically enough, against a wine-dealing corporation in Chicago in which Koch used to be a major investor. Another, though, was against Koch himself when the auctioneer who wrote the sales literature for Christie's successfully sued publisher Random House for libel after it repeated Koch's claims.[67]

Clearly others do not share Koch's skepticism about the origins of the Th.J. bottles, or about the quality of the contents. In fact some guests at a Rodenstock tasting rhapsodized that a 1787 Château d'Yquem from the Jefferson stash had "autumnal aromas of burnt sugar and undergrowth," while another insisted that the oldest (1784) of wines sampled at the event stood out "strange as it seemed, for youthfulness."[68]

While wine-merchants, auction houses, and collectors stand to lose from trophy-wine fakery, or just from stories that it is rampant, others pretend to be unaffected. The director of Château d'Yquem brushed off concerns with the words: "Fakes do not concern the chateau, they concern exchanges between collectors."[69] However the public indifference of elite Bordeaux growers probably hides a private delight. The only way a buyer can be sure is to purchase directly from the original winemaker whose inventory of old treasures increases in value with each major scare.[70] After all, surely a bottle coming from a famous old cellar must be beyond suspicion?

A GAS-TRAUMATIC EXPERIENCE?

Probably the wine most susceptible to fraud is the one most closely associated with conspicuous luxury, even if winophiles turn up their noses at its very name. So, for centuries, did ordinary consumers. The Champagne region was sufficiently far north that the weather often prevented grapes from ripening properly and/or stopped fermentation prematurely. But sometimes, after the wine was already bottled, the warmth of spring reactivated the yeast to fill a bottle with carbon dioxide. Commercializing that process required turning the bottle upside down to keep the gas in place, extracting the cork, then quickly drawing off a sludge of impurities, grape residues and dead yeast without losing too much wine. This was later simplified by freezing the neck so that the crud came out fast in one lump. After that, the wine master would top up the bottle before replacing the cork, perhaps adding some fresh yeast and sugar to restart fermentation.

The story that bubbly white wine was created by frère Dom Pérignon in a Champagne abbey persists, probably because it is so useful for marketing the Moët & Chandon stuff that proudly bears his name. An alternative, less glorious theory suggests that champagne as a distinct trade category was created in London in the seventeenth century when poor-quality wine imported in casks was bottled with added sugar precisely to encourage it to ferment again. Unlike other wines, champagne was from the start a product more of industry than of nature. Merchants struggling to give it sufficient fizz added things like alum and pigeon dung, then had to use especially strong bottles with reinforced corks to avoid premature explosions that could devastate an entire cellar and potentially blind the workers – who took to wearing iron masks. Since the special bottles and corks cost more than the wine itself, from early times they would be collected for reuse, a common practice today for counterfeiters.

Champagne differs in another regard. It is ineluctably associated with celebration; for example, when Mexico's President Carlos Salinas, overseer of one of Mexico's greatest binges of privatization of state assets (from which his brother was reputed to demand 10 percent kickbacks), got together with close friends on New Year's night of 1994 to put away several bottles of Dom Perignon just before receiving a phone call from the army telling them that an anti-capitalist insurgency had broken out in Chiapas State.[71] Particular brands of wines are subject to fad and fashion – Château Pétrus, for example, was known only to an inner circle of winophiliacs until the Kennedy family began to consume it ostentatiously in the 1960s. But champagne as a generic category, almost regardless of brand, is prone to destabilizing shifts of demand, increasing the temptation to pour fake champagne into imitation or recycled bottles when the market gets hot. Since image is the central selling point, most consumers of champagne, even more so than with other wines, have no real idea what to expect after the cork flies across the room to poke out their brother-in-law's eye and they raise their glass in appreciation.[72]

Today, outside of the Champagne region (and probably at more than a few hidden places inside it), the wine is likely fermented in a stainless-steel tank, filtered and bottled under pressure to await refermentation, or perhaps not refermented at all but simply injected with gas by a manufacturer who, in the near future, might be able to collect carbon credits for his effort. The process is undetectable – few wine experts, whatever their other accomplishments, have much luck differentiating genuine champagnes made in France in traditional ways from industrially produced sparkling wines from other countries. However, occasionally someone does catch on, as two defendants in a French champagne scandal found out in 1992.

The project was the brainchild a trained oenologist who was owner of a champagne dealership in Paris and a director of a marketing company. In 1989 they got permission from the Cuban government to bottle wine in a rum factory as long as the product was exported and a cut of the profits went to the Cuban enterprise. With money from France's official farm-loan agency, they bought – through the screen of shell companies – industrial wine coolers, compressors, and, not least, a laser-marking machine identical to the one used by Moët & Chandon. They arranged to export in bulk an Anjou blanc des blancs to Cuba, where it was artificially carbonized in the rum factory and put into bottles identical to the ones for Dom Pérignon. They affixed labels precision-made in South Africa, right down to the identification numbers, invisible to the naked eye, that Moët & Chandon uses to try to stop fraud. Then they sent the "champagne" to a Panama company. From there perhaps as much as 120,000 bottles were sold to American or European distributors. Everything went well until a German dealer claimed that he smelled the champagne and realized it was made from the wrong grape, a story that enhanced his professional reputation while probably covering up for an inside informant.[73]

This was not South Africa's only foray into fake bubbly. One of its major wine co-ops found a way to, first, beat economic sanctions imposed on South Africa during the 1980s, then, in the 1990s, to raise the price of a local product that was almost unknown outside the country. It obtained 250,000 premier-grade bottles from one of France's major manufacturers, filled them with sparkling South African wines, then stuck on false labels bearing French codes. The label designs were personally approved by the co-op's managing director in a memo that instructed the production team to "Remember South Africa must not appear anywhere on any of the packaging materials and neither must the name of the providers."[74]

However, Britain seems to be the real epicentre of champagne fraud. There as the millennium approached, three con artists – with experience peddling high-risk stocks, rare gold coins, and futures on whiskey still in the (empty) barrel – built on false rumours already circulating in the press about a huge shortfall in champagne supply for the pending celebrations ("the biggest party for a thousand years is about to run out of fizz") to bilk British investors into paying £30 per bottle for champagne available in their corner off-license for about £12 a hit. They collected about £4.5 million to support their tastes in fancy cars and luxury apartments.[75] Another British gang did the opposite: it bought cheap French white, steamed off the labels, replaced them with home laser-printer forgeries resembling those of Moët & Chandon and Bollinger, and sold over 100,000 bottles for £5 pounds a bottle (the real stuff could fetch as much as £50), sometimes from the backs of vans at filling stations.[76] In 2002, police raids on the home and factory of a Yorkshire manufacturer yielded thousands of bottles of Spanish sparkling wine relabelled champagne. He was sentenced to eighteen months and ordered to pay £2.3 million. After his release, an unsuccessful foray into currency counterfeiting led to him absconding to Ireland with his fine unpaid.[77]

None of these episodes seems to have much dampened consumer zeal for bubbly white wine with "champagne" on the label. That is why France has put so much diplomatic effort into securing international agreements to protect the name – while corrupting the original concept behind it. Demand had been growing so rapidly that in 2008 France's *Institut national des appellations d'origine* agreed to expand the Champagne growing-region by admitting 40 more communities to its existing 370, not because of soil or climate conditions in the newcomers but because of a commercial supply shortfall. This certainly delighted landowners in the newly designated districts, whose property at a stroke rose in value from about $3,000 to perhaps $1.5 million per hectare.[78]

Granted, the delight of the new French "champagne" producers may have been short-lived, as the economic crisis combined with more competition from foreign sparkling whites led in 2009 to a 30 percent drop in sales for the regal wine, forcing, contrary to one of the central principles of the luxury trade, many of the producers to slash prices.[79] But the market will no doubt recover. And the shift in producing capacity will be permanent.

On the surface this seems like the ultimate debasement of the concept of *terroir*. But perhaps the French had just woken up to the wisdom of Fred Franzia, creator of California's Two Buck Chuck. After he got an appeals court to strike down a law that prevented him from using the word "Napa" on wines when not a single grape had been grown in that valley, he dismissed *terroir* with the words: "Does anybody complicate Cheerios by saying the wheat has to be grown on the side of a mountain and the terroir in North Dakota is better than Kansas and all this horse shit?"[80] Perhaps not with Cheerios. But they certainly do with cigar tobacco; and "horse shit" is exactly the stuff in which the best is grown.

8

Puff Artists: Behind the Smokescreen
of High-End Cigars

Centuries before Cristóbal Colón (slightly misspelled in its English trans-
lation) discovered the Americas, much to the surprise of up to a hundred million people already living there, aboriginals smoked tobacco,
ironically enough, for medicinal purposes. They appreciated it, too, for
its ability to induce hallucinations. Their respect for the plant's powers
led natives in what is now the Bahamas to offer a gift of dried tobacco
to their Spanish visitors, who reciprocated by enslaving or murdering
them all.

Probably the gift was unnecessary. For in the hallucinations department, Christopher Columbus hardly needed help. Sailing under the cut-
ting-edge geophysical theory that gold was engendered in hot climates
and silver in cold, once he made landfall in Cuba, he was convinced
he had reached the mainland of China. Perhaps more propitiously, it
was in Cuba that his men finally figured out that the tobacco they had
received was to be smoked. The world tobacco wars – pipes versus snuff
versus cigars versus cud versus cigarettes, black versus "blonde" leaf,
artisanal producers versus factories, hand rollers versus machine operators, national versus transnational companies, revenue agents versus
smugglers, public-health zealots versus hardcore users, massmarketeers
versus snobs, and, not least, the mighty USA versus a small but defiant
island in its self-proclaimed backyard – were launched, with puff artists
preening and fakers cashing in on the pretense surrounding high-end
cigars at every level.

CIGAR ENVY

The tobacco habit was quickly picked up by Spanish and Portuguese sailors, passed to mariners of other countries, and spread through Europe.
Although in England from the start it was viewed largely as a vice, on the

continent tobacco was more often lauded as a cure for asthma, coughs, headaches, stomach disorders, gout, and much more. The list of medical miracles ascribed by physicians to the leaf – it probably did beat leeches – grew in tandem with the increasingly strident attacks by early versions of today's antismoking crusaders.[1] After the Spanish realized the superior qualities of tobacco grown in the unique climate and soil of Pinar del Río province in northwestern Cuba, they freed the area of otherwise mandatory sugar cultivation, banned local processing in favour of exporting all leaf back to Spain, and made tobacco a royal monopoly. Back then, smuggling tobacco was likely a faster route to a death sentence than smoking it.[2] But, of course, even in relatively wealthy England, life expectancy at the time the tobacco craze began was perhaps thirty-five to forty years, probably not long enough for lung cancer to show up.

As tobacco began to become popular in Europe, it had plenty of detractors, at least among the polite classes. (Given their living conditions, it is doubtful if commoners got too excited about this new insult to their olfactory sensitivities.) King James I of England so detested the stuff that he tried to impose prohibitive levels of taxation, only to be defeated, first by inveterate smokers in Parliament, second by an explosion of smuggling. To the pro-tobacco forces were soon added advocates for England's new Virginia colony. It had shifted its economic base to tobacco cultivation after its dreams of digging for gold collapsed – and it could no longer rely on charity from the aboriginals whose land it was stealing at gunpoint to keep the colony from mass starvation. In any case, the upper crust back home managed to ease royalist opposition to their new habit by shelving their pipes in favour of snuff boxes.

As would happen so often in the future, the military seems to have taken a leading role in spreading tobacco use. Soldiers on all sides in the brutal Thirty Years War that ravaged central Europe in the first half of the seventeenth century gloried in their pipes full of "Indian weed," civilians (females as well as males) soon following suit. Governments of consuming countries, too, soon shared the growing addiction, in their case to the taxes tobacco yielded, provided a government could actually enforce them.

In England efforts to collect customs and excise taxes galvanized the Owlers, a popular name for professional smugglers because of the nocturnal nature of their activities. First emerging in the fourteenth century when England, in an effort to stimulate wool manufacturing at home, heavily taxed the export of raw wool to the Continent, the Owlers, often well armed and well connected, by the seventeenth century had diversified from smuggling wool out to running tobacco (along with tea and brandy) back in. Far from some mysterious, hierarchically controlled

"Mafia," they were a diverse set of small, local gangs who could rely on the discretion of kith and kin or on their ability to ferret out informants and outshoot nosy outsiders, whether representing the Crown or the competition, to ensure that their business remained prosperous.

TEA FOR WHO?

Tobacco was not their sole endeavour. The spread of tobacco was intimately associated with the development of tastes for another exotic and highly taxed drug. Initially England, in its search for a non-alcoholic buzz, favoured chocolate or coffee. But by the mid-seventeenth century, the English coffee house, where much business as well as political debate was conducted, became almost as thick with the fragrance of tea as with the stink of tobacco smoke. Both might have been smuggled into the country, in defiance of heavy excise taxes and, in the case of tea, a legal monopoly held by the British East India Company, by the same gangs using the same boats under the watchful eye of the same crooked customs officers. As late as the mid-eighteenth century, even after the revenue service had been professionalized, the prevailing guesstimate was that about a third of the tobacco consumed in Britain was smuggled. However, that fiscal embarrassment may have been not just equalled but exceeded by tea. With tea duties at a flat rate of 5 shillings per pound, legal tea was effectively priced beyond the range of most people and relegated to a bourgeois and aristocratic privilege, even though those classes, too, were quite prepared to sip contraband. But, in addition, tea was sold extensively in coffee shops that were required to pay a business tax on top of import duties. By the end of the eighteenth century, when seriously armed ships had replaced small boats in running contraband, estimates of the underground import of tea ranged up to two-thirds of total consumption. Smugglers offloaded to smaller craft close to shore; local fishermen unloaded tea cargoes and moved them inland; farmers would hide the stuff in barns and haystacks, and clergymen would store tea in Church crypts and tombs. Although the rival Dutch East India Company was the ultimate source of most of the contraband, even British East India Company captains joined the fun, offloading contraband stuff to smuggling boats before the ships headed on to legal ports to dutifully report the rest of their cargo. Loads impounded by customs might disappear again, either because the smugglers broke into the customs houses or because the officers themselves released the cargo after a little informal import duty was paid. Meanwhile tea shops would evade business taxes by ensuring that their tea bins were refilled with lookalike substances before government inspectors arrived.[3]

In desperation the British Parliament legislated a series of tax cuts, one of which sparked the Boston Tea Party. Although the news always comes as a shock to patriotic Americans, that event was not a revolt against higher taxes on tea but against a massive tax cut that would have put New England merchants, their warehouses stuffed full of contraband, out of business, and therefore been a benefit to ordinary consumers of tea, exactly the class present-day Tea Party types claim to represent. But then, "no tax cuts without representation" is hardly the kind of slogan on which a new country's ideological legitimization could be based.[4]

It was not until the final of the series of tax cuts, in 1784, accompanied by the requirement that the East India Company increase its imports sufficiently to satisfy lower- as well as upper-class demand that the British managed to make a serious dent in tea smuggling – and so lowered the landed price that tea became legally available to all. The East India Company responded by smuggling more opium into China to finance its extra tea purchases; so apparently everyone was happy, except the Chinese – who didn't count in the felicific calculus of the universal benefits of free trade. Anyway back home the main problem had switched to adulteration. A rough official estimate of the amount of "tea" that was really made up of leaves of other plants, some of them poisonous, artificially coloured with things like iron sulphate boiled with sheep's dung, gravel, clay, and, best of all, used leaves, tossed in to increase the weight, put the total at again close to two thirds of legal imports – although that could be just an example of some official recycling a predecessor's wild guess. In what might have been an omen, the same tax-leery entrepreneurs were also capable of producing fake tobacco made from things like safflower and potash, then pressed and dried, neatly combining the vocations of consumer-goods counterfeiter and tax evader in a way worthy of study in any modern business school.[5]

SMOKING OUT TAX EVADERS?

The British were not alone in having official revenues compromised by people in the "quick freight" business. And, once tea duties had been drastically cut, tobacco quickly returned to the top of the list in terms of import tax yields – and their evasion. Since the Spanish, British, and French got an early lock on tobacco plantations in the Caribbean, the Portuguese turned to Brazil. All of its product was to go to special customs warehouses in major ports, supervised by the state tobacco monopoly. Yet ships returning to Portugal, much like those carrying gold and diamonds, might have unreported tobacco hidden in their holds to be offloaded at night, or even during the day when a hefty dose of cash or grog had put revenue agents to sleep. Some consignments, too, were sold while still at sea; others were duly landed and marked for re-export, hence not subject to import duty, then sent to Spanish ports to be promptly diverted back into Portugal. Contraband raw material, though, still had to be processed before it could be sold. Part of that job fell to members of Portugal's ever-enterprising clergy. Royal officials were hesitant to incur the wrath of the Vatican by violating the sanctity of monasteries and convents where snuff was manufactured and pipe tobacco prepared from contraband raw material.[6]

Although cigars (another aboriginal invention) showed up in Spain in the sixteenth century, for a long time they remained rare elsewhere. A preference for cigars over pipes reputedly began to spread to Britain early in the nineteenth century, when soldiers returned from the Iberian campaign of the Napoleonic Wars. During those wars, too, a temporary easing of Spanish control permitted the first large-scale cigar-rolling operations to open in Cuba. By the 1820s, Havana, with about four hundred rolling shops, was already the cigar capital of the world. Ironically, in light of its current status, the Cuban cigar was originally a democratizing force: not only did it make smoking-then-coughing rather than sniffing-then-sneezing respectable again among the upper reaches of society, but it also began to replace the pipe among lower orders – with one difference.[7] By the mid-nineteenth century, when the pipe was relegated to the working class, female smoking went into sharp decline, at least in public in the major urban centres. But with the new male zeal for cigars, most of Europe developed a rolling industry, relying mainly on raw material from the Americas. Hundreds of little cigar-making establishments produced their own informal brands although the elites of Britain and the US still preferred Cuban-rolled. By the time of the railroad age, cigars had become so popular among some (and so loathed by others) that special smoking cars were introduced. Then came another revolution.

One legend places the origin of the cigarette in Spain, when its burgeoning population of beggars started to pick up discarded cigar butts and empty the residue into scraps of paper – at that time made from old cloth rather than from wood pulp. Certainly a roll-your-own cigarette was a far cheaper way to get a nicotine hit than a cigar turned out in a handicraft shop. The tobacco habit spread much further during the American Civil War, probably the first time a government appreciated the virtues of nicotine in keeping soldiers alert and wired while hungry and tired. But the ration handed out on both sides took the form of chewing tobacco. Commercial cigarettes were still relatively expensive and regarded as effeminate. After the Civil War, though, more factories began turning out cigarettes rolled by manual labour. And distinct class lines began to take shape: roll-your-own cigarettes for the Great-Unwashed; factory-made cigarettes for the urban middle class; artisanal hand-rolled cigars for gentlemen quite conscious of their phallic connotations. Then in the early 1880s came another dramatic transformation – the invention of a machine to mass produce cigarettes at a time when cheap wood pulp was replacing rags in paper production. These twin developments allowed tremendous cost savings and led to the concentration of economic power in the hands of two large tobacco trusts, one American and one British, each supreme in its own turf while dividing up the rest of the world between them.

The next important step in the cigarette's march to victory came in 1914–18. During what was then the greatest military mobilization in history, governments competed to buy stocks of tobacco and to distribute cigarettes among the troops. Those soldiers returned home (if they actually did) hooked, albeit some probably found that their new infatuation with the weed was terminated rather quickly by its effects on lungs already damaged by chlorine and mustard gas. Yet even as cigarette consumption took that new leap forward, for the discriminating smoker, the business tycoon touting his own success, or the inveterate snob, Cuban tobacco hand-rolled into cigars retained its reputation.

THE SMOKE RING

Botanical considerations aside, tobacco was very different from sugar, the other major Cuban crop. Sugar was grown on great plantations using, until 1880, slave labour, then processed with heavy machinery. Slave revolts were few and viciously suppressed. By contrast, most Cuban tobacco farmers were small holders who used few slaves; and raw tobacco required skilled labour (almost always by free or freed workers) to turn it into a valuable commodity. While sugar had been kept under the imperial thumb, tobacco planters, along with processors, played a leading role in resistance against Spanish taxes and trade controls from as far back as the early eighteenth century. In the early nineteenth, tobacco workers began to form craft associations to fight wage cuts by owners, establishing a tradition of labour militancy that persisted right up to the 1959 Revolution.

Over the nineteenth century, Spain's economic power in Cuba waned while US influence grew. That shift stamped its imprint on the tobacco business. By the 1830s a small colony of Cuban cigar makers had taken root in Key West, until then just a sand bar surrounded by mangrove, but well located to give manufacturers access to both Cuban leaf and the

US market while freeing them of Spanish taxes and growing labour militancy back home. As so often in the future, tax evasion and union-busting explained more about the dynamics of production than any ideological cant about "consumer preferences" found in economics textbooks. Each subsequent time the US raised duties on foreign manufactured goods, its tobacco companies imported more Cuban leaf and fewer cigars, while more Cuban cigar makers shifted location to the US. Meanwhile, back in Cuba, tobacco planters who freed their slaves took a central role in the Ten Years War (1868–78) against Spain. Although Spanish rule survived the uprising, everyone knew the end was nigh. And Cuban revolutionaries began to openly solicit among émigré tobacco workers in Florida financial contributions toward the next struggle.[8]

During the 1898 revolution, the tobacco sector paid a heavy price, its farms ravaged by curtailment of credit and by imperial reprisals, and its factories drained by recruitment of workers into rebel ranks. When the US took advantage of the struggle to launch the Spanish-American War, gobbling up Cuba along with the Philippines and Puerto Rico, Spain reacted by declaring Cuban tobacco of foreign origin, doubling the tariff level it faced. The US victory permitted emerging US producers to buy up, merge, and shut down Cuban factories, cheered on by Tampa, a city that aspired to replace Havana as the world's cigar capital. No doubt the cheering stopped very quickly as US giants began to wipe out as well small factories producing their own brands at home, including many Cuban-run operations in Florida. The big operators created a new marketing strategy, focusing on a handful of brand names targeted to price categories rather than taste niches. In remaining factories the division of labour intensified along with the pace of work. That trend accelerated in the 1920s with the invention of a new rolling machine that would do for the cigar what had already been done for the cigarette. Big companies could then market their own machine-rolled products made from Cuban leaf for five times the price of the ones containing US tobacco and still undercut genuine Cuban hand-rolled cigars. That category would be increasingly relegated to a wealthy niche market, albeit having to share it with a proliferation of fake "Havana" cigars produced in the US and Europe.[9]

Despite machines dramatically cutting costs, the North American cigar market, unlike that for cigarettes, was unstable. Although the 1920s ought to have been an excellent time for cigars, Hollywood had started to turn out gangster movies featuring cigar-chomping tough guys. That public relations problem persisted until 1940 when the industry lobby, the Cigar Institute of America, persuaded big producers to let their heroes rather than their villains sport the stogies. On the other hand, doctors across the USA were prescribing cigarettes to calm the nerves of patients, and the first open appeals to female users were appearing in mass-media outlets. In the past, any risqué attempts to lure female cigarette smokers had to be indirect – like the picture of a sloe-eyed beauty shooting meaningful sidelong glances at her zoot-suited beau, who was leaning against his roadster with a cigarette between his lips, under the caption "Blow Some My Way."

The Depression and war years were also lean for cigars, while cigarette manufacturers enjoyed the usual military bonanza. The return of general prosperity in the late 1940s did not immediately rebound to the cigar's advantage. In fact during the somewhat egalitarian (compared to the present) decades that followed World War II, cigar smoking seemed a vice more for the fatuous than the cool. Nothing better symbolized the apparently poor prospects of the luxury cigar than the decision of ungrateful British voters to dump Winston Churchill, whose wartime performance, buttressed by frequent brandies, had featured him volubly menacing Britain's enemies (the militantly nonsmoking Hitler and Mussolini) with his omnipresent and preferably Cuban cigar.[10] The postwar electoral landslide put in power the Labour Party led by Clement Attlee. Preferring a contemplative pose with a pipe and a pint, he had given less offense to returning soldiers who, during the war, had brindled at Churchill's posturing with his Romeo y Julieta – perhaps rushed fresh to the UK by corvette ahead of the tankers and freighters that were struggling, often in vain, to get through the U-Boat screen with less urgent cargoes like oil and wheat – when they had not had a decent cigarette for days.

Thus began the Age of the Marlboro Man, or rather men, two of whom died of lung cancer even though the manufacturer, Philip Morris, tried to deny it. Marlboro's success, a microcosm for the industry as a whole, was a brilliant makeover for a type of cigarette that started in the 1920s as a luxury brand, was heavily marketed to newly "liberated" female smokers during the war years, then found another vocation in the 1950s as a symbol of the Great American Outdoors, something that the combined effects of suburbanization, the automobile, and industrial agriculture were rapidly turning into a media fantasy. Swollen by their wartime profits and with boundless confidence that the American Century would last a Millennium, the Virginia Cartel (of five big Anglo-American tobacco companies) set out to conquer the smoking world. In a breathtaking, so to speak, affirmation of the power of mass manipulation, the ultimate sign of middle-class sophistication became not just two Detroit gas guzzlers in every garage but two adult cigarette smokers in every house, with the preteens sneaking a puff out back.

Other profitable innovations followed. The filter, originally introduced for women to avoid having loose tobacco cling to their lipstick,
was repackaged as a means to protect smokers against lung disease,
even though some early filters contained asbestos. This strategy not only
countered mounting health concerns but also cut costs and expanded
sales – filter material was cheaper than the tobacco it replaced; and since
a smoker went for a daily nicotine fix, the industry knew that reducing
the tobacco in each cigarette meant the customer was more likely to buy
a pack of twenty-five than of twenty.[11]

Cigars still had their fan clubs, one of them located in the White House.
Pierre Salinger, former press secretary to President John F. Kennedy,
confirmed that, just before launching the invasion of, and subsequent
embargo on, Cuba, Kennedy recruited for duty from Washington retailers 1,200 prime Cuban stogies. If there was to be gun smoke over the
Bay of Pigs as a mercenary army waddled ashore in battle dress, there
would also be cigar smoke over the White House as a division of pop-
pets paddled around in the swimming pool stripped for action.

Prior to the embargo, virtually every fine cigar in the US (only 5–10
percent of the total sold but accounting for about one third of the money
spent) was either rolled in Cuba or manufactured in the US from Cuban
tobacco. Hence, over the next two decades, cigar smoking in the US ran
up against a shortage of quality stock. It was hit further by fallout from
medical evidence. During the 1970s people increasingly bragged about
kicking the tobacco habit before the habit kicked them. Gone, too, was
an earlier generation of male movie stars shilling for cigar makers as
shamelessly as did the females for De Beers Consolidated, the world
diamond colossus.

Then came the wonder years of the 1980s, aspirations soaring with
the joint progress of stock-market indices and cocaine use. If greed, as
everyone was reassured, was actually good, so must be public exhibition of the take. Cigar smoking revived, really taking off in the 1990s as
gush-up economics triumphed over the trickle-down variety, to the point
where it became hard to deem a sparkling soirée truly complete without
fine cigars to titillate the tongues, sometimes of both sexes. Although
the cigar market was shaken by a glut in the late 1990s, coinciding with
a world financial crisis, things picked up again shortly after.[12] While
never again reaching the frantic pre-1997 growth rate, infatuation with
expensive cigars survived even the sinking of so many careers along
with portfolios into a subprime swamp a decade later. In fact sales of
the top priced cigars, mainly Cuban, served as a leading indicator of the
economic times – dipping sharply during the 2008 crisis, but reviving

as the ranks of millionaires, and the wealth of billionaires, rose during the "recovery."[13]

Many factors account for this new oral fixation: a desire to ostentatiously repudiate the previous era's political correctness; a search for a nicotine hit without the reputational risks of cigarettes; a conviction that metastatic tongue and lip cancer are less miserable ways to die than lung disease, combined with ignorance of the fact that they can be even more lethal; and an industry campaign to associate once again cigar smoke with power, money, and the sweet stink of success. Nor had it done any harm that during most of the 1990s the stogie had another staunch advocate in the White House, even if, to Bill Clinton, sometimes a cigar was not just a cigar.

HUFFING AND PUFFING

When the market soared in the 1990s, it divided roughly into two segments. The first consisted of self-described aficionados who claimed to discern quality and verify origin by taste, smell, and even feel – despite the fact that real Cuban cigars, completely handmade from tobacco that can change in taste from year to year even if grown in the same field, may vary in quality and character from box to box, even cigar to cigar. Lighting up the market are high-profile cigar gurus, featured regularly in glossy trade mags whose covers sport a celebrity-of-the-month caught in the act. These smoke screeners insist, much like the winosaurs whose previous success they emulate, that some types of cigars lose flavour with age, while others peak several months (or even years) after manufacture. Their importance lies not so much in their skill in detecting subtle variations – no doubt some can, although, as professional wine critics have shown, not with the accuracy they may publicly claim. Rather it reflects the fact that overwhelmingly imbibers choose not by taste or scent or feel, but by what is "in." For a fair chunk of high-end buyers the main concern is to pose in public with a cigar equipped with a band attesting to its Cuban hand-rolled origin – much the way winophiliacs worship labels more than the contents of their bottles. In fact cigars get puffed in much the same kind of language. "Tobacco proudly wears until the moment of its death the band of its brand," one of the cigar's preeminent historians declared. "[O]nly in the sacrificial fire does it burn its individuality and convert it to ashes as it ascends to glory." If that is not enough to make any of today's professional wine touts shudder with jealousy or horror, depending on whether their professional insecurities or esthetic sensitivities are more afflicted, the historian gushed further: "there are smokers who smoke their fine cigar to the end without removing the band, which bears witness to the quality of its brand, just as the critical drinker derives greater pleasure from an aged wine if it comes from an old, unopened bottle, coquettishly covered with dust and bearing a gold label indicating the unquestionable aristocracy of its vintage and its origin."[14] So who could fail to be convinced?

Since by far the largest block of puff artists lives in the US, where it is still illegal to import or sell Cuban cigars, inventive means are required to join supply to demand. More is the pity that JFK died so young. What he might have done in Vietnam will be forever debated; but with Cuba he might well have lifted the embargo once his own stash ran short.

Certainly back in Cuba there would have been no lack of willingness to cater to some (but not all) of Kennedy's favourite pastimes. Its Revolution had been led by bearded insurgents eager to clean up Havana of prostitution and gambling but happy to pose for the world's cameras puffing Habanos and slugging back the island's almost-as-famous rum. After Cuba's big tobacco barons had fled, their fields and factories were nationalized (although small-scale plantations were left in private hands), then broken up into small plots and reorganized into state-supervised co-ops. The island's cigar industry soon recovered even with its main former market legally closed. In fact Cuba's most widely acclaimed cigar, the Cohiba, likened by *Cigar Aficionado* magazine with its customary restraint to "a superb main course at a Michelin three-star restaurant," was introduced seven years after Fidel Castro's victory to become, complete with jazzy art-work on its boxes, an international icon of the Revolution's success.

The job of supplying cigars starts in Cuba's prime tobacco fields, mainly in Pinar del Río province, a relatively small area blessed with an excellent climate and sandy loam nourished by 20 million years of erosion from the surrounding mountains, then topped up with organic fertilizers, including horse manure and decaying vegetable matter dredged from nearby lagoons. The fields, grouped in small farms of ten to fifteen acres, are tended by specially skilled farmers who generally work without modern machinery – even ploughing is done with draft animals, although some private plantations use tractors. The necessary inputs are supplied directly by the state according to the quotas set for each plantation. Seeds are graded by hand, then placed in seedbeds. After about six weeks they are transferred to specially humidified and fertilized ground and guarded closely against pests and disease. Harvest begins perhaps six weeks later at the rate of two or three leaves per week from each maturing plant, totally by hand. After it is complete, farmers are free to plant fields with other crops provided they do not deplete the soil of nutrients required for tobacco. That, at least, is the theory. No doubt the reality is a trifle less romantic, not least because farmers are happy to plant corn, harvesting the cob for food and depleting the soil of nutrients, provided state inspectors can be kept in the dark. Privately owned farms claim to be virtuous in complying fully with the regulations while insisting that the worst transgressions against state-dictated rules are the work of nationalized plantations.[15]

After harvest, the leaves are sun-dried over pine racks for another six or seven weeks, sewn into bundles by women working with needles and strings, taken to a fermentation house to be immersed in cedar casks for the tobacco to "sweat" for thirty to forty days, releasing ammonia gas. Next they are classified by size, colour, texture etc. (some slated for wrapper, some for filler, some for binder), rebundled, then perhaps sent to another place of fermentation for a couple months more. After that the tobacco is baled and moved into an aging facility for six to twenty-four months. Then comes preparation and packaging. In the factories, usually in urban centres some distance from the plantations, highly skilled rollers work exclusively by hand with someone reading to them from the daily newspaper, a political tradition that dates back more than a century – though doubtlessly after the tourists have snapped the appropriate photos, some of the rolling shops switch to a background of *son Cubano*, far more likely to inspire today's workforce to greater effort than the text of Fidel's three-hour speeches or Raul's ten-minute ones. Finished cigars are further aged, allowing leaves to "marry" so as to create a more balanced smoke. Then they are laid out according to small colour differences in twin rows separated by a cedar divider in boxes (also of cedar) embossed with logos. A guarantee, printed on parchment, is inserted; and the box is sealed with a warranty stamp. The state monopoly, Habanos S.A., that supervises each of the 222 distinct steps in the process, sells the product to a single distributor in each major customer country, with a small part turned over to state-run outlets catering to tourists inside Cuba.

Not least of Cuba's socialist control measures is a strict limit on the number of large cigars (sought by celebrities abroad), to maintain quality and, of course, to keep up the price. As the Cuban company's vice-president of development explained to that radical pink rag, the *Financial Times*: "Our strategy is to target the high end of the market and … to carve out new space for our clients," a reference to the Cuban corporation's role in promoting smoking lounges and private cigar clubs. He added: "It is all about value-added, collectibles, limited editions, exclusives."[16]

As with all commercial enterprises, there were setbacks. For example, a scandal in France, where, the very day its cigar-puffing self-promoting president told the working population that they had to, in the interests of national financial responsibility, defer their pensions for two years, *Le Canard Enchaîné*, a muckraking satirical newspaper, revealed that France's state secretary for Greater Paris had blown €12,000 in public money in the previous ten months for Upman Magnums, Cohibas, and other fine Cuban products.[17] The minister resigned, complaining that he had been lynched, while reimbursing the government for the €3,500 worth of cigars he had smoked, claiming he had no idea where the rest of the money had gone.[18]

Cuba's commitment to organic and artisanal production forms a dramatic contrast to norms elsewhere. In the last couple of decades, the tobacco frontier has shifted rapidly out of North America to "developing" countries. That trend is ostensibly because tobacco has fallen into disrepute with its clientele shrinking back home as more people kick the habit before the habit kicks them. In fact it is more because tobacco transnationals do a booming business selling in so-called emerging markets while cutting costs drastically by shifting production to places with minimal or nonexistent labour and environmental standards. The result is leaf grown on former rainforest stripped bare of trees, picked by workers shaking from "green tobacco sickness," cured in a corrugated metal shack by burning endangered tropical hardwoods, then machine-rolled in an airless factory by operators with oozing skin lesions from contact dermatitis.

Brazil, for example, still one of the world's greatest leaf producers, loses massive amounts of forest (in the south for a change, rather than in the Amazon) to tobacco. Since it takes about eight kilos of wood to cure one kilo of tobacco, worldwide that means about 600 million trees a year just for curing, not to mention losses from clearing land for planting and from the manufacture of paper, cardboard, and print-advertising materials. Despite the fact that nicotine is itself a natural pesticide (widely used before today's diluted nerve-gases became cheaply available), modern commercial tobacco in its three-month gestation period receives perhaps sixteen doses of toxic, carcinogenic, mutagenic, and probably endocrine-disrupting chemicals, plus ozone-depleting methyl bromide. Although technically tobacco in Brazil and most other poorer countries is produced by independent farmers – Zimbabwe, with plantations dating back to the British colonial era, is the major exception – the big international companies set quotas for each farmer, grade the product, and establish the purchase price, deducting the resulting value of the crop against debts the farmers have incurred for seed, fertilizer, and pesticides, also supplied at prices those companies establish.[19]

Curiously, when the Cuban government dictates prices and quotas, and controls the supply of seed and fertilizers, to its tobacco farmers (who have good incomes, qualify for free social and medical services, and do not have to endure toxic chemicals), it is denounced for Communist authoritarianism. Yet, when Philip Morris does the same thing to its farmers (who can reduce their contact with dangerous pesticides only at the risk of heat stroke from wearing heavy protective clothing, and whose poverty usually requires that their children work beside them), it is lauded as a paragon of free enterprise.

Ironically, just as world cigar demand was soaring in the 1990s, Cuban tobacco faced a major crisis. The collapse of the Soviet Union, which had provided heavy subsidies, forced Cuba to shift resources to food production. Then came an epidemic of blue mould, wiping out nearly half the crop of the special leaf used for wrapping. Inevitably came accusations that the disease was spread by the US as an act of biological warfare, a theory that on the surface seems far-fetched but is difficult to dismiss out of hand, given the long history of sabotage by the US against Cuba.[20] The regime reacted by breeding pest-resistant wrapper leaf and by rationing tobacco to its own people, then among the world's heaviest smokers.[21] No doubt it helped that Fidel himself had quit years before.

On top of falling production (and, briefly, reputation) came competitors in neighbouring countries eager to deprecate Cuban tobacco, a US legal assault on Cuban brands internationally, and an epidemic of counterfeits. Although production recovered by the end of the decade, enough for cigar snobs to worry that too much on the market would take away the mystique, the other three threats remained very much present.

THE CONTRABANDISTAS

After the Revolution, when the old tobacco barons decamped to the Dominican Republic, Honduras, Nicaragua, and Costa Rica, they took with them seeds, skills, and connections. The soil and climate in their new abodes were not nearly as good, and workmanship was well short of Cuban standards; but costs were much lower – a symbol of the whole trend to global outsourcing and its impact on both product quality and the distribution of income.

The barons took something else with them: brand names. The Cuban government continued to produce and market the same brands using tobacco grown by the same methods in the same soil under the same sun by the same farmers, then had it prepared and rolled by the same workers or their immediate successors in the same ways. However, the

US government not only blocked entry of Cuban tobacco, it promoted with foreign-aid funds tobacco produced by émigré Cuban planters in neighbouring countries, who used mechanized methods on inferior soil often saturated by artificial fertilizers and laced with chemical pesticides, then sold their product using the old brand names. Any of their former brands the émigrés did not produce by themselves were first licensed, then sold to US conglomerates. The one exception ought to have been Cohiba, a post-Revolutionary product of a nationalized industry. But the US, while leading a worldwide campaign against infringement of intellectual property rights, blocked Cuba from registering the trademark, then granted to a US company the right to manufacture and market inside the US under that name.[22]

That set the stage for circulation within the US of at least three versions of each major brand: those made openly outside Cuba (whether in neighbouring countries or in the US itself) using the old names; those faked in those same countries or in the US by pasting the elite brand name onto cheap, locally made cigars; and those properly hand-rolled in Cuba in government factories, then smuggled onto the US market.[23] To further complicate matters came a fourth: some cigars (*falsiosos*) are produced in Cuba using genuine tobacco diverted from official outlets. Handicraft manufacturing leads to a lot of waste leaf: sometimes it is used in cigarettes; but it is also smuggled out of the processing plants to roll illegally into cigars. Added to this are the cigars that don't pass quality inspection in official factories. They are diverted legally to the local market, then diverted illegally out of the country. They can be picked up for about $30 a box (more for premium brands) inside Cuba and sold abroad for several hundred or more. The product is packed in real or contrived boxes with proper brand names, then also snuck into the US.

The usual way to smuggle tobacco products, including cigars, around the world is to funnel them legally into so-called free-trade zones (like Panama, Curaçao, or Hong Kong), then pass them to career smugglers who in turn are linked to crooked wholesalers, each with a network of complicit retailers in the target countries, perhaps with street peddlers operating without the inconvenience of licenses or sales taxes at the final stage. That was the technique big US companies used to undermine local competition in countries from which they were were banned, or to force their governments to slash tobacco taxes. Once the national market was flooded by smuggled smokes, the Virginia Cartel could deploy US and UK government muscle in international trade negotiations to "legally" force open the market. That occurred in Latin America in the 1970s, in much of the South East Asia in the 1980s, in Eastern Europe in the 1990s, with China's 350 million-plus smokers now the main target. Takeover of weakened local companies by Anglo-American transnationals frequently followed.

Cuban cigars follow a quite different route. In every country where it exports, Cuba licenses only one distributor and tries to limit the amount sold to keep up the price and maintain reputation. So in places that charge high excise taxes on tobacco products, smuggling is largely the work of "mules" drawn from tens, even hundreds, of thousands of tourists swarming into Cuba to frolic on the beach fronts of highly profitable Italian-, German-, or Spanish-owned hotels while US tourism chains clench their teeth on the sidelines. These petty smugglers can carry back home at least their duty-free allowance, maybe more, and partially finance their trip by selling them at several times acquisition cost.

However, in the US, buying or selling Cuban cigars is not just a tax offense: it is banned under the Trading with the Enemy Act with penalties that by the turn of the millennium could have reached twelve years in prison and $250,000 in fines for an individual, a cool million for a corporation. Still, some take the risk.

Most are ordinary travellers, many of them Florida-based Cubans going back and forth on family visits: they might bring into the US small lots for personal consumption or petty sale. If caught, they are usually subject to little beyond a warning and the distressing sight of their cigars being crushed before their eyes, perhaps a symbol of the pent-up urge of a frustrated official Washington to do likewise to the Cuban regime. This produces a paradoxical situation. Perhaps the most important reason the US maintains the embargo, apart from its impulse to torment countries that don't toe its line (provided they are small and weak enough), is to pander to the anti-Castro Cuban exile community in Florida. Yet it is precisely from that group that the major beneficiaries of Cuban cigar-smuggling (or -faking) are drawn from. Millions of Americans, too, pass through Canada or Mexico on business or holiday; store clerks in both places obligingly repackage cigars for US clients and perhaps remove or replace the bands. The wise buyer just tucks the bands away discretely in their luggage or has the tobacconist mail them separately.

Apart from people sneaking Cuban cigars into the US for their own consumption, casual smugglers from time to time bring back enough to sell to a retailer who, in turn, will resell only to trusted customers. If caught, they might, in addition to losing their cigars, be subject to charges under various tax and customs laws. The more serious offense of Trading with the Enemy was, until recently, almost unknown for the casual smuggler. But there were exceptions. One of them was named Richard Connors.

An Illinois public defender by vocation, Connors had another job on the side: driving into Canada, then flying to Cuba to buy the kind of cigars that fall off the backs of trucks. Returning to Canada by air, he would drive back into the US with his cigars. But, after a nasty divorce, his ex tipped off the feds, supposedly because she was worried that her son was going on one of his smuggling trips. Customs stopped him at the Canadian border, seized forty-six boxes, and temporarily impounded his passport. On subsequent trips he would simply mail his passport home from Canada and cross the border (in pre-Terror War days) with his driver's license as identification. When Connors got cocky enough to write a novel (*Cigar Runner*) glorifying the business, the feds wanted blood. So they persuaded his ex to renew the relationship. Over the next three years she spent weekends at the house, tossing incriminating documents into the garbage, where the feds could pick them up without a search warrant. Besides giving him a thirty-seven-month sentence and $60,000 fine, they seized the house.[24]

Next up the ladder of career success are professionals who service wholesalers or perhaps the elite clientele of high-class restaurants and corporate-executive clubs.[25] The time of greatest danger for this group came in the late 1990s. Amidst predictable stories that drug smugglers who had been working the Caribbean-Florida route were switching to Cuban cigars because the markups were higher and the penalties lighter, senior congressmen, pandering to the Cuba lobby and pressed by the big US cigar makers, pushed through a law to step up enforcement. In addition to customs crackdowns, police began making the front pages by raiding the odd New York or California cigar bar to haul away a few smoke blowers for violating the criminal code, evading taxes, and undercutting US foreign policy, only to have most of them released with the judge simply wagging an admonishing index finger, possibly stained yellow by his most recent Cuban cigar.[26] After all, the defendants in these smuggling and sanctions-busting cases were likely wealthy professionals and "respectable" business types, not street kids selling dime bags of marijuana who could only be properly reformed by several years in prison.

Cuban cigars also enter the US indirectly. They can be purchased via mail order from European or Canadian wholesalers, or off internet sites, although those channels are probably clogged with fakes. Distributors fill credit-card orders, then send the cigars by major courier companies. If cigars enter the US on overnight or two-day delivery, customs pays little attention. Mail-order or internet vendors, too, might replace genuine bands with non-Cuban ones to make life easier for a client. Although the practice would not much bother a genuine aficionado whose main concern is flavour (or so they might claim), it would make a conspicuous consumer cringe. However, that class of imbiber can be appeased if the vendor sends the real bands separately a short time later.

For even larger lots, the best route is probably in the thousands of trucks that cross the borders every day, especially from Mexico into California. Once inside, the cigars will be passed to high-end retailers to resell to trusted clients. However, once the traffic is underground, it is more difficult to separate contraband in the genuine article from a proliferation of fakes.

Counterfeit Cuban cigars were actually pioneered in the US. The early presence of Cuban rollers in Key West encouraged upstarts in New York and Pennsylvania to manufacture from domestic tobacco, then sell "genuine Key West Cuban cigars." In fact the elaborate labels on today's Cuban cigar boxes were first developed in the nineteenth century using heavy machinery to stamp metallic foil into the logo, precisely to combat the proliferation of fakes.[27] Now, too, most counterfeit Habanos (cheap, machine-made cigars wrapped with imitation Cuban bands) are likely made in the US. Next in importance are ones produced in neighbouring countries, exported legally, then reboxed and relabelled. Ironically, there are on the market today even fakes made in Cuba.

The process starts when workers inside official factories collect unused leaves, including floor sweepings and mouldy discards. The tobacco, possibly contaminated by human hair, rodent droppings, and insect remains, is rolled at home or in handicraft shops with a few confederates, those involved always alert to possible police raids. Artisans might wrap the tobacco in dried banana or palm leaf that looks like the official wrapperleaf but has an appalling taste. Workers might also steal bands discarded because of printing errors, or defective boxes that have the advantage of the correct print-face, stamps, codes, and even cedar dividers. The cigars are then sold through peddlers who frequent beach resorts and bistros swarming with tourists on the lookout for cut-rate booze and cheap sex as creeping capitalism, to the delight of Washington, threatens to return Cuba to its pre-Revolutionary status of premier whorehouse of the Caribbean.

The tourists who buy cheap cigars face two possible risks. One is an unfriendly encounter on the way out with Cuban customs officers who can confiscate any cigars that do not have a *factura* (bill of sale) from a state outlet. For some time *facturas* were not difficult to fake. A book of genuine ones might be purchased from sales personnel, copied en masse in an underground print shop, then sold to street suppliers or even to official shops whose staff offered tourists a special discount deal. Today, though, each individually numbered *factura* carries the name of the purchaser with nationality and passport number, where the cigars were bought, and the identity of the clerk who sold them. Still, even without a *factura*, the odds of a customs search of outbound tourists are low.[28] Once past customs, of course, tourists can buy their cigars in duty-free shops without any hassle in every major Cuban airport.

The second, more serious danger is lousy quality. Some unofficial Habanos are real cigars stolen by workers, or diverted to the black market from a worker's own cigar ration. Occasionally a diplomat will request a box from a state distribution outlet, and it gets written into inventory records as two or more, the extra diverted to private sale. Sometimes cigars earmarked as gifts to visiting dignitaries fail to arrive at their official destination or destinatee. These last categories are especially welcome on the parallel market since they have official certificates and serial numbers conforming to the records.[29] However, street vendors routinely use the claim that their offerings have been stolen to explain to gullible tourists why the stuff (probably homemade with no quality control) is so cheap. On the other hand, some illegal shops do turn out reasonably good stuff. Tobacco farmers may divert part of their crop to underground factories that in turn connect to street peddlers or even to international distributors who mix cheap contraband with their official purchases. Thus unofficial Habanos could turn up in duty-free shops elsewhere in Caribbean, or get passed to smugglers to run into the US, particularly to Miami where these well-made Cuban illegals compete directly with cheap US fakes dressed up to look authentic or with legal counterfeits made by US cigar companies in neighbouring countries.

Once in the US, the fake cigars have to be retailed. For small lots destined for the casual market, a tobacconist may simply keep refilling a real (or real-looking) Cuban box with fakes equipped with passable bands. But large lots for sale to more serious smokers need documentation close enough to the real thing to pass a level of scrutiny that varies directly with the sophistication of the consumer and the asking price of the cigar. Using colour copiers, scanners, and laser printers, it is easy to reproduce a band or even imitate a passable one from pictures in *Cigar Aficionado* magazine – whose Counterfeit Gallery might also be useful in seeing what mistakes to avoid. The same is true of the Habanos logo. The guarantee can be run off on a high-quality copier, albeit usually on cardboard rather than authentic parchment. The three branded hallmarks (Habanos S.A., Hecho en Cuba, Totalmente a Mano) burned onto the bottom of a proper box by heat-engraving can be replicated using ordinary inks. Stiff cardboard can substitute for cedar as a divider between two layers of cigars. A reasonable facsimile of the cedar box can be fashioned from plywood. Then comes the job of mimicking the coded ink stamp that reveals where the cigars were made and when they left the factory, as well as any stamps from official distributors in the main customer countries.[30]

For a time the most serious obstacle was the Cuban warranty stamp, applied since 1912 to every box and very difficult to reproduce with photolithography. Digital technologies made copying easier. But in the year 2000 the Cuban government updated the seal with security features of the sort now common on currency notes – microprinting, denser colours that cheaper colour copiers have trouble reproducing, serial numbers, and a hidden watermark. Still, just as with bank notes, where there is a strong enough will, there is a clever enough way. Steady improvement of the taste (if not the safety to workers and the surrounding environment) of Central American and Dominicano tobaccos together with ever fancier digital technologies results now in counterfeits that can pass with increasing frequency as the real thing even among "sophisticated" consumers, although cigar snobs tell a different story.

With the US market served by both counterfeit and contraband, it was bound to occur to someone that the two could be combined. Hardly the model for a remake of *The Godfather*, Joe Hybl was a regular California guy who lost his shirt in a bad hotel investment, then went looking for a way to recoup. A buddy who was an airline pilot offered to pick up Cuban cigars abroad, mail them from some neutral location, and let Hybl find customers. The profits were modest. So they dreamed of bigger deals. Visiting Cuba itself they discovered that they could buy *falsiosos* for $60 a box, and sell them at home for ten times that amount. The only problem was that the boxes often did not pass scrutiny. This was solved when Hybl asked a friend in Spain, the world's largest importer and re-exporter of Habanos, to find him old (genuine) boxes and ship them to Mexico. Hybl and associates made multiple trips to Cuba with large amounts of cash to buy *falsiosos*, sometimes narrowly escaping Cuban police, then flew the cigars to Mexico. However Mexico only permits the import of one box per person. The solution was simple and cheap: they paid off Mexican customs. Then it got simpler and cheaper: they paid off baggage handlers to switch their cargo so that it appeared as domestic rather than international in origin. The cigars were rerouted to Tijuana and housed in a Church where Mexican-made fakes were added to flush out the shipments. The obliging parish priest ran the stogies to a safe house near the border. They were hauled across, partly by illegals bound for work in California, partly in vans driven by friends and associates, to San Diego. Their next destination was the Bay Area, where Hybl delivered to restaurants, tobacco shops, and prominent citizens, or sent them by mail to out-of-state clients. He also ran a parallel operation

peddling to other suppliers, for $3,000 each, books of Cuban cigar labels
that he picked up on the black market for $300 along with special 30th
Anniversary Cohiba ashtrays that cost $50 and resold for $1,000.

Alas, this pioneering effort to expand international cooperation took
place after the cigar glut had led to pressure from the US tobacco companies for a crackdown on the Cuban contraband that threatened their
market for legal counterfeits. Hence the feds launched Operation Smoke
Signal. Officers followed the trail from customers back to retailers, then
back further to one of Hybl's partners – as a lawyer he knew enough to
rat out the others in exchange for immunity. Hybl and four associates
were the first tobacco smugglers (this was pre-Connors) charged under
the Trading with the Enemy Act. The case garnered the desired publicity. The cigar companies were appeased; but in the final analysis all five
defendants, in exchange for guilty pleas, were given probation and some
tax penalties. Meanwhile cops in the know shook their heads at the
waste of resources chasing a few people with no criminal links for smuggling something that was probably resold to local lawyers and judges.[31]

The US cigar companies were also concerned over competition at home
from the proliferation of US-made fakes posing as bona fide Habanos.
But here there was no possible recourse to charges of either smuggling
or trading with some conveniently contrived enemy. (In 1997 a Miami
police detective was charged with fraud for selling Dominican Republic-
made cigars as if they were Cuban.[32]) The main centre of activity is
Florida, particularly among Cuban exiles who, like early generations,
include former cigar workers. Their connections back home provide a
source of genuine boxes and labels to dress up their handiwork. Leading
the fight against counterfeiting was Altadis USA, the US subsidiary of the
Spanish-French tobacco giant, Altadis SA, which is now, ironically, 50
percent owner of Habanos SA and has itself been bought by Imperial
Tobacco, the British half of the original Anglo-American agreement to
divide the world market. Discouraged that Florida state law applied little more than slaps on the wrist to illegal counterfeiters of Cuban cigars,
Altadis, which had the exclusive legal right in the US to counterfeit the
brands, pressed for federal action; and it offered to cover part of the
bill, paying local informants and even putting up the monies for "buy-
and-bust" undercover operations. Its first major success came in 2003
with a raid on a small Miami tobacco shop. The company claimed that
it had shown up with two 25-foot trucks to haul off the fake materials,
then had to swap those for an 18 wheeler. In 2006 a judge slapped an
impossible $900,000 penalty on the store for selling, according to seized
invoices, about $60,000 worth of imitation Montecristos, H. Uppmans,
and Romeo y Julietas.[33]

Equally successful was an elaborate sting mounted jointly by the Miami police, the federal Secret Service, and the US postal inspector's office. All of that cop muscle and taxpayer money targeting criminal masterminds culminated with the arrest of an amateur carpenter who had fled Cuba to the US on a raft eleven years before. He had been making wooden boxes marked "Hecho en Cuba" (just as mementos, he claimed) and filling them with locally made "Don Nobodies" equipped with mock Cuban bands. He was found guilty of trademark violations. Outraged defense lawyers pointed out that the case not only represented a big corporation turning the police into a private enforcement arm (as if that is new) but in effect providing the government of Cuba, the business partner of Altadis SA, with trademark protection. It also argued, quite rightly but to no avail, that Altadis USA was the real counterfeiter since it was using Cuban trademarks in the US to sell non-Cuban tobacco.[34]

There were, and probably still are, legal ways around the ban. For example, the owner of a small cigar company in New Jersey bought from the estate of a Tampa-based cigar maker who had died in the early 1960s (leaving relatives to battle over his will for three decades), 46,000 pounds of genuine Cuban pre-embargo leaf for $2.5 million, or $54.35 per pound. After a tussle with US customs, he started to market cigars that he could advertise legally as made from Cuban tobacco.[35]

Even better, some entrepreneurs have found secret treasure troves of pre-embargo cigars. Back in 1983 the president of a big US tobacco company claimed to have located 200,000 cigars shipped to Spain before the Revolution. He assured potential buyers that they had been kept in a climate-controlled warehouse since 1958 – in other words, for fully a quarter century without anyone apparently being the wiser. Nonetheless he did not expect his treasure trove to simply be sacrificed to epicurean fire. "I'd guess no more than 10 percent of these cigars will ever be smoked. It's like the rarest bottle of wine. There's no occasion good enough to drink it,"[36] a sentiment with which Hardy Rodenstock, the collector-dealer who staged high-profile tastings of, among others, the Thomas Jefferson collection of eighteenth-century Bordeaux, would disagree.

A quarter century later, a cigar bar in Arizona similarly offered clients the opportunity (for $150 to $600 a piece) to puff things like a 1942 H. Upmann Dunhill or a 1949 Montecristo No. 2.[37] No doubt such examples have inspired others in the throbbing heart of the entrepreneurial USA to reproduce passable facsimiles of the old bands, wrap them round suitably "aged" modern cigars, then sell the lot for the appropriate price to people whose taste for forbidden fruit precludes them from ever hollering for the cops. In fact the entrepreneur could even steal a leaf, in a manner of speaking, from the book of wine-snob tricks by inviting their fan club to a gourmet gathering in which another historical cache of an irreplaceable luxury (along with evidence of the fraud) goes up in smoke.

Then, of course, there is the ultimate scam to target the inveterate cigar snob. When Scotland Yard's Art and Antiques Squad claimed to have busted the biggest fake factory in years, one that turned out everything from Noel Coward paintings to automobile memorabilia, the list of its products included two framed cigar labels supposedly from the Allied 1943 Casablanca Conference and signed by a man who was once the Cuban cigar's most renowned shill, Winston Churchill himself.[38]

All of these cons and frauds are tributes to the continued capitalist-market power of socialist Cuba's most prestigious product, despite the best efforts of the US government, Cuban exiles, and jealous competitors.[39] Inherent merit is certainly a major reason. No doubt tradition and hype also play their roles. Also at work is that follow-the-leader-no-matter-how-stupid instinct that seems so firmly implanted in the human genetic code. How else to explain the continuing success of all manner of "luxury" brands today? Add to that the hallucinatory properties of tobacco, of which the Amerindians spoke so highly. In a interview with the publisher of *Cigar Aficionado*, Ron Perelman, US cosmetics billionaire and one-time owner of Consolidated Cigar, laid out his own not-quite-pipe dreams of what he might do once the US embargo ended: "Isn't it every cigar lover's fantasy – like a wine lover's to have a chateau and a vineyard in Bordeaux – to have a factory, a business in Cuba?"[40] On the other hand, at the start of Cuba's own successful antismoking campaign, Fidel Castro suggested that the best thing for anyone to do with cigars was to give a box to their enemies.[41]

9

Afishionados: On Fishy Business in the Fishing Business

Some rave about chocolate-covered ants; others champion bird's nest soup. Those gastronomes who fancy sea food, though, might try London's Fat Duck Restaurant, a Michelin three-star-rated establishment renowned as a world innovator in "molecular gastronomy." Fat Duck's fare included, apart from delicacies like "nitro-scrambled egg and bacon ice cream" and "snail porridge," a "Sound of the Sea" concoction of seafood, foam, and "edible sand" served in a conch shell along with an iPod playing the cadence of waves and seagulls – until the place suddenly shut itself down to figure out why so many of its clients were sending back their meals, from both ends.[1]

Still, in gourmet cuisine, caviar (or, less elegantly, raw unfertilized sturgeon eggs) seems almost beyond challenge – except maybe by glass eels, strictly a niche market especially among those who like to eat their seafood still wriggling.[2] Caviar even featured at the eighty-fifth birthday celebration for Zimbabwe's Robert Mugabe, perpetual winner of presidential (s)elections. Fully "4,000 portions" of the stuff, so the breathless reporting claimed, without specifying how big the portions were: were they 1.8 kilo tins upended bodily down lusty dark throats to the pulsating rhythm of jungle drums, or a tiny lump of eggs delicately perched, to the dazzling swoops and swirls of the Brahms Violin Concerto in D Major, on the edges of milky-white mother-of-pearl serving spoons? According to caviar trade lore, mother-of-pearl is the only substance (except gold) that will not to transmit its own flavour to the eggs. Actually polystyrene is just as neutral – in taste, if not in tastes.

True, the caviar at the Mugabe fête came along with two thousand bottles of champagne, eight thousand lobsters, three thousand ducks, and eight thousand boxes of Ferrero Rocher chocolates, but no "mealie meal," the ground corn on which most of the population subsists. The fact that hundreds of goats, sheep, and cattle were slaughtered to feed the attending masses, who probably appreciated them much more than they would a batch of smelly old fish eggs, never quite caught the headlines. Nor did the lurid accounts that raced around the world identify the type of caviar.[3] However, within the kingdom of caviar, if perhaps not inside the republic of Zimbabwe, the consensus, with few dissenting voices, is that the shimmering black roe of the beluga reign supreme.[4]

Yet what is today deemed a delicacy may have less to do with any science of gastronomy than with the impact of fad on one side and ecological brigandage (turning natural abundance into biological rarity) on the other. After all, at various points in the past caviar has been snubbed as more fit for pigs or peasants than for prigs or princes.[5] And if humanity continues its current course, in the near future the only available wild seafood dish may well be jellyfish soufflé – although the rich and trendy may prefer raw black sea nettle in small slices on a lump of rice.

The oyster, too, has a varied culinary history. Once upon a time it managed, in defiance of today's social conventions and economic "laws," to be both very common *and* highly regarded – rather like the way that, in ages past, gold was the most prized of metals precisely because it was by far the *easiest* to extract and work. Lauded by the rich, but consumed abundantly by the poor, the oyster was transformed into a quasi luxury only after formerly vast beds that had played a vital role keeping water in bays and estuaries clean, were wiped out. People gulped down oysters in massive quantities, none with more enthusiasm than Egypt's 300-pound King Farouq, who supposedly consumed several hundred a week. He died in his Roman exile after another dozen oysters, followed by lobster thermidor, baby lamb, and Monte Bianco (a decadent chocolate desert), all washed down with Coca Cola and topped off with a Cuban cigar.[6] It was probably the Coke that did him in.

The oyster, too, had other strikes against it. Countless millions, perhaps billions, of a non-edible species have been opened and casually discarded over the millennia in a frantic search for pearls. More recently have come massive pollution to finish a job that human predation had started – although in the case of the BP blowout in the Gulf of Mexico, the two worked neatly in tandem – and recurrent plagues that wipe out even cultivated beds.[7]

The oyster's fate has been shared by the abalone, once also phenomenally abundant, particularly along Pacific coasts. For a long time Asian appetites seemed boundless. However the abalone found almost no favour in the West until Americans discovered that the little taste ("subtle flavour") it had could be eradicated completely by deep-frying. At that point its flesh became a delicacy in the US as well, with the advantage over its close culinary rival, Kentucky Fried Chicken, that the abalone (like the oyster) had the alleged side benefit of putting metaphorical lead into aging, sagging pencils.

Because poseurs on both sides of the Pacific now revel in the stuff, the abalone has been plundered to the point of near exhaustion. Sometimes that is the work of recreational divers who take forbidden stocks from prohibited places in restricted seasons; sometimes it is done by professional fishers who exceed quotas; sometimes culprits are fish pirates who grab and run, looting even cultured abalone beds.[8] None of them seem to lack for high-end restaurants eager to buy their stolen goods in the back alley behind the kitchen. If the restaurant is ever queried by the authorities, it can claim that the abalone was purchased from one of the abalone-farming operations that have sprung up in the very places where nature used to provide a cornucopia.[9]

The story is more complex with the bluefin tuna that today sends sushi devotees into raptures. Lauded as the quintessence of Japanese culinary culture, it was actually an outcast from the kitchen even in Japan until after World War II. The change began when the US occupation authorities tried to rebuild the devastated restaurant industry without stimulating a black market in rationed foodstuffs. The answer was to permit use of a fatty junk fish that anglers who were unable to sell it as cat food back in the US had to pay public dumpsites to dispose. Once Japan had been sufficiently irradiated by US TV images to believe that fatty meat was a sign of wealth and luxury, a postwar necessity became a national fad. And once the sushi-sashimi craze swept the world like a virulent form of swine flu, a plague of giant factory ships accompanied by spotter planes descended on the seas to deploy rectangular nets sixty metres deep and up to five kilometres long that could envelop a whole school of tuna, along with everything else in the vicinity, while making a mockery of so-called international regulations by routinely lying about the amount of their catch. Prize adult fish are flown to market, particularly in Japan, where they can fetch at auction up to $400 per pound or more; while smaller tuna enjoy in high-density polyethelene cages a sedentary lifestyle more appropriate to a bond futures trader than a fish evolved to migrate over thousands of miles of ocean – until the juveniles are oleaginous enough to share the fate of their elders.[10]

GONE FISHING?

Many other aquatic species today share the fate of being fished to and even beyond the probable point of no return, although no one is ever sure just where that is located until after the fact. The fishing industry, with ships so large they could swallow a whole pod of blue whales in a gulp, belch lightly, then swallow some more, chats in sunny tones about perpetual abundance. On the other side, some marine scientists speak darkly of Fishmageddon being around the corner, which is quite possibly true, although modifying predictions with an admission of the limitations of their own knowledge of nature's complex relationships is a safer and ultimately more effective policy.[11]

Intensive exploitation of particular areas or particular species has existed for centuries, with baneful results. Europe's conquest of saltwater fisheries probably started in late medieval or early modern times after freshwater stocks started to fall perceptibly. The problem was probably not so much direct overfishing as habitat destruction – the interrelated effects of population growth, intensification of agriculture, deforestation, draining of marshlands, and building dams to power grain mills that fouled or blocked formerly clear rivers and streams. The impact on migratory freshwater fish forced the search into presumed-to-be inexhaustible seas. But in time saltwater species (mammals as well as fish) also faced trouble, with overexploitation as the direct cause.[12]

In the preindustrial age, fisheries used hooked lines, wooden traps, or hand-thrown nets. Damage was gradual and usually invisible. But in the late eighteenth century, after Captain Cook's charts of the South Seas became available to commercial fleets, whalers and sealers descended on the area in search of marine-mammal oil (for industrial lubricants and lighting) or pelts of sea otters and seals (for trade with the Orient). Even with just sailing ships and hand-thrown clubs or harpoons, they managed to exterminate tens of millions of seals and sea lions along with millions of whales in the Antarctic and contiguous parts of the Pacific. Within about fifty years the South Seas marine-mammal "fishery," exploiting one of the greatest concentrations of animal biomass the planet had ever seen, effectively ceased to exist, partly through soaring prices resulting directly from the massive slaughter, partly (and not coincidentally) from the start of the petroleum age, which would wreak its own form of havoc on the oceans. However, that temporary respite to the South Seas gave little pause to a fishing industry busy developing ever more sophisticated means to locate and slaughter other species.[13]

Technological change played a crucial role in the worldwide aquatic disaster to come. Although primitive trawlers (and protests against them) date back to the fourteenth century, the damage increased with the sixteenth century invention of the beam trawl, a large netted bag kept open by a beam and capable of scooping everything in its path. But its impact was still limited by a ship's reliance on wind power. Then came the steam trawler that could not only attack fish en masse but dredge up shellfish and plants from the sea floor, decimating food webs and leaving a marine war zone behind. It was accompanied by the railroad in hauling a greatly expanded catch to ever more distant markets, and by rapid improvement in refrigeration technology. Although for many decades storage requirements for coal restricted the range of steam trawlers, the shift to oil after World War I freed space for fish and liberated hands for massive nets, long lines, and huge trawls.[14]

After World War II came another revolution. Switching from military to civilian production, a government-financed shipbuilding industry quickly replaced fishing boats sunk during the war, then added enormously to numbers, tonnage, and sophistication. Their killing capacity was dramatically enhanced by adapting military technologies to hunt for increasingly scarce fish, guided less by a wizened seadog standing on the bridge in a sou'wester sniffing the breeze for bad weather than by corporate executives in the conference room of their skyscraping headquarters wearing *Amouage Epic Man Eau de Parfum* and who honed their professional skills on Wall Street rather than in a marine biology school. And the targets shifted.

As one species of large ocean predator after another succumbed to intensive fishing, the industry maintained profits by a double dip: it sought species living ever deeper in the sea, including those so distasteful in appearance that they could only be used for filets or fish sticks or, like monkfish, sold with their heads already cut off; and it hauled in ever more small fish that the big ones had formerly preyed upon, most to be pressed into fish oil or ground into fish meal to create feed for the fish farms that were simultaneously spreading.[15] The ever-increasing use of energy-intensive technologies to go deeper while seeking smaller and smaller concentrations of target material bears an obvious kinship to developments in metal mining. But, while mining works with a fixed geological stock, intensive fishing easily creates feedback loops that destroy the biological viability of the target in advance of actual exploitation. Emerging industrial fisheries further ignored the fact that complex ecosystems work best with more, rather than less, constituent species. Depleting one has knockdown effects on others, no matter what "market signals" might say. And once a species is near exhaustion, it is very difficult for it to recover.[16]

The alarm ought to have sounded loud and clear in 1992 with the collapse of perhaps the largest of the world's great fisheries, off the Grand Banks of Newfoundland. Until the 1960s, northern cod were fished inside Canadian territorial waters mainly from small boats – with some foreign trawlers outside – during the spawning season of capelin, the cod's favourite prey. Although Canadian politicians were quick to blame greedy interlopers, particularly Spanish, the beginning of the end was mostly homegrown. In 1977, following a worldwide trend, Canada unilaterally extended its control from the traditional three nautical-mile limit to an exclusive economic zone up to two hundred nautical miles out, taking in the greater part of the Grand Banks. And it turned loose a heavily subsidized – one third of incomes for fishers came from off-season unemployment insurance payments – trawler fleet with quotas that bore no relationship to biological reality. This was backed up by equally subsidized fish-packing plants throughout the traditionally depressed Atlantic Provinces in a typical political fix – a short-term boost for the regional economy leading to a long-term collapse of the fishery after most of the politicians responsible had left office, along with the creation of a powerful pro-fishing-at-all-costs lobby that would fight any future cuts.

Ignoring complaints from inshore fishers and warnings from marine ecologists in favour of sunny extrapolations from flawed data, the Canadian government, pushed by the fishing industry, insisted that there was no lack of cod. Anyway, what could go wrong? The female cod produces seven million eggs; so taking more fish simply meant more food left for more of their offspring to survive and grow – it was just a matter of basic economics. The pattern of increases in licenses and quotas peaked in 1991. The next year the fish virtually vanished. The government imposed a two-year moratorium. Then, taking an apparent abundance of cod in certain bays as a sign of health – and ignoring the fact that certain species under stress band together to give temporarily the appearance of numbers – it reopened the inshore fishery, wiping out the breeding stock on which recovery might have been based. In a panic, it re-imposed a total, this time indefinite ban, leaving cod fishers drawing unemployment insurance while they mended their gear and repaired their boats, waiting in vain for the cod to come back.[17]

Still, it was not all gloom and doom. With top predators gone, crab, shrimp, and lobster populations expanded enormously, the resulting prosperity to those fisheries helping to blunt criticism, particularly since the product sold for so much more per pound. Yet even that was an ecological red flag. As invertebrate populations exploded, they devoured much more zooplankton, creating space for an upsurge in phytoplankton that, in turn, can cause shifts in oceanic chemical cycles. That might further impede recovery of afflicted marine ecosystems and perhaps doom invertebrates to the same ultimate demographic fate as the cod, or so many others, if for different but not unrelated reasons.

Despite that wakeup call, the world fishing industry continued to grow in size, intensity, and technological sophistication. Meanwhile the world's marine authorities snored on the sidelines, arousing themselves up mainly to applaud when governments of major littoral states handed out to their fleets more tax-payer money as a reward for doing such a fine job of conserving nature's bounty.[18]

HOOK, LINE, AND SINKER

For a change, the US was not the worst offender, however high on the most-wanted list it may be. The EU countries had extra centuries to deplete their own fisheries in the Baltic, North, and Mediterranean Seas, and today are responsible for cannibalizing the rest of the world. Spain's politically powerful fleet (about 25 percent of total European fishing capacity) is especially notorious, plundering the seas today with the same kind of arrogant enthusiasm its conquistadores showed in looting the Americas half a millennium ago.[19] The Spanish government defends its fleet's activities on the grounds that seafood consumption is an essential part of national culture – as is bleeding a bull half to death, then, once it is sufficiently weakened, ritually slaughtering it in front of a jeering crowd.[20] South Korea and Japan distinguish themselves, too, at least with respect to their fishing fleets, with the latter also showing a Spanish-type affinity for spearing large mammals, also in the name of national pride.

In general, when rich industrial countries seek seafood as a panacea for an epidemic of heart disease, diabetes, and dementia brought on by overindulgence at home, they condemn to starvation, or to diseases linked to protein deficiency, desperately poor people abroad, particularly on the west and east coasts of Africa, regions already facing calamity from climate change and war. Corrupt or desperate governments, sometimes blackmailed by the World Bank or the WTO, grant to foreigners national fishing permits. In a particularly perverse sequence, the EU heavily subsidizes grain and vegetable production, dumping the surplus below cost on its African "trade partners." Farmers driven out of the market may try to shift into the artisanal fishery, only to face competition from giant European freezer-trawlers. That leaves the locals in places that depend heavily on the seacoasts two options: they can head into dwindling rainforests (already ravaged by illegal loggers feeding tropical hardwood to North American, European, and Asian buyers) to trap bush meat (including that from endangered species); or they can use their fishing boats to sneak into Europe to work as slave labour on fruit and vegetable farms. Those European farms, their costs cut further by savings on wages and social-security charges, can then dump more subsidized produce back into Africa, completing the circle.[21] Europe, its former freshwater fisheries exhausted and its nearby maritime resources polluted beyond recovery, now obtains half its fish from what are still laughingly referred to as "developing countries," much of it landed virtually without inspection in the Canary Islands, a major entrepôt, too, for illegal immigrants.[22]

Meanwhile, on the other side of Africa, the country with the longest shoreline and the richest marine resources, because of a unique upwelling of nutrient-rich water from the depths of the Indian Ocean, is also the one most battered by decades of civil war and foreign invasion. Although Somalia recovered some semblance of stability at the end of the 1990s, a subsequent US-sponsored Ethiopian invasion returned it to political chaos while protracted droughts in the interior drove more nomadic herdsmen and farmers to rely on the artisanal fishery. The problem they faced was that European companies responded to the political vacuum by sending giant trawlers to plunder fishing resources that supported hundreds of thousands of Somalis. The targets were not just small, common fish for the fishmeal market but enormous stocks of spiny lobster, tuna (several types), and shrimp, plus sharks (finned and tossed back to drown, with the fins destined for the Oriental shark-fin soup trade) and coveted reef fish (elsewhere already scarce) like snappers and grouper. In an apt demonstration of what free-market competition is all about, the European ships intruding in inshore waters technically reserved for the domestic artisanal fishery might ram native canoes or, so the locals claim, pour boiling water on their occupants, while other ships took advantage of the chaos to dump toxic and radioactive waste just off the coast. Then, when Somalis take to the seas in small boats, first to try to drive off the trawlers, and later, to hold to ransom foreign ships, the major powers sound the alarm about the upsurge in "piracy" and send their navies to deal with this latest threat from the Islamic Hordes to Judeo-Christian Civilization.[23]

Today's international fishing fleet falls roughly into three classes. Most ships have bona fide registrations and are therefore subject to both national regulations and any international conventions signed by their country of origin. There are also hundreds of privateers flying flags of convenience. Panama remains the favourite for ship registrations – not only does it have the advantage of history and reputation but it also has excellent supporting infrastructure of secret bank accounts and instant corporations. However Liberia, whose business took a knock during its civil wars, has come roaring back. And there are surprising new competitors: the flag of Mongolia, not exactly known for its mighty seafaring tradition, today flies proudly from the masts of North Korean ships.[24]

The key to the use of flags-of-convenience lies in the fact that under international law there is a distinction between the nationality of a ship and that of the owner. The Law of the Sea makes ships subject only to the regulations of their country of registry. Flag-of-convenience jurisdictions compete for that honour by keeping regulations at a minimum, taxes even lower, and maritime unions nonexistent among sailors recruited from poor countries. While most ships flying flags-of-convenience are small and old, their numbers keep growing. After all, when fleets are renewed, most older vessels do not just sail off into a marine sunset or to Pakistani or South Korean shipbreaking yards, institutions that rival dumpsites full of discarded batteries and old computer parts in terms of their menace to both the unfortunates who work there and the surrounding environment. More likely old ships are sold to ply other trades, like immigrant smuggling, gun running, or illegal fishing. Furthermore, modern factory ships, too, might prefer flags-of-convenience to evade safety regulations, fishing quotas, and restrictions on the type of equipment they can use, particularly since they can reflag on the run with nothing more than a satellite-phone call to a representative of the issuing country. There is probably no more compelling example of the cosmopolitan nature of today's fishing business than the possibility of ships using one flag to pick up government subsidies, another to get higher quota, yet another to employ banned fishing gear, and a further one to market the catch.

A final group consists of true pirate vessels that ignore all jurisdictional dictates or international agreements. They have an affinity for areas where civil government has either collapsed or is for sale at a bargain-basement price.[25] They might also turn up to buy catch in places where local fishers use blast or cyanide fishing. Blast-fishing can be done with dynamite bought off the black market near mines or construction sites, or with the same tried and true formula (ammonia fertilizer mixed with diesel fuel) that Timothy McVeigh used to bring down the Oklahoma City federal building in 1996. The cyanide is more likely lifted from the stores of a local gold-mining company.[26]

The difference between the three categories is not so much that one fishes illegally while the other does not. It is more a matter of the proportions of illegal to legal fish they take, and the exact ways in which they bend or break regulations. Despite protestations of corporate good-citizenship and slogans about sustainability, commercially successful fishing ships frequently use techniques that destroy habitat, ruin food webs, and result in gross wastage when they pitch bycatch of poor market value over the side. Modern trawls, for example, go so deep and work under so much pressure that the catch can spend hours dragged around all squashed together, scales stripped off, eyeballs popping out. Needless to add, any unwanted bycatch tossed aside is almost guaranteed to be already dead, or close to that state. The ships are guilty, too, of discarding or losing purse seines (that circle huge areas) and long-lines (with thousands of hooks) that can for years afterward indiscriminately kill marine life, including birds and mammals – they may be chucked because they are old or because they are illegal in the country of destination. Because of the political power of the industry and the flawed nature of data on marine stocks, quotas (where they exist) are likely set above biologically sustainable levels. Yet the "legal" fleet exceeds even its inflated quotas.[27] Excess catch can be offloaded to refrigerated ships at sea, or run into ports with minimal (or corrupt) supervision. Any prohibited or out-of-season species, or juveniles, can be hidden by commingling with legally authorized catch. Or fish can be mislabelled to hide country of origin, production method, or species.

Mislabelling may be just a marketing ploy – it is much easier to sell an orange roughy than a slimehead. A new name might even lead to a market bonanza. For example, for years Vietnam sold its farmed fish in the US as Delta catfish – a sly reference to the Mekong that Americans presumed to mean the Mississippi. When the domestic catfish industry found its markets slipping, it launched a patriotic campaign to convince Americans with the Stars-and-Stripes on their front lawns to shun Commie catfish. When that didn't suffice, it mobilized Southern Congressmen to pass a tariff on foreign sourced catfish and a ban on the use of the very term. So the producers changed the commercial name to basa and engaged in a very successful worldwide marketing campaign. In 2005, US states with their own catfish farms started to ban the newly labelled fish, too, on the grounds that it used an antibiotic not allowed in local fish farms. (The mind boggles at what that might be.) Subsequently, in a burst of law enforcement zeal rarely shown when US ships plunder the oceans, several major fish importers were fined and executives imprisoned for mislabelling Vietnamese farmed catfish to sell on the domestic market.[28]

Even more fish are mislabelled to hide the fact that they have been taken without license or in excess of quota or even from banned species. And mislabelling can be used to con consumers to pay for a more expensive fish than the one they are actually getting. After the near collapse of the Gulf of Mexico fishery for red snapper, highly popular because of its inoffensive taste, the stuff on the North American market shifted, first to "Pacific red snapper" (a group of thirteen species of rockfish with no biological relationship to the true snapper), then more recently to farmed catfish and tilapia. The result has been a string of scandals stretching over many years that may even be getting worse as degree of depletion increases along with prices charged.[29] Grouper, another increasingly sparse "consumer choice," is similarly reported to be a common target of label fraud.[30]

Some in the retail industry try to duck responsibility by insisting that they were fooled by suppliers, a plea that raises questions about whether anyone who cannot tell a rockfish from a rock star ought to be selling seafood. A more credible claim would be that they were just following the US government's lead. In the mid 1970s, federal officials wanted to find more attractive names for things like hogsucker (soon to be butterfish) or dogfish, ratfish or stumpknocker. So it awarded a contract to Chicago-based Brands Group that came up with "edibility profiles" based on a five-point scale that took into account flavour, fattiness, odour, colour, firmness, flakiness, moistness, and coarseness. The idea was to lump all species with similar profiles into groups, then rename them generically or individually. The Feds liked the idea so much that they contracted with the Army Research Laboratory to find a scientific way to measure these characteristics using machinery like the Instron Universal Testing Machine, which compresses, pulls apart, or penetrates the food to produce a "force versus deformation curve." With a nod from professional tasters, the conclusion was that all fish species were potentially marketable, provided the name was right.[31]

Sometimes no label at all works as well as a false one – an illegally caught fish can be processed and introduced onto the market with the singularly informative name: "frozen fish filet."[32] Mislabelling, too, can disguise potentially dangerous fish. While seafood consumption in rich countries grows in part because of its presumed positive impact on human health, oily fish, the most popular in that respect, can now be so contaminated with mercury, PCBs, or flame-retarding chemicals as to have the opposite effect – not to mention all the tiny bits of plastic waste eaten by zooplankton that mount up the food chain until fishermen may soon haul in swordfish steaks already sealed in Saran Wrap.[33]

Not least, mislabelling undermines regulatory efforts, such as they are. Quotas are set according to estimates of stocks; and stocks are calculated by reference to reported catch; the more substitution prior to landing of another species for one that is being depleted, the more inflated will be estimates of those remaining.[34]

All of these problems show up dramatically with respect to one of the newer fads among afishionados. The Patagonian toothfish, a formerly obscure predator in remote oceans, became a consumer rage in the 1980s once it was relabelled Chilean sea bass to appeal to a retail trade already replete with other types of phony "bass." Although that fishery is in theory regulated by the Commission on the Conservation of Antarctic Marine Resources, whose members pledge to accept imports only of legally caught fish, the convention is systematically defeated not just by the activities of nonmembers but by underreporting, commingling, passing fish through a chain of re-exports to hide the trail, processing at sea that disguises the origin of the filets, fraudulent flag-state approvals, and laundering through out-of-the-way ports, plus a fleet that switches flags and home ports at will. While states that want to do the job properly may insist on verifying the location of ships bearing their flags with Vessel Monitoring Systems using GPS equipment, that has proven vulnerable to manipulation. The net result of regulatory efforts for the so-called Chilean sea bass was that by early in the new millennium its stock may have already dropped past the point of biological recovery.[35]

While marine biologists warn that wild seafood may be gone in forty to fifty years, industry cheerleaders reassure the world that there are still great tracts of deep ocean to be raided, assuming their nets and lines can penetrate a progressively thickening layer of polyethylene terephthalate peanut butter jars, polypropylene bottle caps, polystyrene packaging pellets, and polyvinyl chloride sheets.[36] The response in Japan, for example, to rapidly rising costs, the result of requiring heavier and heavier capital investment per unit of fish caught, has been not to allow stocks to recover, but to search for a way of offset fuel costs by building hybrid or biofuel-driven engines for its ships.[37] Anyway ... surely humanity can trust science to find a way. Perhaps by a visionary project financed (naturally) with tax money in which scientists from companies like, for example, BP and Monsanto team-up to bioengineer not a bionic saw fish or a cybernetic swordfish but a self-cloning drillfish spliced with genetic material from a divining rod, which could run on oil spills and bilge waste as it dives down several miles to poke test holes in the ocean floor, solving the twin problems posed by declining oil reserves and by rapidly exhausting fish stocks in a single stroke. Besides, if things get really bad, everyone can take heart that aquaculture is growing by leaps and bounds.

AQUA-FOLLIES

Although aquaculture is one of modern life's premier sins against nature, its roots are ancient. In the Egypt of the Pharaohs, tilapias were raised in ponds; China, three thousand years ago, favoured carp; the same fish, fed on garbage, was raised in early modern Europe; and shrimp cultivation has existed in Southeast Asia for hundreds of years. But these were minor side dishes to the wild fishery. It took centuries of destruction of freshwater habitat, followed by further centuries of intensive mining of the sea combined with rising demand and a modern fundamentalist faith that science could solve all, to spark serious interest in industrial-scale aquaculture. Many species are now farmed. But the leader, by weight and value, is probably the Atlantic salmon, now raised even more commonly on the Pacific. Unlike the tilapia, a fast-growing, quick-breeding vegetarian that thrives in standing bodies of fresh or brackish water, or the carp, a bottom feeder also happy in freshwater ponds and eager to eat all kinds of stuff other fish won't touch, the salmon is highly migratory, needing both fresh and salt water for its life cycle; and it represented the first time that a voracious carnivore was farm-raised for human consumption.[38]

The process starts by cutting open a "ripe" female to extract eggs whose numbers have been artificially boosted by hormone baths and injections, spraying them with milt from a recently killed male, then hatching them in plastic trays in an incubator surrounded by freshwater. Once the fry are weaned, they are exposed to light twenty-four hours a day to stimulate growth. After about a year they are moved into large net-pens in the sea – some the size of several football fields – with the result that bays that would normally support perhaps a few hundred wild salmon could now host to hundreds of thousands of farmed ones. There they are fed ground fishmeal, largely made from anchovies, herring, and mackerel that are among the most heavily fished stocks in the world. In fact they are fished with so much success that their natural predators, be they whales or dolphins or sea birds, can show signs of malnutrition.[39] It takes a minimum of three pounds of fishmeal made from species that are quite edible by humans in their own right to make one pound of salmon flesh. Naturally any chemical toxins in feed-fish bio-accumulate in the salmon – true in wild salmon, too, but with different toxins and probably at a slower rate.

Supposedly to reduce PCB contamination, the salmon-farming industry decided to reduce fishmeal in favour of more soy protein.[40] The real reason was more likely that its own demands sent fishmeal prices soaring, and the US grain companies, desperate for new markets for genetically modified crops, were happy to step into the picture. The dietary change combined with crowding fish into small net-cages results in flabby flesh that, like factory-farmed animals fed soy and corn, contains more saturated fat relative to healthy Omega 3 than in the wild species.

Being fed an artificial diet has another important consequence. Wild salmon feed on krill, tiny crustaceans containing a carotenoid called astaxanthin, from which salmon flesh derives its colour. But the meat of farmed salmon is an unappetizing grey. Hence along with the fish-and-soy meal, salmon are fed a petroleum-derived synthetic. In fact salmon farmers can choose colours along a pink-to-bright red spectrum with no one taking much note that the dye was used in the 1970s as a self-tanner for humans until it was banned as a possible carcinogen. After all, salmon farms can plead that some land-based factory-farms, too, use synthetic astaxanthin to turn egg yolks yellow or ham a reddish tint. Natural astaxanthin costs three to four times as much as the synthetic. And since astaxanthin accounts for 20–30 percent of feed costs, a salmon farmer's "economic" choice is obvious.

Because of confinement so close that feces from one fish pass through the gills of others, pathogens along with them, farmed fish are extremely vulnerable to infections, requiring extensive treatment by antibiotics – which did not prevent the Chilean industry, the heaviest user in the world, from once being wiped out by salmon anemia virus.[41] A more gruesome menace is sea lice. Since wild salmon are widely scattered, the parasites have trouble finding a host; and when an afflicted salmon heads up rivers to spawn in freshwater, the lice die. But farmed salmon densely packed in net-pens can be literally eaten alive. Since the farms are often located near wild-salmon migration routes, sea lice easily jump to wild fish. Like bacteria, sea lice develop resistance, requiring ever greater quantities of ever more powerful poisons. Some biocides used (including varieties banned in agriculture) lodge in the flesh of the salmon; much more is excreted to end up on the ocean floor, killing off shellfish that in normal times would help keep the waters clean. While the fish in the net-pens are not so much swimming as treading water in a pathogen soup, the accumulation of undigested food and feces under the net-pens encourages oxygen-depleting algae blooms. Periodically the organic and chemical waste forces fish farms to migrate and repeat the process elsewhere. Also migrating are the fish themselves. Escapees and descendants of the farmed version of the Atlantic salmon have already heavily repopulated the North Atlantic and are now being found in the Pacific, too, as far away as the Bering Sea.

Bad press and sometimes a bad conscience led some fish farmers to avoid synthetic chemicals or growth hormones, to give salmon more space in the net-pens, to feed them a more natural diet, and to use astaxanthin from seaweed or shrimp shells. While "organic" salmon is certainly an improvement, it is really like keeping a cow locked in a pen and feeding it grass cut from the fields on which it normally would roam and ruminate, while selling its manure to a biofuel manufacturer instead of returning it naturally to the nutrient cycle. Besides, this part of the market is restricted to an elite of consumers with both knowledge and financial means. And there is little to prevent an entrepreneurial wholesaler, perhaps the same one inclined to mislabel farmed salmon as wild, from pushing up the price even further with a phony organic certification.[42] Although from time to time stores in major market countries get spooked by the problems of the farmed salmon business, the scares quickly blow over; and the business continues to grow.

Meanwhile, the wild salmon, whose salvation was one of the main excuses for the rampant expansion of the salmon farming business, continues its long-term decline. (The British Columbia salmon industry's excitement over an exceptionally large 2010 sockeye run, perhaps the largest in a century, will probably turn out to be much like the oil companies trying to insist that an unprecedented July hailstorm in California suffices to refute claims that the Earth's atmosphere is heating up.[43]) In fact so bad has the decline been in recent years that in some places near the Pacific Coast bear populations who rely on its runs as their main source of protein are threatened in turn.[44] The reality is that the only way to protect species in the wild is to protect the wilderness, something that isn't exactly at the top of most government agendas. Instead aquaculture of industrial dimensions continues to spread, growing especially rapidly in one of the places that pioneered its artisanal form.

China, despite the relatively modest size of its own fishing fleet, is today the largest exporter of fish in the world (running at about $35 billion per annum), with the US as its biggest market. Partly that success reflects cheap-labour processing of the catch of other countries, particularly since it can then be re-exported as "made in China," sidestepping international quota restrictions. Partly the remarkable increase in Chinese seafood exports result from a government drive to develop aquaculture, particularly of eels, shrimp, and tilapias, to meet the protein needs of its own people, to generate foreign exchange (as if China needed more), and to give jobs to farmers displaced by rapid urbanization, giant infrastructure projects, and massive soil erosion. But China is polluting even faster than it is producing, fouling water for drinking and irrigation as well as threatening the very success of its own fish farms. Yet, when major polluters are closed by environmental authorities, political pressures sometimes puts them back in business.[45]

The traditional rationalization for fish farming is that it helps to preserve the fish in the wild – as if anyone can point to a positive impact on wild turkey populations from the spread of industrial turkey farms. Apart from the fact that the most popular farmed fish are carnivores feasting off wild fish reduced to fishmeal, the claim is further damaged by the example of tuna farms with their doubly negative impact on the wild species.[46]

Although there are restrictions against taking juveniles, fishermen on the two main migration paths in the Gulf of Mexico and southern Mediterranean capture the small fish without reporting them. They are towed still in the purse seines to fattening farms where they are fed about three times as often as they would eat in the wild. Like salmon or other farmed species, their life in net-pens can only be lengthened by heavy doses of antibiotics. But unlike salmon that require three pounds of small, oily fish like sardines, herrings, and anchovies to produce one pound of body weight gain, with tuna the ratio can be as high as fifteen or twenty to one, although the great scientific breakthroughs in man-ufacturing pellets hyped with synthetic vitamins (especially vitamin E made from petroleum that also "improves" the colour of the flesh) have lowered the ratio closer to eight. So valuable is the product that tuna fat-tening farms are commonly patrolled by armed boats to deter poachers, particularly at night.

That is true, too, in farming operations attempting to cash in on the decimation of another super-luxury fish, the European glass eel.[47] Eels were once so plentiful that peasants in England in the thirteenth century used them by the barrel to pay rent to their ecclesiastical landlords.[48] Although adult eels have never been particularly prized, the price today of baby European eels, transparent in their early phase of life cycle, peaks in Spain where *angula* is a special Christmas delicacy, at about €1,400 a kilo, higher even than in Japan where it is enough of a favou-rite to best the bluefin tuna in price. With a strict migration cycle, from the Sagossa Sea to Southern, then Northern Europe, before moving from salt- to freshwater and changing into the mature yellow eel, the ideal fishing points for juveniles are rivers along the west coasts of Spain, France, and the UK. Led by half a dozen old family businesses in Spain's Basque region, juvenile eels are scooped up en masse, kept in freshwater tanks for a week until a black stripe appears on their back (to distinguish them from those taken already dead, probably poisoned in the river) and usually shipped live. However some are frozen, then sold for a discount that may or may not be passed on to restaurant clients who only see the fish once it is cooked.

Sharply rising prices – glass eels were briefly more expensive than beluga caviar and white truffles – due to the usual combination of gross overexploitation, habitat destruction, and industrial pollution, prompted five reactions: a panic rush of international and national regulations; an upsurge of poaching off-season and in prohibited areas; the substitu-tion of American and Japanese (also transparent when young) for the European eels, usually without telling the buyer; and the invention at least for the Spanish market of a fake called the gula. It is made from passing pollock or other whitefish through a machine that spits out mush shaped like angulas, adding a touch of squid ink on the back and sometimes imitation coal-black eyes and mouth to make them look real.

The fifth reaction was a rush to perfect techniques for the aquaculture of the European eel.[49]

Still, the real money in aquaculture in the future will not be the glass eel or the bluefin tuna. Nor will it even be the Frankensalmon. This "fish" was recently developed in the US to be raised in tanks on land, its growth rate greatly accelerated by splicing in genetic material from the ocean pout, an ugly eel-like creature long shunned because of its propensity to carry parasites but which has the happy property of growing rapidly all year long even in very cold weather.[50] (Unilever, the transnational vendor of food and cosmetic products, already grows antifreeze proteins using the ocean pout's genetic material to "improve" its ice cream.[51]) Instead, the big bucks in aquaculture will come from the increasing success, however temporary, in replacing the Caspian Sea's ravaged sturgeon fishery and the dazzlingly expensive caviar that it yields with a passable farmed version – if for no other reason than to assure that Madonna can continue to have gobs of the stuff follow in a private jet on her concert tours around the world.

ROE BOATS AND STURGEON TRAWLERS

The story begins with a fish that is virtually a living fossil, boasting an ancestry reaching back before the age of the dinosaurs, a potential lifespan of more than a century, and a voracious appetite for other aquatic creatures. Some species, like the beluga, are so large and well armoured as to be themselves free of natural predators, except human beings to the extent they still qualify as "natural." Apart from consuming sturgeon meat and using various bits for everything from traditional Chinese medicine to industrial glues, humans were attracted by its fertility. Eggs of a mature female may account for 8–15 percent of body weight. The recorded champion, caught in 1908, was a sixty-year-old beluga weighing in at nearly a thousand kilograms, whose eggs a century later might have retailed for over $500,000. The ironic process by which sheer fecundity helped to transform the sturgeon from one of the most widespread fish in northern temperate waters into today's few remnants trapped by hydroelectric dams, poisoned by petrochemical sludge, and preyed upon by poachers is commonly referred to as economic development.[52]

The carnage did not occur overnight. As the habit of eating sturgeon roe spread from imperial Russia to Western Europe, and later to North America, first European waterways feeding the Black and Baltic seas, then major rivers of the US were so depleted and polluted as to impede regeneration. (The 300,000 tons of German munitions, including poison gases, dumped in the Baltic by British, US, and Soviet forces at the end of World War II, probably didn't help much either.[53]) Stories about the Austro-Hungarian royal family gleefully firing cannons at migrating schools in the Danube or captains cursing as their boats were blocked by sheer biomass on the Hudson or bars serving free caviar with beer in New York may be exaggerated or even apocryphal; but they make a valid point about the bygone bounty of nature and the modern-day boundlessness of human folly.[54] Indeed, much like the oyster or the aba-lone, caviar became a "luxury" only in response to its growing scarcity – but unlike the bluefin tuna, it did not have or need the benefit of a US army endorsement.

The caviar business begins with the search for a "ripe" female. Since a traumatized female can secrete enzymes that destroy the taste of the eggs and might poison the person eating them, caught sturgeon (of both sexes since they can be visually hard to distinguish) have their bellies quickly ripped open, probably while still alive. Eggs are rinsed, lightly salted, perhaps preserved with borax (forbidden in the US), occasionally pasteurized (to the disapproval of afishionados), then packed in 1.8 kg tins for wholesale trade, later repackaged into smaller tins and jars for retail. Unpasteurized eggs can store for up to six months at $-3°$ Celsius: at higher temperatures, they may putrefy; at lower, they may freeze and rupture. In a proper packing plant, salting is done lightly with a chemi-cally purified, iodine-free marine variety. By contrast, poachers may oversalt with whatever is handy to make eggs better endure long trips hidden in a truck or packed in a suitcase. Even so the load may arrive at a final destination dried out or spoiled, requiring eggs to be artificially rehydrated and perhaps treated with vegetable oils to make them appear (and smell) fit for human consumption.

By the early twentieth century, devastation elsewhere had concentrated the industry on the Caspian Sea. For most of that century, an agreement between Soviet and Iranian state monopolies kept the fishery, if not the fish, healthy. To reduce wastage the USSR banned fishing on the open sea (all fishing had to be conducted on rivers where females spawned); it eliminated bottom-scraping trawlers that destroyed food webs; and it restricted seasons and sizes. Every female caught was numbered; and each tin bore that reference number to permit the caviar to be tracked around the world. Poaching carried a twelve-year prison sentence. Fish stocks seemed sufficient that in the 1980s the USSR let factory ships operate on the Caspian. But, beneath its murky surface, serious prob-lems were stirring.

They actually began to bubble up in the late nineteenth century, along with Caspian oil that spilled into the water to deplete oxygen vital to aquatic life.[55] In the 1950s and 1960s diversion for irrigation dried up parts of the Volga Delta and polluted the rest with pesticides. Hydroelectric dams added PCBs to the toxic brew, interfered with nutrient flow, and ultimately blocked 85 percent of spawning grounds for a fish whose rigid migratory patterns (females spawn in the river where they hatched) and late sexual maturity (six to twenty-five years, depending on the species) make it exceptionally vulnerable to habitat disruption. A massive hatcheries program seemed to resolve the problem in the short run while promising in the long to turn the Caspian into the world's largest polluted fish farm. Then the breakup of the Soviet Union confronted the sturgeon with an enormous new problem.

Out of the ruins, bordering the Caspian, emerged three new countries (Azerbaijan, Kazakhstan, and Turkmenistan) in economic and administrative chaos; while along its own Caspian Coast, Russia itself began to fragment into warlord-run statelets where poachers ran amok. Poaching was further encouraged after Boris Yeltsin's Russia, in another sodden nod toward the magic of the market, cut the maximum prison term for poaching to two years, and introduced fines of the equivalent of $75 per poached fish – when beluga roe was retailing in the US for up to $100 an ounce.

Along the vast Caspian coast with hundreds of rivers, poachers fell into three categories. Many were former fishers or fish-plant employees cast adrift by the foundering of the state-run industry. They operated from shore or small boats, then waited in their villages for middlemen to buy their catch. Resold to smugglers, the caviar was hauled from Astrakhan, former capital of the legal fishery turned latter-day capital of the illegal, further into Russia, mainly for the domestic market, some for international sale. These small poachers were ripe prey for corrupt enforcement agents. A militiaman might capture a poacher, seize the catch, accept a bribe to release the fisher, then take the roe to a specially designated store allowed to deal in confiscated caviar. The store was supposed to transfer it to the state. Alternatively it could pay the militiaman for the caviar, then resell it to a smuggler for several times that sum. Once that smuggler paid off various patrolmen en route, the poached material still came onto the black market with a few extra service charges built into the final price.[56]

More important were open-sea "fishing mafias" with banned trawls. Sometimes they were linked to senior politicians. Sometimes they simply relied on speed or firepower. The problem with the open-sea fishery is that the average take per fish would be by definition much smaller than from rivers where only ripe females went to spawn. Furthermore big poachers who went only after caviar, not sturgeon meat, killed indiscriminately and discarded the carcasses.

Then there were the companies. In an effort to restrict the catch, the government introduced quotas for which only large firms could afford to bid, leaving others to fish sturgeon illegally. Smaller companies might get quota for other species, yet fish for sturgeon. Even licensed companies might take fish in excess of quota or launder roe from poachers. With most hatcheries closed or badly functioning in the immediate post-Soviet period, there was no serious effort to replace fish lost to the black market.

Before it could reach that market, poached caviar had to be processed – professionally by large companies for local elite consumption and export; crudely by small-scale operators for the domestic massmarket and the illegal foreign one. Then it was tinned and labelled. Poachers used fake labels of nonexistent firms or names similar enough to real companies to fool casual inspection; alternatively they might use good copies of genuine labels or real ones stolen from legitimate companies. Best were legitimate labels placed on by a licensed factory that bought caviar from poachers to commingle with legally acquired stock.

While most of the catch probably ended up on the Russian domestic market, in the 1990s an increasing flow seemed to head to Western Europe and especially to the US, which rapidly became the world's premier consumer. In effect the US upper class celebrated the collapse of its former arch-enemy with a consumathon of Russia's most prestigious foodstuff, while in a similar spirit triumphant US-inspired (and sometimes -directed) vulture-capitalists tore chunks out of the dying body of the Soviet economy. The crumbling of control on the northern Caspian coincided with the emigration to the US of ex-Soviet citizens familiar with the caviar trade. The market was encouraged further by an embargo slapped on Iranian caviar by President Reagan in 1987 (long after Iran and the US had broken relations, but just at the start of a US-USSR thaw), in a stroke wiping out 80 percent of Iran's market. It was not lifted until 2000. The result of the Russian caviar binge was such an alarming drop in the sturgeon population that 1998 brought what passes for an international regulatory apparatus shadow-boxing into action.

CITES: FAIR TRADE OR TRADE FAIR?

Fishing today is regulated mainly through a set of regional conventions whose edicts are largely unenforceable. Despite that, councils, like the one supposedly keeping the Patagonian toothfish from going the way of the dodo, are charged with monitoring catch, landings, and types of fishing methods, and applying the usual makeshift guesswork measures ("maximum sustainable yield" or "catch per unit effort") whose main function is to keep the fishing industry going. More serious, genuinely international attempts by countries to cooperate in curbing unrestricted exploitation of all forms of wildlife do exist, particularly the 1973 Convention on International Trade in Endangered Species of Flora and Fauna (CITES).[57] However, those efforts were seriously compromised from the start.

Part of the problem lies in the very nature of international treaties. The usual model for modern environmental treaties in general (although CITES, an older one, had more legitimate roots) is that, once interested NGOs feed a sympathetic media that in turn convinces "the public" (whatever that may mean) in major Western countries that a problem may exist, politicians seize on it to advance their short-term ambitions. What follows next a series of international meetings in which leaders jet off to elegantly newsworthy places, mouth indignant platitudes, get their pictures taken, and leave without really having a clue what they were talking about. In the meantime, senior bureaucrats have been working behind the scenes to placate domestic constituencies, each with different agendas, to produce a grossly watered down version of the original initiative. Subsequently the major powers bribe or browbeat other states to sign on.

But matters hardly stop there. Any treaty – or major modifications in an existing one – has to be ratified by national legislatures, and possibly by lesser jurisdictions in countries with a federal structure, usually requiring further concessions that water down its application. Then regulations have to be penned in each country to implement the law, while signatory governments also have to create an enforcement mechanism. The enforcement agency must be assured adequate powers and resources (and enough freedom from political interference or corruption) to do the job. The results then must be imposed on populations who may well view their governments as venal, abusive, and illegitimate and may consider the treaty to be simply another affront from former colonial powers.

There are examples where such a process worked, sort of – like the Montreal Protocol to phase out ozone depleting substances. In this case the urgency was indisputable, the science beyond serious challenge, the vested interests opposing it relatively weak, and a simple technology fix available for a big part of the problem – as it was then diagnosed and before the California wine and strawberry interests mobilized their muscle. But environmental treaties more commonly turn out to be counterproductive by giving an impression that someone somewhere is on the job, therefore quieting agitation for genuine action while the emergency with which they were supposed to deal gets progressively worse.

The contrary example to the Montreal Protocol is the Kyoto Protocol, which, in the unlikely event it could ever have been seriously implemented, would have had as its main effect not averting climate catastrophe but puffing shares of the nuclear industry and permitting Wall Street or City of London brokers to get rich trafficking in carbon credits.[58]

Unlike some of its successors, CITES was born in an atmosphere more of idealistic concern than of desperate buck-passing. But it, too, gets bogged down in interest-group wrangling. Periodically it gathers "stakeholders" to argue over which species to classify as endangered, a subject that can itself be an issue of contention up to the point where the species vanishes, followed by further contention about why it happened. But, assuming that a species does make the honour list, the question is on which appendix it belongs. Appendix I consists of those so threatened globally as to call for a complete ban on international trade. It permits members of that species to be moved across borders only for scientific and similar purposes accompanied by export permits from the country of origin and import permits from the country of destination. Appendix II consists of those that might soon become endangered without limitations on their trade. It allows commercial exchanges if the country of origin issues an export permit. Appendix III consists of those that are not deemed endangered on a worldwide basis but maybe are within particular countries. Signatories are to assist in their own way the countries struggling to protect the particular species within those countries' borders. Therefore much of the action at CITES events consists (especially if a species is warm and fuzzy-looking) of often bitter and sometimes intractable debates over what goes on which appendix. That may be one reason why CITES lists about nine times as many types of mammals as fish even though fish species outnumber mammal by about the same ratio.[59] In fact a last ditch effort in 2010 to extend CITES protection to the bluefin tuna, a de facto confession that previous fisheries conventions had been a dismal failure, collapsed in the face of concerted opposition from countries with large tuna-fishing fleets and those who were heavy consumers. Japan was in the forefront in both categories with the claim that consumption of bluefin tuna sushi, one of which had sold on the Tokyo market for approximately $125,000, was an essential part of its national culture, presumably on a par with dying from the radiation sickness also bequeathed by the US military.[60]

Yet other species have made the honour list in the past. For example, two types of sturgeon of little commercial value had been placed on Appendix I and four on Appendix II years before the collapse of the beluga. To that latter event CITES responded by adding most remaining species of sturgeon along with related paddlefish to Appendix II. A CITES

II listing did draw some attention to the plight of the sturgeon from a world that has a distinctly limited attention span. But the treaty applied only to international (not domestic) trade, and by definition constrained only member countries, which excluded Azerbaijan and Kazakhstan. The main regulatory requirement was a document specifying origin, size of load, year of harvest, registration number of processing plant, and lot identification number to be shown at both export and import points, then later verified at CITES headquarters. Those who operated completely in the black continued to ignore restrictions; and those running ostensibly legal businesses learned to counterfeit documents, acquire blanks, or make multiple use of single-use certificates. In the event that caviar passed through a third country en route to its final destination, it sufficed for the importer to show not the export certificate from country of origin but just a re-export certificate issued by any transit country.[61]

At first neither CITES requirements nor drastically reduced quotas inside Russia seemed to abate the flow of caviar. Within Russia, where it was an offense to catch without a license but not to sell, caviar reportedly remained available openly at venues ranging from fancy restaurants to street-vendor carts – what they were really selling under the "caviar" label is another matter.[62] And inside the US, the trade simply dove below the surface until a series of dramatic law-enforcement catches pulled it, wriggling and squirming, back into public view.[63]

BAIT-AND-SWITCH?

Smuggling Caspian caviar into the US has a long pedigree. Initially the motive was not to escape CITES restrictions but to evade high customs charges on Soviet (later Russian) product and the embargo on Iranian. For example, in the late 1980s the boss of Aquamar Gourmet Imports arranged for caviar to arrive at JFK airport on SAS or Lufthansa planes – duty-free since it was nominally for re-export – then for empty containers to leave by Pan American. Apparently Pan Am was intrigued enough to itself buy caviar from Aquamar. Not only did the company bill Pan Am full price for beluga on which it had ducked a 30 percent customs charge, it also unloaded both cheaper Caspian sevruga and domestic lumpfish roe in place of beluga onto Pan Am's first-class passengers, then pulled on the same on United Airways and Cathay Pacific. Profits were hidden in Switzerland, safe from trawling expeditions by the US tax service.[64]

By the late 1990s, the objective shifted to evading increasingly tight quotas imposed by Russia on the catch and CITES restrictions on trade. Hence much of the flow to the US began moving indirectly. One favourite transshipment point was Poland. Proximity to Russia along with cozy relations with the US (so that few Polish citizens, unlike Russians, were searched on arrival) made Poland an excellent source for "suitcase caviar." Or so Eugeniusz Koczuk believed. His Gino International became big in the 1980s when Wall Street sharpies targeted airlines for takeover, looted them to pay interest on money borrowed for the buyouts, then forced the crippled hulks to slash costs. The results showed up in drastic cutbacks in staff, as well as the pay of pilots, and a search for things like cheaper caviar to placate first-class passengers irked over delays and mechanical failures. Koczuk's company used couriers – including the deputy chief of the Warsaw police and his wife, a hostess with the Polish national airlines – so that a product that was supposed to be kept at –3° Celsius arrived in New York after alternately freezing in a baggage hold and sweating in a suitcase for a day. To give wholesale buyers an alibi if things went wrong, he repeatedly showed nonreusable CITES documents. He was caught after an anonymous phone call to US customs.[65]

The case unexpectedly collared as well the head of New York airport-based Caspian Star Caviar. Among its accomplishments were under-reporting the weight of caviar imported from Russia via Turkey to reduce import duties, mislabelling osetra caviar as more expensive beluga, mixing Russian with American, and selling protected American paddlefish roe as nonrestricted lumpfish. Its greatest coup was perhaps arranging for a supply of Lake Ontario salmon roe so polluted that it had to be labelled fit only for bait, then, after laundering it through a subsidiary, selling the stuff for human consumption. The downfall came when its boss tried to unload a bad shipment from a Polish supplier onto Eugeniusz Koczuk, who was by then under surveillance by wildlife service officers. They raided the Caspian Star office to discover, among other matters, that its boss also had a habit of reusing nonreusable CITES permits.[66]

Next to fall was Connoisseur Brands Ltd, whose boss also purchased poached caviar from Koczuk's company, including stuff that was frozen or expired. He drained off the rancid fish oil, washed the eggs with salt water, then added walnut or hazelnut oil to disguise the spoilage. Sometimes he mixed in poached American paddlefish roe, then sold it to the usual luxury purveyors. He was caught in a sting when a wildlife officer posing as a purchaser for a gourmet food outlet bought his caviar and subjected it to a DNA test, while yet another posing as a fish poacher taped the company's chief commenting that he did not care if the American paddlefish (whose roe was used to cut the Caspian caviar) was endangered since the punishments were so derisory. He was found guilty of selling illegally caught paddlefish, mislabelling paddlefish as

Russian caviar, purchasing caviar out of suitcases smuggled into the US, using double invoices to minimize import duties, and making false statements to the Fish & Wildlife Service.[67]

While Poland was ideally located for "suitcase caviar," Dubai, favoured by geography and even more by its status as one of the world's great legalized contraband centres, was eminently suited for wholesale trade using fraudulent documents. For example, it became the main turning point for smuggling banned Iranian caviar into the US. Although Iran, unlike the USSR, survived its most political upheaval with the state caviar monopoly intact, poaching does occur, mostly opportunistic and local, sometimes larger scale for export. As in Russia, fishers prepare the roe, then sell it for cash to middlemen who hide it in trucks carrying regular fish to wholesalers in Teheran. There are few road checks; and, in the unlikely event of being caught, the driver pays a small bribe. In Teheran some is delivered to the homes of, or restaurants catering to, the well-to-do; some is sent to the port of Bandar Abbas, then loaded onto planes or fast boats for Dubai, where respectable seafood distributors, the same ones handling Russian contraband, provide the required clearances for re-export.

Although, as a free-trade centre, Dubai has no taxes on goods coming or going, nor a customs check on goods in transit, it is bound by CITES. Hence a Dubai trading company imported poached Russian caviar, bought fraudulent CITES re-export permits from corrupt officials, then resold both the caviar (beluga and sevruga) and the permits to another Dubai company run by the brother-in-law of the head of US Caviar & Caviar. That company pasted onto the tins fake labels pretending they were from a legitimate Russian exporter; and US Caviar & Caviar arranged to print false Russian health certificates, make a phony stamp, and forge the signature of a Russian health official. The caviar with all necessary documents arrived in the US to be resold to restaurants, wholesalers, and gourmet outlets, including airlines for their first-class passengers.

Things went so well that the conspirators got trebly greedy. First they began mislabelling the imported caviar as a lower-quality, lower-price product to reduce import duties, then sold it as the real stuff for full price. Second, they began adulterating the Russian with American lumpfish roe (acquired legally since it is unprotected) at a cost about 1/10 that of beluga. Third, they started to add to the mix roe of endangered American paddlefish and shovelnose sturgeon, bought for cash from domestic poachers. All of that, along with caviar that had been previously frozen, partially cooked, or pasteurized, was sold to the same elite outlets with fake Russian certificates and seals. Things went well until a customs officer at a Washington airport noticed a label peeling off – genuine Russian ones are glued on securely. Both the US Fisheries & Wildlife Service and the FBI were informed. The caviar was subjected to a DNA test; and in 2001 the company and its officers were found guilty of conspiracy, smuggling, submitting false wildlife records, mail fraud, and violations of the Endangered Species Act.[68]

Many of these cases involved a double scam – evading import restrictions on Caspian caviar along with commingling with cheaper and/or poached American roe. However the trick of selling an American species as if it were a Caspian luxury import actually long predated the CITES restrictions. In the late nineteenth century, when the US still had abundant domestic sturgeon, its companies exported to Europe under the name Astrakhan Caviar to fool European consumers into thinking the stuff was Russian, only to have some clever importers ship part of a lot back to the US with a different label making the same claim.[69]

But today, barring a few miraculous sightings in the Hudson River, long used by chemical and electrical companies as an industrial toilet, the east is effectively sturgeon-free. The Mississippi system still hosts paddlefish, subject to various restrictions on size and timing of catch in some states but wide open for exploitation in others, creating an opportunity for poachers to conduct regulation arbitrage. However, the real prize is on the Pacific side, where the white sturgeon can, if left to itself in an unspoiled environment, grow to 20 feet long, live 130 years, and weigh in at 2,000 pounds.[70] Although tentative efforts to limit the catch date back to the early twentieth century, serious conservation efforts began fifty years later, when Washington State wildlife officials became alarmed by a dramatic drop in the average size of egg-bearing females. The state decreed that fish containing roe could be caught only by aboriginals or by licensed fishers, and the roe could be sold only to licensed buyers. Sports fishers were allowed to catch sturgeon but not to sell their eggs, which are not only black like those of the treasured beluga but virtually indistinguishable in taste.

In 1985, Steven Darnell, an amateur fisher, began hanging out with sports anglers, offering to buy their sturgeon roe. No names were given; buys were arranged in cash on back roads or in parking lots; and, since Darnell knew the routine of local wildlife officers, safety was assured. He also began trading with Indians, who trusted him because, unlike buyers for commercial distributors, he never cheated them.[71] Initially his customers were local seafood and gourmet specialty stores. But then he made long-distance contact with Arnold Stürm-Hansen, one of the grand names in American caviar, whose ancestors had shifted their caviar business from Hamburg to New York in response to the collapse of the Elbe River sturgeon. Stürm-Hansen had among his clients the Waldorf-Astoria, the Rainbow Room, and Pan American Airlines, maintaining its high standards in catering to its first-class passengers.[72]

After Darnell purchased caviar, he took it to a room (paid for in cash) in a cheap motel where he and a confederate cleaned and salted it before driving it to Oregon, then shipping it east by courier. Stürm-Hansen relabelled it as beluga to be sold at up to five times the normal price of American roe. To pay Darnell, he wrote out checks to cash, sent an employee to the bank to collect the money, then sent it by courier to post-office boxes in Washington state.[73]

The operation was broken only by a bizarre accident. When a local bank was robbed, the teller activated a device to spill red ink onto some of the bills. A short time later some red-stained cash turned up in the bank deposit of the same motel in which the poachers were working. Police found that two rooms had been rented for cash, one still occupied. After the FBI had watched Darnell and his associate dump empty salt boxes into the trash and the manager had entered their room to discover fishing gear and materials for preparing caviar, the FBI dropped its surveillance but alerted fisheries officials and the Internal Revenue Service. When indicted, Stürm-Hansen pronounced himself "shocked and surprised" that the caviar (which arrived in FedEx boxes from a person whom he had never met, who used false name, and whom he paid in cash) was poached.[74] Although the ring was taken down before the great American caviar binge, it pointed the way for a renewed assault on the Pacific sturgeon a decade or so later.

In 2000 Russia reported that, despite the CITES listing, the legal Caspian catch had dropped from its 1980 level of 12,000 tons of sturgeon yielding 1,000 tons of black caviar for export to 400 tons yielding 45. Pesticide, PCB, and heavy-metal contamination, along with commingling and artificial colouring to make the eggs seem like more expensive versions, reached levels to induce some importers to refuse Russian product. Then came discovery that Caspian sturgeon had effectively stopped breeding in the wild – virtually everything caught had been hatchery reared.[75] Russia reacted in 2002 with a total ban.[76] And internationally pressure mounted to shift the beluga to CITES Appendix I, meaning a complete prohibition in international trade. It was also classified under US law as endangered, permitting domestic criminal prosecutions on top of customs charges.

The US ban on beluga imports outraged imported-caviar merchants, who insisted that the numbers were still too vague to establish that Caspian sturgeon was in trouble.[77] On the other hand, it delighted both environmental activists and American fish-farmers.[78] One Kentucky

farmed-paddlefish angler declared "Kentucky Derby Time." His product, he claimed, tasted like sevruga but at $35 per two-ounce jar was
a real bargain – for consumers, not for the fish. Yet another Kentucky
entrepreneur reacted to the beluga ban by producing trout roe in the
appetizingly natural habitat of an abandoned coal mine.[79] To placate
public qualms, proponents of the new farms insisted that they could
develop techniques to deliver eggs by C-section, rather than by killing
the females – a bogus claim since the only way to keep secretions from
spoiling sturgeon roe is to kill the female, then immediately remove the
eggs. They promised, too, to tweak the reproductive process so that,
much like healthy, happy battery chickens in egg factories programmed
by artificial lights and growth hormones, the fish would be "ripe" faster
and more often, the progress monitored by surgically implanted microchips. The objective was a roe with a "pop" as perfect and a flavour as
buttery as that of wild caviar.[80] That raises the obvious question – why
didn't they just sell popcorn? But presumably that would not satisfy
either first-class passengers of airlines or the huge and ever-growing (in
all senses) cruise-ship clientele shoving mounds of seafood in one orifice
and releasing torrents of toxic waste out another into already plundered
and polluted seas.

Even more delighted were the main California producers of farmed
white sturgeon: "A lot like California wines," one declared proudly,
"we've been able to bring California caviar to international quality."[81]
Apart from his evident ignorance of the environmental impact of industrial-scale wine production, he was apparently unaware that, before
the bays and estuaries of the Golden State were ruined by muck and
mercury from the nineteenth-century gold rush, they had been brim-
ming with healthy sturgeon, rather than the weak, flabby aquacultured
kind. Yet another innovative firm tried to make a mark on the market
with California Kaviar, made from soybeans, presumably unaware that
"Kaviar" is also the name of a defunct rock group and a slang German
term for coprophilia.

However, the Californians were probably less pleased when a giant
fish farm in Abu Dhabi – blessed with capital from its oil wealth, cheap
labour from the Indian subcontinent, and a huge dock for cruise ships
that would, along with its array of luxury hotels, assure a market – set
its sights on an annual production of roe from Siberian sturgeon perhaps
double the entire California total. In these new super-modern fish farms,
the fish were to be given an ultrasound to determine sex, and the females
biopsied with a plastic tube to determine the first moment when the
eggs can be ripped out. After all, as the chef of one of New York's finest

restaurants explained in justifying his decision to switch to farmed roe: "Everyone is thinking more about sustainability."[82]

On the other side of the allegorical high table, the traditional caviar suppliers scoffed at the notion that a US domestic product could ever rival Caspian, or that clients would take to it. Yet curiously, when news had broken of the indictment of US Caviar & Caviar for peddling phony Caspian eggs, an official of Sutton Place Gourmet announced that the company was pulling US Caviar & Caviar products from its shelves while at the same time claiming that the company's actions were not out of fears that its clients could be deceived. "They can tell the difference without any problems," he sniffed.[83] If so, the logical deduction is that the firm's customers so much preferred the paddlefish they had been buying for all those years that they were happy to pay prime beluga prices for it.

The lawyer acting for US Caviar & Caviar seemed to agree, claiming in defense of his client: "No customer has ever complained. No customer has ever sued them, saying they did not get proper goods."[84] That was also the sentiment of Arnold Stürm-Hansen when he insisted in his trial that the white-sturgeon roe he got from Steven Darnell, then resold as beluga, tasted so good that no one was the wiser. Besides, he added, he would never have mislabelled it had he thought a client could actually distinguish the two. Apparently the mislabelling was just to keep his clients happy by making them pay five times the usual price of the domestic stuff.[85]

So today, apart from underground entrepreneurs smuggling in beluga mislabelled by species and place of origin, then peddling it to restaurants through the back door in rich consumer countries, who knows how many distributors hawk paddlefish roe disguised as beluga or sevruga?[86] True, there are colour differences. Lumpfish eggs, for example, are an off-putting grey tone. But, as the salmon-farming industry discovered, a little chemical magic goes a long way. Who knows, too, how many others will follow the footsteps of a couple of former Caspian fish-plant workers? They were arrested in Oregon in 2005 for buying white sturgeon roe from Treaty Indian fishermen with cash, Steven Darnell style, then passing it on to another Russian expat who had contacts with a wealthy private clientele, with several upscale restaurants, and, inadvertently, with some undercover cops.[87] And who knows how much Californian aquacultured white sturgeon roe is sent to New York in legitimate containers, tinned with Russian labels, then sold to wholesalers and restaurants whose clientele will be happy to pay even more than before for something that they think is not just exotic but actually forbidden?[88]

PART FOUR

Invasion of the Biosnatchers

10

Jailbirds: If Parrots Could Really Talk ...

For some people a goofy cocker-spaniel pup, pink tongue lolling out of its cheerfully panting mouth as it drools in anticipation of a doggie biscuit, is strictly nerdsville – compared to a Komodo dragon whose shark-like teeth lie hidden in thick gums until it bares them to chow down on a water buffalo. No doubt some people take pleasure from getting up close and personal with nature's more unusual creations – especially if they can pull it off without any danger of having their blood infected by dengue-bearing mosquitoes while trekking through a tropical rainforest or sucked by leeches while wading through a steamy swamp. But the kick comes less from the animal than from the envy possession of something so beautiful, weird, or scary – or expensive – brings in the eyes of others.[1]

That was not always true. For millennia humans have been fascinated by wildlife, particularly large mammals and exotic birds. However, in ages past, only the super-elite kept wild beasts captive; and the animals were often treated with reverence, even as part of a family, not as objects of public show or private sale. Granted, Roman attitudes were rather less benign, as countless lions and not a few Christians discovered to their dismay. Not that the Christians seem to learn much from the experience. Their attitude that nature existed to be dominated and commoditized helped during colonial times to rationalize a mass slaughter of wildlife abroad, although even then generally only the landed aristocracy collected live specimens (like peacocks to strut about their estates) at home.

A shift in attitudes probably began toward the mid-nineteenth century, or even before, because of the work of a few people with a passion for wildlife. For example, after moving to the US from France early in the nineteenth century, John James Audubon, the illegitimate son of a French privateer and sugar planter who had a slave estate on Haiti, made a commitment to find and paint all the birds of America. Describing a feeling of "intimacy" with birds "bordering on frenzy" he spent years shooting the birds, then hanging them on a wire before painting them. In 2010 a copy of Audubon's *Birds of America*, 1 of only 170 sets known to be in existence, sold at Sotheby's for $9.6 million, a world record for books.[2]

Public awareness was further stoked in the nineteenth century with the emergence of the public zoo and the travelling circus. While there had been grand collections of animals in ancient Egypt and China, or even in the Aztec capital in Mexico, their purpose was to display the power and prestige of the monarch, not to advance zoological knowledge, turn a profit, or entertain the Great Unwashed. True, as Europe "advanced" into modern times, freak shows charged public admission to view abused animals (including deformed humans) in tiny cages. But the first prototype of the modern zoo, the London Zoological Gardens, was not established (by Sir Stamford Raffles, "founder" of Singapore) until the early nineteenth century. Initially admission was only through private subscription by members of the social elite. However, in the 1840s it was opened to anyone who could find a penny for the entrance fee. Others places in Europe, then North America, raced to catch up, their zoos playing the same role as museums in displaying the country's imperial hold over distant lands. The result was the parallel emergence of the first post-Roman worldwide traffic on a large scale in live exotic animals, the ones who survived the trip usually expiring quickly in captivity. Those institutions, along with travelling shows that morphed into circuses, gave the masses a chance to sublimate their fears of nature by tormenting caged beasts or by gawking and laughing as they clumsily performed unnatural antics. Still, personal ownership of wildlife (beyond the occasional small bird) remained unthinkable to most of the population in the North, although aboriginals in South and Central America had long kept parrots or monkeys as pets.[3]

Then came the 1960s and beyond. As lush hills were levelled, old-growth forests slashed, and meandering rivers drained or dammed, to be replaced by boxcar suburbs on squared-off lots covered with perfectly clipped monotonic grass, suddenly demand exploded for exotic "pets," few of which can actually be petted without the risk of losing the offending hand – unless the animals have been defanged, declawed, or otherwise denaturized to satisfy a form of human self-indulgence that is best described as deranged. The fad spread first within North America, Canada, as usual, slavishly mimicking US fashions a bit later, then across Western Europe, then to wealthier parts of East Asia. Although single animals were and still are most in demand, the last few decades have also seen a proliferation of private collectors who specialize in certain categories of flora and fauna with the same zeal that others show for trading cards or snuff movies. The more unusual the species, the greater the thrill from possessing a "living artwork." The craze for exotic animals today even has within its ambit the fantastic fainting goat, whose muscles freeze for ten seconds when it is startled so that fans can gather round to ooh and aah as it collapses onto the ground. Although in natural circumstances that presumably would render a goat somewhat vulnerable to predators, fortunately the International Fainting Goat Association ("offering fast, friendly and reliable service") exists to spread appreciation of the breed and ensure its preservation.[4] So renowned has this exotic animal become that it even inspired a family business specializing in fainting goat brand gelato, strictly organic of course.[5]

Alas, the same law applies to wildlife as to so many playthings of the wannabe rich and famous – the rarer the object, the greater the "value," which in turn prompts a hunt for yet more, further increasing rarity and price. Meanwhile as pressure on the world's wildlife grows, some genius from a "top ten" university economics department will hyperventilate on the op-ed page of the Wall Street Journal about how the free market, left to its own devices, inevitably matches supply to ever-rising demand. Too bad the Yangtze River dolphin never got the benefit of that kind of wisdom, instead of fishermen's nets, hulls of passing ships, and chemical pollutants, before it capitulated to the real law of the market by becoming officially extinct in 2006.[6]

BORN FREE AND DIE?

Exotic wildlife fated for the pet-and-pelt trade (hides or feathers of those who die in transit may be used for ornamental purpose) is culled from almost any habitat, terrestrial or aquatic. It cuts a swathe through sub-Sahara Africa, South East Asia, even Australia, a place doubly blessed with a large and varied population of unique plants and animals and a relatively small number of one particularly destructive primate species. But probably the area most infested by poachers is the Amazon and environs. Colombia, for example, counts 1,850 species of birds, 385 of mammals, and 45,000 of plants – and estimates like that tend to be conservative. Although its government has put the number of animals illegally taken at about 600,000 a year, in reality no one has a clue. Apart from an almost unrivalled biodiversity, Colombia boasts an almost unparalleled history of contraband – coffee, gold, emeralds, cocaine, marijuana, and livestock out; clothes, appliances, booze, tobacco, guns, and precursor chemicals for illegal drugs back in. That augurs as badly for the future of its wildlife (already facing the Colombian government's propensity to blast large areas with US-supplied herbicides in the name of coca eradication) as for its remaining buried treasure of pre-Colum-bian antiquities. Peru, which shares that latter unwelcome attention from modern seekers of ancient gold, can also contest Colombia's claims to top rank in biodiversity rankings, and therefore in variety of species poached; while Brazil's still remaining natural habitat likely propels it to number one spot in sheer scale of losses (twelve million animals per year by a government guess) in spite of what are on paper perhaps the world's toughest restrictions on trade in wildlife.

No matter what the place of origin of a coveted specimen or the dollar value of the particular species, the process of trafficking exotic wildlife is much the same and bears striking similarities to the antiquities trade. Antiquities move mainly from history-rich, economically disadvantaged countries to those that are culturally impoverished (unless "performance art" by its politicians is counted) and financially bloated. Similarly wild-life flows from those amply endowed with "natural capital" to places that got temporarily rich by looting their immediate environment, then desperately sought to maintain their place on the vertical treadmill of contemporary material life by plundering biomass, living as well as dead, from other places.

The trade starts with poor farmers or indigenous hunter-gatherers knowledgeable about habit and habitat, though they may be joined, or pushed off, by professional poachers. The trapper may even be a corrupt wildlife official – when the poacher *is* the gamekeeper, risks of getting caught are particularly low. Those at the bottom of the supply chain receive the least; but since they start (and remain) the poorest, what they get (in cash or kind) may be vital to their existence. Their cut may depend on rarity, condition, and age of the target. It may also be influ-enced by how much the trapper knows about the price that the wildlife will ultimately fetch. However, the buyer is unlikely to enlighten his sup-plier; and the trapper himself may be trapped, if not by the foot, then by the throat, through debt to a local merchant who takes wildlife in pay-ment for goods already advanced, controlling the price of both.

What happens next depends on whether the trapper-cum-poacher takes the animal on his own initiative or to fill an order. If the first, those animals that survive capture may be hauled to the nearest market town and put on display to tempt casual or professional buyers, includ-ing visitors from rich countries on the prowl for personal collections. Because most source countries are relatively poor and have weak public administrations (which likely give low priority to conservation), wildlife officials may be easy to intimidate, bribe, or turn into collaborators. On the other hand, agents charged with protecting nature in financially better-off countries are not always free of the urge to engage in a little well-remunerated extracurricular activity.[7]

If the poacher is working to order, an itinerant trader may collect live animals along with meat and skins, perhaps from several suppliers, then haul them to a location from which they can be moved on by light plane or road to a major urban centre. There they are resold to wildlife dealers, for example in a section of Lima that plays a similar role in animal trafficking as do certain streets in downtown Amsterdam in the sex trade – open displays hinting of what else is on offer while the real action is behind closed doors. At this stage central players probably have a more-or-less legal front. Still at a pinch someone in the market may be able to pick up their choice from itinerant street peddlers – who probably have not a clue about the species they are peddling, how to care for them, or even what to feed them.

Animal breeding farms are also good cover; breeders are usually permitted to stock their operations with a few wild specimens whose numbers magically expand; and poached wildlife can then be peddled as if bred in captivity.[8] The theory that captive breeding reduces pressure on wildlife (rather than stimulating demand at the same time it eases bad consciences) has led some governments to grant breeding licenses to known traffickers who also understand the tricks for getting restricted animals out of the country.[9]

Probably the great majority of animals are smuggled to avoid CITES restrictions – even though they are generally not very restrictive. Countries may establish a quota for Appendix II species based not on biological reality but political convenience – they just assume that the current level of trade is sustainable until they realize in a panic that the animal is facing extinction, then try to rush it onto Appendix I. At that juncture they may run up against opposition from other countries still happily exporting their natural endowment to earn foreign exchange so it can be surrendered to international creditors holding them to ransom or used by their elites for down payments on ivory carvings, leopard skin coats, or teakwood yachts. Animals, even if not on CITES I or II, might also be brought into a country covertly to avoid quarantine costs or quota restrictions.

Whatever the motive, stories abound of eggs of endangered birds stuffed down the front of shirts or small reptiles in coat pockets. (Reptiles have the advantage of surviving much longer without food or water, but their eggs, unlike those of birds, will usually not hatch if removed from their nests.) Larger lots get hidden in everything from hand luggage to commercial containers, where the animals risk dehydration, asphyxiation, or fatal reactions to drugs administered to keep them quiet. Anti-trade activists cite survival rates as low as 10 percent. That must be true. After all, the same scientifically deduced number has been applied to everything from the recovery rate of stolen art to the seizure ratio of smuggled drugs to the percentage of Miami cops on the take to the cut demanded by Raúl Salinas (brother of the former president) on Mexican privatization deals to the number of Ku Klux Klan members acting as FBI informants.[10] Those who insist on the 90 percent death rate also cite extremely high prices paid for smuggled wildlife along with the cold, mercenary instincts of the traffickers, oblivious to the rather obvious contradiction.

No doubt death rates are higher in jobs done by amateurs – along with discovery rates by customs, who can presumably smell rotting carcasses even if their dogs are asleep from sniffing too much marijuana. Industry insiders, by contrast, can use normal methods of transportation while just faking the paperwork. Exotic animals can be, for example, commingled in loads of similar-looking ones subject to fewer (or no) restrictions. Customs officers are unlikely to poke their head or hands into a wire-mesh cage full of common rattlesnakes to check if an endangered king cobra is lurking there. Or the load can simply be mislabelled. No doubt that, too, can sometimes lead to elevated mortality. In 1997 Peru's Ecological Police seized a load of anacondas, water snakes, black crocodiles, black- and red-headed lizards, iguanas, rare turtles, and endangered frogs ("worth an estimated $500,000") packed in boxes marked ornamental fish and bound for California. Of the 1,000 animals, 350 were dead, poisoned by sedatives before they had left the country.[11] That, however, is as much evidence of commercial incompetence as of calculated callousness, and by itself seems to degrade the smuggler's status from pro to what the French call con, something that translates politely into "complete idiot." Occasionally, too, animals can be dyed or pruned or otherwise doctored to make them appear like another species. As in the caviar trade, CITES export permits might have been stolen, counterfeited, altered, reused, or purchased blank from corrupt officials, although in theory security for official permits, as with most documents, has been steadily improving as electronic issue and verification spreads.[12]

The wildlife might take a circuitous route to avoid direct connections between places where poaching is rife and the final-market country, passing through multiple intermediaries, with quantity handled and value per unit rising at each stage. In Southeast Asia, Singapore, with its enormous volume of shipping (defying adequate inspection) and former reputation for blank permits, used to dominate the wholesale traffic. In fact, thanks to its "founder," it was the world's first entrepôt for the wildlife trade. But more recently it seems to have lost that position to Thailand, which, although a CITES signatory, does not enforce rules for wildlife originating from outside its own territory, while its traders have had a reputation for claiming their animals had been declared surplus by zoos in the region. Taiwan, benefiting from its exclusion from international treaties, handles wildlife from Asia heading to North America and exotic animals (or parts thereof) from the Americas eastward bound.[13]

In the Americas, Paraguay acts as a transit point for species from the Amazon, thanks to its generosity with CITES permits and its sometimes make-believe breeding programs. Guyana shares with Paraguay a geographic position backing onto an ecological wonderland without the annoyance of adherence to CITES. Since wildlife in contiguous areas of different countries sharing habitat is much the same, anything poached in Brazil or Venezuela that gets to Guyana is ripe for export, few questions asked. Its neighbour and almost namesake, French Guiana, has even more advantages – since it is officially a *département* of France, anything coming into its territory legally enters the European Union. But of all the transit points, two have stood out, one for the US market, the other for the Western European.

The first is Mexico, whose importance was graphically displayed by one smuggler with ambitions considerably higher than his IQ – he got himself caught by customs at Mexico City International Airport with 18 titi monkeys kidnapped from Peru, two of them dead, stuffed into socks and hidden in a girdle around his waist.[14] From Mexico, wildlife originating in Asia or Latin America (including Mexico's tropical south) can flow into California or Texas in many ways: by small plane using the many private runways on both sides; by road joining the enormous flow of commercial and private vehicles; by foot, when animal couriers mix with thousands of illegal immigrants; even by underground channels, literally. In the late 1980s US agents found their first but not last air-conditioned, electrically lit tunnel under the border. Other tunnels continue to be found, at least ten from 9/11 until late 2010.[15]

The porous nature of the frontier led to a series of USFWS sting operations. One of the biggest, Operation Jungle Trade, netted 660 parrots, reptiles, and jaguars along with an assortment of skins "worth in excess of $600,000," leading to indictments in the US of smugglers and dealers who used local breeding operations as cover.[16] Mexico's role as a way station also made it the place where US federal agents decided to nail "one of the world's largest wildlife dealers," members of a species that government press releases ensure will never be seriously endangered no matter how many are captured in the wild.

Keng Liang Wong ran in Malaysia a wildlife company (and a private zoo) specializing in rare reptiles. He was a regular participant at Repticon, the annual Orlando, Florida, reptile fair, until his first indictment in 1992. He had sources on several continents, some unconventional even for a wildlife smuggler. When thieves cut the wire of a Madagascar breeding facility to make off with seventy-six almost extinct ploughshare tortoises, reputedly half ended up in Keng's inventory. He delivered to clients as promptly as Federal Express ("… provides access to a growing global marketplace …") could ensure, in packages labelled as books or gifts. His couriers might check less vulnerable species with personal luggage on regular flights.

To trap Keng, the feds set up in San Francisco a phony company that spent three years building its reputation as a major dealer. Given that Keng already had a warrant outstanding against him, he was not about to enter the US. So they asked him to come to Acapulco to meet someone who could supply bear bile (popular in traditional Chinese medicine) from Canada. There he explained to undercover agents how effective were the world's wildlife-trade regulations: "I can get anything here from anywhere …. it only depends on how much certain people get paid."[17] He was arrested, imprisoned in Mexico, and, after two years of legal appeals, extradited to the US. It is true, as wildlife agents often lament, that smuggling wildlife does not carry very heavy penalties. But prosecutors in the US can deploy other legal artillery – conspiracy, money laundering, and making false statements to regulators on top of customs or US wildlife law violations. Normally prosecutors simply threaten every possible charge to blackmail a defendant into a plea bargain on some of the lesser ones to avoid costs (and risks) of a lengthy trial followed by appeals. But Keng was charged with just about everything and convicted on most.

Keng was not the only person nailed in what the feds cutely called Operation Chameleon. Others included a man running goliath frogs (the world's largest) out of Cameroon by labelling them as ordinary bullfrogs, accompanying the shipment with a false manifest, then faxing the correct details separately to the customer along with the bill. They included, too, several couriers and US-based reptile dealers. But Keng was king, and the one about whose successful entrapment the feds bragged loudest, before lapsing into an embarassed silence.[18] On his release, Keng got back into business, or rather picked up the reins of a business his wife had continued to run while he was in prison, advertising on the web his claim of $50–100 million worth of sales to the US alone and planning his next big venture, a zoo and a tiger-breeding farm approved by Malaysia's wildlife authorities, who insist that he was framed by the US.[19]

What Mexico is to the US market, the Czech Republic has been to the European. It straddles the border between East and West in Europe, and is well placed to feed Germany, then beyond it, the EU at large. During the Communist era, Czechoslovakia was the Eastern European capital for wildlife breeding, one of the few businesses not tightly controlled by the state, which did, however, closely regulate the movement of exotic species. After the fall of the Communist regime, trade regulations were liberalized and, in a concession to the emerging law of the free-market jungle, the Environmental Inspection Office had its budget slashed. As the country's entrepreneurs ranged the world to collect rare species, breeding stations became excellent cover for poached and smuggled wildlife. Thus a place not exactly renowned for lush rainforests became by the end of the millennium one of the world's largest traders in rare parrots and reptiles.[20] Perhaps embarrassment over recurring scandals caused the Czech Republic to sign CITES and tighten regulations. Seizures of everything from chameleons to conch shells, from tortoises to elephant tusks, shot up. But so did the government's issue of import and export permits. The likely implication was that traffickers were resorting less to false-bottomed suitcases and more to doctored paperwork.[21]

After leaving their places of origin and passing through transit points, exotic animals face arrival formalities in countries of destination. Some airports have special handling facilities. While a smuggler may try to avoid them for fear of meeting personnel trained to detect hidden or mislabelled loads, in places like Miami so many cargos arrive that checks are cursory as long as paperwork seems in order. However, an authentic CITES document may have been illegally obtained; a document may be legally obtained but its information modified; a real document can attest correctly to the nature of a cargo – for the umpteenth time; sometimes a document was originally accurate, but the cargo has been altered en route. Then there are false documents printed on genuine blanks or on high-quality imitations. While CITES now uses security measures similar to those for bank notes, none are beyond the reach of today's counterfeiter. E-verification can only work if computer records are accurate – and someone actually checks. Transshipment points further confuse the trail. Sometimes animals are imported with paperwork indicating they are for re-export, then diverted to domestic trade.[22] As with every controlled or taxed article from antiquities to atomic bombs, the simplest way to avoid regulatory hassles is to mark a load as diplomatic luggage.

Some restricted specimens, of course, are seized on entry. That poses its own dilemmas. Imported exotic animals are by definition alien to the ecology of the country in which they are to be sold, precluding (official) release in the wild even if they are found free of equally exotic diseases. The countries from which they come rarely have the interest or the resources to cover the costs of return. Some impounded animals may end up in public zoos. But few can be so accommodated. Nor is there any guarantee the public zoo will not later sell them to a dealer who in turn supplies every sort of institution from private "petting zoos" to purveyors of exotic meat to research centres where animals are mutilated in the interests of "scientific enquiry," a common euphemism for drug-company profit. In the US, animals taken from smugglers are quarantined at public expense, then, to recover costs, auctioned to licensed wildlife dealers who might be the very people who organized the smuggling, happy to pay a small laundry fee.[23]

If an animal does get past customs checks, its fate depends in part on the method used to smuggle it. If it was simply hidden from sight, it probably ends up in a private collection. The owner may try to acquire passable paperwork after the fact but more likely is just careful about who gets to know. Or perhaps the owner does not bother with an alibi. Few places criminalize ownership of endangered species rather than their import or sale.

Alternatively the animal could be sold covertly to a wildlife dealer who resells it, perhaps to a client knowingly in the market for illegal animals, perhaps to an unsuspecting customer as if it were legal. The animal's subsequent fate depends on who buys it. A collector or breeder may keep it for a while, then, once it has outlived its usefulness, unload it onto the secondary market or into a convenient dumpster.

Someone who just wanted a family pet might find different solutions when minds change. Burmese pythons, for example, were once popular in Florida, epicentre of the US exotic animal business. Their tendency to grow too large (potentially twenty feet and up to two hundred pounds) to be kept at home, along with their propensity to give an owner a big hug to show how much the snakes reciprocate the owner's affection, led to some being discarded in the Everglades. There, despite the area's rapid conversion into a sinking, stinking sewer, they happily breed, free from natural predators, with a population now guesstimated near 100,000 (although that number sounds less the result of a zoological investigation than of a Hollywood horror script in the making). They only seem disconcerted when they bite off more than they can chew or, in this case, dissolve in gastric juices – for example, by trying to swallow an alligator.[24]

If the animal enters in a regular shipment with fake paperwork, it goes through quarantine – reputedly, in the US, those facilities have been sometimes owned by people previously convicted of smuggling, although that is the kind of story opponents of the wildlife trade love to circulate even if they can only cite a single instance in the last fifty years. Once a USFWS agent signs off, the animal can be sold openly.[25] It could end up in the hands of a breeder, collector, or private owner. If the last, the proud buyer can take it home and stick it, covered with colourful wrapping paper and topped by a pretty plastic bow, under the Christmas tree. The joy that the children feel that special morning may be tempered by a quick trip to an emergency room to get Johnny's index finger sewed back on or to stop the bleeding in Jenny's eye. Or perhaps the animal itself must be treated for shock when it realizes that it is now the private property of someone whose previous experience with wild animals consisted of hunting toads with a BB gun.

Collectors are generally more knowledgeable and *may* (no guarantees) treat acquisitions better than would casual owners, not least because they trade back and forth with dealers who also buy, sell, and barter among each other. The result is the emergence of an exotic-animal trafficking network that embraces even publicly funded zoos. For example, in 1998 the reptile curator of San Diego Zoo was caught taking kickbacks from two Florida wildlife dealers who sold to the zoo animals suspected of being smuggled into the country; the curator then sold back to the dealers without authorization supposedly surplus animals for breeding or further resale.[26] Still, the real problem lies not with this or that zoo official taking undercover payments. Rather it is the legal symbiosis between publicly funded institutions and the animal underworld, something particularly large in the US.

Of course, not all exotic animals sought by collectors have to be imported. Take the enterprise of the Bay Area Family Church. It was an affiliate of the Holy Spirit Association for the Unification of World Churches headed by the Reverend Sun Myung Moon, who lauded Jesus as merely a "fisher of men" while proclaiming himself King of the Ocean. Perhaps for that reason Moon's enterprises have included not just a string of newspapers to spread his message and a franchise for exporting assault rifles to drive the points home, along with banks to deposit the take, but also a seafood distribution company and once even a fleet of tuna boats. This particular subsidiary, though, got into the exotic pet business, albeit somewhat elliptically. Its pastor initially used communal fishing expeditions as a conversion tool, then discovered the resale value of leopard sharks. Coveted by collectors for their striking body patterns, the heaviest concentration is off the coast of northern

California. Although, like most of fish in the region, they have accumulated too heavy a toxic load for any sensible person to eat them, the aquarium trade takes such a toll that for many years they have been protected by California statute as well as federal wildlife law. That did not prevent Church converts from hauling in juveniles, keeping them in tanks on the property of Moon's fish-distributing operation, then selling them to local aquariums. Subsequently the Moonie fishers of money sought markets among collectors across the US and Europe, too. Finally three members of the congregation and several aquarium trade distributors pleaded guilty. To avoid prosecution of his umbrella organization, Moon coughed up $500,000 to help restore leopard shark habitat.[27]

However, the usual route is for exotic animals to be brought into the US from abroad, at least initially. Today commercial breeders, medical-research centres, and zoos have been so successful in forcing unnatural rates of reproduction that the US is now in a position to supply some endangered species back to the places from which their forbearers were abducted – but for the fact that few could survive. Although there are laudable exceptions, in general captive breeding, far from assuring survival of endangered species, works with a limited gene pool lacking natural selection pressures to produce animals that have no opportunity to learn behaviour appropriate for what ought to be their natural habitat – that is, in any case, likely to be vanishing quickly. As a result, breeding programs further feed the commercial market.

So do zoos. When a publicly funded institution finds itself with an animal that has, like a fading rock star, lost its drawing power, or with too many offspring, it attempts to find the animal a new home in another zoo, public or private – probably for a price. If there are no takers, it may pass the animal on to a broker (who operates on a commission basis) or a merchant (who buys cheaply in order to resell). The broker or merchant may handle the sale directly or place the animal at one of the exotic-species auctions where bids are anonymous and deals may be closed in cash. Participants include collectors, buyers for other auction houses, retailers, suppliers of medical institutes, even those who plan to acquire animals for a private hunt club or the exotic-meat trade. Some buyers combine several functions. They might run a petting zoo where, after patrons have obligingly fattened up the animals with treats purchased from the owner, the animals are sold off to be slaughtered. The petting zoo might itself be (under a different name) a purveyor of exotic meat, while the owner runs an endangered-species breeding mill on the side. There are many regulations on the books of various levels of government. But in the US the system is so dysfunctional that exotic species may (in some states) have less protection than domestic or farm animals;

and animals can easily disappear along the chain of intermediaries with a little fake (or overlooked) paperwork.[28]

BIRD'S EYE VIEW

While the trade in exotic animals embraces everything from the aardvark to the zorilla (AKA striped polecat), when the main intent is to feed the demand for exotic pets, the most frequent unwilling participant is the parrot. The lure of parrots dates way back. Alexander the Great brought back to Europe parakeets kept as pets by some of the peoples he had conquered; and the ancient Romans also fancied the birds, who, fortunately for Christians, had no appetite for human flesh.[29] Alas, in an allegorical way, the reverse is not true. Today all but 2 of 330 parrot species are on CITES I or II.

There is no denying the parrot's attractions – physical beauty, intelligence, ability to mimic human speech (better than some recent US presidents at press conferences), and longevity, sometimes seventy-five to one hundred years, although that produces the uncomfortable situation that sometimes conscientious owners have to make provision for their parrots in their wills. Reputably the parrot is also very adaptable to human company, although the popularity of African grays in the UK, for example, because they can be trained to carry on lengthy conversations, really speaks volumes about the intelligence of the counterparty to the dialogue – the birds, despite fantasies of their boosters, don't have a clue what most of the sounds they utter actually mean. African grays, of course, have no monopoly on so-called parrot speech. Among the more endearing habits of gold baron Robert Friedland was to teach his collection of rare parrots how to shout inanities at visitors. Romeo, his favourite, would yell: "Help! Let me out! I've been framed! Call my lawyer!"[30]

While birds bred in captivity (easy with only a few species) can be reasonably docile, particularly if the breeder has handfed them in infancy, the intelligence, sociability, and longevity of those taken from the wild make a solitary life in a cage particularly harsh. They might vent their frustrations and strength on the family cat or dog. Failing that, they might turn on themselves. There are tales of pet-store owners deliberately selling wild birds as if captive-bred in the expectation that owners would return them even if the store refused a refund. That way the store resells them, perhaps several times. Nonetheless industry propaganda coupled with television fantasies meant that, starting in the 1970s, demand for parrots as household pets shot up in the US, later spreading to Europe and Japan.[31] Despite CITES restrictions, imports grew dramatically. Although captive breeding also expanded, in the early years of the parrot fad wild birds were cheaper, and, even if poached, once safely inside the market country largely free of legal sanction.

As with every species of wildlife, the process starts with a trapper in a jungle or near-jungle habitat, sometimes a reserve area with poor or corrupt enforcement. Techniques range from foot-trapping with a natural glue from the ficus tree (which risks damaging feathers), nets (which must be strong enough to resist a parrot's powerful beak), or wing shooting (which, even if accurate, may cause lead poisoning). These are supplemented by luring with tame birds. Because most species of parrots mate for life and reproduce slowly, at most one or two chicks per nest per annum, the capture of one adult may permanently affect breeding capacity. Since parrots nest high, returning to the same tree in successive mating seasons, a poacher may cut it down, killing nestlings and destroying future breeding territory.[32]

However, while a fully grown adult looks dramatic, the trade prefers juveniles especially in potential breeding pairs, or eggs for ease of handling – something that presumably precludes cutting down nesting trees unless the objective is scrambled parrot eggs for the exotic cuisine trade. Captive birds follow the usual route to urban centres, to transit countries, then to places of final destination, while passing through the usual chain of intermediaries. Birds physically smuggled are stuffed in pockets, spare tires, hand luggage, or commercial cargos, probably sedated. Apart from games with illegally obtained or falsified or counterfeited permits, birds are themselves altered, for example, to make them appear an Appendix II species when they are really Appendix I. Thus dealers trim the yellow crest-feathers off greater sulphur-crested cockatoos from India and call them white cockatoos. A dye job may work as well. Any alteration must be easily reversible or the animal loses value. Alternatively an Appendix II parrot might be moved into a transit country, receive a re-export permit, and an Appendix I parrot sent abroad in its place. Appendix I parrots could be put in a cage with a load of Appendix II or III birds, with the birds separated after arrival. In addition to CITES certificates, birds on entering the country of destination usually require health certificates from the point of origin, which vets may sell blank to exporters.

With ornithologists in the field becoming more alarmed and anti-trade activists at home denouncing a parrot holocaust, pressures for action (against poaching, not against deforestation, which is wiping out habitat for all birds, including hundreds of northern species) mounted in North America and Europe. Although commercial airlines in the early 1990s agreed to stop carrying live birds, traders just switched to charter-freight companies. In Europe, new legislative restrictions were absent. In the US, by far the biggest market (importing a declared 150,000 wild birds per year), they were not.

The 1992 Wild Bird Conservation Act, passed unanimously by both houses of the US Congress, imposed a moratorium on commercial trade in birds on CITES lists and import quotas on other species based on information from the country of origin. Naturally, there were exceptions: the law still allowed importation of breeding stock, or of captive-bred birds from otherwise banned species, or of wild birds if the authorities in the source country managed them in a "scientifically sustainable" way, or of birds destined for "scientific research" or "zoological display" inside the US.[33] Still, before any imported parrot could be legally sold, it needed a USFWS declaration form in addition to any CITES permit the breed might require. The USA, its officials crowed, had singlehandedly killed off the illegal bird trade.[34]

No doubt it was an important piece of legislation – even if the bill was prompted less by concern for wild parrots than for domestic poultry producers whose chicken flocks were periodically ravaged by imported avian diseases. The priorities were made clear in 1994, when the US Department of Justice announced the sentencing of members of the first big smuggling ring to face justice after passage of the act. The traffickers, it said, had brought "potentially disease-bearing parrots" across the border into Texas to be laundered through a local aviary. "Parrot smuggling," it sternly commented, "transcends greed and stupidity. It has caused untold heartbreak to American poultry farmers and millions of dollars in cost to taxpayers" (presumably for quarantine facilities). It added, apparently as an afterthought, "as well as threatening the existence of endangered animals."[35]

After the act, recorded imports of wild birds into the US plummeted, along with the number of legal importers. Freed of (legal) competition from wild birds, captive breeding shot up. Yet it was never clear how much of the US drop was due to the new law compared to at least some increased vigilance in countries of origin. Several, including Brazil, source of most of the parrots entering the North American market, had theoretically banned wildlife exports nearly a decade before; and recorded imports into the US had already started to fall several years before the WBCA went into effect. However, one more certain effect was to create a class distinction in the parrot market.

The conventional pet trade could rely more on domestic breeders, thanks to techniques of forced reproduction. Since parrots left to themselves produce at most two eggs per year, breeders snatch away eggs for artificial incubation; and captive birds react by laying more. Although

306 this permits doubling or trebling, it stresses females, probably shortens

this permits doubling or trebling, it stresses females, probably shortens their lifespan, and, if the results of aquaculture are any guide, steadily weakens the stock. It also blurs the distinction between aviculture of formerly wild birds and a battery-hen operation run at the expense of domestic ones. It takes little imagination to guess what other "reproductive technologies" breeders hope to employ.

Some people still demand wild birds that behave "more naturally," a trait that has more to do with how long the parrot has had to adapt to human stupidity than whether it was born in the wild or in a breeder's cage. And true collectors will only be satisfied with the rarest of species. Rather than drop out of the search, tighter legislation drives them deeper underground.[36] Most likely the act led to poachers increasingly targeting eggs: they were easy to smuggle, less vulnerable during transport, and almost impossible to trace back to origin once they had hatched.[37] Cover could be further deepened by laundering birds or their eggs through breeding facilities, particularly since breeders normally lend birds to each other, facilitating dispersal of a contraband load. That possibility was forcibly brought to the attention of press, public and politicians by the USFWS in its most spectacular bust, one that just happened to occur when the Wild Bird Conservation Act was in front of Congress.[38]

The case seemed straightforward. Officers had set up an elaborate sting operation using fake quarantine stations and import and brokerage businesses, much as they had to trap Keng, the reptile king, but this time focusing on parrot dealers and breeders in the US and abroad. In the course of enquiries, they picked up a tip from the former operator of a wildlife import business that, several years before, he had purchased poached birds from a well-known breeder. According to the tipster, the supplier had started by buying hot birds to supplement his breeding stock, then began to organize smuggling himself. In this case the shipment included 35 hyacinth macaws – although in the final analysis the target was accused of having, over his career, smuggled at least 186 of them.[39]

The hyacinth macaw is the so-called Rolls Royce of parrots – a nickname that speaks volumes about the mindset of dealers and collectors. Although the largest and to some tastes most spectacular of all parrot species, it is not the most endangered. That honour goes to the Spix's macaw (with the Lear's macaw close behind). For the Spix's macaw, long sought avidly by European collectors, the alarm sounded more than two decades ago with the claim that there may have been only five or so left in the wild, and perhaps twenty-five in zoos around the world. As a result Brazil, with the help of CITES, the World Wildlife Fund, and Tony Silva, president of the American Parrot Association and one of the world's foremost parrot authorities, created a special breeding centre

– albeit it had to get its breeding stock by amnestying (rich and power-ful) people who had previously acquired their birds illegally. Of course, keeping acquisitions safe from other poachers was a challenge. Once, a guard was bribed to steal two chicks, a male and a female, passing them to a dealer who smuggled them to Paraguay, then offered them for sale using papers claiming that they had been hatched in an Asunción zoo. Reputedly a Swiss dealer was ready to pay $40,000 but took the precau-tion of checking the paperwork, then backed off. So the parrots were sold to a German collector for $20,000, who figured to resell them for four times that sum. After a tip-off from the Swiss would-be buyer, the birds ended up in Saõ Paulo Zoo. Alas, the program collapsed without results, and the Spix's macaw was likely extinct in its native habitat by the turn of the millennium.[40]

Although the Spix's macaw tops the list, the hyacinth macaw, too, is critically endangered, something that did not keep Robert Friedland from having one in his collection so it could entertain friends by declar-ing "I can talk. Can you fly?" Its size and beauty makes it a favourite of collectors. Tony Silva himself once said that the bird was worth its weight in gold, words that would come back to haunt him – and dou-bly ironic given the zeal with which gold barons ruin tropical habitat. The fact that it inhabits not deep rainforest but peripheral flooded areas makes it easier to locate and trap. And it is vulnerable during transpor-tation. All of the birds delivered to the dealer who provided the tip to the USFWS reputedly arrived seriously ill, although the target of the sting operation denied that, most to die shortly after.

Then another industry insider, supposedly disgusted by the target's brutal smuggling methods, stepped forward to volunteer his services. Under the guidance of agents, he befriended the target to tape two hun-dred hours of conversation. When the confidential informant asked the target to smuggle endangered wild parrots on his behalf, the target pro-vided details of how it would be done – the animals spirited out of Brazil via Paraguay, brought to Argentina, flown to Mexico, than smuggled across the border hidden in cardboard boxes or stuffed in PVC pipes, a horrifying treatment on which the media later seized.

Yet a third informant, the owner of a quarantine station, reported how he had, on the target's orders, participated in a sort of bait-and-switch scheme. In the US, imported wildlife goes into quarantine under the supervision of an officer of the Department of Agriculture and is held until a USFWS agent clears the load. However, often the Agriculture officer leaves before the USFWS agent turns up. In this case the quaran-tine-station owner and the breeder-smuggler took advantage of the delay to remove the illegal birds and substitute legal ones.[41]

When federal agents presented their evidence to a grand jury, it indicted both the target, then in Spain on business, and his mother who was still in Florida keeping an eye on the target's affairs. The agents raided his house and hauled away what they called smuggling logs describing hundreds of illegal transactions. Then the target returned to face the music. For four years he protested his innocence. But then, following a three-week bargaining session with prosecutors, he pleaded guilty to one count of conspiracy to smuggle and another of filing a false income tax declaration (to hide money earned from selling smuggled birds). In return the feds agreed to reduce the charges against his mother, whose only offense became that she had signed a false tax declaration on his behalf when he was away. It seemed like a triumph for the USFWS. Yet beneath the surface, things were not so clear cut.

First, the defendant was none other than Tony Silva, former president of the American Parrot Association, who was not just a renowned scholar but someone who made public speeches denouncing the illegal trade in parrots. At the time of his indictment, he held the prestigious post of bird curator of Loro Parque in the Canary Islands, a renowned zoo with the world's largest parrot collection. It had also been one of the locations in which an attempt was made to breed the Spix's macaw in hopes of saving it from extinction.[42]

Second, the tip that started the investigation came not from an ordinary wildlife dealer but a man convicted of trafficking cocaine and marijuana ("worth $75 million"), bribing a deputy police chief in Key West, hiring members of the Miami police to collect drug debts, and helping to dismember the body of a federal informant. He was in prison when he provided the information about Silva. Although sentenced to one hundred years, he eventually got out after serving twelve, as a reward for assisting federal authorities in a string of cases against not just Silva but also former confederates in the drug business.[43]

Third, the star informant, who actually wore the wire, had begun working for the USFWS two years before Silva was charged. Among his duties were acquiring illegal birds for the agency to use in its sting operations. In addition to reporting on his conversations about bird smuggling, he told stories about secret meetings to discuss arms-and-drugs deals on behalf of CIA-supported Contra rebels then fighting the Cuban-backed government in Nicaragua. His recording device, the defense later showed in court, could be turned on and off at will, therefore capturing incriminating comments but not necessarily the context that might have changed their meaning. As to the quarantine station owner's claims, Silva later protested that he simply went to assist periodically at the facility, as he did at others, because the owner spoke no Spanish.

Three days into sentencing hearing (Silva's confession had rendered an actual trial unnecessary), Silva tried to withdraw his guilty plea, claiming that he had agreed under duress, that the government had conned him, and that new evidence would help to refute the prosecution claims. The judge refused, then imposed a record sentence of eighty-two months plus a $100,000 fine against a man whom the media were portraying as "a shameless and prolific liar" responsible for the death of "hundreds – perhaps thousands" (the media added shamelessly and prolifically) of birds. The rationalization for the sentence was that Silva was not merely a smuggler but a de facto organized-crime boss. Furthermore government witnesses in the sentencing procedure trotted out the usual magic numbers to establish that Silva had collected $1.3 million in illicit gains, safely over the $1 million threshold that permitted a judge to quadruple the sentence. The trick here seemed to be to take an estimate of the number of birds, then multiply by the highest recorded price such a bird had ever fetched at retail. But rare wildlife is not like soybeans or orange-juice futures. Since every underground transaction is distinct and prices are highly variable, there is no real "market value." The only general reference price available would be from a normal retail transaction involving a legal bird with proper papers, not the covert wholesale price of a smuggled one. Anyway, the IRS agent who investigated the tax evasion for which Silva was also charged indicated finding only $160,000 in unreported income. Still, to clear the slate, Silva's sixty-three-year-old mother was sentenced to twenty-seven months – for signing someone else's falsified tax return.

It did not take long for critics to note similarities between this case and an earlier one. During the Reagan regime, the radical right, convinced that the Fish and Wildlife Service was part of a Bolshevik conspiracy to seize private property (defined to include lakes, forests, rocks, and all species of wildlife), agitated to curb its powers. Meanwhile, the administration, busy putting more public land into the tender care of mining companies and opening more national forests to pulp and paper mills, needed to burnish its green credentials. The new Republican junta had also been elected using War on Crime rhetoric. Its solution to resolving these various political pressures was pure magic. The regulatory and conservation divisions of the wildlife service were rolled back while enforcement was beefed up with money and personnel from the FBI, police forces, and intelligence agencies. Subsequently the USFWS, along with its Canadian counterpart, launched Operation Falcon, to break an allegedly massive racket smuggling North American birds of prey, particularly falcons.[44]

After three years of undercover work, thirty-two falconers and breeders in the US and Canada were charged.[45] But almost every case was either thrown out of court for illegal entrapment (of the people accused, not of the birds) or crumbled during trial. At the Canadian end, the failures included the case against a senior biologist working for the Canadian wildlife service, accused of helping to launder wild-caught falcons through a fake breeding program. After the case collapsed he reappeared as a defense witness for others. In the US, the main result was conviction of a vet who had treated hundreds of injured birds: he was found guilty not of poaching or smuggling or laundering but of interstate transportation without a permit of a bird that came with a proper leg-band and federal permit and had been pressed on him by the undercover operative. In the end the only serious bird-poaching and smuggling operations revealed in the operation seemed to be the work of the wildlife service itself. Birds sold (by the feds) to intermediaries for $5,000 each were reported in press releases as worth $100,000 a head on the black market. When queried about its estimate of four hundred wild birds handled by the falcon black market over the three year investigation, the USFWS claimed that it got the figure from its Canadian counterpart while the Canadian one said it got the number from the Americans.[46]

Given this previous humiliation, could the USFWS have vehemently opposed Tony Silva's request to retract his guilty plea because his case, too, would have been trashed in a proper criminal trial?[47] And given the context, could Tony Silva's laments that he was a political prisoner not be without justification? Publicity sparked by his arrest in 1992 not only consolidated support for the Wild Bird Conservation Act but gave the USFWS a big PR lift. Even though Operation Renegade eventually convicted thirty-five others, its name suggests that from the start it had a prominent parrot breeder and spokesman like Silva in mind.

On the other hand, it is possible to be a political prisoner *and* a smuggler. Silva admitted to smuggling birds into the US, just not to the incidents for which he was charged. His defense was that his activities occurred in the early 1980s, when everyone was doing it, and that the statute of limitations for those particular acts had expired.

After Operation Renegade, parrot breeders claimed a grand conspiracy against their profession (much as had falcon breeders several years before) by out-of-control government agents egged on by radical animal-rights activists. Their tribulations were not confined to the US. Harry Sissen, a prominent British breeder and Tory Party hanger-on, was convicted in 2000 for trafficking in parrots (including six hyacinth and three Lear's macaws) poached in Brazil, then moved to the Czech Republic, where he had bought them to bring back to England with fake papers. Just as Silva portrayed himself as an avicultural Noah, motivated solely by his desire to protect an endangered species, Sissen claimed in his trial that he was "not in it for the money. I'm in it for the birds."[48] After all, he modestly added, "I am the most important breeder of endangered species in the whole of Europe .... I know the best place for the birds is with me because of my record."[49] Given the number of his birds who died after British customs impounded them, it may not have been an idle boast. And it is probably true that some breeders caught poaching are motivated more by the urge to protect the species than just by money.

Later ordered to also pay a £150,000 confiscation order or face another twenty-one months in prison, as Sissen was led from the courtroom in handcuffs, he managed to throw a glass of water at the prosecutor. In his subsequent appeals, he took particular aim at the judge, who allegedly let drug dealers go free while imprisoning someone who, even if guilty, committed the trivial (in Sissen's mind) offense of importing a few birds without correct papers.[50] The judge, though, may well have gotten to the root of the matter when he stated that, "Mr Sissen is a man about which positive things can be said – but he has been carried away by an unwavering sense of knowing best."[51] That affliction, of course, is quite alien to judges.[52]

Meanwhile Tony Silva's attorney went on to greater things in the interest of justice. He was called upon by an old friend, the late Congressman Henry Hyde, to lead the effort in the House of Representatives to impeach President Bill Clinton – not for gutting the welfare system, selling out to the medical-pharmaceutical complex on health care, nor committing mass murder in Iraq and Serbia but for his idiosyncratic taste in custom-flavoured cigars, fortunately not Cuban. After 9/11, that lawyer found a new vocation, denouncing the proliferation of Arab terrorist cells across the US while informing the audiences of radio shock-and-shlock shows that the US federal government had had advanced information about the attacks.[53] Of the Silva case, though, he said one thing that did ring true – the USFWS figured it could get away with its tactics because it "suddenly thought it was the DEA" (Drug Enforcement Administration).

BIRDS OF A FEATHER?

The prosecutor in the Silva case had a similar idea from the opposite perspective. He described to an attentive press that Silva's operation functioned like "an international drug cartel."[54] In a sane world that kind of talk would at a minimum raise eyebrows and maybe induce a belly laugh. But it had serious advantages – for one side.[55] Among law-enforcement agencies the greatest prestige, and with it the most resources and legal powers, go to those facing what the public perceives as the gravest threats. Drugs (by common consensus rather than by common sense) have long been at the top, only recently displaced by the Green Peril – so-called Islamic terrorism. Hence if some police agency or prosecutor could claim with a straight face that the illegal wildlife business has the same organizational structure, uses the same methods, and produces the same level of financial rewards as drug trafficking, that was a pretext to demand, if not the same level of resources, then at least the right to use the same sort of enforcement methods, while coaxing judges and juries to apply the same level of penalties to offenses that they previously refused to take very seriously. Anti-wildlife trade activists joined the game in the hope that by linking the appalling treatment of wild animals to another issue of great social concern, they could mobilize an otherwise indifferent public opinion.[56] (One phrase beloved of those making the link is that the wildlife trade is run by "Mafia-like families.") However, in so doing they degrade a good cause – defending the integrity of the biosphere is far more important than clearing campuses of dime bags of dope.

True, the two rackets occasionally seem to overlap. Heroin has been found in condoms sewn into the bellies of giant goldfish; cocaine has been shoved up the anal cavities of snakes. Yet drugs have also been hidden in everything from cans of paella to packages of frozen shrimp without anyone denouncing a plot by the international wholesale-grocery trade. When wild animals are used as metaphorical mules, they are hardly bound for a pet store when their journey is over. Indeed, far from being smart business, using wildlife as cover for drugs might actually reduce the probability of the dope ever making it to market – it risks drawing scrutiny of wildlife and quarantine officials on top of customs and drug agents. Ultimately the closest analogy in the illegal wildlife business to drug-trade stories of couriers dying in agony after condoms full of merchandise burst in their stomachs is the tale of someone allegedly starting to squirm in front of a customs officer when the nurturing moisture and heat in his crotch makes the reptile eggs stuffed down his pants start to hatch ahead of schedule.[57] Either this was one type of reptile whose eggs could be hatched after removal from the nest, or it was just too good a tale for any reporter to resist.

No doubt, from time to time, someone barters rhino horn for hash. And convicted drug dealers have rematerialized as wildlife merchants. The original informant against Tony Silva was a trafficker who had also run an exotic animal emporium. But Florida offers hospitality to so many participants in both trades that the law of averages dictates an occasional overlap. Probably the most imaginative connection was revealed by a Rio de Janeiro drug gang that kept a couple of caimans, not to stuff them full of dope but to scare their competitors and dispose of the bodies of enemies.[58]

As to what all this is "worth," enforcement agencies, concerned NGOs and agitated reporters cite figures like $10–20 billion per annum for all aspects of the illegal wildlife trade, of which exotic pets are only one part. That number is generally presented, as with similar claims about things like art crime, in the "it is estimated that ..." format, with no information about how, why, or by whom the estimation was done.[59] Along with magic numbers supposedly showing total value come startling claims about the price particular species will fetch, although it is rarely clear if the figure quoted is wholesale or retail, spot or forward, FOB or CIF, with or without an after-sales service contract.[60] That kind of money, overexcited critics claim, makes wildlife trafficking second only to illegal drugs and just ahead of black-market arms in importance. Maybe it is – after all, no one has a clue how big any of them really are. Apart from the danger that artificially puffing potential earnings will attract yet more traffickers (as it probably has with illegal drugs), the very existence of such fatuous numbers reinforces the grotesque notion that nature is to be valued only by what can fetch in bits and pieces on the market.

Although the main danger to wildlife today is habitat loss enhanced by environmental pollution and climate disruption, the result of a human orgy of consumption unprecedented in history and impossible to sustain in the future, the threats are not separable. Habitat loss concentrates remaining members of particular species, rendering them physically more vulnerable to poachers, biologically less capable of replacing losses, and economically more desirable because of their scarcity value. Add to that the sheer impact of human encroachment. Argentina's 180,000 burrowing parrots living in 35,000 nests along 12 kilometres of coastline are now threatened by a tourist industry building holiday homes ever closer to the colony, by people thinking they are communing with nature while blithely tramping through the nesting areas, and by bikes, buggies, and motorized vehicles roaring along the beach and scaring off the young. Meanwhile farmers encroach on already marginal soil, stripping sparse natural vegetation, then kill off parrots who try to feed off seeds and crops.[61] But poachers are certainly eager to complete the work started by agribusiness corporations, forest-product conglomerates, chemical companies, and crude, stupid people.

However, poaching is not the work of giant transnational conspiracies headed by cockatoo-kingpins rolling in cash.[62] Rather, much as with shady activity in art or wine or caviar or so much else, it involves industry insiders, most of whom know and deal with each other, and understand fully the rules as well as how to break them without much risk of getting caught. They in turn try to fill a demand greatly inflated in recent decades by a bio-invasion of the socioeconomic environment by McMultiMillionaires for whom exotic and beautiful animals, rare parrots outstanding among them, are "as coveted as a Ming vase or a Stradivarius."[63] Perhaps so, but rare parrots have the advantage that they are less likely to be fake.

11

The Hunter-Gatherer Society:
From Law of the Jungle to
Maw of the Market

In the late 1950s, a five-minute sequence tagged onto the end of a Walt Disney nature film showed lemmings supposedly in their millions (a camera trick) rushing relentlessly over a cliff and into the sea, an image since embedded irrevocably into the public mind by endless iterations.[1] Of course, the lemmings, specially imported into northern Alberta for the stunt, rather than displaying remarkable stupidity, may have actually shown awesome prescience by anticipating how development of the Athabasca tar sands would convert the region into one huge toxic dumpsite.[2] And the scenario had a more fatal flaw – lemmings do not behave that way. Nor does any other species deliberately march to collective suicide – except perhaps one.

True, species other than humans, by dint of numbers and appetites, do expand their demands on a finite ecosystem niche until their means of sustenance are exhausted and their populations simply collapse. But none of the others are capable of understanding biophysical limits; and their damage is limited in time and space. *Homo saps* can plead neither excuse.

Anthropogenic climate change aside, the most obvious form of human biopredation is the direct takeover of the living space of other species, covering the landscape with urban sprawl and agro-industrial blight. But also important is forcible removal of other species from their natural habitat (be it tundra, savannah, desert, or rainforest) and into the human one (of concrete jungle) by the world trade in wildlife. Much of it is immoral, including the purchase from Inuit tribes of all those lemmings, their transfer into an alien environment, and their slaughter to titillate the folks back home. A big chunk of the trade is also illegal, although the choice of which to be so designated depends more on political expediency than natural justice. Despite modern synthetic-chemical methods and despite (however temporary) success in industrializing biological processes through agriculture, aquaculture, or arboculture, the human appetite for wildlife and its derivatives continues to grow. Each time a particular species is exploited to the point of exhaustion, the human response, as seafaring creatures have found out to their peril, is to simply shift attention to something else somewhere else.

Sometimes wildlife is traded alive, with at least the initial intent to keep it that way. Apart from parrots, although they probably command the most attention, the commerce in exotic pets claims everything from mountain lions to monitor lizards. Sometimes wildlife is traded live with intent to kill it soon after – for example, animals taken to heal the stock-market performance of pharmaceutical companies, to tart up the public face of the cosmetics industry, or to tantalize the taste buds of clients in restaurants offering exotic cuisine. But mostly wildlife is used as raw material. From the wool of the Tibetan antelope comes luxurious "shah-toush" shawls, while crocodile, alligator, ostrich, and various lizard skins decorate high-end handbags and boots.[3] Doctors practicing ancient forms of Asiatic medicine – traditional Chinese medicine (TCM) is the best known – prescribe everything from powdered tiger bone to bear bile. The perfume business processes musk from musk deer or civet cat, ambergris from sperm whales, and castoreum from beavers. The craving for expensive artifacts from its horn has helped (along with TCM) to drive the rhinoceros perilously close to extinction.[4] Mass tourism means mass demand for vulgar trinkets, a factor making a big dent in sea horse populations.[5] Recreational hunting, despite (usually poorly enforced) licensing laws, cuts a swathe through bird populations already dropping dramatically because of habitat loss and agro-industrial chemicals and menaces large mammals whose hides, too, are peddled for ornaments and luxury apparel. To the list of endangered fauna can be added a longer one of threatened flora, less mediagenic but sometimes of greater ecological significance.[6]

Those who supply that demand in the face of legal restrictions are also diverse. They may be peasant farmers to whom some species are a threat to their family's livelihood. They may be trophy hunters eager to hang a tribute to their testosterone levels on their living-room walls. They may be professional poachers operating purely for profit. They may be moonlighting game wardens, motivated by low pay and inferior status in the hierarchy of the government for which they work. They may be insurgent armies who traffic in wildlife to (maybe) finance weapons or (more likely) top up retirement accounts for their leaders. In the US, they may be radical libertarians sure that the Fish & Wildlife Service is part of that nefarious Rockefeller-controlled One World Government conspiracy, or they may be religious wingnuts convinced that ecological carnage will hasten Armageddon.[7]

Penuriousness or macho pride, individual avarice or logistical need, political paranoia or just a theological preference for calling down fire-and-brimstone instead of anguishing over little falling sparrows – the motives vary, the results do not. The products, in whole or in parts, make their way along a marketing chain from poacher to dealer to smuggler, the latter most likely a respectable entrepreneur in the import-export trade, also skilled in the covert movement of restricted or prohibited goods and the clandestine management of the return flow of funds. The exporter will either smuggle outright or pose the restricted or banned species as something not on the endangered lists; may use counterfeit, stolen, or recycled certificates of origin or export licenses; and have partners in jurisdictions that act as laundering or transshipment centres. On arrival at final destination, wildlife and/or its derivatives may pass through a new set of intermediaries, from importer to wholesaler and perhaps to manufacturer, then to retailer. Ultimately the final product is marketed through legitimate businesses ranging from vendors of consumer luxuries to Asian pharmacies to upscale restaurants before reaching its final repose as a tiger-skin rug, a vial of bear bile or the central exhibit in a "safari dinner."

In fact, the probable fate of some species, particularly of certain large mammals, is all the gloomier precisely because they can sate at once several forms of human appetite. Various bits and pieces can serve as trophies (usually the heads), luxury fashion goods (particularly the pelts), material for trendy jewellery (like the teeth and claws), nostrums for body and soul (mainly internal organs and their secretions), or edibles that supposedly work physiological or psychological wonders, with the additional attraction that the bigger and apparently badder the animal, the more tempting it is sizzling on the grill. The very diversity of demand leaves industrial interests, government agencies, and NGOcrats squabbling over whether more damage is done by Western consumatons despoiling the natural world for exotica or by the Yellow Peril ravaging the globe to feed weird tastes in food and medicine, something that seems intolerable when Big Macs and Tylenol are so easy to find. Meanwhile the poisoning of the biosphere, destruction of the rainforests, disruption of the global climate, and degradation of the oceans continue unabated.

FOUR-FOOTED PHARMACY

The tiger is one animal with the misfortune to find a place on everyone's wishlist. Its pelt makes spectacular rugs (especially with the head attached) or coats (better without); its claws and teeth worn around the neck are great to repel uncool suitors in dating bars; choice morsels reputedly confer vitality; and every bit has a role in oriental medicine, some proven, some possible, some absurd.[8] Ground tiger bone does work as an anti-inflammatory, although so does mole rat bone. But using the whiskers to cure a headache seems a bit of a stretch; consuming the blood to increase willpower probably gets the causation in reverse; while tiger tooth is more likely to cause than to cure dramatic sores on a man's penis if the two ever come in contact. On the other hand, the tiger's own penis, dried, then boiled into soup, soaked in wine, or formed into tablets, is supposedly a powerful male aphrodisiac (but what isn't in these days of rising female political power and falling sperm counts?). Since various other tiger parts supposedly work their own medical miracles, almost 20 percent of TCM formulae include tiger extracts, or say they do.[9]

Together, the challenge to hunters of the animal's ferocity, the beauty of its hide and the promises of TCM combined with rapidly shrinking habitat ensured that at the start of the twentieth century perhaps 100,000 animals roamed large tracts of Asia. That was in spite of the mandatory photo-op tiger kills by senior officials of British India and their visiting guests. If they were rich or powerful enough, those companions were assured of bagging a tiger never less than ten feet long, a result guaranteed by the shakiri (native hunting guide) using a tape measure with an eleven inch foot.[10] By the end of the twentieth century there were only a few thousand in total in about 7 percent of former range.

Three of the eight recognized species are already extinct, two on the brink, one dangerously close, and only the Bengal tiger possibly stabilized in sufficient numbers to survive, though that is debatable. Any genuine progress made in India is offset by ongoing pressure in places like Sumatra, where illegal gold-miners and loggers poach wildlife on the side, and Siberia.[11] During the Russian imperial era, the Siberian tiger, hunted especially for skins, faced extinction. Under the Communists, with hunting banned, well-policed reserves created, and the border sealed, wild populations rebounded. With the collapse of Soviet authority, the Siberian tiger – along with the lynx, snow leopard, amur leopard, ibex, goral goat, saiga antelope, black bear, and musk deer – again faced the abyss. Local governments had little power or money, while illegal loggers stripped forest cover and opened roads, reducing habitat and facilitating poaching, particularly with the China border virtually unpoliced.[12] Even now, with Russia stabilized, the race for Siberian oil and timber means that the remaining handful of local tigers have dismal prospects.

Most of the world's wild tigers are now supposedly protected in India and Burma. But nature reserves create small, non-contiguous groups, inhibiting reproduction. Poorly policed reserves, too, function as concentration camps where poachers pose a double danger – direct, given extremely high value of tiger parts, and indirect, by killing off cat food (elk, wild cattle, and deer). Tigers then raid livestock, incurring the wrath of farmers, who surround and intrude increasingly into reserves, with government agencies loath to interfere. That is why India's claim in the 1970s to great success in stemming the collapse of tiger populations turned out to be bogus, the numbers inflated to make politicians look good. Worse, the prior overestimate reduced efforts to protect remaining animals, leading to a series of major poaching scandals. By the new millennium the decline threatened to become a crash there, too, as one reserve after another reported that their tiger populations had vanished, mainly into some trafficker's bank account.[13]

Although professionals supply equipment, and perhaps advance money, most poaching seems to be conducted by villagers near reserves: they know the forest and how to hunt. Since a tiger with its solitary habits and preference for deep jungle is hardly easy prey, it may be poisoned or electrocuted (although that hurts medicinal sales), or bagged by trapping and gunfire. Traders buy dead tigers (and sometimes live cubs) for cash or goods, then resell the animals to distributors who take carcasses to big cities for dismemberment. Some hides are sent to tanneries, sporadically raided by wildlife officers. Parts slated for medicinal use along with some hides are hauled by air or rail to the Himalayas, then carried by foot, yak, or mule, or stuffed inside commercial cargos, through mountain passes, most unguarded or staffed by agents who can be paid off. Mixing tiger bones, for example, with those of other animals can throw off customs searches, assuming an agent actually cares.

One exit route runs through Nepal, the traffic handled by businessmen in the fur and wool trades that form excellent cover. Other routes cross directly into Tibet. Given the virtual extermination of local leopards, some tiger skins remain in Tibet to satisfy a local tradition of using animal skins to trim festive garments. Visitors from China, Europe, and North America, too, shop in Lhasa, Tibet's capital, for pelts banned back home.[14] However, most material moves deeper into China for sale to restaurants, pharmacies, or middlemen who run it abroad.

The same is true for tiger from Burma. For a long time the country hosted healthy populations, especially in Kachin State, homeland to an ethnic minority that had been partially Christianized, armed, then supported in aspirations to independence by the British, particularly since their area hosted gold, gems, rare hardwood, and opium poppy. For the first four decades after Burma's independence, Kachin state remained off-limits to the regime, its wildlife largely intact, while the Kachin independence movement encouraged locals to exploit on a small-scale basis the gold and gemstone riches. But in 1988 the military government attempted to reassert control, and by 1994 the region effectively surrendered. Although the government set up the world's largest tiger reserve, it also sponsored a double alien invasion of the same area – of Burmese in an attempt by the regime to water down Kachin State's ethnic uniqueness, and of large scale gold-mining companies who paid off the military junta to displace artisanal gold miners and who produced the usual ecological disaster zones – meaning, among other things, more bad press for Robert Friedland in the alternative media and NGO sources, despite a post-sanctions attempt to divest his Burmese assets.[15] With or without Canadian gold ventures, though, the opening of the region meant big trouble for wildlife, particularly elephants and tigers, the ivory from the first and almost everything from the second bound mainly for the Chinese market.[16]

China's appetite for tiger imports reflects its population, its growing wealth, the staying power of traditional medicine, and the unpleasant reality that in the 1950s and 1960s Chinese peasants were officially encouraged to treat tigers as livestock-killing vermin. That produced a handy surplus of tiger bone for medicinal purposes. By the 1990s, it was exhausted. Even though China forbade use of wild tiger in medicines, the local supply was partly replaced by poached tigers from India, Burma, and Siberia. The alternative, to raise tigers in captivity, was tried, banned, then tried again to the point where today there are perhaps fifty wild tigers left in China and about four thousand stuck in small cages waiting to be dismembered for TCM, to have skins stuffed for display, or to have choice parts diverted to expensive eateries specializing in "wild flavours."[17] Of course, clients do not always get what they order: in 2005 a police investigation revealed one restaurant serving donkey meat flavoured with tiger urine.[18]

Nor do tiger farms mean less pressure on the wild animals. Legal tiger products keep demand inflated and reduce pressure for alternatives. The cost of poaching a tiger in India or Burma and smuggling it to China is much lower than raising one on a farm. Tiger farms are more useful to launder those caught in the wild.[19]

There's a similar situation in Taiwan.[20] Despite an effort to escape its pariah status by tightening wildlife laws, its continued role as a trafficking hub showed up in 2005 with the seizure of bones representing (supposedly) 5 percent of the remaining tiger population of Sumatra – although obviously no one can be sure of the exact numbers of an animal that leads a solitary existence in the deep jungle.[21] Geography makes South Korea prefer Siberian sources, while Thailand mainly uses Burmese.[22] From all of these countries tiger medicines flow around the world to a growing population of TCM users, expats along with Western converts, even in the face of a ban. So do fakes of those medicines.[23]

With tiger extracts built into pharmaceutical products, smuggling is easy while processing destroys DNA evidence. A false label can be switched back to the real one at point of sale. But that is rarely necessary – TCM pharmacists and their clients are more likely united in knowledge that the product is illegal.[24] But that also invites fakery. A medicine might contain tiger bone so diluted as to be therapeutically useless, or have bones of bear, yak, buffalo, camel, horse, pig, etc. substituted.[25] Similarly in the skin trade, domestic kittens, even stray dogs, could have their fur bleached and artificially coloured to simulate tiger cubs, with claws shaped from things like bovine horn added to the corpse. To fake genitalia, cow's leg tendons can be fashioned into a testicle-like bag; and since a feline penis has barbs, it suffices to make V-shaped surface cuts on the tip of one taken from another suitable animal, then hang it upside down to dry until the edges curl into barb-like projections.[26]

With pressures on the tiger in the wild unrelenting and habitat shrinking, there is probably little prospect of the animal surviving outside zoos and tiger farms. But occasionally rough justice ensues, as in 1992 when a tiger in Sumatra killed two poachers on a reserve, one fishing illegally, the other cutting endangered trees.

Alas, more common is something like an incident in Malaysia in 1998 when a tiger struck by a bus had eyes, tail, lower hind legs, tongue, jaw, and sex organs stripped by the time authorities arrived; or the scene in a Chinese zoo in 2007 when its lone Siberian tiger was found dead with its skin, head, and legs missing; or the eleven Siberian tigers who died in a Chinese wildlife park in 2010, with the possibility that they were deliberately starved so that the staff could sell the parts.[27]

ANOTHER GOLDEN FLEECE?

For decades contraband routes handling tiger parts also serviced movement in the opposite direction of another valuable species. Just fifty years ago, the chiru (Tibetan antelope) ranged in the hundreds of thousands across the harsh Tibetan Plateau. Only in deep winter did it descend to share grazing grounds with livestock. Although chiru were hunted for food, local people were few; and while the antlers were used in TCM, there were ample substitutes. However, the chiru has one evolutionary advantage that threatened its downfall: it survives bitter winters because of an underfleece of extremely fine wool. While other wools are sheared from a living animal, chiru down long enough to weave comes from a dead one, each adult yielding a scant 125–150 grams.

For a time, even that was sustainable. The wool was gathered as a byproduct of the hunt, passed to nomadic traders, then carried into India to Kashmir, epicentre of the Indian handweaving industry, to make shahtoush scarves, prized in northern India as dowry gifts. Then came a dramatic change.

Western interest in shawls made of the feather-light, ultra-warm wool probably began in British India, and from there moved to the London elite. By the 1970s the taste had spread to New York, Paris, and Milan, and the seasonal haunts of their beautiful people, becoming a fashion rage the next decade. A woman's shawl required on average down from three animals, a man's scarf from four. Once rich trend-setters began sporting them under coats like cashmere wraps or over bare shoulders instead of mink stoles (which could attract a shower of rotten eggs from animal-rights activists), the practice among wealthy parasitocrats seeking to one-up each other spread far and fast. When, in the mid-1990s, customers of the main distributor in New York were ordered to appear with their scarves at the Fish and Wildlife Service office, the wife of high-profile political commentator William F. Buckley exclaimed: "I haven't heard of anything so ridiculous in a long time. Some of our friends will have to call a moving van ..."[28]

Simultaneously, the chiru faced a multisided attack on its habitat. Traditional nomadic herders in Tibet gave way to settled livestock farmers who protected scarce grazing land against wild herds. The region's human population grew as China encouraged an influx of Han farmers to water down the ethnic character of Tibet and built modern roads to secure the frontier with India. With farmers and settlers came alluvial gold miners who brought dredging, damming, and mercury pollution. Modern weapons and motor vehicles shifted hunting from entrepreneurial to industrial. By 1977 when the animal was moved to CITES I, there were perhaps 65–75,000 still left. True, China gave the chiru the highest level of protection under its endangered species laws and created a massive reserve in Tibet. However, with demand accelerating, so did poaching. As prices rose, wool poachers no longer focused only on large males in the winter when the coat was thickest, but targeted younger animals and females in the summer as well.[29]

After the animal is killed, the wool is extracted, since it is easier to hide than a whole skin, with the carcass left to rot. Before that wool could reappear as the world's most expensive nappy around the bare bottom of some Hollywood starlet's newly born media-magnet, it followed a circuitous underground route. Some is smuggled directly into India via networks of Tibetan exiles: some goes through Nepal along historic trade and contraband routes. Given very high value in relation to bulk and weight, small loads are profitable.[30] Contraband may be mixed with other wool, including very fine pashmina (also produced by Tibetan nomads) and cashmere, which to the untutored eye and hand look and feel the same. At the borders, tribal peoples reputedly barter shahtoush against other wildlife products like tiger bone, bear gall, and musk deer pods from India, a trade based on tradition, trust, and a shared aversion to outside authority. With larger loads, cash deals arranged directly by wool and wildlife merchants are likely. From there, the product ends up in Kashmir, where a group of politically powerful merchants distribute it to specialists in extended families (women spin and men weave) that have kept the skills for generations.

Despite India's adhesion to the CITES ban, until recently little was done to suppress weaving. Kashmir is technically autonomous; and India, facing a dozen insurgent groups in an area contested with Pakistan, was hesitant to displease the weaving industry. Even if shahtoush was a niche trade, it symbolized the state's prominence in the world fine-wool business when competitors like China were making inroads. Even after India's Supreme Court endorsed the application of Indian wildlife laws to Kashmir, the state's official outlets openly advertised, offering certificates of origin and of authenticity, and (allegedly) fake documents to assist exports.[31]

Once weaving was done, the merchants who handled raw wool sent shawls back to Delhi for local and tourist markets, or for reps of Western haute-couture outlets. Easy to smuggle, shahtoush shawls can be mixed with pashmina and cashmere products and are obviously impervious to X-ray detection. Even after the heat was turned on luxury retailers in the West, shahtoush scarves were reputedly still sold through the upscale equivalent of Tupperware parties in New York, London, and Paris. In Hong Kong high-end shops put shahtoush in their windows.[32]

That rich women strutted about in shahtoush for years after the animal was moved to CITES I reflected a law that banned imports but not domestic trading. Yet few cargoes could be adequately checked; shahtoush was hard to distinguish on casual inspection from other fine wools, particularly once weavers and merchants began to disguise it, by dyeing or by mixing the fibres with other material; and the few customs violations detected could usually be settled by a small fine. Once inside the country of destination, enforcement largely vanished – unless the animal was put on local endangered-species lists. Anti-trade groups did launch a consumer campaign, but it was countered by trade propaganda.

Bergdorf Goodman, the New York luxury retailer renowned for silk bedding and pearl-encrusted baby pillows, reassured its clientele that "The source of the wool is the Mountain Ibex goat of Tibet. After the arduous Himalayan winter is over, the Ibex sheds its down undercoat by scratching itself against low trees and bushes ...."[33]

Hard times for the trade began in 1995 after French customs seized a shipment of shawls to Paris from New York. They had originally been imported by a Hong Kong-based company from a Mumbai supplier for a charity auction to be held at New York's Mayfair Hotel on behalf of the Sloan-Kettering Hospital's Dream Team. The company had agreed to donate $10,000 and a share of profits to making the last wishes of dying children come true – by encouraging the further slaughter of chiru. After a long investigation, the length and care probably reflecting the social class of the targets, in 1999 more than one hundred celebrities and socialites including top fashion designers, supermodels, and patronesses of the arts were given subpoenas to testify at a grand jury investigation and to bring their scarves. Six years after the Mayfair event the Mumbai supplier pleaded guilty to smuggling shawls into the US, and the two women who ran the Hong Kong company pleaded guilty to underreporting the value of the shawls (claiming them to be cashmere) for customs purposes, then re-exporting some to a Paris fashion boutique. None of the women who had bought scarves were charged.[34] But coming after a 1997 London police sting that netted 138 shawls with a retail value set at about $500,000, the affair caused brief revulsion.[35]

International pressure led to action in India, too, during the early years of the new millennium, in the form of enforcement of the ban in Kashmir, financial aid to displaced weavers, busts of shahtoush traders, and a publicized raid on the luxury shop of Delhi's Meridien Hotel.[36] Some weavers shifted to other wools; others went underground. The Kashmiri government protested the loss of livelihood for 100,000 to 500,000 "orphans, the destitute and single-mothers" out of the 100 extended families of specialized, relatively well-to-do shahtoush weavers. Defenders claimed, too, that tales of the chiru being endangered were made-in-China to create a worldwide backlash against shahtoush and clear the way for Chinese domination of the machine-woven pashmina-wool business.[37] Industry pessimists and anti-trade optimists alike predicted the demise of the shahtoush business. However they may both be wrong.

Today, instead of crossing into India via Nepal, some shahtoush seems to transit Central Asia into Pakistan, from there south to Delhi, then north again to Kashmir. Even if the number of weavers has dropped, the trade persists. Apparently now merchants break shawl shipments into smaller packets to distribute widely, minimizing damage from any seizure. Retailers keep shahtoush under the table, doing private deals with foreign clients hustled by cab drivers and travel agents.[38] And the material still moves abroad, no doubt much of it dyed a colour more characteristic of other wools or mixed with commonplace material. In 2005, three decades after the chiru was moved to Appendix I and three years after India had supposedly suppressed the business, Swiss Customs seized 537 shawls, some slated to retail in the $18,000–20,000 range, coming from Hong Kong and Mumbai with customs forms claiming they were pashmina. This, though, was just business as usual with a reverse twist in a luxury-wool trade where pashmina gets sold as shah-toush, machine-woven wools parade as handmade, or materials are claimed to be pure when they are mixed with everything from rabbit fur to acrylic.[39]

Nor is further public sensitization – for example, India's Shawl of Shame campaign featuring pictures of a fashion model handcuffed beside a pile of confiscated wildlife products – likely to have much impact.[40] With the industry fully underground, elite demand for a prohibited product solidly in place, smuggling networks well oiled, and concerns over the chiru swamped by campaigns to save dozens of other species, while its habitat is coveted by mining and oil companies, the fate of the Tibetan antelope is probably sealed as surely, if not as quickly, as that of the tiger, its occasional trade partner. At best it may end up reduced from hundreds of thousands, perhaps millions of free-ranging animals to a few thousand in non-congruous groups confined to the equivalent of open-air zoos and periodically culled in another triumph of "scientific resource-management" over nature.

THE SWEET SMELL OF EX-STINK-TION?

Much the same networks handle traffic in a near-neighbour of the chiru, one whose woes have been as great and started even earlier. True, Western demand for the sexual services of the musk deer has, if not vanished, greatly fallen off in recent decades, not because of a dramatic shift in conscience but because of the magic of the modern lab – producers of luxury perfumes now prefer to poison the habitat of all species with synthetic-chemical waste rather than just to encourage the slaughter of musk deer. However, use of natural musk in TCM as an anti-inflammatory and calmant still takes its toll, and as more luxury perfume producers shift production to Asia, demand may well rise again on that front.[41]

The musk deer is native to much of Central Asia, concentrating in the Himalayas and remote alpine areas of China and Russia. It has one advantage over its only really dangerous predator. Since it is neither cuddly like a koala bear nor dramatic like a tiger, and therefore useless for generating box-office receipts, this shy, solitary, and nocturnally active animal used to hiding in forested slopes is rarely stuck in a concrete-floored cage in broad daylight to be terrorized by louts poking sticks through the bars. However, that plus is more than offset by a huge minus: to attract females, males secrete a scent remarkable for its intensity, persistence, and fixative properties. After the appeal of musk crossed the species barrier to humans, somehow the sexual politics got reversed.

In ages past, fragrances from plants or animals were at least as important for religious or medicinal purposes as for personal adornment. In ancient Egypt, myrrh (a resin from a shrub in southern Arabia and the Horn of Africa) was used to embalm corpses and confer immunity against disease; Sumeria and China thousands of years ago pioneered floral extracts as antiseptics; most major religions used things like frankincense (another resin from the same regions as myrrh) in rituals. The rise of Islam took the craft of fragrances to new heights: musk sometimes scented the mortar used to build mosques, while other extracts were used for personal cleansing demanded by the faith. Still, Mohammed, while praising musk highly, advanced the opinion in the Hadith that "the water's fragrance is better than musk."[42] He might have added that water does not require cruelly killing a harmless little animal whose meat humans do not like and whose pelt humans cannot use (because the hair falls out) to get twenty-five grams of pungent-smelling secretion.

Europe's demand for scents from the Orient took off after the Crusades. The defeated armies returned with knowledge of exotic fragrances, how to distill alcohol (a technique perfected by Muslim alchemists) to dissolve the perfumes, and the manufacture of high-quality bottles. Use of perfume spread among the upper classes, partly because Oriental fragrances reputedly protected against diseases like plague or malaria (literally, "bad air") and partly because Europe had not bathed for about a thousand years.[43] Particularly for people packed into urban areas whose streets might be passable only after the pigs were released to eat the garbage along with stray dogs and the occasional small child, perfume for those who could afford it was the only sure way to cloak the all-pervasive stench. Fragrances were mainly from local flowers. However, among imported ones, musk drew special attention. Initially lauded as an aphrodisiac, it was at other times condemned as immoral, addictive, even poisonous, more for homosexuals and prostitutes than high-class roués and courtesans. Casanova reputedly fainted at the smell, though intense fatigue from his other supposed exploits could have been just as easily to blame.

Musk, though, had another importance. While most essences produce only ephemeral scents, musk was also prized for its powers to maintain other fragrances, and therefore was a key additive to perfumes based on floral extracts. However its rarity, inconsistency of supply, and sky-high price led to a search for synthetics. The first, in the late nineteenth century, was produced accidentally by a chemist attempting to make explosives from coal tar derivatives. The petrochemical age to follow eventually saw hundreds of synthetic musks both to act as powerful fixatives and convey a musk-like fragrance. They were far cheaper than natural musk. That they were non-biodegradable, possibly carcinogenic (with early ones also neurotoxins), and turning up in human fat, mother's milk, and the Great Lakes did not seem to matter very much.[44]

Still, the greater the progress of synthetics, the greater the snob value of natural scents – until 1921. When Chanel No. 5, soon the world's most popular "luxury" perfume, entered a scene dominated by French brands based on mostly locally grown natural fragrances, its creator touted it with the interesting, modernistic claim that only an artificial scent could properly enhance a woman's natural beauty. After World War II, US soldiers took it home to their sweethearts, its popularity soaring there after Marilyn Monroe declared it the only thing she wore in bed at night. Andy Warhol found it as worthy of artistic celebration as Campbell's tomato soup. And one of the perfume's modern advocates breathlessly describes the scent as "regally beautiful ... a radiant chorus of ylang and rose floating like gold leaf on the chalk-white background of aldehydes."[45] The New York Times perfume critic seemed to concur, calmly declaring that it "... hits you like a bank of white-hot searchlights washing the powdered stars at a movie premiere in Cannes on a dry summer night."[46]

However, the real reasons for the triumph of synthetic scents lay not in their aesthetic appeal. Eau de skunk-cabbage would sell by the gallon if Nicole Kidman would do for it the kind of walkabout she did for Chanel No. 5 in the movie *Moulin Rouge*. Rather it was the realization by producers and sellers that, given the impossibility of patenting a product of nature, the only way to sew up "intellectual property rights" was to rely on synthetic molecules. In addition, the French perfume industry, facing rising labour costs after World War II, had two options to maintain its world lead – shift to synthetics for the bulk of its needs and outsource genuine floral essences to countries with more sun and cheaper labour, like Morocco, Southern Italy, Egypt, and later Turkey, India, China, and the Balkans. It did both.[47]

Musk was not out of the game, still figuring as a fixative in top-end perfumes, including Chanel No. 5, in the 1960s, when major perfume makers began to energetically market musk (most of it probably synthetic without that being revealed on the bottle) to both men and women. In the 1970s, luxury perfumes took off again, the most expensive bragging of natural musk content. Combined with ever-rising demand in the Orient both for perfumes (especially Japan) and for medicinal elixirs (particularly China), the result was to push the price of natural musk to peak at $50,000 a kilo.

However, that price hike reflected pending trouble. Although the musk deer, unlike the chiru, is a solitary animal, it usually follows a fixed and well-marked trail to grazing grounds. That allows trappers to construct fence lines along a mountain spur, encircling a large habitat area, but leaving gaps in frequently used paths planted with snare lines, each with multiple traps. When the musk deer treads on a trap, a noose tightens around its leg and jerks it into the air, breaking the bone and/or tearing the muscle and leaving the animal dangling there until it dies or the trapper arrives to kill it. Neither this nor any other hunting method discriminate between sexually mature males and muskless females or young animals. At the same time the musk deer is under further pressure from the encroachment of loggers and of herders who convert habitat into pasture land.[48]

The slaughter virtually wiped out musk deer in some range states, leading the animal to be placed on CITES I in some, CITES II in all others. The countries themselves varied between total internal bans and licensed hunts, even if right next door to each other. That way the "legal" musk trade could play the usual laundering games by smuggling across porous borders or faking certificates of origin. Either way the listings delighted "the king of musk," an Indian trader who ran a worldwide business from Delhi, Hong Kong, and London selling musk from the USSR to top perfume-makers in Europe. The Soviet Union, still hosting large and well-protected herds, had opted out of CITES restrictions. That had convinced the musk king his business would soar. Instead, demand collapsed as luxury perfume-makers shifted ever more to synthetics. They were at least as effective as fixatives and generally much cheaper. Even more importantly, the musk scent itself ceased to be remotely exotic. Synthetic musk was becoming an ingredient in virtually everything present in a bathroom cosmetics cupboard, even in deodorants. Today, if a foodstuff is marked as artificially flavoured, it may contain petroleum-derived musk as well.[49] After all, the label says nothing about whether or not a food product is actually edible. The final blow to the musk-king came when his father, who ran the London end of the business, was murdered and the office ransacked of allegedly $6.5 million worth of musk and bear-bile products. At that point the family began to concentrate on things like cattle gallstones. "I am quite into animal conservation," the de-crowned musk king explained.[50]

In the 1980s, the perfume business took another huge leap up the financial charts and another big lunge down the class ones with the success of Calvin Klein's Obsession. It was to the formerly French-dominated perfume world what California wines were to the previous Bordeaux-Burgundy closed shop. The impact was explained by George Dodd, pioneer in the psychology of scents and himself a perfumer who worked with natural fragrances using old-fashioned methods: "American tastes are dominated by their perfume experiences when they're tiny babies, and get their bums powdered with Johnson's Baby Powder." The result was that fragrances selling well in the US really conjured up not blatant sex – that was what attracted people to the ads, not to the perfume. Rather, ideally for a culture both obsessed with sex and frightened of it, they invoked "cleanliness and innocence."[51] Too bad so many of its perfumes can also invoke skin, neurological, and lung disorders even if they are genuine, and lots more problems if they are high-end fakes, made from cheap chemicals with artificial scents, then packed in genuine-looking packages and bottles.

Meanwhile, freed of the risk of objections from its giant pharmaceutical companies and luxury conglomerates by their very success with synthetics, in 1999 the US, formerly the world's biggest consumer of natural musk perfumes, and India, whose Himalayan musk deer population had been seriously depleted, led a movement for a worldwide ban, while the EU agreed to stop entry of all musk from post-Soviet Russia and from China, two places where the animal seemed particularly threatened by poaching.[52] Luxury perfume makers even in France undertook a final phase-out of natural musk. They, like so many Bordeaux wineries, began to follow the US model. Their specialist perfume makers became simply product divisions of luxury conglomerates; and their perfumes were sold on the basis of celebrity endorsements rather than contents. After all, if someone took note of the fact that "This Is Intimately David Beckham" could be more accurately called benzophenone–3, methyl 2-(4-tetra-butylphenyl) acetate, not only might they hesitate to slap it on their face but some of the more prudent might refuse to even touch the bottle clad in anything short of a radiation suit. The final move to synthetics even affected Chanel No. 5. The only fly in the ointment, if not in the perfume, came with the discovery that it had been using natural musk not from the deer but from a different animal, whose trapping could involve methods just as brutal. So in 1998 the company announced it was also phasing out use of musk from the civet cat.

In fairness, this primitive omnivore that is not really a cat is not yet as seriously endangered as the musk deer, probably because it is more valuable to another luxury trade alive than dead. Although their African cousins are routinely farmed and slaughtered for musk, civet cats on the Indonesian islands of Java, Sumatra, and Sulawesi and in the Philippines climb to the top of coffee plants to swallow ripe berries. After their digestive juices break down the fruit, they excrete the beans in their stool. With a total annual production of no more than one thousand pounds, sometimes much less, the beans retail for $1,500 a kilo, or about $50 a cup, with Western consumaholics raving about the unique flavour.[53] If Chanel No. 5 inspired Andy ("I love plastic. I want to be plastic.") Warhol to depict it on canvas in the 1980s, twenty-five years later, the image of a top-dollar fashion model drenched in that perfume while sipping a demitasse of liquefied civet cat crap, perhaps with a shahtoush shawl over her otherwise bare shoulders, is worthy of the attention of Damien Hirst to rank among his butterfly-wing collages or rotting tiger-shark carcasses.

Even with the virtual elimination of animal musk, both civet and deer, in the West, Asia, led by China, still consumes enormous amounts. China's efforts to either encourage the musk deer to take root in new non-native locations or to milk the glands of farmed deer without killing them have proven largely useless. Meanwhile, its domestic price controls sent increasing amounts of musk poached from its own rapidly falling deer population out of the country, mainly to feed the rival Japanese medicine and perfume market.[54] A new cultural invasion of China by Western perfumes, led by Chanel No. 5, along with the decision of the giant international cosmetics companies to open Chinese subsidiaries that can, if they wish, source natural musk locally, will likely keep the pressure mounting.[55]

Certainly the slaughter of musk deer for TCM is a crime against nature, given that plenty of alternatives exist. However, before the West becomes too holy, it needs to consider whether its self-righteous wrath reflects profound concern about the present-day sins of others or a deep sense of guilt about its own past treatment of wildlife, including the musk deer. Anyway, musk was relatively easy for the West to swear off. It is not even the best natural fixative for perfumes. Among animal-derived substances that honour goes to ambergris from sperm whale intestines. The Western perfume industry used to claim that it collected the stuff from whale vomit – apparently a rapidly diminishing population of sperm whales spends more time puking than eating, sleeping, swimming, and copulating. France, which condemns the slaughter of sperm whales by Japan and Norway, has been hardly reticent about buying the resulting ambergris for a perfume industry that for a time also absorbed about 15 percent of the world's natural musk.

Furthermore, today's reputedly deer musk-shunning luxury perfume industry in the West is happy to test toxic, carcinogenic, and mutagenic chemicals on legions of rats, rabbits, and rhesus monkeys, along with stray or stolen dogs peddled by crooked brokers or unloaded from commercial animal shelters. (Many of those producers who advertise "no animal testing" use ingredients whose safety has been approved by regulators precisely because other companies had tested them on animals before.[56]) These animals endure a miserable, if brief, existence locked in cages to test not just human-lifesaving drugs, for which a case can be occasionally although not very convincingly made, but household cleaners for which there is no justification, and cosmetics, which should provoke unmitigated outrage.[57]

Needless to say, that goes double for the Pentagon, which tests its body armour by strapping it on pigs, then placing them in simulated Humvee transporters before blowing them up – a practice it defends on the grounds that the physiology of pigs is much closer to humans than the rats they used to employ.[58] The Pentagon made no observations about the personality profiles of the victim pigs compared to the humanoid rats who run the test program.

AN UNBEARABLE FATE?

Although exotic beasts in Asia, Africa, and South America are prime targets for biopredation, those of North America have had more than their share of woes. They still do. None suffer more than the bear, who, over the centuries, has played a role in North American (and European) popular culture like that of the tiger in Asian and the lion in African. As a charismatic and carnivorous megabeast it has been variously worshipped, feared, and ridiculed. Few sights are more appalling than of a bear attempting to escape the torment meted out by its trainers by "dancing" on command before a jeering, leering mob – except perhaps a malnourished, diseased animal trapped in a tiny cage on a Chinese bear-bile farm with a rusty catheter in its side. With all five Asian bear species on Appendix I, while North American black bears along with brown ones indigenous to North America, Europe, and Northern Asia on II, it is easy to point an accusing finger at Asia's traditional medical practices. That is also fair – as long as the other nine fingers don't get forgotten.

In North America bears were long hunted for pelts, meat, and fat, sold widely in the nineteenth century as a restorative for hair and as a fragrant oil for perfume and soap. When the bear supply seemed

about depleted in the Eastern US, manufacturers started sourcing from
Canada and the US West. Until well into the twentieth century US officialdom encouraged through subsidies and bounties unrestricted killing by gun, trap, and poison. While now hunters supposedly require
licenses, the carnage continues on both sides of the border. In much
the way, although in reverse direction, that after the Little Big Horn
the Sioux fled a vengeful US army into the Canadian prairies, claiming to be loyal subjects of the Queen, only to be forced back to meet
their fate, so Glacier National Park on the Montana side has its bear
population swollen by grizzly refugees from the Canadian open season. That way, US wildlife authorities can then count them as evidence
of healthy numbers and rationalize yet more hunting licenses on their
side.[59] Only recently have black bears shown any real recovery in North
America, although they are still badly depleted compared to historical
highs. And to this day, brown bears are among the most popular targets
of trophy hunters although they number far fewer than black, have been
eliminated from half or more of their former range states, and are left in
small, isolated pockets in the rest.[60]

Obviously licensed hunting is not alone as a threat to the bear –
although conservationists argue that licenses are granted too freely
while wildlife bureaucrats claim the opposite. On top comes poaching.
In North America traffic accidents are also a big problem, and habitat
loss the biggest of all – without factoring in the collapse of wild salmon
runs on which both black and grizzly bears on the West Coast rely.[61]
However, the various factors are impossible to separate. Clear-cutting
forests and paving over wilderness makes bears and other species more
vulnerable to hunters, licensed or not. And habitat loss along with shortages of salmon, by forcing bears to forage outside their normal turf,
causes humans enjoying pristine nature in Winnebagos, complete with
air conditioners, microwave ovens, and flush toilets, to place panic calls
to park wardens, sometimes leading to the "problem" animal being shot,
even though the bear probably has better reasons than the campers do
to dial for help.

Nor is the North American bear hunt today just for trophies. The net
hosts websites selling bear oil for cooking, soap, native and naturopathic
medicines, lubricants, fuel for lamps, leather conditioning, skin soften-
ers, cosmetic ingredients, aphrodisiacs, and general rejuvenators.[62]

Nonetheless, hunting is certainly encouraged by the fact that the bear
is the only mammal to produce in significant quantity ursodeoxycholic
acid. Extracted as bile from the bear's gallbladder, made into crystals,
dissolved in liquor, molded into capsules and tablets, or mixed in oint-
ments and creams, it is probably second only to tiger parts in the number

of TCM formulations for which it is used. Other parts of the bear are in demand – heads for trophies, hides for rugs, claws and teeth for jewellery, even bear-paw soup as yet another high-priced would-be aphrodisiac. Still, the most consistent target is the gallbladder, preferably from a black bear although most others will do in a pinch.

China's own supply of black bears was long ago decimated, and Russia's made vulnerable by collapse of state authority. Even today poaching for bladders and paws plagues the main Siberian reserves, struggling to hold onto badly underpaid staff in the face of expanding job opportunities in resource extraction – it pays much better to strip forest cover and pollute habitat with oil spills than to protect wildlife. Perhaps worse than the direct impact on bear populations in Siberia is the impact of the thriving bear-parts trade (bear paw as well as bile) across the China border. It opens smuggling links for the Amur tiger and Far Eastern leopard, which are even more endangered.[63] With declining Asian bear populations, the main wild source years ago switched to North America. Although black bear is preferred, rising prices in the 1980s and 1990s accelerated the poaching of all species, even the polar bear, formerly avoided because its bile had a fishy flavour – as if it needed more woes on top of a chemical pollutant load interfering with reproduction and the melting of polar ice.

Even when a hunt is legal, it can cover for illegal activity: a take in excess of quota; a hunt out of the season; a search extended to forbidden areas; and transactions unrecorded to avoid tax. Although a strictly legal hunter might target only mature males, bladder poachers go after them all – bladder size (determining the amount of gall) depends more on diet than on age, sex, or weight of the animal. A legal hunter may collect the head and fur; poachers may just remove the gall-bladders and paws leaving the rest to rot or be eaten by scavengers, destroying the evidence.[64] Then the bladder, dried to reduce size and eliminate odour, takes the usual kind of route through chains of intermediaries, including licensed dealers with access to documents that can be manipulated. Bladders heading to the Orient or Oriental pharmacies in North America have supposedly turned up dipped in chocolate, stuffed in jars of honey, or mixed with perishable foodstuffs. They can go by mail, inside commercial cargoes, or carried in personal luggage, perhaps via third countries (Hong Kong is a favourite) to disguise origin.[65]

Again, illegality covers for fakery. Since larger bladders fetch a higher price per unit than small, they might be injected with plastic beads and lead weights, or artificially coloured to improve appearance and therefore value. Pig bile can be injected into a bear bladder. Alternatively a small amount of bear gall gets injected into a pig bladder to simulate the taste, with the pig gall then coloured with corn-starch, shoe polish, or vanilla. At the Russia-China border, wild boar gallbladders used to be unloaded on Chinese traders until they caught on to the game.

Once in Asia, the bladders go to factories, particularly in China and Taiwan; and from there the products make their way to TCM pharmacies and clinics across the world, including back to North America. All this is aided by a regulatory jungle of conflicting national, state, and provincial laws in North America that facilitate the laundering of bear products poached in one jurisdiction through another. It is aided further by aboriginal peoples who claim the right to hunt and to sell jewellery made from bear teeth and claws openly, while they may peddle bladders illegally on the side.[66] Not least, action is impeded by the fact that estimates about bear populations vary widely, while measures of the extent of poaching, or how much it is worth, are usually wild guesses.[67]

Perhaps because the destination is usually to the inscrutable Orient, all kinds of scary stories have circulated around the trade, like the claim that there were two suitcases of bear gallbladders worth $1 million on the Air India jet blown up by a bomb over the Atlantic in 1985, or that a fridge containing bear bladders provided the motive for a 1991 murder in New York.[68] (It could just as logically be imputed to outraged animal-rights activists.) US wildlife agents contributed a gruesome tale of poachers who not only murdered a rival gang to grab their stash but kept the heads of their erstwhile competitors as trophies. The agents didn't specify whether or not the heads were stuffed and mounted on a wall. These are sometimes combined with fables about "organized crime" infiltrating the business as a sideline to drugs, arms, cigarettes, etc. But rather than bilious barons of bear-bladder crime lurking in the boreal forest, the closest thing to "organized crime" might well have been a hunting club in Los Angeles that offered guided hunts of California black bears for $1,500, with the "club" selling bladders illegally on the side.[69] And probably most typical of the way the traffic is "organized" was the arrest in 2000 of two brothers in British Columbia. One was a bear-trapper from Northern Quebec. The other, a Canadian Armed Forces diver visiting BC from his Alberta base, had asked an Asian-looking fellow in a local nightclub if he knew of anyone interested in bear galls. The diver's new drinking buddy turned out to be an off-duty Royal Canadian Mounted Police officer who informed the BC Environment Ministry's Special Investigations Unit.[70]

Facing severe criticism in the early 1990s, China and Taiwan promoted bear farming on the theory that extracting bile while the bears were alive would reduce pressure on wild stocks. Faced with public revulsion Taiwan was forced to ban the practice; while China tried to better regulate farms, requiring licenses for both farming and trading bear products, and promote techniques that would ostensibly avoid having doped-up animals face a miserable life and early death from infections caused by metal catheters in their gallbladders. The regulations also forced a number of small institutions to merge, creating mega bear farms, each stuffed with five hundred to a thousand animals each. But captive breeding is problematic, so farms had to be stocked with wild bears, particularly since bears on farms rarely survived more than 20 percent of their theoretical lifespan. The result was to encourage more poaching from neighbouring countries, with Russia a growing favourite. Nor did new techniques seem any less debilitating to the animal; and bile farms, given their high mortality rates, developed cozy relationships with nearby restaurants offering, on demand, patrons a piping hot bowl of bear-paw soup (a traditional dish of emperors and noblemen and hence still a status symbol today).[71] Furthermore, TCM purists still insist on bile from a wild animal. And farmed bile, far from just satisfying demand among those less fussy, produced a glut to which manufacturers reacted with bear-bile shampoo, face creams, wine, even soda pop, with the products turning up in departure lounges of China's major airports even while technically banned from international trade.[72]

In the West, those afflicted by political correctness cringe at the prospect that unkind words might lead to them being denounced as cultural imperialists or stooges of Western drug companies in a plot to destroy traditional eastern medicines. Yet the notion of an inevitable conflict between Western "scientific" and Oriental "folk" medicine is a gross oversimplification. Eastern practitioners increasingly use synthetic substitutes; and Western medicine increasingly tries methods that approximate those from the East.[73] The cultural sanctity of traditional Oriental medicine is no better excuse for the atrocities committed against world wildlife than is the macho pride of Western big-game hunters. Furthermore, there is a crucial distinction between cruelty to members of a species and actions throwing its future biological viability into question. Any claim that the Oriental bear-medicine trade alone poses a serious threat to the future existence of a bear species, or several, on a global basis is hard to credit. Even if the bear gallbladder secreted benzene instead of bile, there would be no shortage of Occidental big-game hunters eager to slaughter the animals just for the cheap thrill of the kill.

DON'T LEAVE HOME TO BAG IT

From Afghanistan to Zambia men hunt, but with decreasing frequency. Numbers of subsistence hunters, the only defensible kind, drop fastest, leaving an ever larger share accounted for by "sportsmen." Hunting today is usually (though not always) a luxury item, its avid consumers including top executives of the AIG insurance giant who, right after its bailout by the US Treasury, took a private jet to a seventeenth-century English manor house for a celebratory partridge shoot. After all, they had just taken the pigeons who pay taxes for $123 billion.[74] Anyway, they could cite precedent. Several years before, Vice-President Richard Cheney and nine other gunslinging daredevils visited the plush Rolling Rock Club, where gamekeepers released five hundred pen-raised (i.e., largely tame) pheasants followed by hundreds of mallard ducks so that Cheney and friends could have a blast.[75]

Sports hunting probably reaches its pinnacle of sadism in the fox hunt, finally banned in England in 2004 but still allowed in Ireland. And all across Europe, hunting season brings out packs of predators prowling for bears, wild sheep, elk, chamois deer, and much more, sometimes preceded by horn-blowing flunkeys in eighteenth-century getups.[76] But what makes US hunters special is that they count among the wealthiest, have the most powerful trade organization, pack the heaviest weaponry, seem most prone to sate their bloodlust in "canned hunts," and are probably the only ones who (until recently) could claim tax deductions for their killing sprees. Furthermore, if their most influential lobby, Safari Club International (which declares as its twin objectives the odd combination of "protecting the freedom to hunt and promoting wildlife conservation worldwide"), has its way, ever more women, children, and "physically challenged" people of all races, creeds, colours etc., though not all income levels, will get a real bang out of the sport. To prove this was not just idle talk, in 2007 SCI joined with an Alberta hunting-trip outfitter to donate "a spring bear hunt to a 14 year old boy with MS ...." who, the outfitter enthused "had the dream, will power and courage to go on a bear hunt in Alberta."[77] No doubt it beats hatha yoga or aroma therapy as a cure.

Safari Club International runs a nonprofit sidearm, the Safari Club International Foundation "dedicated to wildlife conservation, outdoor education and humanitarian services" – although how the animals targeted by its members might react to that mission statement is hard to say. That status permits it to issue tax deductions to donors, in effect collecting from the US government to support activities like its presence at CITES meetings to object to further protection to endangered species. It also gets direct government funding for its role the Communal Areas Management Programs for Indigenous Resources (CAMPFIRE) in Zimbabwe, which sells rights to kill an elephant for $10,000 and lobbies for relegalization of the ivory trade.[78] Apart from direct donations, it asks supporters to set up charitable remainder trusts. This tax gimmick was once popular with patrons of the arts because it enabled them to donate a work to a museum or public gallery, take a tax deduction, but keep the thing on display at home until they died. The scam works even better with financial assets. Someone transfers money or securities to a trust that pays a regular income to the donor for the rest of their life, while the donor takes a deduction against taxes spread over several years. Once the donor dies, the trust gives anything left to a pre-designated charity. Not only can the scheme dodge capital-gains taxes, it also permits the donor's estate to evade probate fees on the portion made over to the trust. Of course, it is an open invitation to set up a bogus trust, collect tax deductions, then drain the assets so that, on the donor's demise, there is nothing left for the named-beneficiary institution. But if the operation can be kept sufficiently opaque, the truth emerges only after the donor is dead, at which point presumably not too worried about a prison sentence for tax fraud.[79]

SCI is much more than a convention of hunters, as it showed when George Bush II appointed its former top lobbyist as deputy director of his Fish and Wildlife Service, then promoting the idea of selling off endangered wildlife to private interests in order to better protect them – the animals, not the private interests who, under the Bush Regime, hardly needed more fostering care. Its Political Action Committee raises money to finance campaigns of sympathetic politicians; and it set up a "Hunter Defense Fund" to "protect the freedom to hunt." Its International Wildlife Museum "funds and manages worldwide programs dedicated to wildlife conservation, outdoor education and humanitarian services."[80] As befitting its status, the speaker roster at SCI's annual powwow includes ex-presidents and top military men. Participants include hundreds of concessionaires peddling high-tech hunting gear, tailor-made expeditions to bag the customer's choice, and a fantastic range of options about what to do with the results. At the hands of taxidermists, also well represented, everything from heads to tails, from tips to toes, can be turned into striking displays to grace home and garden. Among the attendees, too, is or at least was Ambush Action Outdoor Products of Texas, specializing in stuff like automatic feeding units that attract deer to a regular routine so that they are, so to speak, sitting ducks when the intrepid hunter rolls up in his SUV. Small wonder its website bragged: "They won't know what hit 'em!"[81] Also present are reps from the thousand or so North American "game ranches," some offering the chance to shoot a penned-up, doped-up animal, perhaps so tame that it is used to being hand fed, then to pose for a heroic photograph of man-the-hunter. Equally present are exotic-animal dealers who buy surplus stock from zoos, broker sales for breeding farms, and provision private "petting zoos," animal shows, and exotic-meat retailers. Not least among attendees are tax-evasion consultants to show rich hunters how to ensure that the job of "protecting their hunting heritage" becomes at least partially a charge on the public purse.[82]

For many years the best scam worked by setting up a private museum whose operating facilities could be in the donor's recreation room. All that was required was to kill an animal, have it stuffed, arrange for an inflated evaluation from cooperative appraisers, then donate it to the "museum," claiming as a tax deduction the trophy's "replacement cost" – i.e., the cost of a new hunting expedition to bag another beast, even if the original kill was the product of a canned hunt.[83] The top choice for appraisals was a Chicago outfit run by a man who had faced previous accusations of tax fraud. He advertised that his strategy was "the ideal solution for duplicate animals, unmounted skins, and when you decide to downsize your collection." And he warned would-be clients that it is foolish to "hunt for an elephant-sized deduction armed with a .22 caliber appraiser." Basing his appraisals on reputation of the taxidermist, specimen condition, rarity, and provenance, he could provide "a liaison between hunters and museums for the placement of these valuable zoological specimens." His appraisals also permitted animal carcasses to be more easily bought and sold like any other collectible.[84]

Nor did the opportunities end there. If the wannabe donor had no museum in mind, the appraiser could help create one. The "museum" in turn might resell surplus trophies for much less than the appraised value, perhaps even back to the original donor – who might also have appointed himself curator.

Granted, the racket was closed after a Humane Society of the United States investigation discovered, among other things, eight hundred "donated" trophies gathering dust in an old railway car. The revised law restricted deductions to the open-market value of the trophy or the cost of mounting.[85] But there are no end of imaginative uses of "donations" – including an instance when a US tycoon and prominent Safari Club International member with a reputation for killing elephants from a helicopter bagged an endangered type of wild sheep in central Asia only to find the law prohibited bringing the stuffed carcass home, except for scientific or "conservation" purposes. So he gave it to the Smithsonian to allow biologists back in the US to "study" it. Since the tycoon had just handed the Smithsonian a (tax deductible) $20 million donation, it was happy to apply for the import license.[86] Fortunately few others have been so inconvenienced. While during the Reagan-Bush era, the government each year gave permission for about two thousand trophies from endangered species to be brought into the country under the guise of aiding scientific research or "conservation," during the Clinton-Gore era, the numbers peaked at more than ten times that level.[87]

With or without a helping hand from the public purse, US hunters tour the world in search of that special kill. One of their favourite destinations is right next door. Canada boasts huge natural expanses, abundant wildlife, minimal enforcement of its own morass of federal and provincial laws, and a long history of pandering to foreign hunters and fishermen. That attitude was suitable captured in Québec in the 1950s, when the provincial government found its big drive to bring in US sportsmen threatened by the murder of three hunters. So it made a public show of locating, convicting, and hanging a local woodsman and prospector on circumstantial or even, some claim, totally contrived evidence, to reassure its US clientele of safety during their open-season execution of bear, deer, and moose.[88]

In Canada aboriginal people, too, are permitted more or less unrestricted hunting, and therefore can hire themselves out as both guides to find game and frontmen if the expedition is caught by a local wildlife officer with kills in excess of quota or out of season. Although Canada holds perhaps two-thirds of the world's remaining polar bears, its efforts to protect them would make Sarah Palin blush.[89] As governor of Alaska she vowed to sue if the federal government tried to put the polar bear on the endangered list, but then, after it went ahead anyway, found other matters pressing on her remarkably underworked mind. Leaders of Canada's Inuk people seemed to agree, protesting that, if Canada followed the US regulatory lead, it would threaten millions of dollars US sports hunters brought into their territories every year.[90] Not surprisingly, reps of Canada's many hunting-and-fishing outfitters turn up at trade fairs in the US to bag potential clients and brag about huge national parks abounding in game and maintained at public expense, with some, no doubt, quietly offering the services of a trans-Canada network of illegal guides, taxidermists, and smugglers.

Still, a trip to Canada to shoot caribou, elk, moose, bear, and wild sheep pales compared to the African Safari Big Five Grand Slam trip to Zimbabwe that permits a hunter to nail a rhino, elephant, leopard, lion, and buffalo in one go. However Grand Slammers need to sign up fast – in the past several years the national government's attempt to shore up crumbling political support by opening wildlife reserves to the landless poor and, more recently, political turmoil combined with an official policy of turning the military loose to feed itself from wildlife has decimated the herds of a country once renowned for its astounding variety and abundance of animals.[91]

But even if they had gotten to Zimbabwe before it collapsed in chaos and cholera, Grand Slammers might have been disappointed by one thing. Missing from the impressive roster is a tiger, a beast not exactly native to Zimbabwe. However, it is to the USA, which now holds maybe five to seven thousand tigers. Perhaps fewer; perhaps many more – no one really knows. But whatever the total, it is likely impressive compared to the presumed (and likely inflated) four to five thousand still living in the Asian wild. In addition the US has plenty of lions, along with a few ligers, their Frankensteinian offspring. About 10 percent (that magic number again) reside in zoos, the rest in roadside menageries, circuses, travelling shows, cat-rescue facilities, and suburban backyards. If the Bengal tigers are ever annihilated on India's reserves, perhaps they can be restocked from US surplus. Better still, the reserves can just be relocated to somewhere in Nevada to catch the attention of a wealthy clientele heading to (but probably not back from) Las Vegas.

Although a regular stream of wild cats gets smuggled into the US, particularly jaguars from South and Central America via Mexico, the real cause of the current glut was that in the 1970s and 1980s zoos overbred tigers to cash in on the drawing power of cubs, then began to sell off the excess (along with adults who had outlived their titillation value) to dealers who in turn serviced commercial breeding farms. There are several thousand licensed breeders and exhibitors in the US (and, no doubt, many more unlicensed) whose operations are overseen by about one hundred Department of Agriculture animal-care inspectors – although obviously the great majority of breeders deal in dogs, domestic cats, and budgies. The strict (on paper) rules regarding how big cats are to be kept is a further incentive to evade registration. Given that life expectancies of wild cats in captivity tend to be short, an owner seeking to sell off an excess can claim that they died of "natural" causes. It is legal to donate the body. So a client pays a broker, the broker gives the breeder or dealer cash, and the breeder-dealer fakes a death, filling out the required forms saying that the body was donated, not to the broker who buys the tiger but to the ultimate client who pays the broker, leaving no money trail between buyer and breeder. Furthermore with medical interventions, some captive cats produce large litters that the breeder underreports, clearing the way to sell off the surplus. Given the shortage of regulatory personnel, there is little chance of an investigation unless there is a tip-off. The result is grist for the canned-hunt, stuffed-trophy, and exotic-meat mills. In fact all three can operate together.

It began when Steven Galecki opened, near Chicago, Funky Monkey Exotics, a "petting zoo" that had trouble getting people to stroke its lamb, goat, or chickens and so diversified into mountain lions and monkeys.

When Galecki put one of his monkeys up for sale, his path crossed that of an organizer of exotic-animal hunts who wanted the monkey as a gift for his wife and also requested a stuffed tiger to promote interest in his safaris. So Galecki arranged to buy and kill a female and cub, then have them stuffed in a growling-mother-protecting-cub mockup to titillate potential clients. The word got out among other hunter types for whom stuffed tigers are a status symbol. Purchased from farms and dealers, the tigers arrived at the "petting zoo," were shot in their cages, then sent off for stuffing. But taking heat from the Department of Agriculture for the condition of his animals, Galecki decided to get out of the business, offering for sale a couple of African lions, some mountain lions, and two black-spotted leopards. At that point his path crossed that of William Kapp, a prison guard who did taxidermy for wealthy buyers on the side. Initially Kapp was interested, but balked at the leopards, not because they were officially listed as endangered but because he did not have the appropriate license. But Galecki reassured Kapp that the law did not apply to donations – so they would just fiddle the federal paperwork appropriately. Kapp, the prison guard-cum-taxidermist also took most of the other big cats to offer to his clients. The two men were soon importing animals from other dealers and breeders. Some taxidermy clients were given the chance to double the pleasure by themselves killing animals in their cages, then have the corpses dragged into an open field in dim light for a photo. In all sixteen tigers, four lions, two cougars, one liger, and one mountain lion were killed, skinned for rugs and trophies, then dismembered for sale as "lion meat," which, unlike tiger, can be legally sold in the US. The exotic-meat dealer also got from Kapp stuff he sold as zebra meat even though the animals from which it came bore a striking resemblance to ordinary donkeys. When a former colleague of Kapp, herself in trouble with the Department of Agriculture, tipped off the authorities, Kapp and fifteen others were arrested and charged under various statutes including the Endangered Species Act and the Lacey Act, prohibiting import and interstate transport of potentially dangerous non-native species. The exotic-meat market was fined and burned down, presumably not by the same people. And its boss was convicted of trafficking in protected animals. However he paid his fine and got back into business as soon as he finished serving his sentence.[92]

Exotic cuisine based on wild animals is hardly unique to the US. In 2008 Brazilian environmental officers discovered 740 skinned and salted alligator corpses in a nature reserve, apparently destined for lunch in regional restaurants.[93] In Japan, blowfish testicles are a rare treat, particularly to those diners who develop paralysis from and consequently get asphyxiated by the toxins. The current British fad of "bush-meat" is probably the result of nostalgia for a long-lost empire combined with an ignorance of history. (One thing the colonial officialdom, exiled far from their "green and pleasant" homeland, insisted upon was a table set not with curried wildebeest and boiled cassava root dished up in hand-carved wooden bowls but with roast beef, Yorkshire pudding, and soggy vegetables on Wiltshire bone china.) But it has reached sufficient proportions to prompt public warnings of the threat of Ebola virus, AIDS, and foot-and-mouth disease, the last raising the spectre of another mass precautionary slaughter of domestic animals even though it does not affect human beings.

However, China's restaurants are notorious for their veritable Noah's Ark of delicacies. In China, wildlife officials have been caught selling live bears to restaurants: the racket was revealed when one bear escaped and ran into a residential area. And the traffic in bear paw, for which cubs are preferred, has produced a black market similar to the one for tiger parts from Indian and Siberian nature reserves.[94] Visitors to Beijing zoo are warned not to feed the animals but are encouraged to eat them at the zoo's restaurant, which offers kangaroo tail, deer's penis, hippo toe, and ant soup.[95] Pangolin (scaly anteater) is another favourite, with a Guangdong chef reporting proudly (and quoted repeatedly in the Western press) on how "We keep them alive in cages until a customer makes an order. Then we hammer them unconscious, cut their throats and drain the blood. It is a slow death. We boil them to remove the scales. We cut the meat into small pieces and use it to make a number of dishes .... Usually the customers take the blood home with them afterwards."[96]

A horrifying image indeed, until someone looks closely at a modern factory farm or abbatoir in the West. At least no one forces the pangolins to eat the entrails or feathers of their deceased kinfolk. Anyway, Chinese dishes come complete with claims about physiological and psychological benefits based on thousands of years of tradition – good or bad, true or false. Those in European and American exotic-food emporia offer but one thing along with their yak patties and alligator sausage – the thrill of eating something weird, with the endangered status of some of the animals on offer (and the consequent high price) making it extra tasty.[97]

12

Goring the Tusk Trade: Mammoth Task, Toothless Law?

The prospect of ending up as the main course at dinner is also a threat to periodically hang over the head, and choicer parts, of the most charismatic of megabeasts – as if the elephant needed more things to prey on a mind that, at least among elder matriarchs, is already exceptional for its long-term memory.[1] A single, mature male of three tons can yield 1,300–1,400 pounds of edible meat. Even the vascular organ weighs in at nearly 50 pounds. That much heart would put to shame a whole army of politicians, sporting cheese-cake smiles and shedding crocodile tears, whose only reason for electoral success is the general public's own startling lack of recall capacity, short term or long.

Ivory-tower ideologues naturally claim that the best way to save the elephant is to consume more of it – after all, the example of chickens shows convincingly that, if there is human demand, there will always be more than enough supply.[2] Although elephant tartar is still not prominently featured at exotic meat counters in the West, enough of an international black market exists today that the meat can fetch more than the tusk, traditionally the main target of poachers. While no one has yet suggested elephant bile to cure sleeping sickness, a result better effected if one of the great beasts inadvertently steps on the head of a snoring tourist curled up beside a campfire, in parts of the Orient elephant joins a long list of meats from other endangered species as an aphrodisiac.[3] And, of course, elephant bits and pieces have been, and are still, in demand for other purposes. Women seeking the ultimate fashion statement might have purses and footwear fashioned from its hide, while men might choose to pass around celebratory Cuban cigars out of humidors made from a baby elephant's foot.

Nonetheless, throughout the ages and across continents, the main target has been the tusks from which humans have fashioned all manner of adornments. Elephant ivory is easy to carve, homogenous and durable, while its inherent beauty grows with time. Ivory carvings have turned up in excavated cave dwellings. In fact in 2009 a cave in Germany yielded the earliest human art form yet discovered, an ivory carving of a woman at least 35,000 years old (the carving, not the woman) and so brazenly voluptuous that it might qualify for one of the 3-D centrefolds (plus geeky glasses) planned by Playboy to compete with proliferating hardcore internet sites.[4] Solomon's throne, too, was reputedly fashioned by Phoenician craftsmen from ivory and gold; ivory icons were perhaps the highest form of Christian art in medieval Europe; ivory fans cooled Chinese imperial courtesans; nimble fingers of piano virtuosi ran glissandi up and down ivory keyboards; billiard balls caromed across felt-topped tables with that uniquely satisfying ivory click; and countless Internet sites now peddle "antique" ivory necklaces, rings, earrings, and pendants. Everyone, it seems, has always loved ivory.[5] Undoubtedly so did the elephants, but their views do not seem to have been taken much into account.

The hunt for ivory is a story of conquest, military and commercial, of people as well as nature. Once Ancient Egypt had wiped out its own elephants, it obtained ivory by plunder, trade, and tribute from Nubia, Somalia, and Ethiopia. Phoenician carvers who set ancient world standards got raw material from both North Africa and Asia, while Indian ivory found its way to artisans in Sumeria by the third millennium BCE. So did the elephant – herds of the Asian variety were reared there to replace local ones hunted to extinction.

However, the Asian elephant was stronger and more trainable, with a value in work and war well beyond that of its relatively small tusks, usually possessed only by males. In Africa elephants roamed in bigger herds, and both sexes had large tusks. Therefore by Roman times ivory came overwhelmingly from Africa. Rome, while slaughtering elephants in wars abroad and games at home, used ivory for everything from a manger from which Caligula fed his favourite horse to artificial teeth, a science the Romans were likely the first to perfect.[6] Any reprieve to the African elephant from the fall of Rome, though, was offset from Asia – in India by bridal ornaments and religious artifacts; in China by everything from palanquins on which high-ranking nobles were carried to audience with the emperor to chopsticks used in the subsequent feast. By the tenth century, Arab carvers complained of a drain of raw material to the Orient.[7]

Yet economics and geography still restricted the toll. Only those at the top of the power ladder possessed ivory carvings, while few outsiders braved the unknown and their own imaginations to pursue tusks into the African interior – until Europeans revolutionized the trade.

INTO AFRICA

First came the Portuguese, seeking ivory to trade in India for spices and cotton. Initially the ivory came from the same parts of West Africa where the Portuguese bartered for gold and slaves. But further south, Angola on the Atlantic Ocean and Mozambique on the Indian were teaming with elephants. For centuries natives had accumulated ivory incidentally to the hunt for meat. Early visitors proclaimed it so abundant that tusks were used for stockades and fences, helping to consolidate the emerging Western illusion that an endless human appetite for the blessings of nature could be balanced by its purported inexhaustibility.[8]

The main Portuguese objective was not to strip Africa's ivory but to break the Muslim-Venetian monopoly of the spice trade. From Zanzibar, then ruled by the Sultan of Oman, Afro-Arab merchants brokered the flow of Indian and Indonesian spices via the Red Sea to Europe, while trading slaves and ivory from the interior. Oman first lost the trade routes to Portugal, then regained them only to lose them again to other European powers. Yet, despite centuries of commercial and military presence, not until well into the nineteenth century did Europeans have any real knowledge of Africa much beyond the coasts. By contrast, Afro-Arab traders, by paying tribute to dominant chiefs, could travel more or less at will, trading for slaves and ivory in areas where Europeans feared disease, wild animals, and hostile native peoples.

If sugar was soon a major threat to the dental health of humans, so it was indirectly to the elephant whose tusks are formed by the same physiological process that produces teeth. Throughout the late seventeenth and eighteenth centuries, Britain and France engaged in a series of wars to control world sugar markets. Sugar required an ever-increasing supply of slaves for West Indian plantations. Captains of slaving vessels got permission from owners to do non-competing business on the side. Ivory was a favourite. African slave-hunters would jointly target villages and nearby elephants. Since tsetse flies were lethal to European horses and oxen, when a village was raided, captives bound for slave markets were used to haul tusks to the coasts. In the past, slaves had formerly been produced incidentally to war, and ivory incidentally to the hunt for meat. Now they became the primary objectives.

Peoples on the east coast of Africa had been long aware of the value of both ivory and slaves; those on the west, too, learned to bargain up prices and demand useful trade goods. Weapons were favourites – they helped to capture slaves and collect ivory, while they made slave-hunters, who had no technology to produce ammunition or repair firearms, more dependent on Europeans. Thus was the link between international gunrunning, civil strife, and ecological brigandage that would turn parts of modern Africa into a charnel house already taking shape by the early seventeenth century.

Even then elephant herds seemed largely intact, except in the far south. There, the only area of sub-Sahara Africa that seemed amenable to temperate agriculture, settlers (first Dutch, then English) slaughtered elephants with enough élan to prompt Africa's first formal conservation law.[9] Elsewhere, though, the interior remained out of bounds to whites; and, even when African hunters received European weapons, their hunt was restrained by animist religious beliefs on the one side and modest demand for European goods on the other. The real problem emerged in the late nineteenth century, with industrialization of demand for ivory and direct involvement of Europeans in its supply.

IVORY AND EMPIRE

As "civilization" advanced, elephants came to be loathed as rapacious raiders with a taste for human food crops and an instinct for when they were ripe. Even after early conservation laws were introduced, elephants, along with other "pests" like hippos and lions, were "fair game." Yet the African elephant was essential to ecosystem health and human prosperity. It spread seeds and recycled nutrients; it reduced bushes and small trees, helping to maintain grasslands necessary for grazing animals, including cattle. As local peoples implicitly understood, the most ecologically efficient human use of most of Africa is a mixture of wildlife and livestock, and a rotation of indigenous food crops among different areas in different seasons. Colonization, and, more recently, rapid human-population growth accompanied by industrial agriculture with alien crops, would upset this symbiosis to the detriment of people, plants, and animals alike.[10]

If the link of ivory and slave-hunting had been central to early European incursions into Africa, the task of suppressing slavery served to rationalize the late nineteenth-century scramble for Africa; while ivory financed everything from exploration to missionary activity. When the British adventurer, Henry Stanley, ventured back into the Dark Continent, which he had first visited during the British Ethiopia campaign, he reported, to public outrage, on native villages wiped out by ivory-and-slave hunters. Much the way ambitious NGOs and sensation-hunting journalists over a century later would spread stories about "Islamic terrorists" trafficking in "blood diamonds" to finance civil wars ravaging West Africa, Stanley wagged an accusing finger at "the Arabs" –forgetting to mention that, notwithstanding the depredations of Afro-Arab slave traders, for centuries slaves had been overwhelmingly bound for British or French sugar colonies or American cotton plantations, and the merchants handling the export of ivory and slaves were predominantly British or imports from British-ruled India.[11]

While Stanley's tales of blood and bondage, burnt villages, and children in chains gave Victorian ladies a fashionable attack of the vapours, other audiences had more manly concerns. In a celebrated 1884 speech to the Manchester Chamber of Commerce, he got down to business. "There are forty million of people beyond the gateway of the Congo, and the cotton spinners of Manchester are waiting to cloth them, Birmingham foundries are glowing with the red metal that will presently be made into iron works for them and the trinkets that shall adorn these dusky bosoms ..." Lest anyone accuse Stanley of thinking only of money, he added: "... and the ministers of Christ are zealous to bring them, the poor benighted heathen, into the Christian fold." The audience broke into cheers.[12]

Others, too, were impressed by Stanley's credentials, including King Leopold of Belgium, who had previously hired him to lead the king's own pre-emptive bid to save the peoples of the Congo basin from the ravages of Afro-Arab slave traders. Once safely under the king's care, the population, rounded up for forced labour on rubber plantations in Belgian-ruled areas (or cocoa ones in French ones), was whipped and mutilated for almost any infraction. In an eerie prelude to the diamond wars in Sierra Leone a century later, native overseers reputedly demonstrated their efficiency by bringing to their white bosses baskets of severed human hands.[13] Nor was there any respite for the elephant. King Leopold concurred with Stanley's assessment that colonization could be financed with ivory. That also cleared grasslands for "civilized" crops. Missionaries blessed the endeavour, using ivory to pay for their own activities while teaching native peoples to forsake heathen deities that prevented them from seeing nature just as more raw material. Then came the "big-game hunters."

Apart from a member of Henry Stanley's own entourage who bought an eleven-year-old girl, then offered her to cannibals so he could record and sketch how she was cooked and eaten, perhaps the most influential of these avid investigators of the zoological features of African wildlife was Theodore Roosevelt.[14] In the course of a single safari, his entourage bagged five thousand mammals, four thousand birds, five hundred fish, and two thousand reptiles for "scientific study" (a useful precedent for Japan's whaling fleet today), then celebrated by dining on elephant-trunk soup.[15] One of Roosevelt's protegés, a Captain Charles Stigand, insisted that elephant hunting is "so vastly superior to all other big-game shooting that, once they [the hunters] have surrendered themselves to its charms, they cannot even treat any other form of hunting seriously" – with one exception. Although in his memoirs, the captain rued the passing of the days when a serious hunter was allowed to blast away without limit or license at anything on four legs, happily he was able to report that it was still possible to get permission from colonial authorities to stalk a much cleverer, though smaller, form of game. After all, Captain Stigand observed, Africans were merely the highest form of animal – while Arabs were the lowest of human being.[16]

Along with big-game hunters for whom the kick came from the act of killing great beasts, and ivory just a bonus for a job well done, came poachers, evading colonial law intended to tax the ivory trade rather than to maintain the biological integrity of wildlife. Natives restricted from taking game from their former hunting grounds engaged in a little "pot poaching" when other meat was scarce. But the real toll was taken by white predators, overwhelmingly British, with high-powered rifles. Perhaps the most important (and prophetic) factor setting off the first twentieth-century animal massacre was the end of the Anglo-Boer War, in which, contrary to the name or standard historical accounts, more blacks than whites died. Discharged British soldiers, filled in equal parts with the urge for more adventure and the arrogance of victory, set off to hunt elephant and seek a legendary elephant graveyard stacked high with old ivory. Perhaps mitigating the impact was their preference for older bulls – their tusks were larger and, being belligerent and unpredictable, they did more to build up the hunter's self-image.[17]

The transformation of ivory from byproduct to primary target transformed economic relations between natives and whites. In the interior, ivory became a currency used by local peoples to trade with Europeans, pay tribute to chiefs, or ransom captured kinfolk. Under European rule, too, taxes were sometimes paid in ivory. Poachers used part of their ivory haul to pay local chiefs for porters, supplies, or even information about anti-poaching patrols – natives shared with poachers an antipathy to colonial officialdom; and when ivory hunters bagged an elephant, native porters got the meat. Meanwhile, scattered through the interior were trading posts, usually run by Portuguese or Indians who stood ready to pay cash (in Belgian francs, British pounds, Portuguese escudos, or a mixture) for poached ivory.[18]

Traders next had to get the ivory to the coast for export. Competition between occupying powers made that easier. So did the existence of a legal ivory trade that could provide cover for poached material. The British in East Africa demanded that white hunters take out licenses and imposed restrictions on take, while natives were required to surrender all ivory at a fixed price, with the ivory periodically put up for auction. Indian merchants in British-ruled Zanzibar, too, had to obtain a license, report which villages they planned to visit, submit equipment to inspection, and pay a tax on ivory before they could legally export it. Once ivory poached in German, Belgian, or Italian-controlled areas paid taxes in the British colonies, it could be commingled with local ivory and legally exported as colonial product.[19]

If hunters provided an ample supply, the market was ready to absorb it. In India, for example, not only was carving an ancient art, but ivory was especially important for weddings. A bride-to-be was decked out in ivory bangles from the wrist to the elbow for a year prior to the event, a practice transcending caste. Increasing population kept demand growing. So did the practice of burning widows along with their ivory bangles on their husband's funeral pyre. If a woman predeceased her husband, her ivory was also cremated along with her corpse. Even after the British suppressed sati, it remained common practice to destroy ivory bangles in a public demonstration of a widow's grief, guaranteeing the slaughter of more elephants.[20]

Meanwhile in North America, as settlement spread, pianos came to grace virtually every middle-class parlour. Its tactile qualities meant that ivory had no serious rival for piano keys: it was just slippery enough to facilitate rapid movement of fingers, but provided enough grip to keep them from sliding off.[21] As a piano aged, the ivory yellowed – harsh white substitutes were, in the eyes of vintage piano collectors, visually dissonant. Although ivory carvings and jewellery were in high demand, especially in Asia, as were ivory cutlery handles, combs, and billiard balls in the West, for decades pianos were the elephant's principal enemy. Every dazzling piano concerto was for elephants a funeral march.[22] Not until the 1920s, with the rise of the movie theatre and the automobile (the first an alternative entertainment form, the second a way to escape the confines of the drawing room) did pressure abate, although not until 1989 did big manufacturers finally agree to stop using it.[23]

POACHERS AND PROFITEERS

With East and West alike gobbling up ivory, colonial governments pushing its export, and farmers encroaching on habitat, the elephant population in the first three-quarters of the twentieth century must have steadily diminished, although no one was keeping track. Traders reported that the price of ivory, while fluctuating from year to year, remained relatively stable over decades. Yet as the fate of ocean ecosystems so well shows, biological scarcity is rarely reflected accurately in economic scarcity until a crisis point is reached, when it is probably too late. In the 1970s, the situation for ivory changed, but from the demand side. Ivory, like gold and diamonds, shot up in price, trebling by the end of the 1970s, then quadrupling in the 1980s after gold and diamonds had tanked. In response, from 1970 to 1989 measured export of raw ivory from Africa totalled 8,000 tons, the product of roughly 500,000 average-sized elephants.

Setting off the 1970s price hikes was a rage for "investment ivory," a bizarre phrase since no one stashes elephant tusks in a safety-deposit box alongside gold bars, bearer shares, and porno pictures of their ex. The real catalyst was hoarding by a clique of traders, particularly in Hong Kong, that set off a perverse dynamic. Higher prices for diamonds or gold meant that more would be extracted; and, while the total geological stock fell, it did so directly in proportion to the amount mined. With wildlife, though, the future supply depended on the present: the more killing in the present, the less available in the future. And expectations of future shortages accelerated the process. The stronger the belief that herds were being decimated, the more assured were hoarders that prices would continue to rise; therefore the more they stockpiled, driving up the price yet more, feeding back to increase the rate of destruction. The trend was accelerated further by the inverse relationship between size of tusk and age: as older elephants were killed off, increasing numbers of younger ones were required to obtain the same weight of ivory. Furthermore, the priority killing of those with larger tusks tilted reproductive advantage to those with smaller, a trend that also demanded more to be "harvested" to secure the same amount of ivory.

These market dynamics were reinforced during the next decade by an explosion of demand in the East. In Japan's soon-to-be-bubble economy, the market soared for "hankos" – signet stamps used for everything from opening a bank account to sending a love letter. Fashioned in the past from wood, stone, and bone, still the preferred material for those with an environmental conscience, during the business boom, ivory, already popular for other types of decorative carving, reputedly came more into vogue, although the overall impact of hanko demand may well have been exaggerated by trade opponents. Perhaps more importantly, Japan hosted the world's two largest piano manufacturers, most of whose production ended up in Europe and North America.[24]

In China, too, there was a dramatic revival. After the Communist Revolution, carving ivory, like jade, had fallen out of favour with carvers fleeing to Hong Kong; and during the Cultural Revolution (1966–76) many of those remaining were sent to work on collective farms. But by the late 1970s the mainland industry recovered; and in the 1980s liberalization and privatization encouraged the spread of family-owned shops turning out material for domestic, tourist, and export markets, a prelude to a demand explosion in the 1990s and beyond. Meanwhile in Taiwan and South Korea, too, wealth was growing, for a time even faster than in China.[25] And Hong Kong shifted from artisans crafting carvings for an elite clientele to mass production of statuettes for export to the West.

With the worldwide expansion of demand came commercialization of poaching. In the early part of the twentieth century local peoples used poison arrows to kill elephants for meat, then traded tusks and hides for supplies. However the more the indigenous population was drawn into a cash-based society, the more objectives reversed: ivory and hides the primary target, with meat a bonus. As the century wore on, although indigenous people might still pick off some elephants opportunistically, ivory-traders contracted in advance, equipping locals with more effective weapons.[26]

The traffic was encouraged from the top of the political ladder. Tanzania paid China for work on the Tanzam Railway partly in ivory. Uganda's Idi Amin used ivory to replenish foreign exchange reserves depleted after he chased out the resident Asians who ran most of the local businesses. President-for-Life-Who-Is-Now-Dead Seko Sese Mobutu of (also former) Zaire, while restricting private trade in ivory, shipped tusks (along with gold, diamonds, and strategic metals) to Belgium to build up Swiss bank accounts and luxury French real estate while the country was so impoverished that its park rangers guided poachers to the best hunting grounds. And a French firm got a monopoly of ivory exports from the Central African Empire of Jean-Bédel Bokassa, the so-called Cannibal Emperor, probably the only thing of which he was not guilty. Apart from trying to deal with nineteen wives, the fifth of whom was a member of a prominent ivory-trading family, Bokassa was also busy exporting uranium and diamonds to placate his political overseers in France – until they sent paratroopers to oust him. Not to fear. After Bokassa's successor took away the ivory monopoly, he began signing "exceptional authorizations" to permit even larger exports of ivory than before.[27]

A second change was militarization. Again there were colonial precedents. During World War I, when the British invaded German East Africa, junior officers took leave with army rifles and squads of black troopers to chase elephants. Some aviators joined the fun, dropping bombs on herds in hopes of returning to pick up any tusks not blown to pieces. The practice had at least tacit encouragement from British authorities content to see ivory poached from German territory to reduce its fiscal base, particularly after the Germans seized Antwerp, then the primary European marketplace for ivory, along with one hundred tons of stored tusks.[28]

In the 1970s and 80s, the old link between irregular warfare, resource looting, and international gunrunning was reconsolidated on a new scale.[29] As central and southern Africa descended into a series of vicious wars, elephants along with rhinos and other big mammals came to be hunted with machine guns, rocket launchers, even helicopter gunships, partly to secure "rations" for the troops, partly perhaps to help finance the war (although insurgents usually had generous outside sponsors), and partly (or mainly?) to top up personal retirement funds. Herds in places like the Sudan and Somalia were effectively obliterated; those in Angola, Mozambique, and Kenya were heavily depleted. A part of Angola formerly known as a wildlife paradise (because people other than native bushmen had been unable to survive its heat and tsetse flies) became for anti-government forces a combination safe house, slaughterhouse, and counting house.[30] The UNITA guerrilla group in Angola reputedly made so much money from wildlife and hardwood that its grateful leader, the so-called Gucci-guerrilla, Jonas Savimbi, once presented South Africa's prime minister with a full-scale AK–47 assault rifle carved from ivory in gratitude for South Africa's assistance, including in running contraband.[31] Across afflicted areas elephant populations may have plummeted to a fifth their former numbers – although no one can be sure. And the ongoing legacy of the 1980s is a continent full of paramilitary bands, some old, some new, who cross borders with impunity, sometimes with official encouragement, to poach in neighbouring countries.[32]

The killing of elephants, whether by local farmers or professional poachers, whether by criminal gangs or irregular army units, was only the start. As before, the ivory had to make its way to urban areas, then by sea or air to processing shops mainly in the Far East, then to final market, East or West. With small-scale operations, a local farmer, usually on his own initiative, kills the animal, then hides the tusks until an itinerant dealer can convey them safely to a collection point to be placed in secret compartments of trucks for delivery to a major city. Then the ivory is passed to well-placed individuals who arrange export. This group in the past has included, in addition to respected businessmen, members of legislatures, senior wildlife officials, diplomatic staff of various embassies, and UN functionaries. In Kenya during the 1970s the government handed out special Collectors' Letters to prominent supporters, including senior officials of the Mau Mau guerrilla group, which had led the country to independence, allowing them to take ivory from dead animals – the letters, duplicated and passed from hand to hand, could be used to launder and export poached ivory.[33] Consistent with a century of history, the roster of traffickers has even included a priest who smuggled out of East Africa ivory mislabelled as wooden carvings to the German monastery that sponsored his mission.[34]

With larger-scale ongoing operations by professional poachers, the initiative started abroad. During the pre-1989 boom, Asian carvers paid a percentage of final value up front to Hong Kong suppliers. Then a Hong Kong firm advanced money, through a local agent, to professional dealers in Africa. The dealers hired poachers, paying them in food and weapons, perhaps with a little cash retainer. From East Africa the ivory might go to Dubai, that festering abscess on the Arabian Peninsula's body politic, hidden in legitimate cargos on regular ships or on dhows, small vessels of the sort that have plied the Indian Ocean for centuries, loading and discharging contraband cigarettes, drugs, booze, gold, or endangered wildlife in creeks and mangrove swamps. From Dubai the ivory headed to Hong Kong, either for local carving or for redistribution throughout South East Asia, with the final product bound for wealthy parts of the world.

When insurgent armies were involved, the loads were larger, costs of detection greater and mechanics of smuggling more sophisticated. So the insurgent ivory business in Mozambique and Angola, along with much of the continent's rhino-horn trade, became linked to Apartheid-era South Africa's counterinsurgency and sanctions-busting apparatus. Its intelligence services arranged for the profits from poached wildlife to be used to purchase smuggled weapons, with senior officers taking a personal rake-off. Contraband moved in military-supply vehicles that local police were either loath or forbidden to inspect, to exit via South African ports to the Orient with the hardwood and ivory to pay for weapons that were smuggled back largely from China. In the rare event that a low-level participant (a civilian contractor or smuggler hired by the military) was caught, penalties were trivial. Meanwhile South Africa could brag that its own herds were well protected in their world-renowned game reserves.[35]

Granted, some poached ivory was intercepted by wildlife services, however underfunded and/or compromised they might have been. But that was scarcely good news for the elephant. The usual practice was to add seizures to official stocks taken from animals that had died a natural death (rather easy to arrange in forest or savannah), been culled to reduce herd size (perhaps because farmers or developers coveted part of the game reserve), or were killed because of "problem" behaviour (typically by young males raised without the restraining influence of older bulls who had been killed off before). Then the ivory might be auctioned, usually with the claim that proceeds went to wildlife conservation, at below normal price or with quantities underreported to buyers pre-selected by bribery or political pressure.[36]

JUST TICKLING THE IVORIES?

It is easy to impute the poaching-smuggling problem to "corruption," as if that were the cause rather than just another consequence of economic degradation, social chaos, and political disintegration. However, weak regulations and poor enforcement reflected the lack not just of resources but of moral authority in poor, multiethnic states where conservation measures carried a colonial-era taint. In fact, the first sustained effort to stop unrestricted killing of game, including female and immature elephants, was the work of the last king of the Ndbele people (who ruled much of what is now Zimbabwe) in a fruitless effort to curb the excesses of white hunters. Once he was overthrown, the prime agricultural land was seized by British colonists from native farmers who were pushed onto marginal land or into wage-work in white-owned mines; the colonial authorities then made all game state property and passed a conservation law to permit them to evict any African landholder deemed in violation.[37]

The first international initiatives dated back to 1900, when major powers carving up Africa agreed to try to save Africa's wild animals if they had "economic value" and were no threat to persons or property, with white male colonists serving as prosecutors, judges, and executioners. African methods of hunting were banned as cruel, conveniently leaving animal populations for white hunters to exploit with rapid-fire rifles, plus, a bit later, the occasional bomb from a British warplane. This convention excluded elephants and rhinos from protection – they (along with lions and zebras) were presumed of no economic value beyond ivory or horn and were a threat to farm property. However, it did restrict size and sex of elephants that could be shot, and imposed rules regarding weight and number of tusks. Still, a convention was not law – it had to be legislated in participating countries, then applied in their colonies. There the typical game warden worked for wealthy white planters, not to protect animals but to keep Africans from "poaching" them. Wildlife reserves, too, were typically in areas used by native hunters and subsistence farmers rather than on land potentially valuable for cash crops grown by white colonists.[38] That remains the practice today where, for example, in Tanzania. There, in a country where hunting brings in a major share of its foreign exchange – an elephant today goes for $15,000 – great game reserves were created by evicting Maasi herders who ended up peddling cheap trinkets to passing buses and vans full of gawkers or selling themselves as cheap labour way off in Zanzibar's booming tourist economy.[39]

The next major chapter was written in 1973 by the creation of CITES. Unlike today's stout defense of things like "intellectual property rights," signatories to wildlife agreements were/are free to opt in and out of particular measures with no sanction. With CITES, as always, the real contest was over the Appendix in which a particular species is placed. Anti-trade forces pushed for the elephant to be placed in Appendix I, a full commercial ban, against traders and big-game hunters who agitated (initially successfully) for III, which implied that any threat to the elephant was local in nature, as was most responsibility for the solution. Governments of affected countries, too, had varying agendas. For example, when Kenya found its prospects of maintaining its status as the world's largest open-air zoo threatened by poachers, it crossed horns with South Africa and Zimbabwe, which supposedly had elephants to burn, or at least to kill, chop up into pieces, and sell abroad.

In 1978, in an attempt to find middle ground, the African elephant was pushed from Appendix III to II. Subsequently ivory could only be traded among member countries accompanied by CITES export permits issued by host governments, few of whom cared much about elephants or had any real capacity to enforce restrictions. In Kenya, for example, the wildlife service, despite rapid growth of tourism, was badly underfunded, riddled with corruption, and hosted a heavy preponderance of office jobs handed out as political patronage compared to field posts whose holders were few, poorly paid, and unequipped to take on heavily armed poachers.[40] Since no international regulations could address burgeoning demand or the spread of civil strife, poaching (at least reports of it) accelerated.

In 1985 rules were again tightened. Subsequently each ivory-producing country was to set a quota reflecting its own estimate of a "sustainable yield"; each tusk was to be given an indelible serial number; all exports were to be accompanied by certificates of origin; and the worldwide movement of raw ivory was to be monitored through a computer system in England, with CITES officers to alert national authorities of discrepancies. Yet serious protection of elephant populations was subverted from the start by individual countries setting "sustainable yields" more by financial than biological criteria. Inflating the size of their remaining herds was all the easier because of the reluctance of elephants to stop at borders for passport checks. And the core idea relied on the fantasy that countries like Somalia or Zaire in the midst of civil breakdown could assess the state of their wildlife, then police their quotas. These avowed

restrictions were accompanied by amnesties for existing hoards, producing a windfall gain to buyers of poached ivory and tempting them to
accumulate more in expectation of the next round.

Then there were the usual difficulties in regulating trade in a commodity in which the legal component was physically indistinguishable from
the illegal. Smuggling sometimes involved hiding a cargo; more often all
it required was faking the paperwork. CITES controls, too, applied only
to raw ivory. So Hong Kong carvers set up plants in non-member states
to do preliminary work on poached tusk, then shipped the stuff home,
openly and legally, for finishing. Those same carving firms were skilled
at commingling contraband with legal ivory.[41] Only sixteen of thirty-five
African parties bothered to comply with the creation of a central registry
to record supposedly indelible serial numbers. And its efficacy became
clear when Britain intercepted at Gatwick Airport a 1.5 ton load from
Zaire whose owner could be identified only as a "Panama investment
company." The tusks bore identical numbers to ones used in an earlier
shipment. After the CITES response was to give permission to a Zairian
embassy official to renumber the tusks with a felt pen, British Customs
cleared the load for re-export to Dubai, probably to be mixed with contraband and shipped on to Hong Kong.[42] In any case, none of the rules
applied to non-members. Some openly sold ivory poached in member
countries, while others with carving industries, like Taiwan, were happy
to receive poached tusks.[43] The evident failure of the new regulations
along with a media campaign in the West featuring pictures of decapi-
tated elephants and stories of park rangers outgunned by machine-gun-
toting poachers fed demands for a full ban on trading.

Some people tried to counter mounting pressures by proving that alternative means existed to save the elephant. One was Bernhard of Lippe-
Biesterfeld, a German count who became prince consort to the queen of
the Netherlands and a man whose passion for big mammals translated
into an urge to shoot them on sight. When World War II broke out, Prince
Bernhard recycled himself from Nazi sympathizer to Allied air-war hero
with a chestfull of medals. After the war he became inspector general of
the Dutch military and a director of numerous arms industries. In those
capacities he made the news again by securing a $1.1 million bribe from
Lockheed Corporation to steer the Dutch military's choice toward its
fighter jets. The scandal led to his de facto dismissal from his government post, most of his corporate boards, and his presidency of the World
Wildlife Fund (now the World Wide Fund for Nature) of which he, with
other business tycoons who had similar notions of "conservation," was a
founding member. Still active in the cause, in 1988 he sold two of his old-
master paintings, donated the money to the WWF, then had the group's

president kick back most of it for a "private project." This consisted of hiring a mercenary company run by a founder of Britain's Strategic Air Services (the elite commando unit that handled dirty operations for British Intelligence) to knock out poachers in Southern Africa. If the plan had worked, it would have sent a message that paramilitary action by ex-spooks and unemployed mercenaries, not a worldwide ban on the ivory trade, was the solution. Much as at the turn of the century, the logic of conservation was to stop native poachers in order to preserve herds for the pleasure of white tourists or licensed hunters with elephant guns. His plan was to have the ex-mercenaries buy ivory and rhino horn from South African and Namibian game-park authorities, then offer it on the black market to infiltrate the networks. But the scheme collapsed in scandal with half of Prince Bernhard's money, and most of the ivory and rhino horn, missing, presumably just mixed with the international flood of contraband that continued as before – until the 1989 CITES decision to elevate the elephant to Appendix I status.[44]

The countdown to the ban featured the usual suspects making the usual claims. Opponents of the trade insisted that in the two previous decades Africa's elephants had plummeted from 1.5–2.0 million to perhaps as low as 600,000. Banning all commercial exchanges eliminated the chance to launder poached ivory by commingling it with legal. Furthermore since noncommercial transfers required both export *and* import permits, with relevant agencies of the two countries required to confirm with each other validity of the documents, much of the burden of enforcement shifted onto places that could more easily afford it, particularly after ivory trafficking became a crime rather than just a customs violation in North America and Western Europe.

The other side was bolstered by a powerful coalition of pro-hunt groups proclaiming their commitment to wildlife welfare and mock NGOs advocating "sustainable development" while denouncing as "imperialist" efforts to deny poor countries the economic benefits of *their* wildlife. Opponents claimed the numbers showing great declines in elephant populations were gross underestimates, that the quota system in place had never been given enough time to do its job, and that holograms and DNA "fingerprinting" sufficed to determine if ivory was poached or legal.[45] The arguments were bogus. Of course, methods of counting animals in the wild are so problematic that they permit those with an agenda to inflate or deflate more or less at will. But no matter what the total, extensive killing, first of large males, then of matriarchs of herds, could upset population profiles and unbalance the complex social life of elephants for generations. As to holograms and DNA tests, any self-respecting credit-card fraudster or currency counterfeiter could

crack the first between beers; and the second was at the time too impre-
cise to be effective.[46]

The quarrel was made worse by deep division between countries. The
US and EC banned imports and domestic trading. But in Hong Kong,
street protests by carvers were so vociferous that Britain retracted its
support for a ban until CITES agreed to an amnesty for all the ivory (estimated at five to six hundred tons) its colony's traders and carvers had
stockpiled. Nor would any Asian member close down domestic trade.
But the most troublesome split was inside Africa.[47]

In the west, herds had largely disappeared before the ivory-price inflation of the 1970s and the wars of the 1980s; in the east, the main problem was entrepreneurial poaching fed further by heavily armed poaching
gangs from Somalia, politically disintegrating into clan-based fiefdoms;
just north of South Africa and its direct sphere of influence, the slaughter
was directly linked to civil war between strong-armed governments and
externally sponsored guerrilla movements; while in South Africa and
contiguous countries where herds were outgrowing habitat, most killing (and the resulting ivory) was officially sponsored. Those countries
protested that a ban punished them for sins of places that "mismanaged"
wildlife. Since proceeds from sale of wildlife products supposedly went
to maintain game reserves, they insisted that a ban actually threatened
the elephant. Of course, their definition of wildlife protection was neatly
captured by South Africa's Kruger National Park, which ran on the side
an abattoir where "surplus" animals were carved up for the exotic-meat
or animal-pelts trade while orphaned ones were sold off, if not for bread,
then for circuses ... or for zoos.[48]

Initially the ban seemed a triumph – prices plummeted and poaching
seemed to dry up. Alas, aside from the fact that many countries were not
signatories, including major consumers like Taiwan and South Korea,
and even those who were members could opt out, as China briefly did,
there were good reasons to temper that optimism.[49] To begin with, much
of the prior runup in prices was probably driven by competitive stockpiling in anticipation of the ban. So the ban triggered an inevitable collapse.[50] After a few years, once hoards had presumably depleted and
black-market prices started to rise, poaching would almost certainly pick
up once more.[51] And that reflected the fact that the CITES ban faced serious problems, some potentially fatal, to the treaty and to the elephants.

FROM RAIN FOREST TO REGULATORY JUNGLE

Even if a country signs a treaty, passes laws, and sets up regulatory agencies, there is no guarantee real enforcement will follow. In Zimbabwe,

for example, when freelance poachers were killed or captured, it might be just because they hadn't paid protection money or were competing with rackets run by army units, politicians, and senior wildlife officers. Poaching by officials could be rationalized as a legal hunt for "rations" to support rangers on duty or as a necessary cull of "problem" animals. And reputedly the country's official stockpile from seizures, culls, and natural deaths was regularly plundered by well-placed political figures for private sale.[52] Nor could Zimbabwe's claim to exceptional virtue in managing its herds survive when, after a nasty 2005 election, the perennial winner, Robert Mugabe, announced Operation Meat, a state-sponsored slaughter of elephants to supply food to starving villages. Once again nature, in the form of elephants, paid the price for human stupidity and cupidity. Among the beneficiaries of this "legal" slaughter were hungry crocodiles on farms turning out high-priced raw material for handbags and shoes gobbled up by *nouveau riche* women in the West.[53]

Nor did CITES actually ban the ivory trade, just the trade in new elephant ivory. Alternative sources of carvable ivory mean not just potential for laundering, but that any improvement for the elephant could be at the expense of things like the frozen corpses of mammoths, probably slated to be an ever larger source (or cover for poached elephant ivory) as the Arctic permafrost melts, all to be marketed, of course, under the name "ethical ivory."[54]

Among the still living, the African hippopotamus has the double disadvantage of herding in a few easily accessible ponds and possessing lower-canine teeth just like elephant ivory. Although smaller size means more limited uses, that did not deter George Washington, whose false teeth were made by colonial America's leading dentist out of hippo ivory and gold. Nor is it an impediment to Chinese traders who set up poaching-cum-smuggling networks reaching from Zambia and ex-Zaire (which formerly had the world's largest hippo concentration) to Hong Kong.[55]

The size disadvantage does not much apply to walrus tusk (upper canines), which may, on a mature male, reach 1.5 metres in length. Long taken incidentally to the hunt for meat and skins by aboriginal peoples in Siberia, Alaska, and the Canadian North, walrus ivory was first made into native artifacts, then came to be preferred in the Orient for certain types of carving, so much so that when Yankee merchants first began to ply the tea trade, they carried walrus ivory to China in exchange. Traditional hunts were limited by both technology (spears) and morality (a spiritual bond between hunter and prey). Supposedly in respect for that tradition, when the US government moved in 1972 to protect the walrus, it exempted natives – they could kill unlimited numbers provided they utilized all parts and traded the tusk (after registering it) only among themselves. But as tourists flooded into Alaska, as world demand for "Eskimo carvings" soared, and as elephant-ivory restrictions spread, the price of walrus ivory shot up. Inuit and Aleut peoples hunted with semi-automatic weapons, targeting the walrus exclusively for ivory and leaving the carcass to rot. The Russian government once complained to the US about thousands of headless corpses washing up on the Siberian coast. Alaskan natives might fail to register tusks or claim they were "fossil" ivory from corpses exposed by melting permafrost. Since the carving industry faced a 20 percent Alaska state tax, aboriginal hunters sold under the table not just to aboriginal carvers but to white ones who turned out imitation native artifacts for tourists, or to white tusk-dealers, possibly proprietors of hunt-and-fish operations. Those dealers passed it on to traders to smuggle to the Orient, sometimes hidden in outgoing cargo, sometimes mislabelled "fossil" ivory. Reputedly carvers in the Far East even started to make imitations of Alaskan native carvings to ship back to North America for sale.[56]

Even the ban on the trade in new elephant ivory was subject to an enormous, perhaps fatal exception. The only way to win support for the ban by the major southern African countries, and some of the Asian manufacturers of ivory, was to pass a special amendment – ironically sponsored by Somalia, a country effectively without government that had long before exterminated its own herds only to emerge as an important export point for ivory poached from its neighbours. This stipulated that any African country could have its elephants downlisted from Appendix I back to II if a panel of experts certified the health of its elephant population and the quality of its anti-poaching, anti-smuggling efforts.[57] Based on that amendment, southern countries, led by Zimbabwe, got permission in 1997 to sell official stockpiles (with the usual promise to use the revenues for conservation) on "once-and-for-all basis" to Japan, whose 200 manufacturers of ivory and 10,000 registered retailers of hankos were more than ready.[58] This "once-for-all" sale was followed in 2008 by another, this time to China as well, where ivory carvers were already soaking up ivory that could only have come from the black market.[59]

In places where most carving occurred, there were further problems. CITES agreements could ban international trade in elephant products, but could say nothing about domestic law. Although in North America and the EU use of new ivory was forbidden, across Asia traditional demand, buttressed by rapidly rising incomes, meant that the carving business expanded even in the face of the ban. Although India followed the West by outlawing new ivory, the business went underground to service a domestic market that manages to blend rising Western-style consumerism with a growing zeal for symbols of Hindu heritage. Plus an increasing numbers of tourists want Indian ivory trinkets, while members of the huge diaspora import Indian cultural artifacts in a public show of commitment to a cultural identity that, if it were really so important, might have prevented them from leaving home in the first place. The result is a continued flow of ivory artifacts and a continued demand for raw material – from poachers who kill wild animals on India's reserves; from legally protected temple beasts with the connivance of religious figures; from private owners who, in defiance of federal law, refuse to register their elephants; or from purloined government stockpiles.[60] That India finally in 2010 gave its elephants the same protected status as tigers seems heartwarming – until account is taken of what that status really meant to the tigers.[61] But most probably comes from Africa. After all, during British rule, Indian ivory merchants dominated the Asian export trade from Zanzibar.

Of course, Indian carvers also learned how to affect certain important economies in their use of raw materials. Since the price of finished ivory statues depends partly on weight, a carving might be filled with mortar, cement, or plaster-of-Paris, which, on drying, matches the consistency, colour, and internal appearance of tusk. Material to be sent overseas could be hidden in other exports or misrepresented, sometimes as antique, sometimes as buffalo bone, a declaration that, to the final buyer's dismay, might turn out to be true.

Meanwhile in the other major Asian producer, a Hong Kong industry built on the post-1949 exodus from the mainland started to move back, partly because China's government encouraged the spread of small, family-owned carving shops (more difficult to monitor than big state-owned factories) and partly because of apparently greater ease of access to poached ivory. Chinese businessmen, like those of Hong Kong a couple decades before, set up factories in the UAE to be closer to the supply.[62]

To carvings from India and China are added those from Taiwan, which briefly banned ivory, then relented under pressure. In Thailand only ivory from domestic elephants was banned, and no one bothered to enforce that. Across a country already notorious for trading in endangered birds, plants, and fish, major hotel souvenir shops openly displayed ivory.[63] Nor did any African country forbid use of something that had long been the most popular raw material for their own cultural industries – and for sale to tourists. Some, too, allowed domestic trade in tusks that could easily be smuggled across borders.

In terms of final market, the ban had limitations even in places prohibiting domestic sale. Some were trivial, like freedom to import ivory as "personal effects" or to continue to sell ivory imported into any member country before the ban – an opportunity to fake dates. "Trophy ivory" was permitted on the grounds that big-game hunters did not slaughter animals en masse. (Whoever dreamed up that one apparently had never heard about Theodore Roosevelt's exploits.) Although trophy ivory in theory could not be openly sold, it can be reported as destroyed in a fire or stolen, then unloaded on the black market. One man who claimed to be the biggest dealer in whole tusk in the US set up a private tax-exempt "museum," then arranged for people with trophy tusks to "donate" them. Of course, that precluded the owner from paying the "donors." So instead he paid them a handsome price for the purchase of pencils or pens.

More serious was the exemption for "antique" ivory, left free to enter EU and North American markets provided it had not been repaired or modified with new ivory. Yet Chinese carvers hundreds of years before had learned to expose new ivory (or even whalebone) to charcoal smoke, then roll it for twenty-four hours in fresh tobacco leaf to give it an antique yellowish veneer.[64] Nineteenth-century Paris was the European centre for mass fakery of Gothic ivory religious carvings, aged by wrapping freshly carved ivory in rabbit skin and burying it until the pelt putrefied.[65] Today Indian carvers put new ivory in the sun to crack the surface a little, then soak it in tea or a henna solution to give it an old-ivory patina, therefore further raising the price they can charge.[66] In many other parts of Asia dealers offer Western tourists "antique ivory" to beat the ban. It might be genuine new ivory artificially aged; it might be buffalo horn sold as old ivory.

Those unable to pick up their Asian ivory artifacts onsite can rely on antique stores proliferating along London's Portobello Road. In the UK, an item claiming to be antique ivory needs only a signed statement from a person purporting to be the original owner to be sold without restriction.[67] Sellers may provide for clients certificates of authenticity that are themselves faked, perhaps in the same Chinese carving shop that produced the artifact, enabling buyers not only to skate through customs but to pull off a coup when they resell the stuff. Inside North America, the object can be resold with an affidavit attesting to its antique status from an art historian, appraiser, or museum curator, the same tribe that do such an excellent job keeping fakes out of art and antiquity collections.[68]

On the other hand, someone doing an authentication might discover that the client has been stuck with simulants like ivorine, ivorote, ivoroid, or ivoride (often lumped together as French- or faux-ivory) – which have been around since the 1930s, along with so-called Hong Kong or Mandarin ivory (a combination of ground alabaster and plastic), Meerschaum (the volcanic clay once so popular in pipes), and ivory nut – or with layers of cloth and bakelite plastic joined under pressure.

Given persistence of demand, effectiveness of the ban depends in good measure on the efficacy of regulation and the probability of serious punishment. The problem here is that while customs in countries that banned import and possession might keep an eye open for whole tusk imported in job lots, it is largely impotent faced with millions of de facto mules carrying small ivory carvings in their personal luggage. Even in the US, the country with perhaps the tightest legal controls and a customs service not exactly known to be polite to visitors or easy on their luggage, sometimes all it takes to beat inspection is a coat of paint. Elephant ivory carvings, too, can be passed off as walrus, hippo, warthog, or mammoth. Elephant ivory has certain characteristic cross-section lines; it responds a certain way to UV radiation; and it can be subjected to DNA analysis. But tests are far from perfect. In any event, there are few wildlife inspectors at airports; and, if present, they are usually overworked checking everything from tins of caviar to crates of anacondas.[69] Meanwhile the internet hosts hundreds of potential sellers, some happy to fake documents. Since most of their material is shipped via international parcel post, it is rarely inspected on arrival. Besides, sellers know enough to leave the word "ivory" (and a return address) off the invoice[70]

Since at least some tusk still makes its way into the US, there is also a domestic carving industry. Like its artistic kinfolk elsewhere in the world, it produces items that resonate with local cultural significance. In India that means wedding bangles, in Japan business-signet stamps, in China delicate little statuettes – in the US one favourite may be ivory gun butts.

In a sense all these problems are inevitable in almost any trade treaty, but applying CITES bans to wildlife implied even more fundamental flaws. First and foremost, there is a huge distinction between the "supply side" response of something produced by human effort and something created by natural forces. If a product is the result of human economic enterprise, a rise in market price will, other things being equal (which they never are), raise total quantity supplied. If a "product" is the result of geological forces, a rise in market price may increase total quantity available to the market obviously without increasing the geological stock, which, to the surprise of economists, will eventually wear down. If the "product" is the result of biological forces, a rise in market price may lead to an actual fall in the biological stock, producing a feedback loop that accelerates the price hike and hastens the decline and eventual extinction of the species. It apparently failed to dawn on architects of the strategy of protecting nature with a trade treaty that the habit of treating nature as a commodity was precisely what caused the problem CITES was supposed to resolve.

Besides, no tool evolved in or slated to be applied by countries with given geopolitical borders is likely to be effective to control exploitation of species whose existence can only be defended within bioregional borders that may bear little or no relationship to those delineated by human geography. This is all the more true since political borders shift with much more frequency and ease than ecological ones.

Furthermore, economic regulations try to govern the terms of competition for resources within one species, namely human beings, not competition between species – humans (with their domestic animals and plants) on one side and virtually the rest of nature on the other.[71] So a CITES trade ban could do nothing to address the problem of the competition of elephants and people for habitat. Much as most of the decimation of forests throughout history has been and still is the result of agricultural clearing rather than cutting trees for commercial sale of the wood, so, too, the (temporary) eclipse of the ivory poacher could easily be offset by a less newsworthy increase of farmers killing elephants to protect crops, herders encroaching onto elephant habitat, or urban developers biting off choice bits of reserve areas for luxury condos or golf courses. These threaten the biological integrity of the herds without invoking the international attention that translate into donations for conservation or pressure on local governments with limited resources and other priorities.

That conflict is abundantly clear in Asia. Its elephants (of less interest to ivory traders or big-game hunters) had been placed on CITES I decades ago. In the wild the Asian elephant lived in smaller, more dispersed herds, making it harder to hunt. Ivory came mainly from domestic males who died of disease, overwork, or old age, or who were culled if domesticated herds got too big. Although India had the largest remaining domestic herds, Burma-Myanmar was a close second, its domestic animals protected not so much by local conservation laws as by the fact that in the country still boasting Asia's greatest remaining forest cover logging until the late twentieth century was still worked largely by domesticated elephants, while its wild herds lived in jungle areas where the government's writ seldom really ran.

However, by the late twentieth century, Burma's religious beliefs, which had protected temple animals, were weakening; trucks were replacing domesticated elephants in logging; the government suppressed or bought off ethnic insurgents in border areas, opening resource lands to exploitation; and an invasion of Thai and Japanese timber companies stripped forest cover from wild herds. Elephant calves, too, were kidnapped to Thailand to join captive girls as tourist attractions – elephants in circuses and zoos, girls in bars and brothels. In Burma, a major centre for ivory carving, it was legal to trade ivory from domestic animals who died of natural causes, providing cover for poaching wild elephants and encouraging owners of domesticated ones to kill them for ivory and hides.[72] Combined with the soaring price of ivory, the result was that, by the end of the 1980s, the Asian elephant, who once roamed in the millions from Mesopotamia to the Malay peninsula, was reduced to a population of perhaps 35,000–55,000 in highly fragmented bands.[73] Even with the usual caveats about accuracy in the numbers, it hardly seems a triumph for a CITES I listing.

Meanwhile, back in Africa, by 2009, ivory poaching, much of it driven by a booming market in ivory carvings in China, revived so much as to prompt a warning from the International Fund for Animal Welfare that within another decade the elephant could be extinct outside its protected reserve areas.[74] Still, the existence of that thriving market led the usual suspects to launch yet another attempt to water down the existing regulations and some African countries to renege on previous agreements. Granted the attempt failed, but only, it seems, at the cost of sacrificing the bluefin tuna – the same CITES gathering that refused permission for yet another "one-off" sale of accumulated stocks of ivory also turned down a proposal to extend Appendix I status to the chronically endangered but much less photogenic fish.

Despite this reprieve, the ultimate fate of the African elephant might soon be little different from that of the North American bison, a handful of herds of dubious biological sustainability in tightly restricted range, surviving by the grace of fickle government handouts and finicky tourist trends while "developers" ogle shrinking habitat with dollar signs lighting up their eyes. Certainly some people genuinely care. But most public lamentations about possible extinction of the elephant in the wild seem motivated less by concern for the integrity of the biosphere or its keystone species than by the need for today's consumaniacs to appease the occasional twinge of environmental conscience without threatening a lifestyle based on obsessive self-gratification.

Coda: From Class Struggle
to Crass Struggle

Spare a tear for the world's ultra-rich in these turbulent times. Take, for example, Australia's former chart-topper, James Packer, who inherited megabucks from his father, a media tycoon, then saw his $6–7 billion stash slashed in half during the 2008 market meltdown. The debacle forced him to put up for sale his $50 million nine-bedroom yacht equipped with its own Aston Martin (in case of icebergs?), to defer delivery of his Boeing Business Jet (lest it, too, crash down in flames?), to sell off a company that operated seventeen cattle-grazing stations (to search for greener pastures elsewhere?), and to begin dumping his media interests in favour of something more in line with contemporary business culture – casinos around the world. Fortunately he could keep his eighteen-hole golf course designed by Aussie superchamp Greg Norman, perhaps to have something constructive to do while waiting for financial skies to clear.[1] They did.

Along came an "economic recovery" that saw sales of "super prime" homes in favourite haunts of the world's ultra-rich bounce back even as foreclosures of ordinary houses continued to climb.[2] This was accompanied by a resurgence of the top-end car market led by Mercedes-Benz, whose Maybach Exelero retails for $6,000,000.[3] Even more reassuring, the Forbes list of billionaires leaped from a mere 793 in 2008 to 1,011 the next year, their total fortunes soaring from $2.4 to $3.6 trillion.[4] That was without factoring in any cash stashed away for a rainy day in the world's rapidly proliferating havens offering instant corporations, coded bank accounts, and offshore trusts. Naturally, their burgeoning wealth had its usual cascade effect. By autumn 2010 the Louis Vuitton flagship emporium on the Champs Elysées in Paris began closing an hour early because it was running so low on stock.[5]

Not least of the signs of the times, Australia's (formerly) richest man got himself a new yacht. Granted, it had a scant four bedrooms and cost only half as much as the old one.[6] But its very existence proved that the world's ultra-rich had the wind back in their polyethylene terephthalate sails. If that isn't a recovery, it will do until the real thing comes along. So who could begrudge them a celebratory bash? And Azeri gezillionaire Telman Ismailov was just the man to stage it.

During late Soviet days, underground entrepreneurs across the Union, including those in Mr Ismailov's remote region of Azerbaijan, were leaders in importing from the West its triple revolution of privatization, deregulation, and "tax reform," a process reaching its logical culmination in the vodkanomics experiments of the Boris Yeltsin era. Perhaps inspired by the late Sam Walton, who in 1992 won both the US Presidential Medal of Freedom for helping America "stem the tide of communism" in Central America and the Golden Star Foreigner's Award of Jiangsu Province, People's Republic of China, for aid to state-owned sweatshops, Mr Ismailov set up in Moscow the Cherkizovsky market complex on federal land that his political friends let him have cheaply.[7] He rented spots to merchants specializing in low-end stuff from China, their prices reduced further by evading import and value-added taxes. Although no one with serious money would be seen near the market, a city with more than a quarter of its population below the poverty line provided ample clients. So did much of Eurasia as shuttle traders arrived in caravans of buses to haul off goods for resale hundreds of miles away. The complex easily outsold rival establishments, some subject to shoot-outs, bombings, and the occasional contract killing of managerial staff, things Sam Walton never had to worry about.[8]

Through all his struggles to create a business empire, Mr Ismailov remained a true party animal. In 2006, when the world economy was still steaming, he threw in Moscow's luxurious Baltschug Kempinski Hotel a New Year's bash featuring three American pop-music idols paid $850,000 to $1,000,000 each for forty-minute performances. Granted, when invited to appear at Mr Ismailov's fiftieth birthday party a couple years later, Jennifer Lopez hiked the fee to $1.5 million. But she had to work harder, publicly bestowing on the celebrant both a ("Happy Birthday") song and a kiss. And in 2009, when Russia faced a collapse of oil prices along with a massive flight of capital, the Azeri business whiz decided to one-up himself with yet another blowout, this one to celebrate the completion of the Mardan Palace, his new luxury hotel near Antalya on Turkey's increasingly posh Mediterranean coast. In a neat summary of the spirit of the times, profits from the sale of contraband and counterfeit products from China to the desperate and destitute were poured into a $1.5 billion monument to enterprise and accomplishment – although party-poopers might prefer to refer to them as ego and waste.

Its opening extravaganza constituted in an allegorical sense a global celebration of that decades-long spendathon by the world's ultra-rich and by those wannabes with the means, at least temporarily, to go along for a gold-plated, diamond-encrusted, caviar-and-champagne ride.

Modeled on Istanbul's Dolmabahçe Palace, the Mardan was touted by luxury travel agents as Europe's most expensive hotel – apparently business wasn't good enough for them to buy a map showing that the place is actually in Asia. That glitch aside, the hotel seems to deserve its title. It features, along with 500,000 suspended crystals and 10,000 square metres of gold leaf, 2,000 floral displays, a 3,200 square metre Italian-marbled lobby with a stained-glass ceiling inspired by Ottoman art, plus a 7,500 square metre spa.[9] That spa boasts a cascading waterfall that stops to allow people with VIP passes to enter and provides artificial snow to cool them down after their exertions. Rooms are decked out in a way that, the hotel asserts, "marks a long-awaited return to the days of opulence" with a tasteful combination of antique furniture and remote-controlled toilets. The Royal suites include their own butlers and plunge pools. Add 11 restaurants featuring about $5 million worth of Hermès crockery, and some 14 bars – one, the Monkey Bar, featuring live monkeys in cages, fit entertainment for any drunken apes at tables.[10]

That, however, was only the beginning of the hotel's salutes to nature. On their way to the discotheque, guests can amble along an elevated walkway past marble animal gargoyles to get an "unobstructed view of a tropical habitat from behind a glass wall" – a futuristic vision if there ever was one. The wooden planked walkway with a thatched roof bisects the exhibit of spider and squirrel monkeys, then leads over a small "river" flowing from a waterfall before arriving at the front steps of a mockup of Cambodia's Angkor Wat temple complex, although without antiquities thieves to provide authenticity. Once persevering guests manage to hack through all that undergrowth, they can enter the Jungle Club to boogie to the primitive pulsations of disco music.[11]

Outside the hotel proper, guests can stroll the fairways of a Jack Nicklaus signature eighteen-hole golf course or just overlook the Mediterranean sparkling with the 12 million metric tons of organic pollutants, 1.5 million of oil, 1.1 million of nitrates, 360,000 of phosphates, 60,000 of detergents, 21,000 of zinc, 3,800 of lead, 2,400 of cadmium, and 100 of mercury, dumped in annually.[12] Perhaps that is why so many chose instead to frolic in a pool that takes half an hour to cross by gondola, assuming boats can get through the one thousand swimmers it was designed to accommodate. The less adventuresome can simply loll on 9,000 tons of sand imported from Egypt, a country that under its current management has little else to offer. (The dangers of mixing sand from one place with that of another with radically different biochemical characteristics are commonly outlined in Environment 101 classes – but apparently haven't penetrated to the level of the top-priced architectural firms planning luxury resorts.) The hotel grounds even feature an outdoor aquarium with an artificial coral reef – a farsighted feature given the rate at which the real ones are dying off in warming, acidifying oceans. In that aquarium, guests can swim with a toothless hound shark, a completely harmless type that in nature lives off invertebrates, just the way many of the guests likely to turn up at such a hotel probably do.

Of course, there was entertainment. Besides the same troupe of overhead aerial dancers that opened the 2008 Beijing Olympics, there were guest appearances by Tom Jones, Paris Hilton, and Mariah Carey. The latter reputedly walked off not just with the post-Jennifer Lopez standard of $1.5 million but with a bonus in the form of a five-carat diamond ring in the shape of her signature butterfly. No doubt she needed it for her subsequent engagement at a "party of the year" birthday celebration for Prince Azim of Brunei, whose father, sultan of the country, boasts the world's largest collection of luxury automobiles, reputedly including five hundred Rolls Royces. For inspiration, guests at the Mardan were treated to a discourse by Sharon Stone, who took to the stage to talk about her mission to aid the world's poor.[13] Meanwhile guests were wowed by about 100 kg of Beluga caviar – the sturgeon had apparently made a dramatic comeback missed completely by marine biologists in Mr Ismailov's home country – washed down with Bollinger and Dom Perignon, hopefully after a forensic investigation of the bottles.[14]

True, Mr Ismailov had his own woes. After leading his guests at the Mardan bash onto the dance floor to be showered with $100 bills, he was denounced publicly by Vladimir Putin for illegally moving abroad bushels of money while Russia was in crisis. The government-controlled media spoke darkly of billions laundered through his Moscow market. When, in summer 2009, that market was officially shut down, it was described by the head of Russia's Investigative Committee as "a state within a state ... It has its own police, its own customs services, its own courts, its own prosecutor and stand-alone infrastructure including brothels."[15] The stern Russian meant that as a denunciation. But, as Mr Ismailov could have countered in his own defense, running a market complex staffed by illegal aliens who unloaded low-end stuff supplied by smugglers on poor customers, then blowing huge sums in public extravaganzas to entertain the nouveau gauche while siphoning off a fortune to a luxury exile – isn't that what free enterprise is supposed to be about? More likely he just insisted that the Russian governing class didn't like him because he was Jewish.[16]

Apart from a slight flare for the theatrical, there was nothing unusual about Mr Ismailov's high-spirited revelry. After centuries, indeed millennia, during which the poor were poor, the rich were rich, and rare the twain would meet, in the 1920s a new culture of mass consumption took root, first in the US, then abroad. Ad men inspired by Sigmund Freud realized that not only does insecurity sell, but competitive buying instills yet more insecurity and therefore acts as its own catalyst. In that way any anger of the working classes that in the past had periodically manifested itself in general strikes, public demonstrations, or even the occasional bombing, could be bought off by giving them the illusion of full participation in economic society on the expenditure side of the market equation. The message was all the easier to broadcast with help from the emerging mass media of glossy magazines and national radio. Far from being a rhetorical invention of fiery-eyed anarcho-syndicalists denouncing "the system," implementation of the notion that collective lower-class discontent could be blunted, even neutralized, by being channelled into consumption was a calculated move, although it went through a few bumps and grinds on the way to success.[17.]

The mirage of masses enjoying a "middle class" existence crashed along with general purchasing power in the 1930s and marked time in the 1940s in the face of wartime and postwar scarcities. Afterward, the Western powers, glancing nervously over their shoulders at Communist regimes in much of the world, determined that the best way to keep their economies on a stable, long-term growth path was not the traditional economic prescription of fostering ever-rising investment. That strategy in the past had translated directly into greater industrial capacity and only indirectly, if at all, into higher incomes to spend on the resulting products. Lacking sufficient purchasing power at home, the result was a scramble for foreign markets, one reason why international capitalism tore itself apart in fratricidal wars in the period before 1919. Continuing such a path therefore ran the risks of another huge mismatch and catastrophic depression that might bring the political and economic status quo to a noisy end. Therefore the new formula was to constantly inflate mass demand by manipulating what John Maynard Keynes, the British economist long hailed as the pin-up saviour of Western capitalism, aptly called "the consumption function," probably without being aware of the term's deeper level of meaning in modern economic society.

Gathering force in the 1950s and 1960s, first in North America, next in Western Europe, then in Japan, and now much beyond, mass-consumption society began in the 1970s to take a pathological new twist as unions were busted, outsourcing to cheap labour havens soared, taxes on upper-income brackets were slashed, and financial behemoths were unleashed, salivating at the prospect of "privatizing" social-security measures and public infrastructure. In response, the affluence-influence-effluence gap began to gape.

That produced something of a dilemma. A mass-consumption economy sustaining a mass-consumption society is only viable if mass purchasing power continues to rise, something rather difficult if earnings for most people stagnate or even fall for decades. The answer was for the Great Unwashed to spend by accumulating debt – first student loans, then credit-card debt, then car loans, then mortgages, then housing "equity" loans, with the odd trip to the local payday-loan company thrown in for good measure – rather than by just relying on income. Growing debts for the lower orders were the flip side of rising assets for the super-rich, whose offspring enjoyed in succession free (to them) education in elite schools, maybe with an American Express "black card" to handle incidentals like skiing the Swiss Alps, a graduation gift of a bright orange Lamborghini Murcielago, then a walk-right-in partnership in daddy's law firm, plus the promise of a neat portfolio of gilt-edged bonds when the old man finally kicks the bucket.[18] Thus did bubble-up economics join the gurgle-down variety to promise a seemingly endless orgy of gleeful spending on both sides of the social divide.

For those on the lower side of the yawning income-and-wealth gap, the lure today is sweat-shop junk with make-believe brand labels whose low price, frequently embellished with a "discount" sticker, assures rapid psychological obsolescence, fast physical deterioration, and the maximum of environmental degradation in its production, distribution, and casual disposal.[19] Politically that formula remains a winner. When times are good, mere bread gives way to double-whoppers-and-fries, and circuses are replaced by interactive porn on one hundred channels, interrupted occasionally by religious wingnuts with both hands outstretched telling flocks waiting to be fleeced how much Jesus loves them. But when things turn rocky, how often is the underclass coaxed into believing that the surest way to salvage a blighted dream is to aid and abet the further destruction of the very things (like decent public services and a progressively redistributive tax-and-transfer system) on which its well-being really depends?

On the other hand, for those laughing all the way to their Geneva-based private bank, the target, apart from "consumer durables" like mansions whose dimensions spread further and faster than an investment banker's paunch or a society matron's hips, includes all manner of high-end stuff bearing elegant, if now long defunct, craft names to conjure up rank and style even if their main attraction is a price absurdly inflated by the combination of pretense and rarity, real or contrived.

Few members of today's parasitocracy seem to care much if their luxury brands are made in Chinese factories belching coal smoke and extruding misery and bear no organic connection to the work of the nineteenth- or early-twentieth-century European craftsmen whose names they still bear. In fact, the main thing those fancy-product names now guarantee is a price out of all proportion to cost that buyers can take as affirmation of their own merits and sellers may interpret as confirmation of an inverse relationship between money and brains.[20] But what else is to be expected when family names once used across generations as a guarantee of quality have, in keeping with the magic of modern markets, become just another "intangible asset" to be "securitized" and peddled from hand to corporate hand?

"Luxury goods" now represent worldwide sales of more than $150 billion per annum, more than 60 percent accounted for by thirty-five brands that in turn are owned by a handful of conglomerates. The business is especially profitable today, not just because of exploding wealth, nor just because the actual work is outsourced to places where both human dignity and environmental integrity are for sale cheaply, thus turning increasing tracts of the world into giant sweatshops built on top of poisoned trash heaps, but because suppliers of luxuries almost never cut prices in response to a soft market. That would make matters worse by subverting the main source of appeal. In fact, the smart strategy when times seem tough is to increase the price, hike the hype, and just wait for bailout funds to flow. But the producers do have one problem – making sure that the very expensive stuff is "real."

Granted, when someone flush with money they likely didn't earn and almost certainly didn't deserve gets conned by a counterfeiter of "luxury" handbags, the populist reflex may be to sympathize with the perpetrator on the rationale that the act represents simply a rip-off of a rip-off. However, it would be a mistake to assume that those responsible are latter-day Robin Hoods – the only redistribution to the poor they are likely to make is through the tip they leave for a waiter or chambermaid at one of the upscale restaurants or fancy hotels where they go to celebrate their coup. As so many "liberal" politicians or NGOcratic do-gooders have yet to learn, in civil-strife situations, including the covert struggle to redistribute overt wealth, it is possible for both parties to be in the wrong.

Fakes also seem rampant today in a high-priced collectibles business populated visibly by dealers, curators, auctioneers, restorers, appraisers, and collectors and much less visibly by thieves, fences, forgers, counterfeiters, and tax evaders, some publicly acclaimed members of the first likely doing double duty from time to time as publicity-shy members of the second. Their apparent proliferation reflects not just the amount of money involved, although that is a major incentive, but also a shift in professional ethics among those who move the markets. In the past the main participants in the legitimate trades were parties who put their family names on the line in a business where intergenerational reputation counted for far more than slick and seductive advertising. Today, though, with financialization of expensive collectibles, be they Old Master paintings or eighteenth-century Sarouq carpets, professional ethics at the high end may owe less to history and tradition than to Wall Street and the City of London, a comparison not intended as either a compliment or a reassurance. After all, what's the difference between peddling a painting of fictionalized ancestry to a consortium of rich collectors and selling a "synthetic collateralized debt obligation" or some equally arcane product of the twisted imaginations of today's finance whizz-kids to a teachers' association pension fund – except that the victims of the first can easily afford to lose the money and that the government will do all in its power to make sure they don't?

There is another thing, too, that complicates the search for bragging rights by today's ultra-rich compared to previous aspirants for a high social status to match their wealth. In the late nineteenth and early twentieth centuries, the ultra-rich had to first build giant factories (apparently with no help from engineers or bricklayers) or create great railways (by bribing legislatures to give them construction subsidies) or metaphorically shoulder axes and shovels to chop down trees or dig for minerals (after governments had booted off aboriginal peoples and waived most royalties and taxes). The fortunes came first – mansions stuffed with art and antiquities along with piles of supposedly old English furniture came later, mainly to flaunt what the owners had accomplished as ruthless business tycoons. But what have today's leveraged buyout artists got to show to their grandchildren as the concrete results of *their* business success? Certainly not the shells of abandoned factories whose production has fled the country in search of ever lower wages and ever looser environmental laws. The Impressionist painting of which they are so proud is useful. But what happens if it gets exposed, a little like the owner, as a David Stein-type fake?

Of course there is one advantage a counterfeit collectible has over a fake luxury product. It can always be donated to a culture palace only open during most people's working hours in return for a fat tax deduction.

In the days of Andrew Carnegie and his cohort there was a sense that exceptional private privilege (even if quite unmerited) conveyed some social responsibility (even if expediently defined). Today, though, "philanthro-capitalists" seek to effectively merge charity with business. This means more than just the first as another scam to cut taxes on the second, or use of a "charitable" foundation to keep control of a corporation out of the hands of raiders. While old-time philanthropists were shameless enough about having buildings, collections, and endowments named after themselves, at least they paid for the honour. Today those seized with the philanthrocratic urge can usually unload onto the general public via tax deductions (as if they needed more) a big chunk of the costs of their own immortalization, as well as setting, through their foundations, public policy by initiatives that conform to their own views about society, culture, and economy. The spread of private "charitable, educational, and religious" foundations therefore confirms the decline of the welfare state and the erosion of an ethic of collective responsibility in favour of *noblesse oblige* handouts to individuals and causes that the donor deems sufficiently worthy or suitably servile. It further reinforces the social superiority of the wealthy donor over the deferential recipient rather than having the Great Unwashed try through collective political action to restrain the power and influence of the ultra-rich. It simultaneously blunts criticism of the profiteering behind so many great fortunes by allowing those who possess them to pose as publicly minded.[21]

Anyway, how much of today's big-buck philanthropy goes to ameliorate conditions of the unfortunate rather than to tart up the leisure of those making the donations? Compare the state of great concert halls in front of which the tuxedo-and-haute-couture step out their Bentleys (Volkswagens by any other name) to hear the Brahms Violin Concerto in D Major played on a several-million-dollar Stradivarius violin (probably fake), to the condition of urban shelters for discarded dogs or derelict humans.[22] While a reasonable case can be made that putting land into a "nature conservancy" to keep it out of the hands of "developers," loggers, or factory farmers, for example, deserves a tax break, by what moral and logical principle does any billionaire deserve to have the general public subsidize something like the Cato Institute, created by the Koch brothers to propagandize for even lower taxes than they already pay and for less government regulation, including, presumably, the sort that led to their own enterprises being so frequently charged with environmental offenses?[23]

Nonetheless, with the almost universal triumph of the notion that everyone is part of the same dysfunctional family of citizen-consumers, what got dumped into the historical trash bin along with disposable diapers and obsolete computer parts is the notion of class conflict – be it slave versus slave-owner, serf versus feudal lord, "independent commodity producer" versus commercial capitalist, proletariat versus bourgeois, or, that most historically enduring struggle, debtor versus creditor, the one that, clichéd dreams of rigor mortis Marxists notwithstanding, is most prominently displayed today. As a result, public exhibitions of gross self-indulgence by the ultra-rich lead not to general outrage and a demand for serious political action but to a populace of electronically lobotomized consumatons hopping into their 4x4s to exercise what has become the ultimate human right – freedom to shop at the discount mall for what they are told is a bargain. From class struggle to crass struggle: that is the defining feature of the times. And the genius of today's political economy has been to convert what used to be a potential life-and-death conflict between haves and have-nots into a minor disagreement between have-lots and wanna-have-mores.

The price of such startling political success, though, has been to unleash a self-propelling growth machine whose capacity for gulping down mountains of raw resources on the one hand, then spitting out great pyramids of toxic waste on the other, long ago overshot by a wide margin the carrying capacity of the biosphere.[24]

No doubt the human and environmental costs of the recent binge of überclass self-indulgence and underclass starry-eyed emulation will eventually sink into skulls so thick that a Neanderthal might grunt with envy – were it not for the fact that the average Neanderthal had a brain 50 percent larger than the human one. But such a belated wakeup is likely to occur only after the economic system, like a colony of algae proliferating in a petri dish, completely consumes its own growth medium and begins to collapse around itself. At that point, in an orgy of mutual recrimination, the ultra-rich will blame the poor for multiplying out of control, their collective appetites along with them; and the poor will blame the super-rich for each having an ecological footprint to match that of the legendary Paul Bunyan whose heavy tread, legend reports, stamped out the basins for North America's Great Lakes. On a material level they will both be right. Currently the world is grossly overpopulated relative to its ability to sustain the collective demands of its most ecologically irresponsible species. However, a few qualifications are in order.

First, if the core problem is human appetites, simple "economic efficiency" suggests the corrective policy that will accomplish the most with the least ought to begin by controlling the social reproduction of the class whose members in per capita terms make the heaviest demands on nature. Heavy taxes on financial speculation, luxury consumption, and inheritance along with drastic reform of laws governing today's pseudo-charities and foundations – the basic tools are in principle simple enough, even if in the current political atmosphere probably impossible to put into action.[25] In theory, they could work both directly and indirectly. The super-wealthy now maintain their position of ascendancy less through recourse to armed force, though in a pinch that is only a bugle call away, than by encouraging the underclass to divert their aspirations and frustrations into a monkey-see, monkey-do-a-little-of-same caricature of behaviour that the very wealthy exhibit.[26] Removing the bad example set by the über-rich *might* have a positive effect in limiting the crudely imitative cravings of the "middle class," although those reflexes may now be so ingrained as to impervious to anything short of an accurately wielded baseball bat.

Second, to the extent that overpopulation per se is an issue, something denied only by those whose hearts have bled so much as to afflict their eyesight, it has been established time and time again that one of the most effective ways to reduce its growth rate is to redistribute income from the upper to the lower rungs of the income and wealth ladder – before kicking the ladder out from under them all. Here, too, a sub-qualification is necessary. Reducing the growth rate does not by itself do what is really necessary – to put world population growth actually into reverse gear. But at least it's a start.

Third, members of the parasitocracy cannot plead, as those in lower-income groups *sometimes* can, that they had no choice. For those at the top, the ultimate deadly sins are not greed and gluttony, the first in piling up wealth thorough the crooked manipulation of paper and politicians, the second in spending it in glitzy, profligate ways – although those, along with envy of social competitors, are certainly prominent on the indictment papers. Rather it is that, while aware of the consequences, they are also indifferent. After all, they will not be the ones to pick up the final tab. They will be proudly ensconced in those mountain-top luxury condos, drinking vintage (?) wines from the former monastery's cellars while the rest of humanity sinks below the surface of an ocean of plastic trash.

Acknowledgments

Although the formal process of writing this book stretches back only two or three years, in a sense I've been working on it for all of my academic life. Even when first taking undergraduate political economy classes, longer ago than I care to remember, I was hoping to find answers to some nagging but then only crudely formulated questions. Translated into today's terms, they would be things like: Why would anyone, except maybe a certified sociopath, embrace with open arms a theology parading as a science that tries to reduce everything, even bits and pieces of nature itself, to a "market price," much less believe the supreme stupidity that since markets are so terribly clever, the prices they set are always "right" or, at worst, require only a little nudge to make them so. Why, in a society premised at least in theory on personal equality, are some obscenely rich and others hopelessly poor, while politicians and their scribes blather on about high tides lifting all boats, apparently even those that have had their hulls ripped open by financial icebergs? Why do those who are so very well off spend their money in such infantile, narcissistic, and damaging (socially and environmentally) ways; and why do so many of the less fortunate insist on doing the same to whatever extent their limited means allow? And why would any individual with even a modicum of common sense believe that it is possible to keep increasing the level of consumption year after year without the economic system that feeds apparently insatiable human appetites grinding to a halt as it runs out of raw materials to shove through the industrial meat-grinder or places to gratuitously dump its garbage?

Nearly half a century after my first economics class, I can formulate the questions much more clearly – and less politely – than I could back then. But, even though they formed the implicit schema within which the main elements of the current book took shape, I still don't have answers that are fully satisfactory. However I've learned that neither does anyone else, although that doesn't stop them from pretending. After all, pretense to knowledge and wisdom that we really don't have is what a large share of academic work is all about today. In fact it probably always has been, just not so transparently. And, to be fair, the social science component of that academic endeavour now has another important function that consumes the greater part of its time and energy – apologizing for the status quo distribution of power and wealth, a function that it performs to near perfection. On the other hand, maybe that isn't so new either.

Over the years I've learned a few other things, too, the influence of which will probably be equally clear in this book. First, after working with governments and quasi-public bodies at various times in various places, I came to appreciate the fundamental wisdom of the advice offered by British journalist, novelist, and political activist Claud Cockburn – don't believe anything until it's officially denied. Second, after so many years trying to think through causes of and prescriptions for society's troubles, I became persuaded by the late twentieth century's most astute philosopher, George Carlin, that the present world is too appalling a mess to be taken completely seriously. Third, after watching the steady descent of political debate into a contest in which the vacuous exchange sunny banalities with the fatuous, I've grown ever more convinced that if pablum is probably not healthy even for babies anymore, given how commercial grains are grown, it is pure poison to feed to what is supposed to be a mature society facing big problems. Besides, the only way to shock somnambulates out of their self-reassuring reveries is a splash of ice-cold reality in the face, though a remarkably large number of them seem immune even to that.

The wide range of subjects this book tackles required soliciting fact and asking opinion from a substantial number of people who have far more expertise than I could possibly muster on any one of the topics covered, let alone all of them. A book project like this is viable only under three conditions. First, the person writing it has to be open to a broad assortment of information from a wide variety of sources even at the risk of being labelled a dilettante, a term I interpret the way it was originally intended, as a compliment. Second, to make that information truly meaningful it has to be placed in context, much like putting a gemstone in a setting to display its attributes in a different light, although in this case the results are not exactly pretty. Third, the author needs to follow the distinctly non-academic rule that it is better to be occasionally wrong about issues that matter than always impeccably correct about things of little or no consequence.

However an apology and explanation is in order: there is one obviously missing chapter dealing with the decimation of the world's forests by the search for precious hardwoods like teak (preferred material for a growing armada of luxury yachts) or rosewood (for everything from expensive guitars to "essential" healing oils) or mahogany (for dining room furniture in elegant townhouses). It was eliminated not because timber poachers, including in that category giant transnational forestry companies, have taken up organic farming. The great forests – east, west, north, south – are still alive with the sound of chainsaws; and the lumber mills that launder the stuff are still hopping to the music of money. Nor was the decision taken because the damage done is not really as irreparable as feared. Just the opposite. Every big-leaf mahogany tree cut in the Brazilian rainforest, for example, can bring down twenty to thirty others of different species along with it, eliminating its own forest cover and therefore precluding its own regeneration in the wild. The chapter is missing simply because of lack of time and space – exactly the problem that led, too, to a chapter on trade and traffic in high-end antiques (furniture, maps, Persian carpets, Stradivarius violins, etc.) also ending up on the cutting-room floor, hopefully to be resurrected in a future edition.

As the ideas in this book took shape, my best teachers have been hordes of my own students who have passed through my courses, some of whom I've thanked in specific chapters. I can only hope that, in light of how much I learned from them, I gave them something of value (in the genuine rather than monetary sense) in return. Once the book was actually in progress, a number assisted with specific parts of the research. They include Matt Brown, Lydia Doll, Matthew Donne, Alex Fraenkel, Adam Ginzburg, Sean Hallisey, Namita Kallianpurkar, Neha Kallianpurkar, Nicholas Krakoff, Craig Milne, Melissa Pang, Daniel Pudjak, Katie Reisman, Brandon Reti, Caitlin Tanner, Alison Withers, and others whom I have no doubt inadvertently overlooked, only to wake up, I suspect, at 4:00 AM some morning long after the book has gone to press with their names racing around my brain.

Many individuals outside my university had important roles in informing or straightening out my thinking on various topics. Special mention goes to: Peter Andreas, always a voice of good sense to bring me back to the point at issue, not always successfully; George Archer, who for decades has tried, sometimes in vain, to keep me from getting too carried away by my own flights of rhetorical fancy; Jacques Courtois, who, although he may disagree with much in this book, is one of the best informed people I know on many of its subjects, maybe the only one who knows something about just about all of them; Alan Green from whom I stole the term "animal underworld" along with some of the information in his disturbing book of the same name; Michael Hudson, who for more than thirty years has been perhaps the sanest voice speaking about a lunatic financial world that, for the most part, is still too crazy to listen; Jennifer Jacquet, whose work on fishy business in the fishing business first hooked me on the subject; Leo Kaklamanos, a special kind of virtuoso who has always been a source of astute observations on art, books, and life itself; Sarah Kamal, who never hesitates to tell me when my opinions are arcane, self-indulgent, or just wrong, even if I usually refuse to admit it, and the only person besides my publisher to suffer through repeated drafts of the manuscript; Azfar Khan, who probably knows better than anyone what the gap between ultra rich and very poor means in human rather than just statistical terms; Rafi Kourouian, my mudīr of Middle Eastern research, who insists on giving credibility to ethnic stereotypes with his Armenian knowledge of diamonds and carpets, and much else; Simon McKenzie for his archeological digs into the underground activities of antiquities traders; Steven Naylor, who, with his professional understanding of musicians and their tools, tuned me in enough to make one of the more unusual chapters possible; Dan O'Meara to whom I regularly turn for information on ivory trafficking or diamond mining or other things that make parts of Africa fascinating for political analysts and miserable for the people living there; Varouj Pogharian, who knows so much about the shady side of things that the world is lucky he chose to be a cop; Fritz Reuter, a master luthier who plays second fiddle to no one in exposing sour notes in the antique violin trade; Pam Ritchie, who illuminated for me hidden facets of the modern gemstones business; Jan Summers and Harold Bedoukian, who told me much that others in their profession might try to sweep under the Persian carpet; and Peter Vadja, who seems to always know what goes on under the hood, in all senses of the term.

There are many more whose help is acknowledged at specific points in the text, including a number of groups and organizations that keep their eyes on issues as varied as corporate malfeasance and environmental degradation. If parts of the book seem on occasion critical of the current proliferation of tax-exempt NGOs, foundations, and institutions, the reader ought to note that for everything like the Environmental Investigative Agency tracking crimes against nature, there is something like a "sound science" institute funded by Big Oil to deny the likelihood of future climate chaos. For everything like Médicins sans frontières, there is something like the former Tobacco Institute, set up back in the 1950s by the Virginia Cartel (of giant Anglo-American tobacco companies) to muddy the link between smoking and lung cancer. I extend my thanks to the (usually badly funded) genuine ones; I extend my hopes to the well-heeled phony ones that their officers get indicted for tax fraud – although they are more likely, given the way the world is run, to finish their careers as high court judges or cabinet ministers in what is left of civil governments.

Thanks as well to the Social Sciences and Humanities Research Council of Canada that supported the background research over several years. I also want to register my appreciation, and say appropriate good-byes, to the late Bruce Trigger, the last of a small group of intellectual giants already established at McGill University when I started there, a group who mentored me through the often confusing early years of an academic career as well as standing as role models to be appreciated and, where possible, emulated in the later years.

Certainly not least, a special word for Philip Cercone, my publisher, and his staff, notably Claude Lalumière, who was once again my editor and sometimes frustrated disciplinarian. It takes a lot of guts in the current political environment for an established university press to publish books like this, or some of its predecessors. Don't think for a moment, Capo, that I am unaware or unappreciative.

Notes

PREAMBLE

1 See Robert H. Frank's *Falling Behind: How Rising Inequality Harms the Middle Class* (Berkeley: University of California, 2007).
2 The most insightful analyses of how this process stretches back for decades are by Michael Hudson; see especially his recent contributions to *Counterpunch* and *Democracy Now*, most reproduced at www.michael-hudson.com.
3 John Kenneth Galbraith, "Recession Economics," *New York Review of Books* 29, no. 1, 4 February 1982.
4 One of the best summaries of recent policy trends is James K. Galbraith, *The Predator State: How Conservatives Abandoned the Free Market and Why Liberals Should Too* (New York: Free Press, 2008).
5 All these numbers need to be treated as only broad indicators. Governments in the West have not for decades tried to do serious investigations of the wealth distribution, probably because they are afraid of what those investigations would show. Measures of the income spread are better but still far from satisfactory. As a result the current gap between production workers and bosses gets cited at anywhere from about 500 to 1,750. I thank Robin Rowley, formerly of McGill University, for cautioning me about the dismal state of wealth data and the problems, ignored by left and right alike, of interpreting income statistics.
6 On Hindery's business dealings, see Geraldine Fabrikant, "Investing IT Enigmatic Architect of Cable Resurgence," *New York Times*, 21 June 1998, and Leslie Cauley, *End of the Line: The Rise and Fall of AT&T* (New York: Free Press, 2005).
7 Cited in Louis Uchitelle, "The Richest of the Rich, Proud of a New Gilded Age," *New York Times*, 15 July 2007.

8 A study by the World Institute for Development Economics Research of
the United Nations University gave the upper 1 percent of the population a mere 40 percent, but that was based on 2000 data – obviously the
situation got much worse over the next several years. For a review of
the data see Tim Jackson, *Prosperity without Growth: Economics for a
Finite Planet* (London: Earthscan, 2009), 5, 221n9. In the US the share
of national income (which usually lags the rise in wealth) for the top 1
percent rose from 6.5 percent of the total in 1980 to 19.5 percent in 2006.
But note the reservations in footnote 5 above. Since wealth data rarely
take account of things like McMansions or art collections, let along offshore bank accounts, if anything they underestimate the wealth gap.

9 There is now an enormous literature on the crisis. Probably the best-
rounded account putting the matter in its political context is Simon
Johnson and James Kwak, *13 Bankers: The Wall Street Takeover and the
Next Financial Meltdown* (New York: Pantheon, 2010). For insights into
the "logic" behind the creation of fatally flawed financial institutions,
see John Cassidy, *How Markets Fail: The Logic of Economic Calamities*
(London: Penguin, 2009). For a thorough account of the mechanics of
the new financial markets by one of the few to have understood them, see
Charles Morris, *The Trillion Dollar Meltdown: Easy Money, High Rollers,
and the Great Credit Crash* (New York: PublicAffairs, 2008). For the public consequences, see Dean Baker, *Plunder and Blunder: The Rise and Fall
of the Bubble Economy* Sausalito California (PoliPointPress, 2009). For a
detailed dissection of the US housing market, see John Talbott, *Contagion:
The Financial Epidemic That Is Sweeping the Global Economy* (Hoboken:
John Wiley, 2009). My favourite is John Lanchester, *IOU: Why Everyone
Owes Everyone and No One Can Pay* (New York: Simon & Schuster,
2010).

10 Throughout 2010, there were massive strikes in various European countries, but not a single government budged from its policy of austerity that
amounted to a program to make workers and social security recipients
pay the cost of massive financial peculation. See, for example, "Analyst
View – European Strikes Unlikely to Shake Governments" *Reuters*, 8
September 2010; Sarah Morris and Gavin Jones, "Special Report: Is There
Power in Europe's Unions?" *Reuters*, 27 September 2010.

11 On the nature of the party, see Robert L. Frank, *Richistan: A Journey
through the American Wealth Boom and the Lives of the New Rich* (New
York: Crown, 2007), and Richard Conniff, *The Natural History of the
Rich: A Field Guide* (New York: W.W. Norton, 2002).

12 The parasitic nature of modern finance is very neatly captured in Michael
Lewis, *The Big Short: Inside the Doomsday Machine* (New York: W.W.
Norton & Co., 2010).

13 See especially Thorstein Veblen's complementary volumes, *The Theory of the Leisure Class: An Economic Study of Institutions* (New York: Macmillan, 1899) and *The Theory of Business Enterprise* (New York: C. Scribner and Sons, 1904).

14 In light of the degree to which "business history" as practiced in today's universities is an exercise in hagiography, it is useful to get a view through the eyes of the era's leading American muckraker, Gustavus Myers, in his 1907 classic *History of the Great American Fortunes* (reprinted New York: Random House, 1937).

15 Cited in Mark Ames, "Top Billionaire Hedge Funder Sees Himself as a Hyena Devouring Wildebeests," *AlterNet*, 21 May 2010.

16 Shawn Tully, "A Reclusive Mogul Bets on the House," *Fortune* 150, no. 5, 6 September 2004.

17 Cited in Julia Mead, "At Home in Versailles on the Atlantic," *New York Times*, 4 July 2004.

18 Cited in Mead, *New York Times*, ibid.

19 Nathan Vardi, "Man with Many Enemies," *Forbes*, 22 July 2002; Emily Thornton et al., "Ira Rennert's House of Debt," *BusinessWeek*, 17 February 2003.

20 See, for example, Guy Adams, "Divided by Origins, United by Wealth: The New Super-Rich," *The Independent*, 8 February 2007; Andrew Buncombe, "A Must-Have Revolution: How Shopping Became India's New Religion," *The Independent*, 6 August 2009; James Fontanella-Khan, "India's Billionaires Outstrip US Counterparts," *Financial Times*, 19 November 2009.

21 Matt Woolsely, "Inside the World's First Billion Dollar Home," *Forbes*, 30 April 2008.

22 "Indian Billionaire's House Plans: Three Helipads, 27 Floors, 600 Staff, and More," *Huffington Post*, 28 March 2008. For more examples, see "Homes of the Billionaires," *Forbes*, 3 November 2009.

23 Asha Krishnakumar, "A Sanitation Emergency," *The Hindu* 20, no. 24, 22 November – 5 December 2003; Vaishnavi C. Sekhar, "Water Contamination in City Touches Alarming Levels: Study," *Times of India* Mumbai, 19 April 2010; Matia Echanove and Rahul Srivastava, "Taking the Slum out of Slumdog," *New York Times*, 21 February 2009. My thanks to Madhav Badami for these references.

24 Robert Frank, "The Wealth Report: The Russians Are Coming – at 40 Knots – Eyeing Record, Tycoon Builds a Bigger Yacht; Challenging the Saudis," *Wall Street Journal*, 12 January 2007. See also Juliet Chung and Guy Chazen, "The Roman Empire," *The Wall Street Journal*, 18 September 2009.

25 Vanessa O'Connell, "The Shrinking of the Fantasy Gift," *The Wall Street Journal*, 7 October 2009. The original depiction at www2.victoriassecret.

com/fantasy/index.html has been removed. Apparently none of the bras actually sold!

26 "Mice, Roaches Close Home of $25,000 Dessert," *Reuters*, 16 November 2007.

27 A similar a pen, a real one, made by Caran d'Ache of Switzerland, sold in 2010 for $265,000; see "Top 13 Most Expensive Pens in The World," *World Interesting Facts: Interesting Facts around the World*, www. worldinterestingfacts.com/wealthy/13-most-expensive-pen-in-the-world. html and www.worldamazingrecords.com/2010/04/world-records-of-most-expensive-luxury.html. There are also rival pens, like the Mont-blanc Boheme Royal made from 18K white gold, set with 1,420 brilliant cut diamonds of total weight 15 carats, available for a more modest $150,000.

28 Lucie Van Den Berg, "The £50,000 Hangover after US Millionaire Was Host of the Ultimate Party," *Daily Mail*, 6 December 2006.

29 The affair led to a court contest between Tours of Enchantment and the NASDAQ chief executive over an unpaid $70,000 portion of the bill. James Doran, "Profit and Loss: Nasdaq Chief Lacks Skills in Economics," *Sunday Times*, 2 December 2006.

30 Adam Sage, "Monaco Lays Out the Red Carpet for the World's Ultra-Rich," *Times of London*, 30 March 2009.

31 Featured on the Formula I Grand Prix, 24 May 2009, lunch at a modest €1,030 without wine or service charges (www.alain-ducasse.com/public_us/restaurants/popup_carte.php?id=179).

32 www.seasonsinstyle.com/Far_East/Thailand/SonevaKiribySixSenses.

33 "Excess Is Back: Luxury Travel Booming Again," *Sydney Morning Herald*, 15 December 2009.

34 "Space Tourist Charles Simonyi Blasts Off to Space aboard Soyuz Rocket," *Daily Telegraph*, 26 March 2009; Reuters, "US Software Mogul Set for Second Space Trip," *New York Times*, 26 March 2009; "Charles Simonyi," *New York Times*, 22 September 2010.

35 See, for example, Rebecca Keegan, "How Much Did Avatar Really Cost?" *Vanity Fair*, 22 December 2009.

36 Kenneth Chang, "In New Space Race, Enter the Entrepreneurs," *New York Times*, 7 June 2010. See also Craig Covault, "Bigelow's Gamble," *Spaceflight Now*, 27 September 2004, www.spaceflightnow.com/news/n0409/27bigelow.

37 www.lanamarks.com/home.htm.

38 Andrew Johnson, "Art, and a Russian Revolution: Soviet and Modern Russian Paintings Are in Demand at Auctions across the World," *The Independent*, 25 April 2010.

39 The image of "Dirty – Jeff on Top" is available at, among many other sites, Adrian Searle, "Sex and Sensibility: Pop Life at Tate Modern," *The Guardian*, 29 September 2009. Google Images has a multitude of variations on the theme.

40 John Harlow "Billionaire Club in Bid to Curb Overpopulation," *Sunday Times*, 24 May 2009.

41 www.saatchi-gallery.co.uk/artists/artpages/tracey_emin_i_got_all.htm.

42 See Richard Brooks, "Tracey Emin: Stuff Your 50 Percent Tax, I'm Taking My Tent to France," *Sunday Times*, 4 October 2009.

43 Stephanie Baker and Tom Cahill, "Uma Thurman No Help to Arpad Busson in Madoff Fraud's Nightmare," *Bloomberg*, 7 January 2009.

44 Louise Armitstead, "Stars Come out for Ark Charity Event," *Daily Telegraph* 6 June 2008; "Jerome Taylor, "What Credit Crisis? Super-Rich Can still Spare £25m for Charity," *The Independent*, 7 June 2008.

CHAPTER ONE

1 www.itechnews.net/wp-content/uploads/2007/10/MacBook-pro-24-carat-Gold-1.jpg.

2 Maybe that's why the godfather of the Melbourne mob arranged for himself a gold-plated casket (modelled on Michael Jackson's) before he was murdered in prison ("Melbourne gangster buried in £18,000 coffin," *The Independent*, 1 May 2010).

3 For a general background, see R.T. Naylor, *Wages of Crime: Black Markets, Illegal Finance, and the Underworld Economy* (Ithaca and Montreal: Cornell University Press and McGill-Queen's University Press, 2004, chapter 5.

4 On the early gold mines, see Bruce Trigger, *Nubia Under the Pharaohs* (Boulder, CO: Westview Press, 1976).

5 Victor Von Hagen, *The Realm of the Incas* (New York: Mentor, 1963). The classic account is William Prescott, *History of the Conquest of Peru* (New York: Harper and Brothers, 1847).

6 See Jacob Lamar, "Out of Africa: Stung by a Ghanaian Smoothy," *Time*, 21 April 1986, and "Out of Africa," *Forbes*, 8 February 1988. There was an investigation ("The Ultimate Con Man") on *60 Minutes*, 29 January 1989, and ongoing controversy ever since.

7 The relationship may be closer than seems at first glance. Just after the 2008 crash, young John's successors, calling themselves Friends of the Oman Ghana Trust Fund, claimed that the trust assets had swollen to nearly three trillion dollars. (See "Oman Ghana Trust Fund now Has Money Nearing THREE TRILLION DOLLARS!" *Bankrupt Banker*, 23

September 2008, bankruptbanker.blogspot.com/2008/09/oman-ghana-
trust-fund-now-has-money.html.

8 Adam Sage, "Economic Uncertainty Means Business Is Booming for Swiss
   Gold Smelters," *Times of London*, 14 November 2009. The uncertainty
   continued into 2010 with the ultra rich piling into gold with the same
   gusto they did champagne and caviar. See Robert Frank, "Uh, Oh! The
   Rich Are Buying Gold Again," *The Wall Street Journal*, 4 October 2010.

9 Richard Tomkins, "International Economy – Gold to Play on Warm Image
   as the 'New Cool,'" *Financial Times*, 11 May 2001.

10 For an indictment of the mining industry in general, in which gold plays
   a starring role, see Earthworks-Oxfam America, *Dirty Metals: Mining,
   Communities and the Environment* (2004).

11 While some of the facts are now challenged, the pioneering early works
   on precious metals in relation to aboriginal societies were by Alex Del
   Mar. See especially his *A History of Monetary Systems* (New York:
   reprint A.M Kelly, 1969) and *A History of the Precious Metals* (reprint
   New York: B. Franklin 1968). Among many more recent treatments, see
   Victor Van Hagen, *The Golden Man: The Quest for El Dorado* (Farm-
   borough: Saxon House 1974), and Marc Cocker, *Rivers of Blood, Rivers
   of Gold: Europe's Conquest of Indigenous Peoples* (New York: Grove
   Press, 1998).

12 See Roy W. Jasrram, *Silver: The Restless Metal* (New York: John Wiley,
   1981), 3–4, where war is described as an instrument for the destruction of
   "obsolete oriental theocracy." Thus the conquests of Alexander the Great
   supposedly meant that "the immense idle reserves of the Archimedean
   Empire were turned to productive use. The flow of new money minted by
   Alexander from captured treasure was to spread prosperity (and incidentally inflation) throughout the conquered lands."

13 On mining frauds, see R.T. Naylor, "The Alchemy of Fraud: Investment
   Scams in the Precious Metal-Mining Business," *Crime, Law & Social
   Change* 47, no. 2, 2007.

14 See, for example, this profile of Goldcorp: "Goldcorp Analysis," *Mining-
   watch Canada*, September 2007, www. miningwatch.ca; and this profile
   of the world's largest gold-mining corporation, Barrick Gold of Toronto:
   Barrick's Dirty Secrets: Communities Worldwide Respond to Gold Mining's Impacts – An Alternative Report, *A Corpwatch Report*, 1 May 2007.

15 There seems more evidence to support the opposite – that at least one rea-
   son for the execution of Jesus, assuming he existed and it really occurred,
   was to put a stop to his proselytizing in favour of tax evasion. See John
   Brown, *The Law of Christ Respecting Civil Obedience: Especially in the
   Payment of Tribute, to Which Are Added Two Addresses on the Voluntary
   Church Controversy* (London: William Ball, 1839, 3rd ed.).

16 A detailed examination of the role of the clergy, specifically in moving
bullion home to Portugal, is in A.J.R. Russell-Wood, "Holy and Unholy
Alliances: Clerical Participation in the Flow of Bullion from Brazil to
Portugal during the Reign of Dom João" *Hispanic American Historical
Review* 80, no. 4, 2000.

17 Norman P. Macdonald, *The Making of Brazil: Portuguese Roots,
1500–1822* (Sussex: Book Guild Ltd, 1996); Bailey W. Diffie, *A History
of Colonial Brazil: 1500–1792* (Malabar: Robert E. Krieger Publishing
Company, 1987); Kenneth Maxwell, *Conflicts and Conspiracies: Brazil
and Portugal 1750–1808* (Cambridge: Cambridge University Press, 1973).

18 See, for example, Grant Smith, *History of the Comstock Lode 1850–1920*
(Reno: State Bureau of Mines, University of Nevada, 1943).

19 There is a chronology of major and minor rushes at "Gold Rush,"
Encyclopedia Britannica, www.britannica.com/EBchecked/topic/237388/
gold-rush

20 On the alleged abuse of judicial processes by Canadian mining companies, see the articles in Montreal's *Le Devoir* newspaper, "Barrick Gold
empêche la publication d'un livre," 25 March 2010; "Barrick Gold met
Ecosociété en demeure de ne plus utiliser l'expression 'poursuite-baillon,'"
23 September 2008; and "Imperial Canada Inc. – La censure d'un ouvrage
jamais paru," 31 March 2010.

21 An early account of conditions in the ongoing Brazilian gold rush is
George Monbiot's *Amazon Watershed* (London: Abacus, 1992).

22 Sahabi Yahaya "Gold Rush Brings Wealth but Kills 400 Children in Nigeria," *The Independent*, 24 October 2010.

23 David Smith, "South African Security Guards Shoot Dead at Least Four
Illegal Miners," *Guardian*, 12 August 2010.

24 These structures are examined by David Cleary in his *Anatomy of the
Amazon Gold Rush* (London: Macmillan, 1990). See also John Barham
"Golden Horde Lays Waste Amazon: Brazil's Uncontrollable Gold Rush,"
Financial Times, 17 December 1988; James Brooke, "Brazil's Outrage
Intensifies as Toll in Massacre Hits 73," *New York Times*, 23 August
1993. See the survey of the Amazon alluvial gold boom by Laura Jarnagin
Pang and Eul-Soo Pang, "The Seamier Side of El Dorado," *Hemisfile:
Perspectives on Political and Economic Trends in the Americas* 7, no. 1,
January-February 1996, and "Golden Rules," *Hemisfile: Perspectives
on Economic and Political Trends in the Americas* 7, no. 2, March-April
1996. On the flesh trade, see Christina Lbel "Teenagers Sold as Sex slaves
in midst of Amazon Jungle," *Sunday Times*, 26 April 1992.

25 "The opening of the Brazilian frontier is just like the American pioneers,
with covered wagons fighting Indians. We don't have horses, we have air-
planes." (Cited in *Globe and Mail*, 30 August 1993.

26 Partly, no doubt, because of Brazil's early practice of cheating miners who did sell to the official buying office by understating the purity of their gold. Twenty years later some are still waiting for restitution (Larry Rohter "Brazilian Miners Wait for Payday after Diet of Bitterness," *New York Times*, 23 August 2004.

27 Andrew Whitley, "American News: Brazilian Gold Fever Prompts Rush to the Hills – Andrew Whitley Explains How Small Prospectors Hold a Key to the Future of Their Country", *Financial Times*, 19 January 1984; James Brooke "This Is El Dorado? Gold and Death in the Jungle," *New York Times*, 30 November 1989.

28 A brief effort by the government to regulate mercury imports did little more than to stimulate a black market, while efforts to provide special closed retorts to restrict mercury loss ran afoul of distances and the fact that most miners are too poor to afford new equipment. Jed Greer, "The Price of Gold," *The Ecologist*, May-June 1993.

29 L.D. Lacerda, "Global Mercury Emissions from Gold and Silver Mining," *Water, Air and Soil Pollution* 97, no. 3–4, July 1997.

30 Marc Lacey, "UN Conference Backs Efforts to Curb Mercury Pollution," *New York Times*, 10 February 2003.

31 Felicity Barringer, "Kenya: Support for Mercury Pact," *New York Times*, 21 February 2009; See also *The Ecologist*, April 2009.

32 On the US, see US Geological Survey, "Mercury Contamination from Historical Gold Mining in California," *Fact Sheet* 2005 – 3014 Ver. 1.1, October 2005.

33 Kathy Marks, "Australian Billionaires Take to the Streets for Tax Protest," *The Independent*, 11 June 2010; Elizabeth Fry "Australia's PM Waters Down Mining Tax," *Financial Times*, 2 July 2010.

34 See Earle Ripley, Robert Redmann, and Adele Crowder, *Environmental Effects of Mining* Delray Beach, Florida: St Lucie Press, 1996, Claudia Gasparrini, *Gold and Other Precious Metals* Berlin: Springer-Verlag, 1993, and "What's Wrong with Gold?" *Project Underground*, 16 February 2002.

35 "Hungary Seeks International Help for Tisza River Cyanide Spill," *Radio Free Europe*, 1 June 2000.

36 Dororthy Kosich, "Hungarian Tailings Spill May Trigger Long-Term Damage to Wildlife, Humans," *Mineweb* 6 October 2010.

37 Milagros Salazar, "Government Generosity Swells Company Profits," *IPS News*, 4 February 2008.

38 Pratap Chatterjee, "Conquering Peru: Newmont's Yanacocha Mine Recalls the Days of Pizarro," *Multinational Monitor* 18, no. 4, April 1997; Michael Riley with Barry Fitzgerald, "Newmont's Midas Touch Is Shaken in Peru but Could Be Stirring in Australia," *The Age*, 14 December 2004;

Jane Perlez et al., "Tangled Strands in Fight over Peru Gold Mine," *New York Times*, 25 October 2005; and "Peru – the Curse of Inca Gold," *Frontline/WORLD* October 2005.

39 For an overview of the issues, see Shanna Langdon "Peru's Yanacocha Gold Mine: The IFC's Midas Touch?" *Project Underground*, September 2000.

40 Andrew Marshall, "Newmont Evacuation from Indonesia Mine after Protests," *Reuters*, 29 June 2007.

41 Donald Greenlees, "Indonesia Clears U.S. Mine Giant of Pollution," *International Herald Tribune*, 25 April 2007; Andrew Trounson, "Indonesia still an Investment Minefield after Gold Giant Cleared," *The Australian*, 30 April 2007.

42 "Newmont Exec Sues New York Times over Indonesian Stories," *Agence France Presse*, 15 May 2007.

43 Kathy Marks, "Deep in the Desert – The Gold Mine That Swallowed a Town," *The Independent*, 6 June 2010.

44 Kevin Andrusiak, "KCGM Gets a Slap on the Wrist for Cyanide Spill," *The Australian*, 28 January 2008.

45 Ean Higgins, "Gold's Failing Tailings," *The Australian*, 16 March 2004.

46 On the lawsuit, see "Robert M. Friedland – Lawsuit Seeks to Establish Full Responsibilities for Costs of Environmental Actions at the Summitville Mine Site in Colorado," PR *Newswire*, 5 May 1999.

47 Jennifer Wells, "Friedland's Environmental Problems," *Macleans*, 9 September 1996

48 For an in-depth look at his early career, see Jacquie McNish, *The Big Score: Robert Friedland and the Voisey's Bay Hustle* (Toronto: Doubleday Canada, 1998), chapter 3: "The Man with the Golden Arm – Mr Robert Friedland Goes to Asia," and *Gravediggers: A Report on Mining in Burma* (MAC: Mines & Communities, www.minesandcommunities.org). For Friedland's rebuttal to his critics, see www.ivanhoe-mines.com/s/Truth AndLies.asp.

49 John Barham, "Commodities and Agriculture: Brazil Tackles Gold Smuggling," *Financial Times*, 25 March 1988; "Guyana Struggles While Gold Is Taken from Its Rain Forest," *Globe and Mail*, 17 May 1990.

50 Desiree Kissoon Jodah "Courting Disaster in Guyana (Cyanide Spills at Guyana's Omai Gold Mine)," *Multinational Monitor*, 1 November 1995; Allan Robinson, "Cambior Cleared in Guyana Spill Inquiry Concludes Miner not Responsible for Discharge of Cyanide into Drinking Water," *Globe and Mail*, 23 January 1996.

51 For a partial profile, see Nathan Vardi, "The Promoter," *Forbes*, 24 November 2003.

52 There is an excellent onsite account of the rebellion in Robert Young
    Pelton, *The Hunter, the Hammer and Heaven*, (Guilford, CT: Lyons Head
    Press, 2002). On early conditions, see *Far Eastern Economic Review*, 19
    September 1975.

53 James P. Sterba, "Chaotic Paradise: An Audacious Rebel Shakes Copper
    Market," *Wall Street Journal*, 3 January 1990.

54 Brin Evans, "Fighting for Their Island," *Sunday Star-Times* (Auckland), 13
    July 1997.

55 Barry FitzGerald, "Bougainville's Copper's Mine Regains Shine," *The Age*,
    27 July 2005.

56 Cited in David Hyndman, "OK Tedi: New Guinea's Disaster Mine," *The
    Ecologist* 18, no. 1, January-February 1988.

57 Sakura Sanders, "Displacement, Poverty and the Global Extractive Indus-
    try: Mining Through Roots," *Counterpunch*, 8 July 2010. For an overview
    of the legal entanglements, see Stuart Kirsch, "An Incomplete Victory at
    Ok Tedi," *Carnegie Council: The Voice for Ethics in International Affairs*,
    6 April 2000.

58 Jed Greer, "The Price of Gold: Environmental Costs of the New Gold
    Rush," *Ecologist* 23, no. 3, May-June 1993. UN Environment Fund,
    Waste from Consumption and Production: the OK Tedi Case, 2002. The
    pollution got so bad, even the Australian senior partner began pressing
    to close the site, only to be opposed by the government and its Canadian
    junior partner.

59 The story of the post-coup corporate carve-up is told in John Pilger, *The
    New Rulers of the World* (New York: Verso, 2002).

60 On the terms of the agreement with Indonesia and the company's own
    expectations, see United States Securities and Exchange Commission Form
    10-K Annual Report Freeport-McMoRan Copper & Gold Inc., 2007,
    www.fcx.com/ir/downloads/FCX200610K.pdf. On the impact on indig-
    enous peoples in general, see Theodore E. Downing et al., "Indigenous
    Peoples and Mining Encounters: Strategies and Tactics," *Mining, Minerals
    and Sustainable Development* no. 57, April 2002. For a critique of Free-
    port's Grasberg operation, see "Risky Business: The Grasberg Gold Mine,"
    An Independent Annual Report on P.T. Freeport Indonesia, 1998, www.
    freewestpapua.org/docs/risky_business.pdf.

61 Jane Perlez and Raymond Bonner, "Below a Mountain of Wealth, a
    River of Waste," *New York Times*, 27 December 2003, and "Gold's
    Other Price: Questionable Moves, Indonesian Operations Tied to Mili-
    tary," *International Herald Tribune*, 28 December 2005; Jane Perlez,
    "The Papuans Say: This Land and Its Ores Are Ours," *New York Times*,
    5 April 2006; Jane Perlez, "Mining Protest Leaves 4 Dead in Indonesia,"
    New York Times, 25 February 2006; "Papua Mine Protestors Hack

Police to Death," *Times of London*, 16 March 2006; "Indonesia: 17 Suspects Jailed in Attacks Killing 3 at World's Largest Gold Mine," *New York Times*, 22 July 2009. "The Environmental Impacts of Freeport-Rio Tinto's Copper and Gold Mining Operation in Papua Jakarta," *Walhi-Indonesian Forum for Environment*, 2006. Thanks to Stephane Abitbol for bringing this to my attention.

62 For a more thorough account, see Naylor, "Alchemy of Fraud" 2006.

63 See Richard Milner, "Shadow of Mafia over Bank Case," *Sunday Times*, 1 January 1978; "Scotland Yard Nipped Gigantic Fraud Plot," *Times of London*, 15 September 1978; "Gold Mine Was Shack in Backwoods," *Times of London*, 16 September 1978, "$228 bn Gold Mine That Never Was," *Times of London*, 17 September 1978; Robert McFadden, "FBI Holds Man Sought by Britain," *New York Times*, 31 March 1979.

64 Shirley Hobbs Scheibla, "Gold Scams – They're Bilking Investors Out of Hundreds of Millions," *Barron's* 5 September 1988; Bruce Ingersoll, "School for Scam: Fraud Is Rife in Market for Pink Sheet Stocks, Securities Officials Say – How Dynapac Sold Shares With Stories of TV Bingo and a Western Gold Mine – Rewards of 'Pump and Dump,'" *Wall Street Journal*, 2 February 1988; Don Clark, "Salesman Says Bye Kids to Canada," *San Francisco Chronicle*, 13 July 1987.

65 Chris Kraul, "Yuba Goldfields Is Now a Burial Ground for Dreams," *Los Angeles Times*, 18 April 1989.

66 For some of the extensive coverage of the Yuba affair, see Frederick M. Muir "Currency Caper: Can Investors Get Any of $150 Million Back from J. David & Co.? – Some Clues May Come Today in Case of Western Firm with List of Elite Clients – The Promise of 40% Returns," *Wall Street Journal*, 21 March 1984; Frederick Muir, "J. David Founder Might Have Fled U.S., Said to Vow Return with Missing Funds," *The Wall Street Journal*, 20 April 1984; and Frederick M. Muir "Arrest, Incarceration of J. David Dominelli Doesn't End Mystery – Where Is the Money Investors Put into J. David & Co? Last Hours on Montserrat," *The Wall Street Journal*, 30 April 1984, "Dominelli Says J. David Investors Likely Lost Money," *The Wall Street Journal*, 24 August 1984.

67 On the legal complications, see "Shareholders Sue to Dissolve Silberman Mining Firm," *Los Angeles Times*, 4 May 1989, and "Yuba Natural Resources: The Troubled Mining Firm ..." *Los Angeles Times*, 23 May 1989, plus further coverage: *Los Angeles Times*, 18 April 1989, 4 May 1989, 22 and 25 September 1990; *Business Week*, 1 May 1989; *New York Times*, 14 August 1994, 27 June 2008. See also Matt Potter "Gold Dust," *San Diego Reader*, 20 May 1999, and "Deductibility of Legal Expenditures as Business Expenses," Richard Silberman v. the United States, no. 93–768, Filed 2 June 1998.

68 Morris Goran, *The Story of Fritz Haber* (Norman: University of Oklahoma Press, 1967), 91.

69 Diane Francis, *Contre-preneurs* (Toronto: Macmillan of Canada, 1988), 35–42; "A Run-up Raises Some Eyebrows," *Business Week*, 21 March 1994; Larry Gurwin, "The Secret Life of JB Oxford," *Time*, 9 December 1996; United States Attorney, Central District of California, "Former JB Oxford Consultant Irving Kott Agrees to Plead Guilty to 2 Felony Offenses and Pay $1 Million," *Press Release 04–062*, 4 May 2004. For the company's own view, see www.answers.com/topic/jb-oxford-holdings-inc?cat=biz-fin.

70 See, for example, Jerry Jackson, "Judge Orders Ex-Goldcor Official to Pay $10.8 million in Gold Scam," *Orlando Sentinel*, 27 November 1991; "Penny Stock Promoter Enters Plea Agreement," SEC *News Digest*, no. 90–74, April 17, 1990. US Securities and Exchange Commission News Release, "Remarks of Commissioner before the North American Securities Administrators Conference," 14 January 1989; Julie Murphy, "Cold Case File: Richard Brown," *Cold Case Files*, News-JournalOnLine, 22 September 2008. William M. Alpert, "Better than Alchemy – How Goldcor, once a Penny Stock, Hit Pay Dirt," *Barron's*, 22 February 1988; David S. Hilzenrath, "SEC Seeks $10.9 Million in Gold Stock Scam; Thousands of Investors Fell for Elaborate Hoax, Agency Says," *Washington Post*, 31 December 1991.

71 "Four Indicted in Alleged Gold Fraud," *Associated Press*, 2 October 1998.

72 Shirley Hobbs Scheibla, "Gold Scams – They're Bilking Investors out of Hundreds of Millions" *Barron's*, 5 September 1988. See also "Receiver Ordered for Orea Mines, Inc. and Orex, Inc.," SEC *News Digest*, 25 March 1988, and "Injunctions Entered against Four 'Gold Mine Defendants,'" SEC *News Digest*, 3 March 1993. For later legal fallout involving one of the company's young salesmen, see Jeff Founds and Christine Perez, "Lawsuits, Bankruptcy Roil Cool Partners Inc.," *Dallas Business Journal*, 10 May 2002.

73 See, for a survey, ALS Chemical, "Salting Solutions," *Minerals Division Newsletter* 7, no. 4.

74 For an excellent account that puts the gold fraud in context, see Robert McGhee, *The Arctic Voyages of Martin Frobisher* (Montreal: McGill-Queens University Press, 2001).

75 Harold Pringle, "A Tale of Fraud and Frobisher's Gold," *New Scientist*, 25 December 1993; Peggy Berkowitz, "Martin Frobisher's Quest for Gold," *University Affairs*, November 1997. Oddly enough, though citing the same University of Ottawa geologist as the *New Scientist* article, this one claims that Frobisher's people overestimated the gold content not by 10,000 but by 260,000 times. On the other hand the *New Scientist* account claims the

original assay reported 1.5 ounces per ton, not 25. In fact, that first figure makes sense only with modern amalgamation techniques.

76 Paul J. Lechler, *Gold from Water (and Other Mining Scams)* (Reno: Nevada Bureau of Mines and Geology, Special Publication, 1997). One justification sometimes offered for remarkable results is that the company uses a unique assay technique no one else possesses. See also Alan Abelson "Smelling Salt" *Barron's*, 26 May 1997.

77 There was extensive coverage of the scandal especially in John Stackhouse, "The Bre-X Scandal Broke All the Rules It May Have Looked like a Model Exploration Camp. But Operations Were Left to Novices, Sample Testing Standards Were Breached and Secrecy Prevailed," *Globe and Mail*, 6 May 1997; Paul Waldie and John Stackhouse, "The Bre-X Scandal Key Site Manager Is Missing," *Globe and Mail*, 7 May 1997; Janet McFarland and Andrew Bell, "The Bre-X Scandal Search Begins for Bre-X Culprits CEO Pledges to Get to Bottom of Tampering Scandal That Wiped Out some Investors' Savings," *Globe and Mail*, 6 May 1997.

78 Of several works on the Bre-X scandal, the best is Douglas Gould and Andrew Willis, *The Bre-X Fraud* (Toronto: McClelland & Stewart, 1997).

79 There is a wealth of information about Barrick at www.corpwatch.org.

80 On the battle for control of the project, see John McBeth "The Battle for Busang," *Far Eastern Economic Review*, 19 December 1996.

81 Gould and Willis, *The Bre-X Fraud*, passim.

82 "Empty Motherlode," *Far Eastern Economic Review*, 10 April 1997; "Bonaza to Bust," *Far Eastern Economic Review*, 24 April 1997; John Stackhouse et al., "Bre-X: The Untold Story Few People in Canada Know the Real Story of How a Group of Geologists Came to Control the Infamous Busang Gold Site and How Promotion of Bre-X Echoed Their Earlier Work in Australia," *Globe and Mail*, 3 May 1997; Paul Waldie "Report Deepens Bre-X Fiasco Bizarre Behaviour of De Guzman Outlined in Text on Alleged Fraud at Busang," *Globe and Mail*, 19 February 1998.

83 Melody Kemp, "Fool's Gold in Indonesia," *Asia Times*, 19 December 2008.

84 "Gold Obtained from a Decayed Stump," *ScienceDaily*, 20 August 2007.

CHAPTER TWO

1 See Jones Jewelers, "Gems of the Famous," jeweler.website2go.com/p.19. html: "We love the lore of jewels, and we like to share it with our shoppers, too."

2 On how ministers were asked in the midst of the economic crisis if money for schools, hospitals, and low-income families could be diverted to meet royal fuel bills, see Robert Verkaik "Queen Tried to Use State Poverty

Fund to Heat Buckingham Palace," *The Independent*, 24 September 2010. Wisely the ministers realized that it would be a public relations disaster if news got out.

3 See, for example, Leslie Field, *The Queen's Jewels: The Personal Collection of Elizabeth II* (New York: Harry Abrams Inc., 1987).

4 The story is told by the person responsible for cataloguing the collection. See M.J. von Larsons (a pseudonym), *An Expert in the Service of the Soviet* (London: Ernest Benn, 1929), translated from the German original.

5 In addition to Field, *The Queen's Jewels,* op. cit., see Suzy Menkes, *The Royal Jewels* (London: Grafton Books, 1985). In such works typically the question of origin is sidestepped with euphemisms like "confiscation."

6 One of the older but still fairly comprehensive accounts is William Jones, *History and Mystery of Precious Stones* (London: Richard Bentley and Son, 1880). See also Frances Rogers and Alice Beard, *5000 Years of Gems and Jewelry* (New York: Frederick A. Stokes, 1940). For a more detailed survey of the geopolitics of gemstone, see R.T. Naylor, "The Underworld of Gemstones," published in three parts *Crime, Law & Social Change* 53, no. 2–4, 2010.

7 Michael Nash, "Famous Jewels and Their Place in History," *British Heritage* 6, 1985, no. 1, 22–33.

8 Colleen DeBaise, "All That Glitters May Be Risky – Gems Attract Investment Setting Record-High Prices – But Could Tarnish Portfolios," *Wall Street Journal*, 26 November 2005

9 "Gemstone Mining Does Not Harm the Environment," SSM gemological consultants assure prospective clients, adding that "Gemstone mining is a profitable and exiting [*sic*] venture," Swenson & Simonet Minerals (www.ssm-kenya.com).

10 True in the good old days. Now, because of a rerouting of traffic, rue St-Denis is a shadow of its former sleazy self (personal observation: April 2010).

11 "Colombia's Emerald-Street Traders Work a $1 Million-a-Day Gold Mine," *Bloomberg Business News*, reprinted *Baltimore Sun*, 20 March 1995. This emerald flea market survived numerous efforts at reform and liberalization of the emerald business. There is a good survey of the history and the ongoing emerald flea market in "Fighting Colombia's Green War: Treasure of the Emerald Forest," *The Independent*, 29 April 2006.

12 Located in the vicinity of Marsa Alam, near the Red Sea Coast. Later the Romans extracted some emeralds from Austria, and centuries later a few came from Swat in what is now Northern Pakistan. But they were minor sources. Gaston Giuliani et al., "Oxygen Isotopes and Emerald Trade Routes Since Antiquity," *Science* 287, no. 5453, 28 January 2000, 631–3.

13 Timothy Ross, "Bloody End of a Drug King," *Sunday Times*, 17 December 1989; "Colombia Issues Warrant for Israeli Who Trained Cartel Squads," *Israeli Foreign Affairs*, October 1989; "Report Claims City Banks Awash in Cash Laundered by Drug Barons," *Observer*, 26 November 1989; Jeff Gerth, "Report Says Mercenaries Aided Colombian Cartels," *New York Times*, 28 February 1991; Shelley Goldman, "Our Man In Medellin," *The Jerusalem Post*, 8 September 1989; US Senate, Committee on Governmental Affairs, Permanent Subcommittee on Investigations, "Arms Trafficking, Mercenaries and Drug Cartels," *Hearings*, 27–8 February 1991.

14 "Israel Television Identifies Soldier in NBC Film pf Colombian Hit Squads as Head of Security Firm US Alarmed at Report of Israelis in Drug Cartel," *The Jerusalem Post*, 24 August 1989.

15 "Arms Exports and Jobs," *Jerusalem Post*, 5 September 1989, Alon Pinkas, "Yair Klein's Firm to Train Civil Administration Staff," *The Jerusalem Post*, 16 September 1991; Geraldine Brooks, "Loose Cannons: Arms Dealers in Israel Operate Quite Openly on the Fringe Law – Yair Klein Is Unprosecuted in Colombia Drug Case Despite Latest Evidence – A History of Latin Intrigue," *Wall Street Journal*, 9 May 1990.

16 "Israel Seeks Release of Officer in Sierra Leone," *Jerusalem Post*, 21 September 1999; James Rupert, "Diamond Hunters Fuel Africa's Brutal Wars; In Sierra Leone, Mining Firms Trade Weapons and Money for Access to Gems," *The Washington Post*, 16 October 1999; "Israeli Who Trained Colombia Guerillas Wins Appeal against Extradition," *Haaretz*, 1 April 2010. Russia released him in November 2010.

17 Francisco Thoumi, *Political Economy and Illegal Drugs in Colombia* (Boulder, CO: Lynne Reinner, 1995), 139–40.

18 See, for example, Diana Jean Schemo, "Bogata Journal: Emeralds' Luster Hides a Darker Side," *New York Times*, 11 April 1998. For more information on the early green wars, see "All Is Not Green That Glitters," *The Economist*, 21 February 1998; Andy Webb-Vidal, "Colombia's Emerald Thieves Face a Less Glittering Future: The Country's Mine Operators Plan to Crack Down on the Murky Gems Trade and Raise the Prices They Fetch," *Financial Times*, 11 May 2004; Daniel Howden, "Treasure of the Emerald Forest," *The Independent*, 29 April 2006.

19 For Carranza's own views on accusations against him, see "Me reuní con el Alemán y Don Berna, pero no avalé acuerdos con paras ni los financié," *El Tiempo*, 7 June 2009, and "Carranza, al banquillio," *El Espectador*, 6 February 2010. The 2009 attack may have been arranged by a powerful narco who resented Carranza's attempts to undermine his authority in the emerald district; see "Declaración de Guerra," *La Semana*, 12 July 2009. On the later attack, see "Risky Business," www.colombianews.tv, 10 March 2010.

20 I am indebted to Nadir Nurmohamed for much of this information. See also Gary Bowersox, "A Status Report on Gemstones from Afghanistan," *Gems & Gemology*, Winter 1985, and "Emeralds of the Panjshir Valley: Afghanistan," *Gems and Gemology*, Spring 1991; Camelia Entekhabi-Farb, "Northern Alliance Veteran Hopes Emeralds Are Key Part of Afghanistan Economic Recovery," *Eurasian Insight*, 14 October 2002; Lisa Ruth, "Gem Smuggling," *The Ganoksin Project*, July/August 2004, www.ganoksin.com/borisat/newam/gem-smuggling.htm.

21 See Jean-Christophe Servant, "Mined Out in Zambia," *Counterpunch*, 29 May 2009, reprinted from *Le Monde diplomatique*.

22 Thanks to a former student whose family was in the business for inside information on the East Africa gem business.

23 I thank Willard Myers for explaining the intricacies of *guanxi*. See also Sterling Seagrave, *Lords of the Rim* (New York: Corgi, 1995) for an excellent treatment of these issues.

24 "Pigeon blood" is an ancient Burmese term for stones coloured a little like pomegranate seeds, compared to "rabbit blood" ones that are darker and somewhat bluish in tint. After the British arrived, Burmese gemologists added "preference of the British" for deep, hot pink, and even "crying Indian" for very dark red.

25 For an excellent overall treatment, see Richard Hughes, *Ruby & Sapphire* (Boulder, Colorado: RWH Publishing, 1997). See also his "Seeing Red: A Guide to Ruby Connoisseurship," *The Guide* 22, no. 2, March-April 2002.

26 Jeremy "Most Expensive Diamond Necklaces," *The Most Expensive Journal*, 30 June 2008, most-expensive.net/diamond-necklaces.

27 Recounted in "Ruby: the King of Gems," *Gemstone Forecaster* 13, no. 1, Spring 1995.

28 See the superb account of Burma's tortured political history in Thant Myint-U, *The River of Lost Footsteps: A Personal History of Burma* (New York, Farrar, Straus and Giroux, 2007). On the looting and its aftermath, see pp. 20–9.

29 Fred Ward, "Rubies and Sapphires," *National Geographic*, October 1991.

30 Robert Genis, "Burma Spinel: One Of the Most Interesting and Misunderstood Gems in the World," *The Gemstone Forecaster* 13, no. 2, Summer 1995; and Robert Genis, "An Interview with the Burma Connection" *The Gemstone Forecaster* 15, no. 3, Fall 1997.

31 Ted Themelis and Damon Poeter, "Out of the Jungle," *Gemkey* Special Report, 6 March 2000.

32 Richard Hughes, "Death of the Thai Ruby," *JewelSiam* 7, no. 4, August-September 1996; Steven Erlanger, "For Khmer Rouge, There's Gold in the Ruby Mines," *The New York Times*, 12 February 1989; Philip Shenon,

"Lingering Shadow – A Special Report; Rebels still Torment Cambodia 20 Years after Their Rampage," *The New York Times,* 6 February, 1995. There is more coverage of the ruby wars in Southeast Asia particularly in the *Far Eastern Economic Review,* for example in "Rubies are Rouge," 7 February 1991, and "Caught in the Act," 23 December, 1993.

33 Seth Mydans, "In Cambodia, Land Seizures Push Thousands of the Poor into Homelessness," *New York Times,* 27 July 2008.

34 This information was given to me by a former resident of the area who, for security reasons, must remain unnamed.

35 Hamza Kondo, "Tanzanian Ruby Find Brings Hope," *Colored Stone,* August 2003.

36 "Kenya: The Ruby Ripoff," *Time,* 14 October 1974. There was further coverage in *Sunday Times,* 29 September 1974; *International Herald Tribune,* 9 December 1974; *New York Times,* 5 October 1974.

37 For example: "Savana Ruby," www.creativegem.com/gem_deals/html/savanda.htm, and "Ruby – The John Saul Ruby Mine," Swala Gem Traders, www.swalagemtraders.com, 6 February 2008.

38 Private information.

39 For general conditions, see Andrew Walsh, "Hot Money and Daring Consumption in a Northern Malagasy Sapphire-Mining Town," *American Ethnologist* 30, no. 2, 2003; and "In the Wake of Things: Speculating in and about Sapphires in Northern Madagascar," *American Anthropologist* 106, no. 2, 2004; and "Nobody Has a Money Taboo," *Anthropology Today* 22, no. 4, August 2006. See also Rosaleen Duffy, "Global Environmental Governance and the Challenge of Shadow States: The Impact of Illicit Sapphire Mining in Madagascar," *Development and Change* 36, no. 5, 17 October 2005.

40 Bilger Burkhard, "The Race for Madagascar's Jewels," *The New Yorker,* 2 October 2006. See also "New Mining Code Outlined," *Africa Energy & Mining,* 17 May 2000; "New Precious Stones License," *African Mining Intelligence,* 30 May 2001; "Madagascar: The (Blue) Gold Rush," *Indian Ocean Newsletter,* 10 April 1999, and "Sapphire Trafficking Rocks the Trade," *Indian Ocean Newsletter,* 6 April 2002.

41 Cited in "How to Enhance a Relationship: Ancient Techniques," *Mining Journal,* 22 December 1995.

42 Richard Hughes, *Ruby & Sapphire* (Boulder CO: RHH Books, 1997), 31, 139.

43 Walter Schumann, *Handbook of Rocks Minerals and Gemstones* (Boston: Houghton Mifflin, 1993), 159.

44 Kurt Nassau, *Gems Made by Man* (Radnor, PA: Chilton Book Company, 1980), 284.

45 www.lightningridge.net.au.

46 See Fred Ward, *Opals* (Bethesda, MD: Gem Books Publishers, 1997).

47 Richard Hughes, "Cloak and Dagger: The Politics of Opticon," *GQ Eye* 1, no. 1, Fall 1998.

48 Hughes, *Ruby*, 127.

49 Richard Harris and Oliver Galibert, "Fracture Filling/Healing of Mong Hsu Ruby," *Australian Gemologist* 20, no. 2, 1998.

50 Colour diffusion can be detected by experts but amateur buyers are regularly taken. See Richard Hughes, "The Sapphire Face-Lift Face-Off Saga," *Gemological Digest* 3, no. 2, 1991; "There's a Rumble in the Jungle," *Gemological Digest* 3, no. 2, 1991; "Vampire Blues: Blue Surface Diffusion Treated Sapphires," *Jewel Siam*, no. 3, May-June 1992; "A Brief History of Heat" *Australian Gemologist* 19, no. 2, 1995.

51 If the stone already possessed the necessary trace impurities inside itself, oxygen alone will suffice, but that has the risk that the colour change will be uneven. See Victoria Gomelsky, "Treated Sapphires Resemble Padparadscha, AGTA Says," *National Jeweler*, 1 February 2002.

52 My thanks to Pierre Akkalian for introducing me to pearls.

53 An interesting early treatment of these issues is in Edwin Streeter, *Pearls and the Pearling Life* (London: George Bell & Sons, 1886).

54 An excellent early account is George Frederick Kunz and Charles Hugh Stevenson, *The Book of Pearl: The History, Art, Science, and Industry of the Queen of Gems* (New York: The Century Company, 1908).

55 See the impressive compendium of information in R.A. Donkin, *Beyond Price, Pearls and Pearl Fishing: Origins to the Age of Discoveries* (Philadelphia: American Philosophical Society, 1998).

56 These industry trends are examined in Fred Ward's *Pearls* (Bethesda: Gem Publishers, 1998).

57 The internet gem seller (www.internetstones.com) raves about a "sensational breakthrough by Scientists at FAU's Harbor Branch Oceanographic Institute" in culturing queen conch pearls. For more on the jewellery trade's view, see David Federman, "Conch Pearl: Pink Pleasure," *Modern Jeweler*, www.modernjeweler.com/web/online/Pearl-Gem-Profiles/Conch-Pearl/3$254.

58 Two useful, if somewhat dated, general overviews are by Nassau, *Gems Made by Man*; and L.H. Yaverbaum (ed.), *Synthetic Gems Production Techniques* (New Jersey; Noyes Data Corp., 1980).

59 Hughes, *Ruby*, 154.

60 See the useful but also somewhat dated survey by Gordon Axon, "Gems: Be on Your Guard," *Consumers' Research*, June 1989.

61 On the absurd hoopla about al-Qa'idah supposedly trading tanzanite, see R.T. Naylor, *Satanic Purses: Money, Myth, and Misinformation in the War on Terror* (Montreal: McGill-Queen's University Press, 2006), 270–3.

See "Tanzanian Government Bans Export of Rough Tanzanite," *Jewellery Business*, August 2005.

62 The news was widely reported. See, for example, "Gem Expert Campbell Bridges Killed by Kenyan Mob after Mining Row," *Times of London*, 13 August 2009. See also *The Independent*, 13 August 2009; *Wall Street Journal*, 3 September 2009; *Daily Nation* (Nairobi), 22 August 2009.

63 See the story about Hasson and his pro golf clients in *Golf Digest*, May 2000, and its "Correction Notice" in its July issue of the same year. Much the same story is told in *Golf Today* ("Jeweler Accused of Defrauding Norman & Nicklaus"), www.golftoday.co.uk/news/yeartodate/news00/jewellryfraud.html.

64 For an in-depth story, see Pam Lambert, "Knave of Diamonds," *People* 53, no. 5, 7 February 2000.

65 There was a long series of articles on the affair in the *Palm Beach Post*: Mary McLachlin, "Collector Claims Gardens Jeweler Bilked Him out of $60 Million," 11 April 1998; Mary McLachlin, "The Shark Feels Bitten by Diamond Dealings," 5 October 1998; Mary McLachlin, "Hasson's Lawyers Trying to Block Trial," 31 October 1999; Mary McLachlin, "Jeweler Jailed on Fraud Charges," 13 April 1999; Mary McLachlin, "Hasson Loses Lawyers, Lawsuit Delay Attempt," 6 May 1999; Mary McLachlin, "Hasson, Ex-Employee Sparred over Hush Money, Inmate Says," 13 February 2000; Mary McLachlin, "Hasson Guilty in Jewel Swindle," 26 February 2000; Mary McLachlin, "Convicted Jewel Dealer Sent to Prison Solitary," 1 April 2000; Mary McLachlin, "Jeweler Gets 40 Years, Ordered to Pay $78 Million Sentence Follows Bizarre Court Scene" 9 June 2000; "Hasson Motion Derided, Dismissed," 3 September 2000; 3 August 2001; 18 June 2003; Mary McLachlin, "Diamond Jack in Prison, but Lawsuits Continue," 2 January 2005. There was also extensive coverage in other newspapers, such as *Cox News Service*, 17 January 1999; *Broward Daily Business Review*, 9 August 1996; "Jury Finds Jeweler to Rich, Famous Guilty on Six Counts of Fraud," *Associated Press*, 25 February 2000; Tom Rhodes, "Gem of a Scam in Palm Beach – An Island of Millionaires, a Confidence Man and a Truckload of Fake Jewelry," *The Toronto Star*, 19 March 2000; Rick Steelhammer, "Jewel Scammer Nabbed When He Visits Mom Florida Convict Violated Supervised Release, Police Say" *Charleston Gazette*, 3 October 2002. On Hasson's interesting associations while in prison, see "Jailed Jeweler Filing Motions to Harass Man He Defrauded" *Miami Herald*, 2 January 2001.

66 Anthony M. DeStefano et al., "False Glitter: Gem-Secured Loans Turn Sour in Europe, Resulting in Big Losses ..." *Wall Street Journal*, 20 August 1985.

67 For the full text see www.govtrack.us/congress/bill.xpd?bill=h110–3890.

68 For an excellent critique of this idiocy, see Myint-U, *River*, 331–44 et passim.

69 See the debate in 1995 at the Athens Conference of the Confederation of Jewelry, Silverware, Diamonds, Pearls and Stones reported in *Jewellery News Asia*, July 1995. "Normal" industry practices were defined to include bleaching of coral or ivory, impregnating stones with a colourless organic solid, or staining things like agate.

70 Thanks to Professor Pamela Ritchie of NASCAD University in Halifax, Nova Scotia, for her comments on this issue.

CHAPTER THREE

1 www.melaniatrump.com/pictures.

2 Floyd Norris, "Trump Sees Act of God in Recession," *New York Times*, 4 December 2008. On Trump's presidential aspirations, see Ben McConville (AP), "Trump Hints He May Run against Obama in 2012," *The Independent*, 9 October 2010.

3 www.melaniatrump.com/press.

4 The whitest pearls were also on his list. Jean-Baptiste Tavernier, *Travels in India* (ed. William Crooke) (reprinted London: Oxford University Press, 1925), 91.

5 Tavernier, *Travels*, 41, 45–8, 48–9, 53. For the history of India's mines, see M. S. Shukla, *History of Gem Industry in Ancient & Medieval India* (Varanasi: Bharat-Bharati, 1972). On royal controls and taxes, see Abdul Aziz, *The Imperial Treasury of the Indian Mughals* (New Delhi: Jayyed Press, 1972), 144–6.

6 There is a huge literature on the diamond trade. Early works include A.C. Austin and Marion Mercer, *The Story of Diamonds* (Chicago: Jewelers Association, 1935); Godehard Lenzen, *History of Diamond Production and the Diamond Trade* (New York: Praeger, 1970); Robert Maillard et al., *Diamonds: Myth, Magic and Reality* (New York: Crown Publishers, 1980). In the 1980s, when the mystique began to be systematically dismantled, there were Timothy Green, *The World of Diamonds* (New York: William Morrow, 19810; David Koskoff, *The Diamond World* (New York: Harper & Row, 1981); Edward Jay Epstein *The Diamond Invention: The Rise and Fall of Diamonds* (New York: Simon and Schuster, 1983). More recently see George Harlow (ed.), *The Nature of Diamonds* (Cambridge: Cambridge University Press, 1998). Of the up-to-date critical books, the most comprehensive is Janine Roberts, *Glitter & Greed: The Secret World of the Diamond Cartel* (New York; The Disinformation Company, 2003).

7 Simon Tolansky, *The Strategic Diamond* (Edinburgh, Oliver & Boyd, 1968), 42.

8 On this, see Robert Proctor, "Anti-Agate: The Great Diamond Hoax and the Semiprecious Stone Scam," *Configurations* 9, no. 3, Fall 2001.

9 This story is commonly cited in the diamond trade. See, for one of many examples, "The History of Diamonds," *Diamond Wholesale Corporation* (White Bison & Son), www.diamondwholesalecorporation.com/diamond-history.html, 12 September 2010. Although this instance may be a classic case of a fact by repetition, the use of diamond powder as an assassination device is well established.

10 Tolansky, *Strategic*, 6–12; Robert Hazen, *The Diamond Makers* (Cambridge: Cambridge University Press, 1999), 2–6, 13.

11 Ulrich Boser, "Diamonds on Demand," *Smithsonian Magazine*, June 2008.

12 In addition to Tavernier's own account, see the recent reconstruction of the interaction of Indian and British societies in William Dalrymple, *White Mughals: Love & Betrayal in Eighteenth-Century India* (London: HarperCollins, 2002), xxxvii-xxxviii, 112.

13 There is good material on the early gold and diamond rushes in C. R. Boxer, *The Golden Age of Brazil 1695–1750* (Berkeley: University of California Press, 1962); Kenneth Maxwell, *Conflicts and Conspiracies: Brazil and Portugal 1750–1808* (Cambridge: Cambridge University Press, 1973); Bailey Diffie, *A History of Colonial Brazil: 1500–1792* (Malabar: Robert E. Kreiger Publishing Company, 1987); and Norman P. Macdonald, *The Making of Brazil: Portuguese Roots, 1500–1822* (Sussex: The Book Guild Ltd, 1996). The shifting regulations and their objectives are explained in Harry Bernstein, *The Brazilian Diamond in Contracts, Contraband and Capital* (Lanham: University Press of America, 1988).

14 Austin and Mercer, *Story*, 19.

15 Bernstein, *Brazilian Diamond*, 69–79.

16 There is a wealth of information on the nineteenth-century diamond and gold rushes in South Africa. A general overview is Geoffrey Wheatcroft, *The Randlords* (London: Weidenfeld & Nicolson, 1985); for the labour question in the gold fields, see Charles van Onselen, *Studies in the Social and Economic History of the Witwatersrand, 1886–1914, Vol. I: New Babylon* (Essex: Longman Publishing Group, 1982), and *Chibaro: African Mine Labour in Southern Rhodesia, 1900–1933* (London: Pluto Press, 1976). On the diamond mines and trades, see William Worger, *South Africa's City of Diamonds, Mine Workers and Monopoly Capitalism in Kimberley, 1867–1895* (New Haven: Yale University Press, 1987); Robert Vicat Turrell, *Capital and Labor in the Kimberley Diamond Fields, 1871–1890* (Cambridge: Cambridge University Press, 1987); and Colin

Newbury, *The Diamond Ring: Business, Politics and Precious Stones in South Africa, 1867–1947* (Oxford: Clarendon Press, 1989).

17 J.T. Muirhead, *Ivory Poaching and Cannibals in Africa* (London: McMillan & Company, 1933), 10–14.

18 Wheatcroft, *Randlords*, 109; Worger, *City*, 134–5; Truell, *Capital*, 5, 175.

19 Maillard, *Diamonds*, 72.

20 See especially David Pallister, Sarah Stewart, and Ian Lepper, *South Africa Inc.: The Oppenheimer Empire* (London: Simon & Schuster, 1987).

21 Worger, *City*, 96, 139–40; Truell, *Capital*, 147–9.

22 Colin Newbury, *The Diamond Ring: Business Politics and Precious Stones and South Africa, 1867–1947* (Oxford: Clarendon Press, 1989), 361, 133.

23 Charles Higham, *Trading with the Enemy: An Expose of the Nazi-"American Money Plot, 1933–1947* (Delacorte Press: New York, 19830, 30, 71.

24 Michael Dynes, "Diamond Rackets Aided the Germans – Wartime Documents Released," *Times of London*, 8 September 1994.

25 Victor Osipov, *Siberian Diamonds* (Moscow: Foreign Languages Publishing House, 1958), 25–7.

26 Green, *Diamonds*, 102; Green, *Smugglers*, 182.

27 The best-known instance was the De Beers economic war against Zaire when it withdrew from cartel marketing arrangements in 1982. See "De Beers Maintains Iron Grip on World's Supply of Diamonds," *Wall Street Journal*, 7 July 1983. See also related story in *The Economist*, 10 January 1987.

28 For the industry view, see World Diamond Council, "Diamond Mining and the Environment Fact Sheet," *Diamond Facts* (World Diamond Council), www.diamondfacts.org/pdfs/media/media_resources/fact_sheets/Diamond_Mining_Environment_Fact_Sheet.pdf, 12 September 2010.

29 There are countless tales of conditions in Namibia. Espstein wrote an early exposé in *Diamond Invention*. See more recently Matthew Hart, "How to Steal a Diamond," *The Atlantic Monthly*, March 1999, and the references to Namibia in Roberts, *Glitter and Greed*, passim. "The Financial Times Reports on the Oranjemund Diamond Mine in Namibia Which is Run by CDM, a De Beers Subsidiary," *Financial Times*, 3 March 1984; "Diamond Company Digs in for Better Cut," *Financial Times*, 24 June 1997; Christopher S. Wren, "Oranjemund Journal; Swapo and De Beers: Are They Engaged to Wed?" *New York Times*, 10 October 1989.

30 On these tactics in Sierra Leone, see Fouad Kamil, *The Diamond Underworld* (London: Allen Lane, 1979); A.W. Cockerill, *Sir Percy Sillitoe* (London: W.H. Allen, 1975); H.L. Van Der Laan, *The Sierra Leone Diamonds* (Oxford: Oxford University Press, 1965); Michael Harbottle, *The Knaves*

of *Diamonds* (London: Seeley, 1976); and Peter Greenhalgh, *West African Diamonds: 1919–1983* (Manchester: Manchester University Press, 1985).

31 According to *Africa Confidential*, 6 November 1992, a now defunct insider political report well fed by various intelligence agencies.

32 Green, *Diamonds*, 189, 223. To this day diamond traders in Antwerp react to occasional tax raids with threats to leave. See Carol Matlack, "Police Raid Diamond Dealers: Are the Diamonds Forever?" *Der Spiegel*, 25 May 2007.

33 On the emergence of the industry, see Aravind Adiga "Uncommon Brilliance: How Did India *Come* to Dominate the Vastly Lucrative Global Market for Cutting and Polishing Diamonds," *Time-Asia Magazine*, 12 April 2004. For a short sketch that may reveal more than its authors intended, see "Historical Gem Cutting Regions: Surat & Gujarat Province, India," *All about Gemstones*, www.allaboutgemstones.com/history_gem_cutting_gujarat.html, 12 September 2010.

34 Roberts, *Glitter*, 52.

35 Private information from a former diamond dealer.

36 Callahan, *Insider Secrets*, 90–4.

37 "India Wants Details on Its Diamond Traders' Arrest in China," *Thaindian News*, 12 January 2010; "Surat Diamond Traders Flay arrest of Indians in China," *Thaindian News*, 12 January 2010 "India again Seeks Access to Jailed Diamond Traders in China" *Hindustan Times*, 3 April 2010; "Indian Diamond Traders May Pull Out of China," *The Financial Express Commodity Online*, 17 January 2010. The spokesman for the Surat Diamond Association insisted it was just a matter of a misunderstanding of the regulations.

38 *Kol Ha'ir*, 14 April 1989; *Yediot Ahronot*, 17 July 1992. There have been other claims that the laundering fee was only 2–3 percent.

39 There is excellent coverage in "Israeli Drug Money Launderers Snared by Sting," *Israeli Foreign Affairs*, 25 June 1993.

40 The apparent relationship between Low and Prushinowski is outlined by Michael Gillard, "City: Dope, Diamonds and Deceit," *Observer*, 21 February 1993. During his five-year sentence for money-laundering ("Rabbi Faces Prison Term on Conspiracy Conviction," *Orlando Sentinel*, 9 April 1994) Low struck a deal with the US Bureau of Prisons to allow him to use a donated Torah scroll in his cell and requiring the prison to accept the donation of twenty-five prayer books for other Jewish inmates ("Imprisoned Rabbi Reaches Settlement with Officials," *Los Angeles Times*, 7 June 1998). On Rabbi Low's affairs, see variously *Los Angeles Times*, 12, 13 and 28 January 1993; *Forward*, 29 January 1993; *The Independent*, 13 January 1993; *Star Tribune*, 13 January 1993.

41 See, for example, Eric Greenberg, "Chassidic Rabbis Implicated in Colombian Drug Trade," *Jweekly.com*, 20 June 1997. See also Larry Neumeister, "Hasidic Sect Shocked by Drug Money Charges against Rabbis," *Associated Press*, 18 June 1997.

42 United States District Court for the Central District of California, *United States v. Naftali Tzi Weisz et al.*, February 2007, First Superseding Indictment CR 06–775 (A). See also "Top US Rebbe Gets Two Years in Jail for Money-Laundering," *Haaretz*, 22 December 2009.

43 Amy Klein, "The Spinka Money Trail – and the Informant Who Brought Them All Down," *The Jewish Journal*, 10 January 2008.

44 The prosecutor at the sentencing hearing announced that "The government concurs with the PSR's (the probation office) assessment that the offense predated Weisz's involvement, having origins generations past, and that it appears to be replicated by a number of other Hasidic organizations throughout the world today. This is a mitigating factor in that Weisz cannot accurately be considered the 'mastermind' of the scheme," cited in Harry Marlyes, "Chasidim and the Spinka Rebbe," *Emes Ve-Emuhah*, 22 December 2009, haemtza.blogspot.com/2009/12/chasidim-and-spinka-rebbe.html, accessed 14 September 2010.

45 United States Attorney for the Southern District of New York, "US Charges Four Diamond District Dealers with Bank Fraud in Massive Check Kiting Scheme," 16 October 2003, and "US Announced Guilty Pleas of Four Diamond District Dealers in Massive Check-Kiting Scheme," 10 June 2004; United States Court of Appeals Second Circuit, *United States of America, Appellee v. David Klein et al.*, decided 5 February 2007. There is a summary in Rob Bates "Dealer and Three Others Convicted of Check Kiting," JCK-*Jewelers Circular Keystone Magazine*, 1 October 2004.

46 "Assets Frozen in Fraud Case," *The Israeli Diamond Industry*, 25 July 2007; See also JCK-*Jewelers Circular Keystone*, 1 September 2007, and "Diamond Dealer Accused of Stealing $3.4 Million in Gems," *Newsday*, 22 April 2008.

47 Kurt Nassau, Shane McClure, Shane Elen, and James Shigly, "Synthetic Moissanite: A New Diamond Substitute," *Gems & Gemology* 33, no. 4, Winter 1997; Tiajinm Lu and James Shigley, "Nondestructive Testing for Identifying Natural, Synthetic, Treated and Imitation Gem Materials," *Materials Evaluation* 58, no. 10, October 2000.

48 Dan Egbert "North Carolina-Based Gemstone Maker Cuts Staff," *News & Observer*, 1 November 2000.

49 Kurt Nassau, *Gems Made by Man* (Radnor, PA: Chilton Book Company, 1980), 233; James Shigley, Reza Abbaschian, and Carter Clarke, "Gemesis Laboratory-Created Diamonds," *Gems & Gemology* 36, no. 4, Winter 2002; Johan Koivula, Maha Tannous, and Karl Schmetzer, "Synthetic

Gem Materials and Simulates in the 1990s," *Gems & Gemology* 36, no. 4, Winter 2000; "A Gem of a Diamond," *The Engineer*, 12 September 2003. For an up-to-date survey of the technology and commerce, see Ulrich Boser, "Diamonds on Demand," *Smithsonian Magazine*, June 2008.

50 See for example, LifeGem (www.LifeGem.com), whose Memorial Diamond "provides a lasting memory that endures just as a diamond does."

51 Thanks to Brandon Reti for research on this topic.

52 *Jewelers' Circular Keystone*, February 1989.

53 "Diamond Test Success for Pegasus," *The Mining Journal*, 17 March 2000.

54 Shipley, *Famous Diamonds*, 4–5.

55 See Whitney Sielaff, "An Honest, Hard Day's Work," *National Jeweler* 98, no. 19, 1 October 2004.

56 John Kidman, "Fake Diamond Scam Smashed in Sydney," *Sydney Morning Herald*, 27 April 2003; Michael Gillard, "Internet Guarantee as Flawed as Gems," *London Evening Standard*, 1 June 2003; Avi Krawitz, "Israeli Diamond Cutters Indicted for $600K Fraud," *Diamonds.net* (Rapaport, n.d.), www.diamonds.net/NewsItem.aspz?ArticleID=21982. GIA filed an international lawsuit alleging counterfeiting against Weisbrot in Israel, and obtained injunctions. "GIA Legal Actions Stop Counterfeit Diamond Grading Reports," *Couture Jeweler* (Neilsen Business Media Inc.), 26 April 2003. See also Rob Bates, "Australian Man Arrested for Using Fake GIA Reports," *JCK Magazine*, 1 June 2003.

57 Jeff Miller, "Pincione vs Vivid, GIA," *Diamonds.net* (Rapaport, n.d.), reprinted in *The Gemstone Forecaster* 23, no. 3, 26 August 2005; "GIA and Pincione Settle Lawsuit," *Modern Jeweler*, 1 February 2006; Rob Bates, "GIA under the Loupe," *JCK-Jewelers Circular Keystone*, January 2006. See also James Doran "Diamond Market Falls Victim to Fraudsters," *Times of London*, 22 December 2005; Anne Zimmerman and Anita Raghavan, "Diamond Group Widens Probe of Bribe Charges," *Wall Street Journal*, 8 March 2006.

58 On the major contours of the affair, see Thomas Kamm, "Fall of Venerable Chaumet Jewelery Firm Shocks France," *Wall Street Journal*, 14 July 1987; Georges Marion and Edwy Plenel, "The Bankrupt Jewellers That Piled Up Some Amazing Debts," *Manchester Guardian*, 8 November 1987; Paul Rambali, "The fall of the house of Chaumet," *Independent on Sunday*, 19 January 1992. "Justice Minister Tied to Jeweler Scandal, *Facts on File*, 13 November 1987. Steven Greenhouse, "A Scandal in French Jewelry," *New York Times*, 14 June 1987.

59 The most complete accounts are by Dave Kaplan and Christian Caryl, "The Looting of Russia," *US News & World Report*, 26 July 1998, and by Peter Byrne, *SF Weekly*, 1 July 1998. See also Federal Bureau of

Investigation, "Golden Ada Company San Francisco, California," www. fbi.gov/hq/cid/orgcrime/casestudies/goldenada.htm, and *Moscow Times*, 13 February 1999.

60 The plan is outlined in *JCK-Jewelers Circular Keystone*, March 1995

61 See Anne Woolner, *Washed in Gold: The Story behind the Biggest Money-Laundering Investigation in US History* (New York: Simon & Schuster, 1994) and Robert Powis, *The Money Launderers: Lessons from the Drug Wars – How Billions of Illegal Dollars Are Washed through Banks and Businesses* (Chicago: Probos Professional Publishing Co., 1992), chapter 5.

62 There is actually a discrepancy between the two accounts mentioned above. Byrne has the spending spree following the second shipment, the $88 million in rough diamonds; Kaplan seems to think it occurred after the first shipment of $90 million worth of valuables from The Closet. This seems to make more sense.

63 Kozlenok later spent four years in prison. "Golden ADA Kingpin Released after Four Years in Jail," *Israel Diamonds*, 1 February 2002.

64 Leonid Nikitinsky, "The End of the Golden ADA," *Moscow News*, 13 February 1997; Mark Whitehouse, "Brilliant Mistake," *Moscow News*, 15 April 1997, 23 June 2001; "Government Still Short of Golden ADA Assets," Izvestia Information Inc – *BizEkon News*, 15 November 2001. On the fate of the participants, see Anastasia Kornya, "Kozlenok Gets Lenient Sentence for Grand Larceny," *Moscow News*, 23 May 2001, and "Convicted Ex-Head of State Precious Metals Committee Asks Supreme Court to Reverse Verdict," *Interfax News Agency*, 21 August 2001. In the final analysis the Supreme Court remitted Kozlenok's sentence and pardoned Bychkov (Leonid Berres, "Supreme Court Remitted Sentences to Diamond Smugglers," *Kommersant*, 15 November 2001).

65 Patti Waldmeir, "De Beers to Spin Off Overseas Interests," *Financial Times*, 7 March 1990.

66 "Diamond Cartel Cuts Up Rough," *Financial Times*, 24 August 1995.

67 Rebecca Bream and Nicol Delgi Innocenti, "De Beers Hopes to Break into US Diamond Market," *Financial Times*, 28 July 2003.

68 R.W. Winder, "The Lebanese in West Africa," *Immigrants and Associations* (The Hague, 1967), L.A. Fallers (ed.).

69 Ian Fleming, *The Diamond Smugglers* (New York: Collier Books, 1964).

70 Fleming, *Smugglers*, 18–9, 33, 37, 42.

71 Fleming, *Smugglers*, 148.

72 When Fleming raised the story of the Soviet diamond discovery, "John Blaize" assured him that "No one's ever seen anything to back that story up" (Fleming, *Smugglers*, 147).

73 The individual, Fouad "Flash Fred" Kamil, told his story in *Diamond Underworld*. It needs to be read with a certain degree of skepticism.

74 The story is outlined in Cockerill, *Sir Percy Sillitoe*.

75 The most influential investigation was "For a Few Dollars More: How al Qaeda Moved into the Diamond Trade," by Global Witness, the NGO that had, since 1998, taken the lead in lobbying for controls on the traffic in diamonds. See also Greg Campbell, *Blood Diamonds: Tracing the Deadly Path of the World's Most Precious Stones* (Boulder, CO: Westview Press, 2002), which takes much the same line.

76 See, for example, "Angola Swoops on Diamond Diggers," BBC *News*, 10 April 2004. The news from Zimbabwe has been much worse, finally prompting efforts to extend the concept of conflict diamonds to places in which police and army brutalize the illegal miners and child labour is extensive (a much more laudable and urgent exercise than inventing tales about Islamic terrorists), but so far without much success.

77 "De Beers: Come Clean to Be Clean," *Global Policy Forum*, 24 March 2000.

78 "De Beers Brands Diamonds," BBC *News*, 4 March 1999.

79 Roberts, *Glitter and Greed*, 326–34.

80 Nor have they stopped. Global Witness still calls on the public to demand from sales staff if they can reassure them that their stones are "conflict-free." On the continued campaign, and its rationalization, see David Howden "Exclusive: The Return of Blood Diamonds," *The Independent*, 25 June 2009. For a review of the "evidence" see Naylor, *Satanic Purses*, chapter 17; For a dissection of accusations made in the American press about al-Qā'idah diamond-dealing, see Christian Dietrich and Peter Danssaert, "Antwerp Blamed, Again," *International Peace Information Service*, 16 November 2001. See also testimony of Christian Dietrich to the Commission d'enquête parlementaire "Grands Lacs" of the Sénat de Belgique, 11 January 2002. He comments, "I cannot imagine that Al Qaida agents would be terribly good in dealing in diamonds unless they could take protection fees from somebody."

81 "Millenium Bras," *The Gemstone Forcaster* 17, no. 4, Winter 1999. There was competition from Triumph International of Germany, which unveiled in Tokyo its own Millenium Bra made from gold thread, hand-woven into fifteenth-century-style "bobbin lace" and strategically decorated with a 15-carat diamond in the centre. It was to sell for only $1.9 million. Incidentally the $6.5 million bra offered 2005 may have been a bargain – the same company priced its Millennium Bra at $10 million.

82 Terri Judd, "Diamond-Encrusted Credit Cards for 'VVIP' Clients," *The Independent*, 15 November 2007.

83 Alan Riding, "Alas, Poor Art Market," *New York Times*, 7 June 2007.
84 James Pomfret, "Rare Blue Diamond to Be Auctioned Off in Hong Kong," *Reuters*, 4 October 2007.

CHAPTER FOUR

1 See, for example, John Noble Wilford, "Full-Figured Statuette, 35,000 Years Old, Provides New Clues to How Art Evolved," *New York Times*, 14 May 2009.
2 Thanks to Ceren Baysan, Sarah el-Fahmy, Melissa Garcia-Lamarca, Laura Kirshner, Sean Hallisey, Stephanie Outerbridge, and Brandon Reti for their research on various aspects of the modern art market. For an excellent overview of its absurdities, see Don Thompson's recent *The $12 Million Stuffed Shark: The Curious Economics of Contemporary Art* (Toronto: Doubleday Canada, 2008).
3 Thomas Hoving, *False Impressions: The Hunt for Big-Time Art Fakes* (New York, 1996), 60–2. This is the de facto professional memoir of the former director of the Metropolitan Museum of Art.
4 On this process, see Stuart Ewen, *All Consuming Images: The Politics of Style in Contemporary Culture* (New York: Basic Books, 1999), 17.
5 Gerald Reitlinger, *The Economics of Taste: The Rise and Fall of the Picture Market 1766–1960* (New York: Holt, Rinehart & Winston, 1961), 39.
6 Keith Middlemas, *The Double Market: Art Theft and Art Thieves* (Middlemas UK: Saxon House, 1975), 2–3.
7 Ewen, *All Consuming*, 27–9.
8 The most comprehensive work on the seedy side of the art market is John Conklin, *Art Crime* (Westport, CT: Praeger, 1994). For a recent updating and refining of some of the analysis and conclusions of Conklin's work, see Simon Mackenzie's "Criminal and Victim Profiles in Art Theft: Opportunity and Repeat Victimization," *Art, Antiquities and Law* 10, no. 4, 2005.
9 See the still very informative work of Gustavus Myer, *History of the Great American Fortunes* (New York: 1907).
10 On these trends, Peter Watson, *From Manet to Manhattan: The Rise of the Modern Art Market* (New York: Random House, 1992).
11 The story is told by the person responsible for cataloguing the collection. See M.J. von Larsons (a pseudonym), *An Expert in the Service of the Soviet* (London: Ernest Benn, 1929), translated from the German original.
12 There are two excellent works on this process. Robert Williams, *Russian Art and American Money 1900–1940* (Cambridge, MA: Harvard

University Press, 1980), and Edward Jay Epstein, *Dossier: The Secret History of Armand Hammer* (New York: Knopf, 1996).

13 Watson, *From Manet to Manhattan*, 243.

14 Roberta Smith, "The Art of the Art Deal: A Portrait of the Old Master," *The New York Times*, 19 November 2004. Oddly, the most recent biography of the Duveens (Meryle Secrest, *Duveen: A Life in Art*, New York: Knopf, 2004) has only a passing mention of this phenomenon.

15 Secrest, *Duveen*, 95–8, 135.

16 Remarkably little of the burgeoning literature on World War II deals with this issue – confirming the proverb that so much history is a fable written by victors. For one exception, see the works of Kenneth Alford: *The Spoils of World War II: The American Military's Role in Sealing Europe's Treasures* (New York: Carol Publishing Group, 1995) and *Nazi Plunder: Great Treasure Stories of World War II* (Mason City: De Capo, 2000).

17 Ulrike Knöfel and Marion Kraske, "Stealing Beauty: Dispute Rages over Austria's Looted Art," *Der Spiegel*, 4 April 2008; Tony Paterson, "The Nazis, the Jewish Banker, and the Battle for Two Priceless Picassos," *The Independent*, 22 August 2008.

18 See the accounts in Robert Frank, *Richistan: A Journey Through the American Wealth Boom and the Lives of the New Rich* (New York: Crown Business, 2007).

19 Of major works on the art market, Middlemas (in *Double Market*, passim), although writing at the very beginning of the art-investment boom, remains one of the few to fully understand the significance of this.

20 Lawrence Malkin, "Why Buy Art? It Is Actually a Lousy Investment," *Connoisseur*, October 1989, and "The Day the Art Market Collapsed," *Connoisseur*, May 1990.

21 Arifa Akbar, "A Multilingual Battle Where Money Talks," *The Independent*, 22 June 2006; Louise Jury, "A Record-Breaking Week of Art Auctions in the Culture Capital," *The Independent*, 8 February 2007; David Usborne; "Record-Breaking Rothko and Bacon Sale Confirms Contemporary Art Market Fever," *The Independent*, 17 May 2007.

22 See the acccount by Jeffrey St Clair, "Fixers Indicated That Hillary Was a Key Player in the Marc Rich Pardon Deal: Bill Clinton and the Rich Women," *Counterpunch* 15, no. 8, 29 May 2008.

23 On the financial absurdities of the art trade, see especially Thompson, *Stuffed Shark*, op. cit, passim.

24 Hoving, *False*, 243.

25 Joshua Levine, "Deco Raiders," *Forbes*, 27 December 2004.

26 See the description of the collecting-investing activities of the Mugrabi family in Erick Konigsberg, "Is Anybody Buying Art These Days," *New York Times*, 27 February 2009.

27 Thompson, *Stuffed Shark*, 38 et passim.

28 James Sterngold, "Some Big Japanese Art Purchases Are under Scrutiny for Scandal," *The New York Times*, 23 April 1991.

29 This is not just ancient history. According to an art expert in Rome cited by Timothy Green, *The Smugglers* (London: Michael Joseph, 1967), 231: "Look, there is no other way that a new American museum can build its collections. Any dealer who smuggles is providing a valuable, albeit illegal, service."

30 This point was made by Karl Meyer in his classic *The Plundered Past* (New York: Atheneum, 1973), 47. It rings even more true today.

31 Yet even with modern stuff, their vetting procedures seem intended mainly to give them an alibi. Thanks to Simon Mackenzie for drawing my attention to the tokenism that often substitutes from true diligence.

32 Middlemas, *Double*, 14–6; Thomas Hoving, "Don't Kick the Stock Ticker," *Connoisseur*, May 1990; Timothy Cone, "The Kindness of Strangers: Restoring Incentives to Be Generous," *Connoisseur*, September 1990.

33 For an example of the legally convoluted consequences, see Her Majesty the Queen (Appellant) v. Robert E. Zelinski et al (Respondents) 2000 DTC 6001 Federal Court of Appeal 10 December 1999, Court File Nos. A–742–96, A–743–96, A –744–96.

34 John L. Hess, *The Grand Acquisitors* (Boston: Houghton Mifflin, 1974), 49.

35 In Canada, the Cultural Property Review Board determines which institutions are eligible to receive donations; it also has the responsibility for certifying something as a bona fide piece of cultural property before it becomes eligible for tax write-offs. That seems a like a good safeguard except that seven of the ten members of the board are dealers, collectors, or curators. In the US, a cultural donation is treated exactly like any other charitable gift; and the sole role of the advisory panel of the IRS (again made up of industry insiders) is to confirm certain appraisals if the IRS is in any doubt – i.e., if it expects they are inflated. Needless to say, since the committee is made up of dealers and museum directors, it is more likely to agree with a high appraisal. My thanks to Sarah el-Fashny for these points.

36 A partial exception is in France, where heirs to big collections can pay estate taxes partly in the form of art directly donated to an accredited public institution (Timothy Cone, "The Kindness of Strangers," *Arts Magazine*, May-September 1990). This does not keep large European museums from soliciting donations from wealthy North Americans.

37 See Daniel Grant, "Tax Write-Offs for Charity Help Giver more than Poor," *Christian Science Monitor*, 23 December 2007.

38 On the mechanics of capital flight to Switzerland in this era, see R.T. Naylor, *Hot Money and the Politics of Debt*, 3rd ed. (Montreal: McGill-Queen's University Press, 2004), chapters 15–16. On the emergence of art mutual-funds in Switzerland, see Middlemas, *Double*, 68.

39 For example the shuffle by Larry Gogosian and his associates that led to a celebrated tax case. See Carol Vogel, "Art Dealer and 3 Others Sued over $26.5 Million in Taxes," *The New York Times*, 20 March 2003; Brooks Barnes, "Deals & Dealmakers: Tax Inquiry Places a Spotlight on Art Dealing, 'Go-Go' Dealer – Beginning as a Messenger, Gagosian Now Handles Multimillion-Dollar Works," *The Wall Street Journal*, 7 March 2003; Phoebe Hoban, "The Artful Dealer," *New York Magazine*, 26 May 2003; *United States of America v. Lawrence Gagosian et al.*, United States District Court Southern District of New York, 19 March 2003. Since it was a civil case, the resolution is confidential; but see "The Fine Art of the Deal," *The Independent*, 2 November 2007.

40 David McKittrick, "Stone Claims Stormont Raid Was 'Art,'" *The Independent*, 23 September 2008; John Lichfield, "On Trial: The Question of What Is Modern Art," *The Independent*, 1 December 2009.

41 "Asceticism as Art," *Wildmind Meditation News*, 13 March 2010.

42 Others catered to the less well-heeled, though at much higher rates. See, for example, Aline Sullivan, "For Art Lovers, Borrowing to Buy Is an Exacting Science," *International Herald Tribune*, 12 December 1992.

43 On theft and fencing of art works, see Middlemas, *The Double Market: Art Theft and Art Thieves*, and Laurence Massey, *Le vol d'oeuvres d'art: une criminalité méconnue* (Bruxelles: Editions Bruyland, 2000).

44 For example, the 2009 theft in Brussels of René Magritte's "Olympia" (David Itzkoff, "Magritte Painting Stolen," *New York Times*, 24 September 2009).

45 A point well made by Simon Mackenzie, "Criminal and Victim Profiles in Art Theft: Motive, Opportunity and Repeat Victimisation," *Art Antiquity and Law* 10, no. 4, 353–70, 2005.

46 Similarly, late in 2007, the Saõ Paulo Museum of Art suffered its first (reported) theft in sixty years, losing a small, undoubtedly real Picasso; it, too, was found abandoned a couple weeks later; and after a major Zurich heist in early 2008, two of the four paintings were dumped in nearby car (Angus MacSwan, "Security Questioned in Picasso Theft in Brazil," *Reuters*, 21 December 2007).

47 "The Fine Art of Stealing an Old Painting," *Financial Times*, 4–5 February 1995.

48 Cited in Stephen Kurkjian, "Masterpieces, Masterminds a Decade Later, Art Theft still Baffles Investigators," *Boston Globe*, 20 December 1999.

49 In Western Europe personal collections are often uninsured to avoid draw-ing possible attention to unpaid wealth taxes (Maria Kielmas, "Dealers and Galleries Turn to Insurance as Thefts Continue to Increase," *Business Insurance*, 29 January 1996).

50 Andrew Murr Kendall Hamilton, "Solving a Monet Mystery: A $17 Million Insurance Scam in Brentwood? (Beverly Hills Doctor Steven G. Cooperman Is Accused of Stealing His Own Paintings)," *Newsweek*, 21 December 1998. Christopher Reed, "Doctor Charged in 'Insurance fraud' after Stolen Art Turns Up," *The Guardian*, 24 November 1998. See US Department of Justice, United States Attorney, Central District of Califor-nia, *Press Release No. 06–061*, 18 May 2006, and *Press Release 07–014*, 31 January 2007. On the law firm, which was probably the most success-ful in the US in winning billions from giant corporations in shareholder class-action suits, see Robert Lenzner and Emily Lambert, "Mr Class Action," *Forbes*, 16 February 2004.

51 Hoving, *False Impressions*, 148.

52 cf. Hoving, *False Impressions*, 86.

53 Elizabeth Nash, "It's Official: 'Goya Work' Was Painted by His Pupil," *The Independent*, 27 June 2008.

54 See, for example, the bitter disputes between Rembrandt experts over which are really his work (Ian Herbert, "Rembrandt 'Copies' Are Authen-tic, Says Expert," *The Independent*, 29 November 2006).

55 Hoving, *False Impressions*, 75.

56 Jonathan Lopez, "A Forger's Masterpiece," *International Herald Tribune*, 11 August 2008.

57 Although there is something of a posthumous personality cult around the Van Meegeren story, a considerably less flattering portrayal can be found in Hoving, *False Impressions*, chapter 12.

58 "German Museum Discovers Prized Monet Is a Fake," *Agence France Presse*, 14 February 2008. To be fair, Monet painted many La Seine scenes, so it was probably easy for a fake to get interspersed with them.

59 "Lucio Fontana," *Review*, 15 March 2000, www.speronewestwater.com.

60 Hoving, *False Impressions*, 106–7. If Hoving is to be believed, the restor-er's only serious challenge in meeting a huge demand for fake Impression-ist works from crooked dealers was Claude Monet, whose colours and tints were too subtle.

61 His story is told by Anne-Marie Stein (and to George Carpozi) in *Three Picassos before Breakfast: Memoirs of an Art Forger's Wife* (New York: Hawthorn Books, 1973). There is a considerably shorter but less flatter-ing version in David Goodrich, *Art Fakes in America* (New York: Viking Press, 1973).

62 John Lichfield, "On Trial: The Question of What Is Modern Art," *The Independent*, 1 December 2009.

63 In one case a gallery sold for $10,000 each print it had bought for $75. See Andrew Decker, "Limited Editions," *ARTnews*, Summer 1988.

64 "The Counterfeiters," *The Independent*, 10 December 2007; plus extensive coverage in *Bolton News*, 17 November 2007, 21 November 2007, 23 January 2009; *Guardian*, 17 November 2007. I thank Roshni Veerapen for research on this topic.

65 Andrew Burnett, "Expert Vigilance the Only Defence in Never-Ending Forgery Battle," *Times* (London), 17 November 2007.

66 Michael Robinson, "The Difficulty of Finding Data," *Connoisseur*, March 1990.

67 Anthony Haden-Guest. "The Double-Dealer," *New York Magazine*, 6 August 2001; "The Great $50 Million Art Swindle," *Forbes*, 2 June 2001; Anthony Haden-Guest, "Art Scandal: Who Is the $50 Million Man?" *Forbes*, 2 August 2001; and Anthony Haden-Guest, "Art Scandal: Cohen's Con Game," *Forbes*, 2 December 2001.

68 Mandarin Trading Ltd V. Guy Wildenstein, Wildenstein & Co. Inc. Index No. 06–602648 New York Supreme Court; Laura Italiano, "Art Dealer Easels out of Lawsuit," *New York Post*, 28 September 2007; Karen Freifield, "Art Dealer Hid Ownership of Gauguin, Inflated Price, Suit Says," *Bloomberg*, 28 July 2006; Beth Bar, "Buyer of Gauguin Painting Loses Suit over High Appraisal," *New York Law Journal*, 27 September 2007, www.law.com. However, some judges dissented that there was a legitimate case that needed to be aired and answered.

69 Marcus Tanner, "Bride of Wildenstein must Pay for Plastic Surgery," *The Independent*, 6 March 1998. See also "Alex Wildenstein," *The Telegraph*, 20 February 2008.

70 See Christopher Mason, *The Art of the Steal: Inside the Sotheby's – Christie's Auction House Scandal* (New York: Berkeley Books, 2004).

71 "Sold!" *Time*, 27 November 1989; Conklin, *Art Crime*, 39–43, 100–7.

72 Interesting details on the evolution of the financial role of the auction house are given in Ben Heller, "The Irises Affair," *Art in America* 78, July 1990.

73 *Antiques Trade Gazette*, 20 November 2008.

74 Jon Ungoed-Thomas and Christopher Owen, "Georgian Furniture 'made from barn planks,'" *Sunday Times*, 6 April 2008; Christopher Owen and Jon Ungoed-Thomas, "Whistleblower Reveals £30m Antiques Scam," and Christopher Mason and Christopher Owen, "Furniture Restorer's Allegations Shake Antiques Trade," *New York Times*, 22 April 2008; "The Feud and the Fakes," *New York Times*, 16 October 2008.

75 Caroline Bankoff, "It Runs in the Family! Two Brothers Both Involved in High-End Antique Fakery," *New York Observer*, 16 October 2008.

76 Cited in *New York Times*, 16 October 2008, op. cit.

77 James Bradshaw "If You Got the Money, She's Got the Monet; Buying Rare Art for Rich Clients Is a Lot like Being a Private Detective with Very Deep Pockets, Tania Buckrell Pos Tells James Bradshaw," *Globe and Mail*, 16 August 2008; Thompson, *Shark*, 159.

78 Department of Justice, United States Attorney Southern District of New York, "US Charges NYC Gallery Owner in Multimillion-Dollar Global Scheme to Steal Real Masterworks and Forged Copies," press release, 10 March 2004.

79 William Sherman, "The Marcos Collection," ARTNews, October 1990. There were some genuinely valuable ones, but they were well hidden. See also *Far Eastern Economic Review*, 29 September 1988.

80 Thompson, *Shark*, 12–14.

81 See for example the review of the contents of the London Ripley's by Thomas Sutcliffe, "The Greatest Freak Show Belongs to Art," *The Independent*, 29 August 2008.

82 Stein, *Three Picassos*, 8, 28, 57.

83 Thompson, *Shark*, 204.

84 For example, the late Hollywood star Kirk Douglas bought from top New York dealers masters such as Picasso, Mondrian, and Chagall, assuming the names were security for the investment. When he tried to resell, dealers trashed the paintings as "fourth rate junk" (Christie Brown, "Welcome, Suckers!" *Forbes*, 25 June 1990).

85 *Insurance Day*, 26 April 2001.

86 For an examination of these issues and assessment as to which approach seems to better suit the objectives of protecting art, see John H. Merryman, "The Good Faith Acquisition of Stolen Art," *Social Sciences Research Network*, 29 October 2007.

87 On the scuttling of UNIDROIT, see "US and UK Art Lobbies Muster to Scupper UNIDROIT Convention," *The Art Newspaper*, no. 51, September 1995.

88 Cited in John McPhee, *The Ransom of Russian Art* (New York: Ferrar, Straus and Giroux, 1994), 78.

89 The story is told in Frances Stonor Saunders, *The Cultural Cold War: The CIA and the World of Arts and Letters* (New York: New Press, 1999).

90 Konstantin Akinsha et al., "The Betrayal of the Russian Avant-Garde," *ARTnews*, February 1996. See also *Forbes*, 3 September 1990.

91 Will Bennet, "After Brush with Law, Artist Puts His Fakes on Show," *The Daily Telegraph*, 7 February 2002; interview with Coli Gleadell, "The

Art Detective the Police Have all but Given Up Trying to Tackle Serious Art ..." *The Daily Telegraph*, 8 July 2002,

92 Peter Landesman, "A 20th-Century Master Scam," *The New York Times*, 18 July 1999; Steve Boggan, "A Fake's Progress," *The Independent*, 15 July 2000.

93 Judith H. Dobrzynski, "New Collectors Are Changing the Market," *The New York Times*, 7 September 1999.

94 Neil Brodie et al., *Stealing History: The Illicit Trade in Cultural Material* (Cambridge: The McDonald Institute for Archeological Research, 2000), 48, 53; Middlemas, *Double*, 15–16.

CHAPTER FIVE

1 In "The Battle for the Past: Comment," *Culture without Context*, no. 13, Autumn 2003, Morag Kersel and Christina Luake critically review the economists' prescription.

2 Probably the most thorough analysis is by Simon Mackenzie, *Going, Going, Gone: Regulating the Market in Illicit Antiquities* (Leicester: Institute of Art and Law, 2005).

3 See, for example, "Taste – Review and Outlook: Cops and Markets," *Wall Street Journal*, 6 February 2004.

4 For survey of the nature of the problem from a legal perspective, see Lisa Borodkin, "The Economics of Antiquities Looting and a Proposed Legal Alternative," *Colombia Law Review* 95, no. 2, March 1995.

5 Karl Deutsch was probably the first to state the proposition in so many words.

6 See an excellent treatment of Roman "globalization" in Bryan Ward-Perkins, *The Fall of Rome: And the End of Civilization* (Oxford: The University Press, 2005), especially chapter 5.

7 "Captured Ghosts Are Sold at Auction," *The Independent*, 9 March 2010.

8 See, for example, Thomas Case, *The Shroud of Turin and the C–14 Dating Fiasco: A Scientific Detective Story* (Cincinnati: White Horse Press, 1996). I thank Hugo Vozak for this and other references.

9 In 2005 a senior scientist at the British Museum shook up the curator-dealer crowd by his frank assessment, similar to that of Thomas Hoving with respect to paintings, that most antiquities on sale in Britain were fakes (Louise Jury, "Art Market Scandal," *The Independent*, 24 May 2005). This followed a report from the Archeological Institute of America claiming that at least 80 percent of ancient West African sculptures on the market were forgeries (Peter Watson. "How Forgeries Corrupt Our Top Museums," *New Statesman*, 25 December 2000.

10 Michael Day, "Cloth of Gold: The glittering return of the Turin Shroud," *The Independent*, 24 March 2010.

11 "Egypt Asks for Rosetta Stone," *Sunday Times*, 6 December 2009.

12 This process was sardonically captured in E.M. Forster's 1920 essay "For the Sake of the Museum," reprinted in his collection *Abinger Harvest* (London: Edward Arnold & Co. 1936).

13 See the details in Henry Morton Stanley's *Coomassie and Magdala: The story of Two British Campaigns in Africa* (London: Marston, Low & Searle, 1874).

14 For details, see Richard Pankhurst, "The Napier Expedition and the Loot from Maqdala," *Presence Africaine*, no. 133–4, 1985, 233–40; Kidane Alemayehu and Konjit Meshesha, "The Last Day of Emperor Tewodros," *EthioMedia: Ethiopia's Premier News and Views Website*, www.ethiomedia.com/newpress/tewodros_last_day.html.

15 See, for example, Peter Conradi, "Ethiopia Asks Queen to Give Back Treasures," *Sunday Times*, 16 February 2004. The controversy is still far from resolved. See Andrew Johnson, "Ethiopia Demands Stolen Crown Back," *The Independent*, 23 November 2008, and Richard Pankhurst, "Ethiopia: The Way in Demand for Restitution of African Artefacts," *New African*, November 2008.

16 For a survey of historical fraud in Near Eastern material, see Oscar White Muscarella, *The Lie Became Great: the Forgery of Ancient Near Eastern Cultures* (Gronigen: Styx Publications, 2000). On the recent epidemic of fake Mali terracottas, see Michel Brent, "Faking African Art," *Archeology Magazine* 54, no. 1, January-February 2001.

17 Check the rationalizations offered by dealers to Simon Mackenzie in his *Going, Going, Gone*, op. cit.

18 On first set of interconnections, see Muscarella's introductory chapter in *Lie Became Great*.

19 Apart from Muscarella (dismissed from the Met for his opinions) and McKenzie, the leaders in denouncing the impact of the trade include Neil Brodie and Colin Renfrew. See in particular Neil Brodie et al., *Stealing History: The Illicit Trade in Cultural Material* {Cambridge: The MacDonald Institute, 2000).

20 They are detailed in the works of Conklin and Massy noted in chapter 4.

21 Kirstin Romey, "Corinth Loot Found under Fresh Fish," *Archeology* 52, no. 6, November-December 1999; Nikos Axarlis "Corinth Antiquities Returned," *Archeology Online Features*, 6 February 2001.

22 I am indebted to Max Watson for introducing me to this subject and its literature. See especially Patrick Geary, *Furta Sacra: Thefts of Relics in the Central Middle Ages* (Princeton: Princeton University Press, 1978); Patrice Boussel, *Des reliques et leur bon usage* (Paris: Balland, 1971); Robert Eke-

lund Jr et al., *The Marketplace of Christianity* (Cambridge, MA: MIT Press, 2008); and Harvey Rachlin, *Lucy's Bones, Sacred Stones & Einstein's Brain*, (New York: Henry Holt, 1996).

23 See Alain Demurger, *Vie et mort de l'ordre du Temple* (Paris: Editions du Seuil, 1989), part 4.

24 For a less-than-pious look at Vatican finances see R.T. Naylor, *Hot Money and the Politics of Debt*, third edition (Montreal: McGill-Queen's University Press, 2004), chapters 5 and 8. On the recent scandal, see Josephine McKenna, "Vatican Bank Reported to Be Facing Money-Laundering Investigation," *Times of London*, 7 December 2009.

25 See Nino Lo Bello, *The Vatican Papers* (London: New English Library, 1984), chapter 18.

26 Thanks to Laura Kirschner for this information.

27 "New York Museum Admits Third of Its Coptic Art Is Fake," *The Independent*, 2 July 2008.

28 Peter Popham, "Symbol of Rome Found to Be 1,000 Years too Young," *The Independent*, 10 July 2008. Muscarella, in *Lie*, 23 et passim, refers to the peer-review process that is supposed to help screen out inaccurate studies as "In many cases the ignorant reviewing the ignorant," a description that applies to much more scholarship than simply bad archeological research.

29 Tony Oram, "Divers Haul Oldest ever Bust of Caesar from Bottom of River in France," *Daily Mail*, 15 May 2008; for the skeptical view, see Maia De La Blaume "A Museum Hails a Caesar, Even if Some Experts Don't Agree," *New York Times*, 30 November 2009.

30 Gregory Curtis, "Base Deception," *The Smithsonian*, October 2003.

31 Michel Brent, "Faking African Art," *Archaeology* 54, no. 1, January–February 2001.

32 The most prestigious are from Oxford University. See Patricia Franklin, *Profits of Deceit: Dispatches from the Front Lines of Fraud* (London: Heinemann, 1990), chapter 3.

33 See Jo Johnson, "Curse of the Pharaoh," *Financial Times*, 22 November 2003.

34 See Vincent Noce, "Drouot: saisies record," *Libération*, 8 December 2009, and "Drouot, serré aux cols," *Libération*, 21 January 2010. See also John Lichfield, "Going, Going, Gone … to the Light-Fingered Porters," *The Independent*, 7 August 2010; and "Les manutentionnaires de l'hôtel Drouot ont été mis en examen," *Le Monde*, 6 August 2010.

35 Cited in Scott Sayare, "Chatter of Swindles and Scams at Auction House," *New York Times*, 26 April 2010. The most likely long-term result of the affair will not be to stop art theft or purge the auction-house inventory of fakes but to bust up France's last remaining workers' co-op, force the

Drouot auctioneers to put an end to their own closed shop, and allow the house to become a publicly traded corporation in which the British and US houses would take shares. It will also give the French government a pretext to slash value-added taxes on sales of art, antiquities, antique furniture, vintage wines, and assorted collectibles, lowering taxes again for the rich in a desperate effort to hang on to the shrinking share of the burgeoning world art market that France, its former centre, still manages to hold.

36 Charles Stanish, "Forging Ahead," *Archeology* 62, no. 3, May/June 2009.

37 The classic work setting off much of the modern debate is Karl Meyer, *The Plundered Past* (New York: Atheneum, 1973).

38 John Hess, *The Grand Acquisitors* (Boston: Houghton Mifflin, 1974), 50.

39 His story, among other things, is recounted in Brian Fagan, *The Rape of the Nile: Tomb Robbers, Tourists and Archeologists in Egypt* (New York: Westview Press, 2004).

40 Hess, *Grand Acquisitors*, 135.

41 For a highly laudatory account from a self-evidently "objective" publishing source, see Lovat Dickson, *The Museum Makers: The Story of the Royal Ontario Museum* (Toronto: Royal Ontario Museum, 1986). See also Geoffrey York, "Book Suggests Musuem's Treasures Smuggled Out of China; Canadian Bishop Shipped Items to Toronto Through Obscure Rail Stations, or in Other Missionaries' Luggage, Author Says," *Globe and Mail*, 19 January 2008. For a less flattering view of some of the museum's financial backers, see R.T. Naylor, *The History of Canadian Business 1867–1914*, third edition (Montreal: McGill-Queen's University Press, 2006).

42 William H. Honan, "Trial to Decide Owner of Mosaics Begins," *The New York Times*, 31 May 1989; William H. Honan, "Clashing Views on Purchaser of Mosaics," *The New York Times*, 6 June 1989; Autocephalous Greek-Orthodox Church of Cyprus and the Republic of Cyprus v. Goldberg & Feldman Fine Arts Inc., and Peg Goldberg; 917 F. 2d 278 U.S. Court of Appeals, 1990 District Court for the Southern District of Indiana; Mark Rose, "Art Theft from Cyprus to Munich," *Archaeology*, 20 April 1998.

43 Mackenzie, *Going Going Gone* 5, 20.

44 Hees, *Grand Acquisitors*, 42.

45 Cited in Atwood, *Stealing History*, 269.

46 "Emmerich-Andre," obituary, *New York Times*, 2 October 2007.

47 This process is graphically described, from official documents, in Tom Segev, *1949: The First Israelis* (New York: The Free Press, 1986), chapter 3, and in Simha Flapan, *The Birth of Israel: Myths and Realities* (New York: Pantheon, 1987), 100–1.

48 Cited in Rachel Shabi, "Faking It," *Guardian*, 20 January 2005.

49 Rachel Shabi, "Faking It," *Guardian*, 20 January 2005.

50 Amy Tiebel, "Dayan Is Accused in Antiquities Plunder," *Associated Press*, 16 June 2006. See also Amiram Barkat, "Moshe Dayan's Antiquities to Be Sold at Bargain Prices in US Auction," *Ha'aretz*, 27 May 2007; *Al-Ahram*, 5–11 June 2007.

51 Claire Soares, "Acropolis Now! A Museum for the Elgin Marbles," *The Independent*, 20 June 2009.

52 Associated Press, "Van Gogh Theft was 'Inside Job,'" *The Independent*, 28 September 2010.

53 Sarah Ktisti, "Lovelorn Cypriots Ravage Historic Tomb of Saint," *The Independent*, 8 August 2009.

54 "Industrial Plant Threatens Agrigento," *The Independent*, 20 November 2008.

55 Stephen Starr, "Turkish History to Sink to Oblivion," *Asia Times*, 8 September 2010.

56 For example, "In exceptional cases an item without provenance may have such an inherently outstanding contribution to knowledge that it would be in the public interest to preserve it" (The ICOM – France – Provenance and Due Diligence requirement). The code of ethics for the American Association of Museums makes no reference to provenance at all (www. aam-us.org/museumresources/ethics/coe.cfm).

57 In one respect, the prime minister was certainly right – it is time to stop singling out the British Museum. The Victoria & Albert reputedly has so much loot from India that it never puts more than about 2 percent of its treasure trove on display at any time (Raja Murthy, "India Wants Its Crown Jewel," *Asia Times*, 5 August 2010).

58 The Metropolitan Museum of Art was, in the 1970s, among those rocked by scandals, as recounted by Heese in *Grand Acquisitors*. The recent Getty scandal established that this is not just a problem of the distant past. And see the notorious example of the privately owned Museum of East Asian Art in Sweden, whose director was caught on tape in 2000 bragging about how he personally smuggled things from China, usually just sticking them in his pockets, or using cigarettes and cash as bribes when necessary (Jenny Doole, "On the Trail of the Tomb Robbers," *Culture without Context*, no. 7, Autumn 2000).

59 See R.T. Naylor, *Wages of Crime: Black Markets, Illegal Finance and the Underworld Economy* (Ithaca, New York: 2004), chapter 3, on the arms black market for an examination of the role of "service costs" in determining black market prices.

60 This is discussed in *Art Journal*, Spring 1971, and *Art in America*, March 1973.

61 Nathaniel C. Nash, "Poor Peru Stands By as Its Rich Past Is Plundered," *New York Times*, 25 August 1993.

62 I am indebted to Nicolas Ferreyros for research on Andean artifact trafficking.

63 Government of Peru V. Benjamin Johnson et al Case No. CV 88–6990-WPG United States District Court for the Central District of California, 29 June 1989.

64 Much of the recovered material was consigned to a local museum that could at least bring some tourist expenditures into the area. The Sipán story was first told in Heinz Plenge, "The Robber's Tale: The True Story," *Connoisseur*, February 1990, then followed soon after by Carl Nagin, "The Peruvian Gold Rush: A Tale of Smugglers, Scoundrels, and Scholars," *Art & Antiques*, May 1990. A recent, much more comprehensive account is Roger Atwood's excellent *Stealing History: Tomb Raiders, Smugglers and the Looting of the Ancient World* (New York: St Martin's Press, 2004).

65 Cui Lili, "Protection of Cultural Relics," *Beijing Review*, 19–25 December 1995,

66 For a good sketch of the situation at the very start of the boom, see Don Cohn, "Buried Treasure," *Far Eastern Economic Review*, 11 June 1992.

67 John Stanmeyer, "Spirited Away," *Asia Magazine*, 20 October 2003.

68 Ron Gluckman, "Re-made in China: The Fine Art of Fakery," *Destinasian*, June 2002.

69 A. Tang, "The Drain of China's Cultural Heritage," *Beijing Review*, 23 May 2005; He Shuzhong, "Illicit Excavation in Contemporary China"; Neil Brodie et al., *Trade in Illicit Antiquities: The Destruction of the World's Archeological Heritage* (Cambridge: The MacDonald Institute for Archeological Research, 2001); Elizabeth Childs-Johnson, "The Three Gorges Dam and the Looting of Archeological Treasures," New York University, 1 May 1998.

70 For well-informed works on jade see those of Richard Harris: "Burma's Jade Mines: An Annotated Occidental History," *Journal of the Geo-Literary Society* 14, no. 1, 1991; (with O. Galibert et al.) "Tracing the Green Line: A Journey to Myanmar's Jade Mines," *Jewelers' Circular – Keystone* 167, no. 11, 1996, 168, no. 1, January 1997; (with Fred Ward) "Heaven and Hell: The Quest for Jade in Upper Burma," *Asia Diamonds* 1, no. 2, September-October 1997; and (with Fred Ward et al.) "Burma Jade: The Inscrutable Gem," *Gems and Gemology* 36, no. 1, Spring 2000.

71 "The King of Stones," *Far Eastern Economic Review*, 9 November 2000.

72 A fascinating account of jade politics is in Adrian Levy and Kathy Scott Clark, *The Stone of Heaven: Unearthing the Secret History of Imperial Green Jade* (Boston: Little Brown, 2001), 118–26.

73 For general background, see Bertil Linter, *Burma In Revolt: Opium and Insurgency since 1948* (Chiang Mai: Silkworm Press, 1994). See also "Jade Is Special, as Are the Risks of Bringing It to Market," *The Smithsonian*, August 1986.

74 See the series of articles on the fraud by Duff Wilson, Sheila Farr, and Brian Joseph in the *Seattle Times* starting 27 January 2003, beginning with Duff Wilson et al., "Buyer beware: All Is Not as advertised at Asian Antiquities Dealer," 27 January 2003. See also US Department of Justice, "Arrest Warrants Issued for Economist and Wife for Their Failure to Appear," United States Attorney, Western District of Washington, press release, 25 February 2003. The gallery later settled the fraud charges with the state attorney general by reimbursing customers and paying a $350,000 fine (Emily Heffter, "Art gallery Settles Fraud Case," *Seattle Times*, 29 October 2005). Thanks to Megan McWhirter for bringing this case to my attention.

75 There is considerable coverage of the China loot issue. See, for example, the blog *A Big Job: Protecting China's Archaeological Heritage*, chiarch. wordpress.com.

76 Andrew Jacobs, "Uneasy Engagements: China Hunts for Art Treasures in US Museums," *New York Times*, 16 December 2009.

77 Karen Mazurkewich, "Late Bidders," *Wall Street Journal*, 14 January 2004, and Karen Mazurkewich, "Treasure Hunt: To Stop the Pillage of Its Historic Art, China Turns to US – Hot Antiquities Market Girds for Crackdown as Beijing Pushes Trade Restrictions – Dealers Go on Buying Spree," *Wall Street Journal*, 2 March 2005.

78 Scott Reyburn and Dune Lawrence, "China-Art Sales May Drop as Bidder Refuses to Pay," *Bloomberg*, 3 March 2009.

79 Republic of Iraq, Ministry of Information, Directorate General of Antiquities, Baghdad, Antiquities Law No. 59 of 1936 and Two Amendments No. 120 of 1974 and No. 164 of 1975.

80 For a detailed account see R.T. Naylor, *Patriots & Profiteers: Economic Warfare, Embargo-Busting and State Sponsored Crime*, third edition (Montreal: McGill-Queen's University Press, 2008), especially the afterword. For good overviews of the looting of Iraq's cultural heritage, see Geoff Emberling and Katharyn Hanson (eds), *Catastrophe: The Looting and Destruction of Iraq's Past* (Chicago: University of Chicago, 2008), and Lawrence Rothfield (ed.), *Antiquities under Siege: Cultural Heritage Protection after the Iraq War* (Plymouth: AltaMira Press, 2008).

81 I thank officials of the Lebanese Directorate General of Antiquities for their courtesy and assistance on these matters.

82 For a summary of some of the rackets see Naylor, *Patriots & Profiteers*, chapter 8.

83 See especially the series of investigations by Robert Fisk, 30 July and 2 August 1991 reproduced at phoenicia.org/feature.html. I thank Assaad Zakka and officials of the Lebanese antiquities directorate for filling me in on some of the details. The figures associated with the terracotta theft are too high to be believed although the actual event itself is fully credible.

84 "A Phoenician Statue for My Coffee Table (Archeological Preservation in Lebanon)," *The Economist*, 3 April 1999.

85 Cited by Reem Haddad, "Too Many Archaelogical Sites in Downtown Beirut to Excavate Them All," *Beirut Daily Star*, reproduced at phoenicia. org/feature.html.

86 See especially the onsite reporting on conditions by Patrick Cockburn, *The Occupation: War and Resistance in Iraq* (London: Verso, 2006).

87 Edmud L. Andrews and Susan Sachs, "Iraq's Slide into Lawlessness Squanders Good Will for US," *New York Times*, 18 May 2003; Neela Banerjee, "Widespread Looting Leaves Iraq's Oil Industry in Ruins," *The New York Times*, 10 June 2003; Edmund L. Andrews, "Iraqi Smugglers Are Brazen and They Don't Stop at Oil," *The New York Times*, 23 June 2003.

88 Kim Sengupta, "Five Years after Fall of Baghdad, All-Day Curfew Is Imposed," *The Independent*, 10 April 2008.

89 Radio Free Europe / Radio Liberty (RFE/RL). 13 July 2004.

90 Luke Harding, "Mosul Descends into Chaos as Even the Museum Is Looted of Treasures," *Guardian*, 12 April 2003.

91 Atwood, *Stealing History*, 267–8. The concern of the ACCP, a lobby group with no real experience in these matters, was to prevent destruction by war of things it intended to liberate for the "free market." See Lawrence Rothfield, "Preserving Iraq's Heritage from Looting," *Antiquities under Siege*, 12–3.

92 See especially Rod Liddle, "The Day of the Jackals," *The Spectator*, 19 April 2003. Accounts differ as to whether the mob came first or after the pros. There seems little disagreement that both operated, and independently.

93 Alan Riding, "Art Experts Mobilize Team to Recover Stolen Treasure and Salvage Iraqi Museums," *The New York Times*, 18 April 2003.

94 For a summary of his investigation, see Matthew Bogdanos "Thieves of Baghdad: The Looting of the Iraq Museum," *Antiquities under Siege: Cultural Heritage Protection after the Iraq War*, Lawrence Rothfield (ed.). For another view, see the description by the former director general of the Iraqi antiquities services and the US archeologist who had taken the lead in trying to prevent war damage – Donny George and McGuire Gibson, "The Looting of the Iraq Museum Complex," *Catastrophe*, op. cit.

95 Andre Emmerich, "Let the Market Preserve Art: What Were All Those Antiquities Doing in Iraq, Anyway?" *Wall Street Journal*, 24 April 2003.

96 Roger Atwood, "Stop, Thieves! Recovering Iraq's Looted Treasures," *Washington Post*, 3 October 2004; Barry Meier and James Glanz, "US Helps Recover Statue and Gives It Back to Iraqis," *The New York Times*, 26 July 2006.

97 Nathaniel Popper, "Defense Lawyer Helps Hip-Hop Artists Beat Their Raps," *Forward*, 6 August 2004.

98 Sandee Brawarsky, "Nitzan Pelman and Joseph Braude," *The New York Times*, 1 April 2007. It was revealed in the trial that Braude had been targeted by customs for special attention, suggesting a tip-off from inside Baghdad by US agents eager for a high-profile homeland bust.

99 See reporting on losses and recoveries, as well as the damage, by the Oriental Institute of the University of Chicago on its Lost Treasures from Iraq website (oi.uchicago.edu/OI/IRAQ/whatsnew.html). A beautiful pictorial account is Milbry Polk and Angela M.H. Schuster, *The Looting of the Iraq Museum, Baghdad: The Lost Legacy of Ancient Mesopotamia* (New York: Harry N. Abrams Inc. 2005).

109 The complex social factors involved are examined in Joanne Farchakh-Bajjaly, "Who Are the Looters at Archeological Sites in Iraq?" *Antiquities under Siege*, and John Russell, "Efforts to Protect Archeological Sites and Monuments in Iraq, 2003–4," *Catastrophe*, op. cit.

101 Mark Fisher, "Tomb Raiders," *The Guardian*, 19 January 2006; Robert Fisk, "It Is the Death of history," *The Independent*, 17 September 2007; Simon Jenkins, "In Iraq's Four-Year Looting Frenzy, the Allies Have Become the Vandals," *The Guardian*, 8 June 2007. Iraq declared it would ask for compensation for the military damage to Ur, Babylon, and Umma Zalalam (Arifa Akbar, "Iraqi Expert Accuses West over Antiquities Trade," *The Independent*, 1 May 2008). See especially the retrospective eyewitness account by John Curtis of the British Museum, "Who Stole Iraq's Priceless Treasures?" *The Sunday Times*, 13 April 2008.

102 Steven Lee Myers, "G.I.'s in Iraq Hope to Heal Sacred Walls," *New York Times*, 19 December 2009.

103 Zainab Bahrani. "In the Fray: British and Swiss Get Tough about Smuggling," *The Wall Street Journal*, 18 February 2004; Steven McElroy, "Looted Antiquities Returned to Iraq," *The New York Times*, 23 June 2008.

104 Orly Blum, "The Illicit Antiquities Trade: An Analysis of Current Antiquities Looting in Israel," *Culture without Context* 11, Autumn 2002.

105 Ozgen Acar and Melik Kaylan, "The Hoard of the Century," *Connoisseur*, July 1988; Ozgen Acar and Melik Kaylan, "The Turkish Connection: An Investigative Report on the Smuggling of Classical Antiquities," *Connoisseur*, October 1990.

106 See Paul Fitzgerald and Elizabeth Gould, *Invisible History: Afghanistan's Untold Story* (San Francisco: City Lights Books, 2009), 243.

107 Nancy Dupree, "Museum under Siege," *Archeology*, 20 April 1998.
108 Rory Stewart, *The Places in Between* (Toronto: Penguin, 2004), 152–3, 159.
109 Fitzgerald and Gould, *Invisible*, 269.
110 Even that was subject to constant revision, depending on which official was speaking and why. See, for example, *New York Times* 23 June 2008.
111 Steven Lee Meyers, "Far from Whole, Iraq Museum That Was Looted Reopens," *New York Times*, 24 February 2009, and the follow-up in Steven Lee Meyers, "Babylon Ruins Reopen in Iraq, to Controversy," *New York Times*, 3 May 2009.

CHAPTER SIX

1 See Jason, "Why Buy An Antique Carpet?" *Educational Articles about Rugs. Antique Rug News from the Nazmiyal Collection*, blog.nazmiyal. com/why-buy-an-antique-carpet/2008/08/01.
2 Ed Welch, "Collecting Investment Grade Antiques," *The Journal of Antiques and Collectibles: America's Fastest Growing Trade Paper*, July 2003.
3 Described in Jessica Rao, "Antiques Can Make Your Portfolio Young Again," CNBC.com, 31 August 2010.
4 The real name is Swedish Central Bank Prize in Economic Science in Honour of the Memory of Alfred Nobel, set up many decades after the genuine Nobel Prizes with the name probably designed in the knowledge that reporters are so prone to simplification that they would just fixate on the last two words and that economists as a tribe are sufficiently desperate for recognition to go along with the fraud. Descendants of Alfred Nobel have protested, to no avail. See Edward Fullbrook (ed.), *Real World Economics: A Post-Autistic Economics Reader* (New York: Anthem Press, 2007), "Part 2: The faux Nobel Prize."
5 Cited in William Finnegan, "A Theft in the Library," *New Yorker* 81, no. 32. The title is a reference to a notorious map thief, not to Arader.
6 For an excellent overview of both some of the history and the technical challenges of detecting fakes, see Wayne G. Sayles, *Classical Deception: Counterfeits, Forgeries and Reproductions of Ancient Coins* (Iola, WI: Krause Publications, 2001).
7 William Jacob, *An Historical Inquiry into the Production and Consumption of the Precious Metals*, vol. 2 (London: John Murray, 1831), 7, 35.
8 Yiannis Androulakis, "How Coins Were Minted," *Coin Minting in the Past, Fleur-de-Coin: Your On-Line Guide to Coin Collecting*, www.fleur-de-coin.com/articles/ancientcoinminting.asp.
9 See, for example, T.F. Reddaway, *The Early History of the Goldsmith's Company 1327–1509* (London: Edward Arnold, 1975).

10 On English silverwork, see Seymour B. Wyler, *The Book of Old Silver* (New York: Crown Publishers, 1937). An alternative theory of the origin of "sterling" is that it comes from Old English "steorling" – meaning a coin with the star sometimes seen stamped on early Norman pennies.

11 See Peter J. Blakewell, *Silver Mining and Society in Colonial Mexico – Zacetas 1546–1700* (Cambridge: Cambridge University Press, 1971); D.A. Brading, *Miners and Merchants in Bourbon Mexico, 1763–1810* (Cambridge: Cambridge University Press, 1971); Arthur Preston Whitaker, *The Huancavelica Mercury Mine: A Contribution to the History of the Bourbon Renaissance in the Spanish Empire, Harvard Historical Monographs 16* (Cambridge: Harvard University Press, 1941); Louisa Schell-Hoberman, *Mexico's Merchant Elite 1590–1660: Silver, State and Society* (Durham: Duke University Press, 1991); Enrique Tandeter, *Coercion and Market: Silver Mining in Colonial Potosí 1692–1826* (Albuquerque: University of New Mexico Press, 1993); Mark Cocker, *Rivers of Blood, Rivers of Gold: Europe's Conquest of Indigenous Peoples* (New York; Grove Press, 1998).

12 Alexander Del Mar, *Money and Civilization* (London: George Bell & Sons, 1886), 44.

13 "Counterfeiter Jailed for Making 14 Million Fake £1 Coins," *Daily Mail*, 23 October 2010. If the number is really accurate, it represents nearly half of the 30 million fake £1 coins made from a nickel-brass compound (perhaps with some lead added to boost electroconductivity to levels acceptable to vending machines) that are reputedly floating around Britain (Martin Hickman, "Thirty Million 1 Pound Coins Are Fake," *The Independent*, 23 September 2008).

14 For one exception, see "Myths, Misunderstandings & Outright Lies," *CMI Gold & Silver*, www.cmi-gold-silver.com/gold-confiscation-1933.html.

15 David E. Sanger, "Fake Coins Embarrass the Japanese," *New York Times*, 8 February 1990; "Commodities and Agriculture: Coin Dealer May Sue Japan's Ministry of Finance," *Financial Times*, 14 March 1991; Kenneth Gooding, "Court Case Revives Row Over 'Forged' Hirohito Coins," *Financial Times*, 24 July 1995.

16 See Ragnar Benson, *Gunrunning for Fun and Profit* (Boulder, CO: Paladin Press, 1986), 2. On their reputed use by Israeli arms-dealers and Mossad agents, see Claire Hoy and Victor Ostrovsky, *By Way of Deception: A Devastating Insider's Portrait of Mossad* (Toronto: Stoddart, 1990), 67.

17 "Coin Con Artists Pick Seniors' Pockets," *Kiplinger Retirement Reports*, September 2007.

18 See, for example, Laurie Goodstein, "Believers Invest in the Gospel of Getting Rich," *New York Times*, 15 August 2009.

19 For example, Craig Smith, *True Wealth*, chapter 3: "End of Times Investing," www.true-wealth.com. This is a legitimate and free service – but the
idea that gold is among the most desirable choices with which to prepare
for Armageddon runs as well through a lot of "Christian" investment
frauds.

20 There is a brief overview and comparison in "Ponzi Schemes: Testimony
of Michael J. Byrne, Chief Counsel, Pennsylvania Securities Commission,"
before the State legislature, 2009. See www.legis.state.pa.us/cfdocs/legis/
TR/transcripts/2009_0157_0001_TSTMNV.pdf.

21 See *United States versus Haywood Eudon Hall*, United States Court of
Appeals for the Eleventh Circuit Case No. 01–14746, 10 November
2003.

22 Michael Fechter, "Ministries May Buy Out Mine Partner," *The Tampa
Tribune*, 26 April 1999; Michael Flechter, "Court to Hear Church-Fraud
Case," *The Tampa Tribune*, 22 January 2001, "Judgment Day For Gerald
Payne," *The Tampa Tribune*, 8 August 2001; Chuck Fager, "Jury Convicts
Greater Ministries of Fraud," *Christianity Today*, 23 April 2001; "Vic-
tims of Church Investment Scam Unlikely to Recover Losses," *Associated
Press*, 14 July 2002; Jeff Testerman, "Jury Convicts Five in Ministries
Scam," *St Petersburg Times*, 13 March 2001.

23 "Matthew Healey, "$7.85 Million for US Coin and Extra for a Stamp,"
New York Times, 23 May 2010.

24 McNall says about the Howard Hughes rumour: "I made no effort to
dispel the myth because it was a great story. And in Los Angeles, a great
story is worth money, whether it's true or not" (Bruce McNall with
Michael D'Antonio, *Fun while It Lasted: My Rise and Fall in the Land of
Fame and Fortune*, New York: Hyperion, 2003, 41).

25 McNall, *Fun*, 43–6; Thomas Hoving, *False Impressions* (New York:
Touchstone, 1997), 286–7.

26 McNall, *Fun*, 64

27 The best source on this is Stephen Fay, *Beyond Greed: The Hunt Family's Bold Attempt to Corner the Silver Market* (New York: Viking Press,
1982). But see also Harry Hurt III, "Silverfinger: The Hunt Brothers'
Story," *Playboy*, September 1980; "Business: Bunker's Busted Silver Bubble," *Time*, 12 May 1980; John A. Jenkins, "The Hunt Brothers: Battling
a Billion-Dollar Debt," *New York Times*, 27 September 1987; Stephan
Labaton, "Trial of Hunt Brothers in Silver Case Begins," *New York Times*,
25 February 1988. There are further details in, variously: *Forbes*, 29 September 1980; *The Economist*, 5 April 1980, 10 April 1980, 6 September
1986; *The Mining Journal*, 7 June 1989, 3 May 1991.

28 On the debacle, see especially Fay, *Beyond Greed*, 168–9.

29 McNall, *Fun*, 55, 64–6, 72.

30 Suzan Mazur, "The Hunt's Hoard on the Auction Block," *The Economist*, 23 June 1990; Geraldine Norman, "Millionaire's Coin Sale Unsettles Money Market," *The Independent*, 10 October 1993.

31 Christie Brown and Lisa Gubernick, "Heads I Win, Tails You Lose," *Forbes*, 5 August 1991.

32 Hand it to McNall, he was the one person who did not give up on himself. When he got out of prison he wrote memoirs (*Fun*, op. cit.) to modestly inform "everyone … how I had turned my intelligence, my nerve and a bit of fraud [bilking banks out of hundreds of millions with phony collateral, trafficking in looted antiquities and conning billionaires in antique coin deals] into a business empire."

33 See "The Importance of Coin Grading," *Professional Coin Grading Service* (Collectors Universe Inc., 1999–2010), www.pcgs.com/thepcgsstory. html.

34 Ray Wiman, "My Coin Collecting: Coin Collecting Made Easier – Grading Services," 2005, www.mycoincollecting.com;

35 Holly Wheelwright with Isaac Rosen, "The Only Way to Invest in Coins GET SERIOUS OR GET RIPPED OFF! Buy Rare, Buy Near-Perfect and Buy American. And Make Yourself an Expert on Price. Or You May Pay Mostly for Hype," CNN *Money*, April 1990.

36 Gregory Couch, "The Rare-Coin Business Feels a New Tarnish," *Los Angeles Times*, 2 September 1990.

37 See Federal Trade Commission v. Security Rare Coin & Bullion Corp., Central Coin Exchange Inc, and William Urlich, United States District Court for the District of Minnesota, Third Division, 11 September 1989, and the appeal by defendants before United States Court of Appeals Eighth Circuit – 931 F.2d 1312 in which the decision of the district court was affirmed.

38 Rob Moll, "Fool's Gold," *Christianity Today*, 1 July 2004.

39 Cited in Jim O'Neill, "East Brunswick Wins Appeal on Restitution in 1991 Stock Fraud Case," *Star-Ledger*, 15 December 2008; Ken Serrano, "UPDATE: Man Who Scammed Gold-Coin Buyers Wins Court Ruling," myCentralJersey.com, 15 December 2008.

40 There is an account of the affair in United States of America Plaintiff vs. Armand DeAngelis et al. Defendants, *Sentencing Memorandum of Defendant Armand DeAngelis* United States District Court, Southern District of Florida, Miami, Florida Case No. 04–20261-CR-Gold. An appeals court upheld the sentence. See also "Securities and Investments," *Fraud Digest*, Miami Florida, www.frauddigest.com/fraud.php?ident+3477.

41 William Power and Michael Siconolfi, "Coin Industry Dealt a Blow by FTC Suit," *Wall Street Journal*, 24 August 1990.

42 In *Coin World*, 26 May 2003.

43 One of the best boiler rooms, based in Toronto in the 1990s, got hold of lists of Americans who had bought coins as an inflation hedge in the 1970s, then offered to find buyers for them, but only if they completed their collection with gemstones – the usual grossly overpriced, heat-treated and flawed variety ("Canadian Gem Scheme Leaves Americans Holding the Stones," *New York Times*, 14 August 1994).

44 Koch admitted that he ought to have used a bit more care but that "it really appealed to all the greed and avarice in me at that time." See Barry Meier "The Case of the Contested Coins: A Modern-Day Battle over Ancient Objects," *New York Times*, 11 January 2009.

45 See Dennis Kroh, "Ancient Coins & Modern Fakes," Address to 99th Annual American Numismatic Association Convention, Seattle, 24 August 1990, at www.mindspring.com/~kroh/Empirecoins/fakes.html.

46 See PCGS, "The Fundamentals of Counterfeit Detection," part 1, 3 January 2000, part 2, 10 January 2000, and "Counterfeit Coin Detection," *Reid Goldsborough*, rg.ancients.info/guide/counterfeits.html.

47 There is a lot of coverage of the issue. See, for example, Richard Giedroyc, "Fake Coins Big Business in China," *Chinese Coins News and Articles*, 4 September 2007, reprinted its 20 October 2008 issue.

48 Reid Goldsborough, "Black Sea Hoard and Other Apollonia Diobol Fakes," *Black Sea Hoard*, www.snible.org/coins/black_sea_hoard.html.

49 Sayles, *Classical Deception*, 62–4.

50 Elana Moya, "Greece Starts Putting Island Land up for Sale to Save Economy," *Guardian*, 24 June 2010.

51 "Spanish Police Arrest Treasure Gang," *The Guardian*, 6 February 2006.

52 "Spain Intercepts US Ship in Treasure Row," *Agence France Press*, 13 July 2007; Cahal Milmo, "Why Is There a Storm Brewing over the Right to Plunder Shipwrecks?" *The Independent*, 3 February 2009.

53 There is an uncritical account in Montieth Illingworth, "Under the Sea: Treasure Hunting," *Cigar Aficionado*, 1 December 1995. Presumably smokers of high-end cigars and collectors of antique gold coins have some things in common.

54 His technique consisted of putting metal tubes into the ocean floor, then using his ship's propellers to blow hundreds of holes averaging twenty to thirty feet across and three to five deep. "Treasure Hunters Are Fined for Destoying Sea Grass in Florida," *New York Times*, 3 August 1997.

55 Jim Carrier, "Hunter Admits Sale of Fake Gold Coins," *New York Times*, 27 November 1998; "New Trouble for a Legend of Key West," *Wall Street Journal*, 2 September 1998; "Treasure Hunter Peddling Fakes," *Daily Record*, 23 November 1998; "Treasure Hunter Mel Fisher Leaves Trail of Gold," *Reuters*, 25 August 2005.

56 Bruce Frankel and Tim Roche "Good as Gold?" *People Magazine* 49, no. 23, 15 June 1998; Evan Perez, "Accused of Selling Fakes, Treasure Hunter Is Fighting the Odds Again," *Associated Press*, 10 May 1998; "Treasure Hunter Calls Fraud Query on Gold Coins a Government Setup," *Associated Press*, 24 April 1998.

57 Rob Hotakainen, "Missouri Man Battles Washington over 2,000 Year Old Coins," *McClatchy Washington Bureau*, 30 November 2007. On the background and work of Wayne Sayles, see ancientcoins.ac and www.accg.us/about/officers/wayne-g-sayles, the Ancient Coin Collectors Guild website. The gist of the anti-repatriation argument is the same as for all antiquities. See Wayne G. Sayles, "Shared Group Identity," ancientcoincollecting.blogspot.com, 2 February 2009.

CHAPTER SEVEN

1 On lead in wine, see James Eisinger, "Early Consumer Protection Legislation – A 17th Century Law Prohibiting Lead Adulteration of Wines," *Interdisciplinary Science Review* 16, no. 1, 1991.

2 Thomas Pellechia, *Wine: The 8000-Year-Old Story of the Wine Trade* (New York: Thunder's Mouth Press, 2006), 10–11, 20, 35.

3 Cited in Christopher Fielden, *Is This the Wine You Ordered, Sir? The Dark Side of the Wine Trade* (London: Christopher Helm, 1989), 5. The author had many years of experience in the trade.

4 For an in-depth history, see Thomas Brennan, *Burgundy to Champagne: The Wine Trade in Early Modern France* (Baltimore: John Hopkins University Press, 1997).

5 Thomas Pellachia, *The 8,000-Year-Old Story of the Wine Trade* (New York: Thunder's Mouth Press, 2006), 66.

6 Tim Unwin, *Wine and the Vine: An Historical Geography of Viticulture and the Wine Trade* (London: Routledge, 1991), 12–14; Pellachia, *Wine*, 125.

7 Fritz Hallgarten, *Wine Scandal* (London: Wiedenfeld and Nicholson, 1986), 12. (The author, whose family had a long history in the wine business, had been pressured by colleagues in the trade not to publish the original version of this book but later decided to revise, update, and publish it anyway.) See also Unwin, *Wine and the Vine*, 277.

8 On the origins of the French system of *appellation d'origine controlée*, see, for example, Nicholas Faith, *The Winemasters* (London: Hamish Hamilton, 19780. Hallgarten's *Scandal* (42 et passim) explains the complexities of the German system.

9 Fielden, *Wine You Ordered*, 66–8, 71.

10 The early history is traced in Laurence Schmeckebier and Francis Eble, *The Bureau of Internal Revenue: Its History, Activities and Organization* (Baltimore: The Johns Hopkins Press, 1923).

11 These issues are dealt with by Mark Thornton, *The Economics of Prohibition* Salt (Lake City: The University of Utah Press, 1991).

12 Loubère, *Wine Revolution*, 17.

13 Loubère, *Wine Revolution*, 25–7. Properly speaking the classification is fourfold: AOC (*vins d'appelation d'origine contrôlée*, with limits on the amount of a particular grape that can be taken from a field): VDSQ (*vins délimités de qualité supérieur*, which allows higher yield from the same grapes); *vins de pays* (coming from outside the AOC region although from the same grape); and *vins de table* (usually mixes).

14 Sarah O'Brien and Jennifer Leczkowski (eds), *Wine Enthusiast* (Philadelphia: Running Press Book Publishers, 2006), 139.

15 Tyler Coleman, *Wine Politics: How Governments, Environmentalists, Mobsters and Critics Influence the Wines We Drink* (Berkeley: University of California Press, 2008), 12–3.

16 See Don and Petie Kladstrup, *Wine & War: The French, the Nazis & the Battle for France's Greatest Treasure* (New York: Broadway Books, 2001).

17 Hallgarten, *Scandal*, 99.

18 Fielden in *Is This the Wine* comments that the result was the grower sold more wine, the merchant got a tacit official endorsement for long-standing fraudulent practices, and the customer probably got an overall better quality of product.

19 Every major work on wine seems to include an account of the affair, but the best, apart from Nicholas Faith, *The Winemasters* (London: Hamish Hamilton, 1978), is by Pierre Bert himself, *In Vino Veritas: l'affaire des vins de Bordeaux* (Paris: Albin Michel, 1975).

20 Surreptitious use of the forbidden grape varieties could only be curbed after the development of a chemical test for pigments present only in the hybrids (Larousse, *Wines and Vineyards of France*, London: Ebury Press, 1990, 94).

21 William Echikson, *A Bordeaux Wine Revolution* (New York: W.W. Norton & Company, Inc., 2004: 22–3).

22 Hallgarten, *Scandal*, 129.

23 "Mafia Blamed for 70 Million Litres of Tainted Italian Wine," *Agence France Press*, 4 April 2008.

24 Hallgarten *Scandal*, 34–9, 52, 67–8. Fielden (*Wine You Ordered*, 78–9) claims that the antifreeze accusations were based on a confusion with ethylene glycol. In fact both can be used in antifreeze. Diethylene glycol, while very sweet to the taste, is toxic – but fortunately only in considerably larger doses than might be added to the typical wine bottle.

25 Walt Bogdanich and Jake Hooker, "From China to Panama, a Trail of Poisoned Medicine," *New York Times*, 6 May 2007; "This Product Made in China ... Badly," *Daily Telegraph*, 8 July 2010.

26 See Vincent Carosso, *The California Wine Industry: A Study of the Formative Years* (Berkely: University of California Press, 1951), and Pellechia, *Wine*, 138; Echikson, *Noble Rot*, 24–6, 78, 84.

27 Examined in Colman, *Wine Politics*, op. cit.

28 On the early unionization drive, see John Dunne, *Delano: The Story of the California Grape Strike* (New York: Farrar, Straus & Giroux, 1967) and George Horwitz, *La Causa: The California Grape Strike* (New York: MacMillan, 1970). For a chronology of the farm worker struggles, see "Cesar Chavez Chronology," www.latinamericanstudies.org/latinos/chavez-chronology.htm. For the fading of the UFA, see James Rainey, "Farm Workers Union Ends 16-Year Boycott of Grapes," *Los Angeles Times*, 22 November 2000.

29 Loubère, *Wine Revolution*, 63.

30 On the improvement, see "American Wine Comes of Age," *Time*, 27 November 1972.

31 Pellachia, *Wine*, 206.

32 Tracie Cone, "Moth Forces Wine Country's Secret into the Open," *Associated Press*, 27 March 2010.

33 Sarah Murray, *Moveable Feasts: From Ancient Rome to the 21st Century, the Incredible Journeys of the Food We Eat* (New York: St Martin's Press, 2007), 149.

34 Cited in Colman, *Wine Politics*, 104.

35 Meraiah Foley, "A Grim Morning After for Australian Wines," *New York Times*, 23 June 2009.

36 Kermit Pattison, "The Scourge of Napa Valley," *Inc.com*, 1 May 2006.

37 Dennis Grimes. "Eagles Nest Winery." *Wine Tasting San Diego*, 2 February 2010; "Worker Died Pruning on Two Buck Chuck Co-owner's Land," *Decanter*, 13 June 2008; Don Santina, "How Maria Fell," *Counterpunch*, 24/26 October 2008.

38 Thanks to Sarah Hartney for this information.

39 Colman, *Wine Politics*, 121, 134.

40 The wiki entry (en.wikipedia.org/wiki/Resveratrol) seems a reasonable and balanced summary.

41 Dorothee Provost et al., "Brain Tumors and Exposure to Pesticides: A Case-Control Study in Southwestern France," *Occupational and Environmental Medicine* 64, no. 8, 2007. See also Northwestern Coalition for Alternatives to Pesticides, "Brain Cancer Linked to Pesticide Exposure," June 2007, www.pesticide.org/hhg/braincancer.html. See the reply to the Pesticide Action Network campaign on wine residues by European

Crop Protection Association – Safely Securing Europe's Food Supply, "The Use of Pesticides in Producing Wine Grapes – Essential and Safe." In their opinion "Campaigners in favour of a ban on pesticides should fully consider the implications – on our wine industry, and European agriculture more generally" but not, apparently, on the health of workers or consumers.

42 Bo Strandeberg and Ronald Hites, "Concentration of Organochloride Pesticides in Wine Corks," *Chemosphere* 44, no. 4, August 2001.

43 "Plastic-Cork Makers Bob Up All Over," *The Free Library by Farlex* (Gardner Publications, 1999), www.thefreelibrary.com/Plastic-Cork+Makers+Bob+ Up+All+Over-a058163435.

44 Robert Parker, cited in Echikson, *Noble Rot*, 93.

45 See especially Elin McCoy, *The Emperor of Wine: The Rise of Robert M. Parker Jr and the Reign of the American Taste* (New York: HarperCollins, 2005), 95–6, and Echikson, *Noble Rot*, chapter 4.

46 McCoy (*Emperor*, 276–7) notes that a class of super-tasters really does exist, blessed with more taste buds on their tongues than ordinary mortals. But appreciation of wine depends more on smell, and all humans have the same number of receptors in their noses.

47 See the report by Adam Sage, "Cheeky Little Test Exposes Wine 'Experts' as Weak and Flat," *Times of London*, 14 January 2002. See also Roger Downey, "Wine Snob Scandal," *Seattle Weekly*, 20 February 2002. On the California experiments, see Jonah Lehrer, "Grape Expectations: What Wine Can Tell Us about the Nature of Reality," *Boston Globe*, 24 February 2008.

48 Stephen Reiss, "Wine Forensics: The Science of Fraud Detection," *Wine Whines*, WineEducation.com, 19 August 2006.

49 Simon Loftus, *Anatomy of the Wine Trade* (London: Sidgwick & Jackson), 143–5, 152–3, 157.

50 Scott Sayare, "Struggling French Pawn Grand Crus," *The Independent*, 13 May 2009.

51 Mahesh Kumar, "Fuelling Up Your Investment Barrel," bmo *InvestorLine*, Fall 2006.

52 US Department of Justice, "Colorado Wine Merchant Arrested in $13 Million Wine Futures Caper," press release, 30 September 2004, and "Colorado Wine Merchant Agrees to Plead Guilty to Federal Fraud Charges in Wine Futures Caper," press release, 14 June 2005; Eric Arnold, "Futures Fraudster Sentenced to Pay $11 Million Restitution, but Avoids Jail," *Wine Spectator*, 13 February 2007; Eric Arnold, "Rare llc Trustee Held Accountable for Wine Futures Sales Gone Wrong," *Wine Spectator*, 23 March 2007.

53 Martin Hickman, "Hundreds of Wine-Lovers Lose Out as 'Posh Farepak' Crashes," *The Independent,* 29 November 2006.

54 Stacy Meichtry, "Swell or Swill? – Top Vineyards Fend Off Bogus Bottles; 'French' Vintages Produced in China," *Wall Street Journal,* 10 August 2006.

55 Scheherazade Daneshkhu, "Asia Demand Drives Hopes of Bordeaux Bonanza," *Financial Times,* 4 June 2010.

56 Bill Schiller, "Fake Icewines from China Put Chill on Canadian Sales; Booze Business Booming for Counterfeiters," *Toronto Star,* 18 August 2007.

57 Peter D. Meltzer, "Single-Owner Cellar Sets New Record, Bringing in Almost $11 Million," *Wine Spectator*, 31 January 2006.

58 In Italy the system is *Denominazione di Origine Controllata e Garanatita* (DOCG – wine from a specific area with strict rules, re: grade, yield, alcohol content, age etc., and tests to prove it); *Denominazione di Origine Controllata* (DOC – similar but permitting more production per hectare); *Indicazione Geografica Tipica* (an intermediate classification, with some blending); and *Vino de Tavola* (VdT – various blends from various areas).

59 "Will the Real Brunello Stand Up?" *Off License News,* 11 July 2008; Eric Asimov, "Fraudulent Brunellos? Shocking!" *New York Times,* 3 April 2008; Peter Wells, "Italy Completes Brunello Inquiry," *New York Times* 7 August 2009; Eric Asimov, "Brunello Inquiry Cites Five Wineries," *New York Times,* 11 August 2009.

60 There was substantial coverage of the scandal. See for example "France Wine Producers Guilty of US Scandal," BBC *News*, 17 February 2010.

61 This is well explained in James Suckling, "A Taste of Deception," *Wine Spectator*, 31 May 1998.

62 Stephen Foley, "Christie's Linked with Counterfeit Wine Scam," *The Independent*, 7 March 2007.

63 Michael Reid, "Label Flaws Uncork Fake Grange Racket," *The Australian*, 18 March 1998; Roger Maynard, "Australia Uncovers Fake Wine Racket," *The Times*, 19 March 1998; "How to Spot a Fake Wine," *The Times,* 18 March 2000; Jeff Collerson, "Beating Vintage Cheats," *Daily Telegraph* Sydney, 7 February 2000; Gadi Hoenig, "Anti-Counterfeiting Technology Could Protect Wine and Profits," *Wine Business Monthly* 9, no. 7, 12 July 2002; Cahal Milmo, "Science Joins the Fight to Sniff Out Wine Fraud," *The Independent*, 17 June 2004; Stacy Meichtry, "Swell or Swill …" *Wall Street Journal,* 10 August 2006; AFP, "Ion Beams Fight against Fraud" ABC *Science*, 3 September 2006.

64 "How to Spot a Fake Wine," *Times of London*, 18 March 2000.

65 Alison Beard, "Investors Are Left with a Bitter Taste – Wine Fraud," *Financial Times*, 8 June 2002.

66 Cited by John Wilke, "Sour Note," *Wall Street Journal*, 1 September 2006.
67 Adam Lechmere "Koch: 'I will keep fighting fraud'" *Decanter.com*, 29
   August 2007; Adam Lechmere, "Broadbent to Sue over Billionaire's Vinegar," *Decanter.com*, 27 July 2009; James Suckling, "A Taste of Deception,"
   Wine Spectator, 31 May 1998; Mitch Frank, "Collector Accuses Chicago Companies of Wine Fraud," *Wine Spectator*, 1 April 2008; Andrew
   Johnson, "Christie's Sells 'Fake' Vintage Wine, Claims Billionaire," *The
   Independent*, 18 April 2010.
68 Cited in John Wilke, "Sour Note," *Wall Street Journal*, 1 September 2006.
69 *Agence France Presse*, 31 October 2006.
70 John Stimpfig, "There's Gold in Those Bordeaux Fields – Huge Demand,
   Short Supplies: Find Wine Investors – and Suppliers – Have Never Had It
   so Good, Says John Stimpfig," *Financial Times*, 10 June 2006.
71 Benjamin Dangl, "A History of el Monstruoso: Mexico City," *Counterpunch*, 6–8 August 2010.
72 Hallgarten, *Wine Scandal*, 102–3, 108; Fielden, *Wine You Ordered*,
   54–60.
73 "'Brut Imperial' Bottlers Watch Their Bubbles Bursting – Fake Moet
   et Chandon Trial," *The Independent*, 18 January 92; Philip Jacobson,
   "Bogus Bubbles Bring a Rum Affair in Cuba to Court – Champagne,"
   Times of London, 18 January 1992; legal proceedings in case No.
   93–82,361 Cour de cassation, Chambre criminelle, 26 Septembre 1994.
74 David Beresford, "Fake Champers Apartheid Style," *Observer*, 8 June
   1997. See also South Africa's *Business Day*, 6 June 1997.
75 Frank J. Prial, "Wine Talk," New York Times, 15 January 1997; Craig
   Dean Sentenced in Millennium Champagne Fraud," *Serious Fraud Office*,
   23 March 2001; "Three jailed for 2m Pound Millennium Champagne
   Scam," *The Independent*, 24 March 2001.
76 Leighton Kitson, "Bubbly Scam Is Taking the Fizz," *Northern Echo*, 24
   November 2000.
77 Alex Marunchak, "The Forger," *Sunday Mirror*, 28 October 2007.
78 Agence France-Presse, "France: Champagne Demand Forces a Bigger
   Vineyard," *New York Times*, 14 March 2008.
79 Jennifer Thompson, "French Drinkers Toast Cheap Champagne," *Financial Times*, 30 December 2009.
80 Cited in Kermit Pattison, "The Scourge of Napa Valley," *Inc.com*, May
   2006.

CHAPTER EIGHT

1 The early history is traced in Egon Caesar Conte Corti, *History of Smoking* (London: George G. Harrap, 1931).

2 For Cuban tobacco in the context of imperial history, see Jean Stubbs, *Tobacco on the Periphery: A Case Study in Cuban Labour History, 1860–1958* (Cambridge: Cambridge University Press, 1985).

3 On the mechanics of smuggling, see J.M. Scott, *The Tea Story* (London: Heinemann, 1964), especially chapter 3.

4 Even the true story is given an unwarranted patriotic tinge by the normally very prescient Thom Hartmann in "The Real Boston Tea Party Was an Anti-Corporate Revolt," www.commondreams.org/view/2009/04/15-10.

5 See n.a., *The History of the Tea Plant from the Sowing of Its Seed to Its Package for the European Market* (London: Lackington, Hughes, Harding, Mavor and Jones, 1820), for details on the extent of smuggling and techniques for faking. I thank Adam Ginzburg for this reference.

6 Jordan Goodman, *Tobacco in History: The Cultures of Dependence* (London: Routledge, 1993), 219.

7 Corti, *History*, 101, 220, 252.

8 Fernando Ortiz, *Cuban Counterpoint: Tobacco and Sugar* (New York: Alfred A. Knopf, 1947), 68, 88, 90–1. For a detailed examination of the growth of the Cuban Florida-based cigar industry, see Robert P. Ingalls and Louis A Perez Jr, *Tampa Cigar Workers: A Pictorial History* (Gainseville: University Press of Florida, 2003), and Stuart Bruce Kaufman, *Challenge & Change: The History of the Tobacco Workers International Union* (Kensington MD: Bakery, Confectionary and Tobacco Workers International Union, 1986).

9 Stubbs, *Periphery*, 9–10, 18.

10 See Peter Welsh, "A Gentleman of History," *Cigar Aficionado*, 7 January 2008, for a Churchillian puff piece. There is now a book entitled *Churchill's Cigar: A Lifelong Love Affair through War and Peace*. I made a point not to read it.

11 An excellent overview of the cigarette business and its machinations is Goodman, *Tobacco in History*. But see also Peter Taylor, *The Smoke Ring: The Politics of Tobacco* (London: Bodley Head, 1984), and Larry White, *Merchants of Death: The American Tobacco Industry* (New York: Beech Tree Books, 1988).

12 For example in 2005 the industry reported sales at more than three times the early 1990s level ("Cigar Industry Enjoying Sales Boom," *Associated Press*, 6 October 2006).

13 Marc Frank, "Cuban Cigar Maker Welcomes Increase in Millionaires," *Financial Times*, 5 July 2010.

14 Ortiz, *Tobacco and Sugar*, 44.

15 Information received onsite at Pinar del Río. On general farm conditions, see also Paul Reid, "The Ultimate Cigar," *Palm Beach Post*, 27 April 1997.

16 Cited in "Cuban Cigar Maker Welcomes Increase in Millionaires," *Financial Times*, 5 July 2010.

17 Ruadhan MacCormaic, "Cigars out as Sarkozy Cuts Perks ahead of Austerity Plan," *The Irish Times*, 26 June 2010.

18 "Christian Blanc: un lynchage sans prevue," *Le Soir* (Brussels), 5 July 2010; "Blanc s'est fait offrir 12 000 euros de cigares par l'État," *L'Express*, 15 June 2010.

19 See Bryan Farrell, "Tobacco Stains: The Global Footprint of a Deadly Crop," *In These Times*, 1 October 2007, and Ellen Hickey and Yenyen Chen, "Tobacco, Farmers and Pesticides: The Other Story," *Pesticide Action Network North America*, May 1998.

20 On the other hand, the US periodically insists that the blue mould that periodically blights its own tobacco crops is blown into the US from Pinar del Río in Cuba (North American Plant Disease Forecast Center, *North Carolina Blue Mold Forecast*, 3 June 2005).

21 "Cuba Rationing Cigarette Sales," *New York Times*. 10 September 1991.

22 Larry Rohter, "Castro's Cigar, a Namesake, and Smell of Trouble," *New York Times*, 7 November 1997.

23 For an overview, see "Touring Pro Bogus Stogies. The Insult: Those Havanas You just Bought Are Fakes. The Injury: Customs May Decide to Bust You Anyway," *Forbes*, 17 November 1997; and James Suckling, "Not the Real Thing: Counterfeits of the Top Cuban Cigar Brands Are Flooding the World Market," *Cigar Aficionado*, Summer 1994.

24 Details of the case are available in United States v. Richard S. Connors Case No. 01–3478 in the United States Court of Appeals for the Seventh Circuit argued 27 October 2005 – 21 March 2006. See also Steven Warmbir, "Cuban Cigar Smuggling Is a Tale, Author Argues; US Says Chicagoan Sneaked Thousands of Them Here in '90s," and Dave Newbart, "Ex-Wife Tells How She Helped Feds Nab Cigar Smuggler," *Chicago Sun-Times*, 22 November 2003.

25 Greg B. Smith, "Stogie Sting Nets 2 More, Feds Say," *New York Daily News*, 8 August 1998.

26 See Glenn Collins, "Illegal Smoke for the 90s, from Cuba," *New York Times*, 8 August 1998.

27 For a selective history, see Loy Glenn Westfall, "Cigar City USA," *Smoke Magazine* 12, no. 4, Fall 2007. Thanks to Sean Hallisey for information about the early anti-counterfeiting efforts.

28 "A Churchill, or Factory-Floor Sweepings?" *The Economist*, 15 March 1997.

29 Private information from someone who finances Cuba trips this way.

30 See Michael Douglas, "Spotting Fake Cuban Cigars," *Smoke Magazine* 3, no. 2, Spring 1998.

31 Jack Boulware, "Holy Cohiba!" *SF Weekly*, 6 October 1999. This view was echoed nearly a decade later by the Government Accountability Office report that the resources put into chasing individual cigar and rum smugglers detracted from serious concerns like anti-terrorism or anti-narcotics actions (Marc Lacey "Report Finds US Agencies Distracted by Focus on Cuba," *New York Times*, 19 December 2007).

32 "An Eye on ... Fags, Drink 'n' Drugs," *The Independant*, 18 November 1997.

33 "Cigar Giant Fights Counterfeit Smokes," *Miami Daily Business Review* 78, no. 47, 15 August 2003.

34 Jay Weaver, "Cigar Firm Funds Probe," *Miami Herald*, 10 October 2006; Jay Weaver, "Hialeah Man Guilty of Selling Fake Cigars," *Miami Herald*, 14 October 2006.

35 Not so laudatory perhaps was the work of another US company that machine-made cigars using local tobacco, adding just a seasoning of Cuban pre-embargo filler so they could be sold under the name "Havana Blend" (www. cigarenvy.com, 14 December 2005)

36 William E. Geist, "Sold: Cigar Boxes of Illegal Cuban Treasures," *New York Times*, 10 December 1983.

37 Burton Bollag, "Seller of Expensive Cigars Stops Buying from Cuba," *New York Times*, 3 January 2008.

38 The trick was to steal genuine letters signed by Lord Mountbatten from Sotheby's, delete and replace the text, and use them to authenticate the fake labels. Information on the breaking of the ring reported in "A Year of Fakers and Thieves," *Times of London*, 21 July 1990.

39 When the son of the Cuban planter credited with creating the Montecristo set up shop in Brazil in 2002 to begin selling what he claimed was the cigar equivalent of a single-malt whiskey, i.e., made from only one type of leaf when most industrial cigars are blends, his proudest claim was that it was supposedly indistinguishable from the best of Cuba (Tony Smith, "Coming Soon to the US: Cuban Cigars Made in Brazil," *The New York Times*, 26 January 2003).

40 "Ron Perelman," www.cigaraficionado.com/Cigar/CA_Profiles/Cigar_Stars_Profile/0,2547,142,00.html.

41 "Cuba Bans Smoking in Public," CBC News, 7 February 2005.

CHAPTER NINE

1 Sarah Lyall, "Illness Strikes Patrons of Fat Duck Restaurant in Britain," *New York Times*, 6 March 2009.

2 Eating them live takes place in Tokyo's famed Tsukiji fish market, but in Spain or France they are fried. See Manny Howard, "Now Swimming onto Menus, Glass Eels," *New York Times*, 30 April 2003.

3 Most accounts, it seems, are copied from Martin Fletcher, "Champagne, Lobster and Caviar: Robert Mugabe Plans Binge in Land of Hunger," *Sunday Times* (London), 10 February 2009.

4 Thanks to several former students (Tara Doolan, Kuroush Sarafzade, Kyle McWhinnie, Arabella Ramsey, Tomek Nishijima, and Alex Fraenkel) who introduced me to the underworld of caviar.

5 For a sketch of how these standards are formulated, and change, see for example, Felipe Fernández-Armesto, *Near a Thousand Tables: A History of Food* (New York: Free Press, 2002).

6 "The Last Supper of King Farouq," *New York Times*, 31 August 2009.

7 The story of the rise and collapse of the once magnificent New York harbour oysters is told in Mark Kurlansky, *The Big Oyster: History on the Half Shell* (New York: Ballantine Books, 2006). Thanks to Daniel Pujdak for introducing me to the ecology of oysters. On the cascade effects of the Gulf blowout, see Dan Barry, "From a Gulf Oyster, a Domino Effect," *New York Times*, 15 July 2010.

8 I thank Katie Reisman for teaching me about abalone poaching. See, for example, Michael Wines, "Poachers' Way of Life Is Endangering the Abalone's," *New York Times*, 3 November 2006.

9 See, for example, the recent crackdown on forty-six restaurants in Melbourne; Australia had until recently one of the last reputedly "sustainable" abalone fisheries in the world ("Black Market Abalone Ring Busted," *The Age*, 12 May 2005). On the similar underground traffic in geoduck (AKA "gooey duck"), the world's largest burrowing clam, see Craig Welch, *Shell Games: Rogues, Smugglers and the Hunt for Nature's Bounty* (New York: William Morrow, 2010). Thanks to Jennifer Jacquet for this reference.

10 I thank Daniel Pujdak for informing me about the bluefin tuna. See especially Sasha Issenberg, *The Sushi Economy: Globalization and the Making of a Modern Delicacy* (New York: Gotham Books, 2008), and Trevor Corson, *The Story of Sushi: An Unlikely Saga of Raw Fish and Rice* (New York: Harper, 2008). On the recent politics of tuna, see Peter Brown, "Sushi Lovers Tense in Tokyo," *Asia Times*, 16 September 2009.

11 Lewis Smith, "No More Fish to Eat in 40 Years," *Times of London*, 3 November 2006.

12 On these developments, see Callum Roberts, *Unnatural History of the Sea* (Washington: Island Press, 2007).

13 Alan Moorehead, *The Fatal Impact: An Account of the Invasion of the South Pacific 1767–1840. Part Three: The Antarctic* (London: Penguin 1968).

14 Roberts, *Unnatural*, chapters 10, 11.

15 William Broad, "From Deep Pacific, Ugly and Tasty, with a Catch," *New York Times*, 10 September 2009; Geoffrey Lean, "Predators Starve as We Plunder Oceans," *The Independent*, 19 April 2009.

16 Alanna Mitchell, *Sea Sick: The Global Ocean in Crisis* (Toronto: McClelland & Stewart, 2009), 130–6.

17 An early serious examination is Pol Chantraine, *The Last Codfish: Life and Death of the Newfoundland Way of Life* (Montreal: Robert David Publishing, 1993). See also Michael Harris, *Lament for an Ocean: The Collapse of the Atlantic Fishery* (Toronto: McClelland & Stewart, 1998); R. Ommery, "One Hundred Years of Fisheries Crisis in Newfoundland," *Acadiensis* 28, no. 2; F. Mason, "The Newfoundland Cod Stock Collapse: A Review and Analysis of Social Factors," *Electronic Green Journal* 1, no. 17.

18 Charles Clover, *The End of the Line: How Overfishing Is Changing the World and What We Eat* (Berkeley, University of California Press: 2008), 94–117; Robert, *Unnatural*, chapter 15.

19 For a small sample of the resources available on Spanish maritime predation, see www.illegal-fishing.info/sub_approach.php?subApproach_id=125. Thanks to Melissa Garcia-Lamarca.

20 The autonomous government of Catalonia took the courageous step in summer 2010 of finally banning the "sport" in its jurisdiction – even if the move was prompted more by nationalism than by humanitarianism ("Catalonia Bans Bullfighting," *The Independent*, 28 July 2010).

21 George Monbiot, "A New Wave of Food Colonialism Is Snatching Food from the Mouths of the Poor," *Guardian*, 26 August 2008, and George Monbiot, "Peter Mandelson Is Bullying the World's Poorest Nations into Following a Development Route That Can't Work," *Guardian*, 8 September 2008.

22 Felicity Lawrence, *Eat Your Heart Out: Why the Food Business Is Bad for the Planet and Your Health* (London: Penguin, 2008), 214; Elisabeth Rosenthal, "Europe's Appetite for Seafood Propels Illegal Trade," *New York Times*, 15 January 2008. The World-Wide Fund for Nature now reckons about 50 percent of Europe's total fish consumption (whether from European or foreign sources) is of illegal origin.

23 For an American view, see Jeffrey Gettleman, "Somali Pirates Tell All: They're in It for the Money," *New York Times*, 1 October 2008; Jeffrey Gettleman, "Somalia's Pirates Flourish in a Lawless Nation," *New York Times*, 31 October 2008; and Jeffrey Gettleman, "For Somali Pirates, Worst Enemy May Be on Shore," *New York Times*, 9 May 2009. There is wide range of considerably deeper reporting around the world. See, for example, Rubrick Biegon, "Somali Piracy and the International Response," *Foreign Policy in Focus*, 29 January 2009; Shashank Bengali, "Somalis Say Illegal Fishing by Foreign Trawlers Drove Them to Piracy," *McClatchy*, 29 April 2009; Daniel Howden, "Somali Piracy: An Insider's View," *The Independent*, 16 June 2009; and "How the Seychelles Became a Pirates' Paradise," *The Independent*, 8 February 2010; Najad Abdullahi,

"Toxic Waste behind Somali Piracy," *Al Jazeera*, 15 April 2009; Mohamed Abshir Waldo, "Somali Piracy: The Other Side of the Coin," *African Prospects*, October 2009.

24 My thanks to Namita Kallianpurkar for work on flags of convenience in illegal fishing.

25 See especially Environmental Justice Foundation, *Pirates and Profiteers: How Pirate Fishing Fleets Are Robbing People and Oceans* (London: 2005); see also Bertrand Le Gallic and Anthony Cox, "An Economic Analysis of Illegal, Unreported and Unregulated Fishing," *Marine Policy*, 15 December 2005.

26 Thanks to Hannah Freeman for some of this information. See C. Pet-Soede et al., "An Economic Analysis of Blast Fishing on Indonesian Coral Reefs," *Environmental Conservation* 26, no. 2, 1999, and Martin Guard and Mwajuma Masaiganah, "Dynamite Fishing in Southern Tanzania," *Marine Pollution Bulletin* 34, no. 10, 1997.

27 For example, the French legal fleet in 2007 had a quota of 4,200 tons of bluefin tuna; its actual catch was probably more than 7,000 (Michael McCarthy, "Is This the End of the Bluefin Tuna?" *The Independent*, 29 November 2008).

28 See, for example, National Oceans and Atmospheric Administration, "Seafood Importer and Associated Corporations Receive Imprisonment and Fines," NOAA news release, 8 January 2007; United States Attorney's Office, Central District of California, "President of Company That Illegally Imported Catfish Sentenced to More than Five Years in Federal Prison," press release, 19 May 2009.

29 See, for example, Y.-H. Peggy Hsieh et al., "Species Substitution of Retail Snapper Filets," *Journal of Food Quality* 18, 1995; Robb Walsh, "Fish Fraud," *Houston* Press, 1 November 2001; Peter Marko et al., "Fisheries: Mislabelling of a Depleted Reef Fish," *Nature*, no. 430, 2004; Douglas Fox, "Imposter Fish," *Conservation*, October-December 2008; Eugene Wong and Robert Hanner, "DNA Barcoding Detects Market Substitution in North American Seafood," *Food Research International* 41, 2008. My thanks to Caitlin Tanner for research on this subject.

30 See, for example, Stephen Nohlgren and Terry Tomalin, "You Order Grouper; What Do You Get?" *St Petersburg Times*, 6 August 2006.

31 Bryan Miller, "Fish with an Image Problem," *New York Times*, 23 September 1981; William Broad, "From Deep Pacific, Ugly and Tasty, with a Catch," *New York Times*, 9 September 2009.

32 See especially Jennifer Jacquet and Daniel Pauly, "Trade Secrets: Renaming and Mislabeling of Seafood," *Marine Policy*, 23 June 2007, and Jennifer Jacquet and Daniel Pauly, "The Rise of Seafood Awareness Campaigns in an Era of Collapsing Fisheries," *Marine Policy* 31, 2007.

33 See David Nicholson-Lord, "Fish, Once Thought the Healthiest of Foods, Is Now Bad for Us," *New Statesman*, 23 August 2004; Stephen Leahy, "Marine Scientists Report Massive 'Dead Zones,'" *Inter Press Service*, 6 October 2006.

34 By the millennium, at a minimum 30 percent of the open-sea fisheries were in a state of collapse, defined as less than 10 percent of their highest recorded level. Within European waters, total fish stocks may be only 5 percent of their former peak (Roberts, *Unnatural*, 195). However, the Environmental Justice Foundation (*Pirates and Profiteers*, passim) puts the percentage of world fish stocks fully or over exploited and depleted at 75 percent.

35 There is an excellent summary in National Environmental Trust, *Black Market for White Gold: The Illegal Trade in Chilean Sea Bass*, 9 January 2004.

36 *Washington Post*, 3 November 2006; *Times of London*, 3 November 2006. The Pacific plastic layer has been notorious for several years. The shock was to recently discover a huge expanse of floating plastic debris in the North Atlantic that may be as great or greater (Steve Connor, "Now Atlantic Is Found to Have Huge 'Garbage Patch,'" *The Independent*, 20 August 2010.

37 Martin Fackler, "Japan Turns to Technology to Lift Fishing Industry," *New York Times*, 26 December 2008.

38 See Terry Lavin, "Introduction," *A Stain upon the Sea: West Coast Salmon Fishing*, Stephen Hume et al. (Madeira Park, BC: Harbour Publishing, 2004). See also Kenneth Weiss, "Fish Farms Become Feedlots of the Sea: Like Cattle Pens, the Salmon Operations Bring Product to Market Cheaply. But Harm to Ocean Life and Possibly Human Health Has Experts Worried," *Los Angeles Times*, 9 December 2002; and Tara Lohan "How Farm-Raised Salmon Are Turning Our Oceans into Dangerous and Polluted Feedlots," *Alternet*, 2 September 2009. Strictly speaking, the shrimp is also a carnivore, but shrimp farming, despite being much older, only reached enormous proportions after the salmon boom began.

39 Geoffrey Lean, "Predators Starve as We Plunder Oceans," *The Independent*, 19 April 2009.

40 Salmon of the Americas, "Feeding Farmed Salmon," *TheFishSite* (5M Enterprises Ltd), www.thefishsite.com/articles/18/feeding-farmed-salmon.

41 Alexei Barrioneuvo, "Facing Deadly Fish Virus, Chile Introduces Reforms," *New York Times*, 4 September 2008.

42 A *New York Times* investigation (Marian Burros, "Stores Say Wild Salmon but Tests Say Farm Bred," 2 August 2008) in the Fulton Market showed six of eight "wild caught" salmon filets tested were farmed.

43 On the uncertainties in prediction, and the fact that an occasional dramatic jump in numbers is hardly inconsistent with long-term overfishing, see Judith Lavoie, "Caution Urged after Huge Sockeye Run: It Would Be Foolish to Consider Numbers a Trend, Commission Told," *Vancouver Sun*, 16 September 2010, and "Record Sockeye Run Smells Fishy to Scientists," *Canadian Press*, 26 August 2010.

44 Mark Hume, "An Ecosystem in Turmoil Puts Its Predators at Risk," *The Globe and Mail*, 18 September 2009.

45 Although inspectors in the US occasionally bar a shipment of Chinese fish, the overwhelming share gets through so that the US now takes 80 percent of its eel and 70 percent its of tilapia from Chinese fish farms (see, for example, David Barboza, "In China, Farming Fish in Toxic Waters," *New York Times*, 15 December 2007).

46 Andrew Revkin, "Tracking the Imperiled Bluefin from Ocean to Sushi Platter," *New York Times*, 3 May 2005; Martin Hickman, "Political Infighting Threatens Survival of the Bluefin Tuna," *The Independent*, 4 September 2009; George Monbiot, "Bluefin Tuna Loses Out Simply Because Scare Fish Make a Profit," *Guardian*, 19 March 2010.

47 In general, see UK Glass Eels, "Suppliers of Glass Eels for Farming and Restocking, Developing a Sustainable Fishery," www.glasseel.com. A good account is "Eel Life History," *Mahalo*, www.mahalo.com/eel-life-history.

48 Bob Sherwood, "UK's Disappearing Eels," *Financial Times*, 27 March 2010.

49 On the emergence of gula, see Mark Kurlansky, "Baby Eels: Look at the Eyes before You Bite," *New York Times*, 27 April 1994. On farming: P. Angelis et al., "Glass Eels Growth in a Recirculating System," *Mediterranean Marine Science* 6, no. 1, 2005.

50 Steve Connor, "A Giant Leap into the Unknown: GM Salmon That Grows and Grows," *The Independent*, 22 September 2010. An attempt to force open a market for fillets from the ocean pout in the US as an emergency World War II measure failed.

51 Julia Moskin, "Can a bit of Arctic Pep Up Ice Cream?" *International Herald Tribune*, 31 July 2006.

52 Two recent accounts are Inga Saffron, *Caviar: The Strange History and Uncertain Future of the World's Most Coveted Delicacy* (New York: Broadway Books, 2002), and Richard Adams Carey, *The Philosopher Fish: Sturgeon, Caviar and the Geography of Desire* (Cambridge, MA: Perseus, 2005). For an analytical overview, see *Roe to Ruin: The Decline of Sturgeon in the Caspian Sea and the Road to Recovery* (a joint publication of the Natural Resources Defense Council, the Wildlife Conservation Society, and SeaWeb, December 2000).

53 Charles Hawley, "Europe's Underwater Chemical Dump," *Der Spiegel*, 30 August 2006. The same problem can be found in certain lakes of reputedly pristine Switzerland. See Tony Paterson, "Switzerland's Explosive War Effort Threatens Environmental Disaster," *The Independent*, 13 September 2009.

54 Carey, *Philosopher Fish*, 123–4 et passim.

55 The problem existed for decades – only by the turn of the millennium was it so appalling that it had to be officially recognized as hazardous for aquatic life ("Caspian Pollution Reaches 'Dangerous" Level,'" *Asia Pulse*, 20 August 2001.

56 Nabi Abdullaev, "Dagestanis Fish for Sturgeon, Caviar, Bribes," *Moscow Times*, 11 October 2000; Julie Bain, "An Unholy Roe," *The New York Times*, 6 August 2000; Jeffrey Tayler, "The Caviar Thugs," *Atlantic Monthly*, June 2001.

57 Eric Hansen, *Orchid Fever: A Horticultural Tale of Love, Lust and Lunacy* (London: Methuen, 2000), 217–8, suggests that the "flora" part was thrown in as an afterthought.

58 On the general record of international environmental treaties, see James Speth, *Red Sky at Morning: America and the Crisis of the Global Environment* (New Haven: Yale University Press, 2004), part 2, although he seems overly positive about CITES in an otherwise negative assessment.

59 George Monbiot, "Feeding Frenzy," *The Guardian*, 3 April 2007.

60 Peter J. Brown, "Sushi Lovers Tense in Tokyo," *Asia Times*, 16 September 2009; Neil MacFarquhar, "Talks to Address Trade in Tuna and Ivory," *New York Times*, 11 March 2010; Paul Bignell, "Ban on Bluefin Tuna Would 'Threaten Japanese Culture,'" *The Independent*, 14 March 2010; George Monbiot, "Bluefin Tuna Loses Out Simply because Scarce Fish Make a Profit," *Guardian*, 19 March 2010.

61 For some of the misuses, see CITES *World*, no. 8, December 2001, 10.

62 Traffic International, "Sturgeons of the Caspian Sea and the International Trade in Caviar," *Traffic Europe*, November 1996. Larger outlets sometimes covered themselves with things like fake certificates of origin claiming it came from Iran, which also justified higher prices. "The Black Market in Black Gold," *The Independent*, 28 December 2007.

63 Details of several are traced in Simon Cooper, "The Caviar Kings," *Seed Magazine*, 16 January 2006.

64 William M. Carley. "First-Class Mystery: Did You Get Sevruga instead of the Beluga? – And if So, Was Mr Garbarino Responsible for the Insult to Jetting Caviar Lovers?" *Wall Street Journal*, 2 December 1987; "Customs Agents Foil Fancy Fish Eggs Scam," UPI, 17 July 1987; "Greenwich Man Faces Fines in Caviar Scheme," *The Hour*, 12 October 1988.

65 Joseph P. Fried, "A Major Importer Is Convicted of Smuggling Caviar into US," *The New York Times*, 4 November 1999: Jen McCaffery, "Bad News Belugas: Roe v. High Grade: Call in the Sturgeon General!" *New York Observer*, 7 August 2000; and phone interview of Special Agent Edward Grace done by Arabella Ramsey. See also *United States of America v. Eugeniusz Koczuk et al.*, United States Court of Appeals for the Second Circuit Docket No. 00–1504 (L) August Term 2000.

66 William Glaberson, "Caviar Seller Faces Charges of Illegal Distribution and False Records," *The New York Times*, 25 May 2002; Charles Laurence, "Caviar Smuggling as Lucrative as Cocaine for US Crime Gangs," *Daily Telegraph*, 10 November 2002; Anita Hamilton, "The Beluga's Blues," *Time*, 13 January 2003. An almost identical operation by a Miami importer – using couriers via Poland, then offering to sell the stuff with phony certificates claiming the roe to be Atlantic lumpfish, was prosecuted the same year (Department of Justice, "Company President Pleads Guilty to Caviar Smuggling Conspiracy," news release, 26 August 2002.

67 Marian Burros, "Unraveling a Caviar Mystery," *The New York Times*, 27 February 2002; US Department of Justice Office of Public Affairs, "Caviar Company and President Convicted in Smuggling Conspiracy," news release, 31 January 2002.

68 Steven Gray, "Alleged Caviar Con Spawns Indictment of Rockville Wholesaler," *The Washington Post*, 20 November 1999; David Snyder, "Md. Caviar Company Admits Smuggling; Fine of $10.4 Million Sets Federal Record," *The Washington Post*, 22 July 2000; US Department of Justice – Environmental Release, "Caviar Dealers Sentenced for Smuggling," 21 February 2001.

69 Carey, *Philosopher Fish*, 14.

70 *Roe to Ruin*, 12.

71 State of Washington Department of Fisheries, Field Services Program, Investigator Paul Buerger to Lt Ron Swatfigure, *Darnell Interview – Electric City*, 18 November 1993.

72 For an approving press biography, see *The Record* (Bergen) 20 March 1988. Six years later (25 September 1994) the newspaper's tone changed rather dramatically.

73 The operation led to the killing of 2,340 white sturgeon, male and female, producing caviar that retailed $2.5 million, of which Darnell collected about $250,000 over five years. For a good summary of the case, see Kit Boss "Caught Fishing – The Trails of a Sturgeon Pirate on the Columbia," *Seattle Times*, 13 March 1994, and Robert Boyle, "The Cost of Caviar," *The Amicus Journal*, Spring 1994. Much of this information came from or was confirmed by Andrew Cohen, agent of the National Marine Fisheries

Service of the Department of Commerce who headed the investigation, to my former student, Tomek Nishijima. See also Andrew Cohen "Sturgeon Poaching and Black Market Caviar: A Case Study," *Environmental Biology of Fishes* 48, 1997.

74 *Bergen Record*, 4 April 1993. When Sturm-Hansen died in 2006, his obituary omitted all references to the conviction ("Paid Notice: Deaths Hansen, Sturm, Arnold," *The New York Times*, 8 January 2006).

75 C.J. Chivers, "Corruption Endangers a Treasure of the Caspian," *The New York Times*, 28 November 2005.

76 "Sturgeon Catch Cut," *The Moscow Times*, 5 October 1999; "Time Is Running Out for Russia's Sturgeon," *Associated Press*, 22 December 2000; "Beluga Sturgeon Now Critically Endangered," *Moscow Times*, 19 March 2009; "Caviar Poaching Pushes Sturgeon to the Brink," *Moscow Times*, 1 July 2010.

77 Carey, *Philosopher*, 84–5.

78 Doug Simpson, "US Caviar Producers Hope for Ban on Caspian Sea Beluga," *Associated Press*, 30 January 2004.

79 Lori Valigra, "Beluga Ban May Breed New Trade: Appalachian Caviar," *National Geographic News*, 26 January 2006.

80 See for example, Julie Bain, "An Unholy Roe," *The New York Times*, 6 August 2000, and CITES *World*, no. 8, December 2001, 13.

81 Carolyn Said, "Beluga Ban Boosts California Caviar / Restrictions on Caspian Sea Imports Give 2 Sturgeon Farms Chance to Corner Market," *San Francisco Chronicle*, 7 January 2006.

82 Jane Black, "The Race to Satisfy Caviar Craving," *The New York Times*, 27 September 2006.

83 Steven Gray, "Alleged Caviar Con Spawns Indictment of Rockville Wholesaler," *The Washington Post*, 20 November 1999.

84 Douglas Frantz, "An Inquiry Finds Roe Impersonating Caviar," *The New York Times*, 19 November 1999.

85 Yet caviar experts seem to fail their own taste tests. And Inga Saffra remarks that "Most caviar dealers are loath to admit it, but when caviar is properly made and eaten fresh, the different brands are as much alike as two kinds of baking soda" (*Strange History*, 152).

86 On smuggling into Canada of Caspian beluga, sevruga, and oestra mislabelled as Amur River kaluga, see "DNA Testing Proves Case of Fishy Caviar Import," *Globe and Mail*, 15 November 2006. Charges against the man responsible, who had denounced the ban as a penalty imposed on responsible consumers instead of lawless producers, were dropped, and his company was fined $3,000. On British restaurants and the back-alley caviar trade, see Martin Hickman, "British Restaurants Using Black Market Caviar," *The Independent*, 25 July 2007.

87 Oddly the problem here was that the team was not greedy enough. The very low price tipped off a client that something was amiss, and that client informed the authorities (Oregon State Police, "Investigation Leads to Arrests for Illegal Trafficking in Sturgeon," news release, 2 February 2005; "Caviar Scheme Leads to Three Arrests," *Seattle Times*, 2 March 2005; Elroy King, "Six Hooked in Sturgeon Trafficking," *The Dalles Chronicle*, 3 March 2005.

88 Vadim Birstein, one of the world's most experienced sturgeon experts, ventured the opinion to Alex Fraenkel in a telephone interview in 2006 that it was already a common practice. He had previously made DNA tests that showed that 30 percent of the caviar on sale in New York during the Russian binge was misrepresented.

CHAPTER TEN

1 Several of my former students introduced me to the world of animal, particularly parrot, smuggling, especially Krystele Bodet, Liam Foran, Monique Garcia, Gure Garmendia, Mike Leithold, and Daniel Martin. Thanks to Mike Davis and Igor Milosavljević for updating me on parrots and lizards, respectively.

2 "The Buzz: Rare Audubon Set Up for Auction," *Globe and Mail*, 10 September 2010; "World's Most Expensive Book Goes Up for Sale," BBC *News*, 9 September 2010.

3 See Terry Glavin's superbly written *Waiting for the Macaws: And Other Stories from the Age of Extinctions* (Toronto: Viking, 2006), 39–42.

4 www.faintinggoat.com.

5 www.faintinggoatseattle.com/fam.php.

6 "China's Rare River Dolphin Now Extinct, Experts Announce," *National Geographic*, 14 December 2006.

7 Reputedly this has been a problem in Australia, for example. See Raymond Hoser, *Smuggled: The Underground Trade in Australia's Wildlife* (Mosman, NSW: Apolloa Books, 1993), and Raymond Hoser, *Smuggled 2: Wildlife Trafficking, Crime and Corruption in Australia* (Doncaster, VIC: Kotabi Publications, 1996). Officials dismiss these books as simply rants, but they are worth a look.

8 As just one of many examples, in 2000 a Miami man pleaded guilty to illegally trafficking rare reptiles under the cover of such a "breeding farm" in Peru (US Department of Justice, "Florida Man Who Trafficked In Protected Species Pleads Guilty," 7 March 2000).

9 This has been true in Peru in the past, for example. See Catherine Elton, "Peru's Eco-police Make Barely a Dent in Trade of Exotic Pets: 30,000 Animals Sold Each Year," *The Christian Science Monitor*, 5 May 1998.

10 The author has a list several pages long of such magic numbers – all 10 percent.

11 "Peruvian Authorities Foil Exotic-Species Smuggling," *Bergen Record*, 26 August 1997.

12 Bolivia in the early 1980s achieved notoriety for handing out presigned blanks to wild-bird dealers (John Turner, "The Deadly Wild-Bird Trade," *Defenders*, November-December 1985).

13 *New Scientist*, 13 April 1991; Dominic Nathan, "13 Cases of Wildlife Smuggling Prosecuted," *The Straits Times*, 6 March 1995.

14 Heidi Blake, "Man Spotted with Mysterious Bulge in His Clothing Had 18 Monkeys up His Jumper," *Daily Telegraph*, 20 July 2010.

15 The most recent in November 2010. See Jack Phillips, "Drug Tunnel under US-Mexico Border Found, Tons of Pot Seized," *The Epoch Times*, 4 November 2010, and Carrie Kahn, "Tunnels under the US-Mexico Border: Big Increase in Discoveries of Smuggler's Routes," *National Public Radio*, 21 November 2010.

16 US Fish and Wildlife Service, "Federal Agents Target Illegal Bird Trade," news release, 29 April 1998; "Operation Jungle Trade, Largest Customs Wildlife Sting," *Federal Wildlife Officer* 11, no. 3, Fall 1998. For a later sting on the Texas border, see *Brownsville Herald*, 17 June 2001.

17 Michael Grunwald, "US Bags Alleged Trafficker in Reptiles; Import Sting Nets Malaysian's Arrest," *The Washington Post*, 16 September 1998.

18 US Fish & Wildlife Services, press release, 14 December 2000; Department of Justice, "Wildlife Dealer Sentenced for Running International Smuggling Ring," Washington, 8 June 2001; "Wildlife Sting Investigation Captures Notorious Animal Smuggler," *AWI Quarterly*, Fall-Winter 1998–99; BBC *Panorama*, "Animal Underworld," 25 February 2001.

19 Bryan Christy, "The Kingpin," *National Geographic*, January 2010.

20 See for example the CTK (Czech News Agency) 20 September 1997 report on a Czech citizen arrested in Peru for trying to make off with apes, tortoises, snakes, and birds. Another Czech couple was notorious for sailing their yacht around the Caribbean to collect rare parrots.

21 "Car Seat Stuffed with Live Parrots," *United Press International*, 24 March 1993; "Central Europe's Parrot Smuggling Scheme Booms," *Inter Press Service*, 21 November 1996. See also *Prague Post*, 8 March 2000, and *Prague Post*, 29 July 2004, where the blame is put on smugglers, not breeders.

22 Charles A Bergman, "The Bust," *Audubon*, May 1991.

23 Once CITES Appendix II and III material is forfeited, it can be sold at auction after sixty days, so it still enters mainstream trade circuits. By contrast Canadian rules stipulate that: "Under no circumstances are goods detained for CITES purposes to be disposed of by public auction" (Canada

Border Services Agency, *Memorandum D 19–7–1, Guidelines and General Information*, Ottawa, 12 June 2001).

24 Stefan Lovgren, "Huge, Freed Pet Pythons Invade Florida Everglades," *National Geographic*, 3 June 2004; "Pet Python Strangles US Toddler," BBC *News*, 2 July 2009; Guy Adams, "Fugitive Pythons Terrorise Florida," *The Independent*, 16 July 2009.

25 Other market countries, too, have passed legislation to stiffen the impact of CITES (which applies only to international trade) by banning domestic sales of endangered species. See, for example, Environment Canada, "Federal Government Moves to Halt Illegal Wildlife Trade," news release, Ottawa, 6 June 1996. What they usually have not done is to criminalize possession.

26 Although only the curator was charged, one of dealers had a prior conviction for animal trafficking, while paperwork for transactions with the other was "inadequate." The curator was found guilty of theft and wire fraud ("Ex-San Diego Zoo Reptile Curator Fined for Rare Animal Trafficking," *Associated Press*, 18 February 2000; see also US Fish & Wildlife Service, *US CI Biennial Report*, 2000–01).

27 See US Department of Justice, "$1.5 Million Partnership Formed to Rehabilitate and Restore Leopard Shark Habitat in San Francisco Bay," press release, 12 February 2007; "Moon's Church to Pay in Shark Poaching," *Los Angeles Times*, 13 February 2007; Marcus Wohlsen, "Shark Poaching Will Cost Moon's Church," *San Diego Union-Tribune*, 13 February 2007; John Coté, "Moon Church Settles Poach Case," *San Francisco Chronicle*, 13 February 2007; "Sharks over the Moon Following Court Ruling," *Traffic: The Wildlife Trade Monitoring Network*, 15 February 2007. My thanks to Chris Coaloa for bringing this case to my attention.

28 See in particular Alan Green, *Animal Underworld: Inside America's Black Market for Rare and Exotic Species* (New York: Public Affairs, 1999). Asked if the situation had improved in the last decade, Mr Green's response was negative.

29 For an excellent overview of the current situation, see Tony Juniper, "EU Wild-Parrot Scandal," *The Ecologist*, 3 January 2009.

30 McNish, *Big Score*, 29; "20 Tycoons [20 Tales]," *Globe and Mail* (based on Peter C. Newman, *Here Be Dragons: Telling Tales of People, Passion and Power*, Toronto: McLelland and Stewart, 2004), www.globeinvestor.com/series/top1000/articles/2004/20tales.html.

31 Michael Allen, "Parrot Smuggling Apes Drug Trade but Isn't as Risky – Birds' Popularity Raises Prices and Endangers Species; Applying a Fowl Disguise," *The Wall Street Journal*, 28 December 1990.

32 *Audubon*, March 1988.

33 US Fish & Wildlife Service, *The Wild Bird Conservation Act, Summary of Effects*, October 1999.

34 Mark Phillips, "The Wild Bird Conservation Act," *Endangered Species Bulletin*, 1 July 1998.

35 US Department of Justice, "Judge Sentences Last Members of Ring Caught Smuggling Potentially Disease-Bearing Endangered Birds into the United States," 9 November 1994.

36 On the continued devastation of Mexican parrots poached for the US market, see "New Report: US Demand Fuelling Illegal Capture and Trade of Certain Endangered Mexican Parrots," *Defenders of Wildlife*, 14 February 2007.

37 A survey of twenty-three neotropical species in fourteen countries in 2001 showed that eggs had been poached from 30 percent of all parrot nests (Timothy Wright and Catherine Toft, "Nest Poaching for Trade", *Psitta-Scene* 13, no. 3, August 2001.

38 I am indebted to former student Daniel Martin for excellent information and analysis of the Silva case.

39 See "Wings of Desire," NBC *News Transcripts*, 4 January 1998.

40 Glavin (*Waiting*, 57–63) comments on the breeding program: that by the time of its collapse "It had degenerated into a private trading club among millionaire Spix fanciers."

41 Deborah Nelson, "Bird Smuggling Worth Millions – Local Expert Is a Suspect in Federal Probe," *Chicago Sun-Times*, 23 October 1994.

42 See Gretchen Reynolds, "Renowned Bird-Lover Tony Silva's Ugly Fall from Grace," *Outside Magazine*, May 1996, and John Tidwell, "Parrots and Profits," *Zoogoer*, November-December 2000.

43 "Drug King Snitches; Out 88 Years Early. US Attorney Cites Extraordinary Help," *Florida Times-Union*, 28 August 2000; "Drug Kingpin Returns to Animal Dealing," *Animal Welfare Institute Quarterly* 50, no. 2, Spring 2001.

44 There is another Operation Falcon currently run by the US Marshals' Office, a national fugitive apprehension program obviously with no connection to the earlier one.

45 US Department of the Interior, "Operation Falcon Exposes North American and European Black Market in Birds of Prey," news release, 29 June 1984.

46 See the account in Paul McKay, *The Pilgrim and the Cowboy* (New York: McGraw-Hill, 1989).

47 See the exchanges and commentary at www.smuggled.com/silva1.htm. The Silva case also bore an odd resemblance to events in Brazil when, in 1990, one of Latin America's leading ornithologists, who boasted of

perhaps the largest private bird collection in the world and, like Silva, had a reputation for publicly denouncing poaching and smuggling, was arrested at an international airport with twenty-two rare parrots, including several hyacinth macaws, without permits. Unlike Silva, he was quietly released (*Sunday Telegraph*, 15 April 1990).

48 Gavin Foster, "Breeder Jailed over Parrot Smuggling, Expert Is Jailed Over," *The Independent*, 15 April 2000; Paul Wilkinson, "Parrot Expert 'Smuggled Rare Macaws,'" *The Times (London)*, 24 March 2000; Neil Sears, "The 24-Carat Parrots; Smuggled Rare Birds Are Worth Even More than Heroin, Jury Is Told," *Daily Mail*, 24 March 2000; "Smuggling Charge Parrot Breeder Weeps in Court," *Press Association Newsfile*, 5 April 2000.

49 "Bird Smuggling Case Family's DNA Test Hopes," *The Northern Echo*, 8 May 1998.

50 Hannah Chapman, "Jailed Breeder's Hunger Protest," *The Northern Echo*, 2 October 2004; Stuart Arnold and Joe Willis, "Prosecutors Debate Appeal against Dealer's Sentence," *The Northern* Echo, 6 January 2006.

51 Echo Staff, "Smuggler Fails in Court Bid to Reclaim Birds," *The Northern Echo*, 10 July 2004.

52 For another view of the Sissen case, see www.ckcbirds.co.uk/harrysissen.htm.

53 For example, his interview on *The Alex Jones Show*, 10 October 2001.

54 Gaylord Shaw, "Champion of Rare Birds Was Secretly Selling Them," *Seattle Times*, 16 February 1997.

55 See, for example, Stuart Winter, "Bird Smugglers Bring In 'Plague,'" *Express on Sunday*, 28 August 2005.

56 Jessica Speart, "Deadly Cargo: The War on Drugs Claims another Victim: Wildlife Used for Smuggling," *Animals Magazine*, November-December 1994, and Adam Roberts, "The Trade in Drugs and Wildlife," *Animals' Agenda* 16, no. 5, November-December 1996.

57 The story is told in *Los Angeles Times*, 3 April 1996. This was not the only case of a smuggler with hot pants. A year before, two men crossing from Mexico into Texas concealed fourteen snakes, stuffing eight of them in their pants, the rest in a toolbox ("Would Be Snake Smugglers Caught with 8 Reptiles Stuffed in Their Pants," *Rocky Mountain News*, 5 August 1995).

58 Felicity Barringer, "Yielding to Conservationists, eBay Will Ban Ivory Sales," *The New York Times*, 21 October 2008.

59 See, for example, Michael Lemonick et al., "Animal Genocide, Mob Style," *Time*, 14 November 1994, and Kevin Hall, "From Amazon to US," *Milwaukee Journal Sentinel*, 19 August 2001. Interestingly, in eight

years time, there was no change in the $10–20 billion "estimate." Silence may partly reflect official embarrassment at the absurdity of the methods used. For example, in the 1980s, to calculate parrots smuggled into the US, the wildlife service extrapolated from a couple of actual cases using numbers from drug smuggling across the US-Mexico border, numbers that are themselves largely guesswork (Judy Franklin, "Aviculture under Fire," *Canadian Parrot Symposium Papers & Articles*, 1997).

60 "Spot" refers to a purchase or sale for immediate delivery; "forward" for future delivery – there can be a wide difference between spot and future prices. FOB means Free on Board or Freight on Board and refers to which party, buyer or seller, fronts the money to load and ship the goods. CIF is an abbreviation of Cost, Insurance and Freight, a term used in commerce when the seller has to arrange and pay for carriage of goods by sea to the port of destination.

61 Daniel Schweimler, "Protecting Argentina's Parrot Colony," *BBC News*, 6 January 2009.

62 See, for example, Stuart Winter, "Bird Smugglers Bring In 'Plague,'" *Express on Sunday*, 28 August 2005.

63 John Tidwell, "Parrots and Profits," *Zoogoer* – Smithsonian National Zooological Park, November-December 2000.

CHAPTER ELEVEN

1 Karl Kruszelnicki, "Lemmings Suicide Myth," *ABC Science*, 27 April 2004 (abc.net.au/science/k2/moments/s1081903.htm).

2 The best examination is William Marsden, *Stupid to the Last Drop: How Alberta Is Bringing Environmnental Armageddon to Canada (and Doesn't Seem to Care)* (Toronto: Random House, 2007). Claims by industry and government that the environment was protected were revealed as nonsense by Environment Canada testing that showed the volume of arsenic, mercury, and lead in the tailings pond increased by 26 percent in the last four years (Nathan Vanderklippe "Tar Sands Toxins Grow Rapidly," *Globe and Mail*, 9 August 2010; Josh Wingrove, "Elevated Level of Toxins Found in Athabaska River," *Globe and Mail*, 30 August 2010).

3 Alexandra Clough, "Lawsuit: Palm Beach's Lana Marks Left Boutique Holding $330,000 Worth of Bags," *Palm Beach Post*, 19 April 2009.

4 It is temporarily stabilized now at very low levels in southern Africa but virtually gone from the north (Amol Rajan and Mike McCarthy, "He's Black, and He's Back! Private Enterprise Saves Southern Africa's Rhino from Extinction," *The Independent*, 17 June 2008).

5 See especially Amanda Vincent, *The International Trade in Sea-Horses* (Traffic International, 1999).

6 For an account of the jungle of wild-plant regulations with specific reference to orchids, see Eric Hansen, *Orchid Fever: A Horticultural Tale of Love, Lust and Lunacy* (London: Methuen, 2000). For an early warning on the often neglected importance of plant varieties, see Harold Koopowitz and Hilary Kaye, *Plant Extinction: A Global Crisis* (Bromley: Christopher Helm, 1983 and 1990).

7 See the novels (based heavily on reality) by Kenneth Goddard who is in his spare time employed at the forensic lab of the Fish & Wildlife Service of the American Interior Department. His full bibliography is at www.kengoddardbooks.com.

8 Thanks to Aaron Garr, Amanda Shah, and Vijeet Jaisinghani for work on this topic.

9 Tiger nose is prescribed for epilepsy and children's convulsions; the teeth for rabies, asthma, and sores on the penis; the eyeballs for malaria, nervousness, or fevers in children, and for treating convulsions and cataracts; the whiskers for toothaches; the brain to cure laziness and pimples; the blood to strengthen the constitution and will-power; the hair to be burnt to drive away centipedes; the flesh for nausea and malaria, improving vitality and toning the stomach and spleen; the fat for addressing vomiting, dog bites, bleeding, and scalp aliments in children; the skin to treat mental illness; the gallstones for weak and watering eyes and abscesses of the hand; the stomach for calming digestive disorders; the bile for convulsions in children; the testes for tuberculosis and lymph node problems; and the tail for skin diseases.

10 Richard Conniff, *The Natural History of the Rich* (New York: W.W. Norton & Company, 2002), 122.

11 On the Sumatra tiger traffic, see Campbell Plowden and David Bowles, "The Illegal Market in Tiger Parts in Northern Sumatra," ORYNX 31, no. 1, January 1997.

12 Daniel Zatz, "Last Favor for a Missing Tiger," *International Wildlife*, July/August 1993.

13 See, for example, Tejbir Singh, "Tragedy of the Tiger," *India Today* 15 August 1992; John F. Burns, "Medical Potions May Doom Tiger to Extinction," *New York Times*, 15 March 1994; Eugene Linden, "Why the Regal Tiger Is on the Brink of Extinction," *Time*, 28 March 1994; Michael McCarthy, "Tigers Fading Fast in Last Stronghold," *The Independent*, 10 April 2007; Andrew Buncombe, "The Face of a Doomed Species," *The Independent*, 31 October 2007, and "The Big Question: Can India's Tigers Be Saved or Are They Doomed to Disappear?" *The Independent*, 16 July 2009.

14 Debbie Banks and Julian Newman, *The Tiger Skin Trail* (EIA, 2004); Environmental Investigation Agency, "Tiger Skin Update," press release, 19

October 2005. In 2003 a single customs raid turned up skins of 31 tigers, 581 leopards, and 778 otters ("Fur Flies over Tiger Plight," *New Zealand Herald*, 18 February 2006).

15 See, for example, "'Toxic Bob' Wastes Burma: Forced Labour and Pollution Rampant at Canadian-Owned Mine," *Canadian Centre for Policy Alternatives Monitor*, March 2001; "Robert Friedland," *SourceWatch: Your Guide to the Names behind the News* (www.sourcewatch.org/index-php?title+RobertFriedland); Gwen Kinkead, "Battling a Toxic Billionaire," *Men's Journal*, 1 December 2009; and much more. On the divestiture, see Dorothy Kosich, "Friedland's Ivanhoe Finds Myanmar Copper Mine Assets Diverstiture Tough Going," *Mineweb*, 4 October 2007.

16 Peter Popham, "Gold in the Lair of the Tiger," *The Independent*, 10 January 2007.

17 Kristin Nowell, *Far from a Cure: The Tiger Trade Revisited* (Cambridge: Traffic International, 2000), viii; Nirmal Ghosh, "The Global Trade in Farmed Tigers: China, CITES and the Fate of the Tiger," *Counterpunch*, 30 May 2007; Andrew Jacobs, "Tiger Farms in China Feed Thirst for Parts," *New York Times*, 13 February 2010.

18 "Roar Deal for Diners," *Daily Telegraph*, 9 September 2005.

19 See Brian Weirum, "Will Traditional Chinese Medicine Mean the End of the Wild Tiger?" *San Francisco Chronicle*, 11 November 2007.

20 Julian Baum, "Wildlife – Asia's Untamed Business," *Far Eastern Economic Review*, 19 August 1993.

21 WWF Canada, "Massive Tiger Bone Seizure," press release, 9 August 2005. Also included were 400 kg of pangolin scales and 1 kg of carved ivory.

22 A. Kumar and "Firoz," "How We Busted the Tiger Gang," *International Wildlife*, July-August 1993; Kenneth Brower, "Devouring the Earth," *Atlantic Monthly*, November 1994; Julian Baum, "Wildlife – Asia's Untamed Business," *Far Eastern Economic Review*, 19 August 1993; Shada Islam, "Environment – Bone Idle: China, Taiwan Face Sanctions over Wildlife Trade," 30 September 1993; EIA, "Thailand's Tiger Economy: Trading Tigers into Extinction," press conference, 12 June 2001.

23 See also Traffic East Asia – Japan, "Japanese Market Survey of Product Containing Tiger Parts and Derivatives," 15 February 1999.

24 Another result may have been a return to earlier techniques, when a TCM formula was specially concocted by a pharmacist or doctor for a particular patient instead of mass produced in more easily policed factories. Thanks to Kimberley Reid, who interviewed a participant in the underground pharmaceutical trade who fled to Canada ahead of a Chinese crackdown and continued in the same business in his new abode.

25 Nowell, *Cure*, 17, 38, 41–3, 51–2, 93.

26 See, for example, "Fake Tiger Skin Recovered," *The Hindu*, 10 July 2005.

27 Novell, *Cure*, 30; "China Closes Zoo Where Siberian Tiger Was Beheaded, 7 Other Tigers Died," *Associated Press*, 26 December 2007; Bill Marsh, "Fretting about the Last of the World's Biggest Cats," *The New York Times*, 7 March 2010.

28 Cited in Bob Colacello, "OK, Lady, Drop the Shawl," *Vanity Fair*, November 1999.

29 IFAW-WTI, *Wrap Up the Trade – An International Campaign to Save the Endangered Tibetan Antelope* (London: 27 June 2001), an extensive onsite investigation. See also Wildlife Conservation Society, "A Petition to List the Tibetan Antelope as an Endangered Species," a thorough examination of current problems of habitat.

30 By 1998 data (probably based on a few reported incidents rather than any systematic average) a herdsman earned the equivalent of $60/kg for raw wool that trades in India $1,250–1,500 before being made into a scarf that can sell for $2,000–30,000 depending on size, workmanship, and purity (i.e., absence of silk, etc.). While the absolute numbers are bound to be different now, the relationship between return to herdsman and retailer is probably not much affected.

31 Inevitably there were stories of shahtoush traders kicking back profits to fund Kashmiri insurgents; see G.K. Singh, "Kashmiri Militants Smuggling Wildlife Products," *The Pioneer*, 8 November 1995. These claims came first from three shahtoush dealers supposedly working as undercover informants for Indian intelligence. More likely they were caught and offered a deal.

32 Judy Mills, "Fashion Statement Spells Death for Tibetan Antelope," *Traffic International*, October 1999.

33 Its clients were further told that they were helping the hard-working Tibetan poor. "A difficult process then commences as local shepherds, called Boudhs, from the region of Changthang, Tibet, climb into the mountains during the three spring months to search for and collect the matted hair." These claims were disproved well before by Dr George Shaller, director for science of the Wildlife Conservation Society. For details, see Bob Colacello, "OK, Lady, Drop the Shawl" *Vanity Fair*, November 1999.

34 US Fish & Wildlife Service, "Shahtoosh Dealers Plead Guilty to Smuggling and Illegal Sale of Tibetan Antelope Shawls," press release, 7 July 2000; Susan Saulny, "Shawls Sold at Charity Event: So Soft, so Rare and so Illegal," *The New York* Times, 3 January 2001.

35 The largest was reportedly twenty feet long and priced at £15,000. But such numbers have to be treated with skepticism (www.met.police.uk/wildlife/new%20site%20docs/docs/shah.htm).

36 "Govt Ready to Grant Rs 50 mn for Kashmir's Shahtoosh Workers," *The Press Trust of India Limited*, 6 August 2002; Wildlife Trust of India, "WTI Helps Indian Customs and DRI Officials Seize 230 kgs of Raw Shahtoosh Wool," press release, 26 September 2002; Maneesh Pandey, "26 Shahtoosh Shawls Seized in Hotel Shop," *The Times of India*, 13 February 2003.

37 "Return of the Shawl" *Hindustan Times*, 8 December 1999; "Cast This Shawl Away," *The Hindu*, 12 August 2001; Neelam Raaj, "And Now 'Pashmina' Chinese Shawls!" *The Times of India*, 11 December 2005.

38 Saurabh Sinha, "Illegal Wildlife Trade Runs away from City," *The Times of India*, 19 November 2002; "21 Shahtoosh Shawls Seized by CBI," *The Times of India*, 23 November 2005; Divya Khanna "Toosh in Your Cupboard!" *The Times of India*, 25 November 2005; "Shahtoosh Smugglers Follow 'Modern Silk Route,'" *Hindustan Times*, 20 November 2005; Amrit Dhillon, "Lethal Cost of Luxury; Kashmiri Weavers and the Tibetan Antelope Have Shared an Uncertain Future since the Global Ban on the Shahtoosh Trade," *South China Morning Post*, 5 November 2005.

39 "Pashmina War," *Business Line*, 2 May 2008.

40 Dilpreet B. Chhabra, "Don't Buy Trouble, Warns TRAFFIC India," *Traffic International*, 29 February 2008.

41 For a comprehensive overview, see Volker Homes, *On the Scent: Conserving Musk Deer – The Uses of Musk and Europe's Role in Its Trade* (Brussels: Traffic Europe, 1999). See also John Pickrell, "Poachers Target Musk Deer for Perfumes, Medicines," *National Geographic News*, 7 September 2004.

42 Juliet Highet, "The Perfumes of Arabia: The Role of Perfumes in the History of the Middle East," *The Middle East*, 10 January 1999.

43 David Phybus, "The History of Aroma Chemistry and Perfume," *The Chemistry of Fragrances: From Perfumer to Consumer*, second edition, Charles Sell (ed.) (Cambridge: Royal Society of Chemistry, 2006).

44 Homes, *Scent*, 41.

45 Cited in Susanah Frankel, "The Chanel No. 5 Story," *The Independent*, 15 October 2008.

46 Susanah Frankel, "The Chanel No. 5 Story," *The Independent*, 15 October 2008.

47 Dana Thomas, *Deluxe: How Luxury Lost Its Luster* (New York: Penguin, 2007), 137.

48 The Biodiversity Research and Training Forum (BRTF), *Report on Conservation of Musk Deer "Moschus chrysogaster" in Annapurna Conservation Area of Mustang District of Nepal (Marpha Village Development Committee (VDC), Mustang)*, submitted to The Rufford Maurice Laing Foundation, UK 2007.

49 Stephen Fowler, "Musk: An Essay," *Juice Magazine*, no. 3, www.epistola. com/sfowler/scholar/scholar-musk.html.

50 Chris Dobson, "Despite Lack of Leads, Son Keeps Up Fight to Bring Businessman's Killers to Justice," *South China Morning Post*, 30 August 1992; Fiona Holland, "Scent of the End for Tigers and Deer," *South China Morning Post*, 17 December 1997.

51 Paul Dalgamo interview with George Dodd in *Sunday Herald*, 9 December 2007. On Dodd's professional credentials, see www.aromasciences. com/our-perfumer.asp.

52 Aarti Aggarwal, "Musk Deer Falling Prety to Poachers," *The Times of India*, 25 May 2000; WWF Factsheet, *Musk Deer* (CITES, 2002).

53 "Coffee from Cats," *Irish Times*, 8 July 2000; Tim Elliot, "Cat's Whiskers," *The Sydney Morning Herald*, 19 February 2008; "Expensive Coffee Comes from Unlikely Source," *Associated Press*, 2 January 2008.

54 Gu Zhong and Li Hui, "Perfuming the World with Scent of China," *Window*, Hong Kong, 24 April 1996; "WWF Warns of Perfume Threat to Musk Deer," *Agence France Presse*, 6 July 1999.

55 www.pr-inside.com/report-on-china-s-perfume-market-r894062.htm; "Skincare Drives the Prestige Beauty Industry in China," *Reuters*, 8 January 2008; "Perfume Makers Pin Their Hopes on China," *International Herald Tribune*, 10 April 2008.

56 Luca Turin and Tania Sanchez, *Perfumes: The A-Z Guide* (New York: Viking Press, 2008), 43.

57 On continued reliance on animal testing, see Erin E. Williams and Margo DeMello, *Why Animals Matter: The Case for Animal Protection* (Amherst: Prometheus Books, 2007), chapter 5.

58 David Usborne, "US Military Blows Up Live Pigs to Test Body Armour," *The Independent*, 9 April 2009.

59 Jeffrey St Clair, "The Bear Minimum," *Counterpunch*, 1 December 2007.

60 See the pioneering investigative works: Traffic Network, "The Bear Facts: The East Asian Market for Bear Gall Bladder," July 1995; Investigative Network and the Humane Society of the United States/Humane Society International, *The Global Underground Trade in Bear Parts* (Washington, 1996); Investigative Network and the Humane Society of the United States/Humane Society International/Humane Society of Canada, *From Forest to Pharmacy: Canada's Underground Trade in Bear Parts* (Toronto, 1996). See also Debra Rose and Andrea Gaski (eds), *Proceedings of the International Symposium on the Trade of Bear Parts for Medicinal Use* (Seattle: Traffic USA World Wildlife Fund, 1994), and, for an excellent update, D. Williamson (ed.), *Proceedings of the 4th International Symposium on the Trade in Bear Parts* (Traffic-East Asia, 2 October 2006), 8–10;

and Amelie Knapp, *Bear Necessities: An Analysis of Brown Bear Management and Trade* (Traffic Europe Report, Brussels: 2006).

61 Chris Darimont and Misty MacDuffee, "New Thinking Needed to Save British Columbia's Salmon and Grizzlies: The Bear Essentials," *Counterpunch*, 8 October 2009.

62 For example, www.naturalist.com/bearfat.htm.

63 Andrew Kramer, "At Russia-China Border, Bear Paws Sell Best," *The New York Times*, 29 June 2010. This article downplays the impact of the trade on brown bear populations whose population, it claims, contrary to what wildlife experts say, is actually rising.

64 This process is traced in the studies cited in note 51, above.

65 *Forest to Pharmacy Global Underground*, 31 et passim; for an update, Nobuo Ishii, "Management of Bears and Utilization of Bear Bile in Japan," *Symposium op. cit.*, Williamson (ed.).

66 On the regulatory impasse see Adam Roberts and Nancy Perry, "Throwing Caution to the Wind: The Global Bear Parts Trade," *Animal Law* (Lewis & Clark Law School, 2000).

67 See Catherine McCracken, Debra Rose, and Kurt Johnson, *Status, Management and Commercialization of the American Black Bear* (Washington: TRAFFIC USA, 1995), and Douglas Williamson, *In the Black: Status Management and Trade of the American Black Bear in North America* (Washington: TRAFFIC North America & World Wildlife Fund, 2002). For a skeptical view of some of the anti-trade claims, see Nova Scotian wildlife officer Tony Nette, "Bear Gallbladders to Sell or Not to Sell," Nova Scotia Department of Natural Resources, 20 August 1998. Claims from one place of astronomical prices for black-market bladders are countered by claims from others that bear carcasses are often found with the bladders intact.

68 A price as high as cocaine, some claim. Barbara Turnbull "Bears Die to Supply Herbal Market," *Toronto Star*, 24 January 1992; Brian McAndrew, "Trade in Bear Parts 'Rivals' Drug Dealing," *Toronto Star*, 2 November 1994; James Barron "Brooklyn Stabbing Death Linked to the Exporting of Animal Parts," *The New York Times*, 22 October 1991. Thus the Humane Society investigation claimed "a significant portion of the illegal trade in bear galls is run by organized criminals who also trade internationally in other highly valued wildlife, drugs and arms." Humane Society of the United States investigation cited in note 60, above.

69 "Police Break Ring of Hunters Selling Bear Parts to Asia," *Agence France Press*, 29 January 1995.

70 I am indebted to Jonathan Freeman for interviewing the officials and supplying details of this case. See also "Bear Parts Jailed," *Canadian Press*, 31

May 2000. Much the same was revealed to be true in Operation SOUP, a Virginia sting operation against bear bladder and paw traffickers that led to twelve arrests and seized three hundred bladders.

71 See, for example, Judy Mills, "Milking the Bear Trade," *International Wildlife*, May-June 1992; J. Ringle, "Battery Farm Bears Milked for Medicine," *Times*, 22 March 1999; Helen Connealy, "Bitter Harvest," *Asia Week*, 15 November 2001; Kati Loeffler et al., "Compromised Health and Welfare of Bears in China's Bear Bile Farming Industry," *AnimalsAsia Foundation*, March 2007.

72 J.A. Mills et al., *The Bear Facts: The East Asian Market for Bear Gall Bladder* (Traffic Network Report, July 1995); Jill Robinson, Gail Cochrane, and Kati Loeffler "Discussion Regarding the Impacts of Bear Bile Farming on Wild Bears in China and Vietnam," *Symposium*, Williamson (ed.). For the positive view of the Chinese bile factory, see Huang Haikui and Li Zhi, "Bear Farming and Bear Conservation in China," *Symposium*, Williamson (ed.). The debate and discussion at the end gives a radically different view.

73 Bee venom to treat arthritis or snake venom for some forms of cancer, and so forth. See, for example, Zoe Cormier, "An Amphibious Assault," *Globe and Mail*, 14 June 2008. The year 2008 saw a breakthrough in malaria treatment using "synthetic biology" to adapt, increase production of, and cheapen an ancient Chinese herbal remedy ("Malaria: A Miracle in the Making Offers Hope to Millions Worldwide," *The Independent*, 4 June 2008). Amelie Knapp, *Bear Necessities: An Analysis of Brown Bear Management and Trade* (Brussels: Traffic Europe Report, 2006).

74 Barry Wigmore, "Fat Cat AIG Bosses Flew to England for £60,000 Partridge Shoot Days after £65bn Bail-Out," *Daily Mail*, 15 October 2008.

75 Wayne Pacelle, "Cheney's Canned Kill," *Humane Society of the United States*, 2004.

76 John Walsh, "The Killing Fields of Europe," *The Independent*, 7 July 2008.

77 Thanks to Sheldon Locking for this information.

78 Williams and DeMello, *Why Animals Matter*, 143.

79 Assuming of course, the scheme is not exposed before. See for example the case of investment guru Wade Cook reported in Dan Richman and Bill Virgin, "Wade Cook, Wife Charged with Tax Fraud: Couple Accused of Hiding $8.9 Million in Income," *Seattle Post Intelligencer*, 2 December 2005, and United States Attorney's Office, Western District of Washington, "Wade Cook Convicted of Tax Evasion, Filing False Tax Returns and Obstructing Justice," 20 February 2007.

80 thewildlifemuseum.org/static/index.cfm?contentID=8.

81 ambushaction.com; recently the website seems to have been deactivated.

82 An astounding description of the annual shindig is in chapter 2 of Matthew Scully, *Dominion: The Power of Man, the Suffering of Animals, and the Call to Mercy* (New York: St Martin's Press, 2002).

83 Williams and DeMello, *Why*, 126; Scully, *Dominion*, 78–81.

84 Marc Kaufman, "Big Game Hunting Brings Big Tax Breaks: Tropy Donations Raise Questions in Congress," *The Washington Post*, 5 April 2005; Humane Society of the United States, "Your Tax Dollars at Work? Hunters Net Hefty Deductions for Trophy Animals," *Wildlife Abuse Campaign: Ending the killing of Animals for Trophies and Pleasure*, www.hsus.org/wildlife_abuse/news/hunting_tax_deductions.html.

85 Humane Society of America, *Congress Shoots Down Taxidermy Tax Scam*, press release, 4 August 2006.

86 "Profile: Dangerous Game; Kenneth Behring, Safari Club International Members and Other Big-Game Hunters still Hunt Endangered or Threatened Animals," ABC News Primetime Thursday, 19 April 2001. Public scandal, not an IRS edict, aborted the scheme.

87 Jeffrey St Clair, "Adventures in the Endangered Skin Trade," *Counterpunch*, 21 June 2008.

88 The controversy over the case refuses to die even if the victim, Wilbert Coffin, has been buried for more than half a century. See, for example, "Was the Wrong Man Hanged?" *The Montreal Gazette*, 11 February 2006. There is an ongoing attempt to have Wilbert Coffin pardoned.

89 Canada is the only range state that permits (in fact delights in encouraging) outsiders to come in to kill its wildlife, and polar bears are the most lucrative targets. (Jerome Taylor, "Bag a Polar Bear for $35,000: The New Threat to the Species," *The Independent*, 20 March 2009).

90 Patrick White, "What Are We Going to Do about Bears," *Globe and Mail*, 14 January 2009.

91 Robin Hammond, "Game Over?" *The Ecologist* 38, no. 5, June 2008.

92 See US Fish and Wildlife Service, "Illinois Exotic Animal Exhibitor Pleads Guilty to Conspiracy for His Role in Trafficking and Killing of Endangered Tigers and Leopard," *US Fish & Wildlife Service News*, 30 August 2002; United States of America, Plaintiff-Appellee v. William R. Kapp, Defendant-Appellant United States Court of Appeals for the Seventh Circuit 419 F. 3d 666 2005. There is a detailed account in Jon Yates and Maurice Possley, "Trophy Slaughter," *Chicago Tribune*, 24 November 2002.

93 "Hundreds of Alligators Slaughtered in Brazil," *Reuters*, 1 April 2008.

94 See Brij Gupta et al., "Trade in Bears and Their Parts in India," *Symposium*, Williamson (ed.).

95 Jonathan Watts, "Hippopotomus on Menu at Beijing Zoo," *The Guardian*, 21 May 2010.

96 Jonathan Watts, "Noah's Ark of 5,000 Rare Animals Found Floating off the Coast of China," *The Guardian*, 26 May 2007.

97 In 2007 the IUCN Red List of species facing the highest threat of extinction hit an all-time high, embracing 25 percent of all mammals, one third of amphibians, and one in eight birds in serious danger (Alison Benjamin, "Extinction Crisis: Who's a Lucky Boy, Then? Parakeet Bucks Trend: Bird's Comeback Is a Rare Success as More Species Are Put on the Danger List," *The Guardian*, 13 September 2007). For an example of exotic meats, see the Superbowl Extravaganza offered by Exotic Meats (exotic-meats.blogspot.com).

CHAPTER TWELVE

1 Science, it seems, has partly confirmed the old proverb that an elephant never forgets, until, of course, it is killed by poachers (Helen Briggs, "Why Elephants Don't Forget," BBC *News*, 19 April 2001).

2 See, for example, mjperry.blogspot.com/2009/05/save-elephants-buy-ivory.html,

3 "Elephant Meat a Commodity for Poachers," *Associated Press*, 7 June 2007; "Taste for Elephant Meat Spreads among Northern Thais," *Associated Press*, 2 June 2000.

4 John Noble Wilford, "Full-Figured Statuette, 35,000 Years Old, Provides New Clues to How Art Evolved," *The New York Times*, 13 May 2009. On the Playboy play, see Gail Dines "3-D Nude Centerforlds? Playboy Tries to Survive in World Filled with Gonzo Porn," *Counterpunch*, 19 May 2010.

5 The classic work is George Frederick Kunz, *Ivory and the Elephant in Art, in Archeology, and in Science* (New York: Doubleday, Page and Co., 1916). For an overview of the illicit trade, see R.T. Naylor, "The Underworld of Ivory," *Crime, Law & Social Change* 42, 2005.

6 James Wynbrandt, *The Excruciating History of Dentistry: Toothsome Tales & Oral Oddities from Babylon to Braces* (New York: St Martin's Press, 1998, 21). In fact, ivory remained in use for dental bridges until well into the nineteenth century (M.D.K. Bremner, *The Story of Dentistry*, Brooklyn: Dental Items Of Interest Publishing Company, 1946, 86, 89).

7 Jack Ogden, *Jewellery of the Ancient World* (New York: Trefoil Books, 1982), 116–19. A highly readable account of the epic of exploitation is Martin Meredith, *Elephant Destiny: Biography of an Endangered Species in Africa* (New York: Public Affairs, 2003). On the role of ivory in Chinese cultural history and the trade in it, see also Berthold Laufer, *Ivory In China* (Chicago: Field Museum of Natural History, University of Chicago: 1925).

8 On the early history and observations of the late-nineteenth- and early twentieth-century trades, see Ernst D. Moore, *Ivory: Scourge of Africa* (New York: Harper & Brothers, 1933). The author was one of Zanzibar's leading ivory traders: this book is apparently a belated attempt to repent his sins. For a fuller history, see Abdul Sheriff, *Slaves, Spices and Ivory in Zanzibar* (Athens: Ohio University Press, 1987).

9 In 1822. See Raymond Bonner, *At the Hand of Man: Peril and Hope for Africa's Wildlife* (New York: Knopf, 1993), 46. This is a good account of the treacherous and sometimes deceitful politics behind the elephant conservation campaigns, though it, like the book by Adams and McShane (see note 10), tends to downplay the long-term impact of the militarization of poaching as a result of regional wars in the critical period.

10 One of the better recent works demystifying a great deal of Western rhetoric is Jonathan S. Adams and Thomas O. McShane, *The Myth of Wild Africa: Conservation without Illusion* (Berkeley: University of California Press, 1996).

11 Moore, *Scourge*, 49; James T. Muirhead, *Ivory Poaching and Cannibals in Africa* (London: Macmillan & Co., 1933), 262; Sheriff, *Slaves*, 35, 41, 47.

12 Actually they cheered quite often, especially when he talked about all the money they could make. See "Address Of Mr H.M. Stanley On England and the Congo and Manchester Trade," Manchester Chamber of Commerce, Special Meeting of Members Held on Tuesday, October 21st, 1884 in the Large Room of the Town Hall, Albert Square, Manchester.

13 Adams, *Myth*, 213–14.

14 *The New York Times* in its review of the posthumous memoirs of the culprit referred to him as "an estimable young English gentleman" – although what follows in the article is a tale of relentless sadism ("Jameson's Own Story," 23 March 1891.

15 Meredith, *Destiny*, 125.

16 See Captain C.H. Stigand, *Hunting the Elephant in Africa* (New York: Macmillan, 1913); chapter 20 is entitled "Stalking the African." The US edition came with a laudatory introduction by Theodore Roosevelt. Lord Baden-Powell also recommended Stigand's work to his newly formed Boy Scouts, a combination child-soldier and children-Crusader corps. After all, according to Baden-Powell, "Football is a good game, but better than it, better than any game, is that of man-hunting" (see the explanatory notes 348 and 349 to the reissue of Baden-Powell's ambiguously entitled *Scouting for Boys*.)

17 See, for example, James T. Muirhead, *Ivory Poaching and Cannibals in Africa* (London: Macmillan & Co., 1933). The author was a former member of one of the most notorious irregular warfare units of the British

Army, a unit whose military duties included stealing livestock from Boer farmers to damage morale and interfere with supplies.

18 Moore, *Scourge*, 166–9 et passim; Muirhead, *Poaching*, 61–2, 225.

19 Moore, *Scourge*, 174–5.

20 Thanks to the late Sardahsan Punhani of Marianopolis College, Montreal, for these insights.

21 Thanks to Steven Naylor, one of my piano-virtuoso brothers, for this observation.

22 A British philanthropist offered a prize for something to replace ivory and prompted discovery of the world's first synthetic plastic; but pianists disliked its feel. William Brock, *The Chemical Tree: A History of Chemistry* (New York: W.W. Norton, 1993), 647–9.

23 Richard Conniff, "When the Music in Our Parlors Brought Death to Darkest Africa," *Audubon Magazine* 89, July 1987.

24 Hisako Kiyono, *Japan's Trade in Ivory After the Tenth Conference of the Parties to CITES* (Traffic International, 2002). By the mid-1980s Japan absorbed more ivory than the US and the EC combined.

25 Caitlin O'Connell-Rodwell and Rob Parry-Jones, *An Assessment of China's Management of Trade in Elephants and Elephant Products* (Traffic International, 2002). By one estimate, demand for ivory carvings in Taiwan and South Korea leapt 1,000 percent from 1979 to 1989.

26 Even the pygmies of Central Africa, among the continent's most isolated populations, felt the effects. Bantu people in French-ruled parts of West Africa sold guns to pygmies inhabiting the rainforest who paid for supplies with ivory and who kept the elephant meat for themselves; and the Bantu intermediaries sold the ivory to French traders (Iain and Oria Douglas Hamilton, *Battle for the Elephants*, New York: Viking, 1992, 156).

27 Malcolm Macpherson, "The Great Elephant Slaughter," *International Wildlife*, March 1974. Oria Douglas-Hamilton "Africa's Elephants: Can They Survive?" *National Geographic Magazine*, November 1980. Naturally most of the press coverage focused on Bokassa's golden throne and diamond-crusted crown. See, for example, "Mounting a Golden Throne," *Time*, 19 December 1977.

28 Moore, *Scourge*, 174–5.

29 This is examined in detail in R.T. Naylor, "Loose Cannons – Covert Commerce and Underground Finance in the Modern Arms Black Market," *Crime, Law & Social Change* 22, 1995, and in Naylor, *Wages of Crime*, chapters 3 and 5.

30 For details on the link to Apartheid-era South Africa, see especially De Wet Potgeiter, *Contraband: South Africa and the International Trade in Ivory and Rhino Horn* (Cape Town: Queillerie, 1995); and R.T. Naylor,

Patriots & Profiteers: Economic Warfare, Embargo Busting and State Sponsored Crime, second ed. (Montreal: McGill Queens University Press, 2008), part 4. This link was officially confirmed after the fall of the regime by the report of Judge Mark Kumleben (see note 35, below). See also Jan Breytenbach, "Slaughter in Paradise: SADF and Ivory smuggling," *Mail & Guardian*, 18 December 1997.

31 Thanks to Dan O'Meara for this and several other points on the underground ivory trade.

32 Jonathan Kaplan and Polly Gahzi, "Elephants Wiped Out to Fund War," *The Observer*, 18 April 1993. Michael Dobbs, "Morocco's War King Hassan Strengthened and Threatened by 10-Year Conflict in Western Sahara," *The Washington Post*, 17 March 1985; Sam Kiley, "SAS Joins Hunt for Elephant Poachers," *The Times of London*, 13 September 1993. Tom Masland and Tom Cadman, "Aiming at the Elephants," *Newsweek*, 13 December 1999.

33 Douglas-Hamilton, *Battle*, 42.

34 Thornton, *Kill*, 91.

35 Republic of South Africa, *Commission of Enquiry into the Alleged Smuggling of and Illegal Trade in Ivory and Rhinocerus Horn in South Africa, Report, 1996*. After the fall of the Apartheid regime, the former Defense minister admitted he had personally given permission to South African military intelligence to open the contraband route.

36 This was observed in Kenya by Richard Leakey and recounted in his *Wildlife Wars* (New York: St Martin's Press, 2001), 40 et passim.

37 Nor was that Nbele king alone in his concerns. In Senegal, mass killing by French soldiers remained a common sport until independence – the survival of its elephants was the work not of European visionaries but of the first president after independence, even if the outbreak of war further north in the old Spanish Sahara and the resulting incursion of armed militia groups undermined his efforts (Douglas-Hamilton, *Battle*, 156).

38 Kunz, *Ivory*, 203–4; Adams, *Myth*, 45, 69; Bonner, *Hand of Man*, 40–2.

39 Thembi Mutch, "Who Needs Africa's Land More: Us or Wildlife?" *The Ecologist*, 29 December 2009.

40 See Leakey *Wildlife Wars*, 65 et passim.

41 Potgeiter, *Contraband*, 109–19; Thornton, *Kill*, 83–6; Merideth *Destiny*, 212–5; Douglas-Hamilton, *Battle*, 300; TED Case Studies Elephant Ivory Ban, 27 October 1999.

42 "500,000 Ecus to Be Given to World Wide Fund for Nature," *The Guardian*, 21 December 1988.

43 Burundi was particularly notorious until it joined CITES in 1988. See Potgeiter, *Contraband*, 108–119.

44 Paul Brown, "Web of Intrigue Foiled Ivory Plot," *The Guardian*, 2 March 1992; "Elephant Victims of Bloodlust Safaris," *The Independent*, 6 January 1996.

45 Marcus Marby and Tara Weingarten, "The Elephant Lobby," *Newsweek*, 8 September 1997. For example, the Sustainable Development Network of Nairobi (John Vidal, "Ivory Vote Sparks New Fears for Elephants," *Guardian*, 13 November 2002). On the problems of collecting data on which a rational policy can be based, see Robin Sharp "The African Elephant: Conservation and CITES," *Orynx* 31, no. 2, April 1997. Some claimed that part of the apparently healthy size in Zimbabwe was because its herds were counted at home, then counted again when they migrated to Botswana (*Africa Confidential*, 6 October 1989).

46 "The Low Price of Dead Elephants – Poacher's Pause," *The Economist*, 2 March 1991; *Science*, 3 March 1995.

47 An excellent source giving (from the anti-trade perspective) the politics of the ban is the Elephant Information Repository at elephant.elehost.com.

48 Described by Leakey, *Wildlife*, 221–2.

49 See Rasmus Heltberg, "Impact of the Ivory Trade Ban on Poaching Incentives: A Numerical Example," *Ecological Economics* 36, 2001.

50 A good examination of the impact of stockpiles on black-market behaviour is in Michael 't Sas-Rolfes, "Elephants, Rhinos and the Economics of the Illegal Trade," *Pachyderm*, no. 24, July-December 1997.

51 The Elephant Trade Information System claimed that poaching declined from 1989 to 1994, then picked up again. However, it bases its information on seizures – in reality the relationship between the volume of poaching and the seizure rate is at best fuzzy; it could be nonexistent. Ed Stoddard, "CITES Seen Approving S. African Ivory Sale," *Reuters*, 18 November 1999; "United Nations Elephant Poaching, Illegal Ivory Trade Figures Disputed by International Coalition," *US Newswire*, 3 April 2000.

52 See Environmental Investigation Agency, "Lethal Experiment: How the CITES-Approved Ivory Sale Led to Increased Elephant Poaching," April 2000. I am indebted to Tarun George for onsite information about Zimbabwe's underground ivory trade that confirms the EIA view.

53 Robin Hammond, "Game Over?" *The Ecologist* 38, no. 5, June 2008.

54 Andrew Osborn, "Russia Digs Up Woolly Mammoth Remains for Guilt-Free Ivory," *Daily Telegraph*, 26 September, 2010.

55 "Uganda Ivory Smuggler Chooses Fine over Prison," *Reuters*, 24 June 2000; Anjan Sundaram, "Congo's Hippos Fast Disappearing – Poachers Blamed for Huge Decline in Hippo Population, but 'animals are for us to eat,' Says One Villager," *Toronto Star*, 12 November 2005.

56 Beck and Cary Anderson, "Off with Their Heads," *Newsweek*, 5 June 1989; Michael Parrish, "Hunting with Gun and Chain Saw: A New

Threat to the Pacific Walrus," *Los Angeles Times*, 22 May 1990; Richard
Ellis, "Walrus Hunters' Bloody Ivory Harvest," *The Sunday Times*, 11
March 1990; "Walrus-Headhunting Ring Uncovered in Alaska, US Agents
Say," *The New York Times*, 15 February 1992; David Hulen, "Old Hunt
Renewed," *Anchorage Daily News*, 26 November 1995, "Head Hunters
Create Serious Concern" 20 July 1996. I am indebted to Laura Kirshner
for excellent work on this issue.

57 Julian Baum, "Asia's Untamed Business," *Far Eastern Economic Review*,
19 August 1993; Shada Islam and Julian Baum, "Bone Idle: China,
Taiwan Face Sanctions over Wildlife Trade," *Far Eastern Economic
Review*, 30 September 1993. Taiwan later imposed its own ban, but soon
relented.

58 I thank Bill Totten for correcting the record for me on hanko use. Contrast this, though, to the claim by the International Fund for Animal
Welfare that across Africa more and more poached ivory seized is already
precut to hanko size , waiting to be finished in Japan.

59 Meera Selva, "Chinese Demand for Ivory Threatens African Elephants,"
The Independent, 5 December 2005; Steve Connor "The Return of
the Elephant Killers," *The Independent*, 27 February 2007; Michael
McCarthy and Colin Brown, "Return of Ivory Trade as Britain Backs
China," *The Independent*, 16 July 2008; Jerome Taylor, "Is It Right to
Sell Ivory, or Does It Just Encourage the Poaching of Elephants?" *The
Independent*, 29 October 2008. On attempts to assess the degree of illegal trade, see www.cites.org/eng/prog/ETIS/index.shtml. The database has
existed since 1992, but it was elevated to official status as a monitoring
tool in 2000. Critics claimed that the system for monitoring illegal killing
was underfunded and especially underreported.

60 Traffic India, *An Assessment of the Domestic Ivory Carving Industry and
Trade Controls in India*, February 2003, 19, 26,

61 Andrew Buncombe, "India's Elephants Finally Given Same Protection as
Tigers," *The Independent*, 2 September 2010.

62 Traffic India, *Assessment*, 22, 23; Yenni Kwok, "SAR Continues to Play
Major Role in Illegal Ivory Trade, Says Watchdog," *South China Morning
Post*, 5 April 2000; "PM's Offer to Quit Rejected," *South China Morning
Post*, 18 April 2000.

63 Nirmal Ghosh, "Wildlife Activists Slam Thailand's Illegal Ivory Trade"
The Straits Times, 27 May 2003.

64 Laufer, *Ivory*, 65.

65 Hoving, *False Impressions*, 84, 132.

66 Traffic India, *Assessment*, 16.

67 International Fund for Animal Welfare, *Elephants on High Street: An
investigation into Ivory Trade in the UK* (London, 2004).

68 US Fish & Wildlife Service, *Asian Elephant Ivory*, Summer 2003. Fake antique ivory carvings come in a well-established hierarchy – those at the top are fashioned from genuine old ivory recarved into something that will fetch a higher price; a little below are those in which damage to the old ivory has been patched up with artificially aged new material, even though its use is technically illegal; toward the middle are facsimiles made entirely from new ivory smuggled from Africa, then artificially aged; at the bottom are those made with substitute materials that, with the right documents, can be unloaded as genuine.

69 Of those ivory objects carvings examined on entry during a five-year period from 1997 to 2001, 22,272 were cleared for import; 2,093 were seized. Remarkably the seizure rate of full tusks is even lower – in that same period, 1,022 pairs of trophy tusks were cleared compared to 8 seized. The Humane Society of the United States, *An Investigation of Ivory Markets in the United States*, 21 October 2002.

70 Thanks to Hari Ramanathan for some of this information.

71 So regulatory measures evolved to deal with manufactured goods and services can hardly cope adequately with "crimes against nature." For the opposite view, see Jason Lowther et al., *Crime and Punishment in the Wildlife Trade* (Traffic International, 2002).

72 An excellent survey is Chris Shepherd, *The Trade in Elephant and Elephant Products in Myanmar* (Traffic International, 2002).

73 "Gun Law in the Elephants' Graveyard," *South China Morning Post*, 8 August 1993.

74 Cahal Milmo, "£20m of Ivory Seized as Poachers Return to Their Prey," *The Independent*, 15 April 2009; James Pomfret and Tom Kirkwood, "Demand for Illegal Ivory Soars in Booming China," *The Independent*, 15 November 2009; Robin McKie, "Asia's Greed for Ivory Puts African Elephant at Risk," *The Observer*, 17 January 2010.

CODA

1 Miriam Steffens, "The Son Sets on Kerry's Media Empire," *Sydney Morning Herald*, 29 October 2008; Nick Leys and Charles Miranda, "James Parker's Shrinking Funds," *Sunday Telegraph* (Sydney), 18 January 2009; Kathy Marks, "Hard-up Billionaire Forced to Sell His Toys," *The Independent*, 19 January 2009.

2 Daniel Thomas, "The Cream Rises Again," *Financial Times*, 16 April 2010.

3 See "Daimler Highlights Luxury Car Recovery," *Financial Times*, 19 April 2010. Not to be scoffed at, though, in 2010 all five Bugatti World Record cars with a top speed of 415 kilometres sold out at the Paris motor show for $2.67 million each.

4 "The World's Billionaires," *Forbes*, 11 March 2009; Matthew Miller and Luisa Kroll, "Bill Gates No Longer World's Richest Man," 3 October 2010. Over the year a record 164 former billionaires returned to the ranking. For a critical look at the people on the list, see Will Hutton, "Don't Celebrate These Billionaires, Be Horrified by Their Existence," *Observer*, 14 March 2010.

5 Scheherazade Daneshkhu, "Luxury Stores Caught Out by Surging Demand," *Financial Times*, 1 October 2010.

6 On his recovery, see James Kirby, "Coming Up Trumps," *The Sunday Age*, 18 October 2009; on the yacht, see "Parker Yacht Makes Waves in Sydney," *Daily Telegraph* (Australia), 24 January 2010. For Packer's response to his critics, see Nick Leys, "Bad Blood Spills Over," *Sunday Telegraph* (Australia), 11 October 2009.

7 Ira Iosebashvili and Nikolaus von Twickel, "The Moscow Mayor, a Market and a Haul of $2bln," *The St Petersburg Times*, 23 June 2009. On the recent firing of Mr Ismailov's main public sponsor, the mayor of Moscow, see Boris Kagarlitsky, "The Battle for Moscow," *Counterpunch*, 1–15 October 2010.

8 "Moscow Market Blast Kills at Least 10," *Radio Free Europe*, 21 August 2006; "Market Explosions Becoming More Frequent," RIA *Novosti*, 22 August 2006; "100 Detained around Cherkivosky Market," *Moscow Times*, 16 July 2009. "Cherkizovsky Framed," *The St Petersburg Times*, 8 June 2010. The Cherkizovsky itself had a major bombing followed by fires that sent traders fleeing en masse into the streets.

9 See, for example, farm4.static.flickr.com/3064/3081620765_276d464d85_o.jpg.

10 Seeing is believing: www.mardanpalace.com.

11 www.icm-corp.com/p-mardan-palace-themed-disco.cfm.

12 Helmut Brückner, "Mediterranean Sea," *Encyclopedia of Global Change*, 1 January 2008. There are many other estimates that show different figures for each pollutant, but they have one thing in common – their enormity. See especially *United Nations Environment Programme State of the Environment and Development in the Mediterranean* – 2009, UNEP, April 2010.

13 Carole Cadwalladr, "Welcome to the Pleasure Dome," *Guardian*, 31 April 2009.

14 See Gostelow, "Mardan Palace Opening," www.kiwicollection.com/wow-travel/industry-insight/mardan-palace-opening. Or as a reporter from Birmingham England, drooled: "Piles of Beluga caviar, vintage Champagne on tap and more lobster than you can shake a crabstick at give the whole weekend an air of unattainable luxury" (Kat Keogh, "Hilton Hotels Are No Match for This Place! Unadulterated Luxury Makes the Mardan

Palace Hotel a Mecca for Hedonists: Greatescape," *Birmingham Evening Mail*, 10 June 2009).

15 On recent turmoil around Ismailov's antics, see Mark Franchetti, "Vladimir Putin Furious over Flaunting Oligarch Telman Ismailov," *The Sunday Times of London*, 28 June 2009; Quentin Fottrell, "Turkish Delight?" *Irish Times*, 16 July 2009; Shaun Walker, "Oligarch Pays for Party That Enraged Putin," *The Independent*, 16 July 2009; "Something Funny Happened on the Way to Cherkizovsky Market," *Wall Street Journal*, 17 July 2009.

16 See Amiram Barkat, "The Village People," *Haaretz*, 29 September 2006; Anna Arutunyan, "Return of the Prodigal Oligarchs," *Moscow News*, 1 March 2010; Vladimir Kozlov, "Cherkizovsky Resurrected," *Moscow News*, 24 May 2010.

17 This phenomenon is discussed in Stuart Ewen's pioneering *Captains of Consciousness: Advertising and the Roots of the Consumer Culture* (New York: Basic Books, 1976, 2001) and his *All Consuming Images: The Politics of Style in Contemporary Culture* (New York: Basic Books, 1988, 1999).

18 The "black card" – properly the Centurion Card – is a great example of marketing imitating artful rumour. The unfounded story of a super-secret card for the super-rich gave birth to a scramble to acquire one, to which American Express responded by creating it, then passing it out to a few high-profile, high-income clients, creating a clamour for like treatment by wannabes and wanna-haves. The clientele isn't even particularly select anymore, except the requirement to be able to pay bills that have to be a minimum size rather beyond the means of an unemployed janitor or a part-time babysitter.

19 This is well analysed in Ellen Shell, *Cheap: The High Cost of Discount Culture* (New York: Penguin, 2009).

20 See Dana Thomas, *Deluxe: How Luxury Lost Its Luster* (New York: Penguin, 2007). Some luxury handbags, for example, are reputed to sell for fifteen to twenty times production cost. Although luxury makers from North America and Europe have long outsourced some production to China, recently a Chinese firm took things to the logical conclusion by purchasing Aquascutum, whose high-end British clientele, including the royal family, dates back 150 years ("Chinese Firm Ready to Swoop on Aquascutum," *Sunday Times*, 24 May 2009).

21 Cf. Peter Wilby, "Philanthropists Aren't Being That Altruistic," *New Statesman*, 19 March 2008.

22 "A $30 million gift to a concert hall," billionaire dissident William Gross observed, "is not philanthropy, it is a Napoleonic coronation"; cited in Stephanie Strom, "Big Gifts, Tax Breaks and a Debate on Charity," *New*

York Times, 7 September 2007. On the donations by the poor, see Frank Grave "America's Poor Are Its Most Generous Givers," *McClatchy Newspapers,* 19 May 2009.

23 See "Koch Industries Environmental Record," www.greenpeace.org/usa/en/campaigns/global-warming-and-energy/polluterwatch/koch-industries/koch-industries-environmental. On Cato Institute funding, see www.cato.org/about.php: "Cato receives approximately 80 percent of its funding through tax-deductible contributions from individuals."

24 Probably the wisest examination of the process is by the doyen of ecological economics, Herman Daly, in his *Beyond Growth: The Economics of Sustainable Development* (Boston: Beacon Press, 1996).

25 Robert H. Frank has long been a leading American advocate of shifting from income to progressive expenditure taxes. See, for example, his "Progressive Consumption Taxation as a Remedy for the US Savings Shortfall," *The Economists' Voice* 2, no. 3, 2005. An even stronger case can be made for it on ecological grounds. But, as the current author (who would add business-cost taxes to the roster of measures) has been finding for at least twenty years, any such pleas fall on conveniently deaf ears, whether they are attached to heads inclined to the left or the right of the political spectrum.

26 An earlier examination of the social and political implications was offered in John Kenneth Galbraith, *The Culture of Contentment* (Boston: Houghton Mifflin, 1992).

Index